Charles Robertson
Boreland.
Muthill

Alex. Nasmyth, pinx.

ROBERT BURNS.

POETICAL WORKS OF ROBERT BURNS, WITH LIFE AND NOTES BY WILLIAM WALLACE, LL.D.

WITH TWENTY-ONE ILLUSTRATIONS FROM ORIGINAL DRAWINGS BY W. D. M'KAY, R.S.A.; C. MARTIN HARDIE, R.S.A.; G. O. REID, R.S.A.; R. B. NISBET, A.R.S.A.; AND G. PIRIE . . . .

LONDON: 38 Soho Square, W.
W. & R. CHAMBERS, LIMITED
EDINBURGH: 339 High Street

Edinburgh:
Printed by W. & R. Chambers, Limited.

Reprinted 1910.

BIOGRAPHICAL SKETCH.

ROBERT BURNS was born on the 25th of January 1759, in a two-roomed clay-cottage built by his father in the village of Alloway, about two miles from the town of Ayr. He came, on the one side, of a family which, he believed, had suffered for the Stuarts; and on the other, of undoubted Covenanting stock. His father, William Burnes, was born on the Kincardineshire estate of Stuart of Inchbeck, who was 'out' in the 'Fifteen,' and his great-grandfather on the mother's side was shot at Aird's Moss.

William Burnes, a gardener, nurseryman, and farmer, was a man of notable character and individuality; wrote for his children a *Manual of Religious Belief;* induced his neighbours to hire a competent teacher, John Murdoch, for their children; and showed his boys—he had seven children in all—both by precept and by practice, how to reason. Agnes Broun, the poet's mother, was an excellent housewife, with no pretensions to education; but it was probably from her that he inherited the lyrical gift. Life was hard with the Burneses. Robert had two and a half years' schooling in Alloway. Then his father, with a view to keeping his children about him, ventured to take the farm of Mount Oliphant, a couple of miles distant from the seven-acre croft he had hitherto cultivated, undertaking to pay forty or forty-five pounds a year for seventy acres of poor land which he could not stock without borrowed money. From the age of nine the boy had none but intermittent school-teaching; but his education was steadily carried on by his father, who taught his boys, in addition to the three 'R's,' geography and the rudiments both of ancient and of natural history, and, as Gilbert, the second son, testified, 'conversed familiarly on all subjects with us as if we had been men.' Possession of a *Complete Letter-Writer* inspired Robert with a strong desire to excel in letter-writing, while it furnished him with 'models by some of the first writers in the language.' The 'latent seeds of poesy' had been cultivated by Betsy Davidson, an 'old maid of his mother's' who was remarkable for her 'ignorance, credulity, and superstition,' but who had 'the largest collection in the country of tales and songs concerning devils, ghosts, fairies, brownies, witches, warlocks, spunkies, kelpies, elf-candles, dead-lights, wraiths, apparitions, cantraips, enchanted towers, giants, and other trumpery.' He read poetry chiefly in 'Selections' and 'Collections,' but secured a copy of *Pope* soon after entering his teens. 'A critic in substantives, verbs, and particles' by ten or eleven, he obtained an introduction to French at fourteen, and made the first of several efforts to overcome a natural distaste by learning Latin.

All the while he was made to work hard; at fifteen he was the principal labourer on the farm; there was little or no social intercourse with neighbours, and what with the overstrain of his young muscles, 'the cheerless gloom of a hermit, with the unceasing toil of a galley-slave,' and anxiety about the future—for the father, with the utmost economy and industry, could not keep his head above water—he was, before he came to manhood, affected with a nervous disorder, which caused him physical suffering and fits of hypochondria through life. But he fell in love in his fifteenth year, and wrote his first song. Two years later he went for a season to a school on a smuggling coast, Kirkoswald, and learned to 'take his glass.' So when in 1777 William Burnes removed to the farm of Lochlea, in Tarbolton parish, Robert at nineteen was well read, 'constantly the victim of some fair enslaver,' and could rhyme.

At Lochlea the circumstances of the family were easier. Burns became a Freemason, started a debating club in Tarbolton, developed the conversational powers which were to impress Edinburgh society, 'thirsted for distinction,' dressed with care, and acquired some notoriety as a champion of heretical as opposed to 'Old Light' opinions (or ultra-Calvinism) in the churchyard colloquies in which he had learned as a mere boy to practise the reasoning faculty so carefully cultivated by his father. He thought of marriage, and, despairing of making a living by farming, spent a season in Irvine learning flax-dressing. The experiment, however, was not successful.

William Burnes died in 1784; and, rescuing some small remains from his embarrassed estate, Robert and Gilbert took the farm of Mossgiel, in the adjoining parish of Mauchline. The poet's life continued to be, on his brother's testimony, frugal and temperate; it must have been so, for he did not earn more than seven pounds a year. But before leaving Lochlea he had for the first time deviated from propriety in his relations with women, and Elizabeth Paton, a servant of his mother's, bore him a daughter. The first genuine determination of his mind towards literary effort, the first appreciation of its usual aims and results, appears in certain entries in his Commonplace Book, which are undated, but may, though not without some hesitation, be ascribed to 1784. There he expressed a strong wish that he might be able to celebrate in verse his native county, associated as it was with many of the actions of 'Glorious Wallace, the Saviour of his Country,' as 'the excellent Ramsay' and 'the still more excellent Fergusson' had celebrated the scenes with which they were familiar. So he made poetry at once the exposition and the sedative of his passions, wrote a welcome to his illegitimate child, and versified epistles to brother-poets in Ayrshire. He fell in love with Jean Armour, daughter of a master-mason in Mauchline. He took sides with the New Lights or liberal clergy against the Old Lights or Highflyers, of whom his own minister in Mauchline, the Rev. William Auld, was one; wrote skits in verse for the cause—'The Twa Herds,' the 'Epistle to John Goldie,' 'Holy Willie's Prayer'—and was encouraged by the countenance and friendship of clergymen who welcomed and appreciated his satiric faculty.

His poems circulated in manuscript; and by 1785, Mossgiel promising to be no more profitable than Lochlea, he had doubtless come to contemplate publishing. Burns was never more productive than at this time, and did the bulk of his best-known work at Mossgiel; it is tolerably safe to set down as the product of the later autumn and early winter these poems: 'To a Mouse,' 'Halloween,' 'Man was Made to Mourn,' 'The Cotter's Saturday Night,' 'Address to the Deil,' 'The Jolly Beggars,' 'To James

Smith,' 'The Vision,' 'The Author's Earnest Cry and Prayer,' 'The Twa Dogs,' 'The Ordination,' and 'Scotch Drink'—the works which formed the foundation of the poet's future fame. Publication was precipitated by the discovery that Jean Armour was soon to become a mother. Burns gave her a writing acknowledging her as his wife, but old Armour would not have him for a son-in-law, and induced his daughter to destroy the document. The poet, rendered desperate, resolved to emigrate to Jamaica as bookkeeper on an estate. Partly to raise money for his passage, he brought out his first volume in the famous Kilmarnock edition, a copy of which was sold in 1898 for five hundred and forty-five guineas. Meantime occurred the still mysterious 'Highland Mary' episode. According to the best hypothesis founded on the few ascertained facts, almost immediately after the breach with the Armour family the poet plighted his troth to Mary Campbell, a Highland maid-servant residing in the neighbourhood, who went home to prepare for marriage, and straightway died, to be apparently forgotten for the moment by Burns (who had never ceased to love Jean), but to live for ever in 'To Mary in Heaven' and other poems.

The appearance of *Poems chiefly in the Scottish Dialect*, although it brought only a few pounds, changed the current of the poet's life. He was induced to abandon the Jamaica scheme, and to proceed to Edinburgh with a view to the publication of a new edition. He set out on 27th November 1786. By this time fairly well accustomed to 'the tables of the great,' he discovered no shyness or awkwardness in his intercourse with the *literati* to whom he was introduced through the mediation of an Ayrshire laird, and he was of course at home among the companions of another rank who got access to him through John Richmond, clerk, an old Mauchline friend whose lodging he shared. Conscious of his power, he met as an equal, and was treated as an equal by, Dugald Stewart, Principal Robertson, Hugh Blair, and Henry Erskine, as well as aristocrats like the Earl of Glencairn. His frank, vigorous, yet modest conversation fascinated the Duchess of Gordon and other ladies of fashion. Creech undertook to publish a new edition for him, and the gentlemen of the Caledonian Hunt were large subscribers. The book put some four hundred or five hundred pounds in his pocket; but

Creech did not promptly come to a settlement. So, after hanging on in Edinburgh for a little, taking stock of his new friends and of the durability of their friendship, delighting the Crochallan Fencibles, a convivial club, with eminently clever verses, and enjoying to the full the social opportunities of the hour, he made a few days' tour of the southern counties.

In the first flush of success he had thought of striking into a new line of life. Adam Smith suggested that he might get a salt-officership, and he did not repudiate the hint of Mrs Dunlop, an Ayrshire lady who was henceforth his most constant correspondent, that he had contemplated buying a commission in the army. Very quickly, however, he determined to live the life to which he had been bred, and on his Border tour he visited Dalswinton, near Dumfries—Mr Miller, the proprietor, having offered him a farm. On his '*éclatant* return,' as he called it, to Mauchline, he was cordially received by Jean Armour, who had borne him twins the previous September, and their relations were restored to the old footing. After a brief stay at Mossgiel, he returned to Edinburgh, only to start on a three weeks' tour in the Highlands, in the course of which he was entertained by the Dukes of Athole and Gordon, and visited his Kincardineshire relatives. Back in the capital, he had to resume the task of badgering Creech for his money; but he would have given it up in December had he not met with an accident which laid him on his back. Simultaneously he fell into a correspondence with a sentimental grass-widow of literary tastes—Mrs Maclehose; the correspondence, carried on in romantic style between 'Sylvander' and 'Clarinda,' ripened into an ardent friendship, and had she been free he might have married her.

But when Burns at last got a settlement with Creech, he returned to Mossgiel in February of 1788; married Jean Armour, who had been turned out of her father's house just before her second accouchement—she bore twins again, but they died immediately after birth; went through a course of instruction in the duties of an Excise officer, having in Edinburgh obtained a promise of a post in the service in case farming failed him again; and took from Miller the farm of Ellisland. Having built his house, the poet took his wife thither, and set himself seriously to make 'conduct' his first aim, while not forgetting his destiny to 'mak' a sang at least' for Scotland or fame. His society was sought by the neighbouring gentry, notably by an enthusiastic antiquary, Mr Riddel of Glenriddel, and he used his pen to help the local Whig politicians. He wrote election verses, and, occasion offering, struck another blow for his old friends, the liberal clergy of Ayrshire. Mrs Dunlop and other friends wrote to and received many letters from him. Captain Riddel and he established a parish library. The struggle for existence was, however, unfavourable to sustained literary effort of the most ambitious kind. The farm was a bad bargain, and before the end of 1789 Burns had applied for and obtained work as an exciseman; and though his beat was in the environment of Ellisland, it covered ten parishes, and involved almost continuous riding. Yet his Muse—he loved the word—was not infertile. He had begun in Edinburgh to contribute to Johnson's *Musical Museum*, and continued to make and adapt songs for that publication. He wrote an 'Ode to the Departed Regency Bill, 1789,' for Stuart's (London) *Star*, and was offered and declined a regular engagement on its staff. He refused also to think of the newly founded Chair of Agriculture in Edinburgh University, for which Mrs Dunlop and Mr Graham of Fintry, one of the Commissioners of Excise, would have pressed his claim. It was in the autumn of 1790 that he composed 'Tam o' Shanter,' which by many critics is regarded as his masterpiece. In the same year Burns committed a breach of conjugal fidelity, his fellow-sinner being Ann Park, servant in a Dumfries inn; but this was nobly forgiven by his wife, who nursed the child of the amour with one of her own.

In November 1791 the poet quitted farming in disgust, sold his stock, and became an exciseman pure and simple. He was appointed to a division in Dumfries at a salary of seventy pounds a year, with perquisites, and within a year this was increased by twenty pounds. He had a good friend in Mr Graham, and soon acquired another in Mr Corbet, one of the Supervisors-General, whom Mrs Dunlop interested in him. His prospects of advancement in his profession were excellent; but his politics now developed into active sympathy with the French Revolutionists. Life went well with him on the whole. He kept on writing songs for Johnson, and more diligently and enthusiastically for Thomson's *Melodies;* struck up a friendship with Mrs Maria Riddel, sister-in-law of his friend the Captain; and was on friendly terms both with the county gentry and the townsfolk. He did not, on his own confession, eschew the tavern; but, according to the emphatic testimony of his wife, his official superior, Supervisor Findlater, and his immediate neighbour Gray, a teacher in the local Academy, he never became habitually intemperate. There is abundant evidence that he was attentive to his official duties; it goes without saying that he was the most careful and affectionate of fathers. But he did not take pains in word or act to conceal his sympathy with French Revolutionists or British Reformers. Although Graham of Fintry remained his steadfast friend, his outspokenness led to a delay in his promotion and to his being 'cut' by a section of Dumfries society; and a rather mysterious quarrel with Mrs Riddel, in which he was more sinned against than sinning, gave him much pain and cost him some friendships. Yet when 'Haughty Gaul' threatened invasion, his patriotic songs rang through the country and brought back any popularity he had lost; and the difference with Mrs Riddel did not last a year. A supervisorship was in sight, and not without reason he looked forward to obtaining, through political influence, a collectorship, which meant 'a life of literary leisure with a decent competence;' but an attack of rheumatic fever in the winter of 1795–96, following in the wake of a severe domestic affliction, proved too much for his constitution. He deliberately prepared for death, and met it calmly—misunderstandings due to delirium deserve no serious consideration—on July 21, 1796.

Sat est vixisse. So Robert Burns, like Walter Scott, might have said of himself. He was not destined to reach the perfection of self-discipline as a man or to realise all his hopes as a poet; but he never abandoned the scheme of self-support and of devotion to art which he deliberately selected in his youth. He resolved to make his living by some craft in which he had rendered himself proficient, while he gave his leisure and his soul to poetry. He adhered to his determination; he died solvent and singing. Poetry to him meant reality, obedience to imperative impulse in the selection of subjects, realism in their treatment, that genius which is equivalent to infinite labour in technical execution, and beyond and above all the search as for hidden treasure of the universal in the particular. Having the strongest of brains and of passions, an ardent ambition which was justified by an accurate inventory of his faculties, a courage which stormed the citadel of every problem in nature and man that came within his ken, and even dared to consider a good song as a greater work than an ambitious but wooden epic, 'words became his slaves;' and, in transcribing his own experiences, he qualified himself as Humanity's ready-reckoner in practical ethics and one of the world's half-dozen lyrists and humorists for whom 'inevitableness' may be claimed. So to the end of time Scotland, recognising that Burns was greater than even his achievement, will love, cherish, and mourn him as her strong man that rejoiced to run his race, her 'Man of Destiny'—nay, even her Prodigal Son whose generation had not the wisdom to kill the fatted calf while yet there was time to make the feast at once a sacrament of brotherhood and a new departure in personal duty and poetic development.

WILLIAM WALLACE.

CONTENTS.

LIST OF ILLUSTRATIONS.

POETICAL WORKS

OF

ROBERT BURNS.

HANDSOME NELL.[1]

TUNE—*I am a man unmarried.*

O once I lov'd a bonie lass,
  Aye, and I love her still;
And whilst that virtue warms my breast,
  I 'll love my handsome Nell.

As bonie lasses I hae seen,
  And mony full as braw; well dressed
But, for a modest gracefu' mien,
  The like I never saw.

A bonie lass, I will confess,
  Is pleasant to the e'e;
But without some better qualities,
  She 's no a lass for me.

But Nelly's looks are blythe and sweet,
  And, what is best of a',
Her reputation is complete,
  And fair without a flaw.

[1] Nelly Kilpatrick, the daughter of Allan Kilpatrick, miller at Parclewan, in Dalrymple parish. Nelly married William Bone, coachman to the Laird of Newark. She died about the year 1820.

She dresses ay sae clean and neat,
Both decent and genteel;
And then there 's something in her gait
Gars ony dress look weel. Makes

A gaudy dress and gentle air
May slightly touch the heart;
But it 's innocence and modesty
That polishes the dart.

'Tis this in Nelly pleases me,
'Tis this enchants my soul;
For absolutely in my breast
She reigns without controul.

I DREAM'D I LAY.

I dream'd I lay where flowers were springing
Gaily in the sunny beam;
List'ning to the wild birds singing,
By a falling, crystal stream:
Straight the sky grew black and daring;
Thro' the woods the whirlwinds rave;
Trees with aged arms were warring,
O'er the swelling drumlie wave. turbid

Such was my life's deceitful morning,
Such the pleasures I enjoy'd;
But lang or noon, loud tempests storming, ere
A' my flowery bliss destroy'd.
Tho' fickle fortune has deceiv'd me—
She promis'd fair, and perform'd but ill,
Of mony a joy and hope bereav'd me—
I bear a heart shall support me still.

TIBBIE, I HAE SEEN THE DAY.

TUNE—*Invercauld's Reel.*

Chorus.—O Tibbie, I hae seen the day
Ye wadna been sae shy;
For laik o' gear ye lightly me, lack—goods—slight
But, trowth, I care na by.

Yestreen I met you on the moor,
Ye spak na, but gaed by like stoure ; dust
Ye geck at me because I 'm poor, mock
But fient a hair care I. not a bit

When comin hame on Sunday last,
Upon the road as I cam past,
Ye snufft and gae your head a cast—
But trowth I care't na by.

I doubt na, lass, but ye may think,
Because ye hae the name o' clink, repute—money
That ye can please me at a wink,
Whene'er ye like to try.

But sorrow tak him that 's sae mean,
Altho' his pouch o' coin were clean,
Wha follows ony saucy quean, wench
That looks sae proud and high.

Altho' a lad were e'er sae smart,
If that he want the yellow dirt,
Ye 'll cast your head anither airt, direction
And answer him fu' dry.

But if he hae the name o' gear, wealth
Ye 'll fasten to him like a brier,
Tho' hardly he, for sense or lear, learning
Be better than the kye.

But, Tibbie, lass, tak my advice :
Your daddie's gear maks you sae nice ;
The deil a ane wad spier your price, ask
Were ye as poor as I.

There lives a lass beside yon park,
I 'd rather hae her in her sark,
Than you, wi' a' your thousan mark ; marks (money)
That gars you look sae high.[1]

[1] Burns, in one of the notes to the collection of his poems and letters known as 'The Glenriddel MSS.,' says, 'This song I composed about the age of seventeen,' and the conjecture has been hazarded that it may be connected with the incident thus alluded to in his autobiography : 'In my seventeenth year, to give my manners a brush, I went to a country dancing school.' Mrs Begg, on the other hand, declared positively that it was in his nineteenth year that he attended the dancing school, and that the Tibbie of the song was Isabella Stein (or Steven), who lived at Little Hill, a farm which marched with Lochlea.

THE RUINED FARMER.—'IT'S O, FICKLE FORTUNE, O!'

TUNE—*Go from my window, Love, do.*

The sun he is sunk in the west,
All creatures retirèd to rest,
While here I sit, all sore beset,
With sorrow, grief, and woe:
And it's O, fickle Fortune, O!

The prosperous man is asleep,
Nor hears how the whirlwinds sweep;
But Misery and I must watch
The surly tempest blow:
And it's O, fickle Fortune, O!

There lies the dear partner of my breast;
Her cares for a moment at rest:
Must I see thee, my youthful pride,
Thus brought so very low!
And it's O, fickle Fortune, O!

There lie my sweet babes in her arms;
No anxious fear their hearts alarms;
But for their sake my heart does ache,
With many a bitter throe:
And it's O, fickle Fortune, O!

I once was by Fortune carest:
I once could relieve the distrest:
Now life's poor support, hardly earn'd,
My fate will scarce bestow:
And it's O, fickle Fortune, O!

No comfort, no comfort I have!
How welcome to me were the grave!
But then my wife and children dear—
O, whither would they go!
And it's O, fickle Fortune, O!

O whither, O where shall I turn!
All friendless, forsaken, forlorn!
For, in this world, Rest or Peace
I never more shall know!
And it's O, fickle Fortune, O!

THE TARBOLTON LASSES.

If ye gae up to yon hill-tap,
Ye 'll there see bonie Peggy;
She kens her father is a laird,
And she forsooth 's a leddy.

There 's Sophy tight, a lassie bright
Besides a handsome fortune:
Wha canna win her in a night,
Has little art in courtin.

Gae down by Faile, and taste the ale,
And tak a look o' Mysie;
She 's dour and din, a deil within, obstinate—dun-coloured
But aiblins she may please ye. perhaps

If she be shy, her sister try,
Ye 'll maybe fancy Jenny;
If ye 'll dispense wi' want o' sense—
She kens hersel she 's bonie.

As ye gae up by yon hillside,
Speer in for bonie Bessy; call in
She 'll gie ye a beck, and bid ye light, courtesy
And handsomely address ye.

There 's few sae bonie, nane sae guid,
In a' King George' dominion;
If ye should doubt the truth o' this—
It 's Bessy's ain opinion!

THE RONALDS OF THE BENNALS.

In Tarbolton, ye ken, there are proper young men,
And proper young lasses and a', man;
But ken ye the Ronalds that live in the Bennals,
They carry the gree frae them a', man. palm

Their father 's a laird, and weel he can spare 't,
Braid money to tocher them a', man; marriage-portion
To proper young men, he 'll clink in the hand count
Gowd guineas a hunder or twa, man.

There 's ane they ca' Jean, I 'll warrant ye 've seen
As bonie a lass or as braw, man;
But for sense and guid taste she 'll vie wi' the best,
And a conduct that beautifies a', man.

The charms o' the min', the langer they shine, mind
The mair admiration they draw, man;
While peaches and cherries, and roses and lilies,
They fade and they wither awa, man.

If ye be for Miss Jean, tak this frae a frien',
A hint o' a rival or twa, man;
The Laird o' Blackbyre wad gang through the fire,
If that wad entice her awa, man.

The Laird o' Braehead has been on his speed,
For mair than a towmond or twa, man; twelvemonth
The Laird o' the Ford[1] will be straught on a board, be stretched in death
If he canna get her at a', man.

Then Anna comes in, the pride o' her kin,
The boast of our bachelors a', man:
Sae sonsy and sweet, sae fully complete, comely
She steals our affections awa, man.

If I should detail the pick and the wale choice
O' lasses that live hereawa, man,
The fau't wad be mine, if she didna shine
The sweetest and best o' them a', man.

I lo'e her mysel, but darena weel tell,
My poverty keeps me in awe, man;
For making o' rhymes, and working at times,
Does little or naething at a', man.

Yet I wadna choose to let her refuse,
Or hae 't in her power to say na, man:
For though I be poor, unnoticed, obscure,
My stomach 's as proud as them a', man.

Though I canna ride in weel-booted pride,
And flee o'er the hills like a craw, man,
I can haud up my head wi' the best o' the breed,
Though fluttering ever so braw, man. brave

[1] Possibly Failford, near Tarbolton.

My coat and my vest, they are Scotch o' the best,
O' pairs o' guid breeks I hae twa, man, breeches
And stockings and pumps to put on my stumps,
And ne'er a wrang steek in them a', man. stitch

My sarks they are few, but five o' them new, shirts
Twal' hundred,[1] as white as the snaw, man,
A ten shillings hat, a Holland cravat;
There are no mony poets sae braw, man.

I never had freens weel stockit in means,
To leave me a hundred or twa, man;
Nae weel-tocher'd aunts, to wait on their drants, well-dowered —long prayers
And wish them in hell for it a', man.

I never was cannie for hoarding o' money, prudent
Or claughtin 't together at a', man; grasping
I 've little to spend, and naething to lend,
But deevil a shilling I awe, man.

* * * *

AH, WOE IS ME, MY MOTHER DEAR.[2]

Paraphrase of Jeremiah, 15th chap., 10th verse.

Ah, woe is me, my Mother dear!
A man of strife ye 've born me;
For sair contention I maun bear;
They hate, revile, and scorn me.

I ne'er could lend on bill or band,
That five per cent. might bless me;
And borrowing, on the tither hand,
The deil a ane wad trust me.

Yet I, a coin-denièd wight,
By Fortune quite discarded;
Ye see how I am, day and night,
By lad and lass blackguarded!

[1] A kind of cloth, woven in a web of twelve hundred divisions.
[2] These verses are given in the Glenriddel MSS., preserved at Liverpool, without any indication as to the date of their composition. An imperfect copy of them was published in 1834 by James Hogg.

MONTGOMERIE'S PEGGY.[1]

Altho' my bed were in yon muir,
Amang the heather, in my plaidie;
Yet happy, happy would I be,
Had I my dear Montgomerie's Peggy.

When o'er the hill beat surly storms,
And winter nights were dark and rainy;
I'd seek some dell, and in my arms
I'd shelter dear Montgomerie's Peggy.

Were I a Baron proud and high,
And horse and servants waiting ready;
Then a' 'twad gie o' joy to me—
The shairin 't with Montgomerie's Peggy.

THE PLOUGHMAN'S LIFE.[2]

As I was a-wand'ring ae morning in spring,
I heard a young ploughman sae sweetly to sing;
And as he was singin', thir words he did say—
There 's nae life like the ploughman's in the month o' sweet May.

The lav'rock in the morning she 'll rise frae her nest,
And mount i' the air wi' the dew on her breast,
And wi' the merry ploughman she 'll whistle and sing,
And at night she 'll return to her nest back again.

THE LASS OF CESSNOCK BANKS.

TUNE—*If he be a Butcher, neat and trim.*

On Cessnock banks a lassie dwells;
Could I describe her shape and mien;
Our lasses a' she far excels,
An' she has twa sparkling rogueish een.

[1] According to Mrs Begg, 'Montgomerie's Peggy' was housekeeper at Coilsfield House, and Burns met her frequently. 'They sat in the same church, and contracted an intimacy together; but she was engaged to another before ever they met.' Burns himself speaks lightly of this intimacy: 'I began the affair merely in a *gaieté de cœur*, and to tell the truth (which would scarcely be believed), a vanity of showing my parts in courtship, particularly my abilities at a *billet-doux*, which I always piqued myself upon, made me lay siege to her.'

[2] This is one of the pieces which were published as Burns's in Cromek's *Reliques*. Gilbert was very doubtful of its genuineness.

She 's sweeter than the morning dawn,
  When rising Phœbus first is seen,
And dew-drops twinkle o'er the lawn;
  An' she has twa sparkling rogueish een.

She 's stately like yon youthful ash,
  That grows the cowslip braes between,
And drinks the stream with vigour fresh;
  An' she has twa sparkling rogueish een.

She 's spotless like the flow'ring thorn,
  With flow'rs so white and leaves so green,
When purest in the dewy morn;
  An' she has twa sparkling rogueish een.

Her looks are like the vernal May,
  When ev'ning Phœbus shines serene,
While birds rejoice on every spray;
  An' she has twa sparkling rogueish een.

Her hair is like the curling mist
  That climbs the mountain-sides at e'en,
When flow'r-reviving rains are past;
  An' she has twa sparkling rogueish een.

Her forehead 's like the show'ry bow,
  When gleaming sunbeams intervene
And gild the distant mountain's brow;
  An' she has twa sparkling rogueish een.

Her cheeks are like yon crimson gem,
  The pride of all the flowery scene,
Just opening on its thorny stem;
  An' she has twa sparkling rogueish een.

Her bosom 's like the nightly snow,
  When pale the morning rises keen;
While hid the murm'ring streamlets flow;
  An' she has twa sparkling rogueish een.

Her lips are like yon cherries ripe
  That sunny walls from Boreas screen—
They tempt the taste and charm the sight;
  An' she has twa sparkling rogueish een.

Her teeth are like a flock of sheep,
  With fleeces newly washen clean,
That slowly mount the rising steep;
  An' she has twa sparkling rogueish een.

Her breath is like the fragrant breeze
  That gently stirs the blossom'd bean,
When Phœbus sinks behind the seas;
  An' she has twa sparkling rogueish een.

Her voice is like the ev'ning thrush
  That sings on Cessnock banks unseen,
While his mate sits nestling in the bush;
  An' she has twa sparkling rogueish een.

But it 's not her air, her form, her face,
  Tho' matching beauty's fabled queen;
'Tis the mind that shines in ev'ry grace,
  An' chiefly in her rogueish een.

WINTER: A DIRGE.

The wintry west extends his blast,
  And hail and rain does blaw;
Or, the stormy north sends driving forth
  The blinding sleet and snaw:
While, tumbling brown, the burn comes down,
  And roars frae bank to brae;
And bird and beast in covert rest,
  And pass the heartless day.

'The sweeping blast, the sky o'ercast,'
  The joyless winter day
Let others fear, to me more dear
  Than all the pride of May:
The tempest's howl, it soothes my soul,
  My griefs it seems to join;
The leafless trees my fancy please,
  Their fate resembles mine!

Thou Power Supreme, whose mighty scheme
  These woes of mine fulfil,
Here, firm, I rest; they must be best,
  Because they are *Thy* will!

Then all I want (O do Thou grant
  This one request of mine!),
Since to *enjoy* Thou dost deny,
  Assist me to *resign*.

A PRAYER,

WRITTEN UNDER THE PRESSURE OF VIOLENT ANGUISH.

O Thou Great Being! what Thou art,
  Surpasses me to know;
Yet sure I am, that known to Thee
  Are all Thy works below.

Thy creature here before Thee stands,
  All wretched and distrest;
Yet sure those ills that wring my soul
  Obey Thy high behest.

Sure Thou, Almighty, canst not act
  From cruelty or wrath!
O, free my weary eyes from tears,
  Or close them fast in death!

But, if I must afflicted be,
  To suit some wise design;
Then man my soul with firm resolves,
  To bear and not repine!

MY FATHER WAS A FARMER.

TUNE—*The Weaver and his shuttle, O.*

My father was a farmer upon the Carrick border,
And carefully he bred me in decency and order;
He bade me act a manly part, though I had ne'er a farthing;
For without an honest manly heart, no man was worth regarding.

Then out into the world my course I did determine;
Tho' to be rich was not my wish, yet to be great was charming:
My talents they were not the worst, nor yet my education;
Resolv'd was I, at least to try, to mend my situation.

In many a way, and vain essay, I courted Fortune's favour;
Some cause unseen still stept between, to frustrate each endeavour;
Sometimes by foes I was o'erpower'd, sometimes by friends forsaken;
And when my hope was at the top, I still was worst mistaken.

Then sore harass'd, and tir'd at last, with Fortune's vain delusion,
I dropt my schemes, like idle dreams, and came to this conclusion—
The past was bad, and the future hid—its good or ill untrièd;
But the present hour was in my pow'r, and so I would enjoy it.

No help, nor hope, nor view had I, nor person to befriend me;
So I must toil, and sweat, and moil, and labour to sustain me;
To plough and sow, to reap and mow, my father bred me early;
For one, he said, to labour bred, was a match for fortune fairly.

Thus all obscure, unknown, and poor, thro' life I'm doom'd to wander,
Till down my weary bones I lay in everlasting slumber;
No view nor care, but shun whate'er might breed me pain or sorrow;
I live to-day as well 's I may, regardless of to-morrow.

But cheerful still, I am as well as a monarch in his palace,
Though Fortune's frown still hunts me down, with all her wonted malice:
I make indeed my daily bread, but ne'er can make it farther:
But as daily bread is all I need, I do not much regard her.

When sometimes by my labour I earn a little money,
Some unforeseen misfortune comes gen'rally upon me;
Mischance, mistake, or by neglect, or my good-natur'd folly:
But come what will, I 've sworn it still, I 'll ne'er be melancholy.

All you who follow wealth and power with unremitting ardour,
The more in this you look for bliss, you leave your view the farther:
Had you the wealth Potosi boasts, or nations to adore you,
A cheerful honest-hearted clown I will prefer before you.

THE DEATH AND DYING WORDS OF POOR MAILIE, THE AUTHOR'S ONLY PET YOWE:

AN UNCO MOURNFU' TALE.

As Mailie an' her lambs thegither,
Were ae day nibblin on the tether,
Upon her cloot she coost a hitch, hoof—cast—loop
An' owre she warsl'd in the ditch: struggled
There groanin, dying, she did lie,
When Hughoc[1] he cam doytin by. walking stupidly

Wi' glowrin een, and lifted han's, staring
Poor Hughoc like a statue stan's;
He saw her days were near-hand ended,
But, waes my heart! he could na mend it!
He gapèd wide, but naething spak—
At length poor Mailie silence brak.

'O thou, whase lamentable face
Appears to mourn my woefu' case!
My dying words attentive hear,
An' bear them to my master dear.

'Tell him, if e'er again he keep
As muckle gear as buy a sheep— money
O, bid him never tie them mair
Wi' wicked strings o' hemp or hair!
But ca' them out to park or hill, drive
An' let them wander at their will:
So may his flock increase, an' grow
To scores o' lambs, and packs o' woo'!

'Tell him, he was a master kin',
An' ay was guid to me an' mine;
An' now my dying charge I gie him—
My helpless lambs, I trust them wi' him.

[1] A neighbour herd-callan.—*B.* In another copy of the poem in the poet's handwriting, a more descriptive note is here given: 'Hughoc was an odd, glowran, gapin' callan, about three-fourths as wise as other folk.'

'O, bid him save their harmless lives
Frae dogs, an' tods, an' butchers' knives! — foxes
But gie them guid cow-milk their fill,
Till they be fit to fend themsel; — provide for
An' tent them duly, e'en an' morn, — care for
Wi' teats o' hay an' ripps o' corn. — handfuls

'An' may they never learn the gaets — ways
Of ither vile, wanrestfu' pets— — restless
To slink thro' slaps, an' reave an' steal — gaps in a fence—tear
At stacks o' pease, or stocks o' kail!
So may they, like their great forbears, — ancestors
For monie a year come thro' the shears:
So wives will gie them bits o' bread,
An' bairns greet for them when they 're dead.

'My poor toop-lamb, my son an' heir, — ram
O, bid him breed him up wi' care;
An' if he live to be a beast,
To pit some havins in his breast! — good manners

'An' warn him—what I winna name,
To stay content wi' yowes at hame; — ewes
An' no to rin an' wear his cloots,
Like ither menseless, graceless brutes. — senseless

'An' neist, my yowie, silly thing, — next—little ewe
Gude keep thee frae a tether string!
O, may thou ne'er forgather up — encounter
Wi' ony blastit, moorland toop;
But ay keep mind to moop an' mell, — nibble—associate
Wi' sheep o' credit like thysel!

'And now, my bairns, wi' my last breath
I lea'e my blessin wi' you baith:
An' when you think upo' your mither,
Mind to be kind to ane anither.

'Now, honest Hughoc, dinna fail
To tell my master a' my tale;
An' bid him burn this cursèd tether,
An', for thy pains, thou'se get my blather.' — bladder

This said, poor Mailie turn'd her head,
An' clos'd her een amang the dead!

POOR MAILIE'S ELEGY.[1]

Lament in rhyme, lament in prose,
Wi' saut tears tricklin down your nose;
Our bardie's fate is at a close,
Past a' remead; remedy
The last sad cape-stane o' his woe 's
Poor Mailie 's dead!

It 's no the loss o' warl's gear,
That could sae bitter draw the tear,
Or mak our bardie, dowie, wear borne down by grief
The mournin weed:
He 's lost a friend an' neebor dear,
In Mailie dead.

Thro' a' the town she trotted by him;
A lang half-mile she could descry him;
Wi' kindly bleat, when she did spy him,
She ran wi' speed:
A friend mair faithfu' ne'er cam nigh him,
Than Mailie dead.

I wat she was a sheep o' sense,
An' could behave hersel wi' mense: good manners
I 'll say 't, she never brak a fence,
Thro' thievish greed.
Our bardie, lanely, keeps the spence inner room
Sin' Mailie 's dead.

Or, if he wanders up the howe, valley
Her livin image in her yowe
Comes bleatin till him, owre the knowe, knoll
For bits o' bread;
An' down the briny pearls rowe roll
For Mailie dead.

[1] It has been pointed out by Mr J. Logie Robertson that Burns's model for this elegy is the 'Epitaph of Habbie Simpson, the Piper of Kilbarchan,' by Robert Sempill, who introduced the stanza in which it is written, and which was a favourite with Ramsay and Fergusson.

She was nae get o' moorlan tips, offspring—rams
Wi' tauted ket, an' hairy hips; matted fleece
For her forbears were brought in ships ancestors
Frae yont the Tweed:
A bonier fleesh ne'er cross'd the clips fleece
Than Mailie's—dead.[1]

Wae worth that man wha first did shape
That vile, wanchancie thing—a raep! ill-omened
It maks guid fellows girn an' gape, make faces
Wi' chokin dread;
An' Robin's bonnet wave wi' crape
For Mailie dead.

O, a' ye bards on bonie Doon!
An' wha on Ayr your chanters tune!
Come, join the melancholious croon dirge
O' Robin's reed!
His heart will never get aboon—
His Mailie 's dead!

JOHN BARLEYCORN—A BALLAD.[2]

There was three kings into the east,
Three kings both great and high,
And they hae sworn a solemn oath
John Barleycorn should die.

They took a plough and plough'd him down,
Put clods upon his head,
And they hae sworn a solemn oath
John Barleycorn was dead.

[1] When preparing the Elegy for the press, Burns substituted this verse for the following, which is interesting for its allusion to Fairlie, where his father had been gardener:

She was nae get o' runted rams,
Wi' woo like goats, and legs like trams:
She was the flower o' Fairlie lambs,
A famous breed;
Now Robin, greetin', chows the hams,
O' Mailie dead.

[2] This is an improvement upon an early song of probably English origin, of which Robert Jameson, in his *Ballads* (2 vols., 8vo, 1808), has given a copy which he obtained from a black-letter sheet in the Pepys Library, Cambridge.

But the cheerful Spring came kindly on,
And show'rs began to fall;
John Barleycorn got up again,
And sore surpris'd them all.

The sultry suns of Summer came,
And he grew thick and strong;
His head weel arm'd wi' pointed spears,
That no one should him wrong.

The sober Autumn enter'd mild,
When he grew wan and pale;
His bending joints and drooping head
Show'd he began to fail.

His colour sicken'd more and more,
He faded into age;
And then his enemies began
To show their deadly rage.

They 've taen a weapon, long and sharp,
And cut him by the knee;
Then ty'd him fast upon a cart,
Like a rogue for forgerie.

They laid him down upon his back,
And cudgell'd him full sore;
They hung him up before the storm,
And turn'd him o'er and o'er.

They fillèd up a darksome pit
With water to the brim,
They heavèd in John Barleycorn—
There let him sink or swim.

They laid him out upon the floor,
To work him further woe;
And still, as signs of life appear'd,
They toss'd him to and fro.

They wasted, o'er a scorching flame,
The marrow of his bones;
But a miller us'd him worst of all,
For he crush'd him 'tween two stones.

And they hae taen his very heart's blood,
And drank it round and round;
And still the more and more they drank,
Their joy did more abound.

John Barleycorn was a hero bold,
Of noble enterprise;
For if you do but taste his blood,
'Twill make your courage rise.

'Twill make a man forget his woe;
'Twill heighten all his joy:
'Twill make the widow's heart to sing,
Tho' the tear were in her eye.

Then let us toast John Barleycorn,
Each man a glass in hand;
And may his great posterity
Ne'er fail in old Scotland!

MARY MORISON.[1]

O, Mary, at thy window be,
It is the wish'd, the trysted hour!
Those smiles and glances let me see,
That make the miser's treasure poor:
How blythely wad I bide the stoure,
A weary slave frae sun to sun,
Could I the rich reward secure,
The lovely Mary Morison.

Yestreen, when to the trembling string
The dance gaed thro' the lighted ha',
To thee my fancy took its wing,
I sat, but neither heard nor saw:

[1] 'Of all the productions of Burns, the pathetic and serious love-songs which he has left behind him in the manner of old ballads are perhaps those which take the deepest and most lasting hold of the mind. Such are the lines to Mary Morison, &c.'—HAZLITT.

C. Martin Hardie, R.S.A.

Yestreen, when to the trembling string
The dance gaed through the lighted ha'.

PAGE 18.

Tho' this was fair, and that was braw,
And yon the toast of a' the town,
I sigh'd, and said amang them a',
'Ye are na Mary Morison.'

O Mary, canst thou wreck his peace,
Wha for thy sake wad gladly die?
Or canst thou break that heart of his,
Whase only faut is loving thee?
If love for love thou wilt na gie,
At least be pity to me shown;
A thought ungentle canna be
The thought o' Mary Morison.

SONG—BONIE PEGGY ALISON.

TUNE—*The Braes o' Balquidder.*

Chorus.—And I 'll kiss thee yet, yet,
And I 'll kiss thee o'er again;
And I 'll kiss thee yet, yet,
My bonie Peggy Alison.

Ilk care and fear, when thou art near,
I ever mair defy them, O!
Young kings upon their hansel[1] throne
Are no sae blest as I am, O!
And I 'll kiss thee yet, yet, &c.

When in my arms, wi' a' thy charms,
I clasp my countless treasure, O!
I seek nae mair o' Heav'n to share
Than sic a moment's pleasure, O!
And I 'll kiss thee yet, yet, &c.

And by thy een sae bonie blue,
I swear I 'm thine for ever, O!
And on thy lips I seal my vow,
And break it shall I never, O!
And I 'll kiss thee yet, yet, &c.

1 'Hansel' means first-fruit of an achievement or a season. 'Hansel throne' may be interpreted as 'maiden throne.'

THE RIGS O' BARLEY.

TUNE—*Corn Rigs.*

Chorus.—Corn rigs, an' barley rigs,
An' corn rigs are bonie :
I 'll ne'er forget that happy night,
Amang the rigs wi' Annie.

It was upon a Lammas night,
When corn rigs are bonie,
Beneath the moon's unclouded light,
I held awa to Annie ;
The time flew by, wi' tentless heed,[1]
Till 'tween the late and early,
Wi' sma' persuasion she agreed
To see me thro' the barley.

The sky was blue, the wind was still,
The moon was shining clearly ;
I set her down, wi' right good will,
Amang the rigs o' barley :
I ken't her heart was a' my ain ;
I lov'd her most sincerely ;
I kiss'd her owre and owre again,
Amang the rigs o' barley.

I lock'd her in my fond embrace ;
Her heart was beating rarely :
My blessings on that happy place,
Amang the rigs o' barley !
But by the moon and stars so bright,
That shone that hour so clearly !
She ay shall bless that happy night
Amang the rigs o' barley.

I hae been blythe wi' comrades dear ;
I hae been merry drinking ;
I hae been joyfu' gath'rin gear ;
I hae been happy thinking :

[1] Many years ago, 'Caleb,' writing in the *Glasgow Citizen*, pointed out that 'tentless heed' is a contradiction in terms, 'tentless' being 'heedless ;' and suggested 'tentless speed.' In the Kilmarnock edition, however, the words stand 'tentless head,' so that 'heed' (the spelling in the 1794 edition) might be a misprint for 'heid.'

But a' the pleasures e'er I saw,
 Tho' three times doubl'd fairly—
That happy night was worth them a'
 Amang the rigs o' barley.

SONG 'COMPOSED IN AUGUST.'

TUNE—*I had a Horse, I had nae mair.*

Now westlin winds and slaught'ring guns
 Bring Autumn's pleasant weather;
The moorcock springs on whirring wings,
 Amang the blooming heather:
Now waving grain, wide o'er the plain,
 Delights the weary farmer;
And the moon shines bright, when I rove at night,
 To muse upon my charmer.

The partridge loves the fruitful fells;
 The plover loves the mountains;
The woodcock haunts the lonely dells;
 The soaring hern the fountains: heron
Thro' lofty groves the cushat roves, wood-pigeon
 The path of man to shun it;
The hazel-bush o'erhangs the thrush,
 The spreading thorn the linnet.

Thus ev'ry kind their pleasure find,
 The savage and the tender;
Some social join, and leagues combine,
 Some solitary wander:
Avaunt, away, the cruel sway!
 Tyrannic man's dominion;
The sportsman's joy, the murd'ring cry,
 The flutt'ring, gory pinion!

But, Peggy dear, the ev'ning's clear,
 Thick flies the skimming swallow;
The sky is blue, the fields in view,
 All fading-green and yellow:
Come let us stray our gladsome way,
 And view the charms of Nature;
The rustling corn, the fruited thorn,
 And ev'ry happy creature.

We 'll gently walk, and sweetly talk,
Till the silent moon shine clearly;
I 'll grasp thy waist, and, fondly prest,
Swear how I love thee dearly:
Not vernal show'rs to budding flow'rs,
Not Autumn to the farmer,
So dear can be as thou to me,
My fair, my lovely charmer![1]

MY NANIE, O.

TUNE—*My Nanie, O.*

Behind yon hills where Stinchar flows,[2]
'Mang moors an' mosses many, O,
The wintry sun the day has clos'd,
And I 'll awa to Nanie, O.

The westlin wind blaws loud an' shill; shrill
The night 's baith mirk and rainy, O;
But I'll get my plaid, an' out I'll steal,
An' owre the hill to Nanie, O.

My Nanie 's charming, sweet, an' young;
Nae artfu' wiles to win ye, O:
May ill befa' the flattering tongue
That wad beguile my Nanie, O.

Her face is fair, her heart is true;
As spotless as she 's bonie, O;
The op'ning gowan, wat wi' dew, daisy
Nae purer is than Nanie, O.

[1] Mrs Begg remembered, about the time of her brother's attachment to Jean Armour, seeing this song, freshly written out, amongst his papers, with the name 'Jeanie' instead of 'Peggy,' and the word 'Armour' instead of 'charmer,' at the end of the first and fifth verses. She therefore suspected that the poet had, through inadvertency, made a mistake in assigning this song to Margaret Thomson. Possibly he may have written the song for Peggy, and only temporarily dethroned her for the sake of a newer love.

[2] Burns subsequently sanctioned the substitution for the 'horribly prosaic' Stinchar, which has local verity in its favour, of the Lugar, a tributary of the Ayr, a name thought to be more euphonious, but which is otherwise unsuitable; yet 'Stinchar' appears in the edition of 1794.

A country lad is my degree,
  An' few there be that ken me, O;
But what care I how few they be?
  I 'm welcome ay to Nanie, O.

My riches a' 's my penny-fee, wages
  An' I maun guide it, cannie, O;
But warl's gear ne'er troubles me, world's wealth
  My thoughts are a'—my Nanie, O.

Our auld guidman delights to view
  His sheep an' kye thrive bonie, O;
But I 'm as blythe that hauds his pleugh,
  An' has nae care but Nanie, O.

Come weel, come woe, I care na by;
  I 'll tak what Heav'n will sen' me, O;
Nae ither care in life have I,
  But live, an' love my Nanie, O.

A PRAYER IN THE PROSPECT OF DEATH.

O Thou unknown, Almighty Cause
  Of all my hope and fear!
In whose dread presence, ere an hour,
  Perhaps I must appear!

If I have wander'd in those paths
  Of life I ought to shun—
As something, loudly, in my breast,
  Remonstrates I have done—

Thou know'st that Thou hast formèd me
  With passions wild and strong;
And list'ning to their witching voice
  Has often led me wrong.

Where human weakness has come short,
  Or frailty stept aside,
Do Thou, All-Good—for such Thou art—
  In shades of darkness hide.

Where with intention I have err'd,
No other plea I have,
But, Thou art good; and Goodness still
Delighteth to forgive.

STANZAS, ON THE SAME OCCASION.

Why am I loth to leave this earthly scene?
Have I so found it full of pleasing charms—
Some drops of joy with draughts of ill between—
Some gleams of sunshine 'mid renewing storms?
Is it departing pangs my soul alarms?
Or death's unlovely, dreary, dark abode?
For guilt, for guilt, my terrors are in arms:
I tremble to approach an angry God,
And justly smart beneath His sin-avenging rod.

Fain would I say, 'Forgive my foul offence!'
Fain promise never more to disobey;
But, should my Author health again dispense,
Again I might desert fair virtue's way;
Again in folly's path might go astray;
Again exalt the brute and sink the man;
Then how should I for heavenly mercy pray,
Who act so counter heavenly mercy's plan?
Who sin so oft have mourn'd, yet to temptation ran?

O Thou great Governor of all below!
If I may dare a lifted eye to Thee,
Thy nod can make the tempest cease to blow,
Or still the tumult of the raging sea:
With that controlling pow'r assist ev'n me,
Those headlong furious passions to confine,
For all unfit I feel my pow'rs to be,
To rule their torrent in th' allowèd line;
O, aid me with Thy help, Omnipotence Divine![1]

[1] Another MS. of this poem contains some variations expressive of deeper contrition than what here appears. After 'Again I might desert fair virtue's way,' comes 'Again by passions would be led astray.' The second line of the last stanza is, 'If one so black with crimes dare call on Thee.'

PARAPHRASE OF THE FIRST PSALM.

The man, in life wherever plac'd,
  Hath happiness in store,
Who walks not in the wicked's way,
  Nor learns their guilty lore!

Nor from the seat of scornful pride
  Casts forth his eyes abroad,
But with humility and awe
  Still walks before his God.

That man shall flourish like the trees,
  Which by the streamlets grow;
The fruitful top is spread on high,
  And firm the root below.

But he whose blossom buds in guilt
  Shall to the ground be cast,
And, like the rootless stubble, tost
  Before the sweeping blast.

For why? that God the good adore,
  Hath giv'n them peace and rest,
But hath decreed that wicked men
  Shall ne'er be truly blest.

THE FIRST SIX VERSES OF THE NINETIETH PSALM VERSIFIED.

O Thou, the first, the greatest friend
  Of all the human race!
Whose strong right hand has ever been
  Their stay and dwelling place!

Before the mountains heav'd their heads
  Beneath Thy forming hand,
Before this ponderous globe itself
  Arose at Thy command;

That Pow'r which rais'd and still upholds
 This universal frame,
From countless, unbeginning time
 Was ever still the same.

Those mighty periods of years
 Which seem to us so vast,
Appear no more before Thy sight
 Than yesterday that 's past.

Thou giv'st the word: Thy creature, man,
 Is to existence brought;
Again Thou say'st, 'Ye sons of men,
 Return ye into nought!'

Thou layest them, with all their cares,
 In everlasting sleep;
As with a flood Thou tak'st them off
 With overwhelming sweep.

They flourish like the morning flow'r,
 In beauty's pride array'd;
But long ere night—cut down, it lies
 All wither'd and decay'd.

EPISTLE TO JOHN RANKINE.

O rough, rude, ready-witted Rankine,
The wale o' cocks for fun an' drinking! — choice
There 's mony godly folks are thinking
 Your dreams and tricks
Will send you Korah-like a-sinkin,
 Straught to auld Nick's.

Ye hae sae mony cracks an' cants, — jokes in conversation—tricks
And in your wicked, drucken rants — frolics
Ye mak a devil o' the saunts, — saints
 An' fill them fou; — drunk
And then their failings, flaws, an' wants
 Are a' seen thro'.

Hypocrisy, in mercy spare it!
That holy robe, O dinna tear it!
Spare 't for their sakes, wha aften wear it—
The lads in black;
But your curst wit, when it comes near it,
Rives 't aff their back. Tears

Think, wicked Sinner, wha ye 're skaithing: harming
It 's just the 'Blue-gown' badge an' claithing [1]
O' saunts; tak that, ye lea'e them naithing
To ken them by,
Frae ony unregenerate heathen
Like you or I.

I 've sent you here some rhymin ware,
A' that I bargain'd for, an' mair;
Sae, when ye hae an hour to spare,
I will expect
Yon sang [2] ye 'll sen 't, wi' cannie care, anxious
And no neglect.

Tho' faith, sma' heart hae I to sing!
My muse dow scarcely spread her wing; can
I 've play'd mysel a bonie spring,
An' danc'd my fill!
I 'd better gaen an' sair't the king served
At Bunker's Hill.

'Twas ae night lately, in my fun,
I gaed a rovin wi' the gun,
An' brought a paitrick to the grun'— partridge
A bonie hen;
And, as the twilight was begun,
Thought nane wad ken.

The poor, wee thing was little hurt;
I straiket it a wee for sport,

[1] Alluding to a blue uniform and badge worn by a select number of privileged beggars in Scotland, usually called King's Bedesmen. Edie Ochiltree, in *The Antiquary*, is an example of the corps. See note 3, p. 35.

[2] A song he had promised the author.—*B.*

Ne'er thinkin they wad fash me for 't; trouble
But, Deil-ma-care!
Somebody tells the poacher-court
The hale affair.

Some auld, us'd hands had taen a note
That sic a hen had got a shot;
I was suspected for the plot;
I scorn'd to lie;
So gat the whissle o' my groat,
An' pay't the fee.

But, by my gun, o' guns the wale, choice
An' by my pouther an' my hail,
An' by my hen, an' by her tail,
I vow an' swear!
The game shall pay, owre moor an' dale,
For this, niest year.

As soon 's the clockin-time is by,
An' the wee pouts begun to cry,
L—d, I 'se hae sportin by an' by,
For my gowd guinea;
Tho' I should herd the buckskin[1] kye
For 't, in Virginia!

Trowth, they had muckle for to blame! In truth
'Twas neither broken wing nor limb,
But twa-three draps about the wame,
Scarce thro' the feathers;
An' baith a 'yellow George' to claim guinea
An' thole their blethers! stand their abuse

It pits me ay as mad 's a hare;
So I can rhyme nor write nae mair;
But pennyworths again is fair,
When time 's expedient:
Meanwhile I am, respected Sir,
Your most obedient.

[1] 'Buckskin' was the nickname given by the Royalists to the American troops in the War of Independence. It has been suggested that 'buckskin kye' really means negroes, and this view finds some support in the fact that Burns subsequently contemplated the possibility of his being 'a poor negro-driver.'

A POET'S WELCOME TO HIS LOVE-BEGOTTEN DAUGHTER.[1]

THE FIRST INSTANCE THAT ENTITLED HIM TO THE VENERABLE APPELLATION OF FATHER.

Thou 's welcome, wean ; mishanter fa' me, child—mishap
If thoughts o' thee, or yet thy mamie,
Shall ever daunton me or awe me, discourage
My bonie lady,
Or if I blush when thou shalt ca' me
Tyta or daddie.

Tho' now they ca' me fornicator,
An' tease my name in kintry clatter, talk throughout the district
The mair they talk, I 'm kent the better,
E'en let them clash ; gossip
An auld wife's tongue 's a feckless matter trifling
To gie ane fash. annoyance

Welcome ! my bonie, sweet, wee dochter,
Tho' ye come here a wee unsought for,
And tho' your comin' I hae fought for,
Baith kirk and queir ;
Yet, by my faith, ye 're no unwrought for—
That I shall swear !

Wee image o' my bonie Betty,
As fatherly I kiss and daut thee, fondle
As dear, and near my heart I set thee,
Wi' as guid will
As a' the priests had seen me get thee
That 's out o' h—ll.

Sweet fruit o' mony a merry dint,
My funny toil is no' a' tint, lost
Sin' thou cam to the warl' asklent, irregularly
Which fools may scoff at ;
In my last plack thy part 's be in 't— the smallest of coins
The better ha'f o' 't. half of it

[1] Burns wrote several versions of this poem, which was first published about the end of last century. In transcribing it in the Glenriddel volume, he omitted the stanza which now stands seventh.

Tho' I should be the waur bestead,
Thou 's be as braw and bienly clad, warmly
And thy young years as nicely bred
Wi' education,
As ony brat o' wedlock's bed, child
In a' thy station.

Lord grant that thou may ay inherit
Thy mither's person, grace, an' merit,
An' thy poor, worthless daddie's spirit,
Without his failins,
'Twill please me mair to see thee heir it,
Than stocket mailens. farms

For if thou be what I wad hae thee,
And tak the counsel I shall gie thee,
I'll never rue my trouble wi' thee—
The cost nor shame o' 't,
But be a loving father to thee,
And brag the name o' 't.

GREEN GROW THE RASHES.[1]

TUNE—*Green grow the Rashes.*

There 's nought but care on ev'ry han',
In every hour that passes, O:
What signifies the life o' man,
An' 'twere na for the lasses, O?

Chorus.—Green grow the rashes, O; rushes
Green grow the rashes, O;
The sweetest hours that e'er I spend,
Are spent among the lasses, O.

The war'ly race may riches chase, worldly
An' riches still may fly them, O;
An' tho' at last they catch them fast,
Their hearts can ne'er enjoy them, O.

[1] This poem may have been composed at Lochlea. The last verse did not appear in the early manuscript copies.

But gie me a cannie hour at e'en, happy
My arms about my dearie, O;
An' war'ly cares, an' war'ly men,
May a' gae tapsalteerie, O! topsy-turvy

For you sae douce, ye sneer at this; grave
Ye 're nought but senseless asses, O:
The wisest man the warl' e'er saw,
He dearly lov'd the lasses, O.

Auld Nature swears, the lovely dears
Her noblest work she classes, O:
Her prentice han' she try'd on man,
An' then she made the lasses, O.[1]

SONG—NO CHURCHMAN AM I.[2]

TUNE—*Prepare, my dear Brethren, to the Tavern let's fly.*

No churchman am I for to rail and to write,
No statesman nor soldier to plot or to fight,
No sly man of business contriving a snare,
For a big-belly'd bottle 's the whole of my care.

The peer I don't envy, I give him his bow;
I scorn not the peasant, tho' ever so low;
But a club of good fellows, like those that are here,
And a bottle like this, are my glory and care.

[1] In this song Burns made an improvement upon an old ditty that was sung to the same air. It has been pointed out that the last admirable verse is formed upon a conceit, which was in print long before the days of Burns, in a comedy entitled *Cupid's Whirligig*, published in 1607. The passage in the comedy is an apostrophe to the female sex, as follows:

'Oh woman ——
—— since we
Were made before ye, should we not love and
Admire ye as the last, and therefore perfect'st work
Of Nature? Man was made when Nature was
But an apprentice, but woman when she
Was a skilful mistress of her art.'

It might be presumed that Burns had no chance of seeing this old play; but it appears that the passage was transcribed in a book which was not very scarce in his time—namely, *The British Muse: a Collection of Thoughts*, by Thomas Hayward, Gent. 4 vols. London, 1738.

[2] It has been conjectured that this song was written by Burns in Irvine. This is possible, as he was admitted an apprentice Mason in July 1781. But the date of its composition is immaterial.

Here passes the squire on his brother—his horse;
There centum per centum, the cit with his purse;
But see you the *Crown* how it waves in the air?
There a big-belly'd bottle still eases my care.

The wife of my bosom, alas! she did die;
For sweet consolation to church I did fly;
I found that old Solomon provèd it fair,
That a big-belly'd bottle 's a cure for all care.

I once was persuaded a venture to make;
A letter inform'd me that all was to wreck;
But the pursy old landlord just waddi'd up stairs,
With a glorious bottle that ended my cares.

'Life's cares they are comforts'[1]—a maxim laid down
By the Bard, what d' ye call him? that wore the black gown;
And faith I agree with th' old prig to a hair;
For a big belly'd bottle 's a heav'n of a care.'[2]

A STANZA ADDED IN A MASON LODGE.

Then fill up a bumper and make it o'erflow,
And honours masonic prepare for to throw;
May every true Brother of the Compass and Square
Have a big-belly'd bottle when harass'd with care.

RANTIN, ROVIN ROBIN.

TUNE—*Dainty Davie.*

There was a lad was born in Kyle,
But whatna day o' whatna style, what
I doubt it 's hardly worth the while
To be sae nice wi' Robin.

Chorus.—Robin was a rovin boy,
Rantin, rovin, rantin, rovin, Reckless or frolicsome
Robin was a rovin boy,
Rantin, rovin Robin!

[1] Young's *Night Thoughts.*
[2] It has been suggested that 'heav'n' is a misprint for 'hav'n,' and that the bottle should be regarded as a port to flee to when troubled. On the other hand, 'heav'n' may be interpreted like 'glory and care,' as a 'dear affliction.'

Our monarch's[1] hindmost year but ane
Was five-and-twenty days begun,
'Twas then a blast o' Janwar' win'
  Blew hansel[2] in on Robin.

The gossip keekit in his loof, — peeped—palm
Quo' scho, 'Wha lives will see the proof, — she
This waly boy will be nae coof: — goodly—fool
  I think we 'll ca' him Robin.'

'He 'll hae misfortunes great an' sma',
But ay a heart aboon them a', — above
He 'll be a credit till us a',—
  We 'll a' be proud o' Robin.'

'But sure as three times three mak nine,
I see by ilka score and line,
This chap will dearly like our kin',
  So leeze me on thee, Robin!'[3] — blessings

ELEGY ON THE DEATH OF ROBERT RUISSEAUX.[4]

Now Robin lies in his last lair,
He 'll gabble rhyme, nor sing nae mair;
Cauld poverty, wi' hungry stare,
    Nae mair shall fear him;
Nor anxious fear, nor cankert care,
    E'er mair come near him.

To tell the truth, they seldom fash'd him, — troubled
Except the moment that they crush'd him;
For sune as chance or fate had hush'd 'em,
    Tho' e'er sae short,
Then wi' a rhyme or sang he lash'd 'em,
    And thought it sport.

Tho' he was bred to kintra-wark, — country-work
And counted was baith wight and stark, — reckoned—vigorous—strong

[1] George II. died in 1760, the year after that of the poet's birth.

[2] A gift for a particular season, or the first money received on a special occasion.

[3] It has been said, but upon no good authority, that there was some foundation in fact for this tale of a gossip—a female tramp, who chanced to be present at the poet's birth—having actually uttered some such prophecies respecting the infant placed in her arms. Similar circumstances attended the birth of Mirabeau.

[4] *Ruisseaux*, Fr. for 'rivulets,' a punning translation of his own name.

Yet that was never Robin's mark
To mak a man;
But tell him, he was learn'd and clark, fit to be considered a scholar
Ye roos'd him then! praised

THE BELLES OF MAUCHLINE.

In Mauchline there dwells six proper young belles,
The pride of the place and its neighbourhood a';
Their carriage and dress, a stranger would guess
In London or Paris they'd gotten it a'.
Miss Miller is fine, Miss Markland's divine,
Miss Smith she has wit, and Miss Betty is braw:
There's beauty and fortune to get wi' Miss Morton,
But Armour's the jewel for me o' them a'.[1]

EPISTLE TO DAVIE,

A BROTHER POET.

While winds frae off Ben-Lomond blaw,[2]
An' bar the doors wi' drivin' snaw,
An' hing us owre the ingle, make us sit close to the fireside
I set me down to pass the time,
An' spin a verse or twa o' rhyme,
In hamely, westlin jingle:

[1] The history of the six belles of Mauchline is as follows: Helen Miller, the first mentioned, daughter of John Miller, of the Sun Inn, Mauchline, married Burns's friend, Dr Mackenzie. Their son, John Whitefoord Mackenzie, a well-known literary and antiquarian collector, died in Edinburgh in the year 1884. Jean Markland was the daughter of George Markland, a Mauchline merchant, and was in 1779, along with her father and mother, charged before the kirk-session with attributing witchcraft to the wife of another local merchant; but the charge broke down. She married, in September 1788, James Findlay, the excise officer in Tarbolton, who was commissioned to instruct Burns in the arts of gauging and excise book-keeping, and who was introduced to her by the poet. Findlay removed to Greenock in 1792, and his wife died there in 1851 at the age of eighty-six. The 'witty' Jean Smith married another friend of Burns, Mr James Candlish, an Edinburgh lecturer on medicine. A tablet erected to her memory in Old Calton Churchyard, Edinburgh, by her son, the Rev. Dr Candlish, the Free Church theologian and ecclesiastical leader, records that she died on 24th January 1854, aged eighty-six. The 'braw' Betty Miller, sister of Helen Miller, became the wife of William Templeton, a merchant in Mauchline. She was born in 1768, married on 8th September 1794, and died at the birth of her first child. To her was addressed Burns's song, 'From thee, Eliza, I must go.' Christina Morton, a native of the parish, with which for several generations her family had been connected, married, on 27th December 1788, Robert Paterson, draper and general merchant, Mauchline, and had four sons and two daughters. Of 'Armour's' history immortality has taken charge.

[2] That is, from the north.

While frosty winds blaw in the drift,
  Ben to the chimla lug,[1]
I grudge a wee the great-folk's gift, — little
  That live sae bien an' snug: — comfortably
    I tent less, and want less — care for
      Their roomy fire-side;
    But hanker, and canker,
      To see their cursed pride.

It's hardly in a body's pow'r,
To keep, at times, frae being sour,
  To see how things are shar'd;
How best o' chiels are whyles in want, — men—sometimes
While coofs on countless thousands rant, — fools—live recklessly
  And ken na how to ware 't; — know—spend
But Davie, lad, ne'er fash your head, — trouble
  Tho' we hae little gear; — wealth
We're fit to win our daily bread,
  As lang's we're hale and fier: — vigorous
    'Mair spier na, nor fear na,'[2] — ask
      Auld age ne'er mind a feg; — fig
    The last o''t, the warst o''t,
      Is only but to beg.[3]

[1] An expressive Scotticism meaning 'in to the very fireside.'

[2] Ramsay.

[3] 'The old-remembered beggar, even in my own time, like the baccoch or travelling cripple of Ireland, was expected to merit his quarters by something beyond an exposition of his distresses. He was often a talkative, facetious fellow, prompt at repartee, and not withheld from exercising his power that way by any respect of persons, his patched cloak giving him the privilege of the ancient jester. To be a *guid crack*—that is, to possess talents for conversation—was essential to the trade of a 'puir body' of the more esteemed class; and Burns, who delighted in the amusement their discourses afforded, seems to have looked forward with gloomy firmness to the possibility of himself becoming, one day or other, a member of their itinerant society. In his poetical works, it is alluded to so often as perhaps to indicate that he considered the consummation as not utterly impossible. Thus, in the fine dedication of his works to Gavin Hamilton, he says:

> "And when I downa yoke a naig,
> Then, Lord be thankit, I can beg."

Again, in his "Epistle to Davie, a brother poet," he states that, in their closing career,

> "The last o''t, the warst o''t,
> Is only but to beg."

And after having remarked, that

> "To lie in kilns and barns at e'en,
> When banes are craz'd, and bluid is thin,
> Is doubtless great distress,"

the bard reckons up, with true poetical spirit, that free enjoyment of the beauties of nature which might counterbalance the hardship and uncertainty of the life even of a mendicant. In one of his prose letters, to which I have lost the refer-

To lye in kilns and barns at e'en,
When banes are craz'd, and bluid is thin,
  Is, doubtless, great distress!
Yet then content could make us blest;
Ev'n then, sometimes, we 'd snatch a taste
  Of truest happiness.
The honest heart that 's free frae a'
  Intended fraud or guile,
However Fortune kick the ba', **ball**
  Has ay some cause to smile;
    An' mind still, you 'll find still,
      A comfort this nae sma'; **small**
    Nae mair then, we 'll care then,
      Nae farther we can fa'. **fall**

What tho', like commoners of air,
We wander out, we know not where,
  But either house or hal', **without—shelter**
Yet nature's charms, the hills and woods,
The sweeping vales, an' foaming floods,
  Are free alike to all.
In days when daisies deck the ground,
  And blackbirds whistle clear,
With honest joy our hearts will bound,
  To see the coming year:
    On braes when we please then,
      We 'll sit an' sowth a tune; **hum**
    Syne rhyme till 't, we 'll time till 't,
      An' sing 't when we hae done.

It 's no in titles nor in rank;
It 's no in wealth like Lon'on bank,
  To purchase peace and rest:

ence, he details this idea yet more seriously, and dwells upon it, as not ill adapted to his habits and powers. As the life of a Scottish mendicant of the eighteenth century seems to have been contemplated without much horror by Robert Burns, the author can hardly have erred in giving to Edie Ochiltree something of poetical character and personal dignity above the more abject of his miserable calling. The class had, in fact, some privileges. A lodging, such as it was, was readily granted to them in some of the outhouses; and the awmous (alms) of a handful of meal (called a gowpen) was scarce denied by the poorest cottager. The mendicant disposed these, according to their different quality, in various bags around his person, and thus carried about with him the principal part of his sustenance, which he literally received for the asking. At the houses of the gentry, his cheer was mended by scraps of broken meat, and perhaps a Scottish "twal-penny," or English penny, which was expended in snuff or whisky. In fact, these indolent peripatetics suffered much less real hardship and want of food than the poor peasants from whom they received alms.'—Sir Walter Scott, *Notes to The Antiquary*.

It 's no in makin muckle, mair; much
It 's no in books, it 's no in lear, learning
To make us truly blest:
If happiness hae not her seat
An' centre in the breast,
We may be wise, or rich, or great,
But never can be blest;
Nae treasures nor pleasures
Could make us happy lang;
The heart ay 's the part ay always
That makes us right or wrang.

Think ye, that sic as you and I,
Wha drudge an' drive thro' wet and dry,
Wi' never ceasing toil;
Think ye, are we less blest than they,
Wha scarcely tent us in their way, notice
As hardly worth their while?
Alas! how aft, in haughty mood,
God's creatures they oppress!
Or else, neglecting a' that 's good,
They riot in excess!
Baith careless and fearless
Of either heaven or hell;
Esteeming, and deeming
It a' an idle tale!

Then let us cheerfu' acquiesce,
Nor make our scanty pleasures less,
By pining at our state:
And, even should misfortunes come,
I, here wha sit, hae met wi' some—
An 's thankfu' for them yet,
They gie the wit of age to youth;
They let us ken oursel;
They make us see the naked truth—
The real guid and ill:
Tho' losses an' crosses
Be lessons right severe,
There 's wit there, ye 'll get there,
Ye 'll find nae other where.

But tent me, Davie, ace o' hearts! note what I say
(To say aught less wad wrang the cartes,
And flatt'ry I detest)—

This life has joys for you and I;
An' joys that riches ne'er could buy;
An' joys the very best.
There 's a' the pleasures o' the heart,
The lover an' the frien';
Ye hae your Meg,[1] your dearest part,
And I my darling Jean!
It warms me, it charms me,
To mention but her name:
It heats me, it beets me, makes me glow with rapture
An' sets me a' on flame!

O all ye Pow'rs who rule above!
O Thou whose very self art love!
Thou know'st my words sincere!
The life-blood streaming thro' my heart,
Or my more dear immortal part,
Is not more fondly dear!
When heart-corroding care and grief
Deprive my soul of rest,
Her dear idea brings relief
And solace to my breast.
Thou Being, All-seeing,
O hear my fervent pray'r;
Still take her, and make her
Thy most peculiar care!

[1] Margaret Orr, a domestic servant to Mrs Stewart of Stair House. The story goes that 'Burns, accompanying his friend on a visit to Stair, on one occasion found some other lasses there who were good singers, and communicated to them some of his songs in manuscript. Chance threw one of these in the way of Mrs Stewart, who, being struck by its elegance and tenderness, resolved to become acquainted with the author. Accordingly, on his next visit to the house, he was asked to go into the drawing-room to see Mrs Stewart, who thus became the first friend he had above his own rank in life.' 'Meg' did not become the wife of 'Davie.' She married John Paton, a shoemaker, and died in 1837. David Sillar, who had removed to Irvine about two years before the 'Epistle' was written, or at all events completed, and started in business as a grocer, published his 'Poems' in 1789. This venture met with neither literary nor financial success, and Sillar became bankrupt. He next tried to obtain literary work in Edinburgh, but failed. Returning to Irvine, he 'opened a school, chiefly for the instruction of young seamen in the science of navigation.' Fortune now smiled upon him, for not only did his school prosper, but through the deaths of three brothers he fell heir to considerable wealth. He entered the Town Council of Irvine, and had served in the magistracy before he died, in 1830, at the age of seventy. 'Intensely parsimonious,' writes one of his biographers, 'he refused to contribute towards the poet's monument on the banks of the Doon; but he loved to discourse on his intimacy with the Bard, and to celebrate each anniversary of his birth.'

All hail; ye tender feelings dear!
The smile of love, the friendly tear,
The sympathetic glow!
Long since, this world's thorny ways
Had number'd out my weary days,
Had it not been for you!
Fate still has blest me with a friend,
In ev'ry care and ill;
And oft a more endearing band—
A tie more tender still.
It lightens, it brightens
The tenebrific scene, dark
To meet with, an' greet with
My Davie, or my Jean!

O, how that *Name* inspires my style!
The words come skelpin, rank an' file, rattling
Amaist before I ken! almost
The ready measure rins as fine,
As Phœbus an' the famous Nine
Were glowrin owre my pen. looking
My spavet Pegasus will limp, spavined
Till ance he's fairly het; heated
And then he'll hilch, and stilt, an' jimp, hobble—limp—jump
And rin an unco fit: at a rapid pace
But least then the beast then
Should rue this hasty ride,
I'll light now, and dight now wipe down
His sweaty, wizen'd hide. withered

DEATH AND DR HORNBOOK,

A TRUE STORY.

Some books are lies frae end to end,
And some great lies were never penn'd:
Ev'n ministers they hae been kenn'd,
In holy rapture,
A rousing whid at times to vend,[1] fib
And nail 't wi' Scripture.

[1] In the earlier editions this line ran 'Great lies and nonsense baith to vend.' In the 1794 edition it appeared as in our text.

But this that I am gaun to tell, going
Which lately on a night befel,
Is just as true 's the Deil 's in hell
Or Dublin city:
That e'er he nearer comes oursel
'S a muckle pity.

The clachan yill had made me canty, village ale—merry
I was na fou, but just had plenty; drunk
I stacher'd whyles, but yet took tent ay staggered at times—care
To free the ditches;
An' hillocks, stanes, an' bushes, kenn'd ay
Frae ghaists an' witches.

The rising moon began to glowre stare
The distant *Cumnock* hills out-owre:
To count her horns, wi' a' my pow'r,
I set mysel;
But whether she had three or four,
I cou'd na tell.

I was come round about the hill,
An' todlin down on *Willie's mill*,[1] tottering
Setting my staff wi' a' my skill,
To keep me sicker; secure
Tho' leeward whyles, against my will, sometimes
I took a bicker. short race

I there wi' *Something* did forgather,
That pat me in an eerie swither; frightened hesitation
An awfu' scythe, out-owre ae shouther,
Clear-dangling, hang;
A three-tae'd leister on the ither fish-spear
Lay, large an' lang.

Its stature seem'd lang Scotch ells twa,
The queerest shape that e'er I saw,
For fient a wame it had ava; Deuce!—belly
And then its shanks,
They were as thin, as sharp an' sma'
As cheeks o' branks.[2]

[1] Tarbolton Mill, situated on the rivulet Fail, about two hundred yards to the east of the village, on the road to Mossgiel; then occupied by William Muir, an intimate friend of the Burns family; it was called *Willie's Mill*, after him. 'Mr William Muir, Tarbolton Mill,' appears in the list of subscribers to the Edinburgh edition of the *Poems*, in which this 'true story' first appeared.

[2] Branks—a kind of wooden frame, forming, with a rope, a bridle for cows.

'Guid e'en,' quo' I; 'Friend, hae ye been mawin, mowing
'When ither folk are busy sawin?' sowing
It seem'd to mak a kind o' stan',
But naething spak;
At length, says I: 'Friend! whare ye gaun?
'Will ye go back?'

It spak right howe,—'My name is *Death*, hollow
'But be na' fley'd.'—Quoth I, 'Guid faith, frightened
'Ye 're may be come to stap my breath;
'But tent me, billie; give heed to me—comrade
'I red ye weel, tak care o' skaith, advise—harm
'See, there 's a gully!' clasp-knife

'Gudeman,' quo' he, 'put up your whittle, knife
'I'm no design'd to try its mettle;
'But if I did, I wad be kittle apt
'To be mislear'd;[1] rude
'I wad na mind it, no that spittle
'Out-owre my beard.'[2]

'Weel, weel!' says I, 'a bargain be 't;
'Come, gies your hand, an' sae we 're gree 't; agreed
'We 'll ease our shanks an' tak a seat— limbs
'Come, gie 's your news;
'This while ye hae been mony a gate, road
'At mony a house.'[3]

'Ay, ay!' quo' he, an' shook his head,
'It 's e'en a lang, lang time indeed
'Sin' I began to nick the thread, cut
'An' choke the breath:
'Folk maun do something for their bread,
'An' sae maun *Death*.

'Sax thousand years are near-hand fled
'Sin' I was to the butching bred, butcher's trade

[1] The phrase 'kittle to be mislear'd' may best be interpreted as 'like to prove an awkward customer.'
[2] The scythe and the beard suggest that the poet had the figure of Time in view, rather than that of Death.
[3] Alluding to a recent epidemical fever.

'An' mony a scheme in vain 's been laid,
'To stap or scar me; stop—scare
'Till ane *Hornbook's*[1] ta'en up the trade,
'And faith! he 'll waur me. worst

'Ye ken *Jock Hornbook* i' the Clachan— village
'Deil mak his king's-hood[2] in a spleuchan!— tobacco-pouch
'He 's grown sae weel acquaint wi' *Buchan*[3]
'And ither chaps,
'The weans haud out their fingers laughin, children
'An' pouk my hips. pluck

'See, here 's a scythe, an' there 's a dart,
'They hae pierc'd mony a gallant heart;
'But Doctor *Hornbook* wi' his art
'An' cursèd skill,
'Has made them baith no worth a f—t,
'D—n'd haet they 'll kill! they will not kill anything

''Twas but yestreen, nae farther gane, yesterday
'I threw a noble throw at ane;
'Wi' less, I'm sure, I've hundreds slain;
'But deil-ma-care, no matter!
'It just play'd dirl on the bane, a short tremulous stroke
'But did nae mair.

'*Hornbook* was by, wi' ready art,
'An' had sae fortify'd the part,
'That when I lookèd to my dart,
'It was sae blunt,
'Fient haet o' 't wad hae pierc'd the heart not a bit
'Of a kail-runt. stalk of green kale

'I drew my scythe in sic a fury,
'I near-hand cowpit wi' my hurry, tumbled over
'But yet the bauld *Apothecary*
'Withstood the shock;
'I might as weel hae try'd a quarry
'O' hard whin rock.

[1] This gentleman, Dr Hornbook, is, professionally, a brother of the sovereign Order of the Ferula; but, by intuition and inspiration, is at once an Apothecary, Surgeon, and Physician.—*R. B., in the first Edinburgh edition.*

[2] 'King's-hood' is the second of the four stomachs of a ruminant. This line may be freely rendered, 'The devil make a pouch of his stomach!'

[3] Buchan's *Domestic Medicine*, then a popular book, and of course a readily available manual for a village doctor. Dr Buchan died in 1808.

'Ev'n them he canna get attended,
'Altho' their face he ne'er had kend it,
'Just —— in a kail-blade, an' send it,
'As soon 's he smells 't,
'Baith their disease, and what will mend it,
'At once he tells 't.

'And tnen a' doctor's saws an' whittles — knives
'Of a' dimensions, shapes, an' mettles,
'A' kind o' boxes, mugs, an' bottles,
'He 's sure to hae;
'Their Latin names as fast he rattles
'As A B C.

'Calces o' fossils, earths, and trees;
'True sal-marinum o' the seas;
'The farina of beans an' pease,
'He has 't in plenty;
'Aqua-fontis, what you please,
'He can content ye.

'Forbye some new, uncommon weapons,
'Urinus spiritus of capons;
'Or mite-horn shavings, filings, scrapings,
'Distill'd *per se;*
'Sal-alkali o' midge-tail-clippings,
'And mony mae.'

'Wae 's me for *Johnie Ged's*[1] *Hole* now,'
Quoth I, 'if that thae news be true!
'His braw calf-ward[2] where gowans grew — daisies
'Sae white and bonie,
'Nae doubt they 'll rive it wi' the plew, — tear it up—plough
'They 'll ruin *Johnie!*'

The creature grain'd an eldritch laugh, — unearthly
And says, 'Ye needna yoke the pleugh,
'Kirkyards will soon be till'd eneugh,
'Take ye na fear:
'They 'll a' be trenched wi' mony a sheugh, — furrow
'In twa-three year.

[1] The parish gravedigger.
[2] The churchyard, which had occasionally been used as an enclosure for calves.

'Whare I kill'd ane, a fair strae death, death in (a straw) bed
'By loss o' blood or want of breath,
'This night I 'm free to take my aith,
'That *Hornbook's* skill
'Has clad a score i' their last claith, grave-cloth
'By drap an' pill. potion

'An honest wabster to his trade, weaver
'Whase wife's twa nieves were scarce weel-bred, fists
'Gat tippence-worth to mend her head,
'When it was sair;
'The wife slade cannie to her bed, slid gently
'But ne'er spak mair.

'A country laird had ta'en the batts, colic
'Or some curmurring in his guts, slight attack of the gripes
'His only son for *Hornbook* sets,
'An' pays him well:
'The lad, for twa guid gimmer-pets, young ewes
'Was laird himsel.

'A bonie lass—ye kend her name—
'Some ill-brewn drink had hov'd her wame;
'She trusts hersel, to hide the shame,
'In *Hornbook's* care;
'*Horn* sent her aff to her lang hame,
'To hide it there.

'That 's just a swatch o' *Hornbook's* way; example
'Thus goes he on from day to day,
'Thus does he poison, kill, an' slay,
'An 's weel paid for 't;
'Yet stops me o' my lawfu' prey,
'Wi' his d—d dirt:

'But, hark! I'll tell you of a plot,
'Tho' dinna ye be speaking o' 't;
'I 'll nail the self-conceited sot,
'As dead 's a herrin:
'Niest time we meet, I 'll wad a groat, wager
'He gets his fairin!' reward

But just as he began to tell,
The auld kirk-hammer strak the bell — struck
Some wee short hour ayont the *twal*, — twelve
Which rais'd us baith: — roused
I took the way that pleas'd mysel,
And sae did *Death*.[1]

EPISTLE TO J. LAPRAIK,[2]

AN OLD SCOTTISH BARD.

While briers an' woodbines budding green,
An' paitricks scraichin loud at e'en, — partridges screeching
An' morning poussie whiddin seen, — hare moving quickly
Inspire my muse,
This freedom, in an unknown frien',
I pray excuse.

[1] It was long believed, on the authority of Lockhart, that the schoolmaster was compelled, through the ridicule occasioned by Burns's satire, to close not only his shop but his school, in consequence of his pupils deserting him. But Mr E. K. Macpherson, Schoolhouse, Tarbolton, writing to the *Burns Chronicle* for 1895, says: 'I have by me an account-book of the funds of Tarbolton session containing the signature of John Wilson as session-clerk of Tarbolton, as late as January 8th, 1793. I believe the poem was pretty well public property in Tarbolton in 1785, so Wilson's skin seems to have been no thinner than that of his modern brethren had need to be.' It may also be noted that Wilson was secretary to the Tarbolton Lodge from 8th August 1782 till some time in 1787. He wrote many of the minutes, and signed two of them as 'Master *pro tempore*,' and a third as 'M. *P. T.*' Wilson left Tarbolton, in consequence, it is said, of a dispute about salary with the heritors, and settled in Glasgow, where he long kept a school for boys and girls. He ultimately became session-clerk of Gorbals parish in the same city. He died on January 13, 1839.

'Gilbert Burns used to relate that Wilson once spoke to him of the poem. He said it was pretty severe in some things; but, on the whole, it was *rather* a compliment. This qualifying "rather" amused Gilbert very much.'—*Letter of Miss Isabella Begg.*

[2] Lapraik is apparently the same name with Lekprevick or Leprevick, honourable in the history of Scottish literature, as having been borne by the printer to James VI., and who in the second half of the sixteenth century published a collected edition of the Scottish statutes. In 1364 David II. confirmed a charter of William de Cunningham, Lord of Carrick, to James de Leprevick, of half the lands of Polkairne, in the parish of Ochiltree, King's Kyle (*Wood's Peerage*, i. 321)—which shows that there were persons of that name at an early period connected with the district. John Lapraik of Dalquhram, in the parish of Muirkirk, was born in 1727, and was therefore bordering on sixty when Burns made his acquaintance. The poet described him as 'a worthy, facetious old fellow, late of Dalfram, near Muirkirk, which little property he was obliged to sell in consequence of some connection in security for some persons concerned in that villainous bubble, the Ayr Bank.' He was thrown into prison for debt, and there wrote—or adapted—the poem which excited the poet's admiration.

On Fasten-e'en we had a rockin,
To ca' the crack and weave our stockin; chat
And there was muckle fun and jokin,
Ye need na doubt;
At length we had a hearty yokin, match
At 'sang about.'

There was ae sang, amang the rest,
Aboon them a' it pleas'd me best,
That some kind husband had addrest
To some sweet wife;
It thirl'd the heart-strings thro' the breast thrilled
A' to the life.

I've scarce heard ought describ'd sae weel,
What gen'rous, manly bosoms feel;
Thought I, 'Can this be Pope, or Steele,
Or Beattie's wark?'
They tauld me 'twas an odd kind chiel
About Muirkirk.

It pat me fidgin-fain to hear 't, excitedly eager
An' sae about him there I spier't; inquired
Then a' that kent him round declar'd
He had *ingine*; genius
That nane excell'd it, few cam near 't,
It was sae fine:

That, set him to a pint of ale,
An' either douce or merry tale, grave
Or rhymes an' sangs he 'd made himsel,
Or witty catches—
'Tween Inverness an' Teviotdale,
He had few matches.

Then up I gat, an' swoor an aith,
Tho' I should pawn my pleugh an' graith, harness
Or die a cadger pownie's death, pedlar
At some dyke-back, back of a wall
A pint an' gill I 'd gie them baith,
To hear your crack. conversation

But, first an' foremost, I should tell,
Amaist as soon as I could spell,
I to the crambo-jingle fell; rhyming
Tho' rude an' rough—
Yet crooning to a body's sel, humming
Does weel enough.

I am nae poet, in a sense,
But just a rhymer like by chance;
An' hae to learning nae pretence;
Yet, what the matter?
Whene'er my muse does on me glance,
I jingle at her.

Your critic-folk may cock their nose,
And say, 'How can you e'er propose,
You wha ken hardly verse frae prose,
To mak a sang?'
But, by your leaves, my learned foes,
Ye 're maybe wrang.

What 's a' your jargon o' your schools—
Your Latin names for horns an' stools?
If honest Nature made you fools,
What sairs your grammars? serves
Ye 'd better taen up spades and shools, shovels
Or knappin-hammers. hammers for breaking stones

A set o' dull, conceited hashes fellows
Confuse their brains in college-classes!
They gang in stirks, and come out asses,
Plain truth to speak;
An' syne they think to climb Parnassus
By dint o' Greek!

Gie me ae spark o' nature's fire,
That 's a' the learning I desire;
Then tho' I drudge thro' dub an' mire pool
At pleugh or cart,
My muse, tho' hamely in attire,
May touch the heart.[1]

[1] 'Great Apollo! if thou art in a giving humour, give me—I ask no more—but one stroke of native humour, with a single spark of thy own fire along with it; and send Mercury, with the *rules and compasses*, if he can be spared, with my compliments to—no matter.'—*Tristram Shandy.*

O for a spunk o' Allan's[1] glee, spark
Or Fergusson's, the bauld an' slee, sly
Or bright Lapraik's, my friend to be,
If I can hit it!
That would be lear eneugh for me, learning
If I could get it.

Now, sir, if ye hae friends enow,
Tho' real friends I b'lieve are few;
Yet, if your catalogue be fu', full
I 'se no insist:
But, gif ye want ae friend that 's true, if
I 'm on your list.

I winna blaw about mysel, boast
As ill I like my fauts to tell;
But friends, an' folk that wish me well,
They sometimes roose me, praise
Tho' I maun own, as mony still
As far abuse me.

There 's ae wee faut they whiles lay to me,
I like the lasses—Gude forgie me!
For mony a plack they wheedle frae me coin
At dance or fair;
Maybe some other thing they gie me,
They weel can spare.

But Mauchline Race[2] or Mauchline Fair,
I should be proud to meet you there:
We 'se gie ae night's discharge to care,
If we forgather; meet
An hae a swap o' rhymin-ware exchange
Wi' ane anither.

The four-gill chap,[3] we 'se gar him clatter, make
An kirsen him wi' reekin water; christen—toddy
Syne we 'll sit down an' tak our whitter,[4]
To cheer our heart;
An' faith, we 'se be acquainted better
Before we part.

1 Allan Ramsay.
2 This was held on the road adjoining Burns's farm of Mossgiel.
3 Chappin, a measure for liquor.
4 A hearty draught of liquor.

Awa ye selfish, warly race,
Wha think that havins, sense, an' grace, — manners
Ev'n love an' friendship should give place
To catch-the-plack! — catch-coin, money-grubbing
I dinna like to see your face,
Nor hear your crack.

But ye whom social pleasure charms,
Whose hearts the tide of kindness warms,
Who hold your being on the terms,
'Each aid the others,'
Come to my bowl, come to my arms,
My friends, my brothers!

But, to conclude my lang epistle,
As my auld pen 's worn to the gristle,
Twa lines frae you wad gar me fissle, — feel lively
Who am most fervent,
While I can either sing or whistle,
Your friend and Servant,
ROBERT BURNESS.

MOSSGIEL, near MACHLINE, *April* 1785.

SECOND EPISTLE TO J. LAPRAIK.

April 21, 1785.

While new-ca'd kye rowte at the stake [1]
An' pownies reek in pleugh or braik,[2] — smoke
This hour on e'enin's edge I take,
To own I'm debtor
To honest-hearted, auld Lapraik,
For his kind letter.

Forjesket sair, with weary legs, — Fatigued
Rattlin the corn out-owre the rigs,
Or dealing thro' among the naigs
Their ten-hours' bite,
My awkwart muse sair pleads and begs
I would na write.

The tapetless, ramfeezl'd hizzie, — heedless—overspent
She 's saft at best an' something lazy:

[1] While the newly-calved cows low, tied to stakes for milking.

[2] Braik, a kind of harrow.—*Burns's Glossary.* More precisely a heavy harrow; a harrow loaded with a log. It is an implement which was at that time much used in Ayrshire and Renfrewshire.

Quo' she, 'Ye ken we 've been sae busy
This month an' mair,
That trowth, my head is grown right dizzie, in truth
An' something sair.'

Her dowff excuses pat me mad ; stupid
'Conscience,' says I, 'ye thowless jade ! feeble
I 'll write, an' that a hearty blaud, effusion
This vera night ;
Sae dinna ye affront your trade,
But rhyme it right.

'Shall bauld Lapraik, the king o' hearts,
Tho' mankind were a pack o' cartes,
Roose you sae weel for your deserts, praise
In terms sae friendly ;
Yet ye 'll neglect to shaw your parts
An' thank him kindly ?'

Sae I gat paper in a blink, moment
An' down gaed stumpie in the ink : went the stumpy pen
Quoth I, 'Before I sleep a wink,
I vow I 'll close it ;
An' if ye winna mak it clink, rhyme
By Jove, I 'll prose it !'

Sae I 've begun to scrawl, but whether
In rhyme, or prose, or baith thegither ;
Or some hotch-potch that 's rightly neither,
Let time mak proof ;
But I shall scribble down some blether nonsense
Just clean aff-loof. off-hand

My worthy friend, ne'er grudge an' carp,
Tho' fortune use you hard an' sharp ;
Come, kittle up your moorland harp rouse
Wi' gleesome touch !
Ne'er mind how Fortune waft and warp ;
She 's but a b—tch.

She 's gien me mony a jirt an' fleg, jerk—kick
Sin' I could striddle owre a rig ; Since—straddle—ridge
But, by the L—d, tho' I should beg
Wi' lyart pow, gray head
I 'll laugh an' sing, an' shake my leg,
As lang 's I dow ! can

Now comes the sax-and-twentieth simmer
I 've seen the bud upo' the timmer,
Still persecuted by the limmer
Frae year to year;
But yet, despite the kittle kimmer, fickle gossip
I, Rob, am here.

Do ye envy the city gent,
Behint a kist to lie an' sklent; chest—deceive
Or purse-proud, big wi' cent. per cent.
An' muckle wame,
In some bit brugh to represent burgh
A bailie's name?

Or is 't the paughty, feudal thane, haughty
Wi' ruffl'd sark an' glancing cane, shirt
Wha thinks himsel nae sheep-shank bane, no unimportant person
But lordly stalks;
While caps and bonnets aff are taen,
As by he walks?

'O Thou wha gies us each guid gift!
Gie me o' wit an' sense a lift,
Then turn me, if Thou please adrift,
Thro' Scotland wide;
Wi' cits nor lairds I wadna shift,
In a' their pride!'

Were this the charter of our state,
'On pain o' hell be rich an' great,'
Damnation then would be our fate,
Beyond remead;
But, thanks to heaven, that 's no the gate
We learn our creed.

For thus the royal mandate ran,
When first the human race began;
'The social, friendly, honest man,
Whate'er he be—
'Tis *he* fulfils great Nature's plan,
And none but he!'

O mandate glorious and divine!
The followers o' the ragged nine [1]—

[1] **Variation in Hogg and Motherwell's edition—'Ragged followers o' the nine'—which is more respectful to the Muses.**

Poor, thoughtless devils—yet may shine
In glorious light;
While sordid sons o' Mammon's line
Are dark as night!

Tho' here they scrape, an' squeeze, an' growl,
Their worthless nievefu' of a soul — handful
May in some future carcase howl,
The forest's fright;
Or in some day-detesting owl
May shun the light.

Then may Lapraik[1] and Burns arise,
To reach their native, kindred skies,
And sing their pleasures, hopes an' joys,
In some mild sphere;
Still closer knit in friendship's ties,
Each passing year!

EPISTLE TO JOHN GOLDIE,[2] IN KILMARNOCK,

AUTHOR OF 'THE GOSPEL RECOVERED.'

August 1785.

O Gowdie, terror o' the whigs,
Dread o' blackcoats and reverend wigs!
Sour Bigotry on his last legs
Girns an' looks back, — scowls
Wishing the ten Egyptian plagues
May seize you quick.

[1] Although Burns wrote a 'Third Epistle to J. Lapraik,' which appears on p. 67, the subsequent history of the Muirkirk poetaster may here be briefly given. He issued in 1788, through Wilson's Kilmarnock press, an octavo volume of verse, bearing the title *Poems on Several Occasions*, and including Burns's 'Third Epistle.' Its literary merit was small, and it failed to attract public attention. Lapraik, who was compelled to give up his property and the mill of Muirsmill, which he had leased in the neighbourhood, removed to Muirkirk about the time of Burns's death. There he kept an inn, and acted as postmaster. He died in 1807.

[2] John Goldie was the son of the miller at Craigmill, on the water of Cessnock, in the parish of Galston, and was born in 1717. He had a natural bent for mechanics, and, while still a young man, removed to Kilmarnock to carry on business as a cabinetmaker. He next became a wine-merchant, but appears to have given up the bulk of his time to scientific (more especially astronomical) investigation and theological speculation, the result of the latter being the publication of his 'Bible' in 1780. In 1808 Goldie published *Conclusive Evidences against Atheism*. He also announced his intention of publishing *A Revise* or *A Reform of the Present History of Astronomy*, but the work never appeared. Goldie, who, according to one of his biographers, 'latterly engaged in mining speculations, and thereby impaired his resources,' died in 1811.

Poor gapin, glowrin Superstition !
Wae 's me, she 's in a sad condition :
Fye ! bring *Black Jock*, her state physician,
To see her water :
Alas, there 's ground for great suspicion
She 'll ne'er get better.

Enthusiasm 's past redemption,
Gane in a gallopin consumption :
Not a' her quacks, wi' a' their gumption, **acuteness**
Can ever mend her ;
Her feeble pulse gies strong presumption,
She 'll soon surrender.

Auld Orthodoxy lang did grapple,
For every hole to get a stapple ; **stopper**
But now she fetches at the thrapple, **catches at the throat**
An' fights for breath ;
Haste, gie her name up in the chapel,
Near unto death.

It 's you an' *Taylor*[1] are the chief
To blame for a' this black mischief ;
But could the L—d's ain folk get leave,
A toom tar barrel **empty**
An' twa red peats wad bring relief,
And end the quarrel.

For me, my skill 's but very sma',
An' skill in prose I 've nane ava' ; **none at all**
But quietlenswise, between us twa, **in a quiet manner**
Weel may ye speed !
And tho' they sud you sair misca', **should—revile**
Ne'er fash your head. **trouble**

E'en swinge the dogs, and thresh them sicker ! **severely**
The mair they squeel ay chap the thicker ; **lay on**
And still 'mang hands a hearty bicker **at intervals ;—draught**
O' something stout ; **invigorating**
It gars an owthor's pulse beat quicker, **makes—author's**
And helps his wit.

[1] Dr John Taylor of Norwich, whose *Scripture Doctrine of Original Sin* was generally accepted as the manual of the New Light rationalism.

There 's naething like the honest nappy ; strong drink
Whare 'll ye e'er see men sae happy,
Or women sonsie, saft and sappy, buxom
'Tween morn and morn,
As them wha like to taste the drappie,
In glass or horn ?

I 've seen me daez't upon a time, dazed
I scarce could wink or see a styme ;[1]
Just ae hauf-mutchkin' does me prime, half-pint
(Ought less, is little,)
Then back I rattle on the rhyme,
As gleg 's a whittle. sharp as a knife

THE TWA HERDS ; OR, THE HOLY TULYIE.[2]

AN UNCO MOURNFU' TALE.

Blockheads with reason, wicked wits abhor,
But fool with fool is barbarous civil war.—POPE.

O a' ye pious godly flocks,
Weel fed on pastures orthodox,
Wha now will keep you frae the fox,
Or worrying tykes ? dogs
Or wha will tent the waifs an' crocks, stragglers—old ewes
About the dykes ?

The twa best herds in a' the wast, west
That e'er ga'e gospel horn a blast
These five an' twenty simmers past—
Oh, dool to tell ! sorrow
Hae had a bitter black out-cast quarrel
Atween themsel.

O, Moodie, man, an' wordy Russell,
How could you raise so vile a bustle ;
Ye 'll see how 'new-light' herds will whistle,
An' think it fine !
The L—'s cause ne'er gat sic a twistle, wrench
Sin' I hae min'.

[1] 'I cannot see a styme'—a popular expression in Scotland, meaning 'I cannot penetrate the darkness in front of me.'
[2] Brawl.

O, sirs! whae'er wad hae expeckit
Your duty ye wad sae negleckit,
Ye wha were ne'er by lairds respeckit
To wear the plaid;
But by the brutes themselves eleckit, elected
To be their guide.

What flock wi' Moodie's flock could rank,
Sae hale and hearty every shank,
Nae poison'd sour Arminian stank pool of standing water
He let them taste;
Frae Calvin's well, ay clear they drank,—
O, sic a feast!

The thummart, willcat, brock, an' tod, foumart or polecat—badger—fox
Weel kend his voice thro' a' the wood, knew
He smell'd their ilka hole an' road,
Baith out and in;
An' weel he lik'd to shed their bluid,
An' sell their skin.

What herd like Russell tell'd his tale;
His voice was heard thro' muir and dale,[1]
He kenn'd the L—'s sheep, ilka tail,
Owre a' the height;
An' saw gin they were sick or hale, if—well
At the first sight.

He fine a mangy sheep could scrub,
Or nobly fling the gospel club,
And 'new-light' herds could nicely drub,
Or pay their skin;
Could shake them o'er the burning dub, pool
Or heave them in.

Sic twa—O! do I live to see 't,
Sic famous twa should disagree't,
And names like 'villain,' 'hypocrite,'
Ilk ither gi'en,
While 'new-light' herds, wi' laughin spite,
Say neither 's lien! lying

[1] There is a literal truth in this line, for a person who sometimes attended Russell's prelections affirmed that, in a favourable state of the atmosphere, his voice, when he was holding forth in the open air at communions, might be heard at a distance of upwards of a mile.

A' ye wha tent the gospel fauld, look to—fold
There 's Duncan[1] deep, an' Peebles[2] shaul', shallow
But chiefly thou, apostle Auld,[3]
We trust in thee,
That thou wilt work them, hot an' cauld,
Till they agree.

Consider, sirs, how we 're beset;
There 's scarce a new herd that we get,
But comes frae 'mang that cursèd set
I winna name;
I hope frae heav'n to see them yet
In fiery flame.

Dalrymple[4] has been lang our fae, foe
M'Gill[5] has wrought us meikle wae, much mischief
An' that curs'd rascal ca'd M'Quhae,[6]
An' baith the Shaws,[7]
That aft hae made us black an' blae, blue
Wi' vengefu' paws.

[1] Dr Robert Duncan, minister of Dundonald. Ordained 1783; died 14th April 1815. Author of a sermon on infidelity.

[2] Rev. William Peebles, of Newton-upon-Ayr. See notes to the 'Holy Fair' and the 'Kirk's Alarm.'

[3] The Rev. William Auld was a younger son of the Laird of Ellanton, in the parish of Symington. He was born in 1709, took his M.A. degree at Edinburgh in 1733, and studied theology at Glasgow and Leyden. After acting for some time as tutor in the family of the laird of Schawfield, he was licensed by the presbytery of Hamilton in 1739, and ordained at Mauchline in 1742. He died on 12th December 1791.

[4] Rev. William Dalrymple, one of the ministers of Ayr. He was the younger son of James Dalrymple, sheriff-clerk of Ayr, and was born on 29th August 1723. He took license in 1745, and was ordained and inducted to the second charge of Ayr in 1756. He was noted for the purity of his life, the serenity of his temper, and the urbanity of his manners. St Andrews University made him a D.D. in 1779, and he was Moderator of the General Assembly in 1781. He died on 28th January 1814, in his ninety-first year. It was he who baptised Burns.

[5] Rev. William M'Gill, one of the ministers of Ayr, colleague of Dr Dalrymple. See note to the 'Kirk's Alarm.'

[6] Rev. William M'Quhae, minister of St Quivox. Born at Wigtown in 1736, he was educated at Glasgow University, and ordained at St Quivox in 1764. He declined the Moderatorship of the General Assembly in 1806, and died in 1823. He was noted for his business aptitude.

[7] Dr Andrew Shaw of Craigie, and Dr David Shaw of Coylton. Dr Andrew was a man of excellent abilities, but extremely diffident—a fine speaker and an accomplished scholar. He was ordained in 1765, and died in 1805. Dr David was a physical prodigy. He was ninety-one years of age before he required an assistant. At that period of life he read without the use of glasses, wrote a neat, small hand, and had not a furrow in his cheek or a wrinkle in his brow. He was Moderator of the General Assembly in 1775. This amiable man died April 26, 1810, in the ninety-second year of his age, and sixty-first of his ministry.

Auld Wodrow[1] lang has hatch'd mischief;
We thought ay, death wad bring relief,
But he has gotten, to our grief,
    Ane to succeed him,
A chield wha 'll soundly buff our beef; rate us
    I meikle dread him. greatly

And mony a ane that I could tell,
Wha fain would openly rebel,
Forby turn-coats amang oursel, besides
    There 's Smith for ane;[2]
I doubt he 's but a grey nick quill, soft quill unfit to be used as a pen
    An' that ye 'll fin'. find

O! a' ye flocks o'er a' the hills,
By mosses, meadows, moors, an' fells,
Come, join your counsel and your skills
    To cowe the lairds, humble
An' get the brutes the power themsels
    To chuse their herds.

Then Orthodoxy yet may prance,
An' Learning in a woody dance, halter
An' that fell cur ca'd 'common-sense,'
    That bites sae sair,
Be banish'd o'er the sea to France:
    Let him bark there.

Then Shaw's an' D'rymple's eloquence,
M'Gill's close nervous excellence,
M'Quhae's pathetic manly sense,
    An' guid M'Math,
Wi' Smith, wha thro' the heart can glance,
    May a' pack aff.

1 There were three brothers of this name, sons of the Church historian, and all ministers—one at Eastwood, their father's charge; the second at Stevenston; and the third, Dr Peter Wodrow, at Tarbolton. Dr Peter is the person named in the poem. He was born in 1715, ordained at Tarbolton in 1738, and died on 17th April 1793. The assistant and successor mentioned in the verse was M'Math, elsewhere alluded to.

2 Rev. George Smith, minister of Galston. He is one of the tent-preachers in the 'Holy Fair.' Here and in the 'Holy Fair' he is claimed as friendly to the New Light party, but he is attacked in the 'Kirk's Alarm.'

EPISTLE TO WILLIAM SIMSON,[1]

SCHOOLMASTER, OCHILTREE.

May 1785.

I gat your letter, winsome Willie;
Wi' gratefu' heart I thank you brawlie; heartily
Tho' I maun say 't, I wad be silly,
An' unco vain,
Should I believe, my coaxin billie, fellow
Your flatterin strain.

But I 'se believe ye kindly meant it,
I sud be laith to think ye hinted unwilling
Ironic satire, sidelins sklented directed sideways
On my poor Musie;
Tho' in sic phraisin terms ye 've penn'd it, flattering
I scarce excuse ye.

My senses wad be in a creel, My head would be turned
Should I but dare a hope to speel, climb
Wi' Allan,[2] or wi' Gilbertfield,[3]
The braes o' fame;
Or Fergusson, the writer-chiel,[4] lad
A deathless name.

(O Fergusson! thy glorious parts
Ill suited law's dry, musty arts!
My curse upon your whunstane hearts,
Ye Enbrugh Gentry! Edinburgh
The tythe o' what ye waste at cartes
Wad stow'd his pantry!) would have filled

[1] William Simson, the elder of the two sons of John Simson, a farmer in Ochiltree, was born in 1758. He was educated for the Church, but became schoolmaster of his native parish, on the post becoming vacant in 1780. Eight years later he became parish schoolmaster of Cumnock, where he died in 1815. His brother, Patrick, who was seven years his junior, succeeded him as parish schoolmaster at Ochiltree, and survived till 1848.

[2] Allan Ramsay, whose 'Gentle Shepherd' appeared in 1725, and who died at the age of seventy-two, the year before Burns was born.

[3] William Hamilton, born about 1665, tenant of Gilbertfield, Lanarkshire, wrote 'Willie was a Wanton Wag' and 'Epistles to Ramsay,' and abridged Blind Harry's 'Wallace;' died 1751.

[4] To Robert Fergusson, poet and law-clerk in Edinburgh (*b.* 1750, *d.* 1774), Burns subsequently did ample justice by every means in his power.

Yet when a tale comes i' my head,
Or lasses gie my heart a screed, rent
As whiles they 're like to be my dead, death
(O sad disease!)
I kittle up my rustic reed; waken
It gies me ease.

Auld Coila[1] now may fidge[2] fu fain,
She 's gotten Poets o' her ain,
Chiels wha their chanters winna hain Youths—spare
But tune their lays,
Till echoes a' resound again
Her weel-sung praise.

Nae Poet thought her worth his while,
To set her name in measur'd style;
She lay like some unkend-of isle
Beside New Holland,
Or where wild-meeting oceans boil
Besouth Magellan. south of

Ramsay an' famous Fergusson
Gied Forth an' Tay a lift aboon; above
Yarrow an' Tweed, to monie a tune,
Owre Scotland rings,
While Irwin, Lugar, Ayr, an' Doon, Irvine
Naebody sings.

Th' Illissus, Tiber, Thames, an' Seine,
Glide sweet in monie a tunefu line!
But, Willie, set your fit to mine, foot
An' cock your crest,
We 'll gar our streams an' burnies shine rivulets
Up wi' the best.

We 'll sing auld Coila's plains an' fells,
Her moors red-brown wi' heather bells,
Her banks an' braes, her dens an' dells,
Where glorious Wallace
Aft bure the gree, as story tells, bore the bell from, or conquered champions
Frae Southron billies.

[1] The Ayrshire district of Kyle, personified under the name of Coila. Burns afterwards assumed Coila as the name of his Muse.

[2] 'Fidge' is a restless movement indicative of great pleasure.

At Wallace' name what Scottish blood
But boils up in a spring-tide flood!
Oft have our fearless fathers strode
By Wallace' side,
Still pressing onward, red-wat shod, ankle-deep in blood
Or glorious dy'd.

O sweet are Coila's haughs an' woods, meadows
When lintwhites chant amang the buds, linnets
And jinkin hares, in amorous whids,[1] dodging
Their loves enjoy,
While thro' the braes the cushat croods wood-pigeon coos
With wailfu' cry!

Ev'n winter bleak has charms to me
When winds rave thro' the naked tree;
Or frosts on hills of Ochiltree
Are hoary gray;
Or blinding drifts wild-furious flee,
Dark'ning the day!

O Nature! a' thy shews an' forms
To feeling, pensive hearts hae charms!
Whether the Summer kindly warms,
Wi' life an' light,
Or Winter howls, in gusty storms,
The lang, dark night!

The Muse, nae Poet ever fand her, found
Till by himsel he learn'd to wander,
Adown some trotting burn's meander,
An' no think lang; find the time tedious
O sweet, to stray an' pensive ponder
A heart-felt sang!

The warly race may drudge an' drive, worldly
Hog-shouther, jundie, stretch an' strive, Jostle with the shoulders—hustle
Let me fair Nature's face descrive, describe from having seen
And I, wi' pleasure,
Shall let the busy, grumbling hive
Bum owre their treasure. Hum

[1] A word expressive of the quick, nimble movements of the hare, which hence is sometimes called a *whiddie* in Scotland.

Fareweel, 'my rhyme-composing brither!'
We 've been owre lang unkenn'd to ither: unknown
Now let us lay our heads thegither,
In love fraternal:
May Envy wallop in a tether, dangle at a rope, or hang
Black fiend, infernal!

While Highlandmen hate tolls an' taxes;
While moorlan herds like guid, fat braxies;[1] moorland
While Terra Firma, on her axis,
Diurnal turns,
Count on a friend, in faith an' practice,
In Robert Burns.[2]

POSTSCRIPT.

My memory 's no worth a preen: pin
I had amaist forgotten clean, almost—absolutely
Ye bade me write you what they mean
By this 'new-light,'
'Bout which our herds sae aft hae been so often
Maist like to fight. almost

In days when mankind were but callans boys
At Grammar, Logic, an' sic talents,
They took nae pains their speech to balance,
Or rules to gie,
But spak their thoughts in plain, braid Lallans, Lowland speech
Like you or me.

In thae auld times, they thought the Moon,
Just like a sark, or pair o' shoon, shirt—shoes
Wore by degrees, till her last roon shred
Gaed past their viewing,
An' shortly after she was done
They gat a new one.

This past for certain, undisputed;
It ne'er cam i' their heads to doubt it,

[1] Dead sheep—a perquisite of the shepherd.
[2] Although Burns signed his name thus in a letter to Thomas Orr in 1782, this is his first notable deviation from 'Burness,' and was probably taken to suit the necessities of rhyme. On April 14, 1786, he made the final change to 'Burns.'

Till chiels gat up an' wad confute it,
An' ca'd it wrang;
An' muckle din there was about it,
Baith loud an' lang.

Some herds, well learn'd upo' the beuk, versed in the Bible
Wad threap auld folk the thing misteuk; insist
For 'twas the auld moon turn'd a neuk, corner
An' out o' sight,
An' backlins-comin, to the leuk, backwards—view
She grew mair bright.

This was deny'd, it was affirm'd;
The herds and hissels were alarm'd: flocks
The rev'rend gray-beards rav'd an' storm'd,
That beardless laddies
Should think they better were inform'd
Than their auld daddies. fathers

Frae less to mair it gaed to sticks; cudgels
Frae words an' aiths to clours an' nicks; blows—cuts
An' monie a fallow gat his licks, got a beating
Wi' hearty crunt; knock
An' some, to learn them for their tricks,
Were hang'd an' brunt. burnt

This game was play'd in monie lands,
An' 'auld-light' caddies bure sic hands, fellows
That faith, the youngsters took the sands
Wi' nimble shanks,
Till Lairds forbad, by strict commands,
Sic bluidy pranks.

But 'new-light' herds gat sic a cowe, humbling
Folk thought them ruined stick-an-stowe, completely
Till now amaist on ev'ry knowe, almost—knoll
Ye 'll find ane plac'd;
An' some, their 'new-light' fair avow,
Just quite barefac'd.

Nae doubt the 'auld-light' flocks are bleatin;
Their zealous herds are vex'd an' sweatin;
Mysel, I 've even seen them greetin in tears
Wi' girnin spite, scowling
To hear the Moon sae sadly lie'd on
By word an' write.

But shortly they will cowe the louns! rascals
Some 'auld-light' herds in neebor touns
Are mind't, in things they ca' balloons,
To tak a flight,
An' stay ae month amang the Moons
An' see them right.

Guid observation they will gie them;
An' when the auld Moon 's gaun to lea'e them,
The hindmost shaird, they 'll fetch it wi' them, fragment
Just i' their pouch,
An' when the 'new-light' billies see them,
I think they 'll crouch!

Sae, ye observe that a' this clatter
Is naething but a 'moonshine matter;'
But tho' dull prose-folk Latin splatter
In logic tulzie, contention
I hope, we Bardies ken some better
Than mind sic brulzie. broil

HOLY WILLIE'S PRAYER.[1]

And Send the Godly in a pet to pray.—POPE.

O Thou that in the heavens does dwell!
Wha, as it pleases best Thysel,
Sends ane to heaven and ten to h—ll,
A' for Thy glory;
And no for ony guid or ill
They 've done before Thee!

[1] Burns, on subsequently making a copy of 'Holy Willie's Prayer' for his friend Glenriddel, prefixed to it the following 'argument,' which should be considered merely as expressing the view taken of Fisher by his New Light opponents in or near Mauchline: 'Holy Willie was a rather oldish bachelor elder, in the parish of Mauchline, and much and justly famed for that polemical chattering which ends in rippling orthodoxy, and for that spiritualized bawdry which refines to liquorish devotion. In a sessional process with a gentleman in Mauchline—a Mr Gavin Hamilton—*Holy Willie* and his priest, Father Auld, after full hearing in the presbytery of Ayr, came off but second best; owing partly to the oratorical powers of Mr Robert Aiken, Mr Hamilton's counsel, but chiefly to Mr Hamilton's being one of the most irreproachable and truly respectable characters in the county. On losing his process, the Muse overheard him [Holy Willie] at his devotions, as follows.'

I bless and praise Thy matchless might,
When thousands Thou hast left in night,
That I am here before Thy sight,
For gifts and grace
A burning and a shining light,
To a' this place.

What was I, or my generation,
That I should get such exaltation ?
I, wha deserv'd most just damnation
For broken laws,
Sax thousand years ere my creation
Thro' Adam's cause.

When frae my mither's womb I fell,
Thou might hae plungèd me in hell,
To gnash my gums, to weep and wail,
In burnin lakes,
Where damnèd devils roar and yell,
Chain'd to their stakes.

Yet I am here, a chosen sample,
To show Thy grace is great and ample ;
I 'm here, a pillar o' Thy temple,
Strong as a rock ;
A guide, a ruler, and example
To a' Thy flock.

O L—d, Thou kens what zeal I bear,
When drinkers drink, an' swearers swear,
An' singin' there, an' dancin' here,
Wi' great and sma' ;
For I am keepit by Thy fear,
Free frae them a'.

But yet, O L—d, confess I must,
At times I 'm fash'd wi' fleshly lust ; **troubled**
And sometimes too in warldly trust
Vile Self gets in
But Thou remembers we are dust,
Defil'd wi sin.

O L—d—yestreen—Thou kens—wi Meg—
Thy pardon I sincerely beg:
O, may 't ne'er be a livin plague,
To my dishonor!
And I 'll ne'er lift a lawless leg
Again upon her!

Besides, I further maun avow,
Wi' Leezie's lass—three times—I trow—
But L—d, that Friday I was fou drunk
When I cam near her;
Or else, Thou kens, Thy servant true
Wad never steer her. meddle with

Maybe Thou lets this fleshly thorn
Buffet Thy servant e'en and morn
Lest he owre proud and high should turn
That he 's sae gifted:
If sae, Thy hand maun e'en be borne
Until Thou lift it.

L—d bless Thy chosen in this place,
For here Thou hast a chosen race;
But G—d confound their stubborn face,
And blast their name,
Wha bring their rulers to disgrace
And public shame.

L—d mind Gaun Hamilton's deserts;
He drinks, and swears, and plays at cartes, cards
Yet has sae mony takin arts popular
Wi' Great and Sma',
Frae G—d's ain Priest the people's hearts
He steals awa.

And when we chasten'd him therefore
Thou kens how he bred sic a splore, disturbance
And set the warld in a roar
O' laughin at us:
Curse Thou his basket and his store
Kail and potatoes.

L—d hear my earnest cry and pray'r
Against that Presbytry of Ayr!
Thy strong right hand, L—d make it bare
Upo' their heads!
L—d visit them and dinna spare,
For their misdeeds!

O L—d, my G—d, that glib-tongu'd Aiken,
My very heart and flesh are quakin,
To think how I sat, sweatin, shakin,
And —— wi' dread,
While Auld, wi' hingin lip gaed sneakin **sneaky**
And hid his head.

L—d in Thy day o' vengeance try him!
L—d visit them wha did employ him!
And pass not in Thy mercy by them,
Nor hear their prayer,
But for Thy people's sake destroy them,
And dinna spare!

But L—d remember me and mine
Wi' mercies temporal and divine;
That I for grace and gear may shine,
Excell'd by nane!
And a' the glory shall be Thine,
AMEN! AMEN!

EPITAPH ON HOLY WILLIE.

Here Holy Willie's sair worn clay
Taks up its last abode;
His saul has ta'en some other way,
I fear, the left-hand road.

Stop! there he is as sure 's a gun,
Poor, silly body, see him;
Nae wonder he 's as black 's the grun,
Observe wha 's standing wi' him.

Your brunstane devilship, I see — brimstone
  Has got him there before ye ;
But haud your nine-tail cat a wee, — hold—for a short time
  Till ance you 've heard my story.

Your pity I will not implore,
  For pity ye have nane ;
Justice, alas ! has gi'en him o'er,
  And mercy's day is gane.

But hear me, Sir, deil as ye are,
  Look something to your credit ;
A coof like him wou'd stain your name, — fool
  If it were kent ye did it.

THIRD EPISTLE TO J. LAPRAIK.[1]

Sept. 13, 1785.

Guid speed an' furder to you, Johny,
Guid health, hale han's, an' weather bony ;
Now when ye 're nickin down fu' cany — cutting
    The staff o' bread, — bread, the 'staff of life'
May ye ne'er want a stoup o' brany — cup
    To clear your head.

May Boreas never thresh your rigs,
Nor kick your rickles aff their legs, — ricks, small stacks
Sendin' the stuff o'er muirs an' haggs — corn—mosses
    Like drivin' wrack ;
But may the tapmast grain that wags
    Come to the sack.

I 'm bizzie too, an' skelpin' at it, — busy—striking
But bitter, daudin showers hae wat it, — pelting—wetted
Sae my auld stumpie pen I gat it
    Wi' muckle wark,
An' took my jocteleg an' whatt it, — knife—whetted, sharpened
    Like ony clark.

[1] First published by Cromek in his *Reliques* (1808).

It 's now twa month that I 'm your debtor,
For your braw, nameless, dateless letter,
Abusin' me for harsh ill nature
On holy men,
While deil a hair yoursel ye 're better,
But mair profane.

But let the kirk-folk ring their bells,
Let 's sing about our noble sel's;
We 'll cry nae jads frae heathen hills — goddesses
To help, or roose us, — praise
But browster wives an' whisky stills, — women who brew or sell malt liquors
They are the muses.

Your friendship, sir, I winna quat it, — give it up
An' if ye mak objections at it,
Then han' in nieve some day we 'll knot it, — fist
An' witness take,
An' when wi' Usquabae we 've wat it, — whisky
It winna break.

But if the beast and branks be spar'd — wooden curbs
Till kye be gaun without the herd, — cows
An' a' the vittel in the yard, — victual, corn
An' theekit right, — thatched
I mean your ingle-side to guard — fireside
Ae winter night.

Then muse-inspirin' aqua-vitæ
Shall make us baith sae blythe an' witty,
Till ye forget ye 're auld an' gatty, — big-bellied
An' be as canty — merry
As ye were nine year less than thretty,
Sweet ane an' twenty!

But stooks are cowpet wi' the blast, — overturned
An' now the sinn keeks in the west, — sun—peeps
Then I maun rin amang the rest,
An' quat my chanter; — leave off rhyming
Sae I subscribe mysel in haste,
Yours, Rab the Ranter.[1]

[1] A sobriquet borrowed from the old Scots song 'Maggie Lauder.'

TO THE REV. JOHN M'MATH,[1]

INCLOSING A COPY OF 'HOLY WILLIE'S PRAYER,' WHICH HE HAD REQUESTED.

Sept. 17, 1785.

While at the stook the shearers cow'r shock—reapers
To shun the bitter blaudin' show'r, beating
Or in gulravage rinnin scow'r hurried scamper—escape
To pass the time,
To you I dedicate the hour
In idle rhyme.

My musie, tir'd wi' mony a sonnet
On gown, an' ban', an' douse black bonnet,[2] grave
Is grown right eerie now she 's done it, frightened
Lest they shou'd blame her,
An' rouse their holy thunder on it
And anathem her. curse

I own 'twas rash, an' rather hardy,
That I, a simple, countra bardie,
Shou'd meddle wi' a pack sae sturdy,
Wha, if they ken me,
Can easy, wi' a single wordie,
Louse h—ll upon me. Let loose

But I gae mad at their grimaces,
Their sighin, cantin, grace-prood faces,
Their three-mile prayers, an' hauf-mile graces,
Their raxin conscience, accommodating
Whase greed, revenge, an' pride disgraces
Waur nor their nonsense. worse

There 's Gau'n,[3] misca'd waur than a beast, reviled
Wha has mair honor in his breast

[1] At that time assistant, and afterwards successor, to the Rev. Peter Wodrow, minister of Tarbolton. He was licensed in 1779, and ordained at Tarbolton on 16th May 1789. He was an excellent preacher, and, like Wodrow, a moderate. He enjoyed the friendship of the Montgomeries of Coilsfield, and of Burns, but unhappily fell into low spirits, in consequence of his dependent situation, and became dissipated. He resigned his charge in 1791, and died in obscurity at Rossul, in the Isle of Mull, December 1825.

[2] 'Gown an' ban'' probably means minister, and 'black bonnet,' elder.

[3] Gavin Hamilton.

Than mony scores as guid 's the priest
Wha sae abus'd him.
An' may a bard no crack his jest
What way they 've used him?

See him, the poor man's friend in need,
The gentleman in word an' deed,
An' shall his fame an' honor bleed
By worthless skellums, wretches
An' not a muse erect her head
To cowe the blellums? bullies

O Pope, had I thy satire's darts
To gie the rascals their deserts,
I 'd rip their rotten, hollow hearts,
An' tell aloud
Their jugglin' hocus-pocus arts
To cheat the crowd.

God knows, I'm no the thing I shou'd be,
Nor am I even the thing I cou'd be,
But twenty times, I rather wou'd be
An atheist clean,
Than under gospel colors hid be
Just for a screen.

An honest man may like a glass,
An honest man may like a lass,
But mean revenge, an' malice fause false
He 'll still disdain,
An' then cry zeal for gospel laws,
Like some we ken.

They take religion in their mouth;
They talk o' mercy, grace an' truth,
For what? to gie their malice skouth scope
On some puir wight,
An' hunt him down, o'er right an' ruth,
To ruin streight. straight

All hail, religion! maid divine!
Pardon a muse sae mean as mine,
Who in her rough imperfect line
Thus daurs to name thee; dares
To stigmatize false friends of thine
Can ne'er defame thee.

Tho' blotch't an' foul wi' mony a stain,
An' far unworthy of thy train,
With trembling voice I tune my strain
To join with those
Who boldly dare thy cause maintain
In spite of foes:

In spite o' crowds, in spite o' mobs,
In spite of undermining jobs,
In spite o' dark banditti stabs
At worth an' merit,
By scoundrels, even wi' holy robes,
But hellish spirit.

O Ayr, my dear, my native ground,
Within thy presbyterial bound
A candid lib'ral band is found
Of public teachers,
As men, as Christians too, renown'd,
An' manly preachers.

Sir, in that circle you are nam'd;
Sir, in that circle you are fam'd;
An' some, by whom your doctrine 's blam'd
(Which gies you honor)
Even, Sir, by them your heart 's esteem'd,
An' winning manner.

Pardon this freedom I have ta'en,
An' if impertinent I 've been,
Impute it not, good Sir, in ane
Whase heart ne'er wrang'd ye,
But to his utmost would befriend
Ought that belang'd ye.

TO A MOUSE,

ON TURNING HER UP IN HER NEST, WITH THE PLOUGH, NOVEMBER 1785.

Wee, sleekit, cowrin, tim'rous beastie, sleek
O, what a panic 's in thy breastie!
Thou need na start awa sae hasty,
Wi' bickering brattle! hasty scamper
I wad be laith to rin an' chase thee, loath
Wi' murd'ring pattle![1]

[1] The stick used to remove clay sticking to the ploughshare.

I 'm truly sorry Man's dominion
Has broken Nature's social union,
An' justifies that ill opinion,
    Which makes thee startle,
At me, thy poor, earth-born companion,
    An' fellow-mortal!

I doubt na, whyles, but thou may thieve ;   sometimes
What then? poor beastie, thou maun live!
A daimen icker in a thrave [1]
    'S a sma' request:
I 'll get a blessin wi' the lave,   remainder
    And never miss 't!

Thy wee bit housie, too, in ruin!
Its silly wa's the win's are strewin!
An' naething, now, to big a new ane,   erect
    O' foggage green!   moss
An' bleak December's winds ensuin,
    Baith snell and keen!   biting

Thou saw the fields laid bare an' waste,
An' weary Winter comin fast,
An' cozie here, beneath the blast,   comfortable
    Thou thought to dwell,
Till crash! the cruel coulter past
    Out thro' thy cell.

That wee bit heap o' leaves an' stibble,   stubble
Has cost thee mony a weary nibble!
Now thou 's turn'd out, for a' thy trouble,
    But house or hald,   Without—holding
To thole the Winter's sleety dribble,   endure—drizzle
    An' cranreuch cauld!   hoar-frost

But Mousie, thou art no thy lane,   not alone
In proving foresight may be vain:
The best-laid schemes o' Mice an' Men
    Gang aft a-gley,   go often wrong
An' lea'e us nought but grief and pain,   leave
    For promis'd joy.

[1] An occasional ear of corn in twenty-four sheaves.

Still thou art blest, compar'd wi' me!
The present only toucheth thee:
But, Och! I backward cast my e'e,
On prospects drear!
An' forward, tho' I canna see,
I guess an' fear!

HALLOWEEN.[1]

The following poem will, by many readers, be well enough understood; but for the sake of those who are unacquainted with the manners and traditions of the country where the scene is cast, notes are added, to give some account of the principal charms and spells of that night, so big with prophecy to the peasantry in the west of Scotland. The passion of prying into futurity makes a striking part of the history of human nature in its rude state, in all ages and nations; and it may be some entertainment to a philosophic mind, if any such honour the author with a perusal, to see the remains of it, among the more unenlightened in our own.—*B.*

Yes! let the Rich deride, the Proud disdain,
The simple pleasures of the lowly train;
To me more dear, congenial to my heart,
One native charm, than all the gloss of art.—GOLDSMITH.

Upon that night, when Fairies light
On Cassilis Downans[2] dance,
Or owre the lays, in splendid blaze, fields
On sprightly coursers prance;
Or for Colean the route is ta'en,
Beneath the moon's pale beams;
There, up the Cove,[3] to stray an' rove
Amang the rocks an' streams
To sport that night.[4]

Amang the bony, winding banks,
Where Doon rins, wimplin, clear, meandering

1 Halloween [All Hallow Eve, or the eve of All Saints' Day] is thought to be a night when witches, devils, and other mischief-making beings are all abroad on their baneful, midnight errands; particularly those aërial people, the fairies, are said, on that night, to hold a grand anniversary.—*B.*

2 Certain little, romantic, rocky, green hills, in the neighbourhood of the ancient seat of the Earls of Cassilis.—*B.*

3 A noted cavern near Colean [Culzean] House, called the Cove of Colean; which, as well as Cassilis Downans, is famed, in country story, for being a favourite haunt of the fairies.—*B.*

4 The use of 'that night,' winding up every stanza in 'Halloween,' may be compared with the similar use of 'that day' in the old Scots poem of 'Christ's Kirk on the Green,' commonly, but on imperfect evidence, attributed to James I. of Scotland, in which every verse has for last line, 'At Christ's Kirk on the Green that day.'

Where Bruce[1] ance rul'd the martial ranks
 An' shook his Carrick spear,
Some merry, friendly, country-folks
 Together did convene,
To burn their nits, an' pou their stocks, — nuts—pull
 An' haud their Halloween — hold
 Fu' blythe that night.

The lasses feat, an' cleanly neat, — trim
 Mair braw than when they 're fine; — looking to greater advantage
Their faces blythe, fu' sweetly kythe, — appear
 Hearts leal, an' warm, an kin': — loyal—kind
The lads sae trig, wi' wooer-babs — spruce—love-knots
 Weel-knotted on their garten; — garters
Some unco blate, an' some wi' gabs, — very bashful—insinuating talk
 Gar lasses' hearts gang startin
 Whyles fast at night.

Then, first an' foremost, thro' the kail, — cabbage-plot
 Their 'stocks'[2] maun a' be sought ance;
They steek their e'en, an' graip an' wale — close—grope—choose
 For muckle anes and straught anes. — large—straight
Poor hav'rel Will fell aff the drift, — half-witted
 An' wander'd thro' the 'bow-kail,'
An' pow't, for want o' better shift, — pulled
 A runt was like a sow-tail,
 Sae bow't that night. — crooked

Then, straught or crooked, yird or nane,
 They roar an' cry a' throu'ther;
The vera wee-things, todlin, rin — tottering
 Wi' stocks out-owre their shouther;
An' gif the custoc 's sweet or sour,
 Wi' joctelegs they taste them; — knives
Syne coziely, aboon the door, — Then comfortably
 Wi' cannie care, they 've plac'd them — gentle
 To lie that night.

[1] The famous family of that name, the ancestors of ROBERT, the great Deliverer of his country, were Earls of Carrick.—*B.*

[2] The first ceremony of Halloween is, pulling a 'stock,' or plant of kail. They must go out, hand in hand, with eyes shut, and pull the first they meet with: its being big or little, straight or crooked, is prophetic of the size and shape of the grand object of all their spells—the husband or wife. If any 'yird,' or earth, stick to the root, that is 'tocher,' or fortune; and the taste of the 'custoc,' that is, the heart of the stem, is indicative of the natural temper and disposition. Lastly, the stems, or, to give them their proper appellation, the 'runts,' are placed somewhere above the head of the door; and the Christian names of people whom chance brings into the house are, according to the priority of placing the 'runts,' the names in question.—*B.*

The lasses staw frae 'mang them a', — stole out
  To pou their stalks o' corn ;[1]
But Rab slips out, an' jinks about, — dodges
  Behint the muckle thorn :
He grippet Nellie hard an' fast ;
  Loud skirl'd a' the lasses ; — screamed
But her tap-pickle maist was lost, — almost
  When kiutlin in the 'Fause-house'[2] — embracing
      Wi' him that night.

The auld Guidwife's weel-hoordet nits[3]
  Are round an' round divided,
An' monie lads and lasses' fates
  Are there that night decided :
Some kindle, couthie, side by side, — agreeably
  An' burn thegither trimly ; — together
Some start awa, wi' saucy pride,
  And jump out-owre the chimlie — fireplace
      Fu' high that night.

Jean slips in twa wi' tentie e'e ; — careful
  Wha 'twas she wadna tell ;
But this is *Jock*, an' this *me*,
  She says in to hersel :
He bleez'd owre her, an' she owre him,
  As they wad never màir part,
Till fuff ! he started up the lum, — chimney
  An' Jean had e'en a sàir heart
      To see 't that night.

Poor Willie, wi' his bow-kail runt,
  Was brunt wi' primsie Mallie ; — prudish
An' Mary, nae doubt, took the drunt, — pet
  To be compar'd to Willie : — associated with

[1] They go to the barnyard, and pull each, at three several times, a stalk of oats. If the third stalk wants the 'top-pickle,' that is, the grain at the top of the stalk, the party in question will come to the marriage-bed anything but a maid.—*B.*

[2] When the corn is in a doubtful state, by being too green or wet, the stack-builder, by means of old timber, &c., makes a large apartment in his stack, with an opening in the side which is fairest exposed to the wind : this he calls a 'fause-house.'—*B.*

[3] Burning the nuts is a favourite charm. They name the lad and lass to each particular nut, as they lay them in the fire, and accordingly as they burn quietly together, or start from beside one another, the course and issue of the courtship will be.—*B.*

Mall's nit lap out wi' pridefu' fling, — leaped
An' her ain fit it brunt it;
While Willie lap, and swoor *by jing*,
'Twas just the way he wanted
To be that night.

Nell had the 'Fause-house' in her min',
She pits hersel an' Rob in;
In loving bleeze they sweetly join,
Till white in ase they 're sobbin: — ashes
Nell's heart was dancin at the view;
She whisper'd Rob to leuk for 't:
Rob, stownins, prie'd her bonie mou, — stealthily—kissed—mouth
Fu' cozie in the neuk for 't, — snugly
Unseen that night.

But Merran sat behint their backs, — Marion
Her thoughts on Andrew Bell;
She lea'es them gashin at their cracks, — engaged in conversation
And slips out by hersel: — alone
She thro' the yard the nearest taks,
An' to the kiln she goes then,
An' darklins grapit for the bauks, — in the dark—searched—cross-beams
And in the 'blue-clue'[1] throws then,
Right fear't that night.

An' ay she win't, an' ay she swat, — winded
I wat she made nae jaukin; — wot, know—delay
Till something held within the pat,
Guid L—d! but she was quakin! — quaking
But whether 'twas the Deil himsel,
Or whether 'twas a bauk-en', — end of a beam
Or whether it was Andrew Bell,
She did na wait on talkin
To spier that night. — inquire

Wee Jenny to her Graunie says, — grandmother
'Will ye go wi' me, Graunie?

[1] Whoever would, with success, try this spell must strictly observe these directions: Steal out, all alone, to the kiln, and, darkling, throw into the 'pot' a clue of blue yarn; wind it in a new clue off the old one; and, towards the latter end, something will hold the thread: demand, 'Wha hauds?' *i.e.*, Who holds? and answer will be returned from the kiln-pot, by naming the Christian and Sirname of your future spouse.—*B.*

I 'll eat the apple at the glass,[1]
  I gat frae uncle Johnie :' — from
She fuff't her pipe wi' sic a lunt, — quantity of smoke
  In wrath she was sae vap'rin, — agitated
She notic't na, an aizle brunt — cinder
  Her braw, new, worset apron — worsted
    Out thro' that night.

'Ye little Skelpie-limmer's face ![2]
  I daur you try sic sportin,
As seek the foul Thief ony place,
  For him to spae your fortune : — foretell
Nae doubt but ye may get a sight !
  Great cause ye hae to fear it ;
For monie a ane has gotten a fright,
  An' liv'd an' di'd deleeret — insane
    On sic a night.

'Ae Hairst afore the Sherra-moor,[3] — a certain harvest
  I mind 't as weel 's yestreen, — yesterday
I was a gilpey then, I 'm sure — young girl
  I was na past fyfteen :
The Simmer had been cauld an' wat,
  An' stuff was unco green ; — corn
An' ay a rantin kirn we gat — jovial harvest-home
  And just on Halloween
    It fell that night

'Our "Stibble-rig"[4] was Rab M'Graen,
  A clever sturdy fallow ;
His Sin gat Eppie Sim wi' wean, — child
  That liv'd in Achmacalla :[5]
He gat hemp-seed,[6] I mind it weel,
  An' he made unco light o' 't ;
But monie a day was by himsel,
  He was sae sairly frighted
    That vera night.'

[1] Take a candle and go alone to a looking-glass ; eat an apple before it, and some traditions say, you should comb your hair all the time ; the face of your conjugal companion, *to be*, will be seen in the glass, as if peeping over your shoulder.—*B.*

[2] A technical term in female scolding.

[3] The battle of Sheriffmuir, near Dunblane, fought in 1715.

[4] The leader of the reapers.

[5] The locality of Achmacalla has never been identified. It has therefore been conjectured that Burns invented the name.

[6] Steal out unperceived, and sow a handful of hemp-seed, harrowing it with anything you can conveniently draw after you. Repeat, now and then—'Hemp-

Then up gat fechtin Jamie Fleck, fighting
An' he swoor by his conscience, swore
That he could saw hemp-seed a peck; sow
For it was a' but nonsense;
The auld guidman raught down the pock, reached—bag
An' out a handfu' gied him; gave
Syne bad him slip frae 'mang the folk, Then—from
Sometime when nae ane see'd him,
An' try 't that night.

He marches thro' amang the stacks,
Tho' he was something sturtin; timorous
The graip he for a harrow taks, dung-fork
An' haurls at his curpin: drags—rear
An' ev'ry now an' then, he says,
'Hemp-seed I saw thee,
An' her that is to be my lass,
Come after me, and draw thee
As fast this night.'

He whistl'd up 'Lord Lenox' March,'
To keep his courage cheary;
Altho' his hair began to arch,
He was sae fley'd an' eerie: frightened
Till presently he hears a squeak,
An' then a grane an' gruntle; groan—grunting noise
He by his shouther gae a keek, look
An' tumbl'd wi' a wintle somersault
Out-owre that night.

He roar'd a horrid murder-shout,
In dreadfu' desperation!
An' young an' auld come rinnin out,
An' hear the sad narration:
He swoor 'twas hilchin Jean M'Craw, halting
Or crouchie Merran Humphie, crook-backed
Till stop! she trotted thro' them a';
An' wha was it but Grumphie the pig
Asteer that night! Moving about

seed I saw thee, hemp-seed I saw thee; and him (or her) that is to be my true love, come after me and pou thee.' Look over your left shoulder, and you will see the appearance of the person invoked, in the attitude of pulling hemp. Some traditions say, 'Come after me, and shaw thee,' that is, show thyself; in which case, it simply appears. Others omit the harrowing, and say, 'Come after me, and harrow thee.'—*B.*

Meg fain wad to the Barn gaen, — would have gone
To winn three wechts o' naething;[1] — corn-baskets
But for to meet the Deil her lane, — all alone
She pat but little faith in:
She gies the Herd a pickle nits, — few
An' twa red cheekit apples,
To watch, while for the barn she sets, — goes
In hopes to see Tam Kipples
That vera night.

She turns the key wi' cannie thraw, — gentle twist
An' owre the threshold ventures;
But first on Sawnie gies a ca', — calls out the name of Satan
Syne bauldly in she enters:
A ratton rattl'd up the wa', — rat
An' she cry'd, L—d preserve her!
An' ran thro' midden-hole an' a', — pool beside the dunghill
An' pray'd wi' zeal an fervour,
Fu' fast that night.

They hoy't out Will, wi' sair advice; — inveigled—persistent
They hecht him some fine braw ane; — promised
It chanc'd the Stack he faddom't thrice,[2]
Was timmer-propt for thrawin;[3]
He taks a swirlie auld moss-oak, — crooked
For some black, grousome Carlin; — horrid-looking old woman
An' loot a winze, an' drew a stroke, — oath
Till skin in blypes cam haurlin — shreds—peeling
Aff 's nieves that night. — off his hands

A wanton widow Leezie was,
As cantie as a kittlen; — lively—kitten
But, Och! that night, amang the shaws, — woods
She got a fearfu' settlin!

[1] This charm must likewise be performed unperceived and alone. You go to the barn, and open both doors, taking them off the hinges if possible; for there is danger that the being about to appear may shut the doors, and do you some mischief. Then take that instrument used in winnowing the corn, which in our country-dialect we call a 'wecht,' and go through all the attitudes of letting down corn against the wind. Repeat it three times, and the third time an apparition will pass through the barn, in at the windy door, and out at the other, having both the figure in question, and the appearance or retinue, marking the employment or station in life.—*B.*

[2] Take an opportunity of going, unnoticed, to a 'bear-stack' [stack of bere or bigg, a kind of barley], and fathom it three times round. The last fathom of the last time, you will catch in your arms the appearance of your future conjugal yoke-fellow.—*B.*

[3] Propped all round with *timber* posts to prevent it from being blown out of shape.

She thro' the whins, an' by the cairn, gorse
An' owre the hill gaed scrievin; careering
Whare three Lairds' lan's meet at a burn,[1]
To dip her left sark-sleeve in,
Was bent that night.

Whyles owre a linn the burnie plays, waterfall—rivulet
As thro' the glen it wimpl't; meandered
Whyles round a rocky scaur it strays; bank of red earth
Whyles in a wiel it dimpl't; eddy
Whyles glitter'd to the nightly rays,
Wi' bickering, dancing dazzle;
Whyles cookit underneath the braes, crept
Below the spreading hazle,
Unseen that night.

Amang the brachens, on the brae, ferns
Between her an' the moon,
The Deil, or else an outler Quey, stray young cow
Gat up an' gae a croon: moan
Poor Leezie's heart maist lap the hool; sheath
Near lav'rock-height she jumpit, nearly as high as a lark's flight
But mist a fit, an' in the pool
Out-owre the lugs she plumpit,
Wi' a plunge that night.

In order, on the clean hearth-stane,
The 'luggies'[2] three are ranged,
And ev'ry time great care is ta'en
To see them duly changed:
Auld uncle John, wha wedlock's joys
Sin' 'Mar's year'[3] did desire,

[1] You go out, one or more, for this is a social spell, to a south-running spring, or rivulet, where 'three lairds' lands meet,' and dip your left shirt-sleeve. Go to bed in sight of a fire, and hang your wet sleeve before it to dry. Lie awake, and, sometime before midnight, an apparition, having the exact figure of the grand object in question, will come and turn the sleeve, as if to dry the other side of it.—*B.*

[2] Take three dishes, put clean water in one, foul water in another, leave the third empty; blindfold a person, and lead him to the hearth where the dishes are ranged; he (or she) dips the left hand: if by chance in the clean water, the future (husband or) wife will come to the bar of matrimony a maid; if in the foul, a widow; if in the empty dish, it foretells, with equal certainty, no marriage at all. It is repeated three times, and every time the arrangement of the dishes is altered.—*B.*

[3] The year 1715, when John Erskine, eleventh Earl of Mar (b. 1675, d. 1732), headed an insurrection in Scotland in the interest of the Pretender, whom he proclaimed king.

Because he gat the toom-dish thrice, empty
He heav'd them on the fire
In wrath that night.

Wi' merry sangs, an' friendly cracks,
I wat they did na weary; know
An' unco tales, an' funnie jokes,
Their sports were cheap an' cheary;
Till butter'd so'ns,[1] wi' fragrant lunt, steam
Set a' their gabs a-steerin; tongues wagging
Syne, wi' a social glass o' strunt, whisky
They parted aff careerin
Fu' blythe that night.[2]

SECOND EPISTLE TO DAVIE,[3]

A BROTHER POET.

AULD NEIBOR,
I'm three times doubly o'er your debtor,
For your auld farrant, frien'ly letter; quaint
Tho' I maun say 't, I doubt ye flatter,
Ye speak sae fair;
For my puir, silly, rhymin, clatter
Some less maun sair. serve

Hale be your heart, hale be your fiddle;
Lang may your elbuck jink an' diddle, elbow
Tae cheer you thro' the weary widdle struggle
O' war'ly cares,
Till bairns' bairns kindly cuddle grandchildren—fondle
Your auld, gray hairs.

But Davie, lad, I'm red ye 're glaikit; informed—inattentive
I'm tauld the Muse ye hae negleckit; told

1 Sowens, with butter instead of milk to them, is always the Halloween Supper.—*B.*

2 The majority of the ceremonies appropriate to Halloween, including all those of an adventurous character, are now disused. Meetings of young people still take place on that evening, both in country and town, but their frolics are usually limited to ducking for apples in tubs of water—a ceremony overlooked by Burns—the lottery of the dishes, and pulling cabbage-stalks.

3 David Sillar, the son of Patrick Sillar, farmer at Spittleside, about two miles distant from Lochlea.

An' gif it 's sae, ye sud be licket — if—so—should—beaten
Until ye fyke ; — move uneasily, from pain
Sic hauns as you sud ne'er be faikit, — hands—spared
Be hain't wha like. — saved from exertion

For me, I 'm on Parnassus brink,
Rivin the words tae gar them clink ; — tearing at—make—rhyme
Whyles daez't wi' love, whyles daez't wi' drink — sometimes bewildered
Wi' jads or masons ; — lasses
An' whyles, but ay owre late, I think
Braw sober lessons. — excellent

Of a' the thoughtless sons o' man,
Commen' me to the Bardie clan ;
Except it be some idle plan
O' rhymin clink,
The devil-haet, that I sud ban, — swear
They ever think.

Nae thought, nae view, nae scheme o' livin',
Nae cares tae gie us joy or grievin' :
But just the pouchie put the nieve in, — pocket—hand
An' while ought 's there, — anything
Then, hiltie, skiltie, we gae scrivin', — helter-skelter—careering
An' fash nae mair. — bother

Leeze me on rhyme ! it 's ay a treasure, — commend me to
My chief, amaist my only pleasure,
At hame, a-fiel, at wark or leisure, — abroad
The Muse, poor hizzie !
Tho' rough an' raploch be her measure, — coarse
She 's seldom lazy.

Haud tae the Muse, my dainty Davie :
The warl' may play you monie a shavie ; — trick
But for the Muse, she 'll never leave ye,
Tho' e'er sae puir,
Na, even tho' limpin wi' the spavie — spavin
Frae door tae door.

SONG—FAREWELL TO BALLOCHMYLE.[1]

The Catrine woods were yellow seen,
  The flowers decay'd on Catrine lee,
Nae lav'rock sang on hillock green,
  But nature sicken'd on the e'e.
Thro' faded groves Maria sang,
  Hersel in beauty's bloom the while;
And ay the wild-wood echoes rang,
  Fareweel the braes o' Ballochmyle.

Low in your wintry beds, ye flowers,
  Again ye 'll flourish fresh and fair;
Ye birdies dumb, in with'ring bowers,
  Again ye 'll charm the vocal air.
But here alas! for me nae mair
  Shall birdie charm, or floweret smile;
Fareweel the bonnie banks of Ayr,
  Fareweel, fareweel! sweet Ballochmyle!

MAN WAS MADE TO MOURN.

A DIRGE.

When chill November's[2] surly blast
  Made fields and forests bare,
One ev'ning, as I wander'd forth
  Along the banks of Ayr,
I spy'd a man, whose aged step
  Seem'd weary, worn with care;
His face was furrow'd o'er with years,
  And hoary was his hair.

[1] Composed on the amiable and excellent family of Whitefoord's leaving Ballochmyle, when Sir John's misfortunes (arising through his connection, as a shareholder, with the banking establishment of Douglas, Heron, & Co., of Ayr) obliged him to sell the estate.—*B.* 'Maria' was Mary Anne Whitefoord, the eldest of Sir John's four daughters. She married Henry Kerr Cranstoun, grandson of William, fifth Lord Cranstoun. Her husband's sister married Professor Dugald Stewart, who subsequently became a friend of Burns, and who was proprietor of the 'Catrine woods' and 'Catrine lee' mentioned in the song. They adjoin Ballochmyle, and are about two miles from Mauchline.

[2] In the Common-place Book, this poem is alluded to under date 'August 1785.' It is possible, therefore, that the 'chill November' alluded to may be the November of 1784.

'Young stranger, whither wand'rest thou?'[1]
   Began the rev'rend Sage;
'Does thirst of wealth thy step constrain,
   Or youthful Pleasures rage?
Or haply, prest with cares and woes,
   Too soon thou hast began
To wander forth, with me, to mourn
   The miseries of man.

'The Sun that overhangs yon moors,
   Out-spreading far and wide,
Where hundreds labour to support
   A haughty lordling's pride;[2]
I've seen yon weary winter-sun
   Twice forty times return;
And ev'ry time has added proofs,
   That Man was made to mourn.

'O Man! while in thy early years,
   How prodigal of time!
Mis-spending all thy precious hours,
   Thy glorious youthful prime!
Alternate Follies take the sway;
   Licentious Passions burn;
Which tenfold force gives Nature's law
   That Man was made to mourn.

'Look not alone on youthful Prime,
   Or manhood's active might;
Man then is useful to his kind,
   Supported is his right.
But see him on the edge of life,
   With cares and Sorrows worn,
Then Age and Want, Oh! ill-match'd pair!
   Show Man was made to mourn.

[1] In the seventh of Shenstone's elegies these lines occur:

'Stranger, amidst this pealing rain,
Benighted, lonesome, whither wouldst thou stray?
Does wealth or power thy weary step constrain?'

Mr J. Logie Robertson, in that portion of his *Furth in Field* entitled 'Burns in a New Aspect,' traces very minutely the influence exercised upon Burns by Goldsmith, Young, Shenstone, Blair, and Beattie.

[2] Variation in Common-place Book—

'Yon sun that hangs o'er Carrick Moors,
That spread so far and wide,
Where hundreds labor to support
The lordly Cassilis' pride.

'A few seem favourites of Fate,
In Pleasure's lap carest;
Yet, think not all the Rich and Great
Are likewise truly blest.
But, Oh! what crowds in ev'ry land,
All wretched and forlorn,
Thro' weary life this lesson learn,
That Man was made to mourn.

'Many and sharp the num'rous ills
Inwoven with our frame!
More pointed still we make ourselves,
Regret, Remorse, and Shame!
And Man, whose heav'n-erected face
The smiles of love adorn,
Man's inhumanity to Man
Makes countless thousands mourn!

'See yonder poor, o'erlabour'd wight,
So abject, mean, and vile,
Who begs a brother of the earth
To give him leave to toil;
And see his lordly fellow-worm
The poor petition spurn,
Unmindful, tho' a weeping wife
And helpless offspring mourn.

'If I'm design'd yon lordling's slave—
By Nature's law design'd—
Why was an independent wish
E'er planted in my mind?
If not, why am I subject to
His cruelty, or scorn?
Or why has man the will and pow'r
To make his fellow mourn?

'Yet, let not this too much, my son,
Disturb thy youthful breast:
This partial view of human-kind
Is surely not the last!
The poor, oppressèd, honest man
Had never, sure, been born,
Had there not been some recompense
To comfort those that mourn!

'O Death! the poor man's dearest friend,
The kindest and the best!
Welcome the hour my aged limbs
Are laid with thee at rest!
The great, the wealthy fear thy blow,
From pomp and pleasure torn;
But, oh! a blest relief for those
That weary-laden mourn!'

THE COTTER'S SATURDAY NIGHT.[1]

INSCRIBED TO R. AIKEN, ESQ.[2]

Let not Ambition mock their useful toil,
Their homely joys, and destiny obscure;
Nor Grandeur hear, with a disdainful smile,
The short and simple annals of the poor.—GRAY.

My lov'd, my honor'd, much respected friend!
No mercenary bard his homage pays;
With honest pride, I scorn each selfish end,
My dearest meed, a friend's esteem and praise:
To you I sing, in simple Scottish lays,
The lowly train in life's sequester'd scene;
The native feelings strong, the guileless ways;
What Aiken in a cottage would have been;
Ah! tho' his worth unknown, far happier there I ween!

November chill blaws loud wi' angry sugh; whistling sound
The short'ning winter-day is near a close;[3]
The miry beasts retreating frae the pleugh;
The black'ning trains o' craws to their repose: crows

[1] Sainte-Beuve, in an article on Aloïsius Bertrand, after quoting that author's description of the interior of a farmhouse, whither he had gone for shelter from a storm, says: 'By the side of this, we may set the poet Burns's famous piece, "The Cotter's Saturday Night." We should then see in what respect, quite apart from poetic form, the latter maintains a great superiority. For, where Bertrand strives, above all, to be picturesque, Burns shows himself—in addition to this—cordial, moral, Christian, patriotic. His episode of Jenny introduces and personifies the chastity of emotion; the Bible, read aloud, casts a religious glow over the whole scene. Then come those lofty thoughts upon the greatness of old Scotland, which is based on such home scenes as this: *Sic fortis Etruria crevit.*' Lockhart has probably given the final word of British criticism upon a poem whose weaknesses are as obvious as its merits, when he said: 'In spite of many feeble lines and some heavy stanzas, it appears to me that even Burns's genius would suffer more in estimation by being contemplated in the absence of this poem, than of any other single poem he has left us.'

[2] Probably the first verse and the inscription to Mr Aiken were added later.

[3] The opening verse of 'The Farmer's Ingle' bears a considerable resemblance to this:

Ha

C. Martin Hardie, R.S.A.

Th' expectant wee-things, toddlin, stacher through
To meet their 'dad,' wi' flichterin' noise and glee.

Page 87.

The toil-worn Cotter frae his labor goes,—
This night his weekly moil is at an end,
Collects his spades, his mattocks, and his hoes,
Hoping the morn in ease and rest to spend,
And weary, o'er the moor, his course does hameward bend.

At length his lonely cot appears in view,
Beneath the shelter of an aged tree;
Th' expectant wee-things, toddlin, stacher through — stagger
To meet their 'dad,' wi' flichterin' noise and glee. — fluttering
His wee bit ingle blinkin bonilie,
His clean hearth-stane, his thrifty wifie's smile,
The lisping infant, prattling on his knee,
Does a' his weary kiaugh and care beguile, — anxiety
And make him quite forget his labor and his toil.

Belyve, the elder bairns come drappin in, — By-and-by
At service out, amang the farmers roun';
Some ca' the pleugh, some herd, some tentie rin — attentively
A cannie errand to a neibor town; — private
Their eldest hope, their Jenny, woman-grown,
In youthfu' bloom—love sparkling in her e'e—
Comes hame; perhaps, to shew a braw new gown,
Or deposite her sair-won penny-fee, — hard-earned wages
To help her parents dear, if they in hardship be.

With joy unfeign'd, brothers and sisters meet,
And each for other's welfare kindly spiers: — inquires
The social hours, swift-wing'd, unnotic'd fleet;
Each tells the uncos that he sees or hears. — news
The parents partial eye their hopeful years;
Anticipation forward points the view;
The mother, wi' her needle and her sheers,
Gars auld claes look amaist as weel 's the new; — Makes—clothes
The father mixes a' wi' admonition due.

Their master's and their mistress's command,
The younkers a' are warnèd to obey;
And mind their labors wi' an eydent hand, — diligent
And ne'er, tho' out o' sight, to jauk or play; — dally

'Whan gloamin' gray out-owre the welkin keeks, — peeps
Whan Bawtie ca's the owsen to the byre, — drives
Whan Thrasher John, sair dung, his barn-door steeks, — jaded—shuts
Whan lusty lasses at the dighting tire: — winnowing
What bangs fu' leal the e'ening's coming cauld, — beats—truly
And gars snaw-tappit winter freeze in vain; — makes
Gars dowie mortals look baith blithe and bauld, — doleful
Nor fleyed wi' a' the puirtith o' the plain; — frightened
Begin, my Muse, and chant in hamely strain.'

'And O! be sure to fear the Lord alway,
And mind your duty, duly, morn and night;
Lest in temptation's path ye gang astray,
Implore His counsel and assisting might:
They never sought in vain that sought the Lord aright!'

But hark! a rap comes gently to the door;
Jenny, wha kens the meaning o' the same,
Tells how a neibor lad came o'er the moor,
To do some errands, and convoy her hame.
The wily mother sees the conscious flame
Sparkle in Jenny's e'e, and flush her cheek;
With heart-struck anxious care, enquires his name,
While Jenny hafflins is afraid to speak; **almost**
Weel-pleas'd the mother hears, it 's nae wild, worthless rake.

Wi' kindly welcome, Jenny brings him ben;
A strappin' youth, he takes the mother's eye;
Blythe Jenny sees the visit 's no ill ta'en; **received**
The father cracks of horses, pleughs, and kye.
The youngster's artless heart o'erflows wi' joy,
But blate an' laithfu', scarce can weel behave; **bashful—hesitating**
The mother, wi' a woman's wiles, can spy
What makes the youth sae bashfu' and sae grave;
Weel-pleas'd to think her bairn's respected like the lave. **child—rest**

O happy love! where love like this is found:
O heart-felt raptures! bliss beyond compare!
I've pacèd much this weary, mortal round,
And sage experience bids me this declare,—
'If Heaven a draught of heavenly pleasure spare—
One cordial in this melancholy vale,
'Tis when a youthful, loving, modest pair
In other's arms, breathe out the tender tale,
Beneath the milk-white thorn that scents the evening gale.'

Is there, in human form, that bears a heart,
A wretch! a villain! lost to love and truth!
That can, with studied, sly, ensnaring art,
Betray sweet Jenny's unsuspecting youth?
Curse on his perjur'd arts! dissembling, smooth!
Are honor, virtue, conscience, all exil'd?
Is there no pity, no relenting ruth,
Points to the parents fondling o'er their child?
Then paints the ruin'd maid, and their distraction wild?

But now the supper crowns their simple board,
  The halesome parritch, chief of Scotia's food; porridge
The sowpe their only hawkie does afford, food—cow
  That, 'yont the hallan snugly chows her cood: porch—cud
  The dame brings forth, in complimental mood,
To grace the lad, her weel-hain'd kebbuck, fell; well-matured cheese—tasty
  And aft he 's prest, and aft he ca's it guid;
The frugal wifie, garrulous, will tell
How 'twas a towmond auld, sin' lint was i' the bell. twelvemonth—flax in flower

The cheerfu' supper done, wi' serious face,
  They, round the ingle, form a circle wide;
The sire turns o'er, with patriarchal grace,
  The big ha'-bible, ance his father's pride: large Bible, that lay in the hall
  His bonnet rev'rently is laid aside,
His lyart haffets wearing thin and bare; gray side-locks
  Those strains that once did sweet in Zion glide,
He wales a portion with judicious care; selects
And 'Let us worship God!' he says with solemn air.

They chant their artless notes in simple guise,
  They tune their hearts, by far the noblest aim;
Perhaps 'Dundee's' wild-warbling measures rise,
  Or plaintive 'Martyrs,' worthy of the name;
  Or noble 'Elgin' beets the heaven-ward flame, fans
The sweetest far of Scotia's holy lays:
  Compar'd with these, Italian trills are tame;
The tickl'd ears no heart-felt raptures raise;
Nae unison hae they, with our Creator's praise.

The priest-like father reads the sacred page,
  How Abram was the friend of God on high;
Or, Moses bade eternal warfare wage
  With Amalek's ungracious progeny;
  Or, how the royal bard did groaning lie
Beneath the stroke of Heaven's avenging ire;
  Or Job's pathetic plaint, and wailing cry;
Or rapt Isaiah's wild, seraphic fire;
Or other holy seers that tune the sacred lyre.

Perhaps the Christian volume is the theme,
  How guiltless blood for guilty man was shed;
How He, who bore in Heaven the second name,
  Had not on earth whereon to lay His head:

How His first followers and servants sped;
The precepts sage they wrote to many a land:
How he, who lone in Patmos banishèd,
Saw in the sun a mighty angel stand,
And heard great Bab'lon's doom pronounc'd by Heaven's command.

Then kneeling down to Heaven's Eternal King,
The saint, the father, and the husband prays:
Hope 'springs exulting on triumphant wing,'[1]
That thus they all shall meet in future days,
There, ever bask in uncreated rays,
No more to sigh, or shed the bitter tear,
Together hymning their Creator's praise,
In such society, yet still more dear;
While circling Time moves round in an eternal sphere.

Compar'd with this, how poor Religion's pride,
In all the pomp of method, and of art;
When men display to congregations wide
Devotion's ev'ry grace, except the heart!
The Power, incens'd, the pageant will desert,
The pompous strain, the sacerdotal stole;
But haply, in some cottage far apart,
May hear, well pleas'd, the language of the soul;
And in His Book of Life the inmates poor enroll.

Then homeward all take off their sev'ral way;
The youngling cottagers retire to rest: **youthful**
The parent-pair their secret homage pay,
And proffer up to Heaven the warm request,
That He who stills the raven's clam'rous nest,
And decks the lily fair in flow'ry pride,
Would, in the way His wisdom sees the best,
For them and for their little ones provide;
But chiefly, in their hearts with grace divine preside.

From scenes like these, old Scotia's grandeur springs,
That makes her lov'd at home, rever'd abroad:
Princes and lords are but the breath of kings,
'An honest man 's the noblest work of God;'

[1] Pope's 'Windsor Forest.'—*B.*

And certes, in fair virtue's heavenly road,
The cottage leaves the palace far behind;
What is a lordling's pomp?—a cumbrous load,
Disguising oft the wretch of human kind,
Studied in arts of hell, in wickedness refin'd!

O Scotia! my dear, my native soil!
For whom my warmest wish to Heaven is sent,
Long may thy hardy sons of rustic toil
Be blest with health, and peace, and sweet content!
And O! may Heaven their simple lives prevent
From luxury's contagion, weak and vile!
Then, howe'er crowns and coronets be rent,
A virtuous populace may rise the while,
And stand a wall of fire around their much-lov'd isle.

O Thou! who pour'd the patriotic tide,
That stream'd thro' Wallace's undaunted heart,[1]
Who dar'd to, nobly, stem tyrannic pride,
Or nobly die, the second glorious part:
(The patriot's God, peculiarly thou art,
His friend, inspirer, guardian, and reward!)
O never, never, Scotia's realm desert;
But still the patriot, and the patriot-bard,
In bright succession raise, her ornament and guard!

ADDRESS TO THE DEIL.

O Prince! O chief of many thronèd pow'rs!
That led th' embattl'd seraphim to war.—MILTON.

O THOU! whatever title suit thee—
Auld 'Hornie,' 'Satan,' 'Nick,' or 'Clootie,'[2]
Wha in yon cavern grim an' sootie,
Clos'd under hatches,
Spairges about the brunstane cootie, — dashes—pail of brimstone
To scaud poor wretches! — scald

Hear me, auld 'Hangie,' for a wee,
An' let poor damnèd bodies be;

[1] This originally read, 'Great, unhappy Wallace' heart.' The change to what appears in the text was made to please Burns's friend and correspondent, Mrs Dunlop.
[2] A Scottish nickname for Satan, from his cloven feet or *cloots*.

I 'm sure sma' pleasure it can gie,
Ev'n to a deil,
To skelp an' scaud door dogs like me, slap—unmanageable
An' hear us squeel!

Great is thy pow'r an' great thy fame;
Far kenn'd an' noted is thy name;
An' tho' yon lowin heugh 's thy hame, burning pit
Thou travels far;
An' faith! thou 's neither lag nor lame, slow
Nor blate, nor scaur. bashful—apt to be scared

Whyles, rangin like a roarin lion,
For prey, a' holes an' corners tryin;
Whyles, on the strong-wing'd tempest flyin,
Tirlin the kirks; Unroofing—churches
Whyles, in the human bosom pryin,
Unseen thou lurks.

I 've heard my rev'rend grannie say,
In lanely glens ye like to stray;
Or where auld ruin'd castles grey
Nod to the moon,
Ye fright the nightly wand'rer's way,
Wi' eldritch croon. weird

When twilight did my grannie summon,
To say her pray'rs, douse, honest woman!
Aft 'yont the dyke she 's heard you bummin,
Wi' eerie drone;
Or, rustlin', thro' the boortrees comin, elder-trees
Wi' heavy groan.

Ae dreary, windy, winter night,
The stars shot down wi' sklentin light, slanting
Wi' you mysel, I gat a fright,
Ayont the lough;
Ye, like a rash-buss, stood in sight, tuft of rushes
Wi' wavin sough. sound

The cudgel in my nieve did shake, fist
Each bristl'd hair stood like a stake,
When wi' an eldritch, stoor 'quaick, quaick,' deep-voiced
Amang the springs,
Awa ye squatter'd like a drake, noisy flight of a wild duck
On whistlin wings.

Let warlocks grim, an' wither'd hags,
Tell how wi' you, on ragweed nags, ragwort
They skim the muirs an' dizzy crags, moors
Wi' wicked speed;
And in kirk-yards renew their leagues,
Owre howket dead. dug-up

Thence, countra wives, wi' toil an' pain,
May plunge an' plunge the kirn in vain; churn
For oh! the yellow treasures taen
By witchin skill;
An' dawtet, twal-pint 'hawkie's' gane petted—cow
As yell 's the bill. milkless as the bull

Thence, mystic knots mak great abuse
On young guidmen, fond, keen an' croose; confident
When the best wark-lume i' the house,
By cantraip wit, magic
Is instant made no worth a louse,
Just at the bit.

When thowes dissolve the snawy hoord, thaws
An' float the jinglin icy boord,
Then, water-kelpies haunt the foord, water-spirits—ford
By your direction,
And 'nighted trav'llers are allur'd benighted
To their destruction.

And aft your moss-traversin 'Spunkies' Will-o'-the-wisps
Decoy the wight that late an' drunk is:
The bleezin, curst, mischievous monkies
Delude his eyes,
Till in some miry slough he sunk is,
Ne'er mair to rise.

When masons' mystic word an' grip
In storms an' tempests raise you up,
Some cock or cat your rage maun stop,
Or, strange to tell!
The youngest 'brither' ye wad whip
Aff straught to hell.

Lang syne in Eden's bonie yard, garden
When youthfu' lovers first were pair'd,
An' all the soul of love they shar'd,
The raptur'd hour—
Sweet on the fragrant flow'ry swaird, sward
In shady bow'r;[1]

Then you, ye auld, snick-drawin dog![2]
Ye cam to Paradise *incog*,
An' play'd on man a cursèd brogue, trick
(Black be your fa'!)
An' gied the infant warld a shog, shake
'Maist ruin'd a'.

D'ye mind that day when in a bizz bustle
Wi' reeket duds, an' reestet gizz, smoked clothes—withered appearance
Ye did present your smootie phiz dirty face
'Mang better folk,
An' sklented on the man of Uzz cast
Your spitefu' joke?

An' how ye gat him i' your thrall,
An' brak him out o' house an' hal',
While scabs an' blotches[3] did him gall,
Wi' bitter claw;
An' lows'd his ill-tongu'd, wicked scaul— scolding wife
Was warst ava?

But a' your doings to rehearse,
Your wily snares an' fechtin fierce,
Sin' that day Michael did you pierce,
Down to this time,
Wad ding a Lallan tongue, or Erse, be too much for—Lowland Scots—Irish Gaelic
In prose or rhyme.

[1] Until Burns's quarrel with the Armours, this verse ran:

'Lang syne, in Eden's happy scene
When strappin Adam's days were green,
And Eve was like my bonie Jean—
My dearest part,
A dancin, sweet, young handsome quean,
O' guileless heart.'

[2] 'Snick-drawin dog' means a person who opens doors by drawing the *sneck* or latch noiselessly.

[3] 'Botches' was the word used in this connection in all editions of Burns's Poems till that of 1794.

An now, auld 'Cloots,' I ken ye 're thinkin,
A certain bardie's rantin, drinkin,
Some luckless hour will send him linkin,
To your black pit;
But, faith! he 'll turn a corner jinkin, dodging
An' cheat you yet.

But fare-you-weel, auld 'Nickie-ben!'
O wad ye tak a thought an' men'!
Ye aiblins might—I dinna ken— perhaps
Still hae a stake:
I 'm wae to think upo' yon den,
Ev'n for your sake!

EPITAPH ON JOHN DOVE,[1]

INNKEEPER, MAUCHLINE.

Here lies Johnie Pigeon;
What was his religion?
Whaever desires to ken,
To some other warl'
Maun follow the carl,
For here Johnie Pigeon had nane!

Strong ale was ablution—
Small beer—persecution,
A dram was '*memento mori;*'
But a full-flowing bowl
Was the saving his soul,
And port was celestial glory.

[1] It seems probable that Dove came originally from Paisley, and that he is the 'Paisley John' of another of Burns's poems. The Whitefoord Arms has been rebuilt, and is now a co-operative store, in two storeys, having on its central chimney this inscription—the work, according to the late Dr Edgar, of 'a local poetaster and worthy elder of the kirk:'

'The house, though built anew,
Where Burns cam weary frae the plough,
To hae a crack wi' Johnny Dow;
O' nights at een,
And whyles to taste the mountain dew
Wi' bonny Jean.'

THE JOLLY BEGGARS:

A CANTATA.

RECITATIVO.

When lyart leaves bestrow the yird, — withered—ground
Or wavering like the bauckie-bird, — bat
Bedim cauld Boreas' blast;
When hailstanes drive wi' bitter skyte, — slanting stroke
And infant frosts begin to bite,
In hoary cranreuch drest; — hoar-frost
Ae night at e'en a merry core — corps, party
O' randie, gangrel bodies,[1] — disorderly, vagrant
In Poosie-Nansie's held the splore, — merry-meeting
To drink their orra duddies: — superfluous rags
Wi' quaffing and laughing,
They ranted an' they sang,
Wi' jumping an' thumping,
The vera girdle [2] rang.

First, niest the fire, in auld red rags,
Ane sat, weel brac'd wi' mealy bags, — girdled with bags for holding the meal
And knapsack a' in order;
His doxy lay within his arm;
Wi' usquebae an' blankets warm — whisky
She blinket on her sodger:
An' ay he gies the tozie drab [3] — tipsy
The tither skelpin kiss, — noisy
While she held up her greedy gab, — mouth
Just like an aumous dish: [4]
Ilk smack still did crack still,
Just like a cadger's whip; — hawker or carrier
Then staggering an' swaggering,
He roar'd this ditty up—

[1] 'Randie-beggars' was long a Scottish equivalent for 'gypsies.'

[2] An iron plate, used in Scottish cottages for baking cakes over the fire.

[3] The late Dr Edgar showed in his *Old Church Life in Scotland* (vol. i.) that the 'tozie drab' may possibly have been 'a vagrant woman called Agnes Wilson, of bad fame in the parish and places whence she came, who for more than six months past has been haunted and entertained by Elizabeth Black and George Gibson,' and who is dealt with in a minute of kirk-session, dated 6th March 1786. He regarded it as absolutely certain, at all events, that Agnes Wilson was the 'jurr' referred to in the humorous poem, 'Adam Armour's Prayer.'

[4] The Scottish beggars used to carry a large wooden dish for the reception of any alms which took the shape of food. The same utensil seems to have once been (if it is not so still) a part of the accoutrements of a Continental beggar. When the revolted Netherlanders, in the sixteenth century, assumed the character of *Les Gueux*, or the Beggars, a beggar's *wooden cup* was one of their insignia.

AIR.

TUNE—*Soldier's Joy.*

I am a son of Mars who have been in many wars,
And show my cuts and scars wherever I come;
This here was for a wench, and that other in a trench,
When welcoming the French at the sound of the drum.
Lal de daudle, &c.

My prenticeship I past where my leader breath'd his last,
When the bloody die was cast on the heights of Abram:[1]
And I servèd out my trade when the gallant game was play'd,
And the Moro[2] low was laid at the sound of the drum.
Lal de daudle, &c.

I lastly was with Curtis among the floating batt'ries,[3]
And there I left for witness an arm and a limb;
Yet let my country need me, with Elliot[4] to head me,
I'd clatter on my stumps at the sound of a drum.
Lal de daudle, &c.

And now tho' I must beg, with a wooden arm and leg,
And many a tatter'd rag hanging over my bum,
I'm as happy with my wallet, my bottle and my callet, trull
As when I used in scarlet to follow a drum.
Lal de daudle, &c.

What tho', with hoary locks, I must stand the winter shocks,
Beneath the woods and rocks, oftentimes for a home,
When the tother bag I sell, and the tother bottle tell,
I could meet a troop of hell, at the sound of a drum.
Lal de daudle, &c.

1 The battle-ground in front of Quebec, where Wolfe fell victorious, September 1759. So called from Maître Abraham, a local pilot.

2 El Moro, the castle which defends the entrance to the harbour of Santiago or St Jago, a small island near the southern shore of Cuba. It is situated on an eminence, the abutments being cut out of the limestone rock. In 1762 the castle was stormed and taken by the British, after which Havana was surrendered with spoil to the value of three millions.

3 'The destruction of the Spanish floating-batteries during the famous siege of Gibraltar in 1782—on which occasion the gallant Captain Curtis rendered the most signal service—is the heroic exploit here referred to.'—MOTHERWELL.

4 George Augustus Eliott, created Lord Heathfield for his gallant and successful defence of Gibraltar during a siege of three years. Born 1717, died 1790.

RECITATIVO.

He ended; and the kebars sheuk, rafters
Aboon the chorus roar;
While frighted rattons backward leuk, rats
An' seek the benmost bore: innermost hole
A fairy fiddler frae the neuk, corner
He skirl'd out, encore!
But up arose the martial chuck, sweetheart
An' laid the loud uproar.

AIR.

TUNE—*Sodger Laddie.*

I once was a maid, tho' I cannot tell when,
And still my delight is in proper young men:
Some one of a troop of dragoons was my daddie,
No wonder I'm fond of a sodger laddie.
Sing, Lal de dal, &c.

The first of my loves was a swaggering blade,
To rattle the thundering drum was his trade;
His leg was so tight, and his cheek was so ruddy,
Transported I was with my sodger laddie.
Sing, Lal de dal, &c.

But the godly old chaplain left him in the lurch;
The sword I forsook for the sake of the church:
He ventur'd the soul, and I risket the body,
'Twas then I prov'd false to my sodger laddie.
Sing, Lal de dal, &c.

Full soon I grew sick of my sanctified sot,
The regiment at large for a husband I got;
From the gilded spontoon to the fife I was ready,
I askèd no more but a sodger laddie.
Sing, Lal de dal, &c.

But the peace it reduc'd me to beg in despair,
Till I met my old boy in a Cunningham fair;
His rags regimental they flutter'd so gaudy,
My heart it rejoic'd at a sodger laddie.
Sing, Lal de dal, &c.

And now I have liv'd—I know not how long,
And still I can join in a cup and a song;
But whilst with both hands I can hold the glass steady,
Here 's to thee, my hero, my sodger laddie.
Sing, Lal de dal, &c.

RECITATIVO.

Poor Merry-Andrew, in the neuk,
Sat guzzling wi' a tinkler-hizzie; tinker-wench
They mind't na wha the chorus teuk,
Between themselves they were sae busy:
At length, wi' drink an' courting dizzy,
He stoiter'd up an' made a face; staggered
Then turn'd, an' laid a smack on Grizzie, kiss
Syne tun'd his pipes wi' grave grimace.

AIR.

TUNE—*Auld Sir Symon.*

Sir Wisdom 's a fool when he 's fou; drunk
Sir Knave is a fool in a session;[1]
He 's there but a prentice I trow,
But I am a fool by profession.

My grânnie she bought me a beuk,
An' I held awa to the school;
I fear I my talent misteuk,
But what will ye hae of a fool?

For drink I would venture my neck;
A hizzie 's the half of my craft; wench
But what could ye other expect,
Of ane that 's avowedly daft? crazy

I ance was ty'd up like a stirk, bullock
For civilly swearing and quaffing;
I ance was abus'd i' the kirk,
For towsing a lass i' my daffin. rumpling—fun

Poor Andrew that tumbles for sport,
Let nae body name wi' a jeer;
There 's even, I 'm tauld, i' the Court
A tumbler ca'd the Premier.

[1] When being tried criminally.

Observ'd ye yon reverend lad
  Mak faces to tickle the mob;
He rails at our mountebank squad,
  It 's rivalship just i' the job.

And now my conclusion I 'll tell,
  For faith I 'm confoundedly dry:
The chiel that 's a fool for himself,
  Guid L—d, he 's far dafter than I.

RECITATIVO.

Then niest outspak a raucle carlin, — stout beldame
Wha kent fu' weel to cleek the sterlin; — steal
For mony a pursie she had hooked,
An' had in mony a well been douked:
Her love had been a Highland laddie,
But weary fa' the waefu' woodie! — gallows
Wi' sighs an' sobs she thus began
To wail her braw John Highlandman

AIR.

TUNE—*O an' ye were dead, Gudeman.*

A Highland lad my love was born,
The lalland laws he held in scorn; — Lowland
But he still was faithfu' to his clan,
My gallant, braw John Highlandman.

CHORUS.

Sing hey my braw John Highlandman!
Sing ho my braw John Highlandman!
There 's not a lad in a' the lan'
Was match for my John Highlandman.

With his philibeg an' tartan plaid, — kilt
An' guid claymore down by his side, — good broadsword
The ladies' hearts he did trepan,
My gallant, braw John Highlandman.
  Sing hey, &c.

We rangèd a' from Tweed to Spey,
An' liv'd like lords an' ladies gay;
For a lalland face he fearèd none,
My gallant, braw John Highlandman.
  Sing hey, &c.

They banish'd him beyond the sea,
But ere the bud was on the tree,
Adown my cheeks the pearls ran,
Embracing my John Highlandman.
Sing hey, &c.

But Och! they catch'd him at the last,
And bound him in a dungeon fast,
My curse upon them every one,
They 've hang'd my braw John Highlandman.
Sing hey, &c.

And now a widow I must mourn
The pleasures that will ne'er return;
No comfort but a hearty can,
When I think on John Highlandman.
Sing hey, &c.

RECITATIVO.

A pigmy scraper wi' his fiddle,
Wha us'd at trystes an' fairs to driddle, cattle fairs—play
Her strappin limb an' gausy middle powerful—buxom
(He reach'd nae higher)
Had hol'd his heartie like a riddle, sieve
An' blawn 't on fire. blown

Wi' hand on hainch, and upward e'e, haunch
He croon'd his gamut, one, two, three, murmured
Then in an arioso key,
The wee Apollo
Set off wi' allegretto glee
His giga solo.

AIR.

TUNE—*Whistle owre the lave o' 't.*

Let me ryke up to dight that tear, reach—wipe
An' go wi' me an' be my dear;
An' then your every care an' fear
May whistle owre the lave o' 't. rest

CHORUS.

I am a fiddler to my trade,
An' a' the tunes that e'er I play'd,
The sweetest still to wife or maid,
Was whistle owre the lave o' 't.

At kirns an' weddins we 'se be there, harvest-homes
An' O sae nicely 's we will fare!
We 'll bowse about till Dadie Care booze
Sing whistle owre the lave o' 't.
I am, &c.

Sae merrily 's the banes we 'll pyke, bones—pick
An' sun oursells about the dyke; wall, fence
An' at our leisure, when ye like,
We 'll whistle owre the lave o' 't.
I am, &c.

But bless me wi' your heav'n o' charms,
An' while I kittle hair on thairms, apply hair to catgut
Hunger, cauld, an' a' sic harms cold
May whistle owre the lave o' 't.
I am, &c.

RECITATIVO.

Her charms had struck a sturdy caird, gipsy
As weel as poor gutscraper; well
He taks the fiddler by the beard,
An' draws a roosty rapier— rusty
He swoor by a' was swearing worth
To speet him like a pliver, spit—plover for roasting
Unless he would from that time forth
Relinquish her for ever:

Wi' ghastly e'e poor tweedledee eye
Upon his hunkers bended, knees
An' pray'd for grace wi' ruefu' face,
An' so the quarrel ended;
But tho' his little heart did grieve,
When round the tinkler prest her,
He feign'd to snirtle in his sleeve, laugh
When thus the caird address'd her:

AIR.

TUNE—*Clout the Caudron.*

My bonie lass, I work in brass,
  A tinkler is my station;
I 've travell'd round all Christian ground
  In this my occupation;
I 've ta'en the gold an' been enroll'd
  In many a noble squadron;
But vain they search'd when off I march'd
  To go an' clout the caudron. mend
    I 've ta'en the gold, &c.

Despise that shrimp, that withered imp,
  With a' his noise an' cap'rin;
An' take a share with those that bear
  The budget and the apron! bag of tools
And *by* that stowp! my faith an' houpe, stoup—hope
  And *by* that dear Kilbaigie,[1]
If e'er ye want, or meet wi' scant,
  May I ne'er weet my craigie. wet—throat
    And by that stowp, &c.

RECITATIVO.

The caird prevail'd—th' unblushing fair
  In his embraces sunk;
Partly wi' love o'ercome sae sair,
  An' partly she was drunk:
Sir Violino, with an air
  That show'd a man o' spunk, mettle
Wish'd unison between the pair,
  An' made the bottle clunk give a hollow sound, as if empty
    To their health that night.

But hurchin Cupid shot a shaft, urchin
  That play'd a dame a shavie— trick
The fiddler rak'd her, fore and aft,
  Behint the chicken cavie. coop

[1] A peculiar sort of whisky so called, a great favorite with Poosie Nansie's clubs.—*R. B.* It was made at Kilbaigie distillery, in the county of Clackmannan.

Her lord, a wight of Homer's craft,[1]
  Tho' limpin wi' the spavie, spavin
He hirpl'd up, an' lap like daft, leaped as if mad
  An' shor'd them *Dainty Davie* promised
    O' boot that night. into the bargain

He was a care-defying blade
  As ever Bacchus listed!
Tho' Fortune sair upon him laid, sorely
  His heart she ever miss'd it.
He had no wish but—to be glad,
  Nor want but—when he thirsted;
He hated nought but—to be sad,
  An' thus the Muse suggested
    His sang that night.

AIR.

TUNE—*For a' that an' a' that.*

I am a Bard of no regard,
  Wi' gentle folks an' a' that;
But Homer like, the glowrin byke, staring multitude
  Frae town to town I draw that.

CHORUS.

For a' that an' a' that,
  An' twice as muckle 's a' that, much
I 've lost but ane, I 've twa behin',
  I 've wife eneugh for a' that. enough

I never drank the Muses' stank, fountain
  Castalia's burn an' a' that;
But there it streams an' richly reams,
  My Helicon[2] I ca' that. call
    For a' that, &c.

Great love I bear to all the fair,
  Their humble slave an' a' that;
But lordly will, I hold it still
  A mortal sin to thraw that. cross
    For a' that, &c.

[1] Homer is allowed to be the oldest ballad-singer on record.—*R. B.*
[2] Here, as elsewhere, Burns speaks of Helicon as a spring.

In raptures sweet this hour we meet,
Wi' mutual love an' a' that;
But for how lang the flie may stang,
Let inclination law that.
For a' that, &c.

Their tricks an' craft hae put me daft,
They 've ta'en me in, an' a' that;
But clear your decks, an' here 's the Sex!
I like the jads for a' that. jades

CHORUS.

For a' that an' a' that,
An' twice as muckle 's a' that,
My dearest bluid, to do them guid,
They 're welcome till 't for a' that.

RECITATIVO.

So sung the bard—and Nansie's wa's walls
Shook with a thunder of applause
Re-echo'd from each mouth!
They toom'd their pocks, they pawn'd their duds, emptied—bags—clothes
They scarcely left to coor their fuds, cover—posteriors
To quench their lowin drouth, burning thirst
Then owre again the jovial thrang crew
The poet did request
To lowse his pack an' wale a sang, open—select
A ballad o' the best;
He, rising, rejoicing,
Between his twa Deborahs,
Looks round him, an' found them
Impatient for the chorus.

AIR.

TUNE—*Jolly Mortals, fill your glasses.*

See the smoking bowl before us,
Mark our jovial, ragged ring!
Round and round take up the chorus,
And in raptures let us sing—

CHORUS.

A fig for those by law protected!
Liberty 's a glorious feast!
Courts for cowards were erected,
Churches built to please the priest.

What is title, what is treasure,
What is reputation's care?
If we lead a life of pleasure,
'Tis no matter how or where.
A fig, &c.

With the ready trick and fable,
Round we wander all the day;
And at night, in barn or stable,
Hug our doxies on the hay.
A fig, &c.

Does the train-attended carriage
Thro' the country lighter rove?
Does the sober bed of marriage
Witness brighter scenes of love?
A fig, &c.

Life is all a variorum,
We regard not how it goes;
Let them cant about decorum,
Who have character to lose.
A fig, &c.

Here 's to budgets, bags and wallets!
Here 's to all the wandering train!
Here 's our ragged brats and callets! children—wenches
One and all cry out, Amen!
A fig, &c.[1]

[1] 'In one or two passages of 'The Jolly Beggars,' the Muse has slightly trespassed on decorum, where, in the language of Scottish song:

"High kilted was she,
As she gaed owre the lee."

Something, however, is to be allowed to the nature of the subject, and something to the education of the poet; and if from veneration to the names of Swift and Dryden, we tolerate the grossness of the one and the indelicacy of the other, the respect due to that of Burns may surely claim indulgence for a few light strokes of broad humour.'—SIR WALTER SCOTT.

'The world of Chaucer is fairer, richer, more significant than that of Burns; but when the largeness and freedom of Burns get full sweep, as in "Tam o' Shanter," or still more in that puissant and splendid production, "The Jolly Beggars," his world may be what it will, his poetic genius triumphs over it. In the world of "The Jolly Beggars" there is more than hideousness and squalor, there is bestiality; yet the piece is a superb poetic success. It has a breadth, truth, and power which make the famous scene in Auerbach's cellar, of Goethe's *Faust*, seem artificial and tame beside it, and which are only matched by Shakespeare and Aristophanes.'—MATTHEW ARNOLD.

'His masterpiece, "The Jolly Beggars," like "The Gueux" of Béranger; but how much more picturesque, varied, and powerful!'—TAINE.

SONG—FOR A' THAT AN' A' THAT.[1]

Tho' women's minds, like winter winds,
May shift, and turn, an' a' that,
The noblest breast adores them maist, most
A consequence I draw that.

Chorus—For a' that an' a' that,
And twice as mickle as a' that;
The bony lass that I loe best love
She 'll be my ain for a' that. own

Great love I bear to all the fair,
Their humble slave, an' a' that,
But lordly will, I hold it still
A mortal sin to thraw that. cross
For a' that, &c.

But there is ane aboon the lave, superior to the rest
Has wit, and sense, an' a' that;
A bonie lass, I like her best,
And wha a crime dare ca' that? call
For a' that, &c.

In rapture sweet this hour we meet,
Wi' mutual love, an' a' that,
But for how lang the flie may stang,
Let inclination law that.
For a' that, &c.

Their tricks and craft hae put me daft,
They 've taen me in, an' a' that;
But clear your decks, and here 's 'The sex!'
I like the jads for a' that. jades
For a' that, &c.

[1] This is an altered version of the Bard's first song in 'The Jolly Beggars;' the next, 'Kissin my Katie,' seems to have been the first draft of the Caird's song. Both appeared in Johnson's *Museum* in 1790.

SONG—KISSIN MY KATIE.

TUNE—*The bob o' Dumblane.*

O merry hae I been teethin a heckle,[1]
An' merry hae I been shapin a spoon;
O merry hae I been cloutin a kettle, mending
An' kissin my Katie when a' was done.
O, a' the lang day I ca' at my hammer,
An' a' the lang day I whistle and sing;
O, a' the lang night I cuddle my kimmer, companion or mistress
An' a' the lang night as happy 's a king.

Bitter in dool I lickit my winnins grief—ate the fruit of—earnings
O' marrying Bess, to gie her a slave:
Blest be the hour she cool'd in her linnens,
And blythe be the bird that sings on her grave!
Come to my arms, my Katie, my Katie,
An' come to my arms and kiss me again!
Drucken or sober, here 's to thee, Katie! drunken
And blest be the day I did it again.

ADAM ARMOUR'S PRAYER.[2]

Gude pity me, because I 'm little!
For though I am an elf o' mettle,
An' can, like ony wabster's shuttle, weaver's
Jink there or here, dodge about
Yet, scarce as lang 's a gude kail-whittle, cabbage-knife
I 'm unco queer. uncommon

An' now Thou kens our woefu' case;
For Geordie's 'jurr' we 're in disgrace,
Because we 'stang'd' her through the place,
An' hurt her spleuchan;
For whilk we daurna show our face dare not
Within the clachan. village

An' now we 're dernd in dens and hollows, concealed
And hunted, as was William Wallace,

[1] Soldering fresh teeth to a flax-dresser's comb.
[2] This poem was first published in the *Edinburgh Magazine* for January 1808.

Wi' constables—thae blackguard fallows,
An' sodgers baith; both
But Gude preserve us frae the gallows,
That shamefu' death!

Auld grim black-bearded Geordie's sel'—
O shake him owre the mouth o' hell! over
There let him hing, an' roar, an' yell hang
Wi' hideous din,
And if he offers to rebel,
Then heave him in.

When Death comes in wi' glimmerin blink,
An' tips auld drucken Nanse the wink, drunken
May Sautan gie her doup a clink
Within his yett,
An' fill her up wi' brimstone drink,
Red-reekin het.

Though Jock an' hav'rel Jean are merry[1]— silly
Some devil seize them in a hurry,
An' waft them in th' infernal wherry
Straught through the lake, straight
An' gie their hides a noble curry
Wi' oil of aik! oak stick

As for the 'jurr'—puir worthless body!
She 's got mischief enough already;
Wi' stanget hips, and buttocks bluidy,
She 's suffer'd sair;
But, may she wintle in a woody, spin round on the gallows
If she wh—e mair!

EPISTLE TO JAMES SMITH.[2]

> Friendship, mysterious cement of the soul!
> Sweet'ner of Life, and solder of Society!
> I owe thee much.—BLAIR.

Dear Smith, the slee'st, pawkie thief, slyest—cunning
That e'er attempted stealth or rief! robbery

[1] 'Jock' and 'hav'rel Jean' (the half-witted 'Racer Jess') were son and daughter of Geordie and Nanse.

[2] James Smith, the son of a Mauchline merchant, and brother of the Jean Smith whose 'wit' was celebrated by Burns, and who married his friend and correspondent, James Candlish, was born in 1765. For a time he was in business as a linen-draper in his native town; but, after 'an affair cognizable by the kirk-session,' started, in partnership with one Miller, a calico-printing manufactory on the banks of the Avon, near Linlithgow. It failed, and Smith migrated to Jamaica, where it is understood he died while still a young man.

Ye surely hae some warlock-breef — spell
Owre human hearts; — over
For ne'er a bosom yet was prief — proof
Against your arts.

For me, I swear by sun an' moon,
An' ev'ry star that blinks aboon, — twinkles
Ye 've cost me twenty pair o' shoon — shoes
Just gaun to see you; — going
An' ev'ry ither pair that 's done, — other
Mair taen I 'm wi' you. — More taken

That auld, capricious carlin, Nature, — hag
To mak amends for scrimpet stature, — stinted
She 's turn'd you off, a human-creature
On her first plan,
And in her freaks, on ev'ry feature
She 's wrote the Man.

Just now I 've taen the fit o' rhyme,
My barmie noodle 's working prime, — excited brain
My fancy yerket up sublime, — tightened
Wi' hasty summon:
Hae ye a leisure-moment's time
To hear what 's comin?

Some rhyme a neibor's name to lash; — neighbour's
Some rhyme (vain thought!) for needfu' cash;
Some rhyme to court the countra clash,[1]
An' raise a din;
For me, an aim I never fash; — think of
I rhyme for fun.

The star that rules my luckless lot,
Has fated me the russet coat,
An' damn'd my fortune to the groat;
But, in requit, — by way of compensation
Has blest me with a random-shot
O' countra wit. — rustic

[1] Get gossiped about in the district.

This while my notion 's taen a sklent, — bend
To try my fate in guid, black prent; — print
But still the mair I 'm that way bent,
Something cries 'Hoolie! — Gently
I red you, honest man, tak tent! — warn—heed
Ye 'll shaw your folly; — show

'There 's ither poets, much your betters,
Far seen in Greek, deep men o' letters, — well-versed
Hae thought they had ensur'd their debtors,
A' future ages;
Now moths deform, in shapeless tatters,
Their unknown pages.'

Then farewell hopes of laurel-boughs,
To garland my poetic brows!
Henceforth I'll rove where busy ploughs
Are whistlin thrang, — busily
An' teach the lanely heights an' howes — lonely hills and dales
My rustic sang. — song

I 'll wander on, wi' tentless heed — utterly careless [1]
How never-halting moments speed,
Till fate shall snap the brittle thread;
Then, all unknown,
I 'll lay me with th' inglorious dead,
Forgot and gone!

But why o' death begin a tale?
Just now we 're living sound an' hale; — strong
Then top and maintop crowd the sail,
Heave Care o'er-side!
And large, before Enjoyment's gale,
Let 's tak the tide.

This life, sae far 's I understand,
Is a' enchanted fairy-land,
Where Pleasure is the magic-wand,
That, wielded right,
Maks hours like minutes, hand in hand,
Dance by fu' light. — full

[1] But see note on p. 20.

The magic-wand then let us wield;
For, ance that five-an'-forty 's speel'd, reached
See, crazy, weary, joyless eild, old age
Wi' wrinkl'd face
Comes hostin, hirplin owre the field, coughing—limping over
Wi' creepin pace.

When ance life's day draws near the gloamin, once—twilight
Then fareweel vacant, careless roamin;
An' fareweel cheerfu' tankards foamin,
An' social noise:
An' fareweel dear, deluding woman,
The joy of joys!

O Life! how pleasant, in thy morning,
Young Fancy's rays the hills adorning!
Cold-pausing Caution's lesson scorning,
We frisk away,
Like school-boys, at th' expected warning,
To joy an' play.

We wander there, we wander here,
We eye the rose upon the brier,
Unmindful that the thorn is near,
Among the leaves;
And tho' the puny wound appear,
Short while it grieves.

Some, lucky, find a flow'ry spot,
For which they never toil'd nor swat; sweated
They drink the sweet and eat the fat,
But care or pain; Without
But haply eye the barren hut
With high disdain.

With steady aim, some fortune chase;
Keen hope does ev'ry sinew brace;
Thro' fair, thro' foul, they urge the race,
An' seize the prey:
Then cannie, in some cozie place, quietly—snug
They close the day.

And others, like your humble servan',
Poor wights! nae rules nor roads observin, no
To right or left eternal swervin,
They zig-zag on;

Till, curst with age, obscure an' starvin,
They aften groan. often

Alas! what bitter toil an' straining—
But truce with peevish, poor complaining!
Is fortune's fickle *Luna* waning?
E'en let her gang!
Beneath what light she has remaining,
Let 's sing our sang.

My pen I here fling to the door,
And kneel, ye Pow'rs! and warm implore,
'Tho' I should wander *Terra* o'er,
In all her climes,
Grant me but this, I ask no more,
Ay rowth o' rhymes. always—abundance

'Gie dreeping roasts to countra lairds, dripping—landed proprietors
Till icicles hing frae their beards; hang
Gie fine braw claes to fine life-guards, handsome
And maids of honor;
An' yill an' whisky gie to cairds, ale—tinkers
Until they sconner. are nauseated

'A title, Dempster[1] merits it;
A garter gie to Willie Pitt;
Gie wealth to some be-ledger'd cit,
In cent. per cent.;
But give me real, sterling wit,
And I'm content.

'While ye are pleas'd to keep me hale,
I'll sit down o'er my scanty meal,
Be 't water-brose or muslin-kail,[2]
Wi' cheerfu' face,
As lang 's the Muses dinna fail don't
To say the grace.'

An anxious e'e I never throws eye
Behint my lug, or by my nose; ear
I jouk beneath Misfortune's blows stoop
As weel 's I may;

[1] George Dempster of Dunnichen, then a conspicuous parliamentary orator and Scottish patriot. He commenced his parliamentary career in 1762, closed it in 1790, and died in 1818, at the age of eighty-two.

[2] 'Water-brose' is a weak porridge made of meal and water without milk or butter. 'Muslin-kail' is broth made without meat.

Sworn foe to sorrow, care, and prose,
I rhyme away.

O ye douce folk that live by rule, serious
Grave, tideless-blooded, calm an' cool,
Compar'd wi' you—O fool! fool! fool!
How much unlike!
Your hearts are just a standing pool,
Your lives, a dyke! wall

Nae hair-brain'd, sentimental traces
In your unletter'd, nameless faces!
In *arioso* trills and graces
Ye never stray;
But *gravissimo*, solemn basses
Ye hum away.

Ye are sae grave, nae doubt ye 're wise;
Nae ferly tho' ye do despise wonder
The hairum-scairum, ram-stam boys, heedless
The rattling squad:
I see ye upward cast your eyes—
Ye ken the road! know

Whilst I—but I shall haud me there— keep
Wi' you I 'll scarce gang ony where— go anywhere
Then, Jamie, I shall say nae mair, no more
But quat my sang, quit
Content wi' you to make a pair,
Whare'er I gang. go

THE VISION.

DUAN FIRST.[1]

The sun had clos'd the winter day,
The curlers quat their roarin play,[2] quitted
And hunger'd maukin taen her way, hungry hare
To kail-yards green, kitchen-gardens
While faithless snaws ilk step betray every
Whare she has been.

[1] *Duan*, a term of Ossian's for the different divisions of a digressive poem. See his Cath-Loda, vol. 2 of M'Pherson's Translation.—*B.*

[2] Curling is the Scottish national ice-game, played with curling-stones on ice, and somewhat resembling the game of bowls. The scene on the ice is an animated one; hence 'roaring play.'

The thresher's weary flingin-tree, — flail
The lee-lang day had tirèd me; — livelong
And when the day had clos'd his e'e, — eye
Far i' the west,
Ben i' the spence,[1] right pensivelie,
I gaed to rest. — went

There, lanely by the ingle-cheek, — solitary
I sat and ey'd the spewing reek, — smoke
That fill'd, wi' hoast-provoking smeek, — cough—fume
The auld clay biggin; — building
An' heard the restless rattons squeak — rats
About the riggin. — rafters

All in this mottie, misty clime, — dusty
I backward mus'd on wasted time,
How I had spent my youthfu' prime,
An' done naething,
But stringing blethers up in rhyme, — idle stories, nonsense
For fools to sing.

Had I to guid advice but harket, — listened
I might, by this, hae led a market,
Or strutted in a bank and clarket
My cash-account;
While here, half-mad, half-fed, half-sarket, — half-clad
Is a' th' amount.

I started, mutt'ring 'blockhead! coof!' — fool
An' heav'd on high my wauket loof, — hardened palm
To swear by a' yon starry roof,
Or some rash aith, — oath
That I henceforth would be rhyme-proof
Till my last breath—

When click! the string the snick did draw; — latch
An' jee! the door gaed to the wa';
An' by my ingle-lowe I saw, — fire
Now bleezin bright, — blazing
A tight, outlandish hizzie, braw, — wench—handsome
Come full in sight.

[1] This was the parlour, or 'ben hoose,' of the farmhouse, and at the end next Mauchline. It contained 'fixed' beds along the back wall.

Ye need na doubt, I held my whisht; kept silence
The infant aith, half-form'd, was crusht; oath
I glowr'd as eerie 's I 'd been dusht,
In some wild glen;[1]
When sweet, like modest Worth, she blusht,
An' steppèd ben. into the inner room

Green, slender, leaf-clad holly-boughs
Were twisted, gracefu', round her brows;
I took her for some Scottish Muse,
By that same token;
And come to stop those reckless vows,
Would soon been broken.

A 'hairbrain'd, sentimental trace'[2]
Was strongly markèd in her face;
A wildly-witty, rustic grace
Shone full upon her;
Her eye, ev'n turn'd on empty space,
Beam'd keen with honor.

Down flow'd her robe, a tartan sheen,
Till half a leg was scrimply seen; barely
An' such a leg! my bonie Jean[3]
Could only peer it;
Sae straught, sae taper, tight an' clean[4]— straight
Nane else came near it. none

Her mantle large, of greenish hue,
My gazing wonder chiefly drew;
Deep lights and shades, bold-mingling, threw
A lustre grand;
And seem'd, to my astonish'd view,
A well-known land.

[1] 'I stared as full of superstitious fear as if I had been thrown to the ground by meeting a being of the other world in some wild glen.'

[2] This expression occurs in the 'Epistle to James Smith,' p. 114.

[3] In the first edition the line stood thus:

'And such a leg! my Bess, I ween.'

Indignation at the conduct of Jean induced him to take the compliment from her and bestow it on Elizabeth Paton. In the first Edinburgh edition, the indignant feeling having subsided, the line was restored as above.

[4] 'Clean' is often used in Scotland to describe a handsome figure or limb—clean-cut. Such is the meaning here intended.

Here, rivers in the sea were lost;
There, mountains to the skies were toss't;
Here, tumbling billows mark'd the coast,
With surging foam;
There, distant shone Art's lofty boast,
The lordly dome.

Here, Doon pour'd down his far-fetch'd floods;
There, well-fed Irwine stately thuds; **Irvine—sounds**
Auld hermit Ayr staw thro' his woods, **stole**
On to the shore;
And many a lesser torrent scuds, **runs rapidly**
With seeming roar.

Low, in a sandy valley spread,
An ancient borough rear'd her head;[1]
Still, as in Scottish story read,
She boasts a race
To ev'ry nobler virtue bred,
And polish'd grace.

By stately tow'r or palace fair,[2]
Or ruins pendent in the air,
Bold stems of heroes, here and there,
I could discern;
Some seem'd to muse, some seem'd to dare,
With feature stern.

My heart did glowing transport feel,
To see a race heroic[3] wheel,
And brandish round the deep-dyed steel,
In sturdy blows;
While, back-recoiling, seem'd to reel
Their suthron foes. **English**

His Country's Saviour,[4] mark him well!
Bold Richardton's[5] heroic swell;

1 Ayr, whose charter dates from the beginning of the thirteenth century.

2 This and the next six stanzas were added in the second edition, for the purpose, apparently, of complimenting Mrs Dunlop of Dunlop and other influential friends of the poet.

3 The Wallaces.—*B.*

4 William Wallace.—*B.*

5 Adam Wallace of Richardton [Riccarton], cousin to the immortal preserver of Scottish independence.—*B.*

The chief, on Sark[1] who glorious fell
In high command;
And he whom ruthless fates expel
His native land.

With secret throes I marked that earth,
That cottage, witness of my birth;
And near I saw, bold issuing forth
In youthful pride,
A Lindsay, race of noble worth,
Famed far and wide.

Where, hid behind a spreading wood,
An ancient Pict-built mansion stood,
I spied, among an angel brood,
A female pair;
Sweet shone their high maternal blood,
And father's air.[2]

An ancient tower[3] to memory brought
How Dettingen's bold hero fought;
Still, far from sinking into nought,
It owns a lord
Who 'far in western'[4] climates fought
With trusty sword.

Among the rest I well could spy
One gallant, graceful, martial boy,
The soldier sparkled in his eye,
A diamond water;
I blest that noble badge with joy
That owned me *frater*.[5]

[1] Wallace, Laird of Craigie, who was second in command, under Douglas, Earl of Ormond, at the famous battle on the banks of Sark, fought in 1448. The glorious victory was principally owing to the judicious conduct and intrepid valour of the gallant Laird of Craigie, who died of his wounds after the action.—*B.*

[2] Sundrum.—*B.* Mr Hamilton of Sundrum was married to a sister of Colonel Montgomerie of Coilsfield. The 'female pair' were Lillias and Margaret Hamilton.

[3] Stair.—*B.*

[4] These words were written over the original in another hand.

[5] Captain James Montgomerie, Master of St James's Lodge, Tarbolton, to which the author has the honour to belong.—*B.*

There, where a sceptr'd Pictish shade
Stalk'd round his ashes lowly laid,[1]
I mark'd a martial race, pourtray'd
In colours strong:
Bold, soldier-featur'd, undismay'd,
They strode along.[2]

Thro' many a wild, romantic grove,[3]
Near many a hermit-fancied cove
(Fit haunts for friendship or for love,
In musing mood),
An aged Judge,[4] I saw him rove,
Dispensing good.

Near by arose a mansion fine,[5]
The seat of many a muse divine;
Not rustic muses such as mine,
With holly crown'd,
But th' ancient, tuneful, laurell'd Nine,
From classic ground.

I mourn'd the card that Fortune dealt,
To see where bonie Whitefoords dwelt;[6]
But other prospects made me melt,
That village near;[7]
There Nature, Friendship, Love! I felt,
Fond-mingling dear!

Hail! Nature's pang, more strong than death!
Warm Friendship's glow, like kindling wrath!

[1] Coilus, King of the Picts, from whom the district of Kyle is said to take its name, lies buried, as tradition says, near the family seat of the Montgomeries of Coilsfield, where his burial-place is still shown.—*B.* The spot pointed out by tradition as the burial-place of Coilus is a small mound marked by a few trees. It was opened May 29, 1837, when two sepulchral urns were found, attesting that tradition has been at least correct in describing the spot as a burial-place, though whose ashes these were it would be difficult to say.

[2] The Montgomeries of Coilsfield. The younger sons of the family were in the army.

[3] Barskimming, the seat of the Lord Justice-clerk.—*B.*

[4] Sir Thomas Miller of Glenlee, who had become Lord Justice-clerk in 1766. In 1788 he became Lord President of the Court of Session. The following year he died, at the age of eighty-two.

[5] Auchinleck.—*B.* The poet here pays a compliment to the Boswell family, and particularly to the biographer of Johnson.

[6] Ballochmyle. The Whitefoords were at this time parting with the property.

[7] Mauchline.

Love, dearer than the parting breath
Of dying friend!
Not even with life's wild devious path
Your force shall end!

The Pow'r that gave the soft alarms,
In blooming Whitefoord's rosy charms,
Still threats the tiny-feathered arms,
The barbèd dart,
While lovely Wilhelmina warms
The coldest heart.[1]

With deep-struck, reverential awe,
The learnèd Sire and Son I saw:[2]
To Nature's God, and Nature's law,
They gave their lore;
This, all its source and end to draw,
That, to adore.

Where Lugar leaves his moorland plaid,[3]
Where lately Want was idly laid,
I markèd busy, bustling Trade,
In fervid flame,
Beneath a Patroness's aid,[4]
Of noble name;

Wild, countless hills I could survey,
And countless flocks as wild as they;
But other scenes did charms display,
That better please,
Where polish'd manners dwelt with Gray[5]
In rural ease.

Where Cessnock pours with gurgling sound,[6]
And Irwine, marking out the bound,
Enamour'd of the scenes around,
Slow runs his race,
A name I doubly honor'd found,[7]
With knightly grace.

1 Wilhelmina Alexander, the 'Bonie Lass of Ballochmyle.'

2 Catrine, the seat of the late Doctor and present Professor Stewart.—*B.* Dr Matthew Stewart (b. 1717, d. 1785) was professor of Mathematics in the university of Edinburgh. His son, Dugald, was born in Edinburgh in 1753, succeeded his father in the mathematical chair in 1775, and ten years later exchanged it for the chair of Moral Philosophy. He retired from active teaching in 1810, and died in Edinburgh in 1828.

3 Cumnock.—*B.*

4 Probably Mrs Stewart herself.

5 Mr Farquhar Gray.—*B.*

6 Auchinskieth.—*B.*

7 Caprington.—*B.* Cunningham of Caprington, Baronet.

Brydon's brave ward,[1] I saw him stand,
Fame humbly offering her hand,
And near his kinsman's rustic band,[2]
With one accord,
Lamenting their late blessed land
Must change its lord.

The owner of a pleasant spot,
Near sandy wilds I last did note,[3]
A heart too warm, a pulse too hot,
At times o'erran;
But large in every feature wrote,
Appeared, the Man.

Brydon's brave ward I well could spy,
Beneath old Scotia's smiling eye;
Who call'd on Fame, low standing by,
To hand him on,
Where many a patriot-name on high
And hero shone.

DUAN SECOND.

With musing-deep, astonish'd stare,
I view'd the heavenly-seeming Fair;
A whispering throb did witness bear
Of kindred sweet,
When with an elder sister's air
She did me greet.

'All hail! my own inspirèd bard!
In me thy native Muse regard;
Nor longer mourn thy fate is hard,
Thus poorly low;
I come to give thee such reward,
As we bestow!

1 Colonel Fullarton.—*B.* Colonel William Fullarton of Fullarton was born in 1754. Educated at Edinburgh University, he travelled under the care of Patrick Brydone (b. 1741, d. 1818), author of *A Tour in Sicily and Malta.* He entered the army, assisted in raising the regiment known as 'Fullarton's Light Horse,' was member for Ayrshire from 1796 to 1803, and subsequently governor of Trinidad. He died in London in 1808. He was the author of an *Account of Agriculture in Ayrshire* and a *View of English Interests in India.*

2 Dr Fullerton.—*B.*

3 Orangefield.—*B.* Mr Dalrymple of Orangefield, near Ayr, was an active patron of Burns.

'Know, the great genius of this land
Has many a light aërial band,
Who, all beneath his high command,
Harmoniously,
As arts or arms they understand,
Their labours ply.

'They Scotia's race among them share:
Some fire the soldier on to dare;
Some rouse the patriot up to bare
Corruption's heart:
Some teach the bard—a darling care—
The tuneful art.

''Mong swelling floods of reeking gore,
They, ardent, kindling spirits pour;
Or, 'mid the venal senate's roar,
They, sightless, stand,
To mend the honest patriot-lore,
And grace the hand.

'And when the bard, or hoary sage,
Charm or instruct the future age,
They bind the wild poetic rage
In energy,
Or point the inconclusive page
Full on the eye.[1]

'Hence, Fullarton, the brave and young;
Hence, Dempster's zeal-inspirèd[2] tongue;
Hence, sweet, harmonious Beattie sung[3]
His "Minstrel" lays;
Or tore, with noble ardour stung,
The sceptic's bays.

'To lower orders are assign'd
The humbler ranks of human-kind,

[1] This stanza does not appear in the Kilmarnock volume: it was added in the second edition.

[2] In first edition:

'Hence, Dempster's truth-prevailing tongue.'

[3] James Beattie (b. 1735, d. 1803), schoolmaster, poet, and professor of Moral Philosophy in Marischal College, Aberdeen, published *Essay on the Nature and Immutability of Truth* in 1770, *The Minstrel* between 1771 and 1774, and the *Evidences of Christian Religion* in 1786.

The rustic bard, the laboring hind,
The artisan;
All chuse, as various they're inclin'd,
The various man.

'When yellow waves the heavy grain,
The threat'ning storm some strongly rein;
Some teach to meliorate the plain,
With tillage-skill;
And some instruct the shepherd-train,
Blythe o'er the hill.

'Some hint the lover's harmless wile;
Some grace the maiden's artless smile;
Some soothe the laborer's weary toil
For humble gains,
And make his cottage-scenes beguile
His cares and pains.

'Some, bounded to a district-space,
Explore at large man's infant race,
To mark the embryotic trace
Of rustic bard;
And careful note each opening grace,
A guide and guard.

'Of these am I—Coila my name:[1]
And this district as mine I claim,
Where once the Campbells,[2] chiefs of fame,
Held ruling pow'r:
I mark'd thy embryo-tuneful flame,
Thy natal hour.

'With future hope I oft would gaze
Fond, on thy little early ways,
Thy rudely caroll'd, chiming phrase,
In uncouth rhymes;
Fir'd at the simple, artless lays
Of other times.

[1] The idea of this visionary being is acknowledged by Burns himself to have been taken from the 'Scota' of Alexander Ross (b. 1699, d. 1784), a Mearns poet and schoolmaster, author of a popular pastoral, much admired by Beattie, entitled 'Helenore; or, The Fortunate Shepherdess' (1768).

[2] The Loudoun branch of the Campbells is here meant. Mossgiel and much of the neighbouring ground was the property of the Earl of Loudoun, for whom Gavin Hamilton acted as factor.

'I saw thee seek the sounding shore,
Delighted with the dashing roar;
Or when the North his fleecy store
Drove thro' the sky,
I saw grim Nature's visage hoar
Struck thy young eye.

'Or when the deep green-mantled earth
Warm cherish'd ev'ry floweret's birth,
And joy and music pouring forth
In ev'ry grove;
I saw thee eye the general mirth
With boundless love.

'When ripen'd fields and azure skies
Call'd forth the reapers' rustling noise,
I saw thee leave their ev'ning joys,
And lonely stalk,
To vent thy bosom's swelling rise
In pensive walk.

'When youthful love, warm-blushing, strong,
Keen-shivering, shot thy nerves along,
Those accents grateful to thy tongue,
Th' adorèd *Name*,
I taught thee how to pour in song,
To soothe thy flame.

'I saw thy pulse's maddening play,
Wild send thee Pleasure's devious way,
Misled by Fancy's meteor-ray,
By passion driven;
But yet the light that led astray
Was light from Heaven.

'I taught thy manners-painting strains,
The loves, the ways of simple swains,
Till now, o'er all my wide domains
Thy fame extends;
And some, the pride of Coila's plains,
Become thy friends.

'Thou canst not learn, nor I can show,
To paint with Thomson's landscape glow;

Or wake the bosom-melting throe,
With Shenstone's art;
Or pour, with Gray, the moving flow
Warm on the heart.

'Yet, all beneath th' unrivall'd rose,
The lowly daisy sweetly blows;
Tho' large the forest's monarch throws
His army-shade,
Yet green the juicy hawthorn grows
Adown the glade.

'Then never murmur nor repine;
Strive in thy humble sphere to shine;
And trust me, not Potosi's mine,
Nor king's regard,
Can give a bliss o'ermatching thine,
A rustic bard.

'To give my counsels all in one,
Thy tuneful flame still careful fan:
Preserve the dignity of Man,
With soul erect;
And trust the Universal Plan
Will all protect.

'And wear thou *this*'—she solemn said,
And bound the holly round my head:
The polish'd leaves and berries red
Did rustling play;
And, like a passing thought, she fled
In light away.[1]

[1] A writer in the *Gentleman's Magazine*, October 1852, expressed his opinion that Burns was indebted for the idea of 'The Vision' to a copy of verses written by the 'melancholy and pensive Wollaston,' so far back as 1681. 'Wollaston's poem was written on the occasion of his leaving, "with a heavy heart," as he says, his beloved Cambridge.' He describes himself as sitting in his own 'small apartment:'

'As here one day I sate,
Disposed to ruminate,
Deep melancholy did benumb,
With thoughts of what was past and what to come.

* * * *

I thought I saw my Muse appear,
Whose dress declared her haste, whose looks her fear;
A wreath of laurel in her hand she bore,
Such laurel as the god Apollo wore.
The piercing wind had backward combed her hair,
And laid a paint of red upon the fair;

A WINTER NIGHT.

Poor naked wretches, wheresoe'er you are,
That bide the pelting of the pityless storm!
How shall your houseless heads, and unfed sides,
Your loop'd and window'd raggedness, defend you
From seasons such as these?—SHAKESPEARE.

When biting Boreas, fell and doure, keen—stern
Sharp shivers thro' the leafless bow'r;
When Phœbus gies a short-liv'd glow'r, stare
Far south the lift, sky
Dim-dark'ning thro' the flaky show'r,
Or whirling drift:

Ae night the storm the steeples rocked, one
Poor Labour sweet in sleep was locked,
While burns, wi' snawy wreaths up-choked, rivulets
Wild-eddying swirl;
Or, thro' the mining outlet bocked, belched
Down headlong hurl:

List'ning the doors an' winnocks rattle, windows
I thought me on the ourie cattle, shivering
Or silly sheep, wha bide this brattle helpless—endure —pelting
O' winter war,
And thro' the drift, deep-lairing, sprattle sinking deep —scramble
Beneath a scaur. cliff

Her gown, which, with celestial colour dyed,
Was with a golden girdle tied,
Through speed a little flowed aside,
And decently disclosed her knee;
When, stopping suddenly, she spoke to me:
"What indigested thought, or rash advice,
Has caused thee to apostatise?
Not my ill-usage, surely, made thee fly
From thy apprenticeship in poetry."

She paused awhile, with joy and weariness oppressed,
And quick reciprocations of her breast,
She spoke again: "What travel and what care
Have I bestowed! my vehicle of air
How often changed in quest of thee!"'

She concludes, like the Muse of Burns, by counselling him to remain true to her and poetry:

'"Suppose the worst, thy passage rough, still I'll be kind,
And breathe upon thy sails behind;
Besides there is a port before:
And every moment thou advancest to the shore,
Where virtuous souls shall better usage find."
Concern and agitation of my head
Waked me; and with the light the phantom fled.'

Ilk happing bird,—wee, helpless thing! hopping
That, in the merry months o' spring,
Delighted me to hear thee sing,
What comes o' thee?
Whare wilt thou cow'r thy chittering wing,
An' close thy e'e? eye

Ev'n you, on murd'ring errands toil'd,
Lone from your savage homes exil'd,
The blood-stain'd roost, and sheep-cote spoil'd,
My heart forgets,
While pityless the tempest wild
Sore on you beats.

Now Phœbe, in her midnight reign the moon, a feminine correlative of Phœbus
Dark-muffl'd, view'd the dreary plain;
Still crouding thoughts, a pensive train,
Rose in my soul,
When on my ear this plaintive strain,
Slow-solemn, stole—

'Blow, blow, ye winds, with heavier gust!
And freeze, thou bitter-biting frost!
Descend, ye chilly, smothering snows!
Not all your rage, as now united, shows
More hard unkindness unrelenting,
Vengeful malice, unrepenting,
Than heaven-illumin'd Man on brother Man bestows![1]

'See stern Oppression's iron grip,
Or mad Ambition's gory hand,
Sending, like blood-hounds from the slip,
Woe, Want, and Murder o'er a land!
Ev'n in the peaceful rural vale,
Truth, weeping, tells the mournful tale,
How pamper'd Luxury, Flatt'ry by her side,
The parasite empoisoning her ear,
With all the servile wretches in the rear,
Looks o'er proud Property, extended wide;

1 Blow, blow, thou winter wind;
Thou art not so unkind
As man's ingratitude. . . .
Freeze, freeze, thou bitter sky;
Thou dost not bite so nigh
As benefits forgot.
—SHAKESPEARE, *As You Like It*, Act II., Scene 7.

And eyes the simple, rustic hind,
Whose toil upholds the glitt'ring show—
A creature of another kind,
Some coarser substance, unrefin'd—
Plac'd for her lordly use thus far, thus vile, below!

'Where, where is Love's fond, tender throe,
With lordly Honor's lofty brow,
The pow'rs you proudly own?
Is there, beneath Love's noble name,
Can harbour, dark, the selfish aim,
To bless himself alone!
Mark maiden-innocence a prey
To love-pretending snares:
This boasted Honor turns away,
Shunning soft Pity's rising sway,
Regardless of the tears and unavailing pray'rs!
Perhaps this hour, in Misery's squalid nest,
She strains your infant to her joyless breast,
And with a mother's fears shrinks at the rocking blast!

'Oh ye! who, sunk in beds of down,
Feel not a want but what yourselves create,
Think, for a moment, on his wretched fate,
Whom friends and fortune quite disown!
Ill-satisfy'd keen nature's clamorous call,
Stretch'd on his straw, he lays himself to sleep;
While thro' the ragged roof and chinky wall,
Chill, o'er his slumbers, piles the drifty heap!
Think on the dungeon's grim confine,
Where Guilt and poor Misfortune pine!
Guilt, erring man, relenting view,
But shall thy legal rage pursue
The wretch, already crushèd low
By cruel Fortune's undeservèd blow?
Affliction's sons are brothers in distress;
A brother to relieve, how exquisite the bliss!'

I heard nae mair, for Chanticleer — no more
Shook off the pouthery snaw, — powdery snow
And hail'd the morning with a cheer,
A cottage-rousing craw. — crow

But deep this truth impress'd my mind—
Thro' all His works abroad,
The heart benevolent and kind
The most resembles God.

YOUNG PEGGY.

TUNE—*Last Time I came o'er the Muir.*

Young Peggy blooms our boniest lass,
Her blush is like the morning,
The rosy dawn, the springing grass,
With early gems adorning:
Her eyes outshine the radiant beams
That gild the passing shower,
And glitter o'er the crystal streams,
And cheer each fresh'ning flower.

Her lips more than the cherries bright,
A richer dye has graced them,
They charm th' admiring gazer's sight,
And sweetly tempt to taste them;
Her smile is as the ev'ning mild,
When feather'd pairs are courting,
And little lambkins wanton wild,
In playful bands disporting.

Were Fortune lovely Peggy's foe,
Such sweetness would relent her,
As blooming Spring unbends the brow
Of surly, savage Winter.
Detraction's eye no aim can gain
Her winning pow'rs to lessen;
And fretful Envy grins in vain
The poison'd tooth to fasten.

Ye Pow'rs of Honor, Love, and Truth,
From ev'ry ill defend her;
Inspire the highly-favor'd youth
The destinies intend her;

Still fan the sweet connubial flame
Responsive in each bosom;
And bless the dear parental name
With many a filial blossom.[1]

SCOTCH DRINK.

Gie him strong drink until he wink,
That's sinking in despair;
An' liquor guid to fire his bluid,
That's prest wi' grief an' care:
There let him bowse, an' deep carouse,
Wi' bumpers flowing o'er,
Till he forgets his loves or debts,
An' minds his griefs no more.

SOLOMON'S PROVERBS, xxxi. 6, 7.

Let other poets raise a frácas — make a to-do
'Bout vines, an' wines, an' drucken Bacchus, — drunken
An' crabbet names an' stories wrack us, — uncouth—torture
An' grate our lug: — ear
I sing the juice Scotch bere can mak us, — barley
In glass or jug.

O thou, my muse! guid auld Scotch drink!
Whether thro' wimplin worms thou jink, — winding—steal
Or, richly brown, ream owre the brink,
In glorious faem, — foam
Inspire me, till I lisp an' wink,
To sing thy name!

Let husky wheat the haughs adorn, — valleys
An' aits set up their awnie horn, — oats—bearded
An' pease and beans, at e'en or morn,
Perfume the plain:
Leeze me on thee, John Barleycorn, — Commend me to
Thou king o' grain!

[1] 'Burns met Miss Kennedy at Mr Hamilton's, where she lived some time. My mother remembers a conversation between Robert and Gilbert, on the *har'st rig*, respecting the young lady and the song which had been written upon her. Gilbert said he did not think quite so much of her. Robert said she had a great deal of wit. One Sarah Weir, who was often about Mr Hamilton's working, and knew them all well, was shearing on the same ridge with my mother. At the poet's remark about the wit of Miss Kennedy, Sarah stopped and asked him if it was not of a shallow kind. The bard only replied with a look of contempt, which greatly amused my mother at the time, and which still remains imprinted on her memory. *Letter of Isabella Begg*, October 1850.

On thee aft Scotland chows her cood, oft—chews—cud
In souple scones, the wale o' food ! supple, flat cakes—choice
Or tumblin in the boiling flood
Wi' kail an' beef ; broth
But when thou pours thy strong heart's blood,
There thou shines chief.

Food fills the wame, an' keeps us leevin ; stomach—living
Tho' life 's a gift no worth receivin,
When heavy-dragg'd wi' pine an' grievin ;
But oil'd by thee,
The wheels o' life gae down-hill, scrievin, go—gliding smoothly
Wi' rattlin glee.

Thou clears the head o' doited Lear ; confused Learning
Thou cheers the heart o' drooping Care ;
Thou strings the nerves o' Labor sair, severe
At 's weary toil ;
Thou ev'n brightens dark Despair
Wi' gloomy smile.

Aft, clad in massy siller weed, often
Wi' gentles thou erects thy head ;[1]
Yet, humbly kind in time o' need,
The poor man's wine ;
His wee drap parritch, or his bread, little drop of porridge
Thou kitchens fine.[2] givest relish to

Thou art the life o' public haunts ;
But thee, what were our fairs and rants ? Without—frolics
Ev'n godly meetings o' the saunts, saints
By thee inspir'd,
When, gaping, they besiege the tents,[3]
Are doubly fir'd.

That merry night we get the corn in,
O sweetly, then, thou reams the horn in !
Or reekin on a New-year mornin smoking hot
In cog or bicker, wooden vessels
An' just a wee drap sp'ritual burn in, whisky
An' gusty sucker ! tasty sugar

[1] As ale in silver mugs, at the tables of the wealthy.
[2] Brisk small-beer used to be a favourite relish to porridge in Scotland.
[3] Sitting round the movable pulpits erected in the open air at parochial celebrations of the communion.—See notes to 'The Holy Fair.'

When Vulcan gies his bellows breath,
An' ploughmen gather wi' their graith, — implements
O rare! to see thee fizz an' freath — froth
I' th' lugget caup! — eared cup, or quaich
Then Burnewin comes on like death — Blacksmith
At ev'ry chaup. — blow

Nae mercy, then, for airn or steel; — iron
The brawnie, bainie, ploughman chiel, — stout—bony—fellow
Brings hard owrehip, wi' sturdy wheel,
The strong forehammer,
Till block an' studdie ring an' reel, — stithy, anvil
Wi' dinsome clamour.

When skirlin weanies see the light, — squalling infants
Thou maks the gossips clatter bright, — makes
How fumblin cuifs their dearies slight; — incapables
Wae worth the name![1]
Nae howdie gets a social night, — midwife
Or plack frae them. — coin

When neibors anger at a plea, — neighbours get angry
An' just as wud as wud can be, — mad
How easy can the barley-brie — malt liquor
Cement the quarrel!
It 's aye the cheapest lawyer's fee,
To taste the barrel.

Alake! that e'er my muse has reason,
To wyte my countrymen wi' treason! — blame
But mony daily weet their weason — wet—throat
Wi' liquors nice,
An' hardly, in a winter season,
E'er spier her price. — ask

Wae worth that brandy, burnin trash!
Fell source o' mony a pain an' brash! — sickness
Twins mony a poor, doylt, drucken hash. — deprives—wearied fellow
O' half his days;
An' sends, beside, auld Scotland's cash
To her warst faes. — worst foes

[1] This and the two following lines run in the edition of 1786:

'Wae worth them for 't!
While healths gae round to him wha, *tight*,
Gies famous sport.'

Ye Scots, wha wish auld Scotland well!
Ye chief, to you my tale I tell,
Poor, plackless devils like mysel! **penniless**
It sets you ill,
Wi' bitter, dearthfu' wines to mell, **meddle**
Or foreign gill.

May gravels round his blather wrench,
An' gouts torment him, inch by inch,
Wha twists his gruntle wi' a glunch **mouth—grumble**
O' sour disdain,
Out owre a glass o' whisky-punch
Wi' honest men!

O whisky! soul o' plays an' pranks!
Accept a bardie's gratefu' thanks![1]
When wanting thee, what tuneless cranks
Are my poor verses!
Thou comes—they rattle i' their ranks
At ither's ——!

Thee, Ferintosh! O sadly lost!
Scotland, lament frae coast to coast!
Now colic grips, an' barkin hoast **cough**
May kill us a';
For loyal Forbes' charter'd boast
Is ta'en awa![2]

1 'Humble thanks' in 1794 edition.

2 For services and expenses on the public account at the Revolution, Forbes of Culloden was empowered, by an Act of the Scottish Parliament in 1690, to distil whisky on his barony of Ferintosh, in Cromartyshire, free of duty. This inconsiderately conferred privilege in time became the source of a great revenue to the family; and *Ferintosh* was at length recognised as something like a synonym for whisky, so much of it was there distilled. By the Act of 1785 dealing with the Scotch distilleries this privilege was declared to be abolished, the Lords of the Treasury being left to make such compensation to the existing Mr Forbes as should be deemed just, or, should they fail to make a satisfactory arrangement, the case was to be decided by a jury before the Scottish Court of Exchequer. The Lords failing to satisfy Mr Forbes, the case was accordingly tried by a jury, November 29, 1785, when it was shown by Mr Henry Erskine, the plaintiff's counsel, that the privilege could be made to yield no less than £7000 a year to the family, though the actual annual gain from it, at an average of the last thirteen years, was but a little more than £1000. He further proved that, while the right was an undoubted piece of property which nothing could justly take away, the family had not failed to deserve it, as they had ever continued useful and loyal servants to the government, Mr Duncan Forbes, the late Lord President, in particular, having spent no less than £20,000 of his private fortune in suppressing the rebellion of 1745-6. The jury surprised the Lords of the Treasury by decreeing the sum of £21,580 for 'loyal Forbes' charter'd boast.'

Thae curst horse-leeches o' th' Excise,
Wha mak the whisky stells their prize! stills
Haud up thy han', Deil! ance, twice, thrice!
There, seize the blinkers!
An' bake them up in brunstane pies brimstone
For poor d—d drinkers.

Fortune! if thou 'll but gie me still
Hale breeks, a scone, an' whisky gill, whole (not ragged) clothes
An' rowth o' rhyme to rave at will, abundance
Tak a' the rest,
An' deal 't about as thy blind skill
Directs thee best.

THE AUTHOR'S EARNEST CRY AND PRAYER

TO THE SCOTCH REPRESENTATIVES IN THE HOUSE OF COMMONS.[1]

Dearest of distillation! last and best—
How art thou lost!—PARODY ON MILTON.

Ye Irish lords, ye knights an' squires,
Wha represent our brughs an' shires, burghs
An' doucely manage our affairs honestly
In parliament,
To you a simple poet's[2] pray'rs
Are humbly sent.

Alas! my roupet muse is hearse! husky—hoarse
Your Honors' hearts wi' grief 'twad pierce, it would
To see her sittin on her ——
Low i' the dust,
And scriechin out prosaic verse, screeching
An' like to brust! burst

Tell them wha hae the chief direction,
Scotland an' me 's in great affliction,
E'er sin' they laid that curst restriction since
On aqua-vitæ;
An' rouse them up to strong conviction,
An' move their pity.

[1] This was written before the Act anent the Scotch distilleries, of session 1786, for which Scotland and the Author return their most grateful thanks.—*B.*

[2] 'Bardie's' in editions prior to 1794.

G. Pirie.

A guid New-Year I wish thee, Maggie!
Hae, there's a ripp to thy auld baggie.

Stand forth an' tell yon Premier youth[1]
The honest, open, naked truth:
Tell him o' mine an' Scotland's drouth, thirst
His servants humble:
The muckle devil blaw ye south, great—blow
If ye dissemble!

Does ony great man glunch an' gloom? grumble
Speak out, an' never fash your thumb! trouble yourself
Let posts an' pensions sink or soom swim
Wi' them wha grant them;
If honestly they canna come, cannot
Far better want them.

In gath'rin votes you were na slack;
Now stand as tightly by your tack:
Ne'er claw your lug, an' fidge your back, scratch your ear—shrug
An' hum an' haw;
But raise your arm, an' tell your crack speech
Before them a'.

Paint Scotland greetin owre her thrissle; weeping—thistle
Her mutchkin stowp as toom 's a whissle; empty
An' d—mn'd excisemen in a bussle,
Seizin a stell, still
Triumphant, crushin 't like a mussel,
Or limpet shell!

Then, on the tither hand, present her— other
A blackguard smuggler right behint her,
An' cheek-for-chow, a chuffie vintner cheek-by-jowl—fat-faced
Colleaguing join,
Pickin' her pouch as bare as winter pocket
Of a' kind coin.

Is there, that bears the name o' Scot,
But feels his heart's bluid rising hot, blood
To see his poor auld mither's pot mother's
Thus dung in staves, driven
An' plunder'd o' her hindmost groat,
By gallows knaves?

[1] William Pitt became Premier at twenty-four, in December 1783.

Alas! I'm but a nameless wight,
Trode i' the mirè out o' sight!
But could I like Montgomeries fight,[1]
Or gab like Boswell,[2] — make speeches
There's some sark-necks I wad draw tight, — shirt
An' tie some hose well.

God bless your Honors! can ye see 't—
The kind, auld, cantie carlin greet, — cheerful old wife—cry
An' no get warmly to your feet, — not—in wrath
An' gar them hear it, — make
An' tell them wi' a patriot-heat,
Ye winna bear it? — won't

Some o' you nicely ken the laws,
To round the period an' pause,
An' wi' rhetòric clause on clause
To mak harangues; — make
Then echo thro' Saint Stephen's wa's — walls
Auld Scotland's wrangs.

Dempster,[3] a true blue Scot I'se warran;
Thee, aith-detesting, chaste Kilkerran;[4] — oath
An' that glib-gabbet Highland baron, — ready-tongued
The Laird o' Graham;[5]
An' ane, a chap that's d—mn'd auldfarran, — fellow—sagacious
Dundas his name:[6]

[1] The poet here alludes to the Montgomeries of Coilsfield, in particular to Hugh, who, born in 1740, entered the army, and served in America. He represented Ayrshire in Parliament from 1784 to 1789, and subsequently in 1796. That year he became (twelfth) Earl of Eglinton, in succession to his cousin Archibald. He died in 1819.

[2] James Boswell of Auchinleck (b. 1740, d. 1795), the biographer of Johnson. He had succeeded to Auchinleck in 1782, and frequently spoke at Ayrshire county meetings.

[3] George Dempster of Dunnichen. See the 'Epistle to James Smith' (p. 113) and 'The Vision' (p. 122).

[4] Sir Adam Fergusson of Kilkerran, born about 1732; died in 1813. He represented the county of Ayr for eighteen years in Parliament, and the city of Edinburgh for four.

[5] The Marquis of Graham, eldest son of the Duke of Montrose, then member for Bedwin, in Wiltshire. He held the offices of President of the Board of Trade, Postmaster-General, and Paymaster of the Forces in Pitt's administration. He succeeded his father as Duke in 1790, and died in 1836, at the age of eighty-one.

[6] The Right Hon. Henry Dundas (b. 1742, d. 1811), Treasurer of the Navy, and M.P. (1774–1787) for Edinburghshire. Created Viscount Melville in 1802.

Erskine,[1] a spunkie Norland billie; — spirited Northern young fellow
True Campbells, Frederick[2] and Ilay;[3]
An' Livistone, the bauld Sir Willie;[4] — bold
An' mony ithers, — others
Whom auld Demosthenes or Tully
Might own for brithers.

See, sodger Hugh, my watchman stented — assigned (parliamentary) representative
If poets e'er are represented;
I ken if that your sword were wanted,
Ye 'd lend a hand;
But when there 's ought to say anent it,
Ye 're at a stand.[5]

Arouse, my boys! exert your mettle,
To get auld Scotland back her kettle;
Or faith! I 'll wad my new pleugh-pettle, — pledge—plough-staff
Ye 'll see 't or lang, — before
She 'll teach you, wi' a reekin whittle, — knife smoking with blood
Anither sang.

This while she 's been in crankous mood, — fretful
Her lost Militia[6] fir'd her bluid;
(Deil nor they never mair do guid,
Play'd her that pliskie!) — trick
An' now she 's like to rin red-wud — run stark mad
About her whisky.

[1] Thomas Erskine (b. 1750, d. 1823), third son of Henry-David, tenth Earl of Buchan, and younger brother of Henry Erskine, who subsequently became a friend and correspondent of Burns. He was called to the English bar in 1778, was returned for Portsmouth in 1783, and became Lord Chancellor in 1806.

[2] Lord Frederick Campbell (b. 1736, d. 1816), second brother of the Duke of Argyll, Lord Clerk-Register for Scotland, and M.P. for the county of Argyll from 1780 to 1799.

[3] Sir Ilay Campbell (b. 1734, d. 1823), eldest son of Archibald Campbell of Succoth, Lord Advocate for Scotland, representative of the Glasgow group of burghs from 1784 to 1789, when he succeeded Sir Thomas Millar as Lord President of the Court of Session.

[4] Sir William Augustus Cunninghame of Milncraig in Ayrshire, and of Livingstone in Linlithgowshire, which he represented from 1774 to 1790. He died in 1828.

[5] This stanza, alluding to the imperfect elocution of Hugh Montgomerie, was omitted from the poem in all editions published by the author.

[6] A militia bill for Scotland was introduced into Parliament in 1782, when the country was in danger of French and Dutch invasion. The Rockingham Ministry, perhaps taking alarm at the attitude of the Irish militia, proposed a clause at the third reading for facilitating enlistment from the designed militia into the army; and the bill, being declined in this form by Dempster and other patriots, was lost.

An' L—d! if ance they pit her till 't, — to it
Her tartan petticoat she 'll kilt,
An' durk an' pistol at her belt, — dirk
She 'll tak the streets,
An' rin her whittle to the hilt, — run—knife
I' the first she meets!

For G—d-sake, sirs! then speak her fair,
An' straik her cannie wi' the hair, — stroke—gently, and with the grain
An' to the muckle house repair, — House of Commons
Wi' instant speed,
An' strive, wi' a' your wit an' lear, — learning
To get remead. — remedy

Yon ill-tongu'd tinkler, Charlie Fox,
May taunt you wi' his jeers an' mocks;
But gie him 't het, my hearty cocks! — hot
E'en cow the cadie! — subdue—fellow
An' send him to his dicing box
An' sportin lady.

Tell yon guid bluid o' auld Boconnock's,[1]
I 'll be his debt twa mashlum bonnocks,[2]
An' drink his health in auld Nanse Tinnock's[3]
Nine times a-week,
If he some scheme, like tea an' winnocks,[4]
Wad kindly seek. — would

Could he some commutation broach,
I 'll pledge my aith in guid braid Scotch, — good broad
He needna fear their foul reproach
Nor erudition,
Yon mixtie-maxtie, queer hotch-potch, — confusedly mixed
The 'Coalition.'[5]

[1] William Pitt's father, the Earl of Chatham, was the second son of Robert Pitt of Boconnock, in the county of Cornwall.

[2] Scones made of a mixture of oatmeal, pease or bean flour, and barley-flour.

[3] A worthy old hostess of the Author's in Mauchline, where he sometimes studies politics over a glass of gude auld 'Scotch Drink.'—*B.* Nanse's story was different. On seeing the poem, she declared that the author had never been but once or twice in her house. A portrait of her was taken by Brooks in 1799, and has been engraved.

[4] Pitt, then Chancellor of the Exchequer, had gained some credit by a measure introduced in 1784 for preventing smuggling of tea by reducing the duty, the revenue being compensated by a tax on windows.

[5] The 'Coalition Ministry,' which included North and Fox, was in power from April to December 1783.

Auld Scotland has a raucle tongue; rough
She 's just a devil wi' a rung; bludgeon
An' if she promise auld or young
To tak their part,
Tho' by the neck she should be strung,
She 'll no desert.

And now, ye chosen Five-and-Forty,[1]
May still your mither's heart support ye;
Then, tho' a minister grow dorty, saucy
An' kick your place,
Ye 'll snap your fingers, poor an' hearty,
Before his face.

God bless your Honors, a' your days,
Wi' sowps o' kail and brats o' claise,[2] spoonfuls of broth—cloth
In spite o' a' the thievish kaes, jackdaws
That haunt St Jamie's!
Your humble poet sings an' prays,
While Rab his name is.

POSTSCRIPT.

Let half-starv'd slaves in warmer skies
See future wines, rich-clust'ring, rise;
Their lot auld Scotland ne'er envies,
But, blythe and frisky,
She eyes her freeborn, martial boys
Tak aff their whisky.

What tho' their Phœbus kinder warms, sun
While fragrance blooms and beauty charms,
When wretches range, in famish'd swarms,
The scented groves;
Or, hounded forth, dishonor arms
In hungry droves!

Their gun 's a burden on their shouther;
They downa bide the stink o' powther; cannot stand—smell
Their bauldest thought 's a hank'ring swither boldest—uncertainty
To stand or rin,
Till skelp—a shot—they 're aff, a' throw'ther, quick!—off—pell-mell
To save their skin.

[1] The representation of Scotland in the Imperial Parliament at this time consisted of forty-five members.

[2] 'Brats' means here coarse cloth or rags. This line is a variant on the common prayer for 'food and raiment.'

But bring a Scotsman frae his hill,
Clap in his cheek a Highland gill,
Say, such is royal George's will,
An' there 's the foe !
He has nae thought but how to kill — no
Twa at a blow.

Nae cauld, faint-hearted doubtings tease him ; — cold
Death comes, wi' fearless eye he sees him ;
Wi' bluidy hand a welcome gies him ;
An' when he fa's, — falls
His latest draught o' breathin lea'es him — leaves
In faint huzzas.

Sages their solemn een may steek, — yes—close
An' raise a philosophic reek, — mist
An' physically causes seek,
In clime an' season ;
But tell me whisky's name in Greek,
I 'll tell the reason.

Scotland, my auld, respected mither ! — mother
Tho' whiles ye moistify your leather, — at times—moisten
Till whare ye sit, on craps o' heather, — crops
Ye tine your dam ; — lose
Freedom and whisky gang thegither ! — go together
Tak aff your dram ! [1]

THE AULD FARMER'S NEW-YEAR MORNING SALUTATION TO HIS AULD MARE, MAGGIE,

ON GIVING HER THE ACCUSTOMED RIPP OF CORN TO HANSEL IN THE NEW-YEAR.

A guid New-year I wish thee, Maggie !
Hae, there 's a ripp to thy auld baggie : — handful—stomach
Tho' thou 's howe-backit now, an' knaggie, — hollow-backed—bony
I 've seen the day
Thou could hae gaen like ony staggie, — colt
Out-owre the lay. — lea

[1] Altered, probably by Mr Fraser Tytler, in 1794, to:

'Till when ye speak, ye aiblins blether, — perhaps talk nonsense
Yet deil mak matter !
Freedom and whisky gang thegither,
Tak aff your whitter.' — a hearty draught of liquor

The alteration has been universally disregarded.

Tho' now thou 's dowie, stiff an' crazy, drooping
An' thy auld hide as white 's a daisie,
I 've seen thee dappl't, sleek an' glaizie,
A bonie gray:
He should been tight that daur't to raize thee, dared—excite
Ance in a day.

Thou ance was i' the foremost rank,
A filly buirdly, steeve an' swank; strong—firm—stately
An' set weel down a shapely shank,
As e'er tread yird; earth
An' could hae flown out-owre a stank, ditch
Like ony bird.

It 's now some nine-an'-twenty year,
Sin' thou was my guidfather's meere; mare
He gied me thee, o' tocher clear, gave—dowry
An' fifty mark;[1]
Tho' it was sma', 'twas weel-won gear, well-earned money
An' thou was stark. strong

When first I gaed to woo my Jenny,
Ye then was trottin wi' your minnie: mother
Tho' ye was trickie, slee, an' funnie, sly
Ye ne'er was donsie; mischievous
But hamely, tawie,[2] quiet, an' cannie,
An' unco sonsie. very plump

That day, ye pranc'd wi' muckle pride, great
When ye bure hame my bonie bride: bore
An' sweet an' gracefu' she did ride,
Wi' maiden air!
Kyle-Stewart I could bragget wide, could have bragged, challenged
For sic a pair.

Tho' now ye dow but hoyte and hobble, can—limp
An' wintle like a saumont-coble, twist and rock—salmon-boat
That day, ye was a jinker noble, runner
For heels an' win'! wind
An' ran them till they a' did wauble, reel
Far, far behin'!

[1] A Scottish coin of the value of 13s. 4d.
[2] That allows itself peaceably to be handled.

When thou an' I were young an' skiegh, high-mettled
An' stable-meals at fairs were driegh, tedious
How thou wad prance, an' snore, an' skriegh, whinny
An' tak the road!
Town's bodies ran, an' stood abiegh, out of the way
An' ca't thee mad. called

When thou was corn't, an' I was mellow, made comfortable by drink
We took the road ay like a swallow:
At brooses[1] thou had ne'er a fellow,
For pith an' speed;
But ev'ry tail thou pay't them hollow,
Whare'er thou gaed.

The sma', droop-rumpl't, hunter cattle drooping at the crupper
Might aiblins waur't thee for a brattle; perhaps beat—short race
But sax Scotch mile, thou try't their mettle, six
An' gar't them whaizle: made—wheeze
Nae whip nor spur, but just a wattle switch
O' saugh or hazle. willow

Thou was a noble 'fittie-lan',' [2]
As e'er in tug or tow was drawn!
Aft thee an' I, in aught hours' gaun, eight hours' work
On guid March-weather,
Hae turn'd sax rood beside our han', six roods
For days thegither.

Thou never braing't, an' fetch't, an' flisket; fretted—raged—kicked
But thy auld tail thou wad hae whisket, lashed
An' spread abreed thy weel-fill'd brisket, breast
Wi' pith an' power;
Till spritty knowes wad rair't an' risket,
An' slypet owre.[3]

When frosts lay lang, an' snaws were deep, long
An' threaten'd labour back to keep,
I gied thy cog a wee bit heap[4]
Aboon the timmer:

[1] A race at a marriage is styled a *broose.*
[2] The near horse of the hindmost pair in the plough.
[3] 'Till hillocks, where the earth was full of tough-rooted plants, would have given forth a cracking sound, and the clods fallen gently over.'
[4] Filled thy measure of corn to overflowing.

I ken'd my Maggie wad na sleep
For that, or simmer. before summer

In cart or car thou never reestet; stood still
The steyest brae thou wad hae fac't it; steepest hill
Thou never lap, an' stenned, an' breastet, leaped—reared
Then stood to blaw;
But just thy step a wee thing hastet, a little—quickened
Thou snoov't awa. pushed on quietly

My 'pleugh' is now thy bairn-time a',
Four gallant brutes as e'er did draw;[1]
Forbye sax mae I've sell't awa, Besides six more
That thou has nurst:
They drew me thretteen pund an' twa, thirteen
The vera warst.

Mony a sair daurg we twa hae wrought, day's work
An' wi' the weary warl' fought! world
An' mony an anxious day, I thought
We wad be beat!
Yet here to crazy age we're brought,
Wi' something yet.

An' think na', my auld trusty servan',
That now perhaps thou's less deservin,
An' thy auld days may end in starvin,
For my last fow, bushel
A heapet stimpart,[2] I'll reserve ane
Laid by for you.

We've worn to crazy years thegither;
We'll toyte about wi' ane anither; move
Wi' tentie care I'll flit thy tether heedful
To some hain'd rig, reserved piece of ground
Whare ye may nobly rax your leather, stretch
Wi' sma fatigue.

[1] Meaning—all the four horses now working in my plough are thy progeny.
[2] A measure—the eighth part of a bushel.

THE TWA DOGS:

A TALE.

'Twas in that place o' Scotland's isle,
That bears the name o' auld 'King Coil,'[1]
Upon a bonie day in June,
When wearing thro' the afternoon,
Twa dogs, that were na thrang at hame, busy
Forgather'd ance upon a time. Met together

The first I'll name, they ca'd him 'Cæsar,'
Was keepet for his Honor's pleasure:
His hair, his size, his mouth, his lugs, ears
Shew'd he was nane o' Scotland's dogs;
But whalpet some place far abroad, whelped
Whare sailors gang to fish for cod. *i.e.* Newfoundland

His lockèd, letter'd, braw brass-collar
Shew'd him the gentleman an' scholar;
But though he was o' high degree,
The fient a pride, nae pride had he; not the least pride
But wad hae spent an hour caressin,
Ev'n wi' a tinkler-gipsey's messan: cur
At kirk or market, mill or smiddie, smithy
Nae tawted tyke, tho' e'er sae duddie, matted-haired dog—unkempt
But he wad stand, as glad to see him,
An' stroan'd on stanes an' hillocks wi' him. stones

The tither was a ploughman's collie— other
A rhyming, ranting, raving billie, fellow
Wha for his friend an' comrade had him,
And in his freaks had 'Luath' ca'd him,
After some dog in Highland sang,[2]
Was made lang syne—Lord knows how lang.

He was a gash an' faithfu' tyke, wise
As ever lap a sheugh or dyke. leaped—ditch or wall
His honest, sonsie, baws'nt face[3] handsome
Ay gat him friends in ilka place; every

[1] 'Kyle,' the name of the middle district of Ayrshire, was traditionally said to derive its name from Coilus, 'king of the Picts,' or 'Old King Cole'—a mere myth. Other derivations are from Gaelic *coille*, 'a wood;' or from *caol*, 'straits,' perhaps referring to the Firth of Clyde.

[2] Cuchullin's dog in Ossian's *Fingal*.—*B.*

[3] Having a white stripe down the face.

His breast was white, his tousie back — shaggy
Weel clad wi' coat o' glossy black;
His gawsie tail, wi' upward curl, — handsome
Hung owre his hurdies wi' a swirl. — hips

Nae doubt but they were fain o' ither, — fond
And unco pack an' thick thegither — very intimate
Wi' social nose whyles snuff'd an' snowket; — sometimes—scented
Whyles mice an' moudieworts they howket; — moles—dug up
Whyles scour'd awa' in lang excursion,
An' worry'd ither in diversion; — each other
Till tir'd at last wi' mony a farce,
They set them down upon their ——,
An' there began a lang digression
About the 'lords o' the creation.'

CÆSAR.

I 've aften wonder'd, honest Luath,
What sort o' life poor dogs like you have;
An' when the gentry's life I saw,
What way poor bodies liv'd ava. — at all

Our laird gets in his rackèd rents,
His coals, his kane,[1] an' a' his stents:[2]
He rises when he likes himsel;
His flunkies answer at the bell;
He ca's his coach; he ca's his horse;
He draws a bonie silken purse,
As lang 's my tail, whare, thro' the steeks, — stitches
The yellow letter'd Geordie keeks. — guinea peeps

Frae morn to e'en it 's nought but toiling,
At baking, roasting, frying, boiling;
An' tho' the gentry first are stechin, — stuffing
Yet ev'n the ha' folk fill their pechan — kitchen-people—belly
Wi' sauce, ragouts, an' sic like trashtrie, — trash
That 's little short o' downright wastrie. — waste
Our whipper-in, wee, blastet wonner, — shrivelled-up wonder
Poor, worthless elf, it eats a dinner,
Better than ony tenant-man
His Honor has in a' the lan':
An' what poor cot-folk pit their painch in, — cottagers—stomach
I own it 's past my comprehension.

[1] Rent in the shape of farm-produce. [2] Assessments.

LUATH.

Trowth, Cæsar, whyles they're fash't eneugh: In truth—sometimes—troubled
A cotter howkin in a sheugh, digging—ditch
Wi' dirty stanes biggin a dyke, building—wall
Baring a quarry, an' sic like;
Himsel, a wife, he thus sustains,
A smytrie o' wee duddie weans, litter, family—little ragged children
An' nought but his han'-daurg, to keep hand's labour
Them right an' tight in thack an' raep.[1]

An' when they meet wi' sair disasters,
Like loss o' health or want o' masters,
Ye maist wad think, a wee touch langer, almost
An' they maun starve o' cauld and hunger:
But how it comes, I never kent yet, knew
They 're maistly wonderfu' contented;
An' buirdly chiels, an' clever hizzies, stalwart men—women
Are bred in sic a way as this is.

CÆSAR.

But then to see how ye're neglecket,
How huff'd, an' cuff'd, an' disrespecket!
L—d man, our gentry care as little
For delvers, ditchers, an' sic cattle;
They gang as saucy by poor folk,
As I wad by a stinking brock. badger

I 've notic'd, on our laird's court-day,—
An' mony a time my heart 's been wae,— sad
Poor tenant bodies, scant o' cash,
How they maun thole a factor's snash; must endure—abuse
He 'll stamp an' threaten, curse an' swear
He 'll apprehend them, poind their gear; make execution on—goods
While they maun stan', wi' aspect humble,
An' hear it a', an' fear an' tremble!

I see how folk live that hae riches;
But surely poor-folk maun be wretches! must—wretched creatures

LUATH.

They 're no sae wretched 's ane wad think.
Tho' constantly on poortith's brink, poverty
They 're sae accustom'd wi' the sight,
The view o' 't gies them little fright.

[1] 'Thack and raep' means here—thatch and straw-rope to bind it.

Then chance and fortune are sae guided,
They 're ay in less or mair provided;
An' tho' fatigu'd wi' close employment,
A blink o' rest 's a sweet enjoyment.
The dearest comfort o' their lives,
Their grushie weans an' faithfu' wives; thriving children
The prattling things are just their pride,
That sweetens a' their fire-side.
An' whyles twalpennie worth [1] o' nappy ale
Can mak the bodies unco happy: very
They lay aside their private cares,
To mind the Kirk and State affairs;
They 'll talk o' patronage an' priests,
Wi' kindling fury i' their breasts,
Or tell what new taxation 's comin,
An' ferlie at the folk in Lon'on. wonder

As bleak-fac'd Hallowmass returns,
They get the jovial, rantin kirns, harvest-home rejoicings
When rural life, of ev'ry station,
Unite in common recreation;
Love blinks, Wit slaps, an' social Mirth shines forth
Forgets there 's Care upo' the earth.

That merry day the year begins,
They bar the door on frosty win's;
The nappy reeks wi' mantling ream, ale smokes—froth
An' sheds a heart-inspiring steam;
The luntin pipe, an' sneeshin mill, puffing out smoke—snuff-box
Are handed round wi' right guid will;
The cantie auld folks crackin crouse, cheery—talking briskly
The young anes ranting thro' the house— frolicking
My heart has been sae fain to see them,
That I for joy hae barket wi' them.

Still it 's owre true that ye hae said too
Sic game is now owre aften play'd;
There 's mony a creditable stock
O' decent, honest, fawsont folk, seemly
Are riven out baith root an' branch, torn
Some rascal's pridefu' greed to quench,

[1] A pennyworth, twelve pence of Scots money being equal to one penny sterling.

Wha thinks to knit himsel the faster
In favor wi' some gentle master,
Wha, aiblins thrang a parliamentin', perhaps busy in Parliament
For Britain's guid his saul indentin'— good

CÆSAR.

Haith, lad, ye little ken about it: Faith—know little
For Britain's guid! guid faith! I doubt it.
Say rather, gaun as Premiers lead him: going
An' saying aye or no 's they bid him:
At operas an' plays parading,
Mortgaging, gambling, masquerading:
Or maybe, in a frolic daft, mad
To Hague or Calais takes a waft,
To mak a tour an' tak a whirl,
To learn *bon ton*, an' see the worl'.

There, at Vienna or Versailles,
He rives his father's auld entails;[1]
Or by Madrid he takes the rout, road
To thrum guitars an' fecht wi' nowt; fight—bullocks
Or down Italian vista startles,
Wh—re-hunting amang groves o' myrtles:
Then bowses drumlie German-water, drinks—turbid mineral-water
To mak himsel look fair an' fatter,
An' clear the consequential sorrows,
Love-gifts of Carnival signoras.

For Britain's guid! for her destruction!
Wi' dissipation, feud an' faction.

LUATH.

Hech man! dear sirs! is that the gate style
They waste sae mony a braw estate! many a fine
Are we sae foughten an' harass'd troubled
For gear to gang that gate at last? wealth—road

O would they stay aback frae courts, away from
An' please themsels wi' countra sports,
It wad for ev'ry ane be better,
The laird, the tenant, an' the cotter!

[1] 'Rives' means literally 'tears.' Burns here doubtless refers to the actions—very common in his day—which were raised in court by the extravagant heirs of entailed Scottish estates, for the purpose of having the entails declared invalid, and so enabling them to burden the estates with debt.

For thae frank, rantin', ramblin' billies,
Fient haet o' them 's ill-hearted fellows; Not a bit
Except for breakin o' their timmer, cutting down their timber
Or speakin lightly o' their limmer, mistress
Or shootin o' a hare or moor-cock,
The ne'er-a-bit they 're ill to poor folk.

But will ye tell me, master Cæsar,
Sure great folk's life 's a life o' pleasure?
Nae cauld nor hunger e'er can steer them, bother
The vera thought o' 't need na fear them.

CÆSAR.

L—d, man, were ye but whyles where I am,
The gentles, ye wad ne'er envy them!
It 's true, they need na starve or sweat,
Thro' winter's cauld, or simmer's heat; cold—summer
They 've nae sair-wark to craze their banes, hard work
An' fill auld-age wi' grips an' granes: groans
But human bodies are sic fools,
For a' their colleges an' schools,
That when nae real ills perplex them,
They mak enow themsels to vex them; enough
An' ay the less they hae to sturt them, trouble
In like proportion, less will hurt them.

A country fellow at the pleugh,
His acre 's till'd, he 's right eneugh;
A country girl at her wheel,
Her dizzen 's done, she 's unco weel;
But gentlemen, an' ladies warst, worst
Wi' ev'n-down want o' wark are curst. work
They loiter, lounging, lank an' lazy;
Tho' deil-haet ails them, yet uneasy; nothing
Their days insipid, dull an' tasteless;
Their nights unquiet, lang an' restless.

An' ev'n their sports, their balls an' races,
Their galloping through public places,
There 's sic parade, sic pomp an' art,
The joy can scarcely reach the heart.

The men cast out in party-matches,
Then sowther a' in deep debauches. reconcile
Ae night they 're mad wi' drink an' wh–ring One
Niest day their life is past enduring. Next
The ladies arm-in-arm in clusters,
As great an' gracious a' as sisters;
But hear their absent thoughts o' ither, each other
They 're a' run deils an' jads thegither. downright devils and wicked women
Whyles, owre the wee bit cup an' platie, Sometimes, over the small cup of tea
They sip the scandal-potion pretty;
Or lee-lang nights, wi' crabbet leuks, livelong—sour
Pore owre the devil's pictur'd beuks; cards
Stake on a chance a farmer's stackyard,
An' cheat like onie unhang'd blackguard. any

There 's some exception, man an' woman;
But this is Gentry's life in common.

By this, the sun was out o' sight,
An' darker gloaming brought the night: twilight
The bum-clock humm'd wi' lazy drone;[1] beetle
The kye stood rowtin i' the loan;[2] cows—lowing
When up they gat, and shook their lugs, got—rose
Rejoic'd they were na *men*, but *dogs*;
An' each took aff his several way,
Resolv'd to meet some ither day.

TO A LOUSE,

ON SEEING ONE ON A LADY'S BONNET AT CHURCH.[3]

Ha! whare ye gaun, ye crowlin ferlie! where are you going?—crawling wonder
Your impudence protects you sairly: marvellously
I canna say but ye strunt rarely, strut dexterously
Owre gauze and lace; over
Tho' faith, I fear, ye dine but sparely in truth
On sic a place.

[1] Compare 'The beetle wheels his droning flight' in Gray's 'Elegy.'

[2] 'Loan' means here an opening between fields of corn near, or leading to, the homestead, where cows are milked.

[3] It is generally understood that this 'lady' was one of the Mauchline 'belles.'

G. Pirie.

The Twa Dogs.

PAGE 144.

Ye ugly, creepin, blastit wonner, worthless creature
Detested, shunn'd by saunt an' sinner, saint
How daur ye set a fit upon her, dare—foot
Sae fine a Lady!
Gae somewhere else and seek your dinner,
On some poor body.

Swith, in some beggar's haffet squattle; Begone—side of the head—sprawl, squat down
There ye may creep, and sprawl, and sprattle scramble
Wi' ither kindred, jumping cattle,
In shoals and nations;
Whare horn nor bane ne'er daur unsettle comb—dare
Your thick plantations.

Now haud you there, ye 're out o' sight, remain
Below the fatt'rils, snug an' tight; ribbon-ends
Na faith[1] ye yet! ye 'll no be right
Till ye 've got on it,
The vera tapmost, tow'ring height
O' Miss's bonnet.

My sooth! right bauld ye set your nose out, bold
As plump and gray as onie grozet; any gooseberry
O for some rank, mercurial rozet, rosin, mercury formed into a paste
Or fell, red smeddum, pungent powder
I 'd gie you sic a hearty dose o' 't, give
Wad dress your droddum! chastise—breech

I wad na been surpris'd to spy would not have been
You on an auld wife's flainen toy; old-fashioned flannel cap
Or aiblins some bit duddie boy, perhaps—little ragged
On 's wyliecoat; under-jacket
But Miss's fine *Lunardi*,[2] fye!
How daur ye do 't?

[1] 'Faith (or haith) ye yet' is best rendered by the English phrase 'confound you!'

[2] Vincenzo Lunardi (b. 1759, d. 1806), secretary to the Neapolitan ambassador in London, and, in his own opinion, 'first aerial traveller in the English atmosphere,' had made a considerable reputation during the years 1784 and 1785 by his balloon ascents in England and Scotland. *An Account of Five Aerial Voyages in Scotland, in a Series of Letters to his Guardian, Gherardo Campagni*, by Vincenzo Lunardi, was published at London in 1786. A fashionable balloon-shaped bonnet was named after him.

O Jenny, dinna toss your head,
An' set your beauties a' abread! — on view
Ye little ken what cursèd speed
The blastie 's[1] makin!
Thae winks and finger-ends, I dread,
Are notice takin![2]

O wad some Pow'r the giftie gie us — gift
To see oursels as ithers see us!
It wad frae monie a blunder free us — from
And foolish notion:
What airs in dress an' gait wad lea'e us, — leave
And ev'n Devotion!

THE ORDINATION.

For sense they little owe to Frugal Heav'n.—
To please the Mob they hide the little giv'n.[3]

Kilmarnock Wabsters, fidge an' claw, — weavers—shrug—scratch
An' pour your creeshie nations; — greasy squadrons
An' ye wha leather rax an' draw, — stretch
Of a' denominations;[4]
Swith to the Laigh Kirk, ane an' a', — Away!—Low Church
An' there tak up your stations;
Then aff to Begbie's[5] in a raw, — row
An' pour divine libations
For joy this day.

[1] 'Blastie' means 'shrivelled-up dwarf.' Here the word is used as a term of contempt.

[2] These two lines may be rendered—'I fear, from the way folk are winking and pointing in your direction, that they see what is the matter.'

[3] In the 'Rob Rhymer' manuscript, 'Ruisseaux' is given below these lines, as if this were the name of their author.

[4] Kilmarnock was then a town of between three and four thousand inhabitants, most of whom were engaged either in the manufacture of carpets and other coarse woollen goods, or in the preparation of leather.

[5] A tavern, now the Angel Hotel, in Market Lane, on the other side of the Marnock Water from the Laigh Kirk. The narrowness of the bridge across which the worshippers had to pass necessitated their straggling 'in a raw.' 'Crookes's' appears in place of 'Begbie's' in the 'Rob Rhymer' manuscript. It is not impossible that 'Crookes's' was, like 'Begbie's,' a tavern in Kilmarnock. On the other hand, Crookes may have been a hospitable member of the Crooks (spelled 'Crookes' and 'Crox') family, which has long been associated with the leather trade in Kilmarnock, and who may have treated his 'leather raxing and drawing' friends to home-brewed ale and porter. There were no licensing acts in these days.

Curst 'Common-sense,' that imp o' h—ll,
  Cam in wi' Maggie Lauder;[1]
But Oliphant aft made her yell,
  An' Russell sair misca'd her;[2] reviled
This day M'Kinlay taks the flail,
  An' he 's the boy will blaud her! slap
He 'll clap a shangan[3] on her tail,
  An' set the bairns to daud her children—bespatter
    Wi' dirt this day.

Mak haste an' turn King David owre, give out for singing one of the Psalms of David
  An' lilt wi' holy clangor; sing
O' double verse come gie us four,
  An' skirl up 'the Bangor:'[4] shriek, sing noisily

[1] A notion prevailed that Mr Lindsay had been indebted for his presentation to his wife, Margaret Lauder, who was popularly believed, but, it now appears, quite erroneously, to have been housekeeper to Lord Glencairn, patron of the living. Mr Lindsay's induction, in 1764, was so much in opposition to the sentiments of the people that it produced a riot, attended by many outrages. Three young men, who had obtained an unenviable notoriety by their violence, were whipped through Ayr, and imprisoned for a month. These circumstances evoked from a shoemaker, named Hunter, a scoffing ballad, to which Burns alludes in his original note on this passage. The violence of the people was so extreme at the attempted induction of Mr Lindsay as to put an effectual stop to the proceedings of the presbytery. The clergy dispersed in terror. A curious anecdote connected with the affair was related by the late William Aiton of Hamilton: 'The minister of Fenwick fled in trepidation, and, mounting his horse, proceeded to ride home, with the fearful scene still occupying his excited imagination. It happened that an English commercial traveller was at the same time leaving the town on his way to Glasgow. He asked the road, which was then somewhat difficult to find, and very bad when it was found. "Keep after that man for the first four miles, and ye cannot go wrong," said the people. The minister, finding a horseman following him very hard, thought it was an outraged Calvinist. He clapped the spurs to his beast, and fled faster than before. The Englishman, fearful to lose his way, put his horse to speed too, and then the affair became a John Gilpin scamper, only with two actors instead of one. At last the poor minister turned down a lane to one of his farmers, on whom he called in desperation to bring out his people and save his life. The Englishman, following close up, rode into the farmyard at the same moment, when, instead of a deadly combat on theological grounds, there took place only an explanation. The whole party enjoyed the joke so much that the farmer insisted on keeping the stranger as his guest for the night, with the minister to help away the toddy.' In the 'Rob Rhymer' manuscript this note is given: 'I suppose the author here means Mrs Lindsay, wife to the late Rev. and worthy Mr Lindsay, as that was her maiden name, I am told. *N.B.*—He got the Laigh Kirk of Kilmarnock.'

[2] The Rev. James Oliphant was minister of Kilmarnock High Church from 1764 to 1774, when he was translated to the parish of Dumbarton. He died in 1818, at the age of eighty-four. He was an 'Auld Light,' like Russell, and possessed of a powerful voice, which enabled him to make the kirk 'yell.'

[3] A stick cleft at one end to put the tail of a dog in, by way of frolic or to frighten him away.

[4] The name of a plaintive psalm-tune, of English origin, which was often sung in Scottish churches. 'Double verse,' in the metrical version of the Psalms, is a stanza of eight lines. 'Four double verses' was twice as much as was usually sung at a time.

This day the Kirk kicks up a stoure,   dust, noise
Nae mair the knaves shall wrang her,   wrong
For Heresy is in her pow'r,
And gloriously she 'll whang her   punish with blows from a strap
Wi' pith this day.

Come, let a proper text be read,
An' touch it aff wi' vigour,
How graceless Ham [1] leugh at his Dad,
Which made Canaan a nigger ;
Or Phinehas [2] drove the murdering blade,
Wi' w——e-abhorring rigour ;
Or Zipporah,[3] the scauldin jad,   scolding vixen
Was like a bluidy tiger,
I' th' inn that day.

There, try his mettle on the creed,
And bind him down wi' caution,
That Stipend is a carnal weed
He taks but for the fashion ;
And gie him o'er the flock, to feed,
And punish each transgression ;
Especial, rams that cross the breed,
Gie them sufficient threshin,   beating
Spare them nae day.

Now auld Kilmarnock cock thy tail,
And toss thy horns fu' canty ;   merrily
Nae mair thou 'lt rowte out-owre the dale,   low—all over
Because thy pasture 's scanty ;
For lapfu's large o' gospel kail   armfuls—greens
Shall fill thy crib in plenty,
An' runts o' grace the pick an' wale,   cabbage-stalks—choice
No gi'en by way o' dainty,   not given
But ilka day.   every

Nae mair by 'Babel's streams' we 'll weep,
To think upon our 'Zion ;'
And hing our fiddles up to sleep,   hang
Like baby-clouts a-dryin :
Come, screw the pegs wi' tunefu' cheep,   chirp
And o'er the thairms be tryin ;   fiddle-strings
Oh, rare ! to see our elbucks wheep,   elbows jerk
And a' like lamb-tails flyin
Fu' fast this day !

[1] Gen. ix. 22.—*R. B.*   [2] Num. xxv. 8.—*R. B.*   [3] Ex. iv. 25.—*R. B.*

Lang Patronage, wi' rod o' airn, iron
  Has shor'd the Kirk's undoin, threatened
As lately Fenwick, sair forfairn, sorely distressed
  Has proven to its ruin:[1] proved
Our Patron, honest man! Glencairn,
  He saw mischief was brewin;
And like a godly elect bairn,
  He 's wal'd us out a true ane, chosen
    And sound this day.

Now Robertson,[2] harangue nae mair,
  But steek your gab for ever: close—mouth
Or try the wicked town of Ayr,[3]
  For there they 'll think you clever;
Or, nae reflection on your lear, learning
  Ye may commence a Shaver; barber
Or to the Netherton[4] repair,
  And turn a carpet-weaver,
    Aff-hand this day. At once

Mutrie[5] and you were just a match,
  We never had sic twa drones:
Auld 'Hornie'[6] did the Laigh Kirk watch,
  Just like a winkin baudrons: cat

[1] Allusion is here made to the long-disputed settlement of the Rev. William Boyd as minister of the parish of Fenwick. The people being prejudiced against him as a moderate, or rather as the nominee of that party, his settlement was resisted as long as possible; but he was at length ordained in the council-chamber of Irvine, June 25, 1782. Mr Boyd afterwards became very popular, and remained in Fenwick till his death in 1828.

[2] The Rev. John Robertson, Mackinlay's colleague, and a moderate. He was inducted in 1765, and died in 1799.

[3] It is probable that Burns did not mean here to libel the community of Ayr as it was in his day. It has been suggested, plausibly enough, that Ayr obtained its reputation for 'wickedness' when it was the centre of such family or clan feuds as that of the Kennedys, which terminated in the 'Auchindraine Tragedy' of 1602. Or Burns may have been thinking of 'godly' John Welsh, who became the first reformed minister of Ayr, and who found 'the place so divided into factions, and filled with bloody conflicts, a man could hardly walk the streets with safety.' In theological 'wickedness,' too, the Ayr of 'D'rymple mild' and his moderate friends could hardly vie with the 'Air toun' of which Wodrow wrote in June 1729: 'On Sabbath, in time of divine worship, men of some character, Mr Charles Cochran, James Dalrymple, clerk, and many others, to the number of seven or eight, instead of worshipping with other Christians, meet in a tavern, and read Woolston's *Discourses on Miracles*, and ridicule all religion.'

[4] A district of Kilmarnock, where carpet-weaving was carried on.

[5] The clergyman whom Mackinlay succeeded, and who had been minister of the second charge of Kilmarnock from 1775 to 1785.

[6] A nickname given to the Devil, from the horns he is supposed occasionally to wear.

And ay he catch'd the tither wretch, other
To fry them in his caudrons: caldrons
But now his honour maun detach, must
Wi' a' his brimstone squadrons,
Fast, fast this day.

See, see auld Orthodoxy's faes foes
She 's swingein thro' the city; whipping
Hark, how the nine-tail'd cat she plays!
I vow it 's unco pretty: very
There, Learning, with his Greekish face,
Grunts out some Latin ditty;
And 'Common Sense' is gaun, she says, going
To mak to Jamie Beattie[1]
Her plaint this day.

But there 's Morality[2] himsel,
Embracing all opinions;
Hear, how he gies the tither yell, other
Between his twa companions;
See, how she peels the skin an' fell,[3]
As ane were peelin onions!
Now there, they 're packèd aff to h—ll,
And banish'd our dominions,
Henceforth this day.

O happy day! rejoice, rejoice!
Come bouse about the porter! pass round
Morality's demure decoys
Shall here nae mair find quarter:
M'Kinlay, Russell, are the boys
That Heresy can torture;
They 'll gie her on a rape a hoyse, rope—hoist
And cowe her measure shorter cut
By th' head some day.

Come, bring the tither mutchkin in, other—measure of whisky equal to a pint
And here 's, for a conclusion,
To ev'ry 'New-light' mother's son,
From this time forth, Confusion:

[1] Doubtless the author of *The Minstrel* and the *Essay on Truth* is meant by Burns. Beattie was a moderate.

[2] The evangelicals constantly reproached the moderates with preaching a 'cold morality,' to the neglect of 'the doctrines of grace.'

[3] 'Fell' means the cuticle immediately below the skin, which tastes bitter.

If mair they deave us wi' their din, deafen
Or Patronage intrusion,
We 'll light a spunk, and, ev'ry skin,[1] brimstone match
We 'll rin them aff in fusion,
Like oil, some day.[2]

ADDRESS
TO THE UNCO GUID, OR THE RIGIDLY RIGHTEOUS.

My son, these Maxims make a rule,
And lump them ay thegither; together
The *Rigid Righteous* is a fool,
The *Rigid Wise* anither:
The cleanest corn that e'er was dight thrashed or winnowed
May hae some pyles o' caff in; grains—chaff
So ne'er a fellow-creature slight
For random fits o' daffin. merriment, folly

SOLOMON.—Eccles. vii. 16.

O ye wha are sae guid yoursel,
Sae pious and sae holy,
Ye 've nought to do but mark and tell
Your Neebour's fauts and folly! faults
Whase life is like a weel-gaun mill, well-going
Supply'd wi' store o' water,
The heapèt happer 's ebbing still, hopper
And still the clap plays clatter.

Hear me, ye venerable Core, folk
As counsel for poor mortals,
That frequent pass douce Wisdom's door grave
For glaikit Folly's portals; careless

1 This may be interpreted, 'We 'll kindle a fire that will melt them, one and all, to nothing,' like 'rendering' the fat of pigs to lard.

2 Mackinlay became a favourite preacher, very much, it is said, in consequence of his 'fine manner;' and had the degree D.D. conferred upon him. On the 6th April 1836 a dinner, presided over by the Provost of Kilmarnock, was given him, on the occasion of his completing the fiftieth year of his ministry. Referring to his famous ordination and the persons present at the subsequent dinner, he said: 'Time, in its sure and silent course, has carried them all away, so that I do not recollect a single individual who was at that dinner who now survives, and in the congregation to which I now minister I cannot recognise above three or four who were members of it when I was ordained.' Dr Mackinlay died on 10th February 1841, at the age of eighty-five. According to a newspaper obituary notice, he was a native of the parish of Douglas, in Lanarkshire, and entered life as 'tutor' in the family of Sir William Cunningham of Windyhill, by whose influence with the Earl of Glencairn he obtained the presentation to the second charge of Kilmarnock.

I, for their thoughtless, careless sakes,
  Would here propone defences,
Their donsie tricks, their black mistakes, — unlucky
  Their failings and mischances.

Ye see your state wi' theirs compar'd,
  And shudder at the niffer, — comparison
But cast a moment's fair regard,
  What maks the mighty differ; — difference
Discount what scant occasion gave,
  That purity ye pride in,
And (what 's aft mair than a' the lave) — often more—rest
  Your better art o' hiding.

Think, when your castigated pulse
  Gies now and then a wallop, — plunge, flourish
What ragings must his veins convulse,
  That still eternal gallop:
Wi' wind and tide fair i' your tail,
  Right on ye scud your sea-way;
But in the teeth o' baith to sail, — both
  It maks an unco leeway. — terrible

See Social-life and Glee sit down,
  All joyous and unthinking,
Till, quite transmugrify'd, they 're grown — transformed
  Debauchery and Drinking:
O would they stay to calculate
  Th' eternal consequences;
Or your more dreaded h—ll to state,
  D—mnation of expences![1]

Ye high, exalted, virtuous Dames,
  Ty'd up in godly laces,
Before ye gie poor *Frailty* names,
  Suppose a change o' cases;
A dear-lov'd lad, convenience snug,
  A treacherous inclination—
But, let me whisper i' your lug, — ear
  Ye 're aiblins nae temptation. — perhaps

[1] These two lines may be interpreted, 'O if they would but pause to set forth the debit and credit sides of the transaction, and consider that damnation in the hell you dread more than they do is the expense of the game they are playing.'

Then gently scan your brother Man,
Still gentler sister Woman;
Tho' they may gang a kennin[1] wrang,
To step aside is human:
One point must still be greatly dark,
The moving *Why* they do it;
And just as lamely can ye mark,
How far perhaps they rue it.

Who made the heart, 'tis *He* alone
Decidedly can try us,
He knows each chord its various tone,
Each spring its various bias:
Then at the balance let 's be mute,
We never can adjust it;
What 's *done* we partly may compute,
But know not what 's *resisted.*

THE INVENTORY.

IN ANSWER TO A MANDATE BY THE SURVEYOR OF THE TAXES.[2]

Sir, as your mandate did request,
I send you here a faithfu' list,
O' gudes an' gear, an' a' my graith, — commodities—wealth—accoutrements, dress
To which I'm clear to gi'e my aith. — oath

Imprimis, then, for carriage cattle,
I hae four brutes o' gallant mettle,
As ever drew afore a pettle. — plough-stick
My *Lan' afore* 's[3] a gude auld *has been*,
An' wight an' wilfu' a' his days been.
My *Lan' ahin* 's[4] a weel gaun fillie,
That aft has borne me hame frae Killie,[5] — often

1 A 'kennin' means 'the least thing,' or 'just as much as you may ken (perceive) and no more,' and is almost identical with the modern 'sensation.'

2 In May 1785, in order to liquidate ten millions of unfunded debt, Pitt made a considerable addition to the number of 'taxed articles,' including female servants. The usual notice in advance was sent by Robert Aiken as tax-surveyor for the district. Dr Currie gave the following heading to the poem: 'Answer to a mandate sent by the Surveyor of the windows, carriages, &c., to each farmer, ordering him to send a signed list of his horses, servants, wheel-carriages, &c., and whether he was a married man or a bachelor, and what children they had.'

3 The fore-horse on the left hand, in the plough.—*B.*

4 The hindmost horse on the left hand, in the plough.—*B.*

5 Kilmarnock.—*B.*

An' your auld burrough mony a time,
In days when riding was nae crime—
But ance whan in my wooing pride
I like a blockhead boost to ride, — behoved
The wilfu' creature sae I pat to,
(L—d pardon a' my sins an' that too!)
I play'd my fillie sic a shavie, — such an ill turn
She 's a' bedevil'd wi' the spavie. — spavin
My *Furr ahin* 's[1] a wordy beast, — worthy
As e'er in tug or tow was trac'd.
The fourth 's a Highland Donald hastie, — quick-tempered Highland pony
A d—d red-wud Kilburnie blastie;[2] — stark-mad
Foreby a Cowt, o' Cowts the wale, — Besides—colt—choice
As ever ran afore a tail.
If he be spar'd to be a beast,
He 'll draw me fifteen pun' at least.— — pounds

Wheel carriages I ha'e but few,
Three carts, an' twa are feckly new; — almost
Ae auld wheelbarrow, mair for token, — more by token
Ae leg an' baith the trams are broken; — One—both—shafts
I made a poker o' the spin'le, — spindle
An' my auld mother brunt the trin'le.— — wheel

For men, I 've three mischievous boys,
Run-de'ils for rantin' an' for noise; — Regular devils—frolic
A gaudsman ane, a thrasher t' other, — driver of horses at the plough
Wee Davock[3] hauds the nowt in fother. — Little—cattle—fodder
I rule them as I ought, discreetly,
An' aften labour them compleatly. — make them do their work thoroughly
An' ay on Sundays duly nightly,
I on the 'Questions' *targe* them tightly; — Shorter Catechism—cross-question
Till, faith, wee Davock 's turned sae gleg, — sharp
Tho' scarcely langer than your leg,
He 'll screed you aff Effectual Calling,[4] — repeat
As fast as ony in the dwalling.—

I 've nane in female servan' station,
(L—d keep me ay frae a' temptation!)

[1] The hindmost horse on the right hand, in the plough.—*B.*

[2] Burns is understood to have bought this horse at Kilbirnie fair, from William Kirkwood, a horse-dealer, who lived at Baillieston, in that neighbourhood.

[3] David Hutcheson, a little child upon Lochlea farm, to whom, according to tradition, Burns was especially attentive, carrying him home from the field on his shoulders, and teaching him English at night. Burns, in fact, took care of 'Wee Davock' till he was old enough to earn a livelihood.

[4] In the Shorter Catechism of the Westminster Assembly of Divines—which used to be known in Scotland as 'The Questions'—*What is Effectual Calling?* is one of the interrogations.

I ha'e nae wife; and that my bliss is,
An' ye have laid nae tax on misses; mistresses
An' then if kirk folks dinna clutch me, kirk-session
I ken the devils dare na touch me.

Wi' weans I'm mair than weel contented, children
Heav'n sent me ane mae than I wanted. one more
My sonsie, smirking, dear-bought Bess,[1] plump
She stares the daddy in her face,
Enough of ought ye like but grace;
But her, my bonny sweet wee lady,
I've paid enough for her already,
An' gin ye tax her or her mither, if
B' the L—d! ye'se get them a' thegither.

An' now, remember Mr Aiken,
Nae kind of licence out I'm takin';
* * * * *
My travel a' on foot I'll shank it, tramp
I've sturdy bearers, Gude be thankit.— God
The Kirk an' you may tak you that,
It puts but little in your pat; pot
Sae dinna put me in your buke,
Nor for my ten white shillings luke.

This list wi' my ain han' I wrote it, own
Day an' date as under notit.
Then know all ye whom it concerns,
Subscripsi huic, ROBERT BURNS.

MOSSGIEL, *February 22d*, 1786.

TO MR JOHN KENNEDY.[2]

Now, Kennedy, if foot or horse
E'er bring you in by Mauchlin corse,[3]
(L—, man, there's lasses there wad force
A hermit's fancy;
An' down the gate in faith they're worse, road—in truth
An' mair unchancy). more dangerous

[1] The poet's child, then living at Mossgiel, and about fifteen months old.

[2] Mr Kennedy subsequently became factor to the Earl of Breadalbane. After holding this post for eighteen years, he retired to Edinburgh, where he died in 1812, at the age of fifty-five.

[3] The market-place of the village, so called from the cross or *corse* that stood there.

But as I 'm sayin, please step to Dow's,[1]
An' taste sic gear as Johnie brews, such liquor
Till some bit callan bring me news little boy
That ye are there ;
An' if ye dinna hae a bouze, convivial meeting
I 'se ne'er drink mair. more

It 's no I like to sit an' swallow,
Then like a swine to puke and wallow ;
But gie me just a true good fallow, fellow
Wi' right ingine, the proper disposition
And spunkie[2] ance to mak us mellow, only
An' then we 'll shine.

Now if ye 're ane o' warl's folk, a worldly person
Wha rate the wearer by the cloak,
An' sklent on poverty their joke, direct
Wi' bitter sneer,
Wi' you nae friendship I will troke. exchange
Nor cheap nor dear.

But if, as I 'm informèd weel,
Ye hate as ill 's the vera deil
The flinty heart that canna feel— cannot
Come, sir, here 's to you !
Hae, there 's my haun, I wiss you weel, hand—wish
An' gude be wi' you. may all go well with you

TO A MOUNTAIN DAISY,

ON TURNING ONE DOWN, WITH THE PLOUGH, IN APRIL 1786.

Wee, modest, crimson-tippèd flow'r, small
Thou 's met me in an evil hour ;
For I maun crush amang the stoure must—dust
Thy slender stem :
To spare thee now is past my pow'r,
Thou bonie gem.

[1] See p. 95.

[2] 'Spunkie' appears to mean here 'whisky.' 'Spunkie ance' may be translated 'just enough of whisky to produce liveliness.'

Alas! it's no thy neebor sweet,
The bonie Lark, companion meet!
Bending thee 'mang the dewy weet! wet
Wi' spreckl'd breast,
When upward-springing, blythe, to greet
The purpling East.

Cauld blew the bitter-biting North cold
Upon thy early, humble birth;
Yet chearfully thou glinted forth peeped
Amid the storm,
Scarce rear'd above the Parent-earth
Thy tender form.

The flaunting flow'rs our Gardens yield,
High shelt'ring woods and wa's maun shield; walls must
But thou, beneath the random bield shelter
O' clod or stane, stone
Adorns the histie stibble-field dry, barren—stubble
Unseen, alane. alone

There, in thy scanty mantle clad,
Thy snawie bosom sun-ward spread, snowy
Thou lifts thy unassuming head
In humble guise;
But now the share uptears thy bed,
And low thou lies!

Such is the fate of artless Maid,
Sweet flow'ret of the rural shade!
By Love's simplicity betray'd,
And guileless trust,
Till she, like thee, all soil'd, is laid
Low i' the dust.

Such is the fate of simple Bard,
On life's rough ocean luckless starr'd!
Unskilful he to note the card[1] chart
Of prudent Lore,
Till billows rage, and gales blow hard,
And whelm him o'er!

[1] Compare Pope's
'Reason the card, but passion is the gale.'

Such fate to suffering Worth is giv'n,
Who long with wants and woes has striv'n,
By human pride or cunning driv'n
To Mis'ry's brink,
Till wrench'd of ev'ry stay but Heav'n,
He, ruin'd, sink!

Ev'n thou who mourn'st the Daisy's fate,
That fate is thine—no distant date;
Stern Ruin's plough-share drives, elate,[1]
Full on thy bloom,
Till crush'd beneath the furrow's weight,
Shall be thy doom!

THE LAMENT.

OCCASIONED BY THE UNFORTUNATE ISSUE OF A FRIEND'S AMOUR.[2]

Alas! how oft does Goodness wound itself!
And sweet Affection prove the spring of Woe.—HOME.

O Thou pale Orb, that silent shines,
While care-untroubled mortals sleep!
Thou seest a wretch that inly pines,
And wanders here to wail and weep!
With Woe I nightly vigils keep,
Beneath thy wan, unwarming beam;
And mourn, in lamentation deep,
How life and love are all a dream.

I joyless view thy rays adorn
The faintly-markèd, distant hill:
I joyless view thy trembling horn,
Reflected in the gurgling rill,
My fondly-fluttering heart, be still!
Thou busy pow'r, Remembrance, cease!
Ah! must the agonizing thrill
For ever bar returning Peace!

No idly-feign'd poetic pains,
My sad, love-lorn lamentings claim;
No shepherd's pipe—Arcadian strains;
No fabled tortures, quaint and tame:

[1] Compare—

'Stars rush and final Ruin fiercely drives
His ploughshare o'er creation.'—YOUNG.

[2] It is hardly necessary to say that the 'friend' was Burns himself.

The plighted faith; the mutual flame;
  The oft attested Pow'rs above;
The promis'd Father's tender name;
  These were the pledges of my love!

Encircled in her clasping arms,
  How have the raptur'd moments flown:
How have I wish'd for fortune's charms,
  For her dear sake, and hers alone!
And must I think it! is she gone,
  My secret heart's exulting boast?
And does she heedless hear my groan?
  And is she ever, ever lost?

Oh! can she bear so base a heart,
  So lost to Honor, lost to Truth,
As from the fondest lover part,
  The plighted husband of her youth!
Alas! Life's path may be unsmooth!
  Her way may lie thro' rough distress!
Then, who her pangs and pains will soothe,
  Her sorrows share and make them less?

Ye wingèd Hours that o'er us past,
  Enraptur'd more, the more enjoy'd,
Your dear remembrance in my breast,
  My fondly-treasur'd thoughts employ'd.
That breast, how dreary now, and void,
  For her too scanty once of room!
Ev'n ev'ry ray of hope destroy'd,
  And not a *Wish* to gild the gloom!

The morn that warns th' approaching day,
  Awakes me up to toil and woe:
I see the hours in long array,
  That I must suffer, lingering, slow.
Full many a pang, and many a throe,
  Keen recollection's direful train,
Must wring my soul, ere Phœbus, low,
  Shall kiss the distant, western main.

And when my nightly couch I try,
  Sore-harass'd out with care and grief,
My toil-beat nerves, and tear-worn eye,
  Keep watchings with the nightly thief:

Or if I slumber, Fancy, chief,
  Reigns haggard-wild, in sore affright:
Ev'n day, all-bitter, brings relief,
  From such a horror-breathing night.

O! thou bright Queen, who o'er th' expanse,
  Now highest reign'st, with boundless sway!
Oft has thy silent-marking glance
  Observ'd us, fondly-wand'ring, stray!
The time, unheeded, sped away,
  While Love's luxurious pulse beat high,
Beneath thy silver-gleaming ray,
  To mark the mutual-kindling eye.

Oh! scenes in strong remembrance set!
  Scenes, never, never, to return!
Scenes, if in stupor I forget,
  Again I feel, again I burn!
From ev'ry joy and pleasure torn,
  Life's weary vale I 'll wander thro';
And hopeless, comfortless, I 'll mourn
  A faithless woman's broken vow.

DESPONDENCY.

AN ODE.

Oppress'd with grief, oppress'd with care,
A burden more than I can bear,
  I set me down and sigh:
O Life! thou art a galling load,
Along a rough, a weary road,
  To wretches such as I!
Dim-backward as I cast my view,
  What sick'ning Scenes appear!
What Sorrows *yet* may pierce me thro',
  Too justly I may fear!
    Still caring, despairing,
      Must be my bitter doom;
    My woes here shall close ne'er,
      But with the closing tomb!

Happy ye sons of Busy-life,
Who, equal to the bustling strife,
No other view regard!
Ev'n when the wishèd *end*'s deny'd,
Yet while the busy *means* are ply'd,
They bring their own reward:
Whilst I, a hope-abandon'd wight,
Unfitted with an *aim*,
Meet ev'ry sad returning night,
And joyless morn the same.
You bustling, and justling,
Forget each grief and pain;
I listless, yet restless,
Find ev'ry prospect vain.

How blest the Solitary's lot,
Who, all-forgetting, all-forgot,
Within his humble cell,
The cavern wild with tangling roots,
Sits o'er his newly-gather'd fruits,
Beside his crystal well!
Or haply, to his ev'ning thought,
By unfrequented stream,
The ways of men are distant brought,
A faint-collected dream:
While praising, and raising
His thoughts to Heav'n on high,
As wand'ring, meand'ring,
He views the solemn sky.

Than I, no lonely Hermit plac'd
Where never human footstep trac'd,
Less fit to play the part,
The lucky moment to improve,
And *just* to stop, and *just* to move,
With self-respecting art:
But ah! those pleasures, Loves, and Joys,
Which I too keenly taste,
The *Solitary* can despise,
Can want, and yet be blest!
He needs not, he heeds not,
Or human love or hate,
Whilst I here must cry here,
At perfidy ingrate!

Oh! enviable, early days,
When dancing thoughtless Pleasure's maze,
To Care, to Guilt unknown!
How ill exchang'd for riper times,
To feel the follies, or the crimes,
Of others, or my own!
Ye tiny elves that guiltless sport,
Like linnets in the bush,
Ye little know the ills ye court,
When manhood is your wish![1]
The losses, the crosses,
That *active man* engage!
The fears all, the tears all,
Of dim-declining *Age!*

TO RUIN.

All hail! inexorable lord!
At whose destruction-breathing word,
The mightiest empires fall!
Thy cruel, woe-delighted train,
The ministers of Grief and Pain,
A sullen welcome, all!
With stern-resolv'd, despairing eye,
I see each aimèd dart;
For one has cut my *dearest tye*,
And quivers in my heart.
Then low'ring, and pouring,
The *Storm* no more I dread;
Tho' thick'ning, and black'ning,
Round my devoted head.

And thou grim Pow'r, by Life abhorr'd,
While Life a *pleasure* can afford,
Oh! hear a wretch's pray'r!
No more I shrink appall'd, afraid;
I court, I beg thy friendly aid,
To close this scene of care!
When shall my soul, in silent peace,
Resign Life's *joyless* day?
My weary heart its throbbings cease,
Cold mould'ring in the clay?

[1] Fairies are often represented as desirous of becoming men.

No fear more, no tear more,
  To stain my lifeless face,
Enclaspèd, and graspèd,
  Within thy cold embrace!

SONG, COMPOSED IN SPRING.

TUNE—*Johnny's Gray Breeks.*

Again rejoicing Nature sees
  Her robe assume its vernal hues,
Her leafy locks wave in the breeze
  All freshly steep'd in morning dews.

Chorus—And maun I still on Menie doat,
    And bear the scorn that 's in her e'e!
  For it 's jet, jet black, an' it 's like a hawk,
    An' it winna let a body be![1]

In vain to me the cowslips blaw,
  In vain to me the vi'lets spring;
In vain to me, in glen or shaw, — wood
  The mavis and the lintwhite sing. — thrush—linnet

The merry Ploughboy cheers his team,
  Wi' joy the tentie Seedsman stalks, — heedful, cautious
But life to me 's a weary dream,
  A dream of ane that never wauks. — awakes

The wanton coot the water skims,
  Amang the reeds the ducklings cry,
The stately swan majestic swims,
  And every thing is blest but I.

[1] Burns, on publishing this song in his first Edinburgh edition, 1787, wrote of the chorus: 'This Chorus is part of a song composed by a gentleman in Edinburgh, a particular friend of the Author's. *Menie* is the common abbreviation of *Mariamne.*' It has been conjectured that the 'particular friend' here alluded to is, like the 'friend' of the 'Lament,' Burns himself. Mr Scott Douglas goes so far as to say that 'the substitution of the name "Menie" for "Jeanie" was a necessary part of the little *ruse* he chose here to adopt.' At the same time, the tone of the chorus jars decidedly with that of the rest of the poem. It is difficult, therefore, to conceive of Burns writing these four lines, however much he may have desired to indicate through them that slighted love was the cause of his misery.

The sheep-herd steeks his faulding slap, *closes—gate in a fence to a sheepfold*
And owre the moorlands whistles shill ; *shrill*
Wi' wild, unequal, wand'ring step,
I meet him on the dewy hill.

And when the lark, 'tween light and dark,
Blythe waukens by the daisy's side, *awakens*
And mounts and sings on flittering wings,
A woe-worn ghaist I hameward glide.[1] *ghost—homeward*

Come Winter, with thine angry howl,
And raging bend the naked tree ;
Thy gloom will soothe my chearless soul,
When Nature all is sad like me !

TO GAVIN HAMILTON, ESQ., MAUCHLINE

(Recommending a Boy).

Mosgaville, *May* 3, 1786.

I hold it, Sir, my bounden duty
To warn you how that Master Tootie,
Alias, Laird M'Gaun,
Was here to hire yon lad away
'Bout whom ye spak the tither day, *spoke—other*
An' wad hae done 't aff han' : *would have—at once*
But lest he learn the callan tricks, *teach—boy*
An' faith I muckle doubt him, *greatly*
Like scrapin' out auld Crummie's nicks,[2]
An' tellin' lies about them ;
As lieve then I 'd have then, *willingly*
Your clerkship[3] he should sair, *serve*
If sae be, ye may be
Not fitted otherwhere.

Altho' I say 't, he 's gleg enough, *sharp*
An' 'bout a house that 's rude an' rough,
The boy might learn to *swear* ;

[1] The resemblance of this verse to a passage in the 'Mountain Daisy' will be observed.

[2] 'Tootie' lived in Mauchline, and dealt in cows. The age of these animals is marked by rings on their horns, which may be cut and polished off, so as to cause the cow to appear younger than she is. 'Crummie' is a name often applied to cows in Scotland.

[3] Gavin Hamilton was known as 'the clerk,' from his acting in this capacity to a number of local courts.

But then wi' *you*, he 'll be sae taught,
An' get sic fair *example* straught, set directly before him
I hae na ony fear. have not
Ye 'll catechise him every quirk, intricate point
An' shore him weel wi' *hell;* threaten
An' gar him follow to the kirk— make
Ay when ye gang yoursel. go
If ye then, maun be then must
Frae hame this comin Friday, next
Then please sir, to lea'e, sir, leave
The orders wi' your lady.

My word of honor I hae gien,
In Paisley John's,[1] that night at e'en,
To meet the 'Warld's worm;'[2]
To try to get the twa to gree, agree
An' name the airles an' the fee, earnest-money
In legal mode an' form:
I ken he weel a *Snick* can draw,[3] play a trick
When simple bodies let him;
An' if a Devil be at a',
In faith he 's sure to get him.
To phrase you an' praise you, flatter
Ye ken your Laureat scorns:
The pray'r still, you share still,
Of grateful MINSTREL BURNS.

EPISTLE TO A YOUNG FRIEND.[4]

May 1786.

I lang hae thought, my youthfu' friend,
A Something to have sent you,
Tho' it should serve nae other end no
Than just a kind memento;

1 Probably the Whitefoord Arms, whose landlord, 'John Dove, vintner,' was understood to have come from Paisley.

2 A term expressive of a mean, avaricious character.

3 See note to the 'Address to the Deil,' p. 94.

4 Andrew Hunter Aiken became a merchant in Liverpool, and prospered. He died in 1831 at Riga, where he held the office of English consul. William Niven of Kirkbride—the 'Willie' of the Kirkoswald anecdotes—used to declare that Burns originally addressed this epistle to him, and it has even been said that the poet 'changed his intention owing to his being informed that his early companion was pervaded by the single idea of how to become rich.' At the same time, Niven never produced a copy of the original 'epistle' addressed to himself. All through the poem, too, the tone of Burns is that of a mentor addressing not a cöeval like Niven, but a much younger man.

But how the subject-theme may gang,
 Let time and chance determine;
Perhaps, it may turn out a Sang;
 Perhaps, turn out a Sermon.

Ye 'll try the world soon, my lad,
 And Andrew dear, believe me,
Ye 'll find mankind an unco squad, strange crew
 And muckle they may grieve ye: much
For care and trouble set your thought,
 Ev'n when your end 's attained;
And a' your views may come to nought,
 Where ev'ry nerve is strained.

I 'll no say men are villains a';
 The real, harden'd wicked,
Wha hae nae check but human law,
 Are to a few restricked: restricted
But Och! mankind are unco weak, very
 An' little to be trusted;
If *Self* the wavering balance shake,
 It 's rarely right adjusted!

Yet they wha fa' in Fortune's strife, fall
 Their fate we should na censure,
For still th' important end of life,
 They equally may answer:
A man may hae an honest heart,
 Tho' Poortith hourly stare him; poverty
A man may tak a neebor's part,
 Yet hae nae cash to spare him.

Ay free, aff han', your story tell, off-hand
 When wi' a bosom crony; companion
But still keep something to yoursel
 Ye scarcely tell to ony.
Conceal yoursel as weel 's ye can well
 Frae critical dissection; from
But keek thro' ev'ry other man look searchingly
 Wi' sharpen'd, sly inspection.

The sacred lowe o' weel-plac'd love, flame
 Luxuriantly indulge it;
But never tempt th' illicit rove,
 Tho' naething should divulge it:

I wave the quantum of the sin,
  The hazard of concealing;
But Och! it hardens a' within,
  And petrifies the feeling!

To catch Dame Fortune's golden smile,
  Assiduous wait upon her;
And gather gear by ev'ry wile — **wealth**
  That 's justify'd by Honor:
Not for to hide it in a hedge,
  Nor for a train-attendant;
But for the glorious privilege
  Of being independent.

The fear o' Hell 's a hangman's whip,
  To haud the wretch in order; — **hold, keep**
But where ye feel your Honor grip,
  Let that ay be your border:
Its slightest touches, instant pause—
  Debar a' side-pretences;
And resolutely keep its laws,
  Uncaring consequences.

The great Creator to revere,
  Must sure become the Creature;
But still the preaching cant forbear,
  And ev'n the rigid feature:
Yet ne'er with Wits profane to range,
  Be complaisance extended;
An Atheist-laugh 's a poor exchange
  For Deity offended!

When ranting round in Pleasure's ring, — **making merry**
  Religion may be blinded;
Or if she gie a random sting, — **give**
  It may be little minded;
But when on Life we 're tempest-driv'n,
  A Conscience but a canker—
A correspondence fix'd wi' Heav'n,
  Is sure a noble anchor!

Adieu, dear, amiable Youth!
  Your heart can ne'er be wanting!
May Prudence, Fortitude, and Truth,
  Erect your brow undaunting!

In ploughman phrase, 'God send you speed'
Still daily to grow wiser;
And may ye better reck the rede, attend to the advice
Than ever did th' Adviser.

ROB[T]. BURNS.

AFTON WATER.[1]

I charge you, O ye daughters of Jerusalem, that ye stir not, nor awake my love—my dove, my undefiled! The flowers appear on the earth, the time of the singing of the birds is come, and the voice of the turtle is heard in our land.—*R. B.*

TUNE—*The Yellow-haired Laddie.*

Flow gently, sweet Afton, among thy green braes, hill-slopes
Flow gently, I 'll sing thee a song in thy praise;
My Mary 's asleep by thy murmuring stream,
Flow gently, sweet Afton, disturb not her dream.

Thou stock dove whose echo resounds thro' the glen,
Ye wild whistling blackbirds in yon thorny den,
Thou green crested lapwing thy screaming forbear,
I charge you disturb not my slumbering Fair.

How lofty, sweet Afton, thy neighbouring hills,
Far mark'd with the courses of clear, winding rills;
There daily I wander as noon rises high,
My flocks and my Mary's sweet Cot in my eye.

How pleasant thy banks and green vallies below,
Where, wild in the woodlands, the primroses blow;
There oft as mild ev'ning weeps over the lea,
The sweet-scented birk shades my Mary and me. birch

Thy crystal stream, Afton, how lovely it glides,
And winds by the cot where my Mary resides;
How wanton thy waters her snowy feet lave,
As, gathering sweet flowerets, she stems thy clear wave.

[1] This song apparently relates to his passion for Mary Campbell, although no reliable facts have been brought forward to decide whether it was partially or entirely written during the continuance of that passion or after her death. A daughter of Mrs Dunlop declared positively that she remembered hearing Burns say it was written upon Mary. If this recollection can be trusted, it must be inferred that the name Afton was adopted in place of Ayr by Burns *euphoniæ gratiâ*, and was suggested to him by the beautiful valley of Glen Afton, near New Cumnock, the paternal property of Mrs Stewart of Stair.

Flow gently, sweet Afton, among thy green braes,
Flow gently, sweet River, the theme of my lays;
My Mary 's asleep by thy murmuring stream,
Flow gently, sweet Afton, disturb not her dream.[1]

THE HIGHLAND LASSIE, O.

Nae gentle dames, tho' ne'er sae fair,[2]
Shall ever be my muse's care;
Their titles a' are empty show;
Gie me my Highland Lassie, O.

Chorus—Within the glen sae bushy, O,
Aboon the plain sae rashy, O, — full of rushes
I set me down wi' right gude will, — sat down
To sing my Highland Lassie, O.

O were yon hills and vallies mine,
Yon palace and yon gardens fine!
The world then the love should know
I bear my Highland Lassie, O.

But fickle fortune frowns on me,
And I maun cross the raging sea; — must
But while my crimson currents flow,
I love my Highland Lassie, O.

Altho' thro' foreign climes I range,
I know her heart will never change,
For her bosom burns with honor's glow,
My faithful Highland Lassie, O.

For her I 'll dare the billow's roar;
For her I 'll trace a distant shore;
That Indian wealth may lustre throw
Around my Highland Lassie, O.

She has my heart, she has my hand,
By secret troth and honor's band!
Till the mortal stroke shall lay me low,
I 'm thine, my Highland Lassie, O.

[1] Burns here translates very accurately the description given in the *Statistical Account* of the parish of New Cumnock, of the junction of the Afton and the Nith: 'Flowing northwards, of local origin, and falling into the Nith, the small stream called the Afton forms a beautiful valley, and is overlooked by richly sylvan banks.'

[2] 'Gentle' is here used in opposition to 'simple.' 'Gentle dames' means ladies of aristocratic birth.

Farewel the glen sae bushy, O!
Farewel the plain sae rashy, O!
To other lands I now must go
To sing my Highland Lassie, O!

WILL YE GO TO THE INDIES, MY MARY?

TUNE—*Will ye go to the Ewe-buchts, Marion?*

Will ye go to the Indies, my Mary,
And leave auld Scotia's shore?
Will ye go to the Indies, my Mary,
Across th' Atlantic's roar?[1]

O sweet grows the lime and the orange,
And the apple on the pine;
But a' the charms o' the Indies
Can never equal thine.

I hae sworn by the Heavens to my Mary,
I hae sworn by the Heavens to be true;
And sae may the Heavens forget me,
When I forget my vow!

O plight me your faith, my Mary,
And plight me your lily-white hand;
O plight me your faith, my Mary,
Before I leave Scotia's strand.

We hae plighted our troth, my Mary,
In mutual affection to join,
And curst be the cause that shall part us!
The hour, and the moment o' time!

FAREWELL TO ELIZA.

TUNE—*Gilderoy.*

From thee, Eliza, I must go,
And from my native shore:
The cruel fates between us throw
A boundless ocean's roar:

[1] The first verse is not to be read as expressing a desire of the poet that Mary should accompany him to the West Indies: the rest of the poem makes the idea of a parting and farewell quite clear. The verse may be accepted simply as a variation of the song whose air was adopted.

But boundless oceans, roaring wide,
  Between my love and me,
They never, never can divide
  My heart and soul from thee.

Farewell, farewell, Eliza dear,
  The maid that I adore!
A boding voice is in mine ear,
  We part to meet no more!
But the latest throb that leaves my heart,
  While Death stands victor by,
That throb, Eliza, is thy part,
  And thine that latest sigh!

ADDRESS OF BEELZEBUB.[1]

To the Right Honorable the Earl of Breadalbine, President of the Right Honorable and Honorable the Highland Society, which met on the 23d of May last, at the Shakespeare, Covent Garden, to concert ways and means to frustrate the designs of FIVE HUNDRED HIGHLANDERS who, as the Society were informed by Mr M'Kenzie of Applecross,[2] were so audacious as to attempt an escape from their lawful lords and masters whose property they were, by emigrating from the lands of Mr M'Donald of Glengary to the wilds of Canada, in search of that fantastic thing—LIBERTY.

Long Life, my lord, an' health be yours,
Unskaith'd by hunger'd Highland boors; **Unharmed**
Lord grant nae duddie, desperate beggar, **ragged**
Wi' dirk, claymore, and rusty trigger,
May twin auld Scotland o' a life **deprive**
She likes—as lambkins like a knife.

Faith, you and Applecross were right
To keep the Highland hounds in sight:
I doubt na! they wad bid nae better, **propose**
Than let them ance out owre the water, **over**
Then up amang thae lakes and seas: **those**
They 'll mak what rules and laws they please:

[1] This poem first appeared in the *Edinburgh Magazine* for February 1818. A copy in the poet's handwriting is in the collection of manuscripts which was the property of the late Mr W. F. Watson, Edinburgh, and is now in the Scottish National Portrait Gallery.

[2] Thomas M'Kenzie of Applecross (a considerable estate in the west of Ross-shire) had a reputation for generosity. Knox, in his *Tour of the Highlands*, written about this very time, mentions an act of M'Kenzie's precisely contrary in its character to the motive which the poet attributes to him. 'Perceiving,' says Knox, 'the bad policy of servitude in the Highlands, Mr M'Kenzie has totally relinquished all the feudal claims upon the labour of his tenants, whom he pays, with the strictest regard to justice, at the rate of sevenpence or eightpence for every day employed upon his works.'

Some daring Hancock, or a Franklin,
May set their Highland bluid a-ranklin;
Some Washington again may head them,
Or some Montgomery, fearless, lead them;
Till (God knows what may be effected
When by such heads and hearts directed),
Poor dunghill sons of dirt an' mire
May to Patrician rights aspire!
Nae sage North now, nor sager Sackville,
To watch and premier o'er the pack vile,— rule
An' whare will ye get Howes and Clintons[1]
To bring them to a right repentance—
To cowe the rebel generation, frighten
An' save the honor o' the nation?

They, an' be d—mn'd! what right hae they
To meat, or sleep, or light o' day?
Far less—to riches, pow'r, or freedom,
But what your lordship likes to gie them?

But hear, my lord! Glengary, hear!
Your hand 's owre light on them, I fear; too
Your factors, grieves, trustees, and bailies, land-stewards—farm-overseers
I canna say but they do gaylies; pretty well
They lay aside a' tender mercies,
An' tirl the hallions to the birses; strip—clowns, worthless fellows—hairy hides
Yet while they 're only poind't and herriet, distrained—plundered
They 'll keep their stubborn Highland spirit:
But smash them! crash them a' to spails, chips
An' rot the dyvors i' the jails! bankrupts

[1] Burns introduces in this poem the names of several of the most prominent figures, both on the British and on the American side, in the War of Independence. The parts played by Franklin (1706–1790), Washington (1732–1799), and Lord North (1732–1792) are too familiar to require detailed description. John Hancock (1737–1793) was President of the Congress of Philadelphia, and is understood to have been the first to sign the Declaration of Independence. Major-general Richard Montgomery (1736–1775), a native of Ireland, and at one time a distinguished soldier in the British army, 'sadly and reluctantly' joined the American side in 1775. He was killed while leading an attack on Quebec on 31st December of that year. George Viscount Sackville (1716–1785) fought at Dettingen and Fontenoy, and fell into disgrace for disobeying orders at the battle of Minden. He was restored to royal favour in 1775, and was Secretary of State for the Colonies during the war. General William Howe (1729–1814) succeeded General Gage in 1775 as commander-in-chief of the British forces in America, commanded at Bunker's Hill, captured New York, defeating Washington at White Plains and Brandywine, but was superseded by Sir Henry Clinton in 1778, because he had not destroyed the American force at Valley Forge. Sir Henry Clinton (1738–1795) captured Charleston two years after being appointed Howe's successor; but after the capitulation of Cornwallis at Yorktown in 1781, he resigned his command and returned to England.

The young dogs, swinge them to the labour; beat
Let wark an' hunger mak them sober! work
The hizzies, if they 're oughtlins faussont, girls—at all handsome
Let them in Drury-lane be lesson'd!
An' if the wives an' dirty brats children
Come thiggin at your doors an' yetts, begging—gates
Flaffin wi' duds, an' grey wi' beese, Fluttering—rags—vermin
Frightin awa' your deucks an' geese, ducks
Get out a horsewhip or a jowler, bulldog
The langest thong, the fiercest growler,
An' gar the tatter'd gipseys pack compel—begone
Wi' a' their bastards on their back!

Go on, my Lord! I lang to meet you, long
An' in my 'house at hame' to greet you;
Wi' common lords ye shanna mingle, shan't
The benmost neuk beside the ingle, innermost corner—fireside
At my right han' assigned your seat,
'Tween Herod's hip an' Polycrate;
Or (if you on your station tarrow), are not satisfied with the position given you
Between Almagro and Pizarro,
A seat, I'm sure ye 're weel deservin 't;
An' till ye come—your humble servant,

BEELZEBUB.

HELL, *June* 1*st*, *Anno Mundi* 5790 [A.D. 1786].

A DREAM.

Thoughts, words, and deeds, the Statute blames with reason;
But surely *Dreams* were ne'er indicted Treason.

On reading, in the public papers, the 'Laureate's Ode,'[1] with the other parade of June 4th, 1786, the Author was no sooner dropt asleep, than he imagined himself transported to the Birth-day Levee; and, in his dreaming fancy, made the following Address.

Guid-mornin to your Majesty!
May heav'n augment your blisses
On ev'ry new birth-day ye see,
A humble poet wishes!

[1] Thomas Warton was then poet-laureate. His ode for June 4, 1786, begins as follows:

'When Freedom nursed her native fire
In ancient Greece, and ruled the lyre,
Her bards, disdainful, from the tyrant's brow
The tinsel gifts of flattery tore,
But paid to guiltless power their willing vow,
And to the throne of virtuous kings,' &c.

My bardship here, at your Levee
  On sic a day as this is,
Is sure an uncouth sight to see,
  Amang thae birth-day dresses — those
    Sae fine this day.

I see ye 're complimented thrang, — assiduously
  By mony a lord an' lady;
'God save the King' 's a cuckoo sang
  That 's unco easy said ay: — very
The poets, too, a venal gang,
  Wi' rhymes weel-turn'd an' ready,
Wad gar you trow ye ne'er do wrang, — make—believe
  But ay unerring steady,
    On sic a day.

For me! before a monarch's face,
  Ev'n there I winna flatter; — won't
For neither pension, post, nor place,
  Am I your humble debtor:
So, nae reflection on your Grace,
  Your Kingship to bespatter;
There 's monie waur been o' the race, — worse—royal family
  And aiblins ane been better — perhaps
    Than you this day.

'Tis very true, my sovereign King,
  My skill may weel be doubted;
But facts are cheels that winna ding, — fellows—will not be beaten
  An' downa be disputed: — cannot
Your royal nest, beneath your wing,
  Is e'en right reft an' clouted, — torn and patched
And now the third part o' the string,
  An' less, will gang about it — go round
    Than did ae day.[1] — at one time

Far be 't frae me that I aspire — from
  To blame your legislation,
Or say, ye wisdom want, or fire,
  To rule this mighty nation:
But faith! I muckle doubt, my sire, — greatly
  Ye 've trusted ministration
To chaps, wha, in a barn or byre — men—cow-house
  Wad better fill'd their station,
    Than courts yon day.

[1] The North American colonies had been lost.

And now ye 've gien auld Britain peace, — given
Her broken shins to plaister;
Your sair taxation does her fleece, — severe
Till she has scarce a tester: — sixpence
For me, thank God, my life 's a lease,
Nae bargain wearing faster,
Or faith! I fear, that, wi' the geese,
I shortly boost to pasture — must needs
I' the craft some day. — field near the house

I 'm no mistrusting Willie Pitt,
When taxes he enlarges,
(An' Will 's a true guid fallow's get,[1] — fellow—son
A name not envy spairges), — befouls
That he intends to pay your debt,
An' lessen a' your charges;
But G— sake! let nae saving fit
Abridge your bonie barges[2]
An' boats this day.

Adieu, my Liege! may Freedom geck — exult
Beneath your high protection;
An' may ye rax Corruption's neck, — stretch
And gie her for dissection!
But since I 'm here, I 'll no neglect,
In loyal, true affection,
To pay your Queen, wi' due respect,
My fealty an' subjection
This great birth-day.

Hail, Majesty most Excellent!
While nobles strive to please ye,
Will ye accept a compliment,
A simple poet gies ye?
Thae bonie bairntime, Heav'n has lent, — family of children
Still higher may they heeze ye — raise
In bliss, till fate some day is sent,
For ever to release ye
Frae care that day.

[1] 'A guid fallow's get' means 'a good fellow's son,' *get* being 'offspring,' 'that which is begotten,' as in 'She was nae get o' moorland tips,' in 'Mailie's Elegy.'

[2] On the supplies for the navy being voted, spring 1786, a Captain Macbride counselled some changes in that force, particularly the giving up of 64-gun ships, which occasioned a good deal of discussion.

For you, young Potentate o' Wales,
  I tell your Highness fairly,
Down Pleasure's stream, wi' swelling sails,
  I'm tauld ye're driving rarely; — told—rapidly
But some day ye may gnaw your nails,
  An' curse your folly sairly, — deeply
That e'er ye brak Diana's pales, — broke the bounds set by the goddess of chastity
  Or rattl'd dice wi' Charlie[1]
    By night or day.

Yet aft a ragged cowt 's been known, — colt
  To mak a noble aiver; — work-horse
So, ye may doucely fill a throne, — soberly
  For a' their clish-ma-claver: — talk
There, him[2] at Agincourt wha shone,
  Few better were or braver;
And yet, wi' funny, queer Sir John,[3]
  He was an unco shaver — a great madcap
    For monie a day.

For you, right rev'rend Osnaburg,[4]
  Nane sets the lawn-sleeve sweeter, — becomes
Altho' a ribban at your lug — ear
  Wad been a dress completer:
As ye disown yon paughty dog — proud
  That bears the keys of Peter,
Then swith! an' get a wife to hug, — away
  Or trowth, ye'll stain the mitre — in truth
    Some luckless day!

Young, royal 'tarry-breeks,' I learn, — sailor
  Ye've lately come athwart her;
A glorious galley,[5] stem and stern,
  Weel rigg'd for Venus' barter;

[1] Charles James Fox, then leader of the Whig Opposition in the House of Commons. He was no favourite of the king's, being believed to be the aider and abetter of 'that ill-advised young man,' the Prince of Wales, afterwards George IV., in his vicious pleasures.

[2] King Henry V.—*B.*

[3] Sir John Falstaff, *vid.* Shakespeare.—*B.*

[4] Frederick, the second son of George, III. (1763–1827), titular bishop of Osnabrück, afterwards Duke of York. The see was held alternately by a Catholic bishop and a secular prince of the house of Brunswick-Luneburg, till it was completely secularised in 1802.

[5] Alluding to the newspaper account of a certain royal sailor's amour.—*B.* The allusion here is to Prince William Henry, third son of George III. (bred for the navy), afterwards William IV., and his marriage to Mrs Jordan, an actress.

But first hang out, that she 'll discern
Your hymeneal charter;
Then heave aboard your grapple-airn,
An', large upon her quarter,
Come full that day.

Ye, lastly, bonie blossoms a',
Ye royal lasses dainty,
Heav'n mak you guid as weel as braw, handsome
An' gie ye lads a-plenty!
But sneer na British boys awa! not—away
For kings are unco scant ay,
An' German gentles are but sma', princes—of small account
They 're better just than want ay
On onie day. any

God bless you a'! consider now,
Ye 're unco muckle dautet; made very much of
But ere the course o' life be through,
It may be bitter sautet: salted
An' I hae seen their coggie fou, dish full
That yet hae tarrow't at it;[1]
But or the day was done, I trow, before—believe
The laggen[2] they hae clautet scraped
Fu' clean that day.

THE HOLY FAIR.

A robe of seeming truth and trust
Hid crafty observation;
And secret hung, with poison'd crust,
The dirk of defamation:
A mask that like the gorget show'd,
Dye-varying on the pigeon;
And for a mantle large and broad,
He wrapt him in *Religion*.

Hypocrisy à-la-Mode.[3]

Upon a simmer Sunday morn, summer
When Nature's face is fair,
I walkèd forth to view the corn,
An' snuff the caller air. fresh

[1] To *tarrow* at food is to linger over it from dislike at it or from want of appetite.
[2] The angle between the side and bottom of a wooden dish.
[3] These lines, like most of the mottoes prefixed to Burns's poems, are probably his own.

N

The rising sun owre Galston muirs — over
Wi' glorious light was glintin;
The hares were hirplin down the furrs, — creeping—furrows
The lav'rocks they were chantin — larks
Fu' sweet that day.

As lightsomely I glowr'd abroad, — with light heart—gazed
To see a scene sae gay,
Three hizzies, early at the road, — wenches
Cam skelpin up the way. — hurrying, walking smartly
Twa had manteeles o' dolefu' black, — mantles
But ane wi' lyart lining; — gray
The third, that gaed a-wee a-back, — held a little aloof
Was in the fashion shining,
Fu' braw that day. — very elegant

The *twa* appear'd like sisters twin,
In feature, form an' claes;
Their visage wither'd, lang an' thin,
An' sour as ony slaes: — sloes
The *third* cam up, hap-step-an'-lowp, — hop-step-and-leap
As light as ony lambie,
An' wi' a curchie low did stoop, — courtesy
As soon as e'er she saw me,
Fu' kind that day.

Wi' bonnet aff, quoth I, 'Sweet lass,
I think ye seem to ken me; — know
I'm sure I've seen that bonie face,
But yet I canna name ye.' — cannot
Quo' she, an' laughin as she spak,
An' taks me by the hands,
'Ye, for my sake, hae gien the feck — bulk
Of a' the ten commands — commandments
A screed some day. — rent

'My name is Fun—your cronie dear,
The nearest friend ye hae;
An' this is Superstition here,
An' that's Hypocrisy.
I'm gaun to Mauchline "Holy fair," — going
To spend an hour in daffin: — sport
Gin ye'll go there, yon runkl'd pair, — If—wrinkled
We will get famous laughin
At them this day.'

Quoth I, 'With a' my heart, I 'll do '
I 'll get my Sunday's sark on, — shirt
An' meet you on the holy spot;
Faith, we 'se hae fine remarkin!'
Then I gaed hame at crowdie-time,[1] — went—breakfast-time
An' soon I made me ready;
For roads were clad, from side to side, — filled
Wi' monie a wearie body, — many
In droves that day.

Here farmers gash, in ridin graith, — sensible—attire
Gaed hoddin by their cotters; — jogging beside
There swankies young, in braw braid-claith, — strapping fellows—fine broadcloth
Are springin owre the gutters.
The lasses, skelpin barefit, thrang, — hastening barefooted—crowded together
In silks an' scarlets glitter;
Wi' sweet-milk cheese, in monie a whang, — large piece
An' farls bak'd wi' butter, — cakes
Fu' crump that day. — hard and brittle

When by the 'plate' we set our nose, — plate for the 'collection' or offertory
Weel heapèd up wi ha'pence,
A greedy glowr 'black-bonnet'[2] throws, — stare
An' we maun draw our tippence. — must bring out—twopence
Then in we go to see the show,
On ev'ry side they 're gathrin;
Some carryin dails, some chairs an' stools, — deals
An' some are busy blethrin — gossiping
Right loud that day.

Here stands a shed to fend the show'rs, — ward off
An' screen our countra gentry;
There 'Racer Jess,'[3] an' twa-three w——s,
Are blinkin at the entry.
Here sits a raw o' tittlin jads, — giggling girls
Wi heavin breasts an' bare neck;
An' there a batch o' wabster lads, — group—weaver
Blackguarding frae Kilmarnock, — Come bent on mischief
For fun this day.

[1] 'Crowdie,' strictly speaking, is meal and cold water mixed together so as to form a thick gruel.

[2] 'Black-bonnet,' a once popular nickname in Scotland for the elder stationed beside the plate at the church door for receiving the offerings of the congregation. Occasionally 'black-bonnet' was applied to the minister himself.

[3] The half-witted daughter of Poosie Nansie, already mentioned. She died in 1813.

Here some are thinkin on their sins,
An' some upo' their claes; upon—clothes
Ane curses feet that fyl'd his shins, one—defiled
Anither sighs an' prays: another
On this hand sits a chosen swatch,[1] sample
Wi' screw'd-up, grace-proud faces;
On that a set o' chaps, at watch,
Thrang winkin on the lasses Busy
To chairs that day.

O happy is that man, an' blest!
Nae wonder that it pride him!
Whase ain dear lass, that he likes best, own
Comes clinkin down beside him! sits down hastily
Wi' arm repos'd on the chair back,
He sweetly does compose him;
Which, by degrees, slips round her neck,
An 's loof upon her bosom, hand
Unkend that day. unnoticed

Now a' the congregation o'er
Is silent expectation;
For Moodie speels the holy door, climbs
Wi' tidings o' dam—ation.[2]
Should *Hornie*, as in ancient days, Satan
'Mang sons o' God present him,
The vera sight o' Moodie's face,
To 's ain het hame had sent him hot
Wi' fright that day.

Hear how he clears the points o' Faith
Wi' rattlin' an' thumpin!
Now meekly calm, now wild in wrath,
He 's stampin, an' he 's jumpin!
His lengthen'd chin, his turn'd-up snout,
His eldritch squeel an' gestures, unearthly squeal

[1] 'Chosen swatch' may be rendered, 'a group of persons who believed themselves to be among the "elect" (chosen) for salvation.'

[2] In the Kilmarnock edition, the word was 'salvation:' it was changed at the suggestion of Dr Hugh Blair of Edinburgh. The Rev. Alexander Moodie was minister of Riccarton, and one of the heroes of 'The Twa Herds.' He was a never-failing assistant at the Mauchline sacraments. In his addresses he dwelt chiefly on the terrors of the law. On one occasion he is credited with having told an audience that they would find the text in John, viii. 44, but it was so applicable to their case that there was no need of his reading it to them. The verse begins: 'Ye are of your father the devil,' &c. Moodie came from the Second Charge of Culross to Riccarton in 1762, and died there in 1799, in his seventy-second year.

O how they fire the heart devout,
  Like cantharidian plaisters — plasters of cantharides, used to produce blisters
    On sic a day!

But hark! the tent has chang'd its voice;
  There 's peace an' rest nae langer;
For a' the real judges rise,
  They canna sit for anger.
Smith opens out his cauld harangues,[1]
  On practice and on morals;
An' aff the godly pour in thrangs, — crowds
  To gie the jars an' barrels
    A lift that day.

What signifies his barren shine,[2]
  Of moral pow'rs an' reason?
His English style, an' gesture fine,
  Are a' clean out o' season.
Like Socrates or Antonine, — Marcus Aurelius Antoninus
  Or some auld pagan heathen,
The *moral man* he does define,
  But ne'er a word o' *faith* in
    That 's right that day.

In guid time comes an antidote
  Against sic poison'd nostrum;
For Peebles, frae the water-fit,[3]
  Ascends the holy rostrum:

[1] Rev. (afterwards Dr) George Smith, minister of Galston—whom the poet introduces in a different feeling, under the appellation of Irvine-side, in 'The Kirk's Alarm,' and who is also mentioned in 'The Twa Herds.' Burns meant on this occasion to compliment him on his rational mode of preaching, but his friends regarded the stanza as calculated to injure his popularity. Dr Smith ministered in Galston from 1778 till his death on 28th April 1823.

[2] See note to 'The Ordination,' p. 156.

[3] The Rev. (afterwards Dr) William Peebles, minister of Newton-upon-Ayr, often called, from its geographical situation, the *Water-fit*. He was in great favour at Ayr among the evangelical party, though much inferior in ability to the moderate ministers of that ancient burgh. 'Robert Hamilton, a crack-pated pauper, who lived long in Ayr, and amused everybody by his droll sayings, one day thus addressed a citizen in the hearing of one of these heretical gentlemen: "I dreamt yesterday I was dead, and at the door o' heaven; and whan I knocked at the door Peter said, 'Wha 's there?' 'It 's me, Mr Robert Hamilton.' 'Whare d' ye come frae?' 'Frae the toon o' Ayr.' 'Get awa wi' ye! Ye canna get in here. There has nane been admitted frae that toon this twa hunner year.' When I gang back, I'll say I'm come frae Prestwick or the Newton"—meaning, in the latter case, that he would have the benefit of the reputation of Mr Peebles's ministrations.' Ordained in 1778, Peebles became a D.D. in 1795, and died in 1825. He published in 1803 a poem, 'The Crisis; or the Progress of Revolutionary Principles,' and, later, a volume of odes and elegies, and another of sermons.

See, up he 's got the Word o' God,
An' meek an' mim has view'd it, primly
While 'Common-sense' has taen the road,
An' aff, an' up the Cowgate[1]
Fast, fast that day.

Wee Miller[2] niest, the Guard relieves, next
An' Orthodoxy raibles, rattles out
Tho' in his heart he weel believes,
An' thinks it auld wives' fables:
But faith! the birkie wants a manse, fellow
So, cannilie he hums them;[3]
Altho' his carnal wit an' sense
Like hafflins-wise o'ercomes him partly
At times that day.

Now, butt an' ben, the change-house fills,[4] public-house
Wi' yill-caup commentators; ale-cup
Here 's crying out for bakes an' gills, biscuits
An' there the pint-stowp clatters; pint-measure
While thick an' thrang, an' loud an' lang, crowded
Wi' Logic an' wi' Scripture,
They raise a din, that, in the end,
Is like to breed a rupture
O' wrath that day.

Leeze me on drink! it gies us mair Commend me to
Than either school or college;
It kindles wit, it waukens lear, rouses—learning
It pangs us fou o' knowledge. crams—full

1 The Cowgate is a lane running off the main street of Mauchline, exactly opposite the entrance to the churchyard. The sense of the passage might be supposed allegorical. But the story goes that Mr Mackenzie, the surgeon of the village, and a friend of Burns, had recently written on some controversial topic under the title of *Common Sense*. On the particular day which Burns is supposed to have had in view, Mackenzie had arranged to join Sir John Whitefoord of Ballochmyle, go to Dumfries House, in Auchinleck parish, and dine with the Earl of Dumfries. Mackenzie, after attending church, and listening to some of the outdoor harangues, was seen to leave the assembly, and go off along the Cowgate, on his way to Ballochmyle, just as Peebles ascended the rostrum.

2 The Rev. Alexander Miller, afterwards minister of Kilmaurs. He was of remarkably low stature, but enormously stout. Burns believed him at the time to belong to the moderate party. This stanza, virtually the most depreciatory in the whole poem, is said to have retarded Miller's advancement. He was ordained at Kilmaurs in 1788, and died in 1804.

3 'Cannilie hums them' may mean 'gently mumbles them'—*i.e.*, the 'auld wives' fables.' Or, if Burns used the word 'hum' in the English slang sense, 'Cannilie hums them' may mean 'dexterously humbugs' the champions of evangelicalism.

4 'But-and-ben' means kitchen and parlour. Here Burns means to say that the whole of the public-house was filled.

Be 't whisky-gill or penny-wheep, very small beer
Or ony stronger potion,
It never fails, on drinkin deep,
To kittle up our notion, enliven our wits
By night or day.

The lads an' lasses, blythely bent
To mind baith saul an' body, both soul
Sit round the table, weel content,
An' steer about the toddy. stir
On this ane's dress, an' that ane's leuk, look
They 're making observations;
While some are cozie i' the neuk, corner
An' forming assignations.
To meet some day.

But now the L—'s ain trumpet touts, sounds
Till a' the hills are rairin, roaring with the echo
And echoes back-return the shouts;
Black Russell [1] is na spairin: sparing
His piercing words, like Highlan swords,
Divide the joints an' marrow; [2]
His talk o' H—ll, whare devils dwell,
Our vera 'sauls does harrow' [3]
Wi' fright that day.

A vast, unbottom'd, boundless pit,
Fill'd fou o' lowin brunstane, flaming brimstone
Whase ragin flame, an' scorchin heat,
Wad melt the hardest whun-stane! whinstone
The half-asleep start up wi' fear,
An' think they hear it roarin,
When presently it does appear,
'Twas but some neebor snorin
Asleep that day.

[1] The Rev. John Russell, at this time minister of the Chapel-of-Ease, Kilmarnock, afterwards minister of Stirling, one of the heroes of 'The Twa Herds.' One of his contemporaries thus described him: 'He was the most tremendous man I ever saw: Black Hugh Macpherson was a beauty in comparison. His voice was like thunder, and his sentiments were such as must have shocked any class of hearers in the least more refined than those whom he usually addressed.' He was ordained in 1774, inducted minister of the West Church, Stirling, in 1800, and died on 28th February 1817.

[2] See Hebrews, iv. 12.

[3] Shakespeare's 'Hamlet' [Act I., sc. v.].—*B.*

'Twad be owre lang a tale to tell — too long
  How monie stories past,
An' how they crouded to the yill, — ale
  When they were a' dismist:
How drink gaed round, in cogs an' caups — wooden dishes of different kinds
  Amang the furms an' benches;
An' cheese an' bread, frae women's laps,
  Was dealt about in lunches, — large pieces
    An' dawds that day. — lumps

In comes a gawsie, gash Guidwife, — buxom—sagacious
  An' sits down by the fire,
Syne draws her kebbuck an' her knife, — Then—cheese
  The lasses they are shyer.
The auld Guidmen, about the *grace*,
  Frae side to side they bother,
Till some ane by his bonnet lays,
  An' gi'es them 't like a tether, — gives it out as if it were a rope
    Fu' lang that day.

Waesucks! for him that gets nae lass, — Alas!
  Or lasses that hae naething!
Sma' need has he to say a grace,
  Or melvie his braw claithing! — soil with meal—fine clothes
O Wives be mindfu', ance yoursel
  How bonie lads ye wanted,
An' dinna, for a kebbuck-heel, — end of a cheese
  Let lasses be affronted
    On sic a day!

Now 'Clinkumbell,' wi' rattlin tow, — rope
  Begins to jow[1] an' croon; — peal—moan
Some swagger hame the best they dow, — can
  Some wait the afternoon.
At slaps the billies halt a blink, — gaps in fences or walls—young men—a short time
  Till lasses strip their shoon: — take off—shoes
Wi' faith an hope, an' love an' drink,
  They 're a' in famous tune
    For crack that day. — talk

How monie hearts this day converts
  O' Sinners and o' Lassies!
Their hearts o' stane, gin night, are gane — before
  As saft as ony flesh is.

[1] 'Jow' includes both the swinging motion and pealing sound of a large bell.

There 's some are fou o' love divine;
 There 's some are fou o' brandy;
An' monie jobs that day begin,
 May end in Houghmagandie — fornication
  Some ither day.

ON A SCOTCH BARD,

GONE TO THE WEST INDIES.

A' ye wha live by sowps o' drink, — spoonfuls
A' ye wha live by crambo-clink, — rhyming
A' ye wha live and never think,
  Come mourn wi' me!
Our billie 's gien us a' a jink,[1]
  An' owre the Sea.

Lament him a' ye rantin core, — merry crew
Wha dearly like a random-splore, — frolic
Nae mair he 'll join the merry roar,
  In social key;
For now he 's taen anither shore, — gone to another country
  An' owre the Sea! — over

The bonie lasses weel may wiss him, — wish him well
And in their dear petitions place him:
The widows, wives, an' a' may bless him
  Wi' tearfu' e'e; — eye
For weel I wat they 'll sairly miss him — well I know—sadly
  That 's owre the Sea!

O Fortune, they hae room to grumble!
Hadst thou taen aff some drowsy bummle, — blunderer
Wha can do nought but fyke an' fumble,
  'Twad been nae plea;
But he was gleg as onie wumble, — sharp—joiner's gimlet
  That 's owre the Sea!

Auld, cantie Kyle may weepers[2] wear,
An' stain them wi' the saut, saut tear: — salt
'Twill mak her poor auld heart, I fear, — make
  In flinders flee: — splinters
He was her Laureat monie a year,
  That 's owre the Sea!

[1] Our brother has eluded us all.
[2] Strips of white muslin placed on a cuff or sleeve as a token of mourning.

He saw Misfortune's cauld *Nor-west* — cold
Lang mustering up a bitter blast; — long
A Jillet brak his heart at last, — jilt
Ill may she be!
So, took a berth afore the mast,
An' owre the Sea.

To tremble under Fortune's cummock, — rod
On scarce a bellyfu' o' drummock, — raw meal and water
Wi' his proud, independent stomach,
Could ill agree;
So, row't his hurdies in a hammock, — rolled—loins
An' owre the Sea.

He ne'er was gien to great misguiding, — addicted to extravagance
Yet coin his pouches wad na bide in; — pockets—remain
Wi' him it ne'er was under hiding;
He dealt it free: — gave it away lavishly
The Muse was a' that he took pride in,
That 's owre the sea.

Jamaica bodies, use him weel, — folk
An' hap him in a cozie biel: — wrap—snug shelter
Ye 'll find him ay a dainty chiel, — good-humoured fellow
And fou o' glee: — full
He wad na wrang'd the vera Deil, — would not have wronged the very devil
That 's owre the Sea.

Fareweel, my rhyme-composing billie! — comrade
Your native soil was right ill-willie; — full of ill-will, unfriendly
But may ye flourish like a lily,
Now bonnilie!
I 'll toast ye in my hindmost gillie, — last gill (of whisky)
Tho' owre the Sea!

A BARD'S EPITAPH.[1]

Is there a whim-inspirèd fool,
Owre fast for thought, owre hot for rule, — too
Owre blate to seek, owre proud to snool, — bashful—submit tamely
Let him draw near;
And owre this grassy heap sing dool, — over—lament
And drap a tear.

[1] It has been conjectured that this poem was written to supersede the 'Elegy on the Death of Robert Ruisseaux,' which appeared (see page 33) in the Commonplace Book, and that he (Burns) originally intended that elegy to have a place in the Kilmarnock edition.

Is there a Bard of rustic song,
Who, noteless, steals the crowds among,
That weekly this area throng,
O, pass not by!
But, with a frater-feeling strong,
Here heave a sigh.

Is there a man whose judgment clear
Can others teach the course to steer,
Yet runs, himself, life's mad career,
Wild as the wave;
Here pause—and, through the starting tear,
Survey this grave.

The poor Inhabitant below
Was quick to learn and wise to know,
And keenly felt the friendly glow,
And softer flame;
But thoughtless follies laid him low,
And stain'd his name!

Reader, attend—whether thy soul
Soars fancy's flights beyond the pole,
Or darkling grubs this earthly hole,
In low pursuit;
Know, prudent, cautious, self-controul
Is Wisdom's root.

A DEDICATION TO GAVIN HAMILTON, ESQ.

Expect na, Sir, in this narration,
A fleechin, fleth'rin Dedication, — begging—flattering
To roose you up, an' ca' you guid, — praise
An' sprung o' great an' noble bluid;
Because ye 're sirnam'd like *His Grace*,[1]
Perhaps related to the race:
Then when I 'm tired—and sae are ye,
Wi' monie a fulsome, sinfu' lie,
Set up a face, how I stop short, — pretence
For fear your modesty be hurt.

[1] The Duke of Hamilton.

This may do—maun do, Sir, wi' them wha
Maun please the Great-Folk for a wamefou ; bellyful
For me ! sae laigh I need na bow, low
For, Lord be thankit, I can plough ;
And when I downa yoke a naig, cannot—horse
Then, Lord be thankit, I can beg ;
Sae I shall say, an' that 's nae flatt'rin,
It 's just *sic Poet* an' *sic Patron.* like poet, like patron

The Poet, some guid Angel help him,
Or else, I fear, some ill ane skelp him ! beat
He may do weel for a' he 's done yet,
But only—he 's no just begun yet.

The Patron (Sir, ye maun forgie me, forgive
I winna lie, come what will o' me),
On ev'ry hand it will allow'd be,
He 's just—nae better than he should be.

I readily and freely grant,
He downa see a poor man want ; cannot bear to
What 's no his ain, he winna tak it ; not—own—won't
What ance he says, he winna break it ;[1]
Ought he can lend he 'll no refus 't, Aught
Till aft his guidness is abus'd ;
And rascals whyles that do him wrang, sometimes—wrong
Ev'n *that*, he does na mind it lang :
As Master, Landlord, Husband, Father,
He does na fail his part in either.

But then, nae thanks to him for a' that ;
Nae godly symptom ye can ca' that ;
It 's naething but a milder feature,
Of our poor, sinfu', corrupt Nature :
Ye 'll get the best o' moral works,
'Mang black Gentoos[2] and pagan Turks, Hindus
Or hunters wild on Ponotaxi,[3]
Wha never heard of Orthodoxy.
That he 's the poor man's friend in need,
The Gentleman in word and deed,

[1] Once he has given his word, he will stand by it.
[2] Burns here uses the popular rendering of the Portuguese *Gentio*, Gentile, applied by old English writers to the natives of India.
[3] 'Ponotaxi' would appear to be a mistake for Cotopaxi.

It 's no thro' terror of D——tion ;
It 's just a carnal inclination.[1]

Morality, thou deadly bane,
Thy tens o' thousands thou hast slain !
Vain is his hope, whose stay an' trust is
In moral Mercy, Truth, and Justice ![2]

No—stretch a point to catch a plack ; farthing
Abuse a brother to his back ;
Steal thro' the winnock frae a w——, window
But point the Rake that taks the door ;
Be to the Poor like onie whunstane, any whinstone
And haud their noses to the grunstane : keep—grindstone
Ply ev'ry art o' legal thieving ;
No matter, stick to sound believing.

Learn three-mile pray'rs, an' half-mile graces,
Wi' weel-spread looves, an' lang, wry faces ; palms
Grunt up a solemn, lengthen'd groan,
And d—— a' parties but your own ;
I 'll warrant then, ye 're nae Deceiver,
A steady, sturdy, staunch Believer.

O ye wha leave the springs o' Calvin,
For gumlie dubs of your ain delvin ! muddy pools—digging
Ye sons of Heresy and Error,
Ye 'll some day squeel in quaking terror,
When Vengeance draws the sword in wrath,
And in the fire throws the sheath ;
When Ruin, with his sweeping besom, brush
Just frets till Heav'n commission gies him :
While o'er the Harp pale Misery moans,
And strikes the ever-deep'ning tones,
Still louder shrieks, and heavier groans !

Your pardon, Sir, for this digression,
I maist forgat my Dedication ; almost forgot
But when Divinity comes 'cross me,
My readers still are sure to lose me.

1 In the first edition there was an additional line here—

'And Och ! that 's nae regeneration !'

2 The sarcasm of this caricature of moderatism with its 'cold morality,' from the high evangelical point of view, has not been perceived by some of Burns's critics. Thus, M. Taine, who doubts whether any one has 'better spoken the language of rebels and levellers than Burns,' finds in these four lines 'hatred to cant and return to nature.'

So, Sir, you see 'twas nae daft vapour; foolish impulse
But I maturely thought it proper,
When a' my works I did review,
To dedicate them, Sir, to *You:*
Because (ye need na tak it ill) take
I thought them something like yoursel.

Then patronize them wi' your favor,
And your petitioner shall ever——
I had amaist said, *ever pray,* almost
But that 's a word I need na say:
For prayin I hae little skill o 't,
I 'm baith dead-sweer, an' wretched ill o 't; altogether unwilling—clumsy at it
But I 'se repeat each poor man's pray'r, I 'll
That kens or hears about you, Sir— knows

'May ne'er Misfortune's growling bark, angry
Howl thro' the dwelling o' the Clerk!
May ne'er his gen'rous, honest heart,
For that same gen'rous spirit smart!
May Kennedy's far-honor'd name[1]
Lang beet his hymeneal flame, fan
Till Hamiltons, at least a diz'n, dozen
Are frae their nuptial labors risen:
Five bonie lasses round their table,
And sev'n braw fellows, stout an' able, fine
To serve their King an' Country weel, well
By word, or pen, or pointed steel!
May Health and Peace, with mutual rays,
Shine on the ev'ning o' his days;
Till his wee, curlie John's ier-oe,[2]
When ebbing life nae mair shall flow, more
The last, sad, mournful rites bestow!'

I will not wind a lang conclusion,
With complimentary effusion:
But whilst your wishes and endeavours
Are blest with Fortune's smiles and favours,
I am, Dear Sir, with zeal most fervent,
Your much indebted, humble servant.

[1] Mrs Hamilton was a Kennedy.

[2] Great-grandchild: literally, a grandchild's heir, from *oe*, a grandchild, and *eer*, an heir.

But if (which Pow'rs above prevent)
That iron-hearted carl, Want, fellow
Attended, in his grim advances,
By sad mistakes, and black mischances, misfortunes
While hopes, and joys, and pleasures fly him,
Make you as poor a dog as I am,
Your 'humble servant' then no more ;
For who would humbly serve the Poor ?
But, by a poor man's hopes in Heav'n !
While recollection's pow'r is giv'n,
If, in the vale of humble life,
The victim sad of Fortune's strife,
I, thro' the tender-gushing tear,
Should recognise my Master dear,
If friendless, low, we meet together,
Then, sir, your hand,—my Friend and Brother !

THE FAREWELL.

TO THE BRETHREN OF ST JAMES'S LODGE, TARBOLTON.

TUNE—*Good-night and joy be wi' you a'.*

Adieu ! a heart-warm, fond adieu !
Dear brothers of the *mystic tie !*
Ye favour'd, ye *enlighten'd* few,
Companions of my social joy !
Tho' I to foreign lands must hie,
Pursuing Fortune's slidd'ry ba', slippery ball
With melting heart, and brimful eye,
I'll mind you still, tho' far awa.

Oft have I met your social Band,
And spent the chearful, festive night ;
Oft, honor'd with supreme command,
Presided o'er the *Sons of Light :*
And by that *Hieroglyphic* bright,
Which none but *Craftsmen* ever saw !
Strong Mem'ry on my heart shall write
Those happy scenes when far awa !

May Freedom, Harmony and Love,
Unite you in the *grand Design,*
Beneath th' Omniscient Eye above,
The glorious *Architect* Divine !

That you may keep th' *unerring line*,
  Still rising by the *plummet's law*,
Till *Order* bright completely shine,
  Shall be my pray'r when far awa.

And *You*,[1] farewell! whose merits claim
  Justly that *highest badge* to wear!
Heav'n bless your honor'd, noble Name,
  To *Masonry* and *Scotia* dear!
A last request permit me here,
  When yearly ye assemble a',
One *round*, I ask it with a *tear*,
  To him, *the Bard, that's far awa.*

YE SONS OF OLD KILLIE.

TUNE—*Shawn-boy*, or *Over the water to Charlie.*

Ye sons of old Killie, assembled by Willie,
  To follow the noble vocation;
Your thrifty old mother has scarce such another
  To sit in that honourèd station.
I've little to say, but only to pray,
  As praying 's the ton of your fashion;
A prayer from the Muse you well may excuse,
  'Tis seldom her favourite passion.

Ye powers who preside o'er the wind and the tide,
  Who markèd each element's border;
Who formèd this frame with beneficent aim,
  Whose sovereign statute is order:—
Within this dear mansion, may wayward Contention
  Or witherèd Envy ne'er enter;
May secrecy round be the mystical bound,
  And brotherly Love be the centre!

[1] The masonic official alluded to here was at one time believed to have been Major-General (then Captain) James Montgomerie (a younger brother of Colonel Hugh Montgomerie of Coilsfield), who was Grand Master of the lodge, while the poet was Depute Master. The Rev. J. C. Higgins of Tarbolton states positively, however, in his *Life of Robert Burns* (Appendix C) that the person alluded to was William Wallace, Sheriff of Ayrshire, and Grand Master of St David's Lodge. The same view is taken by James Marshall, the author of 'A Winter with Robert Burns,' and is supported by the fact that the Sheriff's name is 'to Scotia dear.' A third suggestion, that Sir John Whitefoord is referred to, may be dismissed.

THE LASS O' BALLOCHMYLE.

TUNE—*Ettrick Banks.*

'Twas even—the dewy fields were green,
On every blade the pearls hang;[1]
The Zephyr wantoned round the bean,
And bore its fragrant sweets alang:
In every glen the mavis sang, thrush
All nature listening seemed the while,
Except where green-wood echoes rang,
Amang the braes o' Ballochmyle.

With careless step I onward strayed,
My heart rejoiced in nature's joy,
When musing in a lonely glade,
A maiden fair I chanced to spy:
Her look was like the morning's eye,
Her air like nature's vernal smile,
Perfection whispered, passing by,
'Behold the lass o' Ballochmyle!'

Fair is the morn in flowery May,
And sweet is night in Autumn mild;
When roving thro' the garden gay,
Or wandering in the lonely wild;
But woman, nature's darling child!
There all her charms she does compile;
Even there her other works are foil'd
By the bonny lass o' Ballochmyle.

O had she been a country maid,
And I the happy country swain,
Tho' sheltered in the lowest shed
That ever rose on Scotland's plain!
Thro' weary winter's wind and rain,
With joy, with rapture, I would toil;
And nightly to my bosom strain
The bonny lass o' Ballochmyle.

Then pride might climb the slipp'ry steep;
Where fame and honours lofty shine;
And thirst of gold might tempt the deep,
Or downward seek the Indian mine;

[1] *Hang*, Scotticism for *hung*.

Give me the cot below the pine,
  To tend the flocks or till the soil,
And every day have joys divine
  With the bonny lass o' Ballochmyle.

EXTEMPORE EPISTLE TO GAVIN HAMILTON, ESQ.[1]

[STANZAS ON 'NAETHING.']

To you, Sir, this summons I've sent,
  Pray whip till the pownie is fraething; pony—frothing
But if you demand what I want,
  I honestly answer you—naething.

Ne'er scorn a poor Poet like me,
  For idly just living and breathing,
While people of every degree
  Are busy employed about—naething.

Poor Centum-per-centum may fast,
  And grumble his hurdies their claithing; posteriors—clothing
He'll find, when the balance is cast,
  He's gane to the devil for—naething.

The courtier cringes and bows,
  Ambition has likewise its plaything;
A coronet beams on his brows:
  And what is a coronet?—naething.

Some quarrel the Presbyter gown, dispute about
  Some quarrel Episcopal graithing,[2]

[1] This poem was given a place in the Glenriddel collection. Professor Jack of Glasgow University, in one of the very interesting papers which he contributed in 1878–79 to *Macmillan's Magazine* on 'Burns's Edinburgh Common-place Book,' in which the 'Stanzas' appear, ingeniously argues that they may have been written on February 24, 1788, the day after its author's return from Edinburgh to Mauchline, and to Jean (he supposes her to be the 'feminine whig'), for whom—then *enceinte* for the second time—he took a room; on which day also he wrote to Mrs Maclehose contrasting her with the uneducated girl who had been so faithful to him. Professor Jack thinks Burns sent these verses to Gavin Hamilton before calling upon him. 'Kissed her and promised her—naething' undoubtedly expresses the feeling—happily but a temporary feeling—which Burns then had towards Jean. But the positive declaration, 'And now I must mount on the wave,' so different from the vague fear expressed in the letter to Clarinda, that the Indies must be his lot, appears to make it certain that the poem was written when he saw nothing for it but exile to Jamaica.

[2] 'Graithing' literally means 'harness.' Here Burns uses it, not quite respectfully, to indicate vestments.

But every good fellow will own
  Their quarrel is all about—naething.

The lover may sparkle and glow,
  Approaching his bonie bit gay thing:
But marriage will soon let him know
  He 's gotten a buskit up naething. dressed

The Poet may jingle and rhyme
  In hopes of a laureate wreathing,
And when he has wasted his time
  He 's kindly rewarded with naething.

The thundering bully may rage,
  And swagger and swear like a heathen;
But collar him fast, I 'll engage,
  You 'll find that his courage is naething.

Last night with a feminine whig,
  A Poet she could na put faith in,
But soon we grew lovingly big,
  I taught her, her terrors were naething.

Her whigship was wonderful pleased,
  But charmingly tickled wi' ae thing;
Her fingers I lovingly squeezed,
  And kissed her and promised her—naething.

The priest anathèmas may threat,—
  Predicament, Sir, that we 're baith in;[1]
But when honour's reveillé is beat,
  The holy artillery 's naething.

And now, I must mount on the wave,
  My voyage perhaps there is death in:
But what is a watery grave?
  The drowning a Poet is naething.

And now, as grim death 's in my thought,
  To you, Sir, I make this bequeathing:
My service as long as ye 've aught,
  And my friendship, by G—, when ye 've naething.

[1] Burns here alludes to the prolonged 'persecution' of Gavin Hamilton by Mr Auld and the Mauchline kirk-session.

THE FAREWELL.

The valiant, in himself, what can he suffer?
Or what does he regard his single woes?
But when, alas! he multiplies himself,
To dearer selves, to the lov'd tender fair,
To those whose bliss, whose beings hang upon him,
To helpless children,—then, Oh then he feels
The point of misery festering in his heart,
And weakly weeps his fortune like a coward:
Such, such am I!—undone!
THOMSON'S *Edward and Eleanora.*

Farewell, old Scotia's bleak domains,
Far dearer than the torrid plains,
Where rich ananas [1] blow!
Farewell, a mother's blessing dear!
A brother's sigh! a sister's tear!
My Jean's heart-rending throe!
Farewell, my Bess! tho' thou 'rt bereft
Of my paternal care,
A faithful brother I have left,
My part in him thou 'lt share!
Adieu too, to you too,
My Smith, my bosom frien';
When kindly you mind me,
O then befriend my Jean!

What bursting anguish tears my heart;
From thee, my Jeany, must I part!
Thou, weeping, answ'rest—'No!'
Alas! misfortune stares my face,
And points to ruin and disgrace,
I for thy sake must go!
Thee, Hamilton, and Aiken dear,
A grateful, warm adieu!
I, with a much-indebted tear,
Shall still remember you!
All-hail then, the gale then,
Wafts me from thee, dear shore!
It rustles, and whistles
I 'll never see thee more!

[1] Burns here refers to the *Ananassa sativa,* whose fruit is the anana or pine-apple, and which is indigenous to the West Indies, whither he was about to proceed. Possibly the allusion was suggested by Thomson's

'Witness thou, best anana, thou the pride
Of vegetable life.'

THE CALF.

To the Rev. Mr [James Steven], on his Text, *Malachi*, iv. 2—'And ye shall go forth, and grow up, as CALVES of the stall.'

Right, sir! your text I'll prove it true,
Tho' Heretics may laugh;
For instance, there's yoursel just now, — yourself
God knows, an unco *Calf!* — a great

And should some Patron be so kind,
As bless you wi' a kirk, — present you to a living
I doubt na, Sir, but then we'll find, — not
Ye're still as great a *Stirk.* — young bullock

But, if the Lover's raptur'd hour
Shall ever be your lot,
Forbid it, ev'ry heavenly Power,
You e'er should be a *Stot!* — ox

Tho', when some kind, connubial Dear
Your But-and-ben adorns, — two-roomed dwelling
The like has been that you may wear
A noble head of *horns.*

And, in your lug, most reverend James, — ear
To hear you roar and rowte, — bellow
Few men o' sense will doubt your claims
To rank amang the *Nowte.* — cattle

And when ye're number'd wi' the dead,
Below a grassy hillock,
Wi' justice they may mark your head—
'Here lies a famous *Bullock!*'[1]

[1] In *Scots Lore* (Glasgow) for February 1895, page 112, appeared a communication entitled 'A Burns Parallel,' from Mr J. J. Elliott. The parallel is of 'The Calf' to an epitaph in Latin which appears in Camden's *Remains Concerning Britain* (1674 edition, page 499). The following is the paraphrase by the 'Translatour:'

'All Christian men in my behalf
Pray for the soul of Sir John Calf.
O cruel death, as subtle as a Fox
Who would not let this Calf live till he had been an Oxe,
That he might have eaten both brambles and thorns,
And when he came to his father's years might have worn horns.'

The bovine metaphor, Mr Elliott points out, did not receive that freedom of treatment which it afterwards met with in the Scottish poet's *jeu d'esprit.*

NATURE'S LAW—A POEM.

HUMBLY INSCRIBED TO GAVIN HAMILTON, ESQ.

Great Nature spoke; observant man obey'd.—POPE.

Let other heroes boast their scars,
The marks of sturt and strife;
And other poets sing of wars,
The plagues of human life;
Shame fa' the fun; wi' sword and gun
To slap mankind like lumber!
I sing his name, and nobler fame,
Wha multiplies our number.

Great Nature spoke, with air benign,
'Go on, ye human race;
This lower world I you resign;
Be fruitful and increase.
The liquid fire of strong desire
I've pour'd it in each bosom;
Here, on this hand, does Mankind stand,
And there is Beauty's blossom.'

The Hero of these artless strains,
A lowly bard was he,
Who sung his rhymes in Coila's plains,
Wi' meikle mirth an' glee; much
Kind Nature's care had given his share
Large, of the flaming current;
And, all devout, he never sought
To stem the sacred torrent.

He felt the powerful, high behest
Thrill, vital, thro' and thro';
And sought a corresponding breast,
To give obedience due:
Propitious Powers screen'd the young flow'rs,
From mildews of abortion;
And lo! the bard—a great reward—
Has got a double portion!

Auld cantie Coil may count the day, happy Kyle
As annual it returns,
The third of Libra's equal sway,
That gave another Burns,[1]

[1] Robert Burns, who was born on 3d September 1786—the sun enters the sign of Libra in September—and died at Dumfries 14th May 1857. Although he wrote some passable verses, he did not justify his father's prediction.

With future rhymes, an' other times,
  To emulate his sire;
To sing auld Coil in nobler style,
  With more poetic fire.

Ye Powers of peace, and peaceful song,
  Look down with gracious eyes;
And bless auld Coila, large and long,
  With multiplying joys;
Long may she stand to prop the land,
  The flow'r of ancient nations;
And Burnses spring, her fame to sing,
  To endless generations!

WILLIE CHALMERS.

Wi' braw new branks in mickle pride, *handsome—bridle—great*
  And eke a braw new brechan, *in addition—horse-collar*
My Pegasus I 'm got astride,
  And up Parnassus pechin; *panting*
Whiles owre a bush wi' downward crush, *over*
  The doited beastie stammers; *stupid—stumbles*
Then up he gets, and off he sets,
  For sake o' Willie Chalmers.

I doubt na, lass, that weel kenn'd name *well-known*
  May cost a pair o' blushes;
I am nae stranger to your fame,
  Nor his warm urgèd wishes.
Your bonie face, sae mild and sweet,
  His honest heart enamours,
And faith ye'll no be lost a whit,
  Tho' wair'd on Willie Chalmers. *spent*

Auld Truth hersel might swear ye're fair,
  And Honour safely back her;
And Modesty assume your air,
  And ne'er a ane mistak her:
And sic twa love-inspiring een *such eyes*
  Might fire even holy palmers;
Nae wonder then they 've fatal been
  To honest Willie Chalmers.

I doubt na fortune may you shore *offer*
  Some mim-mou'd pouther'd priestie, *precise in speech—powdered clergyman*
Fu' lifted up wi' Hebrew lore, *made conceited by*
  And band upon his breastie:

But oh! what signifies to you
  His lexicons and grammars;
The feeling heart 's the royal blue,
  And that 's wi' Willie Chalmers.

Some gapin', glowrin countra laird — goggling—landed proprietor
  May warsle for your favour; — strive
May claw his lug, and straik his beard, — scratch—ear—stroke
  And hoast up some palaver: — cough—nonsense
My bonie maid, before ye wed
  Sic clumsy-witted hammers, — fellows
Seek Heaven for help, and barefit skelp — barefoot—run off
  Awa wi' Willie Chalmers.

Forgive the Bard! my fond regard
  For ane that shares my bosom,
Inspires my Muse to gie 'm his dues,
  For deil a hair I roose him. — I don't flatter him in the least
May powers aboon unite you soon, — above
  And fructify your amours,
And every year come in mair dear — more
  To you and Willie Chalmers.

REPLY TO AN EPISTLE

RECEIVED FROM A TAILOR.[1]

What ails ye now, ye lousie b—h,
To thresh my back at sic a pitch?
Losh man! hae mercy wi' your natch, — needle
    Your bodkin 's bauld, — sharp
I did na suffer half sae much
    Frae Daddie Auld.

[1] Thomas Walker, a tailor living at Pool, near Ochiltree. He was a friend of William Simson, the schoolmaster, to whom Burns addressed a poetical epistle. Walker, like Simson, could write verses. Seeing how successful his friend had been in 'drawing' Burns, he thought to do likewise, and sent the poet a long-winded epistle containing twenty-six stanzas. Burns took no notice of it. On the appearance of the Kilmarnock edition, Walker made another attempt to attract the poet's attention, and, by attacking him in the character of a moral censor, succeeded. A comparison of his MS. with the 'Epistle from a Tailor,' as printed by Stewart, shows that Simson, who reduced the original from twenty-one to ten stanzas, was almost as much responsible for the composition as Walker himself. An absurd theory was mooted after his death that Simson was also author of the 'Reply;' he never disputed the attribution of the verses to Burns in Stewart's publication. Besides, they proclaim themselves as by the same hand that wrote the 'Epistle to John Rankine.'

What tho' at times, when I grow crouse, merry
I gie their wames a random pouse,
Is that enough for you to souse thrash
Your servant sae? so
Gae mind your seam, ye prick-the-louse,
An' jag-the-flae.

King David, o' poetic brief, reputation
Wrocht 'mang the lasses sic mischief such
As fill'd his after-life wi' grief,
An' bloody rants, frolics
An' yet he 's rank'd amang the chief
O' lang-syne saunts. ancient saints

And maybe, Tam, for a' my cants, perhaps—tricks
My wicked rhymes, an' drucken rants,
I 'll gie auld cloven Clooty's haunts Satan
An unco slip yet,
An' snugly sit amang the saunts, saints
At Davie's hip yet.

But fegs! the Session says I maun faith!—must
Gae fa' upo' anither plan Go fall
Than garrin lasses cowp the cran
Clean heels owre body,
And sairly thole their mither's ban sorely bear
Afore the howdy. midwife

This leads me on to tell, for sport,
How I did wi' the Session sort—
Auld Clinkum at the inner port the old bellman—door
Cry'd three times, 'Robin!
Come hither lad, an' answer for 't,
Ye 're blam'd for jobbin'!'

Wi' pinch I put a Sunday's face on,
An' snoov'd awa before the Session— sneaked
I made an open, fair confession,
I scorn'd to lie;
An' syne Mess John, beyond expression, then—the minister
Fell foul o' me.

A fornicator lown he call'd me, worthless fellow
An' said my fau't frae bliss expell'd me; fault
I own'd the tale was true he tell'd me,
'But what the matter?

(Quo' I) I fear unless ye geld me,
I 'll ne'er be better!'

'Geld you! (quo' he) an' what for no? why not
If that your right hand, leg or toe
Shou'd ever prove your sp'ritual foe,
You shou'd remember
To cut it aff—an' what for no
Your dearest member?'

'Na, na (quo' I), I 'm no for that,
Gelding 's nae better than 'tis ca't, called
I 'd rather suffer for my faut,
A hearty flewit, blow
As sair owre hip as ye can draw 't!
Tho' I should rue it.

'Or, gin ye like to end the bother,
To please us a', I 've just ae ither,
When next wi' yon lass I foregather, meet
Whate'er betide it,
I 'll frankly gie her 't a' thegither,
An' let her guide it.'

But, sir, this pleas'd them warst ava, worst of all
An' therefore, Tam, when that I saw,
I said 'Gude night,' and cam' awa,
And left the Session;
I saw they were resolvèd a'
On my oppression.

TAM SAMSON'S ELEGY.[1]

An honest man 's the noblest work of God.—POPE.

When this worthy old Sportsman went out last muir-fowl season, he supposed it was to be, in Ossian's phrase, 'the last of his fields;' and expressed an ardent wish to die and be buried in the muirs. On this hint the Author composed his Elegy and Epitaph.—*R. B.*, 1787.

Has auld Kilmarnock seen the Deil?
Or great Mackinlay[2] thrawn his heel? sprained his ankle

[1] Thomas Samson was one of the poet's Kilmarnock friends—'a seedsman of good credit, a zealous sportsman, and a good fellow.'

[2] A certain preacher, a great favourite with the million. See 'The Ordination,' stanza ii.—*B.*

Or Robertson[1] again grown weel,
To preach an' read?[2]
'Na, waur than a'!' cries ilka chiel, worse—each
'*Tam Samson*'s dead!'

Kilmarnock lang may grunt an' grane, groan
An' sigh, an sab, an' greet her lane, sob—cry in solitude
An' cleed her bairns, man, wife, an' wean, clothe—children (inhabitants)
In mourning weed;
To Death she 's dearly pay'd the kane, rent in kind
Tam Samson 's dead!

The Brethren o' the mystic 'level'
May hing their head in wofu' bevel, hang—slope
While by their nose the tears will revel,
Like ony bead;
Death 's gien the Lodge an unco devel, heavy blow
Tam Samson 's dead!

When Winter muffles up his cloak,
And binds the mire[3] like a rock;
When to the loughs the Curlers flock,[4] lochs
Wi' gleesome speed,
Wha will they station at the *cock*?
Tam Samson 's dead!

He was the king of a' the Core, [corps] the whole of the curling fraternity
To guard, or draw, or wick a bore,
Or up the rink like *Jehu* roar,
In time o' need;
But now he lags on Death's *hog-score*,
Tam Samson 's dead![5]

[1] Another preacher, an equal favourite with the few, and who was at that time ailing. For him also, see 'The Ordination,' stanza ix.—*B.*

[2] For a minister to read his sermons, as was frequently done by members of the moderate school, was, and still is, often a cause of great unpopularity in Scotland.

[3] *Mire*, pronounced as a dissyllable—*mi-ar.*

[4] Oddly enough, these lines are quoted at page 154 of Mr Phil Robinson's *The Poets' Birds* (Chatto & Windus, London, 1883) as a description, not of *curlers*, but of *curlews!* It is thus that Tam Samson and his friends appear in Mr Robinson's pages:

'To the lochs the Curlew flocks
Wi' gleesome speed.'

[5] In this verse are several terms of the curler's art. The *hog-score* is a line crossing the course, or rink, near its extremity: a stone which does not pass it is held as disgraced, and is set aside.

Now safe the stately Sawmont sail, salmon
And Trouts bedropp'd wi' crimson hail, spots
And Eels weel kend for souple tail, well-known—supple
And Geds for greed, pikes
Since dark in Death's *fish-creel* we wail fish-basket
Tam Samson dead!

Rejoice, ye birring Paitricks a'; partridges
Ye cootie[1] Moorcocks, crousely craw; boldly crow
Ye Maukins, cock your fud fu' braw, hares—tail quite confidently
Withoutten dread; Without
Your mortal Fae is now awa, foe—away
Tam Samson 's dead!

That woefu' morn be ever mourn'd
Saw him in shootin graith adorn'd, dress
While pointers round impatient burn'd,
Frae couples freed; From
But, Och! he gaed and ne'er returned! went
Tam Samson 's dead!

In vain Auld age his body batters;
In vain the Gout his ancles fetters;
In vain the burns cam down like waters, rivulets—floods
An acre braid! broad
Now ev'ry auld wife, greetin, clatters old woman—weeping—calls out
'Tam Samson 's dead!'

Owre mony a weary hag he limpit, trench-like depression in a peat-moss
An' ay the tither shot he thumpit, always—other
Till coward Death behind him jumpit,
Wi' deadly feide; enmity
Now he proclaims, wi' tout o' trumpet, blast
Tam Samson 's dead!

When at his heart he felt the dagger,
He reel'd his wonted bottle-swagger,
But yet he drew the mortal trigger
Wi' weel-aim'd heed;
'L—d, five!' he cry'd, an' owre did stagger; over
Tam Samson 's dead?

1 A term applied to those fowls whose legs are clad with feathers.—JAMIESON.

Ilk hoary Hunter mourn'd a brither; Every—brother
Ilk Sportsman-youth bemoan'd a father;
Yon auld gray stane, amang the heather,
Marks out his head,
Whare *Burns* has wrote, in rhyming blether, nonsense
Tam Samson's dead!

There, low he lies, in lasting rest;
Perhaps upon his mould'ring breast
Some spitefu' muirfowl bigs her nest, builds
To hatch an' breed:
Alas! nae mair he 'll them molest! no more
Tam Samson 's dead![1]

When August winds the heather wave,
And Sportsmen wander by yon grave,
Three vollies let his mem'ry crave
O' pouther an' lead, powder
Till Echo answer frae her cave, from
Tam Samson 's dead!

Heav'n rest his saul, whare'er he be! soul
Is th' wish o' mony mae than me: many more
He had twa fauts, or maybe three, faults—perhaps
Yet what remead? remedy
Ae social, honest man want we: One—miss
Tam Samson 's dead!

THE EPITAPH.

Tam Samson's weel-worn clay here lies,
Ye canting Zealots, spare him!
If Honest Worth in Heaven rise,
Ye 'll mend or ye win near him. before—get

PER CONTRA.

Go, Fame, an' canter like a filly
Thro' a' the streets an' neuks o' *Killie*,[2] nooks
Tell ev'ry social, honest billie fellow
To cease his grievin,

[1] This verse first appeared in the 1793 edition.
[2] 'Killie' is a phrase the country-folks sometimes use for the name of a certain town in the West [Kilmarnock].—*B.*

For yet, unskaith'd by Death's gleg gullie, unharmed—sharp knife
Tam Samson's livin! [1]

[1] Tam Samson's house still stands almost opposite to the entrance to Kay Park, where the Mauchline road, by which Burns was in the habit of entering Kilmarnock, turned to the left and descended the slope towards Tankard Ha' Brae, and opened into Sandbed Street. The interior of the house, including a low-roofed kitchen on the ground floor, and an upper room, to which access was had only by a stair, and which was used as an office, is still preserved. It is understood that Burns and Samson often met in the 'Bowling-green House,' a tavern kept by Alexander Patrick—commonly known as 'Sandy Paitrick'—the nurseryman's son-in-law. This house, which was situated in a lane at the head of the Faegate, where it joined the no longer existing Back Street, was widely celebrated for its home-brewed ale, which, from the wooden vessels in which it was served, was popularly known as 'caup ale.' 'Bowling-green House' is associated with the following anecdote, often told by another Kilmarnock intimate of Burns, William Parker, of Assloss House, about a mile north from Kilmarnock, on the road to Fenwick:

'At a jovial meeting one evening in Kilmarnock, at which Burns, Mr Parker, and Mr Samson were present, the poet, after the glass had been circulated pretty freely, said "He had indited a few lines, which, with the company's permission, he would read to them." The proposal was joyfully acceded to, and the poet immediately read aloud his inimitable "Tam Samson's Elegy"—

"Has auld Kilmarnock seen the Deil?" &c.

The company was convulsed with laughter, with the exception of one individual—the subject, *videlicet*, of the verses. As the burden, "Tam Samson's dead," came round, Tam twisted and turned his body into all variety of postures, evidently not on a bed of roses. Burns saw the bait had taken, and fixing his keen black eyes on his victim (Sir Walter Scott says that Burns had the finest eyes in his head he had ever seen in mortal), mercilessly pursued his sport with waggish glee. At last flesh and blood could stand it no longer. Tam, evidently anything but pleased, roared out vociferously, "Ou ay, but I'm no deid yet!" Shouts of laughter followed from the rest, and Burns continued to read, ever and anon interrupted with Tam's "Ay, but I'm no deid yet!" After he had finished, Burns took an opportunity of slipping out quietly, and returned in a few minutes with his well-known

"PER CONTRA.

Go, Fame, an' canter like a filly
Thro' a' the streets an' neuks o' Killie,
Tell ev'ry social, honest billie
To cease his grievin,
For yet, unskaith'd by Death's gleg gullie,
Tam Samson's livin!"

Tam was propitiated. Like the "humble auld beggar" in our humorous old Scotch ballad, "He helpit to drink his ain dregie," and the night was spent in the usual joyous manner where Burns was the presiding genius.'

The monument to Samson, a slab in the burial-ground of the Laigh Kirk, Kilmarnock, contains the following inscription:

'THOMAS SAMSON,
Died the 12th December 1795,
Aged 72 years.

Tam Samson's weel-worn clay here lies,
Ye canting Zealots spare him!
If Honest Worth in Heaven rise,
Ye'll mend or ye win near him.—BURNS.'

Oddly enough, Samson, who died in 1795; Robertson, who died in 1798; and Mackinlay, who died in 1841, and who are all mentioned in the first stanza of the elegy, are buried within a few feet of each other.

TO MR M'ADAM, OF CRAIGEN-GILLAN,[1]

IN ANSWER TO AN OBLIGING LETTER HE SENT IN THE COMMENCEMENT OF MY POETIC CAREER.

Sir, o'er a gill I gat your card, — got—note
I trow it made me proud; — assure you
See wha taks notice o' the bard! — who takes
I lap and cry'd fu' loud. — leaped

Now deil-ma-care about their jaw, — chaff
The senseless, gawky million; — foolish
I 'll cock my nose aboon them a', — above
I 'm roos'd by Craigen-Gillan! — praised

'Twas noble, Sir; 'twas like yoursel, — yourself
To grant your high protection:
A great man's smile ye ken fu' well, — know
Is ay a blest infection. — always

Tho', by his[2] banes who in a tub — bones
Match'd Macedonian Sandy! — Alexander the Great
On my ain legs thro' dirt and dub, — own—pool
I independent stand ay— — always

And when those legs to gude, warm kail, — good—broth
Wi' welcome canna bear me; — cannot
A lee dyke-side,[3] a sybow-tail, — onion
And barley-scone shall cheer me. — cake of barley-meal

Heaven spare you lang to kiss the breath — long
O' mony flow'ry simmers! — summers
And bless your bonie lasses baith, — both
I 'm tauld they 're loosome kimmers! — told—lovable girls

[1] It has been conjectured that this poem was written before the issue of the Kilmarnock edition, and early in 1786. It is impossible to settle the date on internal evidence. Burns included it in the Glenriddel collection, and stated that it was 'wrote in Nanse Tinnock's, Mauchline.'

[2] Diogenes.

[3] 'Lee dyke-side' means the shelter afforded by the side of a dyke, or stone wall made without mortar. It is possible that Burns intended in this allusion to convey a compliment to the Laird of Craigen-Gillan, who had obtained a reputation in the district for the strength of the 'dykes,' or stone fences, which he encouraged his tenants and neighbours to erect. The Dalmellington *dykes* were long famous.

And God bless young Dunaskin's[1] laird,
The blossom of our gentry!
And may he wear an auld man's beard,
A credit to his country.

LYING AT A REVEREND FRIEND'S HOUSE[2] ONE NIGHT, THE AUTHOR LEFT THE FOLLOWING

VERSES

IN THE ROOM WHERE HE SLEPT:—

O Thou dread Pow'r, who reign'st above!
I know Thou wilt me hear;
When for this scene of peace and love,
I make my pray'r sincere.

The hoary Sire—the mortal stroke,
Long, long be pleas'd to spare;
To bless his little filial flock,
And show what good men are.

She, who her lovely Offspring eyes
With tender hopes and fears,
O bless her with a Mother's joys,
But spare a Mother's tears!

Their hope, their stay, their darling youth,
In manhood's dawning blush;
Bless him, Thou God of love and truth,
Up to a Parent's wish.

The beauteous, seraph Sister-band,
With earnest tears I pray,
Thou know'st the snares on ev'ry hand,
Guide Thou their steps alway.

[1] Dunaskin was a small property north-west of Dalmellington, which had been purchased by Mr M'Adam. His son, who became Colonel M'Adam of Craigen-Gillan, was 'young Dunaskin's laird.'

[2] Loudon manse, the residence of the Rev. George Lawrie, who received the degree of D.D. from the University of Glasgow in 1791, and died in 1799, in his seventy-eighth year. This song was apparently intended as part of a lyric description of the festivities at Loudon manse. The manuscript, in the poet's handwriting, was long in the possession of Louisa Lawrie.

R. B. Nisbet, A.R.S.A.

The gloomy night is gath'ring fast,
Loud roars the wild, inconstant blast.

PAGE 215.

When soon or late they reach that coast,
O'er life's rough ocean driven,
May they rejoice, no wand'rer lost,
A family in Heaven!

SONG.

TUNE—*Irvine's Bairns are bonnie a'.*

The night was still, and o'er the hill
The moon shone on the castle wa'; wall
The mavis sang, while dew-drops hang thrush—hung
Around her on the castle wa'.

Sae merrily they danced the ring
Frae eenin till the cock did craw; evening—crow
And aye the ower-word o' the spring refrain, burden—tune
Was Irvine's bairns are bonnie a'.

FAREWELL, THE BONIE BANKS OF AYR.

TUNE—*Roslin Castle.*

I composed this song as I conveyed my chest so far on my road to Greenock, where I was to embark in a few days for Jamaica. I meant it as my farewell dirge to my native land.—*R. B.*

The gloomy night is gath'ring fast,
Loud roars the wild, inconstant blast,
Yon murky cloud is foul with rain,
I see it driving o'er the plain;
The Hunter now has left the moor,
The scatt'red coveys meet secure,
While here I wander, prest with care,
Along the lonely banks of Ayr.

The Autumn mourns her rip'ning corn
By early Winter's ravage torn;
Across her placid, azure sky,
She sees the scowling tempest fly:
Chill runs my blood to hear it rave,
I think upon the stormy wave,
Where many a danger I must dare,
Far from the bonie banks of Ayr.

'Tis not the surging billow's roar,
'Tis not that fatal, deadly shore;
Tho' Death in ev'ry shape appear,
The Wretched have no more to fear:
But round my heart the ties are bound,
That heart transpierc'd with many a wound;
These bleed afresh, those ties I tear,
To leave the bonie banks of Ayr.

Farewell, old Coila's hills and dales,
Her heathy moors and winding vales;
The scenes where wretched Fancy roves,
Pursuing past, unhappy loves!
Farewell, my friends! farewell, my foes!
My peace with these, my love with those—
The bursting tears my heart declare,
Farewell, the bonie banks of Ayr!

THE BRIGS OF AYR.

A POEM.[1]

INSCRIBED TO JOHN BALLANTINE, ESQ., AYR.

The simple Bard, rough at the rustic plough,
Learning his tuneful trade from ev'ry bough;
The chanting linnet, or the mellow thrush,
Hailing the setting sun, sweet, in the green thorn bush;
The soaring lark, the perching red-breast shrill,
Or deep-ton'd plovers, grey, wild-whistling o'er the hill;
Shall he, nurst in the Peasant's lowly shed,
To hardy Independence bravely bred,
By early Poverty to hardship steel'd,
And train'd to arms in stern Misfortune's field,
Shall he be guilty of their hireling crimes,
The servile, mercenary Swiss[2] of rhymes?
Or labour hard the panegyric close,
With all the venal soul of dedicating Prose?
No! though his artless strains he rudely sings,
And throws his hand uncouthly o'er the strings,

[1] In a beautiful manuscript of this poem, now in the possession of the Earl of Rosebery, the title is given as 'The Brigs of Ayr, a True Story.'

[2] Swiss soldiers were in the habit of hiring themselves to any country that chose to pay for their services, and, as was shown at the fall of the Bastille in 1789, fought well.

He glows with all the spirit of the Bard,
Fame, honest fame, his great, his dear reward.
Still, if some Patron's gen'rous care he trace,
Skill'd in the secret, to bestow with grace;
When Ballantine befriends his humble name,
And hands the rustic stranger up to fame,
With heartfelt throes his grateful bosom swells,
The godlike bliss, to give, alone excels.

'Twas when the stacks get on their winter-hap, covering
And thack and rape secure the toil-won crap; thatch and straw-rope—crop
Potatoe-bings are snuggèd up frae skaith heaps—from danger
Of coming Winter's biting, frosty breath;
The bees, rejoicing o'er their summer-toils,
Unnumber'd buds an' flow'rs' delicious spoils,
Seal'd up with frugal care in massive waxen piles,
Are doom'd by man, that tyrant o'er the weak,
The death o' devils, smoor'd wi' brunstane reek: smothered—brimstone smoke
The thundering guns are heard on ev'ry side,
The wounded coveys, reeling, scatter wide;
The feather'd field-mates, bound by Nature's tie,
Sires, mothers, children, in one carnage lie:
(What warm, poetic heart but inly bleeds,
And execrates man's savage, ruthless deeds!)
Nae mair the flow'r in field or meadow springs; No more
Nae mair the grove with airy concert rings,
Except perhaps the Robin's whistling glee,
Proud o' the height o' some bit half-lang tree: little half-grown
The hoary morns precede the sunny days,
Mild, calm, serene, wide-spreads the noontide blaze,
While thick the gossamour waves wanton in the rays.

'Twas in that season, when a simple Bard,
Unknown and poor, Simplicity's reward,
Ae night, within the ancient brugh of *Ayr*, One—burgh
By whim inspir'd, or haply prest wi' care, perhaps
He left his bed, and took his wayward route,
And down by *Simpson's* [1] wheel'd the left about:
(Whether impell'd by all-directing Fate,
To witness what I after shall narrate; [2]

[1] A noted tavern at the Auld Brig end.—*B.*
[2] In a MS. copy, here occur two lines omitted in print:

'Or penitential pangs for former sins
Led him to rove by quondam Merran D—n's.

Or whether, rapt in meditation high,
He wander'd out he knew not where nor why).
The drowsy *Dungeon-clock*[1] had number'd two,
And *Wallace-tow'r*[2] had sworn the fact was true:
The tide-swoln Firth, with sullen-sounding roar,
Through the still night dash'd hoarse along the shore:
All else was hush'd as Nature's closèd e'e; eye
The silent moon shone high o'er tow'r and tree:
The chilly frost, beneath the silver beam,
Crept gently, crusting-o'er the glittering stream.—

When, lo! on either hand the list'ning Bard,
The clanging sugh of whistling wings is heard; rustle
Two dusky forms dart thro' the midnight air,
Swift as the *Gos*[3] drives on the wheeling hare;
Ane on th' *Auld Brig* his airy shape uprears, One
The ither flutters o'er the *rising piers*: other
Our warlock Rhymer instantly descry'd wizard
The Sprites that owre the *Brigs of Ayr* preside. over
(That Bards are second-sighted is nae joke,
And ken the lingo of the sp'ritual folk; know the language of spirits
Fays, Spunkies, Kelpies, a', they can explain them, will-o'-the-wisps—water-spirits
And ev'n the vera deils they brawly ken them.) well know
Auld Brig appear'd of ancient Pictish race,
The vera wrinkles Gothic[4] in his face: very
He seem'd as he wi' Time had warstl'd lang, wrestled
Yet teughly doure, he bade an unco bang. toughly obstinate—withstood a heavy stroke
New Brig was buskit in a braw new coat, dressed
That he, at Lon'on, frae ane Adams,[5] got;
In's hand five taper staves as smooth 's a bead,
Wi' virls an' whirlygigums at the head. rings—useless ornaments

1 The clock on the steeple of the Tolbooth or Old Jail of Ayr, which stood in the centre of the Sandgate. The whole structure was removed in 1826, from its having been found an obstruction to traffic.

2 The clock in the Wallace Tower—an old baronial tower at the corner of High Street and Mill Vennel, which had originally belonged to the Cathcarts of Corbieston, but had been acquired by the Town Council in 1673. How it came to be styled the Wallace Tower is not accurately known. It was replaced in 1834 by a handsome Gothic tower, 113 feet high, and has in its front a statue of Wallace.

3 The goshawk, or falcon.—*B.*

4 This would almost seem to suggest that Burns held, with Pinkerton, that the Picts were Teutons, and spoke a Gothic dialect.

5 The celebrated Robert Adam was the architect of the New Bridge. At all events, it appears from Ayr burgh accounts that he was paid for a plan of a bridge which he had supplied. There is a local tradition that Alexander Steven, mason, who built the structure, was also its architect. Robert Adam was the second son of William Adam of Maryborough, near Kinross. He was born in Kirkcaldy in 1728, and died in 1792. He is buried in Westminster Abbey. His father and four brothers were all architects.

The Goth was stalking round with anxious search,
Spying the time-worn flaws in ev'ry arch ;
It chanc'd his new-come neebor took his e'e, neighbour—eye
And e'en a vex'd and angry heart had he !
Wi' thieveless sneer to see his modish mien, cold
He, down the water, gies him this guid-een— good-evening

AULD BRIG.

I doubt na, frien', ye 'll think ye 're nae sheepshank,[1]
Ance ye were streekit o'er frae bank to bank ! Once—stretched—from
But gin ye be a Brig as auld as me, if—old
Tho' faith that day,[2] I doubt, ye 'll never see,
There 'll be, if that date[2] come, I 'll wad a boddle, wager a half-farthing
Some fewer whigmeleeries i' your noddle. whims—head

NEW BRIG.

Auld Vandal ! ye but show your little mense, manners
Just much about it wi' your scanty sense ;
Will your poor, narrow foot-path of a street,
Where twa wheel-barrows tremble when they meet,
Your ruin'd, formless bulk o' stane and lime, stone
Compare wi' bonie *Brigs* o' modern time ?
There 's men o' taste wou'd tak the *Ducat-stream*,[3]
Tho' they should cast the vera sark and swim, strip to the skin
E'er they would grate their feelings wi' the view
Of sic an ugly, Gothic hulk as you.

AULD BRIG.

Conceited gowk ! puff'd up wi' windy pride ! fool
This mony a year I've stood the flood an' tide ; many
And tho' wi' crazy eild I 'm sair forfairn, old age—sadly enfeebled
I 'll be a *Brig* when ye 're a shapeless cairn ![4] heap of stones

[1] No contemptible or worthless thing.

[2] In the first Edinburgh edition (1787) these words are transposed.

[3] A noted ford, just above the Auld Brig.—*B.* It was the only passage to the town before the Auld Brig was built. During the storms of winter and spring the ford was the scene of much loss of life.

[4] The sinister prophecy of the Auld Brig was fulfilled to the letter. In 1877 the New Brig was so injured by floods that the arch at the south end fell. The whole structure was pulled down, and stood revealed 'a shapeless cairn.' It was rebuilt at a cost of £15,000, yet, in 1881-1882, £2000 more had to be spent in repairing it. Its weakness lay in its foundations, which, as events proved, were not—at all events at the south end—laid on solid rock. It used to be believed in Ayr that Burns gained his knowledge of this weakness from the master of the

As yet ye little ken about the matter, know
But twa-three winters will inform ye better. two or three
When heavy, dark, continued, a'-day rains, whole-day
Wi' deepening deluges o'erflow the plains;
When from the hills where springs the brawling *Coil*,
Or stately *Lugar's* mossy fountains boil,
Or where the *Greenock* winds his moorland course,
Or haunted Garpal[1] draws his feeble source,
Arous'd by blust'ring winds an' spotting thowes, thaws
In mony a torrent down his sna-broo rowes; snow-broth rolls
While crashing ice, borne on the roaring speat, flood
Sweep dams, an' mills, an' brigs, a' to the gate; out of the way
And from *Glenbuck*,[2] down to the *Ratton-Key*,[3]
Auld *Ayr* is just one lengthen'd, tumbling sea;
Then down ye'll hurl, deil nor ye never rise!
And dash the gumlie jaups up to the pouring skies, muddy splashing waves
A lesson sadly-teaching, to your cost,
That Architecture's noble art is lost!

NEW BRIG.

Fine *architecture*, trowth I needs must say't o''t, in truth
The L—d be thankit that we've tint the gate o''t; lost—way
Gaunt, ghastly, ghaist-alluring edifices, ghost
Hanging with threat'ning jut like precipices;
O'er-arching, mouldy, gloom-inspiring coves,
Supporting roofs fantastic, stony groves;
Windows and doors in nameless sculptures drest,
With order, symmetry, or taste unblest;
Forms like some bedlam Statuary's dream,
The craz'd creations of misguided whim;

works or foreman builder on the New Brig, who was a personal friend, and so was enabled to prophesy from knowledge. This view gains some countenance from the fact that Burns, while he speaks of the 'rising' piers, yet alludes contemptuously to the columns as 'five taper staves,' and even to the open balusters over each arch as 'virls and whirlygigums,' thus, to all appearance, indicating an intimate acquaintance with the structure as it was when completed. This, however, he could have obtained from a drawing of the bridge—such a drawing as he might see in the hands of the master of works. The foundations of the Auld Brig were found in 1892 to have been so injured that steps had to be taken to secure its stability also.

1 The banks of Garpal Water is one of the few places in the West of Scotland, where those fancy scaring beings, known by the name of *Ghaists*, still continue pertinaciously to inhabit.—*B.* The streams mentioned in these few lines are tributaries of the Ayr.

2 The source of the river Ayr.—*B.* The village of Glenbuck is situated amid the hills of Muirkirk parish, in the east of Ayrshire, and less than a mile from the Lanarkshire border.

3 A small landing-place above the large key.—*B.*

Forms might be worshipp'd on the bended knee,
And still the *second dread command*[1] be free,
Their likeness is not found on earth, in air, or sea.
Mansions that would disgrace the building taste
Of any mason reptile, bird or beast:
Fit only for a doited monkish race, stupid
Or frosty maids forsworn the dear embrace,
Or Cuifs of later times, wha held the notion fools
That sullen gloom was sterling, true devotion:
Fancies that our guid Brugh denies protection,[2] burgh
And soon may they expire, unblest wi' resurrection!

AULD BRIG.

O ye, my dear-remember'd, ancient yealings, contemporaries
Were ye but here to share my wounded feelings!
Ye worthy Proveses, an' mony a Bailie, provosts
Wha in the paths o' righteousness did toil ay;
Ye dainty Deacons, an' ye douce Conveeners,[3] worthy—sedate
To whom our moderns are but causey-cleaners; street-sweepers
Ye godly Councils wha hae blest this town; have
Ye godly Brethren o' the sacred gown,
Wha meekly gie your hurdies to the smiters, posteriors
And (what would now be strange),[4] ye godly Writers:
A' ye douce folk I've borne aboon the broo, sedate—above—water
Were ye but here, what would ye say or do!
How would your spirits groan in deep vexation,
To see each melancholy alteration;
And agonising, curse the time and place
When ye begat the base, degenerate race! begot
Nae langer Rev'rend Men, their country's glory, No longer
In plain braid Scots hold forth a plain braid story! broad
Nae langer thrifty citizens, an' douce,
Meet owre a pint, or in the Council-house;
But staumrel, corky-headed, graceless Gentry, half-witted
The herryment and ruin of the country; spoliation
Men three-parts made by tailors and by barbers,
Wha waste your weel-hain'd gear on d——'d new brigs and
harbours! carefully hoarded wealth

[1] The Second Commandment forbids the making of 'likenesses' of anything in 'the heaven above,' &c. But it was not violated in the case of the uncouth figures alluded to by 'New Brig,' as these were not 'likenesses' of existing things.

[2] An allusion to the moderatism of the Ayr clergy.

[3] 'Deacon' and 'convener' are officials of a trade guild.

[4] A hit at the 'easy professions' of the Ayr *writers* or solicitors known to Burns.

NEW BRIG.

Now haud you there! for faith ye've said enough, hold
And muckle mair than ye can mak to through.[1] much more—make good
As for your Priesthood, I shall say but little,
Corbies and *Clergy* are a shot right kittle:[2]
But, under favor o' your langer beard,
Abuse o' Magistrates might weel be spar'd: well
To liken them to your auld-warld squad, antiquated
I must needs say, comparisons are odd.[3]
In Ayr, *Wag-wits* nae mair can hae a handle more—have
To mouth 'a Citizen,' a term o' scandal:[4]
Nae mair the Council waddles down the street,
In all the pomp of ignorant conceit;
Men wha grew wise priggin owre hops an' raisins, higgling over
Or gather'd lib'ral views in Bonds and Seisins: sasine
If haply Knowledge, on a random tramp,
Had shor'd them with a glimmer of his lamp, threatened
And would to Common-sense for once betray'd them,
Plain, dull Stupidity stept kindly in to aid them.

What further clishmaclaver might been said, palaver
What bloody wars, if Sprites had blood to shed,
No man can tell; but, all before their sight,
A fairy train appear'd in order bright:
Adown the glittering stream they featly danc'd;
Bright to the moon their various dresses glanc'd:
They footed o'er the wat'ry glass so neat,
The infant ice scarce bent beneath their feet:
While arts of Minstrelsy among them rung,
And soul-ennobling Bards heroic ditties sung.

[1] Inserted here in MS. copy:

'That's aye a string auld doited Graybeards harp on,
A topic for their peevishness to carp on.'

[2] This may be rendered—'Ravens and ministers are troublesome creatures to shoot at.'

[3] In Lord Rosebery's manuscript these two lines run:

'To even them to your auld-warld bodies,
I needs must say "Comparisons are odious."'

In this case Burns's second thoughts would not appear to have been his best.

[4] These lines mean—'Wags can no longer make "citizen" or "councillor" a term of opprobrium—they are so much superior to the stupid tradesmen who used to fill the office.'

O had M'Lauchlan,[1] thairm-inspiring sage, catgut
Been there to hear this heavenly band engage,
When thro' his dear Strathspeys they bore with Highland rage;
Or when they struck old Scotia's melting airs,
The lover's raptur'd joys or bleeding cares;
How would his Highland lug been nobler fir'd, ear
And ev'n his matchless hand with finer touch inspired!
No guess could tell what instrument appear'd,
But all the soul of Music's self was heard;
Harmonious concert rung in every part,
While simple melody pour'd moving on the heart.

The Genius of the Stream in front appears,
A venerable Chief advanc'd in years;
His hoary head with water-lilies crown'd,
His manly leg with garter-tangle bound.
Next came the loveliest pair in all the ring,
Sweet Female Beauty hand in hand with Spring;
Then, crown'd with flow'ry hay, came Rural Joy,
And Summer, with his fervid-beaming eye:
All-cheering Plenty, with her flowing horn,
Led yellow Autumn wreath'd with nodding corn;
Then Winter's time-bleach'd locks did hoary show,
By Hospitality with cloudless brow:
Next follow'd Courage, with his martial stride,
From where the Feal wild-woody coverts hide;[2]
Benevolence, with mild, benignant air,
A female form, came from the tow'rs of Stair;[3]
Learning and Worth in equal measures trode,
From simple Catrine, their long-lov'd abode:[4]
Last, white-rob'd Peace, crown'd with a hazel wreath,
To rustic Agriculture did bequeath
The broken, iron instruments of death;
At sight of whom our Sprites forgat their kindling wrath. forgot

[1] A well-known performer of Scottish music on the violin.—*B.* 'James M'Lauchlan, a Highlander, had been once footman to Lord John Campbell at Inveraray. He came to Ayrshire in a fencible regiment, and was patronised by Hugh Montgomerie of Coilsfield (afterwards Earl of Eglintoun), who was himself both a player and a composer. Matthew Hall used to accompany M'Lauchlan over a wide extent of country, for the purpose of playing at gentlemen's houses, and even in Edinburgh and Glasgow on great occasions. In one week, to use Hall's words, they have passed twenty-six parish kirks, and returned to Ayr on Friday to a ball, never getting to bed till Saturday night.'—*Ballads and Songs of Ayrshire.*

[2] We have here a compliment to Montgomerie of Coilsfield—Sodger Hugh—alluded to in the preceding note. Coilsfield, as has already been noted, is situated on the Fail (Faile or Feal), a tributary of the Ayr.

[3] A compliment to Mrs Stewart of Stair. See 'Epistle to Davie.'

[4] A compliment to Professor Dugald Stewart.

EXTEMPORE VERSES ON DINING WITH LORD DAER.

This wot ye all whom it concerns,
I Rhymer Robin, alias Burns,
October twenty-third,
A ne'er to be forgotten day,
Sae far I sprachled up the brae, clambered—hill
I dinner'd wi' a Lord.

I 've been at druken writers' feasts, drunken
Nay, been bitch-fou 'mang godly priests,
Wi' reverence be it spoken;
I 've even join'd the honor'd jorum, convivial meeting
When mighty Squireships of the quorum,[1]
Their hydra drouth did sloken. thirst—slake

But wi' a Lord!—stand out my shin,[2]
A Lord—a Peer—an Earl's son,
Up higher yet, my bonnet;
An' sic a Lord!—lang Scotch ells twa, six feet high
Our Peerage he o'erlooks them a',
As I look o'er my sonnet.

But O for Hogarth's magic pow'r
To show Sir Bardy's willyart glow'r, bewildered gaze
An' how he star'd an' stammer'd,
When goavin, as if led wi' branks, moving stupidly—bridle
An' stumpin on his ploughman shanks, legs
He in the parlour hammer'd. moved about clumsily

I sidling shelter'd in a nook,
An' at his Lordship steal't a look
Like some portentous omen;
Except good-sense and social glee,
An' (what surprised me) modesty,
I markèd nought uncommon.

I watch'd the symptoms o' the Great,
The gentle pride, the lordly state,
The arrogant assuming;
The fient a pride, nae pride had he,[3]
Nor sauce, nor state, that I could see, insolence
Mair than an honest ploughman. more

[1] Burns here evidently alludes to the Commissioners of Supply, or some other board or committee representing the country gentlemen of Ayrshire.

[2] Compare Allan Ramsay's 'burnt side of your shin.'

[3] 'Devil a bit of pride had he' is the modern slang equivalent for this line.

Then from his Lordship I shall learn,
Henceforth to meet with unconcern
One rank as weel 's another; well
Nae honest worthy man need care
To meet with noble youthful Daer,
For he but meets a brother.[1]

EPISTLE TO MAJOR LOGAN.

Hail, thairm-inspirin, rattlin Willie! catgut
Tho' fortune's road be rough an' hilly
To every fiddling, rhyming billie, fellow
We never heed,
But take it like the unback'd filly,
Proud o' her speed.

When, idly goavin, whyles we saunter; staring stupidly —sometimes
Yirr! fancy barks, awa we canter, off
Up hill, down brae, till some mischanter, slope—accident
Some black bog-hole,
Arrests us, then the scathe an' banter
We 're forced to thole. endure

Hale be your heart! hale be your fiddle! stout
Lang may your elbuck jink and diddle, elbow—jog
To cheer you through the weary widdle struggle
O' this wild warl', world
Until you on a crummock driddle, walking-staff—move slowly
A grey hair'd carl.[2]

[1] Basil William Hamilton Douglas, Lord Daer, second son of the fourth Earl of Selkirk, was born in the same year as Burns. He attended classes in Edinburgh University, boarded with Dugald Stewart, and took a keen interest in philosophical and socio-political questions, contributing to the *Proceedings of the Speculative Society of Edinburgh* (of which he was a member) essays on 'The Origin and Nature of Rights' and 'Grounds and Tendency of the Benevolent System of Philosophy.' When Burns met him he had just returned from France, where he had cultivated the society of some of the men who afterwards figured in the Revolution (particularly Condorcet), and had contracted their sentiments. As a consequence, he became a keen advocate of parliamentary reform in this country, and regarding the interpretation of the Articles of Union, which prevented the eldest sons of Scottish peers from sitting in parliament, to be doubtful, tried the question in the law courts, but without avail. He died in November 1794, leaving the succession to his younger brother, Thomas, fifth Earl of Selkirk, who was also a friend of Dugald Stewart, but is chiefly remembered for his emigrating large numbers of Highlanders to Canada in 1812, and so founding the Red River Settlement, now Manitoba.

[2] Compare this stanza with No. 2 of the 'Second Epistle to Davie,' p. 81.

Come wealth, come poortith, late or soon, poverty
Heaven send your heart-strings ay in tune,
And screw your temper-pins aboon, up
(A fifth or mair,) more
The melancholious, lazy croon
O' cankrie care. peevish

May still your life from day to day,
Nae 'lente largo' in the play,
But 'allegretto forte' gay,
Harmonious flow,
A sweeping, kindling, bauld strathspey— bold
Encore! Bravo!

A blessing on the cheery gang
Wha dearly like a jig or sang,
An' never think o' right an' wrang
By square an' rule,
But, as the clegs o' feeling stang, gadflies—sting
Are wise or fool.

My hand-waled curse keep hard in chase chosen
The harpy, hoodock, purse-proud race, miserly
Wha count on poortith as disgrace;
Their tuneless hearts,
May fireside discords jar a base bass
To a' their parts! all

But come, your hand, my careless brither, brother
I' th' ither warl', if there 's anither, other—another
An' that there is, I 've little swither doubt
About the matter;
We, cheek for chow, shall jog thegither, cheek by jowl—together
I 'se ne'er bid better. I shall never desire

We've faults and failings—granted clearly,
We're frail backsliding mortals merely,
Eve's bonie squad,[1] priests wyte them sheerly blame—entirely
For our grand fa'; fall
But still, but still, I like them dearly—
God bless them a'!

[1] The lovely daughters of Eve.

Ochon for poor Castalian drinkers, — Alas—poets
When they fa' foul o' earthly jinkers! — sprightly girls
The witching, curs'd, delicious blinkers
Hae put me hyte, — Have—mad
And gart me weet my waukrife winkers, — made—wet—sleepless eyelids
Wi' girnin spite. — agonised envy

But by yon moon!—and that 's high swearin—
An' every star within my hearin!
An' by her een wha was a dear ane! — eyes—one
I 'll ne'er forget;
I hope to gie the jads a clearin, — clear up accounts with the girls
In fair play yet.

My loss I mourn, but not repent it;
I 'll seek my pursie whare I tint it; — purse—lost
Ance to the Indies I were wonted,[1] — Once
Some cantraip hour, — witching
By some sweet elf I 'll yet be dinted;
Then *vive l'amour!*

Faites mes baissemains respectueusè,
To sentimental sister Susie,
And honest Lucky; no to roose you, — praise
Ye may be proud,
That sic a couple fate allows ye,
To grace your blood.

Nae mair at present can I measure,
An' trowth my rhymin ware 's nae treasure; — And in truth
But when in Ayr, some half-hour's leisure,
Be 't light, be 't dark,
Sir Bard will do himself the pleasure
To call at Park.

ROBERT BURNS.

MOSSGIEL, 30*th October* 1786.

ADDRESS TO EDINBURGH.

Edina! Scotia's darling seat!
All hail thy palaces and tow'rs
Where once beneath a Monarch's feet
Sat Legislation's sov'reign pow'rs!

[1] 'Wonted' may be a reduplicated past form of the Scotch verb 'win,' signifying 'reach,' 'get.' In any case, the line means 'once I had reached the Indies.'

From marking wildly-scatt'red flow'rs,
  As on the banks of Ayr I stray'd,
And singing, lone, the ling'ring hours,
  I shelter in thy honor'd shade.

Here Wealth still swells the golden tide,
  As busy Trade his labours plies;
There Architecture's noble pride
  Bids elegance and splendor rise;
Here Justice, from her native skies,
  High wields her balance and her rod;
There Learning, with his eagle eyes,
  Seeks Science in her coy abode.

Thy sons, Edina, social, kind,
  With open arms the Stranger hail;
Their views enlarg'd, their lib'ral mind,
  Above the narrow, rural vale:
Attentive still to Sorrow's wail,
  Or modest Merit's silent claim;
And never may their sources fail!
  And never Envy blot their name!

Thy Daughters bright thy walks adorn,
  Gay as the gilded summer sky,
Sweet as the dewy, milk-white thorn,
  Dear as the raptur'd thrill of joy!
Fair Burnet[1] strikes th' adoring eye,
  Heav'n's beauties on my fancy shine;
I see the Sire of Love on high,
  And own His work indeed divine!

There, watching high the least alarms,
  Thy rough, rude Fortress gleams afar;
Like some bold Vet'ran, gray in arms,
  And mark'd with many a seamy scar:

[1] 'Miss Elizabeth Burnet, second daughter of Lord Monboddo, is frequently mentioned by Burns with great admiration, and most justly, for she was remarkably handsome and a very amiable young woman. She had one great personal defect, however—her teeth were much decayed and discoloured—but fortunately she had a very small mouth, and took care not to open it much in mixed company. She was, moreover, what is not noticed (either by the Poet or his Biographers), herself a poetess and a very clever woman.'—From 'MSS. Recollections of Burns and Others, written by Alexander Young, Esq. of Harburn, W.S., Edinburgh,' contained in the Laing Collection, Edinburgh University Library.

The pond'rous wall and massy bar
  Grim-rising o'er the rugged rock,
Have oft withstood assailing War,
  And oft repell'd th' Invader's shock.

With awe-struck thought and pitying tears
  I view that noble, stately Dome,
Where Scotia's kings of other years,
  Fam'd heroes! had their royal home:
Alas, how chang'd the times to come!
  Their royal Name low in the dust!
Their hapless Race wild-wand'ring roam!
  Tho' rigid Law cries out ''twas just!'

Wild beats my heart to trace your steps
  Whose ancestors, in days of yore,
Thro' hostile ranks and ruin'd gaps
  Old Scotia's bloody lion bore:
Ev'n I who sing in rustic lore,
  Haply my Sires have left their shed,
And fac'd grim Danger's loudest roar,
  Bold-following where your Fathers led!

Edina! Scotia's darling seat!
  All hail thy palaces and tow'rs
Where once beneath a Monarch's feet
  Sat Legislation's sov'reign pow'rs!
From marking wildly-scatter'd flow'rs,
  As on the banks of Ayr I stray'd,
And singing, lone, the lingering hours,
  I shelter in thy honor'd shade.

TO A HAGGIS.

Fair fa' your honest, sonsie face, — Fair fall=Good luck to —jolly, well-favoured
Great Chieftain o' the Puddin-race!
Aboon them a' ye tak your place, — Above
    Painch, tripe, or thairm: — paunch—intestines
Weel are ye wordy o' a grace — worthy
    As lang 's my arm.

The groaning trencher there ye fill,
Your hurdies like a distant hill, — buttocks
Your pin[1] wad help to mend a mill — would
In time o' need,
While thro' your pores the dews distil
Like amber bead.

His knife see Rustic-labour dight, — clean, wipe
An' cut you up wi' ready sleight,
Trenching your gushing entrails bright
Like onie ditch; — any
And then, O what a glorious sight,
Warm-reekin, rich! — steaming

Then, horn for horn they stretch an' strive, — horn-spoon
Deil tak the hindmost, on they drive, — last
Till a' their weel-swall'd kytes belyve — swelled stomachs by-and-by
Are bent like drums;
Then auld Guidman, maist like to rive, — almost—burst
'Bethankit' hums. — murmurs 'God be thanked'

Is there that owre his French *ragout*, — over
Or *olio* that wad staw a sow, — would surfeit
Or *fricassee* wad mak her spew
Wi' perfect sconner, — disgust
Looks down wi' sneering, scornfu' view
On sic a dinner? — such

Poor devil! see him owre his trash,
As feckless as a wither'd rash, — feeble—rush
His spindle shank a guid whip-lash, — thin leg—good
His nieve a nit; — closed fist—nut
Thro' bluidy flood or field to dash, — bloody
O how unfit!

But mark the Rustic, haggis-fed,
The trembling earth resounds his tread;
Clap in his walie nieve a blade, — large fist
He'll mak it whissle; — whistle
An' legs, an' arms, an' heads will sned — lop off
Like taps o' thrissle. — tops of thistles

[1] The wooden pin used to fix the opening in the bag. The haggis is a dish composed of minced offal of mutton, mixed with oatmeal and suet, and boiled in a sheep's stomach.

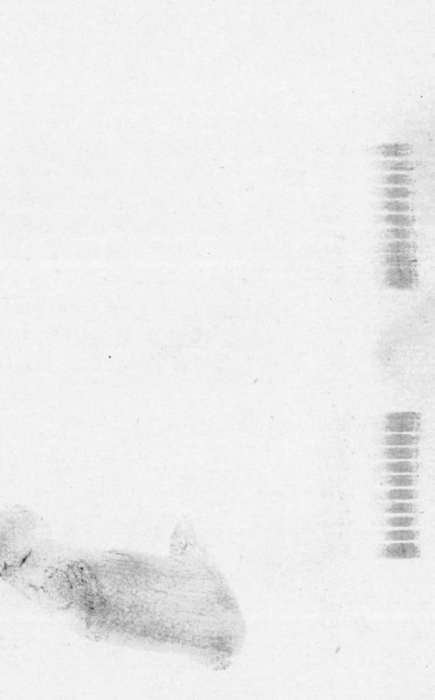

G. O. Reid, A.R.S.A.

Fair fa' your honest, sonsie face,
Great chieftain o' the puddin-race!

PAGE 229.

Ye Pow'rs wha mak mankind your care
And dish them out their bill o' fare,
Auld Scotland wants nae skinking ware — thin stuff
That jaups in luggies; — splashes in bowls
But if ye wish her gratefu' prayer,
Gie her a Haggis![1] — Give

TO MISS LOGAN,[2]

WITH BEATTIE'S POEMS FOR A NEW-YEAR'S GIFT, JAN. 1, 1787.

Again the silent wheels of time
Their annual round have driv'n,
And you, tho' scarce in maiden prime
Are so much nearer Heav'n.

No gifts have I from Indian coasts
The infant year to hail;
I send you more than India boasts,
In Edwin's simple tale.

Our Sex with guile and faithless love,
Is charg'd, perhaps too true;
But may, dear Maid, each Lover prove
An Edwin still to you.

[1] In the *Caledonian Mercury*, and in the *Scots Magazine* for January 1787, in the Poet's Corner of which it also appeared, the last verse ran thus:

'Ye Powers wha gie us a' that's gude, — give
Still bless Auld Caledonia's brood
Wi' great John Barleycorn's heart's blude
In staups and luggies; — stoups and bowls
And on our board that King o' food,
A glorious Haggis.'

There are various traditions as to the origin of the poem. One is that Burns produced it almost in its entirety when at dinner in the house of his friend, Andrew Bruce, merchant, Castlehill, Edinburgh. Another is that the original last verse was given by Burns as a 'grace' to a dinner, of which a haggis formed a part, in the house of a friend, said to be a Mr Morison, cabinet-maker, in Mauchline. But that a haggis was in these days regarded as a luxury to be sighed for may be gathered from this allusion in the Life of Dr Lawson of Selkirk: 'If I were a king, I do not know that I should live very much differently from what I do—only, perhaps, I would have a haggis oftener to dinner' (*Life and Times of George Lawson, D.D.*, by the Rev. John Macfarlane, LL.D.; Edinburgh, 1862).

[2] The 'sentimental sister Susie' of Major Logan, to whom the poet had addressed an epistle on the 30th October of the preceding year.

TO MRS SCOT,[1]

GUIDWIFE OF WAUKHOPE-HOUSE, ROXBURGHSHIRE.

GUIDWIFE,
I mind it weel in early date, — well
When I was beardless, young and blate, — bashful
An' first cou'd thresh the barn,
Or haud a yokin at the pleugh— — do a day's ploughing
An' tho' forfoughten sair eneugh, — fatigued sore enough
Yet unko proud to learn: — very
When first amang the yellow corn
A man I reckon'd was,
An' with the lave ilk merry morn — rest—each
Could rank my rig and lass:[2] — strip of land
Still shearing and clearing
The tither stookèd raw, — one row of stooks or shocks after another
With clavers and haivers — gossip and nonsense
Wearing the time awa: — away

Ev'n then a wish (I mind its pow'r)—
A wish that to my latest hour
Shall strongly heave my breast:
That I for poor auld Scotland's sake
Some useful plan or book could make,
Or sing a sang at least. — song
The rough bur-thistle spreading wide — spear-thistle
Amang the bearded bear,
I turn'd my weeding heuk aside, — hook
An' spar'd the symbol dear:
No nation, no station
My envy e'er could raise:
A Scot still, but blot still, — without dishonour
I knew nae higher praise. — no

But still the elements o' sang
In formless jumble, right an' wrang,
Wild floated in my brain;

[1] Mrs Scot, daughter of Mr David Rutherford, 'counsellor' in Edinburgh, was born there in 1729. She was 'rather advanced' in life, says a biographer, when she married Walter Scot, a country gentleman in Roxburghshire. She died in 1789. Under the title of *Alonzo and Cora, with other Original Poems*, her literary remains were published in 1801. The volume contained her epistle to Burns, and also the Poet's reply.

[2] When he was allotted a 'rig' to 'shear' and a girl to 'gather' after him.

'Till, on that harste I said before, harvest
My partner[1] in the merry core, company
  She rous'd the forming strain:
I see her yet, the sonsy quean, buxom lass
  That lighted up my jingle, rhyme
Her pauky smile, her kittle e'en, artful—fascinating eyes
  That gar'd my heartstrings tingle: made
    So tichèd, bewitchèd, 'ticed = enticed
      I rav'd ay to mysel;
    But bashing and dashing, abashed—cast down
      I kenn'd na how to tell. knew not

Health to the sex! ilk guid chiel says, each good fellow
Wi' merry dance in winter-days,
  An' we to share in common;
The gust o' joy, the balm of woe, spice
The saul o' life, the heav'n below, soul
  In rapture-giving woman.
Ye surly sumphs who hate the name, fools
  Be mindfu' o' your mither: mother
She, honest woman, may think shame
  That ye 're connected with her:
    Ye 're wae men, ye 're nae men woeful (poor creatures)—no
      That slight the lovely dears:
    To shame ye, disclaim ye,
      Ilk honest birkie swears. Each—fellow

For you, na bred to barn and byre, not—cow-house
Wha sweetly tune the Scottish lyre,
  Thanks to you for your line:
The marled plaid ye kindly spare of mixed colours
By me should gratefully be ware— worn
  'Twad please me to the Nine.
I 'd be mair vauntie o' my hap more proud—wrap
  Douce hingin owre my curple, Decently hanging over—haunches
Than ony ermine ever lap, any—hung in folds
  Or proud imperial purple.
    Fareweel then, lang heal' then long health
      An' plenty be your fa'; lot
    May losses and crosses
      Ne'er at your hallan ca'. door call

R. Burns.

March 1787.

[1] 'Handsome Nell.'

VERSES INTENDED TO BE WRITTEN BELOW A NOBLE EARL'S PICTURE.

Whose is that noble, dauntless brow?
And whose that eye of fire?
And whose that generous, Princely mien
Ev'n rooted Foes admire?

Stranger, to justly show that brow,
And mark that eye of fire,
Would take *His* hand, whose vernal tints
His other Works inspire.[1]

Bright as a cloudless Summer-sun,
With stately port he moves;
His guardian Seraph eyes with awe
The noble Ward he loves.

Among th' illustrious Scottish Sons,
That Chief thou may'st discern,
Mark Scotia's fond-returning eye,
It dwells upon GLENCAIRN.

BALLAD ON THE AMERICAN WAR.

TUNE—*Killiecrankie.*

When Guilford [2] good our Pilot stood,
An' did our hellim thraw, man, — helm turn
Ae night, at tea, began a plea — lawsuit
Within America, man:
Then up they gat the maskin-pat,[3]
And in the sea did jaw, man, — dash
An' did nae less, in full Congress,
Than quite refuse our law, man.

[1] In the MS. of this poem now in the Museum of the City Chambers, Edinburgh, the last word of stanza second is 'admire:' it is probable that the Poet intended to write 'inspire.'

[2] Frederick North, second Earl of Guilford, better known as Lord North.

[3] Tea-pot. Mask = brew. The allusion is to the Boston tea-riots of 1773.

Then thro' the lakes Montgomery[1] takes,
I wat he was na slaw, man, slow
Down Lowrie's Burn[2] he took a turn,
And Carleton did ca' man: drive
But yet, whatreck, he, at Quebec, notwithstanding
Montgomery-like[3] did fa', man, fall
Wi' sword in hand, before his band,
Amang his en'mies a', man.

Poor Tammy Gage within a cage
Was kept at Boston-ha', man,[4]
Till Willie Howe took o'er the knowe went over the hill
For Philadelphia,[5] man:
Wi' sword an' gun he thought a sin
Guid Christian bluid to draw, man; blood
But at New-York, wi' knife an' fork,
Sir Loin he hackèd sma',[6] man. small

Burgoyne gaed up like spur an' whip, went
Till Fraser brave did fa', man;
Then lost his way, ae misty day, one
In Saratoga shaw,[7] man. wood
Cornwallis fought as lang 's he dought, dared
An' did the Buckskins claw, man;[8] Virginians beat
But Clinton's glaive, frae rust to save, sword—from
He hung it to the wa', man.

Then Montague, an' Guilford too,
Began to fear a fa', man;
And Sackville doure, wha stood the stoure grimly determined—brunt of the struggle
The German Chief[9] to thraw man: thwart

[1] General Richard Montgomery invaded Canada (autumn 1775) and took Montreal, the British commander, Sir Guy Carleton, retiring before him. In an attack on Quebec he was less fortunate, being killed while leading his men.

[2] 'Lowrie's Burn,' a name for the St Lawrence.

[3] A compliment to the Montgomeries of Coilsfield.

[4] General Gage, governor of Massachusetts, was cooped up in Boston by General Washington during the later part of 1775 and early part of 1776. In consequence of his inefficiency, he was replaced in October of that year by General Howe.

[5] General Howe removed his army from New York to Philadelphia in the summer of 1777.

[6] Alluding to a *razzia* made by orders of Howe at Peekskill, March 1777, when a large quantity of cattle belonging to the Americans was destroyed.

[7] General Burgoyne surrendered his army to General Gates, at Saratoga, on the Hudson, October 1776.

[8] Alluding to the active operations of Lord Cornwallis in Virginia in 1780, which ended, however, in the surrender of his army at Yorktown, October 1781, while vainly hoping for reinforcement from General Clinton at New York.

[9] The commander of the Hessian auxiliaries.

For Paddy Burke, like ony Turk,
Nae mercy had at a', man;
An' Charlie Fox threw by the box, aside
An' lows'd his tinkler jaw, man. loosed

Then Rockingham took up the game;
Till Death did on him ca', man; call
When Shelburne meek held up his cheek
Conform to Gospel law, man:
Saint Stephen's boys, wi' jarring noise,
They did his measures thraw, man, thwart
For North an' Fox united stocks,
An' bore him to the wa', man.[1]

Then Clubs an' Hearts were Charlie's cartes: cards
He swept the stakes awa', man,
Till the Diamond's Ace, of Indian race,
Led him a sair *faux pas*, man:[2]
The Saxon lads, wi' loud placads, cheers
On Chatham's Boy did ca', man;
An' Scotland drew her pipe, an' blew
'Up, Willie,[3] waur them a', man!' vanquish

Behind the throne, then, Granville 's gone,
A secret word or twa, man;
While slee Dundas[4] arous'd the class astute
Be-north the Roman wa', man:
An' Chatham's wraith, in heav'nly graith, ghost's garb
(Inspirèd Bardies saw, man,)
Wi' kindling eyes, cry'd 'Willie, rise!
Would I hae fear'd them a', man?'

But, word an' blow, North, Fox and Co.
Gowff'd[5] Willie like a ba', man, Struck

[1] Lord North's administration was succeeded by that of the Marquis of Rockingham, March 1782. On the death of the latter, in the succeeding July, Lord Shelburne became prime-minister, and Fox resigned his secretaryship. Under Shelburne, peace was restored, January 1783. By an alliance between Lord North and Fox, however, he was soon after forced to resign in favour of his rivals, the heads of the celebrated Coalition.

[2] Fox's famous India Bill, by which his Ministry was brought to destruction, December 1783.

[3] 'Up an' waur them a', Willie,' a Jacobite song on the battle of Sheriffmuir, was then popular in Scotland.

[4] Henry Dundas, afterwards Viscount Melville, was at this period accounted Pitt's 'Grand Vizier for Scotland.'

[5] This is the only line in Burns which can be construed as an allusion to the now universally popular game of golf.

Till Suthron raise, an' coost their claise — cast off—clothes
Behind him in a raw, man: — row
An' Caledon threw by the drone, — bagpipe
An' did her whittle draw, man; — sword
An' swoor fu' rude, thro' dirt an' blood, — swore
To mak it guid in law, man.[1] — good

EXTEMPORE IN THE COURT OF SESSION.

TUNE—*Killiecrankie.*

LORD ADVOCATE.[2]

He clench'd his pamphlets in his fist,
He quoted and he hinted,
Till, in a declamation-mist,
His argument he tint it: — lost
He gapèd for 't, he grapèd for 't, — groped
He fand it was awa, man; — found—away
But what his common sense came short,
He ekèd out wi' law, man.

MR ERSKINE.[3]

Collected, Harry stood a wee, — for a short time
Then open'd out his arm, man;
His lordship sat wi' ruefu' e'e, — eye
And ey'd the gathering storm, man:
Like wind-driv'n hail it did assail,
Or torrents owre a lin, man; — over—waterfall
The BENCH sae wise lift up their eyes,
Half-wauken'd wi' the din, man. — wakened

[1] To the new parliament called by Pitt, after his accession to office, in the spring of 1784, Scotland sent an extraordinarily large number of sympathisers with the young minister.

[2] Sir Ilay Campbell, son of Archibald Campbell of Succoth, clerk of session, born in 1734; called to the Bar in 1757; Solicitor-General for Scotland in 1783; Lord Advocate and M.P. for Glasgow in 1784; appointed Lord President of the Court of Session in 1789; resigned office and made a baronet in 1808; died at Garscube, near Glasgow, in 1823.

[3] Henry Erskine, second son of Henry David, tenth Earl of Buchan, born in Edinburgh in 1746; called to the Bar in 1768; Lord Advocate in 1783; Dean of Faculty in 1786; Dean of Faculty and member for the Dumfries Burghs in 1806–1807; died at his seat of Amondell, West Lothian, in 1817.

A FRAGMENT.

TUNE—*Dainty Davie.*

I.

There was a birkie born in Kyle, lively fellow
But what na day, o' what na style,
I doubt it 's hardly worth the while
To be sae nice wi' Davie.
Leeze me on thy curly pow,[1]
Bonie Davie, daintie Davie;
Leeze me on thy curly pow,
Thou 'se ay my daintie Davie.[2]

II.

Our Monarch's hindmost year but ane
Was five an' twenty days begun,
'Twas then a blast o' Janwar win'
Blew hansel in on Davie.

III.

The Gossip keekit in his loof, peeped—palm
Quo she, wha lives 'll see the proof, Quoth
This walie boy will be nae coof, goodly—fool
I think we 'll ca' him Davie. call

IV.

He 'll hae misfortunes great an' sma',
But ay a heart aboon them a'; above
He 'll gie his Daddie's name a blaw,
We 'll a' be proud o' Davie.

V.

But sure as three times three maks nine,
I see by ilka score an' line every
This chap will dearly like our kin', fellow—kind, sex
So leeze me on thee, Davie.

VI.

Guid faith, quo she, I doubt you, Sir,
Ye 'll gar the lasses lie aspar; make
But twenty fauts ye may hae waur, faults—worse
So blessins on thee, Davie.[3]

[1] 'Leeze me:' an expression of affection = Dear to me is thy curly head.
[2] Thou 'se (idiom) = Thou is (art) *or* Thou shalt be.
[3] Cf. this version, written two years after the immortal 'There was a Lad,' with the popular version, p. 32.

PROLOGUE SPOKEN BY MR WOODS[1] ON HIS BENEFIT NIGHT,[2]

Monday, 16*th April* 1787.

When, by a generous Public's kind acclaim,
That dearest meed is granted—honest fame;
When *here* your favour is the *actor's* lot,
Nor even the *man* in *private life* forgot;
What breast so dead to heav'nly Virtue's glow
But heaves impassion'd with the grateful throe?
 Poor is the task to please a barb'rous throng,
It needs no Siddons'[3] powers in Southern's song;
But here, an ancient nation fam'd afar,
For genius, learning high, as great in war—
Hail, CALEDONIA, name for ever dear!
Before whose sons I'm honour'd to appear!
Where every science—every noble art
That can inform the mind, or mend the heart,
Is known; as grateful nations oft have found
Far as the rude barbarian marks the bound.
Philosophy,[4] no idle pedant dream,
Here holds her search by heaven-taught Reason's beam;
Here History[5] paints, with elegance and force,
The tide of Empire's fluctuating course;
Here Douglas[6] forms wild Shakespeare into plan,
And Harley[7] rouses all the God in man.
When well-form'd taste and sparkling wit unite
With manly lore, or female beauty bright

[1] William Woods (*circa* 1751–1802) first appeared on the stage (the Haymarket, Edinburgh, according to one biographer; the Haymarket, London, according to another) in 1771. His career was almost entirely confined to the Scottish capital, he having been a member of the Edinburgh Company of Players for thirty-one years. He was an intimate friend of Robert Fergusson, and is said to have regularly taken him into the theatre and given him a free seat. He retired from the stage in April 1802, and set up as a teacher of elocution. He died in December following, and is buried in Calton Burying-ground.

[2] The play on this night was Shakespeare's *The Merry Wives of Windsor*.

[3] Mrs Siddons had made her début in Edinburgh in 1784. She had returned again in the following year. On both occasions the town was thrown into an extraordinary state of excitement. Mrs Siddons revisited the Scottish capital in July 1788, the first piece in which she played being *Douglas*, taking the character of Lady Randolph. Her representation of Isabella in *The Fatal Marriage* of the dramatist 'Honest Tom Southerne' (1660–1746) was very celebrated.

[4] In Professors Dugald Stewart of Edinburgh and Thomas Reid of Aberdeen.

[5] The allusion here is to David Hume and William Robertson.

[6] John Home's *Douglas*, which was first performed in Edinburgh in 1757. Here Burns must be regarded as complimenting the friends of his friends, not as deliberately giving Home a superior position among dramatists to Shakespeare.

[7] Henry Mackenzie's *Man of Feeling*.

(Beauty, where faultless symmetry and grace
Can only charm us in the second place)—
Witness my heart, how oft with panting fear,
As on this night, I 've met these judges here!
But still the hope Experience taught to live,
Equal to judge—you 're candid to forgive.
No hundred-headed Riot here we meet
With decency and law beneath his feet;
Nor Insolence assumes fair Freedom's name:
Like CALEDONIANS, you applaud or blame.

O Thou dread Power! whose empire-giving hand
Has oft been stretch'd to shield the honour'd land!
Strong may she glow with all her ancient fire;
May every son be worthy of his sire;
Firm may she rise with generous disdain[1]
At Tyranny's, or direr Pleasure's, chain;
Still self-dependent in her native shore,
Bold may she brave grim Danger's loudest roar,
Till Fate the curtain drop on worlds to be no more.

ADDRESS TO WILLIAM TYTLER, ESQ.

Revered defender of beauteous Stuart,[2]
Of Stuart, a name once respected;
A name which to love was the mark of a true heart,
But now 'tis despised and neglected.

Tho' something like moisture conglobes in my eye,
Let no one misdeem me disloyal:
A poor friendless wand'rer may well claim a sigh,
Still more, if that wand'rer were royal.

[1] In the original draft the closing five lines are as follows:

'May never sallow Want her bounty stint,
Nor selfish maxim dare the sordid hint;
But may her virtues ever be her prop;
Thou her best stay, and Thou her surest hope,
Till Fate on worlds the eternal curtain drop.'

[2] William Tytler (b. 1711, d. 1792) was the son of a Writer to the Signet in Edinburgh. He was himself trained to the legal profession, and practised as a Writer to the Signet from 1744 till his death. He had published, in 1759, *An Enquiry, Historical and Critical, into the Evidence against Mary Queen of Scots* (2 vols.), which was a defence against what its author believed to be the calumnies of Robertson and Hume. It was sufficiently popular to be translated into French in 1772. Alexander Fraser Tytler, Lord Woodhouselee, was a son of William Tytler; Patrick Fraser Tytler, the historian, a grandson.

My fathers that name have rever'd on a throne:
  My fathers have fallen to right it;
Those fathers would spurn their degenerate son,
  That name should he scoffingly slight it.

Still in prayers for King George I most heartily join,
  The Queen, and the rest of the gentry:
Be they wise, be they foolish, is nothing of mine,
  Their title 's avow'd by my country.

But why of that epocha make such a fuss,
  That gave us th' Electoral stem?
If bringing them over was lucky for us,
  I 'm sure 'twas as lucky for them.[1]

But loyalty, truce! we 're on dangerous ground:
  Who knows how the fashions may alter?
The doctrine, to-day, that is loyalty sound,
  To-morrow may bring us a halter!

I send you a trifle, a head of a bard,[2]
  A trifle scarce worthy your care;
But accept it, good Sir, as a mark of regard,
  Sincere as a saint's dying prayer.

Now life's chilly evening dim shades on your eye,
  And ushers the long dreary night:
But you, like the star that athwart gilds the sky,
  Your course to the latest is bright.

WILLIE'S[3] AWA'.

Auld chuckie[4] Reekie 's[5] sair distrest, — sore
Down droops her ance weel burnish'd crest, — once
Nae joy her bonie buskit nest — decorated
    Can yield ava, — at all
Her darling bird that she lo'es best— — loves
    Willie, 's awa.

[1] In Currie's edition (1800) lines 2–4 of this verse are omitted. Their place is supplied by asterisks.
[2] A portrait of the Poet, engraved by Beugo.
[3] William Creech, the Poet's publisher, who had just gone to London.
[4] Literally, a hen; secondarily, a familiar term of address:
  'Gin ony sour-mou'd girning bucky
  Ca' me conceited keckling chucky.'—Ramsay.
[5] Literally, smoky; a familiar sobriquet for Edinburgh.

O Willie was a witty wight,
And had o' things an unco' sleight, uncommon knowledge
Auld Reekie ay he keepit tight, kept
And trig an' braw: neat—handsome
But now they 'll busk her like a fright— dress
Willie 's awa!

The stiffest o' them a' he bow'd;
The bauldest o' them a' he cow'd; boldest
They durst nae mair than he allow'd, dared—more
That was a law:
We 've lost a birkie weel worth gowd: fellow—gold
Willie 's awa!

Now gawkies, tawpies, gowks,[1] and fools,
Frae colleges and boarding schools, From
May sprout like simmer puddock-stools summer toad-stools
In glen or shaw; wood
He wha could brush them down to mools— the dust
Willie 's awa!

The brethren o' the Commerce-Chaumer[2]
May mourn their loss wi' doolfu' clamour; doleful
He was a dictionar and grammar
Amang them a';
I fear they 'll now make mony a stammer:
Willie 's awa!

Nae mair we see his levee door[3] No more
Philosophers and poets pour,
And toothy critics by the score,
In bloody raw! row
The adjutant o' a' the core— corps
Willie 's awa!

Now worthy Gregory's Latin face;
Tytler's and Greenfield's modest grace;

1 'Gawky,' a simpleton; 'tawpy,' usually applied to an indolent, spiritless woman; 'gowk,' literally, the cuckoo—secondarily, a fool.

2 The Chamber of Commerce in Edinburgh, of which Creech was secretary.

3 Creech lived on familiar terms with many of the literary Scotsmen of his day. His house, in one of the elevated floors of a tenement in the High Street, accessible from a wretched alley called Craig's Close, was frequented in the mornings by company of that kind, to such an extent that the meeting used to be called *Creech's Levee.* Burns here enumerates as attending it, Dr James Gregory (1753–1821), Alexander Fraser Tytler, afterwards Lord Woodhouselee (1747–1813), Rev. William Greenfield, Henry Mackenzie, and Dugald Stewart.

M'Kenzie, Stewart, such a brace
As Rome ne'er saw;
They a' maun meet some ither place, must—other
Willie 's awa!

Poor Burns ev'n 'Scotch drink' canna quicken, cannot
He cheeps like some bewilder'd chicken chirps
Scar'd frae its minnie and the cleckin mother—brood
By hoodie-craw; carrion crow
Grief 's gien his heart an unco kickin, given—sad
Willie 's awa!

Now ev'ry sour-mou'd girnin' blellum, sour-mouthed, scowling chatterer
And Calvin's folk,[1] are fit to fell him;[2]
Ilk self-conceited critic skellum[3] Every
His quill may draw:
He wha could brawlie ward their 'bellum'— bravely resist their violence
Willie 's awa!

Up wimpling stately Tweed I 've sped, winding
And Eden scenes on crystal Jed,
And Ettrick banks now roaring red
While tempests blaw; blow
But every joy and pleasure 's fled—
Willie 's awa!

May I be Slander's common speech;
A text of Infamy to preach;
And lastly, streekit out to bleach stretched
In winter snaw; snow
When I forget thee, WILLIE CREECH,
Tho' far awa!

May never wicked Fortune touzle him! ruffle, toss
May never wicked men bamboozle him!
Until a pow as auld 's Methusalem head—old—Methuselah
He, canty, claw! cheerful
Then to the blessed New Jerusalem
Fleet wing awa!

[1] Here again Burns indulges in a hit at the evangelicals.
[2] Angry enough to knock him down.
[3] A term of contempt:

'She tauld thee weel thou was a skellum.'—*Tam o' Shanter*.

ON INCIVILITY SHOWN HIM AT INVERARAY.

Whoe'er he be that sojourns here,
I pity much his case—
Unless he come to wait upon
The Lord *their* God, 'His Grace.'

There 's naething here but Highland pride,
And Highland scab and hunger;
If Providence has sent me here,
'Twas surely in an anger.

ON READING IN A NEWSPAPER AN ACCOUNT OF

THE DEATH OF JOHN M'LEOD, ESQ.,

BROTHER TO A YOUNG LADY, A PARTICULAR FRIEND OF THE AUTHOR'S.[1]

Sad thy tale, thou idle page,
And rueful thy alarms:
Death tears the brother of her love
From Isabella's arms.

Sweetly deckt with pearly dew
The morning rose may blow;
But cold successive noontide blasts
May lay its beauties low.

Fair on Isabella's morn
The sun propitious smil'd,
But, long ere noon, succeeding clouds
Succeeding hopes beguil'd.

Fate oft tears the bosom chords
That Nature finest strung:
So Isabella's heart was form'd,
And so that heart was wrung.

Dread Omnipotence alone
Can heal the wound He gave;

[1] This poem is entered in the Glenriddel volume of poetry, with note: 'This poetic compliment, what few poetic compliments are, was from the heart.'

Can point the brimful grief-worn eyes
To scenes beyond the grave.

Virtue's blossoms there shall blow,
And fear no withering blast;
There Isabella's spotless worth
Shall happy be at last.

ON THE DEATH OF SIR JAMES HUNTER BLAIR.

The Performance is but mediocre, but my grief was sincere. The last time I saw the worthy, public-spirited man—A MAN he was! How few of the two-legged breed that pass for such, deserve the designation!—he pressed my hand, and asked me with the most friendly warmth if it was in his power to serve me; and if so, that I would oblige him by telling him how. I had nothing to ask of him; but if ever a child of his should be so unfortunate as to be under the necessity of asking any thing of so poor a man as I am, it may not be in my power to grant it, but, by G—, I shall try!!!—*R. B., in Glenriddel MSS.*

The lamp of day, with ill-presaging glare,
Dim, cloudy, sunk beyond the western wave;
Th' inconstant blast howl'd through the darkening air,
And hollow whistled in the rocky cave.

Lone as I wander'd by each cliff and dell,
Once the lov'd haunts of Scotia's royal train;[1]
Or mus'd where limpid streams, once hallow'd, well,[2]
Or mould'ring ruins mark the sacred Fane.[3]

Th' increasing blast roar'd round the beetling rocks,
The clouds, swift-wing'd, flew o'er the starry sky,
The groaning trees untimely shed their locks,
And shooting meteors caught the startled eye.

The paly moon rose in the livid east,
And 'mong the cliffs disclos'd a stately Form
In weeds of woe, that frantic beat her breast,
And mix'd her wailings with the raving storm.

Wild to my heart the filial pulses glow,
'Twas Caledonia's trophied shield I view'd:
Her form majestic droop'd in pensive woe,
The lightning of her eye in tears imbued.

[1] The Queen's Park, at Holyrood House. [2] St Anthony's Well.
[3] St Anthony's Chapel.

Revers'd that spear, redoubtable in war,
Reclined that banner, erst in fields unfurl'd,
That like a deathful meteor gleam'd afar,
And brav'd the mighty monarchs of the world.

'My patriot son fills an untimely grave!'
With accents wild and lifted arms she cried—
'Low lies the hand that oft was stretch'd to save,
Low lies the heart that swell'd with honest pride!

'A weeping country joins a widow's tear,
The helpless poor mix with the orphan's cry;
The drooping arts surround their patron's bier,
And grateful science heaves the heartfelt sigh.

'I saw my sons resume their ancient fire;
I saw fair freedom's blossoms richly blow:
But ah! how hope is born but to expire!
Relentless fate has laid their guardian low.

'My patriot falls, but shall he lie unsung,
While empty greatness saves a worthless name?
No; every Muse shall join her tuneful tongue,
And future ages hear his growing fame.

'And I will join a mother's tender cares,
Thro' future times to make his virtues last:
That distant years may boast of other Blairs'—
She said, and vanish'd with the sweeping blast.

TO MISS FERRIER,[1]

ENCLOSING THE 'ELEGY ON SIR J. H. BLAIR.'

Nae heathen name shall I prefix
Frae Pindus or Parnassus:
Auld Reekie dings them a' to sticks, knocks—shivers
For rhyme-inspiring lasses.

Jove's tunefu' dochters three times three daughters
Made Homer deep their debtor:
But, gi'en the body half an e'e, given—eye
Nine Ferriers wad done better! would

1 Eldest daughter of Mr Ferrier, and afterwards the wife of General Graham.

R. B. Nisbet, A.R.S.A.

The Birks of Aberfeldy
(*Falls of Moness*).

PAGE 248.

Last day my mind was in a bog,
  Down George's Street I stoited: staggered
A creeping cauld prosaic fog cold
  My very senses doited. stupefied

Do what I dought to set her free, could
  My saul lay in the mire: soul
Ye turned a neuk—I saw your e'e— corner
  She took the wing like fire!

The mournfu' sang I here enclose, song
  In gratitude I send you;
And [wish and] pray in rhyme sincere,
  A' gude things may attend you! good

VERSES

WRITTEN 'WITH MY PENCIL OVER THE CHIMNEY-PIECE IN THE PARLOUR OF THE INN AT KENMORE, AT THE OUTLET OF LOCH TAY.'

Admiring Nature in her wildest grace,
These northern scenes with weary feet I trace;
O'er many a winding dale and painful steep,
Th' abodes of covey'd grouse and timid sheep,
My savage journey, curious, I pursue,
Till fam'd Breadalbane opens to my view.—
The meeting cliffs each deep-sunk glen divides,
The woods, wild-scatter'd, clothe their ample sides;
Th' outstretching lake, imbosomed 'mong the hills,
The eye with wonder and amazement fills;
The Tay meand'ring sweet in infant pride;
The palace rising on its verdant side;
The lawns wood-fring'd in Nature's native taste;
The hillocks dropt in Nature's careless haste;
The arches striding o'er the new-born stream;
The village glittering in the noontide beam—

* * * *

Poetic ardors in my bosom swell,
Lone-wand'ring by the hermit's mossy cell:
The sweeping theatre of hanging woods;
Th' incessant roar of headlong tumbling floods—

* * * *

Here Poesy might wake her heav'n-taught lyre,
And look through Nature with creative fire;
Here, to the wrongs of Fate half reconcil'd,
Misfortune's lighten'd steps might wander wild;
And Disappointment, in these lonely bounds,
Find balm to soothe her bitter, rankling wounds:
Here heart-struck Grief might heav'nward stretch her scan,
And injur'd Worth forget and pardon man.

* * * *

THE BIRKS OF ABERFELDY.

TUNE—*The Birks of Abergeldie.*

Chorus—Bonny lassie, will ye go,
Will ye go, will ye go,
Bonny lassie, will ye go
To the Birks of Aberfeldy? — birches

Now Simmer blinks on flowery braes, — Summer glances
And o'er the crystal streamlets plays,
Come, let us spend the lightsome days
In the birks of Aberfeldy.

The little birdies blythely sing,
While o'er their heads the hazels hing, — hang
Or lightly flit on wanton wing
In the birks of Aberfeldy.

The braes ascend like lofty wa's, — hills—walls
The foamy stream deep-roaring fa's, — falls
O'erhung wi' fragrant-spreading shaws, — foliage
The birks of Aberfeldy.

The hoary cliffs are crown'd wi' flowers,
White o'er the linns the burnie pours, — cascades—stream
And rising, weets wi' misty showers — wets
The birks of Aberfeldy.

Let Fortune's gifts at random flee,
They ne'er shall draw a wish frae me; — from
Supremely blest wi' love and thee
In the birks of Aberfeldy.

THE HUMBLE PETITION OF BRUAR WATER[1] TO THE NOBLE DUKE OF ATHOLE.

My Lord, I know your noble ear
  Woe ne'er assails in vain;
Embolden'd thus, I beg you 'll hear
  Your humble slave complain
How saucy Phœbus' scorching beams,
  In flaming summer-pride,
Dry-withering, waste my foamy streams,
  And drink my crystal tide.

The lightly-jumping, glowrin' trouts — staring
  That thro' my waters play,
If, in their random, wanton spouts, — darts
  They near the margin stray;
If, hapless chance! they linger lang, — long
  I 'm scorching up so shallow
They 're left the whitening stanes amang
  In gasping death to wallow.

Last day I grat wi' spite and teen, — wept—vexation
  As Poet Burns came by,
That, to a Bard, I should be seen
  Wi' half my channel dry:
A panegyric rhyme, I ween,
  Even as I was, he shor'd me; — threatened
But had I in my glory been,
  He, kneeling, wad ador'd me. — would

Here, foaming down the skelvy rocks, — shelvy
  In twisting strength I rin; — run
There, high my boiling torrent smokes,
  Wild-roaring o'er a linn: — face of a precipice

[1] 'The first object of interest that occurs upon the public road after leaving Blair, is a chasm in the hill on the right hand, through which the little river Bruar falls over a series of beautiful cascades. Formerly, the Falls of the Bruar were unadorned by wood; but the poet Burns, being conducted to see them (September 1787) after visiting the Duke of Athole, recommended that they should be invested with that necessary decoration. Accordingly, trees have been thickly planted along the chasm, and are now far advanced to maturity. Throughout this young forest a walk has been cut, and a number of fantastic little grottos erected for the convenience of those who visit the spot. The river not only makes several distinct falls, but rushes on through a channel, whose roughness and haggard sublimity adds greatly to the merits of the scene, as an object of interest among tourists.'—R. Chambers's *Picture of Scotland*. Most of the 'fragrant birks' planted in answer to Burns's 'humble petition' have been blown down by gales.

Enjoying large each spring and well
  As Nature gave them me,
I am, altho' I say 't mysel, — myself
  Worth gaun a mile to see. — going

Would, then, my noble master please
  To grant my highest wishes?
He 'll shade my banks wi' tow'ring trees,
  And bonie spreading bushes.
Delighted doubly then, my Lord,
  You 'll wander on my banks,
And listen mony a grateful bird — many
  Return you tuneful thanks.

The sober laverock, warbling wild, — lark
  Shall to the skies aspire;
The gowdspink, Music's gayest child, — goldfinch
  Shall sweetly join the choir;
The blackbird strong, the lintwhite clear, — linnet
  The mavis mild and mellow; — thrush
The robin pensive Autumn cheer
  In all her locks of yellow.

This, too, a covert shall ensure
  To shield them from the storm;
And coward maukin sleep secure, — hare
  Low in her grassy form:
Here shall the shepherd make his seat,
  To weave his crown of flow'rs;
Or find a shelt'ring, safe retreat,
  From prone-descending show'rs.

And here, by sweet, endearing stealth,
  Shall meet the loving pair,
Despising worlds, with all their wealth,
  As empty, idle care:
The flow'rs shall vie in all their charms
  The hour of heav'n to grace,
And birks extend their fragrant arms — birches
  To screen the dear embrace.

Here haply, too, at vernal dawn
  Some musing bard may stray,
And eye the smoking, dewy lawn,
  And misty mountain grey;

Or, by the reaper's nightly beam,
 Mild-chequering thro' the trees,
Rave to my darkly dashing stream,
 Hoarse-swelling on the breeze.

Let lofty firs, and ashes cool,
 My lowly banks o'erspread,
And view, deep-bending in the pool,
 Their shadows' wat'ry-bed:
Let fragrant birks, in woodbines drest,
 My craggy cliffs adorn;
And, for the little songster's nest,
 The close embow'ring thorn.

So may, Old Scotia's darling hope,
 Your little angel band
Spring, like their fathers, up to prop
 Their honour'd native land!
So may, thro' Albion's farthest ken,
 To social-flowing glasses
The grace be—'Athole's honest men,
 And Athole's bonie lasses!'

VERSES

WRITTEN WITH A PENCIL, STANDING BY THE FALL OF FYERS, NEAR LOCH-NESS.

Among the heathy hills and ragged woods
The foaming Fyers pours his mossy floods;
Till full he dashes on the rocky mounds,
Where, thro' a shapeless breach, his stream resounds
As high in air the bursting torrents flow,
As deep recoiling surges foam below,
Prone down the rock the whitening sheet descends,
And viewless Echo's ear, astonished, rends.
Dim seen, through rising mists and ceaseless show'rs,
The hoary cavern, wide-surrounding, low'rs.
Still thro' the gap the struggling river toils,
And still, below, the horrid caldron boils.—

* * * *

ON CASTLE GORDON.

Streams that glide in orient plains,
Never bound by winter's chains;
Glowing here on golden sands,
There commix'd with foulest stains
From tyranny's empurpled hands:
These, their richly gleaming waves,
I leave to tyrants and their slaves;
Give me the stream that sweetly laves
The banks by Castle Gordon.

Spicy forests, ever gay,
Shading from the burning ray
Hapless wretches sold to toil,
Or the ruthless native's way,
Bent on slaughter, blood and spoil:
Woods that ever verdant wave,
I leave the tyrant and the slave,
Give me the groves that lofty brave
The storms, by Castle Gordon.

Wildly here, without controul,
Nature reigns and rules the whole;
In that sober pensive mood,
Dearest to the feeling soul,
She plants the forest, pours the flood;
Life's poor day I'll musing rave,
And find at night a sheltering cave,
Where waters flow and wild woods wave,
By bonie Castle Gordon.[1]

THE BONIE LASS OF ALBANIE.[2]

TUNE—*Mary, weep no more for me.*

My heart is wae, and unco wae, sad
To think upon the raging sea,
That roars between her gardens green
And th' bonie lass of Albanie.

[1] Designed to be sung to 'Morag,' a Highland tune of which Burns was extremely fond.—CURRIE.

[2] It has been conjectured in some quarters that it was the death of the young Pretender, on the 31st January 1788, that induced Burns to write 'The Bonie Lass of Albanie,' and Mr R. B. Drummond of Perth has thus ingeniously

This lovely maid's of noble blood
  That ruled Albion's kingdoms three;
But Oh, Alas, for her bonie face!
  They hae wrang'd the lass of Albanie.

In the rolling tide of spreading Clyde
  There sits an isle of high degree;[1]
And a town of fame whose princely name
  Should grace the lass of Albanie.[2]

But there is a youth, a witless youth
  That fills the place where she should be;[3]
We'll send him o'er to his native shore,
  And bring our ain sweet Albanie. **own**

Alas the day, and woe the day,
  A false Usurper wan the gree, **won—superiority, victory**
That now commands the towers and lands,
  The royal right of Albanie.

attempted to fix the actual date and circumstances of its conception: 'On the 18th February 1788 Burns left Edinburgh for Mossgiel. On his way he spent a night at Glasgow with his friend Broun, and one at Paisley with Mr Patterson; and on the morning of the 20th he left Paisley on foot, and walked over the Gleniffer Braes to Dunlop House, the seat of his constant and attached friend Mrs Dunlop, where he remained two days. From Dunlop House he walked to Kilmarnock, where he arrived on the afternoon of the 22nd. The road from Dunlop to Kilmarnock passes over the ridge of Cunningham, from whence, on a clear day in February, the view is extensive and interesting. The poet saw to the north-west the little Island of Bute, nestling on the bosom of the silver-grey firth, and sheltered by the mountains of Arran and the mainland. Away to the south, as far as the eye could reach, he could see long stretches of the Ayr and the Nith, bounded by the mountains of Galloway, the scene of "Mary's Dream." The situation, coupled with the poet's newly-excited grief for the exiled Stuarts, found utterance in the following song.' This view may be correct. In a volume of manuscripts which was long in the possession of Mr Benjamin Nightingale, London, however, the song follows the lines written on the inn window at Stirling. It was first printed from the Nightingale manuscripts, in vol. vi. (1843) of *Bentley's Miscellany*. It is believed to have been submitted to Allan Cunningham, when he was preparing his edition of Burns for the press, and that he declined to insert it on the ground that 'George IV. and the Duke of York were too recently deceased, and their brother William IV. then occupied the throne.'

[1] Bute.

[2] Rothesay, the county town of Bute, gave a title to the eldest son of the king of Scotland (Duke of Rothesay).

[3] The 'witless youth' was the then Prince of Wales, afterwards George IV., who was born in 1762, and had, in the first three years after attaining his majority, accumulated debts to the amount of half-a-million. 'It was in 1787,' Professor Jack has pertinently pointed out in *Macmillan's Magazine* (May 1879), 'that Parliament granted him £160,000 to pay them. In the same year he repudiated Mrs Fitzherbert under the advice of his friend, Charles James Fox. She afterwards received a pension of £8000 a year from the royal family. The position of the Prince of Wales was discussed in the debates on the regency (December 1787–March 1788) which arose on the apparently permanent disablement of King George III.'

We 'll daily pray, we 'll nightly pray,
On bended knees most ferventlie,
That the time may come, with pipe and drum
We 'll welcome home fair Albanie.[1]

ON SCARING SOME WATER-FOWL IN LOCH-TURIT.

This was the production of a solitary forenoon's walk from Oughtertyre-house. I lived there, Sir William's guest, for two or three weeks, and was much flattered by my hospitable reception. What a pity that the mere emotions of gratitude are so impotent in this world! 'Tis lucky that, as we are told, they will be of some avail in the world to come.—*R. B., Glenriddel MSS.*

Why, ye tenants of the lake,
For me your wat'ry haunt forsake?
Tell me, fellow-creatures, why
At my presence thus you fly?
Why disturb your social joys,
Parent, filial, kindred ties?—
Common friend to you and me,
Nature's gifts to all are free:
Peaceful keep your dimpling wave,
Busy feed, or wanton lave;
Or, beneath the sheltering rock,
Bide the surging billow's shock.

Conscious, blushing for our race,
Soon, too soon, your fears I trace.
Man, your proud usurping foe,
Would be lord of all below:
Plumes himself in Freedom's pride,
Tyrant stern to all beside.

The eagle, from the cliffy brow,
Marking you his prey below,
In his breast no pity dwells,
Strong Necessity compels.
But Man, to whom alone is giv'n
A ray direct from pitying Heav'n,

[1] The Duchess of Albany went to live with her father immediately after her legitimation. He left her his heiress, but she survived him less than two years, dying on the 14th November 1789. Her story is told very fully in Alfred von Reumont's monograph, *Die Gräfin von Albany,* and by Professor Jack in *Macmillan's Magazine* for May 1879.

Glories in his heart humane—
And creatures for his pleasure slain.

In these savage, liquid plains,
Only known to wand'ring swains,
Where the mossy riv'let strays,
Far from human haunts and ways;
All on Nature you depend,
And life's poor season peaceful spend.

Or, if man's superior might
Dare invade your native right,
On the lofty ether borne,
Man with all his pow'rs you scorn;
Swiftly seek, on clanging wings,
Other lakes and other springs;
And the foe you cannot brave,
Scorn at least to be his slave.

BLYTHE WAS SHE.[1]

TUNE—*Andro and his Cutty Gun.*

Chorus—Blythe, blythe and merry was she,
Blythe was she but and ben;[2]
Blythe by the banks of Earn,
And blythe in Glenturit glen.

By Oughtertyre grows the aik, oak
On Yarrow banks, the birken shaw; birch-woods
But Phemie was a bonier lass
Than braes o' Yarrow ever saw.

Her looks were like a flow'r in May,
Her smile was like a simmer morn; summer
She trippèd by the banks o' Earn
As light 's a bird upon a thorn.

[1] Euphemia, daughter of Mr Mungo Murray of Lintrose, a beautiful girl of eighteen, known in the district as 'The Flower of Strathmore.' Burns made her the subject of this pastoral song.

[2] Literally, in both rooms of the house; here, throughout the house.

Her bonny face it was as meek
  As ony lamb upon a lee; any—lea
The evening sun was ne'er sae sweet so
  As was the blink o' Phemie's e'e. eye

The Highland hills I 've wander'd wide,
  And o'er the Lawlands I hae been; Lowlands
But Phemie was the blythest lass
  That ever trode the dewy green.

A ROSE BUD BY MY EARLY WALK.

TUNE—*The Shepherd's Wife.*

A rose bud by my early walk
Adown a corn-inclosèd bawk,[1]
Sae gently bent its thorny stalk,
    All on a dewy morning.
Ere twice the shades o' dawn are fled,
In a' its crimson glory spread,
And drooping rich the dewy head,
    It scents the early morning.

Within the bush her covert nest
A little linnet fondly prest,
The dew sat chilly on her breast
    Sae early in the morning.
She soon shall see her tender brood,
The pride, the pleasure o' the wood,
Amang the fresh green leaves bedew'd,
    Awauk the early morning. Awake

So thou, dear bird, young Jeany fair,
On trembling string or vocal air
Shall sweetly pay the tender care
    That tents thy early morning. guards
So thou, sweet Rose bud,[2] young and gay,
Shalt beauteous blaze upon the day,
And bless the Parent's evening ray
    That watch'd thy early morning.

[1] An open space in a cornfield.
[2] Miss Cruikshank, to whom the next poem is addressed. The 'Rosebud' became, in 1804, wife of James Henderson, a legal practitioner at Jedburgh. There she died in 1835. Her husband survived her four years.

TO MISS CRUIKSHANK, A VERY YOUNG LADY.

WRITTEN ON THE BLANK LEAF OF A BOOK PRESENTED TO HER BY THE AUTHOR.

Beauteous rose-bud, young and gay,
Blooming on thy early May,
Never may'st thou, lovely Flow'r,
Chilly shrink in sleety show'r!
Never Boreas' hoary path,
Never Eurus' pois'nous breath,
Never baleful stellar lights,
Taint thee with untimely blights!
Never, never reptile thief
Riot on thy virgin leaf!
Nor even Sol too fiercely view
Thy bosom blushing still with dew!

May'st thou long, sweet crimson gem
Richly deck thy native stem;
Till some ev'ning, sober, calm,
Dropping dews, and breathing balm,
While all around the woodland rings
And ev'ry bird thy requiem sings;
Thou, amid the dirgeful sound,
Shed thy dying honours round,
And resign to Parent Earth
The loveliest form she e'er gave birth.

WHERE, BRAVING ANGRY WINTER'S STORMS.

TUNE—*Neil Gow's Lamentation for Abercairny.*

Where, braving angry winter's storms,
  The lofty Ochils rise,
Far in their shade my Peggy's [1] charms
  First blest my wondering eyes;
As one who by some savage stream
  A lonely gem surveys,
Astonish'd, doubly marks it beam
  With art's most polish'd blaze.

[1] In this and the following poem the reference is to a girl of the name of Margaret Chalmers.

Blest be the wild, sequester'd shade,
And blest the day and hour,
Where Peggy's charms I first survey'd,
When first I felt their pow'r!
The tyrant death with grim controul,
May seize my fleeting breath,
But tearing Peggy from my soul
Must be a stronger death.

MY PEGGY'S FACE, MY PEGGY'S FORM.

My Peggy's face, my Peggy's form,
The frost of Hermit age might warm;
My Peggy's worth, my Peggy's mind,
Might charm the first of human kind.
I love my Peggy's angel air,
Her face so truly, heavenly fair,
Her native grace so void of art,
But I adore my Peggy's heart.

The lily's hue, the rose's dye,
The kindling lustre of an eye;
Who but owns their magic sway!
Who but knows they all decay!
The tender thrill, the pitying tear,
The generous purpose, nobly dear,
The gentle look that rage disarms,
These are all immortal charms.

THE BANKS OF THE DEVON.

How pleasant the banks of the clear winding Devon,
With green-spreading bushes, and flow'rs blooming fair!
But the bonniest flow'r on the banks of the Devon
Was once a sweet bud on the braes of the Ayr.[1]
Mild be the sun on this sweet blushing Flower
In the gay, rosy morn, as it bathes in the dew;
And gentle the fall of the soft vernal shower
That steals on the evening each leaf to renew!

[1] Charlotte, daughter of Gavin Hamilton, was born on the banks of the Ayr. She was now living at Harvieston, on the banks of the Devon.

O spare the dear blossom, ye orient breezes
  With chill, hoary wing as ye usher the dawn!
And far be thou distant, thou reptile that seizest
  The verdure and pride of the garden or lawn!
Let Bourbon exult in his gay, gilded Lilies,
  And England triumphant display her proud Rose;
A fairer than either adorns the green vallies
  Where Devon, sweet Devon, meandering flows.

ON THE DEATH OF LORD PRESIDENT DUNDAS.[1]

Lone on the bleaky hills, the straying flocks
Shun the fierce storms among the sheltering rocks;
Down foam the rivulets, red with dashing rains,
The gathering floods burst o'er the distant plains;
Beneath the blast the leafless forests groan,
The hollow caves return a sullen moan.

Ye hills, ye plains, ye forests and ye caves,
Ye howling winds, and wintry-swelling waves,
Unheard, unseen, by human ear or eye,
Sad to your sympathetic scenes I fly;
Where to the whistling blast and waters' roar
Pale Scotia's recent wound I may deplore.

O heavy loss thy Country ill could bear!
A loss these evil days can ne'er repair!
Justice, the high vicegerent of her God,
Her doubtful balance ey'd and sway'd her rod;
Hearing the tidings of the fatal blow
She sank abandon'd to the wildest woe.

Wrongs, Injuries, from many a darksome den,
Now gay in hope explore the paths of men.
See from his cavern grim Oppression rise,
And throw on Poverty his cruel eyes;
Keen on the helpless victim see him fly,
And stifle, dark, the feebly-bursting cry.
Mark ruffian Violence, distain'd with crimes,
Rousing elate in these degenerate times;

[1] Robert Dundas of Arniston, elder brother of Viscount Melville, was born 1713, appointed Lord President of the Court of Session in 1760, and died December 13, 1787, after a short illness.

View unsuspecting Innocence a prey,
As guileful Fraud points out the erring way:
While subtle Litigation's pliant tongue
The life-blood equal sucks of Right and Wrong.
Hark, injur'd Want recounts th' unlisten'd tale,
And much-wrong'd Mis'ry pours th' unpitied wail!

Ye dark, waste hills, ye brown, unsightly plains,
Congenial scenes! ye soothe my mournful strains:
Ye tempests, rage; ye turbid torrents, roll;
Ye suit the joyless tenor of my soul:
Life's social haunts and pleasures I resign,
Be nameless wilds and lonely wanderings mine,
To mourn the woes my Country must endure,
That wound degenerate ages cannot cure.

SYLVANDER TO CLARINDA.

IN ANSWER TO HER STANZAS—EXTEMPORE.

When dear Clarinda, matchless fair,
  First struck Sylvander's raptur'd view,
He gaz'd, he listen'd, to despair
  Alas! 'twas all he dar'd to do.

Love, from Clarinda's heavenly eyes,
  Transfix'd his bosom thro' and thro';
But still in Friendship's guarded guise,
  For more the demon fear'd to do.

That heart, already more than lost,
  The imp beleaguer'd all *perdue;*
For frowning Honor kept his post,
  To meet that frown he shrunk to do.

His pangs the Bard refus'd to own,
  Tho' half he wish'd Clarinda knew:
But Anguish wrung th' unweeting groan—
  Who blames what frantic Pain must do?

That heart, where motley follies blend,
  Was sternly still to Honor true:
To prove Clarinda's fondest friend,
  Was what a Lover sure might do.

The Muse his ready quill employ'd,
  No nearer bliss he could pursue;
That bliss Clarinda cold deny'd—
  'Send word by Charles how you do!'

The chill behest disarm'd his muse,
  Till Passion all impatient grew:
He wrote, and hinted for excuse
  ''Twas 'cause he 'd nothing else to do.'

But by those hopes I have above!
  And by those faults I dearly rue!
The deed, the boldest mark of love,
  For thee that deed I dare to do!

O, could the Fates but name the price
  Would bless me with your charms and you!
With frantic joy I 'd pay it thrice,
  If human art or power could do!

Then take, Clarinda, friendship's hand,
  (Friendship, at least, I may avow;)
And lay no more your chill command,
  I 'll write, whatever I 've to do.

BIRTHDAY ODE FOR 31ST DECEMBER 1787.[1]

Afar the illustrious Exile roams
  Whom kingdoms on this day should hail;
An inmate in the casual shed,
On transient pity's bounty fed,
  Haunted by busy memory's bitter tale!
Beasts of the forest have their savage homes,
  But He who should imperial purple wear
Owns not the lap of earth where rests his royal head!
  His wretched refuge, dark despair,
While ravening wrongs and woes pursue,
And distant far the faithful few
  Who would his sorrows share.

False flatterer, Hope, away!
  Nor think to lure us as in days of yore:
We solemnize this sorrowing natal day
  To prove our loyal truth—we can no more,

[1] Birthday of Prince Charles Edward.

And owning Heaven's mysterious sway,
Submissive, low adore.
Ye honored, mighty Dead,
Who nobly perished in the glorious cause,
Your King, your Country, and her laws,
From great Dundee, who smiling Victory led,
And fell a Martyr in her arms,
(What breast of northern ice but warms!)
To bold Balmerino's undying name,
Whose soul of fire, lighted at Heaven's high flame,
Deserves the proudest wreath departed heroes claim:
Not unrevenged your fate shall lie,
It only lags, the fatal hour,
Your blood shall, with incessant cry,
Awake at last th' unsparing Power;
As from the cliff, with thundering course
The snowy ruin smokes along
With doubling speed and gathering force,
Till deep it, crushing, whelms the cottage in the vale!
So Vengeance' arm, ensanguin'd, strong,
Shall with resistless might assail,
Usurping Brunswick's pride shall lay,
And Stewart's wrongs and yours, with tenfold weight, repay.

Perdition, baleful child of night!
Rise and revenge the injured right
Of Stewart's royal race:
Lead on the unmuzzled hounds of hell,
Till all the frighted echoes tell
The blood-notes of the chase!
Full on the quarry point their view,
Full on the base usurping crew,
The tools of faction, and the nation's curse!
Hark how the cry grows on the wind;
They leave the lagging gale behind,
Their savage fury, pityless, they pour;
With murdering eyes already they devour;
See Brunswick spent, a wretched prey,
His life one poor despairing day,
Where each avenging hour still ushers in a worse!
Such havock, howling all abroad,
Their utter ruin bring;
The base apostates to their God,
Or rebels to their King.

R. B. Nisbet, A.R.S.A.

On the Nith, Ellisland.

PAGE 270.

A FAREWELL TO CLARINDA

ON LEAVING EDINBURGH.

Clarinda, mistress of my soul,
The measured time is run!
The wretch beneath the dreary pole
So marks his latest sun.

To what dark cave of frozen night
Shall poor Sylvander hie,
Deprived of thee, his life and light—
The sun of all his joy?

We part—but by those precious drops
That fill thy lovely eyes!
No other light shall guide my steps
Till thy bright beams arise.

She, the fair sun of all her sex,
Has blest my glorious day;
And shall a glimmering planet fix
My worship to its ray?

M'PHERSON'S FAREWELL.

TUNE—*M'Pherson's Rant.*

[The freebooter James M'Pherson was a bastard of the Invereshie family by a Gypsy mother. Of great personal strength, and an excellent violinist, he had held the counties of Aberdeen, Banff, and Moray in fear for some years, when, with his Gypsy followers, he was seized by Duff of Braco, ancestor of the Duke of Fife, and tried before the Sheriff of Banff (November 7, 1700). In the prison, while he lay under the sentence of death, he composed a song and an appropriate air, the former commencing thus:

I've spent my time in rioting,
Debauched my health and strength;
I squandered fast as pillage came,
And fell to shame at length.
But dantonly, and wantonly, defiantly
And rantingly I'll gae; go
I'll play a tune, and dance it roun' round
Beneath the gallows-tree.

When brought to the place of execution, at the cross of Banff (November 16), he played the tune on his violin, and then asked if any friend was present who would accept the instrument as a gift at his hands. No one coming forward, he snapped the fiddle across his knee, and threw away the fragments; after which he submitted to the executioner.[1] Burns's verses were designed as an improvement on those ascribed to the freebooter, and were set to the same air.]

Farewell, ye dungeons dark and strong,
The wretch's destinie!

[1] Cramond's *Annals of Banff;* New Spalding Club, 1892.

M'Pherson's time will not be long
On yonder gallows-tree.
Chorus—Sae rantingly, sae wantonly,
Sae dauntingly gaed he; defiantly went
He play'd a spring, and danc'd it round tune
Below the gallows-tree.

O what is death but parting breath?
On many a bloody plain
I've dar'd his face, and in this place
I scorn him yet again!

Untie these bands from off my hands
And bring to me my sword;
And there's no a man in all Scotland
But I'll brave him at a word.

I've liv'd a life of sturt and strife; violence
I die by treacherie:
It burns my heart I must depart
And not avengèd be.

Now farewell, light, thou sunshine bright,
And all beneath the sky!
May coward shame distain his name, stain
The wretch that dares not die![1]

STAY, MY CHARMER, CAN YOU LEAVE ME?

TUNE—*An Gille dubh ciar dhubh.*

Stay, my charmer, can you leave me?
Cruel, cruel to deceive me!
Well you know how much you grieve me:
Cruel charmer, can you go!

By my love so ill-requited,
By the faith you fondly plighted,
By the pangs of lovers slighted,
Do not, do not leave me so!

[1] It is interesting to know that 'M'Pherson's Rant' was played once at Chelsea to Tennyson. 'I never hear it,' Carlyle wrote afterwards (1844) to Edward FitzGerald, 'without something of emotion—poor Macpherson; though the artist hates to play it. Alfred's face grew darker, and I saw his lip slightly quivering.'

STRATHALLAN'S LAMENT.[1]

Thickest night surround my dwelling!
Howling tempests o'er me rave!
Turbid torrents, wintry swelling,
Roaring by my lonely cave.
Crystal streamlets gently flowing,
Busy haunts of base mankind,
Western breezes softly blowing,
Suit not my distracted mind.

In the cause of Right engagèd
Wrongs injurious to redress,
Honor's war we strongly wagèd,
But the heavens deny'd success:
Ruin's wheel has driven o'er us,
Not a hope that dare attend,
The wide world is all before us—
But a world without a friend!

THE YOUNG HIGHLAND ROVER.

TUNE—*Morag.*

Loud blaw the frosty breezes, blow
The snaws the mountains cover, snows
Like winter on me seizes,
Since my young Highland Rover[2]
Far wanders nations over.

Chorus—Where'er he go, where'er he stray,
May Heaven be his warden:
Return him safe to fair Strathspey
And bonie Castle-Gordon!

The trees now naked groaning,
Shall soon wi' leaves be hinging, hanging
The birdies dowie moaning, dolefully
Shall a' be blythely singing,
And every flower be springing.

[1] William Drummond, fourth Viscount Strathallan, was killed at Culloden, 1746. His name, with that of his eldest son James, was included in a Bill of Attainder passed in the same year. James became fifth Viscount, and died in 1766. It was most probably into the mouth of the latter that the poet put the 'Lament.'

[2] Prince Charles Stuart.

Chorus—Sae I 'll rejoice the lee-lang day, livelong
When by his mighty Warden
My youth 's return'd to fair Strathspey
And bonie Castle-Gordon.

RAVING WINDS AROUND HER BLOWING.

TUNE—*M'Grigor of Ruara's Lament.*

I composed these verses on Miss Isabella M'Leod of Raasay, alluding to her feelings on the death of her sister, and the still more melancholy death (1786) of her sister's husband, the late Earl of Loudon, who shot himself out of sheer heart-break at some mortifications he suffered, owing to the deranged state of his finances.—*B*.

Raving winds around her blowing,
Yellow leaves the woodlands strowing,
By a river hoarsely roaring
Isabella stray'd deploring.
Farewell, hours that late did measure
Sunshine days of joy and pleasure;
Hail, thou gloomy night of sorrow,
Cheerless night that knows no morrow.

O'er the Past too fondly wandering,
On the hopeless Future pondering,
Chilly Grief my life-blood freezes,
Fell Despair my fancy seizes.
Life, thou soul of every blessing,
Load to Misery most distressing,
Gladly how would I resign thee,
And to dark Oblivion join thee!

MUSING ON THE ROARING OCEAN.

TUNE—*Druimion Dubh.*

I composed these verses out of compliment to a Mrs M'Lauchlan, whose husband is an officer in the East Indies.—*B*.

Musing on the roaring ocean
Which divides my love and me;
Wearying Heav'n in warm devotion
For his weal where'er he be.

Hope and Fear's alternate billow
Yielding late to Nature's law,
Whisp'ring spirits round my pillow
Talk of him that 's far awa.

Ye whom Sorrow never wounded,
Ye who never shed a tear,
Care-untroubled, joy-surrounded,
Gaudy Day to you is dear.

Gentle Night, do thou befriend me;
Downy Sleep, the curtain draw;
Spirits kind, again attend me,
Talk of him that 's far awa!

TO CLARINDA.

Fair Empress of the Poet's soul,
And Queen of Poetesses,
Clarinda, take this little boon,
This humble pair of glasses;

And fill them up with generous juice,
As generous as your mind,
And pledge me in the generous toast
'The whole of humankind!'

'To those who love us!' second fill,
But not to those whom we love:
Lest we love those who love not us.
A third, 'To thee and me, love!'

THE CHEVALIER'S LAMENT.

The small birds rejoice in the green leaves returning,
The murmuring streamlet winds clear thro' the vale,
The hawthorn trees blow in the dews of the morning,
And wild scattered cowslips bedeck the green dale:

But what can give pleasure, or what can seem fair,
While the lingering moments are numbered wi' care?
No flowers gayly springing, nor birds sweetly singing,
Can soothe the sad bosom of joyless despair.

The deed that I dared, could it merit their malice?
A king and a father to place on his throne:
His right are these hills, and his right are these vallies
Where the wild beasts find shelter, but I can find none.

But 'tis not my sufferings, thus wretched, forlorn,
My brave gallant friends, 'tis your ruin I mourn;
Your deeds proved so loyal in hot bloody trial,
Alas! can I make you no sweeter return!

EPISTLE TO HUGH PARKER.

In this strange land, this uncouth clime,
A land unknown to prose or rhyme:
Where words ne'er crost the muse's heckles,[1]
Nor limpet in poetic shackles: — limped
A land that prose did never view it,
Except when drunk he stacher't thro' it; — staggered
Here, ambush'd by the chimla cheek, — chimney=fireside
Hid in an atmosphere of reek, — smoke
I hear a wheel thrum [2] i' the neuk, — corner
I hear it—for in vain I leuk. — look
The red peat gleams, a fiery kernel,
Enhuskèd by a fog infernal:
Here, for my wonted rhyming raptures,
I sit and count my sins by chapters;
For life and spunk like ither Christians, — spirit—other
I'm dwindled down to mere existence,
Wi' nae converse but Gallowa' bodies,[3] — no—folk
Wi' nae kend face but Jenny Geddes.[4] — known
Jenny, my Pegasean pride!
Dowie she saunters down Nithside, — Sadly
And ay a westlin leuk she throws — look westwards
While tears hap o'er her auld brown nose! — drop
Was it for this, wi' canny care — gentle
Thou bure the Bard through many a shire? — bore
At howes or hillocks never stumbled, — hollows
And late or early never grumbled?
O, had I power like inclination,
I'd heeze thee up a constellation, — raise
To canter with the Sagitarre, — Sagittarius
Or loup th' ecliptic like a bar, — leap over
Or turn the pole like any arrow,
Or, when auld Phebus bids good-morrow,

[1] Hackles—an instrument for dressing flax.

[2] 'Thrum' = sound of a spinning-wheel in motion.

[3] Ellisland, although in Dumfriesshire, is situated near the borders of the Stewartry of Kirkcudbright, which, with Wigtownshire, forms the district known as Galloway.

[4] His mare.

Down the zodiac urge the race,
And cast dirt on his godship's face:
For I could lay my bread and kail — broth
He 'd ne'er cast saut upo' thy tail. — salt
Wi' a' this care and a' this grief,
And sma', sma' prospect of relief, — small
And nought but peat reek i' my head, — smoke
How can I write what ye can read?
Tarbolton, twenty-fourth o' June,
Ye 'll find me in a better tune;
But till we meet and weet our whistle,[1] — wet
Tak this excuse for nae epistle. — Take—nae epistle= what is not an epistle

June 1788. ROBERT BURNS.

I LOVE MY JEAN.

TUNE—*Miss Admiral Gordon's Strathspey.*

Of a' the airts the wind can blaw, — directions—blow
I dearly like the west,
For there the bonie Lassie lives,
The Lassie I lo'e best: — love
There 's wild-woods grow, and rivers row, — roll
And mony a hill between;[2]
But day and night my fancy's flight
Is ever wi' my Jean.

I see her in the dewy flowers,
I see her sweet and fair;
I hear her in the tunefu' birds,
I hear her charm the air:

[1] 'Weet our whistle' means 'have a friendly drink.'

[2] The commencement of this stanza is usually given—'There wild woods grow,' &c., as implying the nature of the scenery in the west. In Wood's *Songs of Scotland* the reading is—

'Though wild woods grow and rivers row,
Wi' mony a hill between,
Baith day and night,' &c.,—

evidently an alteration designed to improve the reasoning of the verse. It appears that both readings are wrong, for in the original manuscript (Burns's contribution to Johnson), now in the British Museum, the line is written: 'There 's wild woods grow,' &c., as in the text. The idea is not new in verse:

——————'ἐπειὴ μάλα πολλὰ μεταξὺ
Οὔρεά τε σκιόεντα, θάλασσά τε ἠχήεσσα.'

Iliad i., 156–7.

There 's not a bonie flower that springs
By fountain, shaw, or green ; wood
There 's not a bonie bird that sings,
But minds me o' my Jean.[1]

O, WERE I ON PARNASSUS HILL.

TUNE—*My love is lost to me.*

O, were I on Parnassus hill,
Or had o' Helicon [2] my fill,
That I might catch poetic skill
To sing how dear I love thee.
But Nith maun be my Muses' well, must
My Muse maun be thy bonie sel',[3] self
On Corsincon I 'll glow'r and spell, gaze
And write how dear I love thee !

[1] These stanzas appeared in the third volume of Johnson's *Museum.* Burns's note upon it afterwards was: 'This song I composed out of compliment to Mrs Burns. *N.B.*—It was in the honeymoon.' Two additional stanzas were some years afterwards produced by a John Hamilton, music-seller in Edinburgh. They are generally sung by way of lengthening the song, but their inferiority to Burns's lines is painfully obvious :

O blaw, ye westlin winds, blaw saft, blow—west—softly
Amang the leafy trees ; Among
Wi' gentle gale, frae muir and dale, from
Bring hame the laden bees ; home
And bring the lassie back to me,
That 's ay sae neat and clean : so—handsome
Ae blink o' her wad banish care, One—would
Sae charming is my Jean.

What sighs and vows, among the knowes, hillocks
Hae pass'd atween us twa ! two
How fain to meet, how wae to part, sorry
That day she gaed awa ! went away
The Powers aboon can only ken above—know
(To whom the heart is seen)
That nane can be sae dear to me none
As my sweet, lovely Jean.

[2] British poets have from a very early period been unwilling to content themselves with *Mount* Helicon as the haunt of the Muses, and its fountains Aganippe and Hippocrene. Montgomerie, in *The Cherry and the Slae*, has 'at fontaine Helicon ;' and the song, 'Declare ye banks of Helicon' (probably Montgomerie's ; see Cranstoun's edition for the Scottish Text Society, 1887), points the same way. Spenser has 'Parnasse . . . whence floweth Helicon the learned well,' a usage expressly defended in a gloss. Nor was he the only English poet to write thus. It has been pointed out that Pausanias describes a small stream called Helicon north of Mount Olympus, which, however, seems to have had no special connection with the Muses. See *Notes and Queries*, 4th series, ii., 243-475.

[3] A writer in *Notes and Queries* has pointed out a similar idea to this in Propertius :

'Non hæc Calliope, non hæc mihi cantat Apollo,
Ingenium nobis ipsa puella facit.'

Then come, sweet Muse, inspire my lay!
For a' the lee-lang simmer's day — livelong summer's day
I couldna sing, I couldna say, — could not
How much, how dear, I love thee.
I see thee dancing o'er the green,
Thy waist sae jimp, thy limbs sae clean,[1] — neat
Thy tempting lips, thy roguish een— — eyes
By Heaven and Earth I love thee!

By night, by day, a-field, at hame,
The thoughts o' thee my breast inflame;
And ay I muse and sing thy name,
I only live to love thee.
Tho' I were doom'd to wander on
Beyond the sea, beyond the sun,
Till my last weary sand was run,
Till then—and then I love thee!

WRITTEN IN FRIARS' CARSE HERMITAGE.

(FIRST VERSION.)

Thou whom Chance may hither lead,
Be thou clad in russet weed,
Be thou deckt in silken stole,
Grave these maxims on thy soul.

Life is but a Day at most;
Sprung from Night—in Darkness lost:[2]
Hope not Sunshine every hour,
Fear not Clouds will ever lour.
Happiness is but a name,
Make Content and Ease thy aim.
Ambition is a meteor-gleam;
Fame, a restless idle dream;
Pleasures, insects on the wing
Round Peace, the tenderest flower of Spring;
Those that sip the dew alone,
Make the Butterflies thy own;
Those that would the bloom devour,
Crush the Locusts, save the Flower.

1 'Clean,' in this relation, means 'well shaped, handsome.'
2 Compare Epicurus's ἀταραξία καὶ ἀπονία.

For the Future be prepar'd,
Guard, wherever thou can'st guard;
But thy Utmost duly done,
Welcome what thou canst not shun.
Follies past, give thou to air;
Make their Consequence thy care.
Keep the name of Man in mind,
And dishonour not thy kind.
Reverence, with lowly heart,
Him whose wondrous Work thou art;
Keep His Goodness still in view,
Thy trust, and thy example too.
Stranger, go! Heaven be thy guide!
Quod the Beads-mane of Nithe-side.

WRITTEN IN FRIARS-CARSE HERMITAGE, ON NITH-SIDE.

(SECOND VERSION.)

Thou whom chance may hither lead,
Be thou clad in russet weed,
Be thou deckt in silken stole,
Grave these counsels on thy soul.

Life is but a day at most,
Sprung from night—in darkness lost:
Hope not sunshine ev'ry hour,
Fear not clouds will always lour.

As Youth and Love with sprightly dance
Beneath thy morning star advance,
Pleasure with her siren air
May delude the thoughtless pair:
Let Prudence bless Enjoyment's cup,
Then raptur'd sip, and sip it up.

As thy day grows warm and high,
Life's meridian flaming nigh,
Dost thou spurn the humble vale?
Life's proud summits would'st thou scale?

Check thy climbing step, elate,
Evils lurk in felon-wait : hiding with felonious intent
Dangers, eagle-pinioned, bold,
Soar around each cliffy hold,
While cheerful peace, with linnet song,
Chants the lowly dells among.

As thy shades of ev'ning close,
Beck'ning thee to long repose ;
As life itself becomes disease,
Seek the chimney-nook of ease.
There ruminate with sober thought
On all thou 'st seen, and heard, and wrought ;
And teach the sportive younkers round,
Saws of experience, sage and sound.
Say, man's true, genuine estimate,
The grand criterion of his fate,
Is not, art thou high or low ?
Did thy fortune ebb or flow ?
Did many talents gild thy span ?
Or frugal Nature grudge thee one ?
Tell them, and press it on their mind,
As thou thyself must shortly find,
The smile or frown of aweful Heav'n,
To Virtue or to Vice is giv'n.
Say, to be just, and kind, and wise—
There, solid self-enjoyment lies ;
That foolish, selfish, faithless ways
Lead to be wretched, vile and base.

Thus resign'd and quiet, creep
To thy bed of lasting sleep :
Sleep, whence thou shalt ne'er awake,
Night, where dawn shall never break,
Till Future Life, future no more,
To light and joy the good restore,
To light and joy unknown before.

Stranger, go ! Heav'n be thy guide !
Quod the Beadsman of Nith-side.[1] Quoth

[1] 'Quod Dunbar' is printed at the end of many of Dunbar's poems. So also with many of the poems of other 'makkars.'

TO MR ALEXANDER CUNNINGHAM,[1]

WRITER, ST JAMES' SQUARE, EDINBURGH.

ELLISLAND, NITHSDALE, *July 27th*, 1788

MY GODLIKE FRIEND—
Nay, do not stare,
You think the phrase is odd-like;
But 'God is Love' the saints declare,
Then surely thou art God-like.

And is thy ardour still the same?
And kindled still at ANNA?
Others may boast a partial flame,
But thou art a volcano!

Ev'n Wedlock asks not love beyond
Death's tie-dissolving portal;
But thou, omnipotently fond,
May'st promise love immortal!

Thy wounds such healing powers defy,
Such symptoms dire attend them,
That last great antihectic try—
MARRIAGE perhaps may mend them.

Sweet Anna has an air—a grace
Divine, magnetic, touching;
She talks, she charms—but who can trace
The process of bewitching?

FIRST EPISTLE TO ROBERT GRAHAM, ESQ., OF FINTRY,

REQUESTING A FAVOR.[2]

When Nature her great Masterpiece designed,
And framed her last, best work, the Human-mind,
Her eye intent on all the various plan,
She formed of various parts the various man.

[1] Cunningham became a W.S. in 1798, but later joined an uncle as jeweller. He died in 1812. 'Anna' was Miss Anne Setwart, daughter of John Stewart of East Craigs. Shortly after the date of writing this, she became wife of Mr Forrest Dewar, surgeon in Edinburgh, Cunningham's rival. Although Cunningham married four years later, it is said that he never completely recovered from the shock occasioned by this disappointment.

[2] The favour requested was received almost a year later.

Then first she calls the USEFUL MANY forth—
Plain, plodding Industry, and sober Worth:
Thence Peasants, Farmers, native sons of earth,
And Merchandise' whole genus take their birth,
Each prudent Cit a warm existence finds,
And all Mechanics' many-aproned kinds.
Some other rarer Sorts are wanted yet,
The lead and buoy are needful to the net:
The *Caput mortuum* of strong Desires
Makes a material for mere Knights and Squires;
The Martial Phosphorus is taught to flow;
She kneads the lumpish Philosophic Dough,
Then marks th' unyielding mass with grave Designs,
Law, Physics, Politics, and deep Divines:
Last, she sublimes th' Aurora of the Poles,
The flashing elements of Female Souls.

The ordered System fair before her stood,
Nature, well pleased, pronounced it very good;
But ere she gave creating labour o'er,
Half-jest, she tried one curious labour more.
Some spumy, fiery, *ignis fatuus* matter,
Such as the slightest breath of air might scatter,
With arch-alacrity and conscious glee
(Nature may have her whim as well as we;
Her Hogarth-art, perhaps she meant to show it)
She forms the thing, and christens it—a Poet.

Creature, tho' oft the prey of Care and Sorrow,
When blest today, unmindful of tomorrow;
A being form'd t' amuse his graver friends,
Admir'd and prais'd—and there the wages ends;
A mortal quite unfit for Fortune's strife,
Yet oft the sport of all the ills of life;
Prone to enjoy each pleasure riches give,
Yet haply wanting wherewithal to live;
Longing to wipe each tear, to heal each groan,
Yet frequent all-unheeded in his own.

But honest Nature is not quite a Turk,
She laugh'd at first, then felt for her poor work:
Pitying the propless Climber of mankind,
She cast about a Standard-tree to find;

And to support his helpless woodbine state,
Attach'd him to the generous, truly great:
A title, and the only one I claim,
To lay strong hold for help on bounteous GRAHAM.

Pity the tuneful Muses' hapless train,
Weak, timid Landsmen on life's stormy main!
Their hearts no selfish stern absorbent stuff
That never gives—tho' humbly takes enough;
The little Fate allows, they share as soon,
Unlike sage, proverb'd Wisdom's hard-wrung boon:
The world were blest did bliss on them depend,
Ah, that the Friendly e'er should want a friend!
Let Prudence number o'er each sturdy son
Who life and wisdom at one race begun,
Who feel by reason, and who give by rule,
(Instinct 's a brute, and Sentiment a fool!)
Who make poor 'will do' wait upon 'I should:'
We own they 're prudent, but who owns they 're good?
Ye Wise-Ones, hence! ye hurt the social eye!
God's image rudely etch'd on base alloy!
But come ye who the godlike pleasure know,
Heaven's attribute distinguish'd—to bestow;
Whose arms of love would grasp the human race:
Come *thou* who giv'st with all a courtier's grace,
(*Friend of my life*, true Patron of my rhymes!)
Prop of my dearest hopes for future times.

Why shrinks my soul, half-blushing, half-afraid,
Backward, abash'd, to ask thy friendly aid?
I know my need, I know thy giving hand,
I tax thy friendship at thy kind command;
But there are such who court the tuneful Nine—
Heavens! should the branded character be mine!
Whose *verse* in manhood's pride sublimely flows,
Yet vilest reptiles in their begging *prose*.
Mark, how their lofty independent spirit
Soars on the spurning wing of injur'd Merit!
Seek you the proofs in *private life* to find?
Pity the best of words should be but wind!
So, to heaven's gates the lark's shrill song ascends,
But grovelling on the earth the carol ends.
In all the clamorous cry of starving want,
They dun Benevolence with shameless front;

Oblige them, patronise their tinsel lays,
They persecute you all your future days!
Ere my poor soul such deep damnation stain,
My horny fist assume the plough again,
The pie-bald jacket let me patch once more,
On eighteen pence a week I 've liv'd before.
Tho', thanks to Heaven! I dare even that last shift,
I trust, meantime, my boon is in thy gift;
That plac'd by thee upon the wish'd-for height,
Where Man and Nature fairer in her sight,
My Muse may imp[1] her wing for some sublimer flight.

THE FÊTE CHAMPÊTRE.

TUNE—*Killiecrankie.*

O wha will to Saint Stephen's House — who
  To do our errands there, man?
O wha will to Saint Stephen's House
  O' th' merry lads of Ayr, man?
Or will we send a man o' law?
  Or will we send a sodger? — soldier
Or him wha led o'er Scotland a' — all
  The meikle Ursa-Major?[2] — great

Come, will ye court a noble lord,
  Or buy a score o' lairds, man? — landholders
For worth and honour pawn their word,
  Their vote shall be Glencaird's, man.
Ane gies them coin, ane gies them wine, — One gives
  Anither gies them clatter; — Another—glib talk
Annbank, wha guess'd the ladies' taste,
  He gies a Fête Champêtre.

When Love and Beauty heard the news,
  The gay green-woods amang, man;
Where, gathering flowers, and busking bowers, — decking
  They heard the blackbird's sang, man: — song

[1] Both Spenser and Shakespeare speak of 'imping' one's wings in the sense of strengthening them, fitting them for flight.

[2] That is, James Boswell. The allusion is to the well-known joke of the elder Boswell, who, hearing his son speak of Johnson as a great luminary, quite a constellation, said, 'Yes, *Ursa Major.*'

A vow, they seal'd it with a kiss,
  Sir Politics to fetter;
As theirs alone, the patent bliss,
  To hold a Fête Champêtre.

Then mounted Mirth on gleesome wing,
  O'er hill and dale she flew, man;
Ilk wimpling burn, ilk crystal spring, Each winding
  Ilk glen and shaw she knew, man: wood
She summon'd every social sprite
  That sports by wood or water,
On th' bonie banks o' Ayr to meet,
  And keep this Fête Champêtre.

Cauld Boreas wi' his boisterous crew Cold
  Were bound to stakes like kye, man; cattle
And Cynthia's car, o' silver fu', full
  Clamb up the starry sky, man: Climbed
Reflected beams dwell in the streams,
  Or down the current shatter;
The western breeze steals thro' the trees
  To view this Fête Champêtre.

How many a robe sae gaily floats! so
  What sparkling jewels glance, man,
To Harmony's enchanting notes,
  As moves the mazy dance, man:
The echoing wood, the winding flood,
  Like Paradise did glitter
When angels met, at Adam's yett, gate
  To hold their Fête Champêtre.

When Politics came there, to mix
  And make his ether-stane, man![1]
He circled round the magic ground,
  But entrance found he nane, man: none
He blush'd for shame, he quat his name, quitted
  Forswore it, every letter,
Wi' humble prayer to join and share
  This festive Fête Champêtre.

[1] This is an allusion to a very ancient superstition, referred to the Druids, which represents adders as forming annually from their slough certain little annular stones of streaked colouring, which are occasionally found, but which are in reality beads fashioned and used by our early ancestors. They were believed to act as charms.

THE DAY RETURNS, MY BOSOM BURNS.

TUNE—*Seventh of November.*

The day returns, my bosom burns,
  The blissful day we twa did meet:
Tho' winter wild in tempest toil'd,
  Ne'er summer-sun was half sae sweet.
Than a' the pride that loads the tide,
  And crosses o'er the sultry line;
Than kingly robes, than crowns and globes,
  Heav'n gave me more—it made thee mine!

While day and night can bring delight,
  Or nature aught of pleasure give;
While joys above my mind can move,
  For thee, and thee alone, I live!
When that grim foe of life below
  Comes in between, to make us part,
The iron hand that breaks our band,
  It breaks my bliss—it breaks my heart!

MRS FERGUSSON OF CRAIGDARROCH'S LAMENTATION FOR THE DEATH OF HER SON,

AN UNCOMMONLY PROMISING YOUTH OF EIGHTEEN OR NINETEEN YEARS OF AGE.[1]

'Fate gave the word, the arrow sped,'
  And pierced my Darling's heart;
And with him all the joys are fled
  Life can to me impart!

By cruel hands the Sapling drops,
  In dust dishonored laid:
So fell the pride of all my hopes,
  My age's future shade.

[1] 'Died here on Monday last [Nov. 19, 1787] James Fergusson, Esq., younger of Craigdarroch. The worth of this truly amiable and much-lamented youth can best be estimated by a sketch given of him on his leaving Glasgow College in May last: "Of all the young men of this age I have ever known, he is by much the most promising. His abilities are equal to anything he chooses to undertake. His understanding is clear and penetrating, and readily comprehends the most abstract subjects. His memory is retentive. He speaks with fluency and perspicuity; he writes with neatness and accuracy. No one can exceed him in the assiduity of his application, and he persists in it with the utmost steadiness, in spite of every allurement. United with all these shining qualifications, he discovers the most gentle temper, simple manners, and the amiable modesty of youth."'—*Newspaper Obituary.*

The mother-linnet in the brake
  Bewails her ravished young;
So I, for my lost Darling's sake,
  Lament the liveday long.

Death, oft I've fear'd thy fatal blow;
  Now, fond, I bare my breast;
O, do thou kindly lay me low
  With him I love, at rest!

THE LAZY MIST HANGS FROM THE BROW OF THE HILL.

The lazy mist hangs from the brow of the hill,
Concealing the course of the dark winding rill;
How languid the scenes, late so sprightly, appear
As Autumn to Winter resigns the pale year.
The forests are leafless, the meadows are brown,
And all the gay foppery of summer is flown:
Apart let me wander, apart let me muse
How quick Time is flying, how keen Fate pursues.

How long I have liv'd—but how much liv'd in vain;
How little of life's scanty span may remain;
What aspects Old Time, in his progress, has worn;
What ties cruel Fate in my bosom has torn;
How foolish, or worse, till our summit is gain'd!
And downward, how weaken'd, how darken'd, how pain'd!
Life is not worth having with all it can give,
For something beyond it poor man sure must live.

I HAE A WIFE O' MY AIN.

I hae a wife o' my ain, — have—own
  I'll partake wi' naebody; — nobody
I'll tak cuckold frae nane, — take—from none
  I'll gie cuckold to naebody.

I hae a penny to spend,
  There—thanks to naebody;
I hae naething to lend,
  I'll borrow frae naebody.

I am naebody's lord,
  I 'll be slave to naebody;
I hae a gude braid sword,
  I 'll tak dunts frae naebody. — blows

I 'll be merry and free,
  I 'll be sad for naebody;
If naebody care for me,
  I 'll care for naebody.[1]

AULD LANG SYNE.[2]

Should auld acquaintance be forgot, — old
  And never brought to mind?
Should auld acquaintance be forgot,
  And auld lang syne! — days of long ago

Chorus—For auld lang syne, my dear,
    For auld lang syne,
  We 'll tak a cup[3] o' kindness yet
    For auld lang syne.

And surely ye 'll be your pint stowp! — tankard
  And surely I 'll be mine!
And we 'll tak a cup o' kindness yet,
  For auld lang syne.

We twa hae run about the braes,
  And pou'd the gowans fine: — pulled
But we 've wander'd mony a weary fitt, — many—foot
  Sin' auld lang syne. — Since

We twa hae paidl'd in the burn — waded
  Frae morning sun till dine: — dinner-time
But seas between us braid hae roar'd — broad
  Sin' auld lang syne.

[1] On the 28th of November 1788 the *Edinburgh Advertiser* noted that 'Burns, the *Ayrshire Bard*, is now enjoying the sweets of retirement at his farm. Burns, in thus retiring, has acted wisely. Stephen Duck, the *Poetical Thresher*, by his ill-advised patrons, was made a parson. The poor man, hurried out of his proper element, found himself quite unhappy; became insane; and with his own hands, it is said, ended his life. Burns, with propriety, has resumed the *flail*—but we hope he has not thrown away the *quill*.'

[2] The melody to which the song is now sung was composed by William Shield, and forms part of the overture to his opera *Rosina* (1783).

[3] 'Some sing *kiss* in place of *cup*.'—Note in Johnson's *Museum*.

And there 's a hand, my trusty fiere! friend
 And gie 's a hand o' thine! give
And we 'll tak a right gude-willie [1] waught draught
 For auld lang syne.

MY BONIE MARY.[2]

Go, fetch to me a pint o' wine,
 And fill it in a silver tassie, cup
That I may drink, before I go,
 A service to my bonie lassie:
The boat rocks at the Pier o' Leith,
 Fu' loud the wind blaws frae the Ferry, blows from
The ship rides by the Berwick-Law,[3]
 And I maun leave my bonie Mary. must

The trumpets sound, the banners fly,
 The glittering spears are rankèd ready,
The shouts o' war are heard afar,
 The battle closes deep and bloody:
It 's not the roar o' sea or shore
 Wad make me langer wish to tarry; Would—longer
Nor shouts o' war that 's heard afar,
 It 's leaving thee, my bonie Mary!

ELEGY ON THE YEAR 1788.

For Lords or Kings I dinna mourn, don't
E'en let them die—for that they 're born!
But oh, prodigious to reflec'!
A *Towmont*, Sirs, is gane to wreck! twelvemonth
O *Eighty-eight*, in thy sma' space
What dire events hae taken place!
Of what enjoyments thou hast reft us!
In what a pickle thou hast left us!

[1] Gude-willie = with good-will.
[2] This song may be effectively sung to one of the numerous settings of the 'Highland Laddie,' to be found in Johnson's *Musical Museum*.
[3] North Berwick Law, a conical hill near the shore of the Firth of Forth, very conspicuous at Edinburgh, from which it is distant about twenty miles. The Ferry is Queensferry.

C. M. Hardie, R.S.A.

We twa hae paidl't in the burn
Frae morning sun till dine.

PAGE 281.

The Spanish empire 's tint a head,[1] lost
An' my auld teethless Bawtie 's[2] dead;
The tulzie 's teugh 'tween Pitt an' Fox, fight is tough
An' oor gudewife's wee birdy cocks: small
The tane is game, a bluidy devil, one
But to the hen-birds unco civil; very
The tither 's dour, has nae sic breedin', other—obstinate
But better stuff ne'er claw'd a midden!

Ye ministers, come mount the pupit, pulpit
An' cry till ye be hearse an' roupit, hoarse with shouting
For *Eighty-eight* he wish'd you weel,
An' gied you a' baith gear an' meal: gave money
E'en mony a plack and mony a peck, coin
Ye ken yoursels, for little feck. know—value, consideration

Ye bonny lasses, dight your e'en, dry—eyes
For some o' you hae tint a frien':
In *Eighty-eight*, ye ken, was taen
What ye 'll ne'er hae to gie again.

Observe the very nowt an' sheep, cattle
How dowff an' dowie now they creep; dull—sad
Nay, even the yirth itsel does cry, earth
For Embro wells are grutten dry.[3] Edinburgh—wept

O *Eighty-nine!* thou 's but a bairn, child
An' no owre auld, I hope, to learn! too
Thou beardless boy, I pray tak care,
Thou now has got thy Daddy's chair,
Nae hand-cuff'd, mizl'd, hap-shackl'd *Regent*,[4] muzzled—foot-bound
But, like himsel, a full free agent.
Be sure ye follow out the plan
Nae waur than he did, honest man!— worse
As muckle better as you can. much

January 1, 1789.

[1] Charles III., king of Spain, died 13th December 1788.

[2] A generic familiar name for a dog in Scotland.

[3] The Edinburgh newspapers of the day contain references to a scarcity of water in consequence of severe frost.

[4] The king having shown symptoms of unsound mind in November, the country was at this time agitated by discussions as to the propriety of appointing a regent. Pitt and his party were for restricting the power of the proposed regent—the Prince of Wales.

ROBIN[1] SHURE IN HAIRST.

I gaed up to Dunse — went
To warp a wab o' plaiden, — web—woollen cloth
At his daddie's yett — gate
Wha met me but Robin?

Chorus—Robin shure in hairst, — sheared—harvest
I shure wi' him:
Fient a heuk had I, — Never a reaping-hook
Yet I stack by him.

Was na Robin bauld,
Tho' I was a cotter,
Play'd me sic a trick,
And me the Eller's dochter? — elder's daughter

Robin promis'd me
A' my winter vittle; — food
Fient haet he had but three — Not a thing
Goose-feathers and a whittle! — knife

EXTEMPORE TO CAPTAIN RIDDEL,

ON RETURNING A NEWSPAPER.[2]

ELLISLAND: *Monday Even:*

Your News and Review, Sir, I've read through and through, Sir,
With little admiring or blaming:
The Papers are barren of home-news or foreign,
No murders or rapes worth the naming.

Our friends the Reviewers, those Chippers and Hewers,
Are judges of mortar and stone, Sir;
But of MEET OR UNMEET, in a FABRIC complete,
I'll boldly pronounce they are none, Sir.

My Goose-quill too rude is to tell all your goodness
Bestowed on your servant, The Poet;
Would to God I had one like a beam of the Sun,
And then all the World, [Sir,] should know it!

ROBT. BURNS.

[1] His friend Robert Ainslie, an Edinburgh Writer to the Signet.
[2] The MS. of this is now in the Liverpool Public Library.

CALEDONIA, A BALLAD.

TUNE—'*Caledonian Hunt's delight*'—*Mr Gow's.*

There was on a time, but old Time was then young,
That brave Caledonia, the chief of her line,
From some of your northern deities sprung,
(Who knows not that brave Caledonia 's divine?)
From Tweed to the Orcades was her domain,
To hunt or to pasture, or do what she would;
Her heavenly relations there fixèd her reign,
And pledged her their godheads to warrant it good.

A lambkin in peace, but a lion in war,
The pride of her kindred the Heroine grew;
Her grandsire, old Odin, triumphantly swore,
'Who e'er shall provoke thee th' encounter shall rue!'
With tillage or pasture at times she would sport,
To feed her fair flocks by her green rustling corn;
But chiefly the woods were her fav'rite resort,
Her darling amusement the hounds and the horn.

Long quiet she reigned, till thitherward steers
A flight of bold eagles from Adria's strand:[1]
Repeated, successive, for many long years
They darkened the air and they plundered the land.
Their pounces were murder, and horror their cry,
They 'd ravag'd and ruin'd a world beside;
She took to her hills and her arrows let fly,
The daring invaders they fled or they died.

The Camelon savage disturb'd her repose[2]
With tumult, disquiet, rebellion and strife;
Provok'd beyond bearing, at last she arose,
And robb'd him at once of his hopes and his life:

[1] The Romans.

[2] Burns, who had spoken of Camelon, near Falkirk, as the capital of the Picts, was, like his contemporaries, accustomed to regard the Scots alone as the forefathers of the later Scottish nation, and the Picts, accordingly, as aliens and enemies. Bellenden's *Croniclis,* the vernacular version of Boece's history, repeated in many popular forms, describes at length the siege, capture, and destruction of Camelon by Kenneth Macalpin (referred to A.D. 839) as the final subversion and practical extirpation of the Picts, and their disappearance from history. This is, of course, wholly unhistorical. In most editions of Burns's poems 'Camelon savage' appears as 'Cameleon savage,' which is unintelligible.

The Anglian lion, the terror of France,
  Oft prowling ensanguin'd the Tweed's silver flood;
But, taught by the bright Caledonian lance,
  He learnèd to fear in his own native wood.

The fell Harpy-raven took wing from the North,[1]
  The scourge of the seas and the dread of the shore;
The wild Scandinavian boar[2] issu'd forth,
  To wanton in carnage and wallow in gore:
O'er countries and kingdoms their fury prevail'd,
  No arts could appease them, no arms could repel;
But brave Caledonia in vain they assail'd,
  As Largs[3] well can witness and Loncartie[4] tell.

Thus bold, independent, unconquer'd and free,
  Her bright course of glory for ever shall run;
For brave Caledonia immortal must be—
  I'll prove it from Euclid as clear as the sun:
Rectangle-triangle the figure we'll chuse,
  The Upright is Chance and old Time is the Base;
But brave Caledonia 's the Hypothenuse;
  Then, Ergo, she 'll match them, and match them always.[5]

ODE

SACRED TO THE MEMORY OF MRS OSWALD OF AUCHENCRUIVE.[6]

Dweller in yon dungeon dark,
Hangman of creation, mark!
Who in widow-weeds appears,
Laden with unhonoured years,

[1] The Danes.

[2] The Norsemen.

[3] Alexander III. defeated Haco at Largs 1263.

[4] Kenneth III., according to Boece (but no earlier authority), defeated the Danes with slaughter at Luncarty, four miles from Perth, in 990.

[5] Allusion is here made to Euclid's familiar proposition, according to which in a right-angled triangle the square of the hypotenuse is always equal to the squares of the two other sides.

[6] 'Dec. 6, 1788, died at her house in Great George Street, Westminster, Mrs Oswald, widow of Richard Oswald, Esq. of Auchencruive' (*Magazine Obituary*). Richard Oswald, youngest son of the Rev. George Oswald of Dunnet, settled in London and acquired great wealth as a merchant and, afterwards, as a Government contractor during the Seven Years' War. He purchased Auchencruive (parish of St Quivox, Ayrshire), the ancient seat of the Cathcarts, about 1759, and lived there until his death in 1784. He had married Mary Ramsay (only daughter and heiress of Alexander Ramsay, of Jamaica), through whom he had acquired large estates in America and the West Indies. On his death she removed to London, and died there. It was while her body was being taken to St Quivox, to be laid beside that of her husband, that the cortège stopped overnight at Sanquhar. Auchencruive is still in the possession of the Oswald family.

Noosing with care a bursting purse,
Baited with many a deadly curse?

STROPHE.

View the wither'd beldam's face—
Can thy keen inspection trace
Aught of Humanity's sweet, melting grace?
Note that eye, 'tis rheum o'erflows—
Pity's flood there never rose.
See those hands, ne'er stretch'd to save,
Hands that took—but never gave.
Keeper of Mammon's iron chest,
Lo, there she goes, unpitied and unblest
She goes, but not to realms of everlasting rest!

ANTISTROPHE.

Plunderer of Armies! lift thine eyes
(A while forbear, ye tort'ring fiends),
Seest thou whose step, unwilling, hither bends?
No fallen angel, hurl'd from upper skies!
'Tis thy trusty, *quondam Mate*,
Doom'd to share thy fiery fate—
She, tardy, hell-ward plies.

EPODE.

And are they of no more avail,
Ten thousand glitt'ring pounds a-year?
In other worlds can Mammon fail,
Omnipotent as he is here?
O, bitter mock'ry of the *pompous bier*,
While down the wretched *vital part* is driv'n!
The cave-lodg'd beggar, with a conscience clear,
Expires in rags, unknown, and goes to Heav'n.

TO MR JOHN TAYLOR.[1]

With Pegasus upon a day
Apollo, weary flying,
Thro' frosty hills the journey lay,
On foot the way was plying.

[1] The MS. of this, with Sloan's letter attached, is now in Alloway Cottage.

Poor, slip-shod, giddy Pegasus
  Was but a sorry walker,
To Vulcan then Apollo gaes
  To get a frosty calker.[1]

Obliging Vulcan fell to wark,
  Threw by his coat and bonnet;
And did Sol's business in a crack,
  Sol pay'd him with a sonnet.

Ye Vulcan's Sons of Wanlockhead,
  Pity my sad disaster!
My Pegasus is poorly shod,
  I'll pay you like my Master.

ODE TO THE DEPARTED REGENCY-BILL, 1789.

ELLISLAND, 17*th March* 1789.

Daughter of Chaos' doting years!
Nurse of ten thousand hopes and fears!
Whether thy airy, unsubstantial Shade
(The rights of sepulture now duly paid)
Spread abroad its hideous form
On the roaring Civil Storm,
Deafening din and warring rage
Factions wild with factions wage;
Or under ground, deep-sunk, profound,
  Among the demons of the earth,
With groans that make the mountains shake,
  Thou mourn thy ill-starred, blighted birth;
Or in the uncreated Void
  Where seeds of future-being fight,
With lessen'd step thou wander wide,
  To greet thy Mother—Ancient Night,[2]
And as each jarring, monster mass is past,
Fond recollect what once thou wast:
In manner due, beneath this sacred oak,
Hear, Spirit, hear! thy presence I invoke!

    By a Monarch's heaven-struck fate!
    By a disunited State!

[1] A horse is said in Scotland to be 'frosted' or 'sharpened' when it is rough-shod for frosty weather, by having the edges at the front of the shoes—the calks, calkins, calkers, or caulkers—turned over so as to grip on slippery ground.
[2] Milton's 'chaos and ancient night' again.

By a generous Prince's wrongs!
By a Senate's strife of tongues!
By a Premier's sullen pride,
Louring on the changing tide!
By dread Thurlow's powers to awe,
Rhetoric, blasphemy and law!
By the turbulent ocean,
A Nation's commotion!
By the harlot-caresses
Of borough-addresses!
By days few and evil!
Thy portion, poor devil!
By Power, Wealth, Show! the gods by men adored!
By Nameless Poverty! (Their hell abhorred!)
By all they hope! By all they fear!
Hear!!! And Appear!!!

Stare not on me, thou ghastly Power;
Nor grim with chained defiance lour:
No Babel-structure would I build
Where, Order exil'd from his native sway,
Confusion may the REGENT-sceptre wield,
While all would rule and none obey:
Go! to the world of Man relate
The story of thy sad, eventful fate!
And call Presumptuous Hope to hear,
And bid him check his blind career,
And tell the sore-prest sons of Care,
Never, never to despair![1]

Paint CHARLES's speed on wings of fire,
The object of his fond desire,
Beyond his boldest hopes, at hand:
Paint all the triumph of the Portland Band:[2]
Mark how they lift the joy-exulting voice;
And how their numerous Creditors rejoice:
But just as hopes to warm enjoyment rise,
Cry CONVALESCENCE! and the vision flies.

Then next portray a darkening twilight gloom
Eclipsing, sad, a gay, rejoicing morn,
While proud Ambition to th' untimely tomb
By gnashing, grim, despairing fiends is borne:

[1] From *The Masque of Alfred*, by James Thomson and David Mallet.

[2] The (third) Duke of Portland was nominal head of the 'Coalition Ministry' of 1783, of which 'Charles' (Charles James Fox) was the chief member.

Paint ruin, in the shape of high D[undas],
Gaping with giddy terror o'er the brow;
In vain he struggles, the Fates behind him press,
And clamorous hell yawns for her prey below:
How fallen *That*, whose pride late scaled the skies!
And *This*, like Lucifer, no more to rise!
Again pronounce the powerful word;
See Day, triumphant from the night, restored.

Then know this truth, ye Sons of Men!
(Thus end thy moral tale)
Your darkest terrors may be vain,
Your brightest hopes may fail.

STANZAS OF PSALMODY.[1]

KILMARNOCK, *April* 30.

MR PRINTER—In a certain *Chapel* not fifty leagues from the market-cross of this good town, the following stanzas of Psalmody, it is said, were composed for, and devoutly sung on, the late joyful solemnity, on the 23rd inst.

O, sing a new song to the Lord!
Make, all and every one,
A joyful noise, ev'n for the king
His Restoration.

The sons of Belial in the land
Did set their heads together;
Come, let us sweep them off, said they,
Like an o'erflowing river.

They set their heads together, I say,
They set their heads together:
On right, and left, and every hand,
We saw none to deliver.

Thou madest strong two chosen Ones,
To quell the Wicked's pride:
That Young Man,[2] great in Issachar
The burden-bearing Tribe.

[1] Thursday, 23rd April 1789, was appointed a day of public thanksgiving for the recovery of the king. Burns looked on the 'whole business as a solemn farce of pageant mummery,' and composed these 'Stanzas of Psalmody.'

[2] William Pitt.

C. M. Hardie, R.S.A.

Go, fetch to me a pint o' wine,
And fill it in a silver tassie.

PAGE 282.

And him, among the Princes chief
  In our Jerusalem,
The Judge that 's mighty in Thy law,[1]
  The Man that fears Thy name.

Yet they, even they, with all their might,
  Began to faint and fail;
Even as two howling, ravening wolves
  To dogs do turn their tail.

Th' Ungodly o'er the Just prevail'd,
  For so Thou hadst appointed,
That Thou might'st greater glory give
  Unto Thine own Anointed.

And now Thou hast restor'd our State,
  Pity our kirk also,
For she by tribulations
  Is now brought very low!

Consume that High-Place, PATRONAGE,
  From off thine holy hill;
And in Thy fury burn the book
  Even of that man M'Gill.[2]

Now hear our Prayer, accept our Song,
  And fight Thy Chosen's battle:
We seek but little, Lord, from Thee,
  Thou kens we get as little.

DUNCAN M'LEERIE.

DELIA, AN ODE.[3]

Fair the face of orient day,
  Fair the tints of op'ning rose;
But fairer still my Delia dawns,
  More lovely far her beauty shows.

[1] Edward Thurlow, then Lord Chancellor. Pitt and 'fighting Thurlow' had opposed (for personal and party reasons) the appointment of a regent armed with all the powers of a king.

[2] *Essay on the Death of Jesus Christ*, by William M'Gill.

[3] This ode is usually included in Burns's works; but, from its lack of force and true feeling, many critics have suspected it was not his composition.

Sweet the lark's wild warbled lay,
Sweet the tinkling rill to hear;
But, Delia, more delightful still
Steal thine accents on mine ear.

The flower-enamour'd busy bee
The rosy banquet loves to sip;
Sweet the streamlet's limpid laps
To the sun-brown'd Arab's lip.

But, Delia, on thy balmy lips
Let me, no vagrant insect, rove;
O let me steal one liquid kiss,
For, oh! my soul is parched with love!

SKETCH.

INSCRIBED TO CHARLES JAMES FOX, ESQ.

How Wisdom and Folly meet, mix and unite;
How Virtue and Vice blend their black and their white;
How Genius, th' illustrious father of fiction,
Confounds rule and law, reconciles contradiction—
I sing: If these mortals, the critics, should bustle,
I care not, not I—let the critics go whistle!

But now for a patron, whose name and whose glory
At once may illustrate and honor my story.

Thou first of our orators, first of our wits,
Yet whose parts and acquirements seem mere lucky hits,
With knowledge so vast and with judgment so strong,
No man with the half of 'em e'er went far wrong;
With passions so potent and fancies so bright,
No man with the half of 'em e'er went quite right;
A sorry, poor, misbegot son of the muses,
For using thy name offers fifty excuses.

Good L—d, what is man! for as simple he looks,
Do but try to develop his hooks and his crooks;
With his depths and his shallows, his good and his evil,
All in all he 's a problem must puzzle the devil.

On his one ruling passion Sir Pope [1] hugely labours,
That, like th' old Hebrew walking-switch, eats up its neighbours:

[1] Pope's *Essay on Man.*

Mankind are his show-box—a friend, would you know him?
Pull the string, ruling passion the picture will shew him.
What pity, in rearing so beauteous a system,
One trifling particular, *truth*, should have miss'd him;
For, spite of his fine theoretic positions,
Mankind is a science defies definitions.

Some sort all our qualities, each to its tribe,
And think human nature they truly describe;
Have you found this or t' other? there 's more in the wind,
As by one drunken fellow his comrades you 'll find.
But such is the flaw, or the depth of the plan,
In the make of that wonderful creature call'd Man;
No two virtues, whatever relation they claim,
Nor even two different shades of the same,
Though like as was ever twin brother to brother,
Possessing the one shall imply you 've the other.

But truce with abstraction, and truce with a Muse
Whose rhymes you 'll perhaps, Sir, ne'er deign to peruse:
Will you leave your justings, your jars and your quarrels,
Contending with Billy[1] for proud-nodding laurels?
My much-honor'd Patron, believe your poor poet,
Your courage, much more than your prudence, you show it:
In vain with Squire Billy for laurels you struggle;
He 'll have them by fair trade, if not, he will smuggle:
Not cabinets even of kings would conceal 'em,
He 'd up the back-stairs, and by G— he would steal 'em!
Then feats like Squire Billy's you ne'er can achieve 'em;
It is not, out-do him—the task is, out-thieve him!

ON SEEING A WOUNDED HARE LIMP BY ME,

WHICH A FELLOW HAD JUST SHOT AT.

Inhuman man! curse on thy barb'rous art,
And blasted be thy murder-aiming eye;
May never pity soothe thee with a sigh,
Nor ever pleasure glad thy cruel heart!

Go live, poor wanderer of the wood and field,
The bitter little that of life remains!
No more the thickening brakes and verdant plains
To thee shall home, or food, or pastime yield.

[1] William Pitt.

Seek, mangled wretch, some place of wonted rest,
No more of rest, but now thy dying bed!
The sheltering rushes whistling o'er thy head,
The cold earth with thy bloody bosom prest.

Oft as by winding Nith I, musing, wait
The sober eve, or hail the cheerful dawn,
I'll miss thee sporting o'er the dewy lawn,
And curse the ruffian's aim and mourn thy hapless fate.[1]

TO JAMES TENNANT OF GLENCONNER.

Auld comrade dear and brither sinner,
How's a' the folk about Glenconner?
How do you this blae eastlin wind — raw—easterly
That's like to blaw a body blind?
For me, my faculties are frozen,
My dearest member nearly dozen'd. — benumbed
I've sent you here, by Johnie Simson,[2]
Twa sage philosophers to glimpse on:
Smith, wi' his sympathetic feeling,[3]
An' Reid, to common sense appealing.
Philosophers have fought and wrangled,
An' meikle Greek an' Latin mangled, — much
Till wi' their logic-jargon tir'd,
And in the depth of science mir'd,
To common-sense they now appeal,
What wives and wabsters see and feel. — weavers
But, hark ye, friend! I charge you strictly,
Peruse them, an' return them quickly—
For now I'm grown sae cursed douce — sedate
I pray and ponder butt the house: — i.e. in the kitchen

[1] Allan Cunningham mentions that the poor hare whose sufferings excited this burst of indignation on the part of the poet was shot by a lad named James Thomson, son of a farmer near Ellisland. Burns, who was near the Nith at the moment, execrated the young man, and threatened to throw him into the water.

[2] 'Johnie Simson,' whom, as 'poor Simson,' James Tennant is asked in the fourth last line of the poem to 'assist,' is believed to have been a dancing-master. The object of the epistle was to induce 'the miller' to take Simson round the parish, and introduce him to possible patrons. The result, according to tradition, was 'the biggest dancing-class ever known in Ochiltree.'

[3] Adam Smith's *Theory of the Moral Sentiments* was published in 1759; *An Inquiry into the Human Mind, on the Principles of Common Sense*, by Thomas Reid, D.D., in 1764.

My shins, my lane, I there sit roastin', alone
Perusing Bunyan, Brown an' Boston,[1]
Till by an' by, if I haud on, hold
I'll grunt a real gospel groan:
Already I begin to try it,
To cast my e'en up like a pyet magpie
When by the gun she tumbles o'er
Flutt'ring an' gasping in her gore:
Sae shortly you shall see me bright,
A burning an' a shining light.

My heart-warm love to guid auld Glen,
The ace an' wale of honest men: choice
When bending down wi' auld grey hairs
Beneath the load of years and cares
May He who made him still support him,
An' views beyond the grave comfort him;
His worthy fam'ly, far and near,
God bless them a' wi' grace and gear! goods

My auld schoolfellow, preacher Willie;
The manly tar, my mason-Billie; Freemason crony
An' Auchenbay, I wish him joy—
If he's a parent,[2] lass or boy,
May he be *dad* and Meg the *mither*,
Just five-and-forty years thegither! together
An' no forgetting wabster Charlie,
I'm tauld he offers very fairly;
An' Lord, remember singing Sannock,
Wi' hale breeks, saxpence an' a bannock;[3] whole trousers—scone
An' next, my auld acquaintance, Nancy,
Since she is fitted to her fancy,
An' her kind stars hae airted till her directed to
A good chiel wi' a pickle siller; fellow—some money
My kindest, best respects, I sen' it
To cousin Kate an' sister Janet:

[1] Bunyan's *Pilgrim's Progress*, *The Self-interpreting Bible* of Rev. John Brown of Haddington (1722–87), and *The Fourfold State* of Rev. Thomas Boston of Ettrick (1676–1732), used to be found in every pious Scottish household.

[2] Supporters of the view that the 'Epistle' was written at Mossgiel find further confirmation in these two lines, which they maintain were written in anticipation of the birth (15th May 1786) of John Tennant's first child, Jane. The report goes that when Burns was engaged on its composition he heard that a messenger had arrived at Mauchline from Auchenbay, which was three miles distant, for a midwife.

[3] 'Fortune! if thou'll but gie me still
Hale breeks, a scone, an' whisky gill.'—*Scotch Drink*.

Tell them, frae me, wi' chiels be cautious, — lads
For, faith, they 'll aiblins fin them fashious: — possibly—troublesome
To grant a heart is fairly civil,
But to grant a maidenhead 's the devil;
An' lastly, Jamie, for yoursel,
May guardian angels tak a spell,
An' steer you seven miles south o' hell:
But, first, before you see heaven's glory,
May ye get monie a merry story,
Monie a laugh and monie a drink,
And aye eneugh o' needfu' clink. — money

Now fare ye well an' joy be wi' you:
For my sake this I beg it o' you,
Assist poor Simson a' ye can,
Ye 'll fin' him just an honest man;
Sae I conclude, and quat my chanter,[1] — quit
Yours, saint or sinner,

Rob the Ranter.[2]

1 Chanter is part of a bagpipe.

2 The various allusions to the Tennant family in this poem may here be explained. Its head, 'Guid Auld Glen,' is, of course, John Tennant (1726–1810), farmer in Glenconner, from 1769 to 1780 factor for the Ochiltree property of Elizabeth, Countess of Glencairn, and the friend both of Burns and of his father. He was thrice married, and the James Tennant to whom this epistle is addressed was one of the sons of the first marriage. He was five years Burns's senior, and having taken the mill at Ochiltree, was popularly known as 'the miller.' 'My auld schoolfellow, preacher Willie,' was William Tennant (1758–1813), the eldest son of 'Auld Glen' by his second wife. Trained for the ministry of the Church of Scotland, he became chaplain to the forces in India, published two works based on his experiences there—*Indian Researches* and *Thoughts on the Effects of the British Government on the State of India*, and returned to Glenconner, where he died. The 'manly tar, my mason-Billie,' was David Tennant (1762–1839), third son of Glenconner. He entered the merchant service, and so distinguished himself in privateering against the French that he was offered a knighthood. He died in Swansea. 'Auchenbay' was John Tennant (1760–1853), Glenconner's second son by his second wife. Having tried business, first as a shipbuilder and then as a distiller, he leased the farm of Auchenbay in Ochiltree parish. He became noted as a skilful and successful agriculturist, and before he died purchased the estate of Creoch, in his native parish. 'Meg the mither' was his wife, Margaret Colville, whom he married in 1785, and who died in 1823. 'Wabster Charlie' was Charles Tennant (1768–1838), Glenconner's fourth son by his second wife. Sent by his father to Kilbarchan to learn weaving, he entered the bleaching business, and ultimately became founder of the chemical-works at St Rollox, Glasgow, the senior partner in the firm owning which is (1900) his descendant, Sir Charles Tennant of The Glen, Innerleithen. 'Singing Sannock' is understood to be Robert Tennant (1774–1841), sixth son of Glenconner by his second wife. He also entered the bleaching business, and died in Ireland. 'My auld acquaintance, Nancy,' was Agnes Tennant, eldest daughter of Glenconner. In 1785 she married George Reid of Barquharie, on whose pony Burns rode into Edinburgh. According to the family tombstone in Ochiltree churchyard, she died on 14th June 1787. 'Cousin Kate' was Katherine, daughter of Alexander Tennant, a younger brother of Glenconner. 'Sister Janet' was Janet Tennant (1766–1843), second daughter of Glenconner. She married Andrew Paterson, of Ayr, and died there.

THE KIRK'S ALARM—A BALLAD.

TUNE—*Come rouse, brother Sportsmen.*

Orthodox, Orthodox, who believe in John Knox,
 Let me sound an alarm to your conscience :
There 's a heretic blast has been blawn i' the west,
 That 'what is not sense must be nonsense,'
 Orthodox! That 'what is not sense must be nonsense.'

Doctor Mac,[1] Doctor Mac, ye should stretch on a rack,
 To strike evil-doers wi' terror;
To join Faith and Sense, upon any pretence,
 Was heretic, damnable error,
 Doctor Mac! 'Twas heretic, damnable error.

Town of Ayr,[2] town of Ayr, it was rash, I declare,
 To meddle wi' mischief a-brewing;
Provost John is still deaf to the Church's relief,
 And orator Bob[3] is its ruin,
 Town of Ayr! Yes orator Bob is its ruin.

D'rymple mild,[4] D'rymple mild, tho' your heart 's like a child,
 And your life 's like the new-driven snaw,

[1] Dr M'Gill was a Socinian or Unitarian in principle, though not a student of the works of Socinus, none of which he had ever read. He was a strange mixture of simplicity and stoicism. He seldom smiled, but often set the table in a roar by his quaint remarks. He was inflexibly regular in the distribution of his time: he studied so much every day, and took his walk at the same hour in all sorts of weather. He played at golf a whole twelvemonth without the omission of a single week-day, except the three on which there were religious services at the time of the Communion. His views of many of the dispensations of Providence were widely different from those of the bulk of society. A friend told him of an old clergyman, an early companion of his own, who, having entered the pulpit in his canonicals, and being about to commence service, fell back and expired in a moment. Dr M'Gill clapped his hands together, and said, 'That was very desirable; he lived all the days of his life.' The morning after a domestic calamity of the most harrowing kind, the reverend doctor, to the surprise of his flock, officiated in church with his usual serenity. He conversed on self-murder with the coolness of a Roman philosopher.

[2] When Dr M'Gill's case first came before the Synod, the magistrates of Ayr published an advertisement in the newspapers, bearing warm testimony to the excellence of the defender's character and to their appreciation of his services as a pastor.

[3] It is scarcely necessary to say that 'Provost John' is John Ballantyne, and 'orator Bob' Robert Aiken.

[4] Rev. Dr William Dalrymple, senior minister of the collegiate charge of Ayr—a man of extraordinary benevolence. It is related that one day, meeting an almost naked beggar in the country, he took off his coat and waistcoat, gave the latter to the poor man, then put on his coat, buttoned it up, and walked home. He died in 1814.

Yet that winna save ye, old Satan must have ye,
For preaching that three 's ane and twa,
D'rymple mild! For preaching that three 's ane and twa.

Calvin's sons, Calvin's sons, seize your spiritual guns,
Ammunition ye never can need;
Your hearts are the stuff will be powder enough,
And your skulls are a storehouse o' lead,
Calvin's sons, and your skulls are a storehouse o' lead.

Rumble John,[1] Rumble John, mount the steps with a groan,
Cry, the book is with heresy cramm'd;
Then lug out your ladle, deal brimstone like aidle, muck-water
And roar every note o' the Damn'd,
Rumble John, and roar every note o' the Damn'd.

Simper James,[2] Simper James, leave the fair Killie dames,
There 's a holier chase in your view;
I 'll lay on your head that the Pack ye 'll soon lead,
For Puppies like you there 's but few,
Simper James, for Puppies like you there 's but few.

Singet Sawnie,[3] Singet Sawnie, are ye herding the Penny, singed—hoarding
Unconscious what danger awaits?
With a jump, yell and howl, alarm every soul,
For Hannibal 's just at your gates,
Singet Sawnie! For Hannibal 's just at your gates.

Poet Willie,[4] Poet Willie, gie the Doctor a volley,
Wi' your 'liberty's chain' and your wit;
O'er Pegasus' side ye ne'er laid a stride,
Ye only stood by where he sh—,
Poet Willie! Ye only stood by where he sh—.

Barr Steenie,[5] Barr Steenie, what mean ye? what mean ye?
If ye 'll meddle nae mair wi' the matter,
Ye may hae some pretence, man, to havins and sense, man, manners
Wi' people that ken you nae better,
Barr Steenie! Wi' people that ken you nae better.

1 Rev. John Russell, celebrated in 'The Holy Fair.'

2 Rev. James Mackinlay, minister of Kilmarnock, the hero of 'The Ordination.'

3 Rev. Alexander Moodie, of Riccarton, one of the heroes of 'The Twa Herds.'

4 Rev. William Peebles (see note. p. 187) had excited some ridicule by a line in a poem on the Centenary of the Revolution:

'And bound in *Liberty's* endearing *chain*.'

5 Rev. Stephen Young, minister of Barr, 1780–1819.

Jamie Goose,[1] Jamie Goose, ye hae made but toom roose empty boast
O' hunting the wicked Lieutenant;
But the Doctor 's your mark, for the L—d's holy ark,
He has cooper'd and ca'd a wrang pin in, driven
Jamie Goose! He has cooper'd and ca'd a wrang pin in.

Davie Bluster,[2] Davie Bluster, for a saunt if ye muster,
It 's a sign they 're no nice o' recruits;
Yet to worth let 's be just, Royal Blood ye might boast—
If the Ass were the king o' the brutes,
Davie Bluster! If the Ass were the king o' the brutes.

Cessnock-side,[3] Cessnock-side, wi' your turkey-cock pride,
O' manhood but sma' is your share:
Ye 've the figure, it 's true, even your faes maun allow, foes
And your friends darena say ye hae mair,
Cessnock-side! And your friends darena say ye hae mair.

Muirlan' Jock,[4] Muirlan' Jock, whom the Lord gave a stock
Would set up a tinkler in brass;
If ill manners were wit, there 's no mortal so fit
To prove the poor Doctor an ass,
Muirlan' Jock! To prove the poor Doctor an ass.

Andrew Gowk,[5] Andrew Gowk, ye may slander the book,
And the book nought the waur, let me tell ye: worse

[1] Rev. James Young became minister of New Cumnock in 1757, and died in 1795.

[2] Rev. David Grant was minister of Ochiltree from 1786 till his death in 1791.

[3] Rev. George Smith, Galston. This gentleman is praised as friendly to Common Sense in 'The Holy Fair.' The offence which was taken at that compliment probably embittered the poet against him.

[4] Rev. John Shepherd, minister of Muirkirk from 1775 till his death in 1799. The statistical account of Muirkirk contributed by this gentleman to Sir John Sinclair's work is very well written. He had, however, an unfortunate habit of saying rude things, which he mistook for wit, and thus laid himself open to Burns's satire.

[5] Dr Andrew Mitchell, minister of Monkton from 1775 till 1811. He perhaps 'looked big,' because he was the son of Hugh Mitchell, laird of Dalgain, in the eastern part of Ayrshire, and his mother was one of the Campbells of Fairfield. He himself was laird of Avisyard, in the neighbourhood of Cumnock. Extreme love of money and a strange confusion of ideas characterised this clergyman. In his prayer for the Royal Family he would express himself thus: 'Bless the King—His Majesty the Queen—Her Majesty the Prince of Wales.' The word chemistry he pronounced in three different ways—*hemistry*, *shemistry*, and *tchemistry*—but never by any chance in the right way. Notwithstanding the antipathy he could scarcely help feeling towards Burns, one of the poet's comic verses would make him laugh heartily, and confess that, 'after all, he was a droll fellow.' He died in 1811, aged eighty-six.

Tho' ye 're rich and look big, yet lay by hat and wig,
And ye 'll hae a *calf's head* o' sma' value,
Andrew Gowk! And ye 'll hae a *calf's head* o' sma' value.

Daddie Auld,[1] Daddie Auld, there 's a tod i' the fauld, fox—fold
A tod meikle waur than the Clerk;[2] much worse
Tho' ye do little skaith, ye 'll be in at the death, harm
For if ye canna bite, ye can bark,
Daddie Auld! For if ye canna bite, ye can bark.

Poet Burns, Poet Burns, wi' your priest-skelping turns, hitting
Why desert ye your auld native Shire?
Tho' your Muse is a gipsy, yet were she even tipsy,
She could ca' us nae waur than we are,
Poet Burns! She could ca' us nae waur than we are.

Holy Will,[3] Holy Will, there was wit in your skull,
When ye pilfer'd the alms o' the poor;
The timmer is scant when ye 're ta'en for a saint, timber
Wha should swing in a rape for an hour, rope
Holy Will! Ye should swing in a rape for an hour.

PRESENTATION STANZAS.

Factor John, Factor John, whom the Lord made alone,
And ne'er made another thy peer,
Thy poor servant, the Bard, in respectful regard,
Presents thee this token sincere,
Factor John.[4] He presents thee this token sincere.

Afton's Laird! Afton's Laird, when your pen can be spared,
A copy of this I bequeath,
On the same sicker score as I mention'd before,
To that trusty auld worthy, Clackleith,
Afton's Laird! To that trusty auld worthy, Clackleith.

[1] Rev. Mr Auld, of Mauchline.
[2] Mr Gavin Hamilton.
[3] William Fisher, whom Burns had already immortalised. It has never been proved that 'Holy Willie' did 'pilfer' the alms-box.
[4] It does not seem certain whether 'Factor John' was John M'Murdo, chamberlain to the Duke of Queensberry; John Kennedy, factor to the Earl of Dumfries; or John Tennant of Glenconner, who was for some time factor to the Earl of Glencairn.

TO ROBERT GRAHAM, ESQ., OF FINTRY,

ON RECEIVING A FAVOUR, 10TH AUGUST 1789.

I call no goddess to inspire my strains,
A fabled Muse may suit a bard that feigns;
Friend of my life! my ardent spirit burns,
And all the tribute of my heart returns,
For boons accorded, goodness ever new,
The gift still dearer, as the Giver You.
Thou Orb of day! thou other Paler Light!
And all ye many sparkling stars of night!
If aught that Giver from my mind efface;
If I that Giver's bounty e'er disgrace;
Then roll, to me, along your wand'ring spheres
Only to number out a villain's years!
I lay my hand upon my swelling breast,
And grateful would, but cannot, speak the rest.

WILLIE BREW'D A PECK O' MAUT.

O Willie brew'd a peck o' maut, malt
  And Rob and Allan cam to pree; taste
Three blyther hearts, that lee-lang night, livelong
  Ye wad na found in Christendie.

Chorus—We are na fou, we 're nae that fou, full [drunk]
  But just a drappie in our e'e; drop—eye
 The cock may craw, the day may daw, dawn
  And ay we 'll taste the barley bree. brew, juice

Here are we met, three merry boys,
  Three merry boys, I trow, are we;
And mony a night we 've merry been,
  And mony mae we hope to be! more

It is the moon, I ken her horn,
  That 's blinkin' in the lift sae hie; heavens—high
She shines sae bright to wyle us hame, lure
  But, by my sooth, she 'll wait a wee! a while

Wha first shall rise to gang awa,
  A cuckold, coward loun is he! fellow
Wha last beside his chair shall fa',
  He is the King amang us three!

THE WHISTLE.

In the train of Anne of Denmark, when she came to Scotland with our James the Sixth, there came over also a Danish gentleman of gigantic stature and great prowess, and a matchless champion of Bacchus. He had a little ebony Whistle, which, at the commencement of the orgies, he laid on the table; and whoever was last able to blow it, everybody else being disabled by the potency of the bottle, was to carry off the Whistle as a trophy of victory. The Dane produced credentials of his victories, without a single defeat, at the courts of Copenhagen, Stockholm, Moscow, Warsaw, and several of the petty courts in Germany; and challenged the Scots Bacchanalians to the alternative of trying his prowess or else of acknowledging their inferiority. After many overthrows on the part of the Scots, the Dane was encountered by Sir Robert Lawrie of Maxwelton, ancestor to the present worthy baronet of that name; who, after three days' and three nights' hard contest, left the Scandinavian under the table,

And blew on the Whistle his requiem shrill.

Sir Walter, son to Sir Robert before mentioned, afterwards lost the whistle to Walter Riddel of Glenriddel, who had married a sister of Sir Walter's.[1]—*R. B.* The whistle being now in the possession of Captain Riddel, Burns's neighbour at Friars' Carse, it was resolved that he should submit it to an amicable competition between himself and two other descendants of the conqueror of the Scandinavian —namely, Alexander Fergusson of Craigdarroch, and Sir Robert Lawrie of Maxwelton, then M.P. for Dumfriesshire.

I sing of a Whistle, a Whistle of worth,
I sing of a Whistle, the pride of the North,
Was brought to the court of our good Scottish King,
And long with this Whistle all Scotland shall ring.

Old Loda,[2] still rueing the arm of Fingal,
The god of the bottle sends down from his hall—
'This Whistle 's your challenge, to Scotland get o'er,
And drink them to Hell, Sir! or ne'er see me more!'

Old poets have sung and old chronicles tell
What champions ventur'd, what champions fell:
The son of great Loda was conqueror still,
And blew on the Whistle their requiem shrill.

Till Robert, the lord of the Cairn and the Scaur,[3]
Unmatch'd at the bottle, unconquer'd in war,
He drank his poor god-ship as deep as the sea;
No tide of the Baltic e'er drunker than he.

[1] It is evidently to the first baronet that the legend recorded by Burns refers, as his successor's successor was a son, Sir Walter, a contemporary of Walter Riddel of Glenriddel. The story had probably some such foundation as that described, though Burns's dates are wrong.

[2] See Ossian's Caric-thura.—*B.*

[3] The Cairn, a stream in Glencairn parish, on which Maxwelton House is situated; the Skarr, a similar mountain-rill, in the parish of Penpont; both are affluents of the Nith.

G. O. Reid, A.R.S.A.

It is the moon, I ken her horn.

PAGE 301.

Thus Robert, victorious, the trophy has gain'd;
Which now in his house has for ages remain'd;
Till three noble chieftains, and all of his blood,
The jovial contest again have renew'd.

Three joyous good fellows, with hearts clear of flaw:
Craigdarroch, so famous for wit, worth, and law;
And trusty Glenriddel, so skill'd in old coins;
And gallant Sir Robert, deep-read in old wines.

Craigdarroch began, with a tongue smooth as oil,
Desiring Glenriddel to yield up the spoil;
Or else he would muster the heads of the clan,
And once more, in claret, try which was the man.

'By the gods of the ancients!' Glenriddel replies,
'Before I surrender so glorious a prize
I'll conjure the ghost of the great Rorie More,[1]
And bumper his horn with him twenty times o'er.'

Sir Robert, a soldier, no speech would pretend,
But he ne'er turn'd his back on his foe or his friend;
Said—'Toss down the Whistle, the prize of the field,'
And, knee-deep in claret, he'd die ere he'd yield.

To the board of Glenriddel our heroes repair,
So noted for drowning of sorrow and care;
But for wine and for welcome not more known to fame
Than the sense, wit and taste, of a sweet lovely dame.

A bard was selected to witness the fray,
And tell future ages the feats of the day;
A bard who detested all sadness and spleen,
And wish'd that Parnassus a vineyard had been.

The dinner being over, the claret they ply,
And ev'ry new cork is a new spring of joy;
In the bands of old friendship and kindred so set,
And the bands grew the tighter the more they were wet.

Gay Pleasure ran riot as bumpers ran o'er;
Bright Phœbus ne'er witness'd so joyous a core, company
And vow'd that to leave them he was quite forlorn,
Till Cynthia hinted he'd see them next morn.

[1] See Johnson's *Tour to the Hebrides*.—*B.*

Six bottles a-piece had well wore out the night,
When gallant Sir Robert, to finish the fight,
Turn'd o'er in one bumper a bottle of red,
And swore 'twas the way that their ancestors did.

Then worthy Glenriddel, so cautious and sage,
No longer the warfare ungodly would wage:
A high Ruling Elder to wallow in wine![1]
He left the foul business to folks less divine.

The gallant Sir Robert fought hard to the end;
But who can with Fate and quart bumpers contend?
Though Fate said, a hero shall perish in light;
So uprose bright Phœbus—and down fell the knight.

Next uprose our Bard, like a prophet in drink:—
'Craigdarroch, thou 'lt soar when creation shall sink!
But if thou would flourish immortal in rhyme,
Come—one bottle more—and have at the sublime!

'Thy line, that have struggled for freedom with Bruce,
Shall heroes and patriots ever produce:
So thine be the laurel and mine be the bay;
The field thou hast won, by yon bright God of Day!'

PRESENTATION STANZA:

But one sorry quill—and that worn to the core;
No paper—but such as I shew it;
But such as it is, will the good Laird of Torr
Accept—and excuse the poor Poet?[2]

[1] Glenriddel, who was a ruling-elder—all the lay elders are ruling-elders—represented the Presbytery of Dumfries in the Assembly from 1789 till 1793.

[2] The following statement was made in 1851 by William Hunter of Cockrune, in the parish of Closeburn, who at the time of the drinking contest was a servant at Friars' Carse: 'Burns,' he said, 'was present the whole evening. He was invited to attend the party, to see that the gentlemen drank fair, and to commemorate the day by writing a song. I recollect well that when the dinner was over, Burns quitted the table, and went to a table in the same room that was placed in a window that looked south-east; and there he sat down for the night. I placed before him a bottle of rum and another of brandy, which he did not finish, but left a good deal of each when he rose from the table after the gentlemen had gone to bed. . . . When the gentlemen were put to bed, Burns walked home without any assistance, not being the worse of drink. When Burns was sitting at the table in the window, he had pen, ink, and paper, which I brought to him at his own request. He now and then wrote on the paper, and while the gentlemen were sober, he turned round often and chatted with them, but drank none of the claret which they were drinking. . . . I heard him read aloud several parts of the poem, much to the amusement of the three gentlemen.' Doubts have been cast upon the accuracy of Hunter's statement, and it is by no means improbable that after the lapse of many years his memory may have played

TO MARY IN HEAVEN.

TUNE—*Captain Cook's Death, &c.*

Thou ling'ring star, with less'ning ray,
That lov'st to greet the early morn,
Again thou usher'st in the day
My Mary from my soul was torn.
O Mary! dear departed Shade!
Where is thy place of blissful rest?
See'st thou thy Lover lowly laid?
Hear'st thou the groans that rend his breast?

That sacred hour can I forget:
Can I forget the hallow'd grove
Where, by the winding Ayr, we met
To live one day of parting love!
Eternity can not efface
Those records dear of transports past;
Thy image at our last embrace,
Ah, little thought we 'twas our last.

Ayr, gurgling, kiss'd his pebbled shore,
O'erhung with wild-woods, thickening green;
The fragrant birch and hawthorn hoar
Twin'd amorous round the raptur'd scene;
The flowers sprang wanton to be prest,
The birds sang love on every spray,
Till too, too soon the glowing west
Proclaim'd the speed of wingèd day.

him false, especially in regard to the object of Burns's presence on the evening. His statement is now of interest chiefly as an indication of Burns's reputation for sobriety—at all events as sobriety was understood in those days. All his Ellisland servants without exception gave the same testimony. Thus Elizabeth Smith, who was in his service in 1788-89, testified that she saw her master only once affected with liquor—at the New Year. In this connection, also, the following may be quoted from Mrs Burns's reminiscences: 'Mrs B. remembers the circumstances about the Whistle—that, as she heard them related, the Bard, tho' present at the contest, came home in his ordinary trim. Tho' he drank, perhaps, like some others, he was not required to keep pace with the champions. The song was composed soon after the drinking bout; and Captain Riddel frequently called to see how he was coming on with it'—'that is,' writes Dr Hately Waddell, 'with the finished copy.' The statement of Miss Isabella Begg to Dr Robert Chambers on this subject was as follows: 'My grandmother was at Ellisland when the "Whistle" was contended for. In his letter of 14th August 1789 to his brother William the poet mentions his mother; in another, 10th November same year, he says: "My mother is returned, now that she has seen my boy, Francis Wallace, fairly set to the world." Now my mother (Mrs Begg) always said her mother said that Robert was at the dinner, and that he returned quite sober from the contest.'

Still o'er these scenes my mem'ry wakes
And fondly broods with miser-care;
Time but th' impression stronger makes,
As streams their channels deeper wear:
My Mary, dear departed Shade!
Where is thy place of blissful rest?
See'st thou thy Lover lowly laid?
Hear'st thou the groans that rend his breast?

TO DR BLACKLOCK.[1]

ELLISLAND, *21st Oct.* 1789.

Wow, but your letter made me vauntie! — elated
And are ye hale, and weel, and cantie? — in good health—merry
I ken'd it still your wee bit jauntie — jaunt
Wad bring ye to:
Lord send you ay as weel 's I want ye,
And then ye 'll do!

The ill-thief blaw the Heron[2] south! — devil
And never drink be near his drouth! — thirst
He tauld mysel, by word o' mouth,
He 'd tak my letter;
I lippen'd to the chiel in trouth, — trusted—fellow
And bade nae better. — desired

But, aiblins, honest Master Heron — perhaps
Had, at the time, some dainty fair one
To ware his theologic care on — spend
And holy study;
And tired o' sauls to waste his lear on, — learning
E'en tried the body.

But what d 'ye think, my trusty fier? — friend
I'm turn'd a gauger—Peace be here!
Parnassian queens, I fear, I fear
Ye 'll now disdain me,
And then my fifty pounds a year
Will little gain me!

[1] In reply to a letter in rhyme from Dr Blacklock.

[2] Robert Heron, son of a weaver, born at New Galloway in 1764. He passed through the University of Edinburgh, supporting himself by writing for booksellers. His works comprise a *History of Scotland*, *Journey through the Western Counties of Scotland*, *Life of Burns* (the first Life published). He was imprisoned for debt in Newgate, where he died (of fever), 1807.

Ye glaiket, gleesome, dainty damies — giddy
Wha, by Castalia's wimplin' streamies, — winding
Lowp, sing, and lave your pretty limbies, — Jump
Ye ken, ye ken — know
That strang necessity supreme is
'Mang sons o' men.

I hae a wife and twa wee laddies—
They maun hae brose and brats o' duddies: — hasty pudding—suits of clothes
Ye ken yoursels my heart right proud is—
I need na vaunt—
But I'll sned besoms—thraw saugh woodies, — cut—twist—willow withes
Before they want.

Lord help me thro' this warld o' care!
I'm weary sick o 't late and air! — early
Not but I hae a richer share
Than mony ithers;
But why should ae man better fare,
And a' men brithers?

Come, Firm Resolve, take thou the van,
Thou stalk o' carl-hemp [1] in man!
And let us mind faint heart ne'er wan — won
A lady fair:
Wha does the utmost that he can,
Will whyles do mair. — sometimes—more

But to conclude my silly rhyme
(I'm scant o' verse and scant o' time),
To make a happy fire-side clime
To weans and wife— — children
That 's the true pathos and sublime
Of human life.

My compliments to sister Beckie;
And eke the same to honest Lucky:
I wat she is a daintie chuckie [2]
As e'er tread clay;
And gratefully, my gude auld cockie,
I'm yours for ay.

ROBERT BURNS.

[1] Carl-hemp or churl-hemp, the name given (on the erroneous assumption that it was the male plant) to what is really the female plant of hemp, the robuster and coarser of the two. 'You have a stalk of carle hemp in you' is a proverb—'spoken to sturdy and stubborn boys.'—KELLY'S *Scottish Proverbs.*

[2] Chuckie, a familiar term for a hen, used for a darling, 'a duck.'

ON CAPTAIN GROSE'S[1] PEREGRINATIONS THRO' SCOTLAND,

COLLECTING THE ANTIQUITIES OF THAT KINGDOM.

Hear, Land o' Cakes, and brither Scots
Frae Maidenkirk[2] to Johnny Groat's—
If there 's a hole in a' your coats,
I rede you tent it: warn—attend to it
A chield 's amang you takin' notes, fellow
And faith he 'll prent it:

If in your bounds ye chance to light
Upon a fine, fat, fodgel wight, plump
O' stature short but genius bright,
That 's he, mark weel—
And wow! he has an unco sleight uncommon skill
O' cauk and keel. chalk(s) and ruddle

By some auld, houlet-haunted biggin, owl—building
Or kirk deserted by its riggin, roof
It 's ten to ane ye 'll find him snug in
Some eldritch part, eerie
Wi' deils, they say, Lord safe 's! colleaguin conferring
At some black art.

Ilk ghaist that haunts auld ha' or chamer Each—hall—chamber
Ye gipsy-gang that deal in glamour, sorcery
And you, deep-read in hell's black grammar,
Warlocks and witches:
Ye 'll quake at his conjúring hammer,
Ye midnight bitches!

[1] Francis Grose, son of a jeweller who had left Switzerland and settled at Richmond, was born at Greenford, Middlesex, about 1731, and studied as an artist, but having spent a fortune left him by his father, took to writing, chiefly on antiquities. He published *Antiquities of England and Wales* (4 vols. 1773–1778), and when he made the acquaintance of Burns was engaged in a similar work on Scotland. The latter work was published 1789–91 (2 vols.), and included Burns's 'Tam o' Shanter'—written for it. He subsequently visited Ireland, with a similar purpose, but had only started work at Dublin when he died (1791). He has been described as a sort of antiquarian Falstaff. His other works deal with philological and miscellaneous subjects.

[2] Maidenkirk is an inversion of the name Kirkmaiden, in Wigtownshire, the most southerly parish in Scotland.

It 's tauld he was a sodger bred,
And ane wad rather fa'n than fled ; would have fallen
But now he 's quat the spurtle-blade quitted—sword
And dog-skin wallet, sporran
And taen the—*Antiquarian trade*,
I think they call it.

He has a fouth o' auld nick-nackets : abundance
Rusty airn caps, and jinglin jackets iron—jack-armour
Wad haud the Lothians three in tackets keep—shoe-nails
A towmont gude ; twelvemonth
And parritch-pats and auld saut-backets porridge-pots—salt-boxes
Before the Flood.

Of Eve's first fire he has a cinder ;
Auld Tubalcain's fire-shool and fender ; shovel
That which distinguishèd the gender
O' Balaam's ass ;
A broomstick o' the witch of Endor,
Weel shod wi' brass. with brass ferrule

Forbye, he 'll shape you aff fu' gleg Besides—smartly
The cut of Adam's philibeg ; kilt
The knife that nicket Abel's craig cut—throat
He 'll prove you fully
It was a faulding jocteleg,[1] folding clasp-knife
Or lang-kail gullie. knife for cutting greens

But wad ye see him in his glee
(For meikle glee and fun has he), much
Then set him down, and twa or three
Gude fellows wi' him ;
And *port*, O *port !* shine thou a wee, for a short time
And then ye 'll see him !

Now, by the Pow'rs o' verse and prose !
Thou art a dainty chield, O Grose !— fine fellow
Whae'er o' thee shall ill suppose,
They sair misca' thee ; badly slander
I 'd take the rascal by the nose,
Wad say 'Shame fa' thee.' befall

[1] The etymology of this word is doubtful. It used to be derived from *Jacques de Liège*, assumed to be the name of the maker. But the word is doubtless akin to the English *jackalegs*, *jacklag-knife*, and *jack-knife*.

VERSES ON CAPTAIN GROSE.[1]

Ken ye aught o' Captain Grose?
Igo and ago,
If he 's amang his friends or foes?
Iram, coram, dago.

Is he to Abra'm's bosom gane?
Igo and ago,
Or haudin Sarah by the wame?
Iram, coram, dago.

Is he South or is he North?
Igo and ago,
Or drownèd in the river Forth?
Iram, coram, dago.

Is he slain by Hielan' bodies?
Igo and ago,
And eaten like a wether-haggis? — sheep's haggis
Iram, coram, dago.

Where'er he be, the Lord be near him!
Igo and ago,
As for the deil, he daur na steer him, — dare not disturb
Iram, coram, dago.

But please transmit th' inclosèd letter,
Igo and ago,
Which will oblige your humble debtor,
Iram, coram, dago.

So may ye hae auld stanes in store,
Igo and ago,
The very stanes that Adam bore,
Iram, coram, dago.

So may ye get in glad possession,
Igo and ago,
The coins o' Satan's coronation!
Iram, coram, dago.

[1] Sent with a letter to Adam de Cardonnel, a brother antiquary.

ELECTION BALLAD FOR WESTERHA'.

TUNE—*Up and waur them a'.*

The Laddies by the banks o' Nith
Wad trust his Grace[1] wi' a', Jamie;
But he 'll sair them as he sair'd the king— served
Turn tail and rin awa, Jamie.

Chorus—Up and waur them a', Jamie,[2] baffle
Up and waur them a';
The Johnstones hae the guidin o 't,[3]
Ye turncoat Whigs, awa!

The day he stude his country's friend,
Or gied her faes a claw, Jamie, foes—stroke
Or frae puir man a blessin' wan,
That day the Duke ne'er saw, Jamie.

But wha is he, his country's boast?
Like him there is na twa, Jamie;
There 's no a callant tents the kye boy—herds—cows
But kens o' Westerha', Jamie.

To end the wark, here 's Whistlebirk,[4]
Long may his whistle blaw, Jamie;
And Maxwell true, o' sterling blue;
And we 'll be Johnstones a', Jamie.

[1] William, third Earl of March (born 1725), succeeded his cousin as fourth (and last) Duke of Queensberry in 1778. Almost his whole life he was a patron and supporter of the turf, and was most successful in his speculations. He held the office of lord of the bedchamber to George III. from 1760 till 1789, when he was dismissed because of his supporting the claim of the Prince of Wales. He died in 1810, having possessed a peerage for eighty years.—'Old Q. will ever stand conspicuous in the annals of this country as one who reached the height of notoriety without having done more than one single act worthy of a nation's praise. The much-vaunted contributions to the "Patriotic Fund" excepted, nothing remains.'

[2] 'Up and waur them a', Willie,' is an old Border song.

[3] A Border proverb, significant of the great local power of this family in former times.

[4] Alexander Birtwhistle, merchant at Kirkcudbright, and provost of the burgh. A contemporary chronicle notices him as carrying on a brisk foreign trade from that little port.

THE FIVE CARLINS,

AN ELECTION BALLAD.

The five burghs are here represented in figurative characters: Dumfries, as Maggy by the banks o' Nith; Lochmaben, as Marjory o' the mony Lochs; Annan, as Blinkin Bess of Annandale; Kirkcudbright, as Whisky Jean of Galloway; and Sanquhar, as Black Joan frae Chrichton-Peel.

There was five Carlins in the South, **old women**
  They fell upon a scheme,
To send a lad to London town
  To bring them tidings hame.

Nor only bring them tidings hame,
  But do their errands there;
And aiblins gowd and honor baith **possibly gold**
  Might be that laddie's share.

There was Maggy by the banks o' Nith,
  A dame wi' pride eneugh;
And Marjory o' the mony Lochs,
  A carlin auld and teugh. **tough**

And Blinkin Bess of Annandale,
  That dwelt near Solway-side;
And Whisky Jean, that took her gill,
  In Galloway sae wide.

And Black Joan frae Crichton-Peel,
  O' gipsy kith and kin:
Five wighter Carlins were na found **more powerful**
  The South Countrie within.

To send a lad to London town,
  They met upon a day;
And mony a Knight, and mony a Laird,
  That errand fain wad gae.

O mony a Knight, and mony a Laird,
  This errand fain wad gae;
But nae ane could their fancy please,
  O ne'er a ane but twae.

The first ane was a belted Knight,[1]
  Bred of a Border-band;
And he wad gae to London town,
  Might nae man him withstand.

[1] Sir James Johnston.

And he wad do their errands weel,
  And meikle he wad say; much
And ilka ane about the court every
  Wad bid to him Gude-day.

Then niest cam in a Soger youth,[1] next—soldier
  Wha spak wi' modest grace,
And he wad gae to London town,
  If sae their pleasure was.

He wad na hecht them courtly gifts, promise
  Nor meikle speech pretend;
But he would hecht an honest heart,
  Wad ne'er desert his friend.

Then, wham to chuse and wham refuse,
  At strife thir Carlins fell; these
For some had Gentlefolks to please,
  And some wad please themsel.

Then out spak mim-mou'd Meg o' Nith, prim-mouthed
  And she spak up wi' pride,
And she wad send the Soger youth,
  Whatever might betide.

For the auld Gudeman o' London court[2]
  She didna care a pin;
But she wad send the Soger youth,
  To greet his eldest son.[3]

Then up sprang Bess o' Annandale,
  And a deadly aith she 's ta'en,
That she wad vote the Border Knight,
  Though she should vote her lane: alone

For far-aff fowls hae feathers fair,
  And fools o' change are fain;
But I hae tried this Border Knight,
  And I'll try him yet again.

Says Black Joan frae Crichton-Peel,
  A Carlin stoor and grim, austere
The auld Gudeman, and the young Gudeman,
  For me may sink or swim:

1 Captain Miller. 2 The king. 3 The Prince of Wales.

For fools will prate o' right and wrang,
While knaves laugh them to scorn;
But the Soger's friends hae blawn the best,
So he shall bear the horn.

Then Whisky Jean spak owre her drink,
Ye weel ken, kimmers a', gossips
The auld Gudeman o' London court,
His back 's been at the wa';

And mony a friend that kiss'd his caup
Is now a fremit wight; estranged
But it 's ne'er be said o' Whisky Jean—
We 'll send the Border Knight.

Then slow raise Marjory o' the Lochs,
And wrinkled was her brow,
Her ancient weed was russet gray,
Her auld Scots bluid was true;[1]

There 's some great folk set light by me,
I set as light by them;
But I will send to London town
Wham I like best at hame. Whom

Sae how this weighty plea may end, lawsuit
Nae mortal wight can tell;
God grant the King and ilka man
May look weel to himsel!

THE BLUE-EYED LASSIE.[2]

I gaed a waefu' gate yestreen, road—yester-evening
A gate, I fear, I 'll dearly rue:
I gat my death frae twa sweet een, eyes
Twa lovely een o' bonie blue.
'Twas not her golden ringlets bright,
Her lips, like roses wat wi' dew, wet
Her heaving bosom, lily-white—
It was her een sae bonie blue.

[1] This verse was a favourite with Sir Walter Scott, who used to recite it with good effect.

[2] Jean, the only daughter of Rev. Andrew Jaffray, Lochmaben. This song was printed in Johnson's *Museum*, with an air composed by Riddel of Glenriddel. It was set by George Thomson to the tune of 'The Blathrie o' 't.'

She talk'd, she smil'd, my heart she wyl'd, beguiled
  She charm'd my soul I wist na how;
And ay the stound, the deadly wound, pang
  Cam frae her een sae bonie blue.
But, 'spare to speak, and spare to speed,'[1]
  She'll aiblins listen to my vow: perhaps
Should she refuse, I'll lay my dead death
  To her twa een sae bonie blue.

SKETCH—NEW-YEAR'S DAY.

TO MRS DUNLOP.

  This day, Time winds th' exhausted chain,
To run the twelvemonths' length again:
I see the old, bald-pated fellow,
With ardent eyes, complexion sallow,
Adjust the unimpair'd machine,
To wheel the equal, dull routine.

  The absent lover, minor heir,
In vain assail him with their prayer;
Deaf as my friend, he sees them press,
Nor makes the hour one moment less.
Will you (the Major's[2] with the hounds;
The happy tenants share his rounds;
Coila's fair Rachel's[3] care to-day,
And blooming Keith's engaged with Gray)
From housewife cares a minute borrow—
That grandchild's cap will do to-morrow—
And join with me a-moralizing—
This day's propitious to be wise in.
First, what did yesternight deliver?
'Another year is gone for ever.'
And what is this day's strong suggestion?
'The passing moment's all we rest on!'
Rest on—for what? what do we here?
Or why regard the passing year?
Will Time, amus'd with proverb'd lore,
Add to our date one minute more?

[1] A proverbial expression, meaning 'If you don't speak, you'll never come any speed,' and equivalent to the English 'Faint heart never won fair lady.'

[2] Andrew, *fourth* son of Mrs Dunlop, had passed through the American war, and attained the rank of major. He died, unmarried, in 1804.

[3] Rachel, *fourth* daughter of Mrs Dunlop, was making a sketch of Coila; Keith was Mrs Dunlop's *fifth* daughter.

A few days may—a few years must—
Repose us in the silent dust.
Then, is it wise to damp our bliss?
Yes—all such reasonings are amiss!
The voice of Nature loudly cries,
And many a message from the skies,
That something in us never dies:
That on this frail, uncertain state
Hang matters of eternal weight:
That future-life in worlds unknown
Must take its hue from this alone;
Whether as heavenly glory bright,
Or dark as Misery's woeful night.

Since then, my honor'd first of friends,
On this poor being all depends;
Let us th' important *now* employ,
And live as those who never die.
Tho' you, with days and honors crown'd,
Witness that filial circle round
(A sight life's sorrows to repulse,
A sight pale Envy to convulse),
Others now claim your chief regard;
Yourself, you wait your bright reward.

PROLOGUE FOR MR GEORGE S. SUTHERLAND.

SPOKEN AT THE THEATRE, DUMFRIES, ON NEW-YEAR'S DAY EVENING.

No song nor dance I bring from yon great city,
That queens it o'er our taste—the more 's the pity:
Tho', by the bye, abroad why will ye roam?
Good sense and taste are natives here at home:
But not for panegyric I appear,
I come to wish you all a good New Year!
Old Father Time deputes me here before ye,
Not for to preach, but tell his simple story:
The sage, grave Ancient cough'd, and bade me say,
'You 're one year older this important day,'
If *wiser*, too—he hinted some suggestion,
But 'twould be rude, you know, to ask the question;
And, with a would-be-roguish leer and wink,
Said—'Sutherland, in one word, bid them THINK!'

Ye sprightly youths, quite flush with hope and spirit,
Who think to storm the world by dint of merit,
To you the dotard has a deal to say,
In his sly, dry, sententious, proverb way!
He bids you mind, amid your thoughtless rattle,
That the first blow is ever half the battle;
That tho' some by the skirt may try to snatch him,
Yet by the forelock is the hold to catch him;
That whether doing, suffering or forbearing,
You may do miracles by persevering.

Last, tho' not least in love, ye youthful fair,
Angelic forms, high Heaven's peculiar care!
To you old Bald-pate smooths his wrinkled brow,
And humbly begs you 'll mind the important—NOW!
To crown your happiness he asks your leave.
And offers bliss to give and to receive.

For our sincere, tho' haply weak endeavours,
With grateful pride we own your many favours;
And howsoe'er your tongues may ill reveal it,
Believe our glowing bosoms truly feel it.

MY LOVELY NANCY.[1]

TUNE—*The Quaker's Wife.*

Thine am I, my faithful fair,
  Thine, my lovely Nancy;
Ev'ry pulse along my veins,
  Ev'ry roving fancy.

To thy bosom lay my heart,
  There to throb and languish:
Tho' despair had wrung its core,
  That would heal its anguish.

Take away those rosy lips
  Rich with balmy treasure;
Turn away thine eyes of love,
  Lest I die with pleasure.

[1] This poem was sent to George Thomson in 1793. It has been surmised, therefore, that it was not written till that year, and that the editor of the Clarinda correspondence inserted it, without authority, in place of 'To Mary in Heaven.' In support of this view, however, no reliable evidence has been brought forward.

What is life when wanting love?
Night without a morning:
Love 's the cloudless summer sun
Nature gay adorning.

PROLOGUE FOR MR SUTHERLAND ON HIS BENEFIT-NIGHT.

What needs this din about the town o' Lon'on,
How this new play an' that new sang is comin'?
Why is outlandish stuff sae meikle courted? much
Does nonsense mend, like whisky, when imported?
Is there nae poet, burning keen for fame,
Will try to gie us sangs and plays at hame? give
For Comedy abroad he needna toil,
A fool and knave are plants of every soil;
Nor need he hunt as far as Rome and Greece
To gather matter for a serious piece;
There 's themes enow in Caledonian story enough
Would shew the Tragic Muse in a' her glory.

Is there no daring bard will rise, and tell
How glorious Wallace stood, how, hapless, fell?
Where are the Muses fled that could produce
A drama worthy o' the name o' Bruce?
How here, even here, he first unsheath'd the sword
'Gainst mighty England and her guilty lord;
And after mony a bloody, deathless doing,
Wrenched his dear country from the jaws of ruin!
O for a Shakspeare or an Otway scene
To draw the lovely, hapless Scottish Queen!
Vain all th' omnipotence of female charms
'Gainst headlong, ruthless, mad Rebellion's arms:
She fell, but fell with spirit truly Roman,
To glut the vengeance of a rival woman:
A woman—though the phrase may seem uncivil—
As able and as cruel as the devil!
One Douglas lives in Home's immortal page,[1]
But Douglasses were heroes every age:
And though your fathers, prodigal of life,
A Douglas followed to the martial strife,
Perhaps, if bowls [2] row right, and Right succeeds,
Ye yet may follow where a Douglas leads!

[1] *Douglas, a Tragedy*, by John Home. [2] If bowls (in the game) roll.

As ye hae generous done, if a' the land
Would take the Muses' servants by the hand;
Not only hear, but patronise, befriend them,
And where ye justly can commend, commend them;
And aiblins, when they winna stand the test, perhaps—will not
Wink hard and say 'The folks hae done their best!'
Would a' the land do this, then I'll be caition caution, security
Ye'll soon hae poets o' the Scottish nation
Will gar Fame blaw until her trumpet crack, make
And warsle Time, and lay him on his back! wrestle with

For us and for our stage should ony spier, inquire
'Wha's aught thae chiels maks a' this bustle here?'[1] fellows
My best leg foremost, I'll set up my brow,
We have the honour to belong to you!
We're your ain bairns, e'en guide us as ye like, own children—treat us
But like gude mithers, shore before you strike. warn
And gratefu' still I hope ye'll ever find us,
We've got frae a' professions, sets, and ranks:
God help us! we're but poor—ye'se get but thanks ye shall
For a' the patronage and meikle kindness. much, great

TIBBIE DUNBAR.

TUNE—*Johnny M'Gill.*[2]

O wilt thou go wi' me, sweet Tibbie Dunbar?
O wilt thou go wi' me, sweet Tibbie Dunbar?
Wilt thou ride on a horse or be drawn in a car
Or walk by my side, O sweet Tibbie Dunbar?

I care na thy daddie his lands and his money; I don't care for
I care na thy kin, sae high and sae lordly;
But say thou wilt hae me, for better, for waur, worse
And come in thy coatie, sweet Tibbie Dunbar. in thy petticoat (*i.e.* without dowry)

THE GARDENER WI' HIS PAIDLE.

TUNE—*The Gardener's March.*

When rosy May comes in wi' flowers,
To deck her gay, green-spreading bowers,
Then busy, busy are his hours,
The Gardener wi' his paidle. small hoe

[1] 'To whom do these fellows belong who are making all this bustle here?'—'Wha's aught' means 'who owns.'

[2] The air has been claimed as Irish.

The crystal waters gently fa',
The merry birds are lovers a',
The scented breezes round him blaw,
The Gardener wi' his paidle.

When purple morning starts the hare
To steal upon her early fare,
Then thro' the dews he maun repair, must
The Gardener wi' his paidle.

When day, expiring in the west,
The curtain draws of Nature's rest,
He flies to her arms he lo'es the best,
The Gardener wi' his paidle.

HIGHLAND HARRY.[1]

TUNE—*Highlander's Lament.*

My Harry was a gallant gay,
Fu' stately strade he on the plain;
But now he 's banish'd far away,
I'll never see him back again.

Chorus—O for him back again!
O for him back again!
I wad gie a' Knockhaspie's land
For Highland Harry back again!

When a' the lave gae to their bed, rest
I wander dowie up the glen; sad
I set me down and greet my fill, weep
And ay I wish him back again.

O were some villains hangit high,
And ilka body had their ain! every

[1] Of this song Burns says in the Glenriddel notes: 'The oldest title I ever heard to this air was "The Highland Watch's Farewell to Ireland." The chorus I picked up from an old woman in Dunblane; the rest of the song is mine.' It is evident that the poet has understood the chorus in a Jacobite sense, and written his own verses in that strain accordingly. Peter Buchan has, nevertheless, affirmed 'that the original song related to a love attachment between Harry Lumsdale, the second son of a Highland gentleman, and Mrs Jeanie Gordon, daughter to the Laird of Knockespock, in Aberdeenshire. The lady was married to her cousin, Habichie Gordon, a son of the Laird of Rhynie; and some time after, her former lover having met her and shaken her hand, her husband drew his sword in anger, and lopped off several of Lumsdale's fingers, which Highland Harry took so much to heart that he soon after died.'—See Hogg and Motherwell's edition of Burns, ii. 197.

Then I might see the joyfu' sight,
  My Highland Harry back again.

Sad was the day and sad the hour
  He left me on his native plain,
An' rush'd, his sair-wrang'd Prince to join,
  But oh, he ne'er cam back again!

Strong was my Harry's arm in war,
  Unmatch'd on a' Culloden plain;
But Vengeance mark'd him for his ain,
  For oh, he ne'er cam back again!

O for him back again!
  The auld Stuarts back again!
I wad gie a' my faither's land
  To see them a' come back again.[1]

BEWARE O' BONIE ANN.[2]

AIR—*Ye Gallants Bright.*

Ye gallants bright, I rede you right — advise
  Beware o' bonie Ann;
Her comely face sae fu' o' grace,
  Your heart she will trepan: — steal
Her een sae bright, like stars by night,
  Her skin is like the swan;
Sae jimply lac'd her genty waist, — tightly—lady-like, graceful
  That sweetly ye might span.

Youth, grace and love attendant move,
  And pleasure leads the van:
In a' their charms, and conquering arms,
  They wait on bonie Ann.
The captive bands may chain the hands,
  But love enslaves the man:
Ye gallants braw, I rede you a'
  Beware o' bonie Ann.

[1] The two closing verses do not appear in Johnson's *Museum*. They are given in a MS. of the song—though not in Burns's hand—now in the British Museum.

[2] 'I composed this song out of compliment to Miss Ann Masterton, the daughter of my friend Allan Masterton, the author of the air "Strathallan's Lament" and two or three others [including 'O, Willie brew'd a peck o' maut' *and* 'The Braes o' Ballochmyle'] in this work [*Scots Musical Museum*].'—*Burns.* Ann Masterton married a medical man of the name of Derbishire, who resided first in Bath and subsequently in London.

JOHN ANDERSON, MY JO.[1]

TUNE—*John Anderson, my Jo.*

John Anderson, my jo, John, — love, darling
When we were first acquent,
Your locks were like the raven,
Your bonie brow was brent; — unwrinkled
But now your brow is beld, John, — bald
Your locks are like the snaw;
But blessings on your frosty pow, — white head
John Anderson, my jo.

John Anderson, my jo, John,
We clamb the hill thegither; — climbed
And mony a canty day, John, — happy
We 've had wi' ane anither;
Now we maun totter down, John:
And hand in hand we 'll go,
And sleep thegither at the foot,
John Anderson, my Jo.

THE BATTLE OF SHERRAMOOR.[2]

TUNE—*Cameron Rant.*

'O cam ye here the fight to shun,
Or herd the sheep wi' me, man?
Or were ye at the Sherra-moor,
Or did the battle see, man?'
'I saw the battle, sair and teugh,
And reekin-red ran mony a sheugh; — ditch
My heart, for fear, gae sough for sough,
To hear the thuds, and see the cluds — knocks—clouds
O' Clans frae woods, in tartan duds, — clothes
Wha glaum'd at kingdoms three, man. — grasped

[1] Improved from an old song. Additional verses, by William Reid of Glasgow, appear in *Poetry Original and Selected*, but are worthless.

[2] 'This was written about the time our bard made his tour to the Highlands, 1787.'—*Currie.* Gilbert Burns entertained a doubt if the song was by his brother; but for this scepticism we can see no just grounds. In this instance Burns has pruned and paraphrased a more diffuse song on the same subject, which is understood to have been the composition of Rev. John Barclay (1734-1798), minister of the Church of Scotland, and founder of a small sect called 'Bereans' or 'Barclayites.'

'The red-coat lads, wi' black cockauds,
  To meet them were na slaw, man,
They rush'd and push'd, and blude outgush'd,
  And mony a bouk did fa', man: heavy body
The great Argyle led on his files,
I wat they glanc'd for twenty miles,
They hough'd the Clans like nine-pin kyles, nine-pin pieces
They hack'd and hash'd, while braid-swords clash'd,
And thro' they dash'd, and hew'd and smash'd
  Till fey men died awa, man. doomed

'But had ye seen the philibegs
  And skyrin tartan trews, man, shining, showy—tight-fitting trousers
When in the teeth they dar'd our Whigs
  And covenant Trueblues,[1] man:
In lines extended lang and large,
When baig'nets o'erpower'd the targe, bayonets
And thousands hasten'd to the charge,
Wi' Highland wrath they frae the sheath
Drew blades o' death, till, out o' breath,
  They fled like frighted dows, man.' doves

'Oh how deil, Tam, can that be true? in the devil's name
  The chace gaed frae the north, man;
I saw mysel they did pursue
  The horse-men back to Forth, man;
And at Dunblane, in my ain sight,
They took the brig wi' a their might, bridge
And straught to Stirling wing'd their flight:
But, cursèd lot! the gates were shut;
And mony a huntit, poor Red-coat,
  For fear amaist did swarf, man.' almost—swoon

'My sister Kate cam up the gate
  Wi' crowdie unto me, man; oatmeal porridge
She swoor she saw some rebels run
  Frae Perth and to Dundee, man;
Their left-hand General had nae skill;
The Angus lads had nae gude will
That day their neebors' blude to spill,
For fear, by foes, that they should lose
Their cogs o' brose,[2] they scar'd at blows
  And hameward fast did flee, man.

[1] The Covenanters carried a 'Blue Banner,' and were therefore called 'True blues.'
[2] Basins of hasty-pudding. The phrase was synonymous for means and substance, wealth.

'They 've lost some gallant gentlemen
  Amang the Highland clans, man;
I fear my Lord Panmure is slain,
  Or in his en'mies' hands, man;
Now wad ye sing this double fight,
Some fell for wrang and some for right;
And mony bade the world gude-night;
Say, pell and mell, wi' muskets' knell
How Tories fell and Whigs to hell
  Flew off in frighted bands, man!'

BLOOMING NELLY.[1]

On a bank of flowers, in a summer day,
  For summer lightly drest,
The youthful, blooming Nelly lay,
  With love and sleep opprest;
When Willie, wand'ring thro' the wood,
  Who for her favour oft had sued;
He gaz'd, he wish'd, he fear'd, he blush'd,
  And trembled where he stood.

Her closèd eyes, like weapons sheath'd,
  Were seal'd in soft repose;
Her lip, still as she fragrant breath'd,
  It richer dy'd the rose;
The springing lilies, sweetly prest,
  Wild-wanton, kiss'd her rival breast;
He gaz'd, he wish'd, he fear'd, he blush'd,
  His bosom ill at rest.

Her robes light-waving in the breeze,
  Her tender limbs embrace;
Her lovely form, her native ease,
  All harmony and grace;
Tumultuous tides his pulses roll,
  A faltering, ardent kiss he stole;
He gaz'd, he wish'd, he fear'd, he blush'd,
  And sigh'd his very soul.

[1] The rather 'broad' original of this, by Theobald, finds a place in Ramsay's *Tea-table Miscellany*.

As flies the partridge from the brake
  On fear-inspirèd wings,
So Nelly starting, half-awake,
  Away affrighted springs;
But Willie follow'd—as he should,
  He overtook her in the wood;
He vow'd, he pray'd, he found the maid
  Forgiving all and good.

MY HEART'S IN THE HIGHLANDS.[1]

TUNE—*Failte na Miosg.*[2]

Farewell to the Highlands, farewell to the north,
The birth-place of Valour, the country of Worth;
Wherever I wander, wherever I rove,
The hills of the Highlands for ever I love.

Chorus—My heart 's in the Highlands, my heart is not here;
My heart 's in the Highlands, a-chasing the deer;
A-chasing the wild-deer and following the roe,
My heart 's in the Highlands, wherever I go.

Farewell to the mountains high-cover'd with snow;
Farewell to the straths and green vallies below;
Farewell to the forests and wild-hanging woods;
Farewell to the torrents and loud-pouring floods.

[1] In this song Burns caught up the single streak of poetry which existed in a well-known old stall song entitled 'The Strong Walls of Derry,' and which commences thus:

The first day I landed, 'twas on Irish ground,
The tidings came to me from fair Derry town,
That my love was married, and to my sad wo,
And I lost my first love by courting too slow.

After many stanzas of similar doggerel, the author breaks out, as under an inspiration, with the one fine verse, which Burns used as a basis for his own beautiful ditty:

My heart 's in the Highlands, my heart is not here;
My heart 's in the Highlands a-chasing the deer;
A-chasing the deer, and following the roe—
My heart 's in the Highlands, wherever I go.

[2] It must not be supposed, from the Gaelic names given as tunes for his songs, that Burns or his neighbours in Ayrshire or Dumfriesshire knew that language. Though some kind of Gaelic seems to have been spoken in the extreme south of Ayrshire till the beginning of the eighteenth century, Kyle, Burns's country, and Nithsdale were a part of the old Welsh-speaking kingdom of Strathclyde until 'Lowland Scotch' or northern English established itself there.

THE BANKS OF NITH.

TUNE—*Robie donna Gorach.*

The Thames flows proudly to the sea,
 Where royal cities stately stand ;
But sweeter flows the Nith, to me,
 Where Comyns ance had high command :
When shall I see that honor'd Land,
 That winding Stream I love so dear !
Must wayward Fortune's adverse hand
 For ever, ever keep me here ?

How lovely, Nith, thy fruitful vales,
 Where bounding hawthorns gayly bloom ;
And sweetly spread thy sloping dales,
 Where lambkins wanton through the broom.
Tho' wandering, now, must be my doom,
 Far from thy bonie banks and braes,
May there my latest hours consume,
 Amang the friends of early days !

TAM GLEN.

My heart is a-breaking, dear Tittie, sister
 Some counsel unto me come len', lend
To anger them a' is a pity—
 But what will I do wi' Tam Glen ?

I 'm thinking, wi' sic a braw fellow handsome
 In poortith I might mak a fen': poverty—shift
What care I in riches to wallow,
 If I maunna marry Tam Glen ! mustn't

There 's Lowrie the laird o' Dumeller—
 'Gude-day to you'—brute ! he comes ben :
He brags and he blaws o' his siller— money
 But when will he dance like Tam Glen !

My Minnie does constantly deave me mother—pester
 And bids me beware o' young men :
They flatter, she says, to deceive me,
 But wha can think sae o' Tam Glen !

My daddie says gin I 'll forsake him — if
He 'd gie me gude hunder marks ten:
But, if it 's ordain'd I maun take him, — must
O wha will I get but Tam Glen!

Yestreen at the Valentines' dealing,[1]
My heart to my mou gied a sten; — mouth—bound
For thrice I drew ane without failing,
And thrice it was written 'Tam Glen!'

The last Halloween[2] I was waukin — watching
My droukit sark-sleeve, as she ken, — wet—sleeve of a garment
His likeness cam up the house staukin, — stalking
And the very grey breeks o' Tam Glen![3] — trousers

Come, counsel, dear Tittie! don't tarry;
I'll gie you my bonie black hen
Gif ye will advise me to marry — If
The lad I loe dearly, Tam Glen.

ELEGY ON WILLIE NICOL'S MARE.

Peg Nicholson[4] was a good bay mare
As ever trode on airn; — iron
But now she 's floating down the Nith,
And past the Mouth o' Cairn.[5]

Peg Nicholson was a good bay mare,
And rode thro' thick and thin;
But now she 's floating down the Nith,
And wanting even the skin.

Peg Nicholson was a good bay mare,
And ance she bore a priest;
But now she 's floating down the Nith
For Solway fish a feast.

[1] Distributing sweethearts or valentines by lot.
[2] All-Hallow Eve. [3] See note, *Halloween*, p. 80.
[4] In burlesque allusion, it may be presumed, to the insane woman, Margaret Nicholson, who made an attempt to stab George III. with a knife, August 1786.
[5] Strictly speaking, it is the Cluden and not the Cairn that flows into the Nith at Lincluden. Cairn offered a tempting rhyme, and its use is not absolutely wrong. The Cairn proper, which for a portion of its course forms one of the boundaries of the parish of Dunscore, is joined below a picturesque fall at what is known as Rauten Bridge by the Auld Water of Cluden. Below the confluence the river takes the name of the smaller stream.

Peg Nicholson was a good bay mare,
And the priest he rode her sair:
And much oppressed and bruised she was,
——As priest-rid cattle are.[1]—&c. &c.

WRITTEN TO A GENTLEMAN WHO HAD SENT THE POET A NEWSPAPER, AND OFFERED TO CONTINUE IT FREE OF EXPENSE.

Kind Sir—I've read your paper through,
And faith, to me, 'twas really new!
How guessed ye, Sir, what maist I wanted?
This mony a day I've grain'd and gaunted — groaned—yawned
To ken what French mischief was brewin
Or what the drumlie Dutch were doin; — dull
That vile doup-skelper, Emperor Joseph,
If Venus yet had got his nose off;
Or how the collieshangie works — contention
Atween the Russians and the Turks;[2]
Or if the Swede, before he halt,
Would play anither Charles the Twalt;[3] — Twelfth
If Denmark, any body spak o' 't;
Or Poland, wha had now the tack o' 't; — lease
How cut-throat Prussian blades were hingin; — hanging, dangling
How libbet Italy was singin; — eunuch
If Spaniard, Portuguese or Swiss
Were sayin or takin aught amiss;
Or how our merry lads at hame
In Britain's court kept up the game:
How Royal George, the Lord leuk o'er him!
Was managing St Stephen's quorum;
If sleekit Chatham Will was livin, — smooth Pitt
Or glaikit Charlie got his nieve in; — rash Fox—fist
How daddie Burke the plea was cookin,
If Warren Hastings' neck was yeukin;[4]

[1] Nicol, to whom the mare belonged, had been educated for the Scotch ministry.

[2] Turkey had declared war (1787) against Russia because of arrogant claims by the latter. Austria sided with Russia; the Turks were ultimately defeated and forced to sue for peace (1791).

[3] Gustavus III. had attracted considerable notice in 1789 by his vigorous (though latterly unsuccessful) measures against Russia, and the arrest of many of his nobility who disapproved of his measures.

[4] Itching, as a premonition of death on the gallows.

How cesses, stents and fees were rax'd, rates—taxes—raised
Or if bare a—— yet were tax'd;
The news o' Princes, dukes and earls,
Pimps, sharpers, bawds and opera-girls;
If that daft buckie, Geordie Wales, Prince of Wales
Was threshin still at hizzies' tails; hussies'
Or if he was grown oughtlins douser, any more sedate
And no a perfect kintra cooser: country stallion
A' this and mair I never heard of,
And but for you I might despair'd of:
So, gratefu', back your news I send you,
And pray a' gude things may attend you!

THE GOWDEN LOCKS OF ANNA.

TUNE—*Banks of Banna.*

Yestreen I had a pint o' wine,[1]
A place where body saw na;
Yestreen lay on this breast o' mine
The gowden locks of Anna.

The hungry Jew in wilderness,
Rejoicing o'er his manna,
Was naething to my hiney bliss honey
Upon the lips of Anna.

Ye Monarchs, take the East and West,
Frae Indus to Savannah!
Gie me within my straining grasp,
The melting form of Anna.

There I 'll despise Imperial charms:
An Empress or Sultana,
While dying raptures in her arms,
I give and take with Anna!

Awa, thou flaunting God o' Day!
Awa, thou pale Diana!

[1] Referring to 'Anna'—Anne Park, niece of Mrs Hyslop, landlady of the Globe Tavern, Dumfries—Allan Cunningham writes, 'She was accounted beautiful by the customers at the inn, when wine made them tolerant in matters of taste; and, as may be surmised from the song, had other pretty ways to render herself agreeable to them than the serving of wine.'

Ilk Star, gae hide thy twinkling ray
When I 'm to meet my Anna.

Come in thy raven plumage, Night,
(Sun, Moon and Stars withdrawn a' ;)
And bring an angel-pen to write
My transports wi' my Anna.

POSTSCRIPT.

The Kirk an' State may join an' tell
To do sic things I maunna : mustn't
The Kirk an' State may gae to h——,
And I 'll gae to my Anna.

She is the sunshine o' my e'e,
To live but her I canna ; without
Had I on earth but wishes three,
The first should be my Anna.

I MURDER HATE.[1]

I murder hate by field or flood,
Tho' glory's name may screen us ;
In wars at home I 'll spend my blood,
Life-giving wars of Venus :
The deities that I adore
Are social Peace and Plenty ;
I 'm better pleased *to make one more*,
Than be the death of twenty.

I would not die like Socrates,
For all the fuss of Plato ;
Nor would I with Leonidas ;
Nor yet would I with Cato.
The Zealots of the Church or State
Shall ne'er my mortal foes be,
But let me have bold Zimri's fate,
Within the arms of Cozbi ![2]

[1] The first eight lines of this song, which was inserted by Burns in the Glenriddel volume immediately after 'The Gowden Locks of Anna,' were inscribed by him with a diamond pen on the window-pane of a bedroom in the Globe Tavern.
[2] See Numbers xxv. 8-15.

SECOND EPISTLE TO ROBERT GRAHAM, ESQ., OF FINTRY, ON THE ELECTION FOR THE DUMFRIES STRING OF BOROUGHS, ANNO 1790.

Fintry, my stay in worldly strife,
Friend o' my Muse, Friend o' my Life,
Are ye as idle 's I am?
Come then, wi' uncouth, kintra fleg — country vagary
O'er Pegasus I 'll fling my leg,
And ye shall see me try him.

But where shall I go rin a ride, — run
That I may splatter nane beside? — splash
I wad na be uncivil:
In manhood's various paths and ways
There 's ay some doytin body strays, — stupid person
And *I* ride like the devil.

Thus I break aff wi' a' my birr, — with all my dash
An' down yon dark, deep alley spur,
Where Theologics daunder: — stroll
Alas! curst wi' eternal fogs,
And damn'd in everlasting bogs,
As sure 's the creed I 'll blunder!

I 'll stain a band or jaup a gown[1] — splash
Or rin my reckless, guilty crown
Against the haly door:[2] — holy
Sair do I rue my luckless fate
When, as the Muse an' Deil wad hae 't,
I rade that road before.

Suppose I take a spurt, and mix
Amang the wilds o' Politics—
Elector and elected,
Where dogs at Court (sad sons of bitches!)
Septennially a madness touches,
Till all the land 's infected.

[1] Minister's pulpit-gown and bands.
[2] Burns means that he will attack the clergy.

All hail! Drumlanrig's haughty Grace,
Discarded remnant of a race
Once godlike—great in story;
Thy forbears' virtues all contrasted, forefathers
The very name of Douglas blasted,
Thine that inverted glory!

Hate, envy, oft the Douglas bore,
But thou hast superadded more,
And sunk them in contempt;
Follies and crimes have stain'd the name,
But, Queensberry, thine the virgin claim
From aught that 's good exempt!

I 'll sing the zeal Drumlanrig[1] bears
Who left the all-important cares
Of princes and their darlings;
And, bent on winning borough-towns,
Cam shaking hands wi' wabster-louns, weavers
And kissin barefit carlins. barefooted hussies

Combustion thro' our Boroughs rode,
Whistling his roaring pack abroad
Of mad, unmuzzled lions;
As Queensberry Buff and Blue[2] unfurled,
And Westerha' and Hopetoun[3] hurled
To every Whig defiance.

But cautious Queensberry left the war—
Th' unmanner'd dust might soil his Star,
Besides, he hated *Bleeding*:
But left behind him heroes bright,
Heroes in Cæsarean fight
Or Ciceronian pleading.

O for a throat like huge Mons-Meg,[4]
To muster o'er each ardent Whig
Beneath Drumlanrig's banner!

The Duke of Queensberry ('Old Q') was also Earl of Drumlanrig and Sanquhar.

2 The livery of Fox.

3 James, third Earl of Hopetoun (1741–1817), then one of the sixteen representative peers of Scotland. In 1809 he was created Baron Hopetoun of Hopetoun.

4 A piece of ordnance of extraordinary size (for its time), made in the reign of James IV. of Scotland, about the end of the fifteenth century, and still exhibited in Edinburgh Castle. The diameter of the bore is twenty inches.

Heroes and heroines commix,
All in the field of Politics,
To win immortal honor.

M'Murdo[1] and his lovely spouse
(Th' enamour'd laurels kiss her brows!)
Led on the Loves and Graces:
She won each gaping Burgess' heart,
While he, sub rosa, play'd his part
Among their wives and lasses.

Craigdarroch[2] led a light-arm'd core, corps
Tropes, metaphors and figures pour
Like Hecla streaming thunder:
Glenriddel,[3] skill'd in rusty coins,
Blew up each Tory's dark designs,
And bar'd the treason under.

In either wing two champions fought:
Redoubted Staig,[4] who set at nought
The wildest savage Tory;
While Welsh,[5] who never flinch'd his ground,
High-wav'd his magnum-bonum[6] round
With Cyclopean fury.

Miller[7] brought up th' artillery ranks,
The many-pounders of the Banks,
Resistless desolation!
While Maxwelton,[8] that baron bold,
'Mid Lawson's[9] port entrench'd his hold,
And threaten'd worse damnation.

To these what Tory hosts oppos'd,
With these what Tory warriors clos'd,
Surpasses my descriving:
Squadrons, extended long and large,
With furious speed rush to the charge,
Like furious devils driving.

[1] The Duke's chamberlain.
[2] Alexander Fergusson of Craigdarroch, victor in the Whistle-contest.
[3] Riddel of Glenriddel. [4] The Provost of Dumfries.
[5] Sheriff of the county.
[6] Magnum-bonum is the trade name for a large-sized barrel-pen.
[7] Patrick Miller of Dalswinton, father of the Whig candidate. He had been a banker in Edinburgh.
[8] Sir Robert Lawrie of Maxwelton, M.P. for Dumfriesshire.
[9] Lawson, a local wine-merchant.

What Verse can sing or Prose narrate
The butcher deeds of bloody Fate
Amid this mighty tulyie! conflict
Grim horror girn'd, pale Terror roar'd, scowled
As Murder at his thrapple shor'd, throat—threatened
And Hell mix'd in the brulyie. broil

As Highland craigs by thunder cleft,
When lightnings fire the stormy lift, firmament
Hurl down with crashing rattle;
As flames among a hundred woods,
As headlong foam a hundred floods,
Such is the rage of battle.

The stubborn Tories dare to die;
As soon the rooted oaks would fly
Before th' approaching fellers:
The Whigs come on like ocean's roar
When all his wintry billows pour
Against the Buchan Bullers.[1]

Lo, from the shades of Death's deep night,
Departed Whigs enjoy the fight,
And think on former daring:
The muffled Murtherer of Charles[2]
The Magna Charta flag unfurls—
All deadly gules its bearing. red in blazonry

Nor wanting ghosts of Tory fame:
Bold Scrimgeour[3] follows gallant Graham;[4]
Auld Covenanters shiver!
Forgive! forgive! much-wrong'd Montrose!
Now Death and Hell engulph thy foes,
Thou liv'st on high for ever.

Still o'er the field the combat burns:
The Tories, Whigs, give way by turns;
But Fate the word has spoken:

[1] The 'Bullers of Buchan' is a shaft or well in the rocks on the Aberdeenshire coast, near Peterhead, having an opening to the sea at the bottom. The sea, raging in it at certain states of the tide, gives it the appearance of a pot or boiler; hence the name.

[2] 'Charles I. was executed by a man in a mask.'—*R. B.*

[3] John Scrimgeour, third Viscount Dudhope, fought with Charles II. at Worcester. He was made Earl of Dundee at the Restoration, and died in 1668, without issue, when the title became extinct.

[4] John Graham, the great Marquis of Montrose.

For Woman's wit and strength o' Man,
Alas! can do but what they can—
The Tory ranks are broken.

O that my een were flowing burns! eyes—brooks
My voice, a lioness that mourns
Her darling cubs' undoing!
That I might greet, that I might cry, weep
While Tories fall, while Tories fly
From furious Whigs pursuing!

What Whig but melts for good Sir James—
Dear to his Country, by the names
Friend, Patron, Benefactor!
Not Pulteney's wealth can Pulteney save;[1]
And Hopetoun falls, the generous, brave;
And Stewart, bold as Hector.[2]

Thou, Pitt, shalt rue this overthrow,
And Thurlow growl a curse of woe,
And Melville melt in wailing:
How Fox and Sheridan rejoice!
And Burke shall sing 'O Prince, arise
Thy power is all-prevailing!'

For your poor friend, the Bard, afar
He only hears and sees the war,
A cool Spectator purely!
So, when the storm the forest rends,
The Robin in the hedge descends,
And sober chirps securely.

Now, for my friends' and brethren's sakes,
And for my native Land o' Cakes,
I pray with holy fire:
Lord, send a rough-shod troop o' Hell
O'er a' wad Scotland buy or sell, who would
And grind them in the mire!!!

[1] Sir James Johnstone's younger brother, William (afterwards fifth baronet of Westerhall), had married Frances Pulteney, and through her acquired the vast estates of William Pulteney, Earl of Bath, the eminent statesman. Sir William Johnstone is said to have been one of the richest men in the British Empire on his death in 1805.

[2] Stuart of Hillside.

ELEGY ON CAPTAIN MATTHEW HENDERSON,[1]

A GENTLEMAN WHO HELD THE PATENT FOR HIS HONOURS IMMEDIATELY FROM ALMIGHTY GOD![2]

'Should the poor be flattered?'—SHAKESPEARE.[3]

O Death! thou tyrant fell and bloody!
The meikle devil wi' a woodie — halter
Haurl thee hame to his black smiddie — Drag—smithy
O'er hurcheon hides, — hedgehog
And like stock-fish come o'er his studdie — strike—anvil
Wi' thy auld sides!

He 's gane, he 's gane! he 's frae us torn,
The ae best fellow e'er was born! — one
Thee, Matthew, Nature's sel shall mourn
By wood and wild,
Where, haply, Pity strays forlorn,
Frae man exil'd.

Ye hills, near neebours o' the starns, — stars
That proudly cock your cresting cairns!
Ye cliffs, the haunts of sailing yearns, — eagles
Where Echo slumbers!
Come join ye, Nature's sturdiest bairns, — children
My wailing numbers!

Mourn, ilka grove the cushat kens! — every—wood-pigeon
Ye hazly shaws and briery dens! — hazel coppices
Ye burnies, wimplin down your glens — brooks—winding
Wi' toddlin din,

[1] He is described in the Burial Register of Greyfriars' Church, in the graveyard of which he lies, as 'Captain Matthew Henderson of Tannochside; buried 27th Nov. 1788.' He had on the death of his father, David Henderson, succeeded both to the estate of Tannochside in Lanarkshire and to Tannoch in Ayrshire. Financial embarrassments, however, caused by luxurious living in Edinburgh, compelled him to part with his estates, as well as with certain tenements at the head of Carrubber's Close, Edinburgh, and when Burns knew him his chief means of subsistence was a pension of £300 from Government. In his youth he had served as a lieutenant in the Earl of Home's Regiment, but had obtained a Civil Service appointment of some value, which he held till his retirement. He was fifty-one at the time of his death.

[2] From a copy of the MS. which is now in the possession of Mr A. C. Lamb, of Dundee.

[3] *Hamlet*, Act III. scene ii. line 64.

Or foaming, strang, wi' hasty stens, leaps
Frae lin to lin! cascade

Mourn, little harebells o'er the lea;
Ye stately foxgloves, fair to see;
Ye woodbines, hanging bonilie
In scented bow'rs;
Ye roses on your thorny tree,
The first o' flowers!

At dawn, when ev'ry grassy blade
Droops with a diamond at his head;
At ev'n, when beans their fragrance shed
I' th' rustling gale;
Ye maukins, whiddin thro' the glade; hares—skipping
Come join my wail!

Mourn, ye wee songsters o' the wood;
Ye grouse that crap the heather bud;
Ye curlews, calling thro' a clud; cloud
Ye whistling plover;
And mourn, ye whirring paitrick brood: partridge
He 's gane for ever!

Mourn, sooty coots and speckled teals;
Ye fisher herons, watching eels;
Ye duck and drake, wi' airy wheels
Circling the lake;
Ye bitterns, till the quagmire reels
Rair for his sake! Roar

Mourn, clam'ring craiks, at close o' day, corncrakes, landrails
'Mang fields o' flow'ring clover gay!
And when ye wing your annual way
Frae our cauld shore,
Tell thae far warlds wha lies in clay, those
Wham we deplore.

Ye houlets, frae your ivy bow'r owls
In some auld tree or eldritch tow'r, haunted
What time the moon, wi' silent glow'r, stare
Sets up her horn,
Wail thro' the dreary midnight hour
Till waukrife morn! wakeful

O rivers, forests, hills and plains!
Oft have ye heard my canty strains: cheery
But now, what else for me remains
But tales of woe?
And frae my een the drapping rains eyes
Maun ever flow. Must

Mourn, Spring, thou darling of the year!
Ilk cowslip cup shall kep a tear; Each—catch
Thou, Simmer, while each corny spear
Shoots up its head,
Thy gay, green, flow'ry tresses shear
For him that 's dead!

Thou Autumn, wi' thy yellow hair,
In grief thy sallow mantle tear!
Thou, Winter, hurling thro' the air
The roaring blast,
Wide o'er the naked world declare
The worth we 've lost!

Mourn him, thou Sun, great source of light!
Mourn, Empress of the silent night!
And you, ye twinkling starnies bright, little stars
My Matthew mourn!
For through your orbs he 's taen his flight—
Ne'er to return.

O Henderson! the man! the brother!
And art thou gone, and gone for ever?
And hast thou crost that unknown river,
Life's dreary bound?
Like thee where shall I find another
The world around?

Go to your sculptur'd tombs, ye Great,
In a' the tinsel trash o' state!
But by thy honest turf I'll wait,
Thou man of worth!
And weep the ae best fellow's fate
E'er lay in earth!

THE EPITAPH.

Stop, passenger! my story 's brief,
And truth I shall relate, man:
I tell nae common tale o' grief,
For Matthew was a great man.

If thou uncommon merit hast,
Yet spurn'd at Fortune's door, man;
A look of pity hither cast,
For Matthew was a poor man.

If thou a noble sodger art — soldier
That passest by this grave, man;
There moulders here a gallant heart,
For Matthew was a brave man.

If thou on men, their works and ways,
Canst throw uncommon light, man;
Here lies wha weel had won thy praise,
For Matthew was a bright man.

If thou at Friendship's sacred ca'
Wad life itself resign, man;
Thy sympathetic tear maun fa',
For Matthew was a kind man.

If thou art staunch, without a stain,
Like the unchanging blue, man;
This was a kinsman o' thy ain,
For Matthew was a true man.

If thou hast wit, and fun, and fire,
And ne'er gude wine did fear, man;
This was thy billie, dam and sire, — comrade
For Matthew was a queer man.

If ony whiggish, whingin sot, — peevish
To blame poor Matthew dare, man;
May dool and sorrow be his lot, — grief
For Matthew was a rare man.

But now his radiant course is run,
For Matthew's was a bright one;
His soul was like the glorious sun,
A matchless, Heav'nly light, man.

TAM O' SHANTER:

A TALE.[1]

'Of Brownyis and of Bogillis full is this Buke.'

GAWIN DOUGLAS.

When chapman billies leave the street, — packman fellows
And drouthy neebors neebors meet; — thirsty
As market days are wearing late,
An' folk begin to tak the gate; — road
While we sit bousing at the nappy, — ale
An' gettin fou and unco happy, — full, mellow—very
We think na on the lang Scots miles,[2]
The mosses, waters, slaps, and stiles, — bogs—gaps
That lie between us and our hame,
Whare sits our sulky sullen dame,
Gathering her brows like gathering storm,
Nursing her wrath to keep it warm.

This truth fand honest Tam o' Shanter, — found
As he frae Ayr ae night did canter:
(Auld Ayr, wham ne'er a town surpasses
For honest men and bonny lasses).

O Tam! hadst thou but been sae wise
As taen thy ain wife Kate's advice!
She tauld thee weel thou was a skellum, — rogue
A blethering, blustering, drunken blellum;[3]
That frae November till October
Ae market-day thou was na sober;

1 Gilbert Burns wrote: 'The antiquary and the poet were "unco-pack and thick thegither." Robert requested of Captain Grose, when he should come to Ayrshire, that he would make a drawing of Alloway Kirk, as it was the burial-place of his father, where he himself had a sort of claim to lay down his bones when they should be no longer serviceable to him; and added, by way of encouragement, that it was the scene of many a good story of witches and apparitions, of which he knew the captain was very fond. The captain agreed to the request, provided the poet would furnish a witch story, to be printed along with it. "Tam o' Shanter" was produced on this occasion, and was first published in Grose's *Antiquities of Scotland*.' Grose's *Antiquities* was published in April 1791 with this acknowledgment: 'To my *ingenious* friend Mr Robert Burns I have been variously obligated; he was not only at the pains of marking out what was worthy of notice in Ayrshire, the county honoured by his birth, but he also wrote expressly for the work the *pretty tale* annexed to Alloway Church.'

2 A mile Scots was longer than an English or imperial mile.

3 An idle-talking fellow.

That ilka melder[1] wi' the miller — every
Thou sat as lang as thou had siller; — money
That every naig was ca'd a shoe on — shod
The smith[2] and thee gat roaring fou on;
That at the L—d's house, ev'n on Sunday,
Thou drank wi' Kirkton Jean till Monday.[3]
She prophesy'd that, late or soon,
Thou wad be found deep drown'd in Doon;
Or catch'd wi' warlocks in the mirk — wizards—darkness
By Alloway's auld haunted kirk.

Ah, gentle dames! it gars me greet — makes—weep
To think how mony counsels sweet,
How mony lengthen'd, sage advices
The husband from the wife despises!

But to our tale:—Ae market night,
Tam had got planted unco right;
Fast by an ingle, bleezing finely, — fire
Wi' reaming swats, that drank divinely; — foaming—new ale
And at his elbow, Souter Johnny, — Cobbler
His ancient, trusty, drouthy crony; — thirsty
Tam lo'ed him like a very brither;
They had been fou for weeks thegither.
The night drave on wi' sangs and clatter;
And ay the ale was growing better:
The Landlady and Tam grew gracious
Wi' favours secret, sweet and precious:

[1] 'The quantity of meal ground at the mill at one time.'—JAMIESON.

[2] 'Oct. 22, 1823 [died] at Doonfoot Mill, Mr David Watt, miller, in the sixty-eighth year of his age. He was school-fellow with the celebrated Robert Burns, and the last person baptised in Alloway Kirk.'—*Magazine obituary.* According to local tradition, the name of the miller celebrated in the poem was Hugh Broun, a relative of the poet on the mother's side, and he lived in what is now the farmhouse of Ardlochan, then known as Damhouse. There also, according to the same authority, lived John Niven 'the smith,' who was the first person that manufactured wheel-carts in that part of the district of Carrick—cars or sledges having been previously used, which were dragged over the ground, without the intervention of wheel and axletree.

[3] In Scotland, the village where a parish-church is situated is usually called the Kirkton. A certain Jean Kennedy, who, with her sister Ann, kept a reputable public-house in the village of Kirkoswald, is here alluded to. The author of *The Real 'Souter Johnny,'* says: 'Although, from the way in which she is introduced in the Tale, Jean's character may appear in a doubtful colour, she was notwithstanding, as well as her younger sister, a woman of staid and peaceable habits, and of genteel and respectable exterior. Jean, being the elder sister, had the charge of the "public" department of household duties, so that those "drouthy neebors" who frequented the house regarded it in that light, as hers.' This house was known as 'The Leddies' House,' and is believed to be indicated in the previous line by 'L—d's House,' which met the exigencies of rhythm better than the village nickname.

The Souter tauld his queerest stories;
The landlord's laugh was ready chorus:
The storm without might rair and rustle, roar
Tam did na mind the storm a whistle.

Care, mad to see a man sae happy,
E'en drown'd himself amang the nappy;
As bees flee hame wi' lades o' treasure, loads
The minutes wing'd their way wi' pleasure:
Kings may be blest, but Tam was glorious,
O'er a' the ills o' life victorious!

But pleasures are like poppies spread,
You seize the flow'r, its bloom is shed;
Or like the snow falls in the river,
A moment white—then melts for ever;[1]
Or like the borealis race
That flit ere you can point their place;
Or like the rainbow's lovely form
Evanishing amid the storm.
Nae man can tether time or tide;
The hour approaches Tam maun ride; must
That hour, o' night's black arch the key-stane,
That dreary hour he mounts his beast in;
And sic a night he taks the road in
As ne'er poor sinner was abroad in.

The wind blew as 'twad blawn its last; would have
The rattling show'rs rose on the blast;
The speedy gleams the darkness swallow'd;
Loud, deep, and lang, the thunder bellow'd:
That night a child might understand
The Deil had business on his hand.

Weel mounted on his gray mare, Meg,
A better never lifted leg,
Tam skelpit on thro' dub and mire, rattled—puddle
Despising wind, and rain, and fire;
Whiles holding fast his gude blue bonnet;
Whiles crooning o'er some auld Scots sonnet; humming
Whiles glow'ring round wi' prudent cares gazing
Lest bogles catch him unawares: hobgoblins

[1] Candidior nivibus, tunc cum cecidere recentes,
In liquidas nondum quas mora vertit aquas.
OVID, *Amor*. iii. 5.

Kirk-Alloway was drawing nigh,[1]
Whare ghaists and houlets nightly cry. owls

By this time he was 'cross the ford,
Whare in the snaw the chapman smoor'd; smothered

[1] 'Alloway Kirk, with its little enclosed burial-ground, stands beside the road from Ayr to Maybole, about two miles from the former town. The church has long been roofless, but the walls are pretty well preserved, and it still retains its bell at the east end. Upon the whole, the spectator is struck with the idea that the witches must have had a rather narrow stage for the performance of their revels, as described in the poem. The inner area is now divided by a partition-wall, and one part forms the family burial-place of Mr Cathcart of Blairston. The "winnock-bunker in the east," where sat the awful musician of the party, is a conspicuous feature, being a small window divided by a thick mullion. Around the building are the vestiges of other openings, at any of which the hero of the tale may be supposed to have looked in upon the hellish scene. Within the last few years, the oaken-rafters of the kirk were mostly entire, but they have now been entirely taken away, to form, in various shapes, memorials of a place so remarkably signalised by genius. It is necessary for those who survey the ground in reference to the poem, to be informed that the old road from Ayr to this spot, by which Burns supposed his hero to have approached Alloway Kirk, was considerably to the west of the present one, which, nevertheless, has existed since before the time of Burns. Upon a field about a quarter of a mile to the north-west of the kirk is a single tree enclosed with a paling, the last remnant of a group which covered

"the cairn
Whare hunters fand the murdered bairn;"

and immediately beyond is

"the ford,
Whare in the snaw the chapman smoored"

(namely, a ford over a small burn which soon after joins the Doon)—being two places which Tam o' Shanter is described as having passed on his solitary way. The road then made a sweep towards the river, and, passing a well which trickles down into the Doon, where formerly stood a thorn on which an individual, called in the poem "Mungo's mither," committed suicide, approached Alloway Kirk upon the west. These circumstances may here appear trivial, but it is surprising with what interest any visitor to the real scene will inquire into and behold every part of it which can be associated, however remotely, with the poem of "Tam o' Shanter." The churchyard contains several old monuments, of a very humble description, marking the resting-places of undistinguished persons who formerly lived in the neighbourhood, and probably had the usual hereditary title to little spaces of ground in this ancient cemetery. Among those persons rests William Burness, father of the poet, over whose grave the son had piously raised a small stone, recording his name and the date of his death, together with the short poetical tribute to his memory which is copied in the works of the bard. But for this monument, long ago destroyed and carried away piecemeal, there is now substituted one of somewhat finer proportions. But the churchyard of Alloway has now become fashionable with the dead as well as the living. Its little area is absolutely crowded with modern monuments, referring to persons many of whom have been brought from considerable distances to take their rest in this doubly consecrated ground. Among these is one to the memory of a person named Tyrie, who, visiting the spot some years ago, happened to express a wish that he might be laid in Alloway Churchyard, and, as fate would have it, was interred in the spot he had pointed out within a fortnight. Nor is this all; for even the neighbouring gentry are now contending for departments in this fold of the departed, and it is probable that the elegant mausolea of rank and wealth will soon be jostling with the stunted obelisks of humble worth and noteless poverty.'—*Chambers's Edinburgh Journal*, 1833.

And past the birks and meikle stane — birches—big
Whare drunken Charlie brak 's neck-bane;
And thro' the whins, and by the cairn — gorse—pile of stones
Whare hunters fand the murder'd bairn; — child
And near the thorn, aboon the well, — above
Whare Mungo's mither hang'd hersel.
Before him Doon pours all his floods,
The doubling storm roars thro' the woods;
The lightnings flash frae pole to pole;
Near and more near the thunders roll:
When, glimmering thro' the groaning trees,
Kirk-Alloway seem'd in a bleeze;
Thro' ilka bore the beams were glancing; — every cranny
And loud resounded mirth and dancing.

Inspiring bold John Barleycorn!
What dangers thou canst make us scorn!
Wi' tippenny [1] we fear nae evil;
Wi' usquabae we 'll face the devil! — whisky
The swats sae ream'd in Tammie's noddle,
Fair play, he car'd na deils a boddle.[2]
But Maggie stood right sair astonish'd,
Till, by the heel and hand admonish'd,
She ventur'd forward on the light;
And, vow! Tam saw an unco sight! — in sooth!—marvellous

Warlocks and witches in a dance;
Nae cotillion brent new frae France, — brand-new
But hornpipes, jigs, strathspeys and reels,
Put life and mettle in their heels.
A winnock-bunker in the east, — window-recess
There sat auld Nick, in shape o' beast;[3]

[1] A weak kind of beer, which was sold at 2d. the Scots pint, equal to two quarts.

[2] With fair play, he thought, he didn't care a halfpenny.

[3] 'The origin of this grotesque poetic conceit,' writes Mr James Tennant, Hillend Gardens, Glasgow, great-grandson of 'Auld Glenconner,' 'is as follows: When our great-grandfather was at Corton, Bridge of Doon, a Highland bullock went amissing from one or other of the neighbouring pastures, strayed into the Kirk Yard, passed into the Kirk, could nowhere be found, and went half-mad with hunger. A day or so after, some woman body passing the Kirk looked in and was saluted with a fearful roar, and seeing a pair of huge horns projecting above the seats in which the animal had become entangled, she fled in terror and raised the alarm that the Deil was in the Kirk. My grandfather, who was a youngster of perhaps thirteen or fourteen, was curious to see his "Majesty," and recognising in him the missing bullock, gave the necessary information, and was present when the beast was extricated. Robert Burns was a boy of perhaps eight or ten, and hearing the terrible story of the Kirk being invaded by "Clootie," had it fixed in his mind, and afterwards wove it into the world-known story of "Tam

A towzie tyke, black, grim and large, — shaggy dog
To gie them music was his charge:
He screw'd the pipes and gart them skirl — made—scream
Till roof and rafters a' did dirl. — vibrate
Coffins stood round, like open presses, — cupboards
That shaw'd the dead in their last dresses;
And, by some devilish cantraip sleight, — weird trick
Each in its cauld hand held a light—
By which heroic Tam was able
To note upon the haly table
A murderer's banes, in gibbet-airns; — irons
Twa span-lang, wee, unchristen'd bairns;
A thief new-cutted frae a rape, — from a rope
Wi' his last gasp his gab did gape; — mouth
Five tomahawks wi' blude red-rusted;
Five scymitars wi' murder crusted;
A garter which a babe had strangled;
A knife a father's throat had mangled—
Whom his ain son o' life bereft—
The grey hairs yet stack to the heft; — stuck to the handle
Wi' mair of horrible and awefu',
Which ev'n to name wad be unlawfu'.

As Tammie glowr'd, amaz'd and curious, — stared
The mirth and fun grew fast and furious:
The piper loud and louder blew,
The dancers quick and quicker flew:
They reel'd, they set, they cross'd, they cleekit, — took hands
Till ilka carlin swat and reekit, — witch—steamed
And coost her duddies to the wark, — threw off—clothes
And linket at it in her sark! — set to it—shift

Now Tam, O Tam! had thae been queans, — these—young women
A' plump and strapping in their teens!
Their sarks, instead o' creeshie flannen, — greasy flannel
Been snaw-white seventeen hunder linnen!—[1]

o' Shanter." In taking "Nick" out of the Kirk one of his horns was knocked off and was taken to Corton. When the family removed to Glenconner the horn was brought with them, and was long used as a bolting tube for giving medicine to cattle. Many years after, the sexton and town-crier in Ochiltree (Peter Kennet) being in want of a horn for making the village proclamations, and for blowing through the village in the early morning to waken the villagers—clocks then being few—the old Alloway "Clootie" horn was then given to him, fitted with a silver mouthpiece, and used for years to call up the villagers to their daily work.' The horn passed through various hands, and is now (1901) the property of Sir Charles Tennant.

[1] 'The manufacturer's term for a fine linen, woven in a reed of 1700 divisions.' —CROMEK.

Thir breeks o' mine, my only pair, — These
That ance were plush, o' gude blue hair,
I wad hae gi'en them off my hurdies — buttocks
For ae blink o' the bonie burdies! — birds

But wither'd beldams, auld and droll,
Rigwoodie [1] hags wad spean [2] a foal,
Lowping and flinging on a crummock, — Leaping—stick with a crooked head
I wonder didna turn thy stomach.

But Tam kend what was what fu' brawlie: — quite well
There was ae winsome wench and wawlie, — comely
That night enlisted in the core — corps
(Lang after kend on Carrick shore:
For mony a beast to dead she shot, — death
And perish'd mony a bonny boat,
And shook baith meikle corn and bear, — much barley
And held the country-side in fear).
Her cutty sark, o' Paisley harn, — short shift—coarse linen
That while a lassie she had worn,
In longitude tho' sorely scanty,
It was her best, and she was vauntie.— — proud of it
Ah! little kend thy reverend grannie,
That sark she coft for her wee Nannie, — bought
Wi' twa pund Scots ('twas a' her riches), — 3s. 6d. English
Wad ever grac'd a dance of witches! [3]

But here my Muse her wing maun cour — fold
Sic flights are far beyond her pow'r;
To sing how Nannie lap and flang — leaped—kicked
(A souple jade she was and strang),
And how Tam stood like ane bewitch'd
And thought his very een enrich'd;
Even Satan glowr'd, and fidg'd fu' fain, — gazed and hitched his shoulders in glee
And hotch'd and blew wi' might and main, — squirmed

[1] Usually interpreted as worthy of the gallows; but this is very doubtful. *Rigwoodie* is the chain or rope which crosses the saddle of a horse's harness to support the shafts of a cart; hence it also means *durable, tough, stubborn*, and so may here mean simply *withered, wizened*.

[2] Would wean a foal through sheer fright.

[3] A woman, named Katie Steven or Stein, who lived a solitary life at Laighpark, in the parish of Kirkoswald, and died there in 1816, is thought to have been the personage represented under the character of Cutty-sark. She enjoyed the reputation of being a good fortune-teller, and was rather a favourite guest among her neighbours; yet with others, who knew her less, she was reputed a witch, addicted to the practices described in the poem. She is also said to have been an accomplice of the Carrick smugglers, and to have been a receiver of contraband goods.

G. Pirie.

The carlin claught her by the rump,
And left poor Maggie scarce a stump.

xa

PAGE 347.

Till first ae caper, syne anither, then
Tam tint his reason a' thegither lost—altogether
And roars out 'Weel done, Cutty-sark!'
And in an instant all was dark;
And scarcely had he Maggie rallied,
When out the hellish legion sallied.

As bees bizz out wi' angry fyke, fret
When plundering herds assail their byke; herd-boys—nest
As open pussie's mortal foes, the hare's
When, pop! she starts before their nose;
As eager runs the market-crowd,
When 'Catch the thief!' resounds aloud;
So Maggie runs—the witches follow,
Wi' mony an eldritch skreech and hollow. frightful

Ah, Tam! Ah, Tam! thou 'll get thy fairin! reward, treat
In hell they 'll roast thee like a herrin!
In vain thy Kate awaits thy comin!
Kate soon will be a woefu' woman!
Now, do thy speedy utmost, Meg,
And win the key-stane [1] of the brig; reach
There, at them thou thy tail may toss:
A running stream they dare na cross.
But ere the key-stane she could make,
The fient a tail she had to shake! No tail had she
For Nannie, far before the rest,
Hard upon noble Maggie prest,
And flew at Tam wi' furious ettle: endeavour
But little wist she Maggie's mettle—
Ae spring brought off her master hale, whole
But left behind her ain grey tail:
The carlin claught her by the rump, clutched
And left poor Maggie scarce a stump.

Now, wha this tale o' truth shall read,
Ilk man and mother's son, take heed:
Whene'er to drink you are inclin'd,
Or cutty sarks run in your mind,
Think! ye may buy the joys o'er dear,
Remember Tam o' Shanter's mare.

[1] It is a well-known fact that witches, or any evil spirits, have no power to follow a poor wight any farther than the middle of the next running-stream. It may be proper likewise to mention to the benighted traveller, that when he falls in with *bogles*, whatever danger may be in his going forward, there is much more hazard in turning back.—*B.*

ON THE BIRTH OF A POSTHUMOUS CHILD, BORN IN PECULIAR CIRCUMSTANCES OF FAMILY-DISTRESS.

Sweet flow'ret, pledge o' meikle love — much
And ward o' mony a prayer,
What heart o' stane wad thou na move,
Sae helpless, sweet and fair!

November hirples o'er the lea, — limps
Chill, on thy lovely form;
And gane, alas! the shelt'ring tree
Should shield thee frae the storm!

May He, who gives the rain to pour
And wings the blast to blaw,
Protect thee frae the driving show'r,
The bitter frost and snaw!

May He, the friend of woe and want,
Who heals life's various stounds, — pangs
Protect and guard the mother plant
And heal her cruel wounds!

But late she flourish'd, rooted fast,
Fair on the summer morn,
Now feebly bends she in the blast—
Unshelter'd and forlorn.

Blest be thy bloom, thou lovely gem,
Unscath'd by ruffian hand!
And from thee many a parent-stem
Arise to deck our Land![1]

ELEGY

ON THE LATE MISS BURNET OF MONBODDO.

Life ne'er exulted in so rich a prize
As Burnet, lovely from her native skies;
Nor envious Death so triumph'd in a blow
As that which laid th' accomplish'd Burnet low.

[1] This poem was first published in the *Scots Magazine* for December 1793.

Thy form and mind, sweet Maid, can I forget!
In richest ore the brightest jewel set!
In thee, high Heaven above was truest shown,
As by His noblest work the Godhead best is known.

In vain ye flaunt in summer's pride, ye groves!
 Thou crystal streamlet with thy flowery shore,
Ye woodland choir that chant your idle loves,
 Ye cease to charm: Eliza is no more!

Ye heathy wastes, immix'd with reedy fens;
 Ye mossy streams, with sedge and rushes stor'd;
Ye rugged cliffs, o'erhanging dreary glens,
 To you I fly—ye with my soul accord.

Princes, whose cumbrous pride was all their worth,
 Shall venal lays their pompous exit hail;
And thou, sweet Excellence! forsake our earth
 And not a Muse with honest grief bewail!

We saw thee shine in youth and beauty's pride,
 And Virtue's light, that beams beyond the spheres;
But like the sun eclips'd at morning-tide
 Thou left'st us, darkling in a world of tears.

The Parent's heart that nestled fond in thee,
 That heart how sunk, a prey to grief and care!
So deckt the woodbine sweet yon aged tree;
 So, rudely ravish'd, left it bleak and bare!

LAMENT OF MARY QUEEN OF SCOTS, ON THE APPROACH OF SPRING.

Now Nature hangs her mantle green
 On every blooming tree,
And spreads her sheets o' daisies white
 Out o'er the grassy lea;
Now Phœbus cheers the crystal streams
 And glads the azure skies:
But nought can glad the weary wight
 That fast in durance lies.

Now laverocks wake the merry morn, larks
  Aloft on dewy wing;
The merle, in his noontide bow'r, blackbird
  Makes woodland echoes ring;
The mavis mild wi' many a note thrush
  Sings drowsy day to rest:
In love and freedom they rejoice,
  Wi' care nor thrall opprest.

Now blooms the lily by the bank,
  The primrose down the brae; slope
The hawthorn 's budding in the glen
  And milk-white is the slae: sloe
The meanest hind in fair Scotlànd
  May rove their sweets amang;
But I, the Queen of a' Scotlànd,
  Maun lie in prison strang. Must

I was the Queen o' bonie France,
  Where happy I hae been;
Fu' lightly rase I in the morn,
  As blythe lay down at e'en:
And I 'm the sov'reign of Scotlànd,
  And mony a traitor there!
Yet here I lie in foreign bands
  And never-ending care.

But as for thee, thou false womàn,
  My sister and my fae, foe
Grim vengeance yet shall whet a sword
  That thro' thy soul shall gae! go
The weeping blood in woman's breast
  Was never known to thee,
Nor th' balm that draps on wounds of woe
  Frae woman's pitying e'e.

My son! my son! may kinder stars
  Upon thy fortune shine;
And may those pleasures gild thy reign
  That ne'er wad blink on mine! shine
God keep thee frae thy mother's faes
  Or turn their hearts to thee;
And where thou meet'st thy mother's friend,
  Remember him for me!

O! soon, to me, may summer-suns
  Nae mair light up the morn!
Nae mair to me the autumn winds
  Wave o'er the yellow corn!
And in the narrow house o' death
  Let winter round me rave;
And the next flow'rs that deck the spring
  Bloom on my peaceful grave.

THERE'LL NEVER BE PEACE TILL JAMIE COMES HAME.

By yon castle wa', at the close of the day,
I heard a man sing, tho' his head it was grey;
And as he was singing, the tears down came,—
There 'll never be peace till Jamie comes hame.

The Church is in ruins, the State is in jars,
Delusions, oppressions and murderous wars,
We dare na weel say 't, but we ken wha 's to blame,—
There 'll never be peace till Jamie comes hame.

My seven braw sons for Jamie drew sword,
And now I greet round their green beds in the yerd; earth
It brak the sweet heart of my faithfu' auld dame,—
There 'll never be peace till Jamie comes hame.

Now life is a burden that bows me down,
Sin I tint my bairns and he tint his crown; lost
But till my last moments my words are the same,—
There 'll never be peace till Jamie comes hame.

LAMENT FOR JAMES, EARL OF GLENCAIRN.

The wind blew hollow frae the hills,
  By fits the sun's departing beam
Look'd on the fading yellow woods
  That wav'd o'er Lugar's winding stream:
Beneath a craigy steep, a Bard,
  Laden with years and meikle pain, much
In loud lament bewail'd his lord,
  Whom death had all untimely taen.

He lean'd him to an ancient aik, oak
Whose trunk was mould'ring down with years;
His locks were bleachèd white with time,
His hoary cheek was wet wi' tears;
And as he touch'd his trembling harp,
And as he tun'd his doleful sang,
The winds, lamenting thro' their caves,
To echo bore the notes alang:

'Ye scatter'd birds that faintly sing,
The reliques of the vernal quire!
Ye woods that shed on a' the winds
The honours of the agèd year!
A few short months, and, glad and gay,
Again ye 'll charm the ear and e'e;
But nocht in all revolving time
Can gladness bring again to me.

'I am a bending agèd tree,
That long has stood the wind and rain;
But now has come a cruel blast,
And my last hold of earth is gane:
Nae leaf o' mine shall greet the spring,
Nae simmer sun exalt my bloom;
But I maun lie before the storm, must
And ithers plant them in my room.

'I 've seen sae mony changefu' years,
On earth I am a stranger grown:
I wander in the ways of men,
Alike unknowing and unknown:
Unheard, unpitied, unreliev'd,
I bear alane my lade o' care,
For silent, low, on beds of dust,
Lie a' that would my sorrows share.

'And last, (the sum of a' my griefs!)
My noble master lies in clay;
The flow'r amang our barons bold,
His country's pride, his country's stay:
In weary being now I pine,
For a' the life of life is dead,
And hope has left my agèd ken,
On forward wing for ever fled.

'Awake thy last sad voice, my harp!
The voice of woe and wild despair!
Awake! resound thy latest lay,
Then sleep in silence evermair!
And thou, my last, best, only friend,
That fillest an untimely tomb,
Accept this tribute from the Bard
Thou brought from fortune's mirkest gloom. darkest

'In Poverty's low barren vale,
Thick mists, obscure, involv'd me round;
Though oft I turn'd the wistful eye,
Nae ray of fame was to be found:
Thou found'st me, like the morning sun
That melts the fogs in limpid air:
The friendless Bard and rustic song
Became alike thy fostering care.

'O! why has worth so short a date,
While villains ripen grey with time!
Must thou, the noble, gen'rous, great,
Fall in bold manhood's hardy prime!
Why did I live to see that day—
A day to me so full of woe?
O! had I met the mortal shaft
Which laid my benefactor low!

'The bridegroom may forget the bride
Was made his wedded wife yestreen;
The monarch may forget the crown
That on his head an hour has been;
The mother may forget the child
That smiles sae sweetly on her knee;
But I'll remember thee, Glencairn,
And a' that thou hast done for me!'

LINES SENT TO SIR JOHN WHITEFOORD, BART. OF WHITEFOORD, WITH THE FOREGOING POEM.

Thou, who thy honour as thy God rever'st,
Who, save thy mind's reproach, nought earthly fear'st,
To thee this votive off'ring I impart,
The tearful tribute of a broken heart.

The *Friend* thou valued'st, I the *Patron* lov'd;
His worth, his honour, all the world approved.
We 'll mourn till we, too, go as he has gone,
And tread the shadowy path to that dark world unknown.

THIRD EPISTLE TO ROBERT GRAHAM, ESQ. OF FINTRY.

5th October 1791.

Late crippl'd of an arm, and now a leg;
About to beg a pass for leave to beg;
Dull, listless, teas'd, dejected and deprest
(Nature is adverse to a cripple's rest);
Will generous Graham list to his Poet's wail
(It soothes poor Misery, hearkening to her tale)
And hear him curse the light he first survey'd
And doubly curse the luckless rhyming trade.

Thou, Nature! partial Nature! I arraign;
Of thy caprice maternal I complain:
The lion and the bull thy care have found,
One shakes the forests, and one spurns the ground;
Thou giv'st the ass his hide, the snail his shell;
Th' envenom'd wasp, victorious, guards his cell;
Thy minions kings defend, control, devour,
In all th' omnipotence of rule and power.
Foxes and statesmen subtile wiles ensure;
The cit and polecat stink, and are secure;
Toads with their poison, doctors with their drug,
The priest and hedgehog in their robes, are snug;
Ev'n silly woman has her warlike arts,
Her tongue and eyes—her dreaded spear and darts.

But Oh! thou bitter step-mother and hard,
To thy poor, fenceless, naked child—the Bard!
A thing unteachable in world's skill,
And half an idiot too, more helpless still:
No heels to bear him from the op'ning dun;
No claws to dig, his hated sight to shun;
No horns, but those by luckless Hymen worn,
And those, alas! not Amalthea's horn;
No nerves olfact'ry, Mammon's trusty cur,
Clad in rich Dulness' comfortable fur;

In naked feeling and in aching pride,
He bears th' unbroken blast from ev'ry side:
Vampyre booksellers[1] drain him to the heart,
And scorpion Critics cureless venom dart:

Critics—appall'd, I venture on the name;
Those cut-throat bandits in the paths of fame;
Bloody dissectors, worse than ten Monroes:[2]
He hacks to teach, they mangle to expose.

His heart by causeless wanton malice wrung,
By blockheads' daring into madness stung;
His well-won bays, than life itself more dear,
By miscreants torn, who ne'er one sprig must wear;
Foil'd, bleeding, tortur'd in th' unequal strife,
The hapless Poet flounders on thro' life:
Till, fled each hope that once his bosom fir'd,
And fled each Muse that glorious once inspir'd,
Low sunk in squalid, unprotected age,
Dead, even resentment for his injur'd page,
He heeds or feels no more the ruthless Critic's rage!

So, by some hedge, the gen'rous steed deceas'd,
For half-starv'd snarling curs a dainty feast,
By toil and famine wore to skin and bone,
Lies, senseless of each tugging bitch's son.

O Dulness! portion of the truly blest!
Calm shelter'd haven of eternal rest!
Thy sons ne'er madden in the fierce extremes
Of Fortune's polar frost, or torrid beams.
If mantling high she fills the golden cup,
With sober selfish ease they sip it up:
Conscious the bounteous meed they well deserve,
They only wonder 'some folks' do not starve.
The grave sage hern thus easy picks his frog,
And thinks the Mallard a sad, worthless dog.
When disappointment snaps the clue of hope,
And thro' disastrous night they darkling grope,
With deaf endurance sluggishly they bear,
And just conclude 'that fools are fortune's care.'
So, heavy, passive to the tempest's shocks,
Strong on the sign-post stands the stupid ox.

[1] This, of course, refers to Creech.

[2] Alluding to the eminent anatomist, Professor Alexander Monro, of Edinburgh University.

Not so the idle Muses' mad-cap train;
Not such the workings of their moon-struck brain:
In equanimity they never dwell;
By turns in soaring heav'n or vaulted hell.

I dread thee, Fate, relentless and severe,
With all a poet's, husband's, father's fear!
Already one strong hold of hope is lost:
Glencairn, the truly noble, lies in dust
(Fled, like the sun eclips'd as noon appears,
And left us darkling in a world of tears).
O! hear my ardent, grateful, selfish pray'r!
Fintry, my other stay, long bless and spare!
Thro' a long life his hopes and wishes crown,
And bright in cloudless skies his sun go down!
May bliss domestic smooth his private path;
Give energy to life; and soothe his latest breath,
With many a filial tear circling the bed of death!

POEM ON PASTORAL POETRY.

Hail, Poesie! thou Nymph reserv'd!
In chase o' thee what crowds hae swerv'd
Frae common sense, or sunk enerv'd
'Mang heaps o' clavers; — nonsense
And och! o'er aft thy joes hae starv'd, — too oft thy sweethearts
'Mid a' thy favors!

Say, Lassie: why thy train amang,
While loud the trump's heroic clang,
And sock or buskin skelp alang — move briskly along
To death or marriage,
Scarce ane has tried the shepherd-sang
But wi' miscarriage?

In Homer's craft Jock Milton thrives;
Æschylus' pen Will Shakespeare drives;
Wee Pope, the knurlin, 'till him rives — crooked fellow —clutches
Horatian fame;
In thy sweet sang, Barbauld, survives
Even Sappho's flame.

But thee, Theocritus, wha matches?
They 're no herd's ballats, Maro's catches;[1]
Squire Pope but busks his skinklin patches[2] smartens up—shining, showy
O' heathen tatters:
I pass by hunders, nameless wretches, hundreds
That ape their betters.

In this braw age o' wit and lear, learning
Will nane the Shepherd's whistle mair more
Blaw sweetly in its native air
And rural grace;
And wi' the far-fam'd Grecian share
A rival place?

Yes! there is ane: a Scottish callan! lad
There 's ane: come forrit, honest Allan! forward
Thou need na jouk behint the hallan, crouch behind the partition
A chiel sae clever; fellow
The teeth o' time may gnaw Tantallan,[3]
But thou 's for ever.

Thou paints auld Nature to the nines,
In thy sweet Caledonian lines;
Nae gowden stream thro' myrtles twines, winds
Where Philomel,
While nightly breezes sweep the vines,
Her griefs will tell!

In gowany glens thy burnie strays daisy-clothed—brooklet
Where bonnie lasses bleach their claes, clothes
Or trots by hazelly shaws and braes slopes
Wi' hawthorns gray,
Where blackbirds join the shepherd's lays
At close o' day.

Thy rural loves are nature's sel; self
Nae bombast spates o' nonsense swell; floods
Nae snap conceits, but that sweet spell
O' witchin love,
That charm that can the strongest quell,
The sternest move.

1 Virgil's *Eclogues* are not the ballads or songs of real shepherds.
2 Cf. *purpurei panni*, 'purple patches.'
3 A massive castle near North Berwick.

SENSIBILITY.

Sweet Sensibility how charming,
  Thou, my Friend, canst truly tell;
But how Distress, with horrors arming!
  Thou, Alas! hast known too well!

Fairest Flower, behold the lily,
  Blooming in the sunny ray:
Let the blast sweep o'er the valley,
  See it prostrate on the clay.

Hear the Woodlark charm the forest,
  Telling o'er his little joys:
But, Alas! a prey the surest
  To each pirate of the skies.

Dearly bought the hidden treasure
  Finer Feelings can bestow:
Chords that vibrate sweetest pleasure
  Thrill the deepest notes of woe.

ADDRESS TO THE SHADE OF THOMSON,

ON CROWNING HIS BUST AT EDNAM, ROXBURGHSHIRE, WITH BAYS.

While virgin Spring by Eden's flood
  Unfolds her tender mantle green,
Or pranks the sod in frolic mood,
  Or tunes Eolian strains between;

While Summer, with a matron grace,
  Retreats to Dryburgh's cooling shade,
Yet oft, delighted, stops to trace
  The progress of the spikey blade;

While Autumn, benefactor kind,
  By Tweed erects his agèd head,
And sees, with self-approving mind,
  Each creature on his bounty fed;

While maniac Winter rages o'er
  The hills whence classic Yarrow flows,

Rousing the turbid torrent's roar,
Or sweeping, wild, a waste of snows:

So long, sweet Poet of the Year!
Shall bloom that wreath thou well has won;
While Scotia, with exulting tear,
Proclaims that THOMSON was her son.

LOVELY DAVIES.[1]

TUNE—*Miss Muir.*

O how shall I, unskilfu', try
The Poet's occupation?
The tunefu' powers, in happy hours,
That whispers inspiration,
Even they maun dare an effort mair
Than aught they ever gave us,
Or they rehearse, in equal verse, Ere
The charms o' lovely Davies.

Each eye, it cheers when she appears,
Like Phebus in the morning,
When past the show'r, and every flower
The garden is adorning:
As the wretch looks o'er Siberia's shore,
When winter-bound the wave is;
Sae droops our heart when we maun part
Frae charming, lovely Davies.

Her smile 's a gift frae 'boon the lift, sky
That maks us mair than princes;
A scepter'd hand, a king's command,
Is in her darting glances:
The man in arms 'gainst female charms,
Even he her willing slave is;
He hugs his chain, and owns the reign
Of conquering, lovely Davies.

[1] Deborah Davies, a beautiful *petite* young Englishwoman, was a relative of the Riddels, and connected by the marriage of a sister with the family of Kenmure in Kirkcudbrightshire. Burns afterwards celebrated Miss Davies still more effectively in a much finer and more tender song, 'The Bonie Wee Thing,' which has had the good fortune to be associated with one of the most beautiful of Scottish airs.

My Muse to dream of such a theme,
Her feeble powers surrender;
The eagle's gaze alone surveys
The sun's meridian splendor:
I wad in vain essay the strain,
The deed too daring brave is;
I'll drop the lyre, and mute, admire
The charms o' lovely Davies.

THE BONIE WEE THING.

TUNE—*Bonnie Wee Thing.*

Wishfully I look and languish
In that bonie face o' thine;
And my heart it stounds wi' anguish — throbs
Lest my wee thing be na mine.

Chorus—Bonie wee thing, cannie wee thing, — dainty
Lovely wee thing, was thou mine;
I wad wear thee in my bosom,
Lest my jewel I should tine. — lose

Wit and Grace and Love and Beauty,
In ae constellation shine; — one
To adore thee is my duty,
Goddess o' this soul o' mine!

A FRAGMENT:

ON GLENRIDDEL'S FOX BREAKING HIS CHAIN.[1]

Thou, Liberty, thou art my theme:
Not such as idle Poets dream
Who trick thee up a Heathen goddess
That a fantastic cap and rod has:
Such stale conceits are poor and silly;
I paint thee out, a Highland filly,
A sturdy, stubborn, handsome dapple,
As sleek 's a mouse, as round 's an apple,
That when thou pleasest can do wonders;
But when thy luckless rider blunders,

[1] The only MS. of this known to exist is the Glenriddel MS. at Liverpool.

Or if thy fancy should demur there,
Wilt break thy neck ere thou go further.

These things premis'd, I sing a fox
Was caught among his native rocks
And to a dirty kennel chained—
How he his liberty regained.

Glenriddel, a Whig without a stain,
A Whig in principle and grain,
Could'st thou enslave a free-born creature,
A native denizen of nature?
How could'st thou, with a heart so good
(A better ne'er was sluiced with blood),
Nail a poor devil to a tree,
That ne'er did harm to thine or thee?

The staunchest Whig Glenriddel was,
Quite frantic in his country's cause;
And oft was Reynard's prison passing,
And with his brother-Whigs canvassing
The Rights of Men, the Powers of Women,
With all the dignity of Freemen.

Sir Reynard daily heard debates
Of Princes', kings' and Nations' fates;
With many rueful, bloody stories
Of tyrants, Jacobites and Tories:
From liberty how angels fell
That now are galley-slaves in hell;
How Nimrod first the trade began
Of binding Slavery's chains on man;
How fell Semiramis, G—d d—mn her![1]
Did first, with sacrilegious hammer,
(All ills till then were trivial matters!)
For Man dethroned forge hen-peck fetters;
How Xerxes, that abandoned Tory,
Thought cutting throats was reaping glory,
Until the stubborn Whigs of Sparta
Taught him great Nature's Magna Charta;
How mighty Rome her fiat hurl'd
Resistless o'er a bowing world,

[1] Semiramis, queen of Ninus, and with him a fabled founder of the Assyrian empire, was said to have obtained leave from her husband to rule for five days; and having obtained supreme power, cast the unlucky Ninus into prison, or, according to another story, put him to death. At any rate, her subsequent fame threw that of Ninus into the shade.

And kinder than they did desire,
Polished mankind with sword and fire;
With much, too tedious to relate,
Of Ancient and of Modern date,
But ending, still, how Billy Pitt,
(Unlucky boy!) with wicked wit,
Has gagg'd old Britain, drained her coffer,
As butchers bind and bleed a heifer.

Thus wily Reynard, by degrees,
In kennel listening at his ease,
Suck'd in a mighty stock of knowledge,
As much as some folks at a college:
Knew Britain's rights and constitution,
Her aggrandisement, diminution,
How fortune wrought us good from evil;
Let no man, then, despise the devil,
As who should say, 'I ne'er can need him,'
Since we to scoundrels owe our freedom.

* * * * *

TO JOHN MAXWELL, ESQ., OF TERRAUGHTY, ON HIS BIRTHDAY.

Health to the Maxwells' vet'ran Chief!
Health, ay unsour'd by care or grief:
Inspir'd, I turn'd Fate's sibyl leaf,
This natal morn,
I see thy life is stuff o' prief, — proof
Scarce quite half-worn:

This day thou metes threescore eleven,
And I can tell that bounteous Heaven
(The second sight, ye ken, is given — know
To ilka Poet) — every
On thee a tack o' seven times seven — term, lease
Will yet bestow it.

If envious buckies view wi' sorrow — gallants
Thy lengthen'd days on this blest morrow,
May Desolation's lang-teeth'd harrow,
Nine miles an hour,
Rake them, like Sodom and Gomorrah,
In brunstane stoure. — brimstone dust

But for thy friends, and they are mony,
Baith honest men and lasses bonie,
May couthie Fortune, kind and cannie, comfortable—frugal
In social glee,
Wi' mornings blythe and e'enings funny
Bless them and thee!

Fareweel, auld birkie! Lord be near ye, good fellow
And then the Deil, he daurna steer ye: dare not touch
Your friends ay love, your faes ay fear ye,
For me, shame fa' me, befall
If neist my heart I dinna wear ye next
While BURNS they ca' me.

SONG.

TUNE—*Rory Dall's Port.*

Ae fond kiss, and then we sever; One
Ae fareweel, and then for ever!
Deep in heart-wrung tears I'll pledge thee,
Warring sighs and groans I'll wage[1] thee.

Who shall say that Fortune grieves him
While the star of hope she leaves him?
Me, nae cheerful twinkle lights me:
Dark despair around benights me.

I'll ne'er blame my partial fancy,
Naething could resist my Nancy:
But to see her was to love her;
Love but her, and love for ever.

Had we never lov'd sae kindly!
Had we never lov'd sae blindly!
Never met—or never parted,
We had ne'er been broken-hearted.

Fare-thee-weel, thou first and fairest!
Fare-thee-weel, thou best and dearest!
Thine be ilka joy and treasure, every
Peace, Enjoyment, Love and Pleasure!

[1] 'Wage' is here obviously used with the archaic sense, *stake, pledge.* The old dramatists were partial to this usage of the word. The fourth stanza of this song was placed by Byron at the head of his poem, 'The Bride of Abydos.'

Ae fond kiss, and then we sever!
Ae fareweel, Alas, for ever!
Deep in heart-wrung tears I 'll pledge thee,
Warring sighs and groans I 'll wage thee.

SONG.

To an old Scots tune.

Behold the hour, the boat, arrive!
My dearest Nancy, Oh, fareweel!
Sever'd frae thee can I survive,
Frae thee wham I hae lov'd sae weel!
Endless and deep shall be my grief,
Nae ray o' comfort shall I see
But this most precious, dear belief:
That thou wilt still remember me!

Alang the solitary shore
Where fleeting sea-fowl round me cry,
Across the rolling, dashing roar,
I'll westward turn my wistful eye:
'Happy, thou Indian grove,' I'll say,
'Where now my Nancy's path shall be!
While thro' your sweets she holds her way,
O tell me does she muse on me!!!'

SONG.

To a charming plaintive Scots air.

Ance mair I hail thee, thou gloomy December! Once more
Ance mair I hail thee wi' sorrow and care:
Sad was the parting thou makes me remember,
Parting wi' Nancy, Oh, ne'er to meet mair!

Fond lovers' parting is sweet, painful pleasure,
Hope beaming mild on the soft parting hour,
But the dire feeling, Oh, farewell for ever!
Anguish unmingled and agony pure!

Wild as the winter now tearing the forest,
Till the last leaf o' the summer is flown,
Such is the tempest has shaken my bosom,
Since my last hope and last comfort is gone!

Still as I hail thee, thou gloomy December,
Still shall I hail thee wi' sorrow and care,
For sad was the parting thou makes me remember,
Parting wi' Nancy, Oh, ne'er to meet mair!

SONG OF DEATH.[1]

Scene—A Field of Battle—Time of the day, evening—The wounded and dying of the victorious army are supposed to join in this song.

AIR—*Oran an Aoig.*

Farewell, thou fair day, thou green earth and ye skies,
Now gay with the broad-setting sun!
Farewell, loves and friendships, ye dear, tender ties!
Our race of existence is run.
Thou grim king of terrors, thou life's gloomy foe,
Go, frighten the coward and slave!
Go, teach them to tremble, fell tyrant! but know
No terrors hast thou to the Brave!

Thou strik'st the dull peasant, he sinks in the dark,
Nor saves e'en the wreck of a name;
Thou strik'st the young hero, a glorious mark!
He falls in the blaze of his fame.
In the field of proud Honor, our swords in our hands,
Our king and our country to save,
While victory shines on life's last ebbing sands,
O! who would not die with the Brave!

O MAY, THY MORN WAS NE'ER SAE SWEET.

O May, thy morn was ne'er sae sweet
As the mirk night o' December! dark
For sparkling was the rosy wine,
And secret was the chamber;
And dear was she I dare na name,
But I will ay remember;
And dear was she I dare na name,
But I will ay remember.

[1] 'The circumstance that gave rise to these verses was—looking over with a musical friend M'Donald's collection of Highland airs, I was struck with one, an Isle of Skye tune, entitled "Oran an Aoig," or "The Song of Death," to the measure of which I have adapted my stanzas.'—*B.*

And here 's to them that, like oursel,
Can push about the jorum! liquor
And here 's to them that wish us weel:
May a' that 's gude watch o'er them!
And here 's to them, we dare na tell,
The dearest o' the quorum!
And here 's to them, we dare na tell,
The dearest o' the quorum!

MY NANIE'S AWA.

TUNE—*There 'll never be peace till Jamie comes hame.*

Now in her green mantle blythe Nature arrays,
And listens the lambkins that bleat o'er the braes, slopes
While birds warble welcome in ilka green shaw;
But to me it 's delightless—my Nanie 's awa.

The snawdrap and primrose our woodlands adorn,
And violets bathe in the weet o' the morn:
They pain my sad bosom, sae sweetly they blaw,
They mind me o' Nanie—and Nanie 's awa.

Thou lav'rock that springs frae the dews of the lawn lark
The shepherd to warn o' the grey-breaking dawn,
And thou mellow mavis that hails the night-fa', thrush
Give over for pity—my Nanie 's awa.

Come Autumn, sae pensive, in yellow and grey,
And soothe me wi' tidings o' Nature's decay:
The dark, dreary Winter and wild-driving snaw
Alane can delight me—now Nanie 's awa.

WANDERING WILLIE.

Here awa, there awa, wandering Willie,
Now tired with wandering, haud awa hame; make for home
Come to my bosom, my ae only dearie,
And tell me thou bring'st me my Willie the same.

Loud blew the cauld winter winds at our parting;
It was na the blast brought the tear in my e'e:
Now welcome the simmer, and welcome my Willie,
The simmer to nature, my Willie to me.

Ye hurricanes, rest in the cave o' your slumbers!
O how your wild horrors a lover alarms!
Awaken ye breezes! row gently ye billows! roll
And waft my dear laddie ance mair to my arms.

But if he 's forgotten his faithfullest Nannie,
O still flow between us, thou wide-roaring main;
May I never see it, may I never trow it,
But, dying, believe that my Willie 's my ain![1] own

THE DEIL'S AWA WI' TH' EXCISEMAN.[2]

TUNE—*The Looking-glass.*

The deil cam fiddlin thro' the town,
And danc'd awa wi' th' Exciseman;
And ilka wife cries 'Auld Mahoun,[3] every
I wish you luck o' the prize, man.'

Chorus—The deil 's awa, the deil 's awa,
The deil 's awa wi' th' Exciseman,
He 's danc'd awa, he 's danc'd awa,
He 's danc'd awa wi' th' Exciseman.

We 'll mak our maut and we 'll brew our drink,
We 'll laugh, sing and rejoice, man!
And mony braw thanks to the meikle black deil hearty—big
That danc'd awa wi' th' Exciseman.

There 's threesome reels, there 's foursome reels,
There 's hornpipes and strathspeys, man,
But the ae best dance e'er cam to the Land
Was 'The deil 's awa wi' th' Exciseman.'

1 This song appears to have had a prototype in an old one of which two stanzas have been preserved:

Here awa, there awa, here awa, Willie,
Here awa, there awa, here awa hame;
Lang have I sought thee, dear have I bought thee,
Now I hae gotten my Willie again.

Through the lang muir I have followed my Willie,
Through the lang muir I have followed him hame,
Whatever betide us, nought shall divide us,
Love now rewards all my sorrow and pain.

2 The song is supposed to be sung by smugglers and their sympathisers.

3 An old form of *Mahomet*, identified with the devil.

BONIE LESLEY.[1]

O saw ye bonie Lesley
As she gaed o'er the Border?
She 's gane, like Alexander,
To spread her conquests farther!

To see her is to love her,
And love but her for ever:
For Nature made her what she is,
And never made anither!

Thou art a queen, fair Lesley,
Thy subjects, we before thee;
Thou art divine, fair Lesley,
The hearts o' men adore thee.

The Deil he could na scaith thee — harm
Or aught that wad belang thee: — should belong to
He 'd look into thy bonie face
And say—'I canna wrang thee!'

The Powers aboon will tent thee, — above—watch
Misfortune sha'na steer thee: — shall not molest
Thou 'rt like themsel' sae lovely
That ill they 'll ne'er let near thee.

Return again, fair Lesley,
Return to Caledonie!
That we may brag we hae a lass
There 's nane again sae bonie!

CRAIGIEBURN WOOD.[2]

Sweet closes the evening on Craigieburn wood,
And blythely awaukens the morrow;
But the pride of the spring in the Craigieburn wood
Can yield me nothing but sorrow.

[1] Miss Lesley Baillie became Mrs Robert Cumming of Logie in 1799, and died in Edinburgh, July 1843.

[2] 'This song was composed on a passion which a Mr Gillespie, a particular friend of mine, had for a Miss Lorimer, afterwards Mrs Whelpdale. The young lady was born at Craigieburn wood. The chorus is part of an old foolish ballad.' —*R. B. in Glenriddel Notes.*

Chorus—Beyond thee, dearie, beyond thee, dearie, Beyond=Beside
And O! to be lying beyond thee,
O sweetly, soundly, weel may he sleep
That 's laid in the bed beyond thee!

I see the spreading leaves and flowers,
I hear the wild birds singing;
But pleasure they hae nane for me,
While care my heart is wringing.

I can na tell, I maun na tell, must
I daur na for your anger; dare
But secret love will break my heart
If I conceal it langer.

I see thee gracefu', straight and tall,
I see thee sweet and bonie;
But Oh, what will my torments be
If thou refuse thy Johnie!

To see thee in another's arms,
In love to lie and languish,
'Twad be my dead, that will be seen, death
My heart wad brust wi' anguish.

But, Jeanie, say thou will be mine,
Say thou loes nane before me;
And a' my days o' life to come
I 'll gratefully adore thee.

FRAE THE FRIENDS AND LAND I LOVE.[1]

AIR—*Carron Side.*

Frae the friends and Land I love,
Driv'n by Fortune's felly spite;
Frae my best Belov'd I rove,
Never mair to taste delight: more
Never mair maun hope to find must
Ease frae toil, relief frae care;
When Remembrance wracks the mind,
Pleasures but unvail despair.

[1] 'Burns says of this song in his *Glenriddel Notes*: "I added the last four lines by way of giving a turn to the theme of the poem, such as it is." The whole song, however, is in his own handwriting, and I have reason to believe it is all his own.'—*Stenhouse.*

Brightest climes shall mirk appear, dark
  Desert ilka blooming shore, every
Till the Fates, nae mair severe,
  Friendship, Love and Peace restore.
Till Revenge, wi' laurell'd head,
  Bring our Banished hame again;
And ilk loyal, bonie lad each
  Cross the seas and win his ain. recover—own

O MEIKLE THINKS MY LUVE O' MY BEAUTY.[1]

TUNE—*My Tocher's the Jewel.*

O meikle thinks my Luve o' my beauty, much
  And meikle thinks my Luve o' my kin;
But little thinks my Luve, I ken brawlie know well
  My tocher 's the jewel has charms for him. dowry
It 's a' for the apple he 'll nourish the tree,
  It 's a' for the hiney he 'll cherish the bee,
My laddie 's sae meikle in love wi' the siller, money
  He canna hae luve to spare for me.

Your proffer o' luve 's an airle-penny, earnest money
  My tocher 's the bargain ye wad buy;
But an ye be crafty, I am cunnin, if
  Sae ye wi' anither your fortune may try.
Ye 're like to the timmer o' yon rotten wood,
  Ye 're like to the bark o' yon rotten tree,
Ye 'll slip frae me like a knotless thread,
  And ye 'll crack your credit wi' mae nor me. more than

WHAT CAN A YOUNG LASSIE DO WI' AN AULD MAN?[2]

TUNE—*What can a Young Lassie do wi' an Auld Man?*

What can a young lassie, what shall a young lassie,
  What can a young lassie do wi' an auld man?
Bad luck on the penny that tempted my minnie mother
  To sell her poor Jenny for siller an' lan'! money

[1] Although this song is ascribed to Burns in the *Museum*, the fifth and sixth lines of the first stanza and the four closing lines are old.

[2] Below the MS. of this song, which is in the British Museum, the author has noted the following directions to Johnson: 'Dr Blacklock's set of the tune is bad: I here enclose a better. You may put Dr B.'s song after these verses or you may leave it out, as you please. It has some merit; it is miserably long.'

Bad luck on the penny that tempted my minnie
To sell her poor Jenny for siller an' lan'!

He 's always compleenin frae mornin to e'enin,
He hoasts and he hirples the weary day lang; coughs—limps
He 's doylt and he 's dozin, his blude it is frozen,— worn-out—dull-witted
O dreary 's the night wi' a crazy auld man!
He 's doylt and he 's dozin, his blude it is frozen,—
O dreary 's the night wi' a crazy auld man!

He hums and he hankers, he frets and he cankers,[1]
I never can please him, do a' that I can;
He 's peevish, and jealous o' a' the young fellows,—
O, dool on the day I met wi' an auld man! woe
He 's peevish and jealous o' a' the young fellows,—
O, dool on the day I met wi' an auld man!

My auld auntie Katie upon me taks pity,
I 'd do my endeavour to follow her plan;
I 'll cross him and wrack him until I heart-break him,
And then his auld brass will buy me a new pan.
I 'll cross him and wrack him until I heart-break him,
And then his auld brass will buy me a new pan.[2]

HOW CAN I BE BLITHE AND GLAD?[3]

TUNE—*The Bonny Lad that 's far awa.*

O how can I be blythe and glad,
Or how can I gang brisk and braw, well clad
When the bonie lad that I loe best
Is o'er the hills and far awa!

It 's no the frosty winter wind,
It 's no the driving drift and snaw;
But ay the tear comes in my e'e,
To think on him that 's far awa.

My father pat me frae his door,
My friends they hae disown'd me a';
But I hae ane will tak my part,
The bonie lad that 's far awa.

[1] He is sullen and restless, fretful and peevish.
[2] This phrase is borrowed from the old song 'Auld Rob Morris.'
[3] 'He took the first line, and even some hints of his verses, from an old song in Herd's collection, which begins, "How can I be blithe or glad, or in my mind contented be?"'—*Stenhouse.* The song at once suggests Jean Armour's treatment by her family.

A pair o' glooves he bought to me,
And silken snoods he gae me twa; hair-ribbons
And I will wear them for his sake,
The bonie lad that 's far awa.

O weary winter soon will pass
And spring will cleed the birken shaw;[1] clothe
And my young babie will be born,
And he 'll be hame that 's far awa.

I DO CONFESS THOU ART SAE FAIR.[2]

I do confess thou art sae fair
I wad been o'er the lugs in luve— ears
Had I na found the slightest prayer
That lips could speak thy heart could muve.
I do confess thee sweet, but find
Thou art sae thriftless o' thy sweets—
Thy favours are the silly wind
That kisses ilka thing it meets. every

See yonder rosebud, rich in dew,
Amang its native briers sae coy,
How sune it tines its scent and hue soon—loses
When pu'd and worn a common toy! pulled
Sic fate ere lang shall thee betide: Such
Tho' thou may gayly bloom a while,
Yet sune thou shalt be thrown aside
Like ony common weed and vile.

YON WILD MOSSY MOUNTAINS.

TUNE—*Yon Wild Mossy Mountains.*[3]

Yon wild, mossy mountains sae lofty and wide
That nurse in their bosom the youth o' the Clyde,

[1] 'Birken shaw' = a piece of land at the foot of a hill, and covered with birches.

[2] Altered into Scots by Burns, from an English poem by Sir Robert Aytoun, private secretary to Mary and Anne, Queens of Scotland. 'I do think I have improved the simplicity of the sentiments by giving them a Scots dress.—R. B.'

[3] 'This tune is by Oswald: the song alludes to a part of my private history which it is of no consequence to the world to know.'—*Burns in Glenriddel Notes.* Highland Mary has been claimed as the heroine of this song. But it may refer to one of Burns's mysterious excursions to Lanarkshire in 1787.

Where the grouse lead their coveys thro' the heather to feed,
And the shepherd tents his flock as he pipes on his reed: watches

Not Gowrie's rich valley nor Forth's sunny shores
To me hae the charms o' yon wild, mossy moors;
For there, by a lanely, sequesterèd stream,
Resides a sweet Lassie, my thought and my dream.

Amang thae wild mountains shall still be my path, those
Ilk stream foaming down its ain green, narrow strath, Every—valley
For there, wi' my Lassie, the day-lang I rove,
While o'er us, unheeded, flie the swift hours o' Love.

She is not the fairest, altho' she is fair;
O' nice education but sma' is her share;
Her parentage humble as humble can be;
But I loe the dear Lassie because she loes me.

To Beauty what man but maun yield him a prize, must
In her armour of glances, and blushes, and sighs;
And when Wit and Refinement hae polish'd her darts,
They dazzle our e'en as they flie to our hearts.

But Kindness, sweet Kindness, in the fond-sparkling e'e
Has lustre outshining the diamond to me;
And the heart beating love as I'm clasp'd in her arms,
O, these are my Lassie's all-conquering charms.

O FOR ANE AN' TWENTY, TAM.[1]

TUNE—*The Moudiewort.*

They snool me sair and haud me down, snub—hold
And gar me look like bluntie, Tam; make—a stupid
But three short years will soon wheel roun',
And then comes ane and twenty, Tam.

[1] 'The subject of this song had a real origin: a young girl having been left some property by a near relation, and at her own disposal on her attaining majority, was pressed by her relations to marry an old rich booby. Her affections, however, had previously been engaged by a young man, to whom she had pledged her troth when she should become of age, and she of course obstinately rejected the solicitations of her friends to any other match. Burns represents the lady addressing her youthful lover in the language of constancy and affection.'—*Stenhouse.*

Chorus—An' O, for ane and twenty, Tam!
And hey, sweet ane and twenty, Tam!
I'll learn my kin a rattlin sang
An I saw ane and twenty, Tam. — If=once

A gleib o' lan', a claut o' gear, — piece—hoard—wealth
Was left me by my Auntie, Tam;
At kith or kin I need na spier — ask
An I saw ane and twenty, Tam.

They'll hae me wed a wealthy coof, — fool
Tho' I mysel hae plenty, Tam;
But, hearst thou, laddie! there's my loof: — palm (of the hand)
I'm thine at ane and twenty, Tam.

BESSY AND HER SPINNIN-WHEEL.

TUNE—*The Sweet Lass that Loes Me.*

O leeze me on my spinnin-wheel, — Dear to me is
And leeze me on my rock and reel; — distaff
Frae tap to tae that cleeds me bien, — clothes—comfortably
And haps me fiel and warm at e'en! — wraps—cosy
I'll set me down and sing and spin,
While laigh descends the simmer sun, — low
Blest wi' content and milk and meal,
O leeze me on my spinnin-wheel!

On ilka hand the burnies trot — every—brooks
And meet below my theekit cot; — thatched
The scented birk and hawthorn white
Across the pool their arms unite,
Alike to screen the birdie's nest
And little fishes caller rest: — cool
The sun blinks kindly in the biel — shelter, shed
Where blythe I turn my spinnin-wheel.

On lofty aiks the cushats wail, — oaks—wood-pigeons
And Echo cons the doolfu' tale; — woeful
The lintwhites in the hazel braes, — linnets—banks
Delighted, rival ither's lays;
The craik amang the claver hay, — corncrake—clover
The paitrick whirrin o'er the ley, — partridge fluttering—grass land
The swallow jinkin round my shiel, — flitting—cottage
Amuse me at my spinnin-wheel.

C. Martin Hardie, R.S.A.

Blythe Bessie, in the milking shiel.

PAGE 376

Wi' sma' to sell and less to buy,
Aboon distress, below envy, Above
O wha wad leave this humble state
For a' the pride of a' the great?
Amid their flairing, idle toys,
Amid their cumbrous, dinsome joys, noisy
Can they the peace and pleasure feel
Of Bessy at her spinnin-wheel?

NITHSDALE'S WELCOME HAME.[1]

The noble Maxwells and their powers
Are coming o'er the border,
And they 'll gae big Terregles towers build
And set them a' in order.
And they declare, Terregles fair
For their abode they chuse it:
There 's no a heart in a' the land
But 's lighter at the news o 't.

Tho' stars in skies may disappear
And angry tempests gather,
The happy hour may soon be near
That brings us pleasant weather:
The weary night o' care and grief
May hae a joyfu' morrow;
So dawning day has brought relief,
Fareweel our night of sorrow.

THE COUNTRY LASS.

TUNE—*The Country Lass.*

In simmer, when the hay was mawn
And corn wav'd green in ilka field, every
While claver blooms white o'er the lea clover—grass land
And roses blaw in ilka bield! sheltered spot

[1] Written when Lady Winifred Maxwell Constable, the descendant of the forfeited Earl of Nithsdale, returned to Scotland and rebuilt Terregles House, in the Stewartry of Kirkcudbright. Mrs Burns in her memoranda states that her husband, when at Ellisland, dined there once or twice. Captain Riddel of Glenriddel furnished the air to which Burns composed the verses.

Blythe Bessie, in the milking shiel, hut
Says—'I'll be wed come o't what will;'
Out spak a dame in wrinkled eild— old age
'O' gude advisement comes nae ill.

'It's ye hae wooers mony ane,
And lassie, ye're but young, ye ken; know
Then wait a wee, and cannie wale a short time—cautious choose
A routhie[1] butt, a routhie ben:
There's Johnie o' the Buskie-glen,
Fu' is his barn, fu' is his byre;
Tak this frae me, my bonie hen,
It's plenty beets the luver's fire.' fans

'For Johnie o' the Buskie-glen
I dinna care a single flie;
He lo'es sae weel his craps and kye, cattle
He has nae loove to spare for me:
But blythe's the blink o' Robie's e'e, glance
And weel I wat he lo'es me dear; know
Ae blink o' him I wad na gie
For Buskie-glen and a' his gear.' wealth

'O thoughtless lassie, life's a faught: fight, struggle
The canniest gate the strife is sair; most prudent way—severe
But ay fu-han't is fechtin best:[2]
A hungry care's an unco care. heavy
But some will spend and some will spare,
And wilfu' folk maun hae their will;
Syne as ye brew, my maiden fair, Accordingly
Keep mind that ye maun drink the yill.' ale

'O gear will buy me rigs o' land money
And gear will buy me sheep and kye;
But the tender heart o' leesome loove gladsome
The gowd and siller canna buy:
We may be poor, Robie and I,
Light is the burden Loove lays on;
Content and Loove brings peace and joy—
What mair hae Queens upon a throne?'

[1] 'Routhie' = well-filled, comfortable. 'Butt and ben,' the two rooms of a cottage.
[2] It is best to fight with a full hand.

FAIR ELIZA.[1]

Turn again, thou fair Eliza!
  Ae kind blink before we part; glance
Rew on thy despairing Lover: Repent thy coldness to
  Canst thou break his faithfu' heart?
Turn again, thou fair Eliza!
  If to love thy heart denies,
For pity hide the cruel sentence
  Under friendship's kind disguise!

Thee, sweet maid, hae I offended?
  My offence is loving thee:
Canst thou wreck his peace for ever
  Wha for thine wad gladly die?[2]
While the life beats in my bosom,
  Thou shalt mix in ilka throe: every
Turn again, thou lovely maiden,
  Ae sweet smile on me bestow.

Not the bee upon the blossom
  In the pride o' sinny noon; sunny
Not the little sporting fairy
  All beneath the simmer moon;
Not the Poet, in the moment
  Fancy lightens in his e'e,
Kens the pleasure, feels the rapture,
  That thy presence gies to me.

O LUVE WILL VENTURE IN.[3]

TUNE—*The Posie.*

O luve will venture in where it daur na weel be seen,
O luve will venture in where wisdom ance hath been;

[1] Burns composed this song to a Highland air which he found in Macdonald's collection. In the original manuscript the name of the heroine is Rabina, which he is understood to have afterwards changed to Eliza, for reasons of taste. Stenhouse states that the verses were designed to embody the passion of a Mr Hunter, a friend of the poet, towards a Rabina of real life, who, it would appear, was loved in vain, for the lover went to the West Indies, and died there soon after his arrival.

[2] The similarity of these two lines to the familiar ones in 'Mary Morrison' will at once strike the reader.

[3] In his *Glenriddel Notes*, Burns says he took down the air and the old words of this song from the singing of a country girl. He subsequently explained to Thomson that this 'country girl' was his wife.

But I will down yon river rove, amang the wood sae green,
  And a' to pu' a posie to my ain dear May. all to pull

The primrose I will pu', the firstling o' the year,
And I will pu' the pink, the emblem o' my Dear;
For she 's the pink o' womankind, and blooms without a peer:
  And a' to be a posie to my ain dear May.

I 'll pu' the budding rose when Phebus peeps in view,
For it 's like a baumy kiss o' her sweet, bonie mou; balmy—mouth
The hyacinth for constancy wi' its unchanging blue:
  And a' to be a posie to my ain dear May.

The lily it is pure and the lily it is fair,
And in her lovely bosom I 'll place the lily there;
The daisy 's for simplicity and unaffected air:
  And a' to be a posie to my ain dear May.

The hawthorn I will pu', wi' its locks o' siller gray, silver
Where like an agèd man it stands at break o' day,
But the songster's nest within the bush I winna tak away: will not
  And a' to be a posie to my ain dear May.

The woodbine I will pu' when the e'ening star is near,
And the diamond draps o' dew shall be her een sae clear;
The violet 's for modesty, which weel she fa's to wear:[1]
  And a' to be a posie to my ain dear May.

I 'll tie the posie round wi' the silken band o' luve,
And I 'll place it in her breast, and I 'll swear by a' abuve,
That to my latest draught o' life the band shall ne'er remuve:
  And this will be a posie to my ain dear May.

THE BANKS O' DOON.

[ORIGINAL VERSION.]

Sweet are the banks—the banks o' Doon,
  The spreading flowers are fair,
And everything is blythe and glad,
  But I am fu' o' care. full of

[1] Which she rightly has, as her lot, to wear; which she has a good right to wear.

Thou 'll break my heart, thou bonie bird
That sings upon the bough;
Thou minds me o' the happy days
When my fause Luve was true: false
Thou 'll break my heart, thou bonie bird,
That sings beside thy mate;
For sae I sat, and sae I sang,
And wist na o' my fate.

Aft hae I rov'd by bonie Doon,
To see the woodbine twine;
And ilka bird sang o' its Luve, every
And sae did I o' mine;
Wi' lightsome heart I pu'd a rose
Upon its thorny tree;
But my fause Luver staw my rose, stole
And left the thorn wi' me:
Wi' lightsome heart I pu'd a rose cheerful
Upon a morn in June;
And sae I flourished on the morn,
And sae was pu'd or' noon. pulled ere

THE BANKS O' DOON.

[LATER VERSION.]

TUNE—*Caledonian Hunt's Delight.*

Ye banks and braes o' bonie Doon,
How can ye bloom sae fresh and fair!
How can ye chant, ye little birds,
And I sae weary fu' o' care!
Thou 'll break my heart, thou warbling bird
That wantons thro' the flowering thorn:
Thou minds me o' departed joys,
Departed, never to return.

Aft hae I rov'd by bonie Doon,
To see the rose and woodbine twine;
And ilka bird sang o' its luve, every
And fondly sae did I o' mine;
Wi' lightsome heart I pu'd a rose,
Fu' sweet upon its thorny tree;
And my fause luver staw my rose, false
But, ah! he left the thorn wi' me.

WILLIE WASTLE.

TUNE—*The Eight Men of Moidart.*

Willie Wastle dwalt on Tweed,
The spot they ca'd it Linkumdoddie;[1]
Willie was a wabster gude — weaver
Cou'd stown a clue wi' ony bodie;
He had a wife was dour and din, — sulky—ill-coloured
O, Tinkler Maidgie was her mither:
Sic a wife as Willie had—
I wad na gie a button for her!

She has an e'e, she has but ane,
The cat has twa the very colour;
Five rusty teeth forbye a stump, — besides
A clapper tongue wad deave a miller; — deafen
A whiskin beard about her mou, — mouth
Her nose and chin they threaten ither: — one another
Sic a wife as Willie had—
I wad na gie a button for her!

She 's bow-hough'd, she 's hem-shin'd,[2] — bandy-legged
Ae limpin leg a hand-breed shorter; — One—hand-breadth
She 's twisted right, she 's twisted left,
To balance fair in ilka quarter: — every
She has a hump upon her breast,
The twin o' that upon her shouther:
Sic a wife as Willie had—
I wad na gie a button for her!

Auld baudrons by the ingle sits, — cat—fireside
An' wi' her loof her face a-washin; — paw
But Willie's wife is nae sae trig: — dainty
She dights her grunzie wi' a hushion;[3] — wipes—mouth
Her walie nieves like-midden-creels, — huge fists—manure panniers
Her face wad fyle the Logan Water: — pollute
Sic a wife as Willie had—
I wad na gie a button for her!

[1] An imaginary place. It has been averred that Willie was in reality a farmer near Ellisland, with an unattractive wife. 'Cunningham says the name of Willie Wastle's wife is lost; I could tell him who it was, but there is no use in opening old sores.'—*Extract from a Letter of Mrs Renwick (Jane Jaffray) to her Sister, Nov.* 13, 1838.

[2] With shins of shape of hems, or hames, two hinged pieces of iron or wood of a horse's collar to which the traces are fastened.

[3] Footless stocking worn on the arm.

BONIE BELL.

The smiling Spring comes in rejoicing,
  And surly Winter grimly flies;
Now crystal clear are the falling waters,
  And bonny blue are the sunny skies.
Fresh o'er the mountains breaks forth the morning,
  The ev'ning gilds the Ocean's swell;
All creatures joy in the sun's returning,
  And I rejoice in my Bonie Bell.

The flowery Spring leads sunny Summer,
  And yellow Autumn presses near;
Then in his turn comes gloomy Winter,
  Till smiling Spring again appear:
Thus seasons dancing, life advancing,
  Old Time and Nature their changes tell;
But never ranging, still unchanging,
  I adore my Bonie Bell.[1]

THE GALLANT WEAVER.

TUNE—*The Weavers' March.*

Where Cart[2] rins rowin to the sea, rolling
By mony a flow'r and spreading tree,
There lives a lad, the lad for me,
  He is a gallant Weaver.
Oh, I had wooers aught or nine, eight
They gied me rings and ribbons fine;
And I was fear'd my heart would tine, be lost
  And I gied it to the Weaver. gave

My daddie sign'd my tocher-band dowry-bond
To gie the lad that has the land,
But to my heart I'll add my hand,
  And gie it to the Weaver.
While birds rejoice in leafy bowers,
While bees delight in opening flowers,
While corn grows green in simmer showers,
  I'll love my gallant Weaver.[3]

[1] 'Bonie Bell' is one of the few heroines of Burns for whom an original has not been suggested.

[2] Paisley stands on the river Cart.

[3] This song will at once suggest Jean Armour's visit to Paisley in 1786, and the offer of marriage said to have been made to her by Robert Wilson, the well-to-do weaver.

THE DEUK'S DANG O'ER MY DADDIE.[1]

The bairns gat out wi' an unco shout, — children—great
  'The deuk 's dang o'er my daddie, O!' — duck has knocked down
'The fien-ma-care,' quo' the feirrie auld wife, — devil-ma-care —sturdy
  'He was but a paidlin body, O! — dawdling
He paidles out, and he paidles in,
  An' he paidles late and early, O!
This seven lang years I hae lien by his side,
  An' he is but a fusionless carlie, O.' — pithless—little man

'O haud your tongue, my feirrie auld wife, — hold
  O haud your tongue, now Nansie, O;
I 've seen the day, and sae hae ye,
  Ye wad na been sae donsie, O. — saucy
I 've seen the day ye butter'd my brose, — put butter in my hasty porridge
  And cuddled me late and early, O;
But downa-do 's come o'er me now, — 'am-not-able'= failure of strength
  And Oh, I find it sairly, O!'

SHE'S FAIR AND FAUSE.[2]

TUNE—*She 's Fair and Fause.*

She 's fair and fause that causes my smart, — false
  I lo'ed her meikle and lang; — much
She 's broken her vow, she 's broken my heart,
  And I may e'en gae hang:
A coof cam in wi' routh o' gear, — fool—abundance of goods
  And I hae tint my dearest dear; — lost
But woman is but warld's gear,
  Sae let the bonie lass gang. — go

Whae'er ye be that woman love,
  To this be never blind:
Nae ferlie 'tis tho' fickle she prove, — wonder
  A woman has 't by kind: — nature

[1] Charles Kirkpatrick Sharpe supplied from a manuscript in his possession some of the old words which Burns modified. His first four lines are easily traced in:

The bairns they a' set up the cry,
  'The deuk 's dang o'er my daddie, O;'
'There's no mickle matter,' quo' the gudewife,
  'He 's ay been a daidlin body, O.'

[2] This song was probably suggested to Burns by the love disappointment of his friend Alexander Cunningham.

O woman lovely, woman fair!
An angel-form 's faun to thy share, fallen
'Twad been o'er meikle to gien thee mair[1]—
I mean an angel-mind.

MY WIFE'S A WINSOME WEE THING.

I never saw a fairer,
I never lo'ed a dearer,
And neist my heart I'll wear her, next
For fear my jewel tine. be lost

Chorus—She is a winsome wee thing, agreeable
She is a handsome wee thing,
She is a loesome wee thing,[2]
This dear wee wife o' mine.

The world's wrack we share o' 't, misfortune
The warstle and the care o' 't, wrestling
Wi' her I'll blythely bear it,
And think my lot divine.

HIGHLAND MARY.

TUNE—*Katherine Ogie.*

Ye banks and braes and streams around
The castle o' Montgomery!
Green be your woods, and fair your flowers,
Your waters never drumlie: muddy
There Simmer first unfauld her robes,
And there the langest tarry;
For there I took the last Fareweel
O' my sweet Highland Mary.

How sweetly bloom'd the gay, green birk, birch
How rich the hawthorn's blossom,
As underneath their fragrant shade
I clasp'd her to my bosom!
The golden Hours on angel wings
Flew o'er me and my Dearie;
For dear to me as light and life
Was my sweet Highland Mary.

1 It would have been too much to have given thee more.
2 Manuscript—'She is a winsome wee thing.' The alteration was by Thomson.

Wi' mony a vow and lock'd embrace,
 Our parting was fu' tender;
And, pledging aft to meet again,
 We tore oursels asunder;
But oh! fell Death's untimely frost,
 That nipt my Flower sae early!
Now green 's the sod and cauld 's the clay
 That wraps my Highland Mary!

O pale, pale now those rosy lips
 I aft hae kiss'd sae fondly!
And clos'd for ay the sparkling glance
 That dwalt on me sae kindly!
And mouldering now in silent dust
 That heart that lo'ed me dearly!
But still within my bosom's core
 Shall live my Highland Mary!

THE RIGHTS OF WOMAN:

An Occasional Address spoken by Miss Fontenelle[1] on her Benefit-Night. [Nov. 26, 1792.][2]

While Europe's eye is fix'd on mighty things:
The fate of empires and the fall of kings;
While quacks of state must each produce his plan;
And even children lisp *The Rights of Man;*
Amid this mighty fuss just let me mention
The Rights of Woman merit some attention.

First, in the sexes' intermix'd connection,
One sacred Right of Woman is *protection:*
The tender flower that lifts its head, elate,
Helpless must fall before the blasts of fate,
Sunk on the earth, defac'd its lovely form,
Unless your shelter ward th' impending storm.

Our second Right—but needless here is caution,
To keep that right inviolate 's the fashion:

1 Miss Fontenelle, a lively little actress, who played 'Little Pickle' in *The Spoiled Child*, and other such characters. Burns admired Miss Fontenelle's performances and wrote poems both for her and about her. She appeared as early as December 26, 1789, in Edinburgh, when she acted in *A Confederacy*.

2 The bill of the night announces *The Country Girl* as the play, and that, thereafter, 'Miss Fontenelle will deliver a new Occasional Address, written by Mr Robert Burns, called "The Rights of Woman."'—*Dumfries Times.*

Each man of sense has it so full before him,
He 'd die before he 'd wrong it—'tis *decorum:*
There was, indeed, in far less polish'd days,
A time when rough rude man had naughty ways:
Would swagger, swear, get drunk, kick up a riot,
Nay, even thus invade a lady's quiet.
Now, thank our stars! these Gothic times are fled;
Now well-bred men—and you are all well-bred—
Most justly think (and we are much the gainers)
Such conduct neither spirit, wit nor manners.[1]

For Right the third, our last, our best, our dearest,
That right to fluttering female hearts the nearest;
Which even the Rights of Kings, in low prostration,
Most humbly own—'tis dear, dear *admiration!*
In that blest sphere alone we live and move;
There taste that life of life—immortal love.
Smiles, glances, sighs, tears, fits, flirtations, airs,
'Gainst such an host what flinty savage dares—
When awful Beauty joins with all her charms,
Who is so rash as rise in rebel arms?

But truce with kings and truce with constitutions,
With bloody armaments and revolutions;
Let Majesty your first attention summon,
Ah! *ça ira!* THE MAJESTY OF WOMAN!

TO MISS FONTENELLE, ON SEEING HER IN A FAVOURITE CHARACTER.

Sweet naïveté of feature,
Simple, wild, enchanting elf,
Not to thee, but thanks to nature,
Thou art acting but thyself.

Wert thou awkward, stiff, affected,
Spurning nature, torturing art;
Loves and graces all rejected,
Then indeed thou 'dst act a part.

[1] An ironical allusion to the annual saturnalia of the Caledonian Hunt at Dumfries.

THE LEA-RIG.

TUNE—*The Lea-Rig.*

When o'er the hill the eastern star
  Tells bughtin-time [1] is near, my jo,
And owsen frae the furrow'd field — oxen
  Return sae dowf and weary, O; — dull, spiritless
Down by the burn, where birken buds — birch
  Wi' dew are hangin' clear, my jo,
I'll meet thee on the lea-rig,
  My ain kind Dearie, O.

At midnight hour, in mirkest glen, — darkest
  I'd rove, and ne'er be eerie, O, — frightened
If thro' that glen I gaed to thee, — went
  My ain kind Dearie, O;
Altho' the night were ne'er sae wild,
  And I were ne'er sae weary, O,
I'll meet thee on the lea-rig,
  My ain kind Dearie, O.

The hunter lo'es the morning sun,
  To rouse the mountain deer, my jo;
At noon the fisher seeks the glen
  Alang the burn to steer, my jo:
Gie me the hour o' gloamin grey.
  It maks my heart sae cheery, O,
To meet thee on the lea-rig,
  My ain kind Dearie, O.

AULD ROB MORRIS.

There's Auld Rob Morris that wons in yon glen, — dwells
He's the King o' gude fellows and wale o' auld men; — choice
He has gowd in his coffers, he has owsen and kine, — gold—oxen
And ae bonie lassie, his darling and mine.

She's fresh as the morning, the fairest in May;
She's sweet as the ev'ning amang the new hay;
As blythe and as artless as the lambs on the lea,
And dear to my heart as the light to my e'e.

[1] Time to drive the sheep into the *bughts* or folds.

But oh! she 's an Heiress (auld Robin 's a laird),
And my daddy has nought but a cot-house and yard; garden
A wooer like me maunna hope to come speed, must not
The wounds I must hide that will soon be my dead. death

The day comes to me, but delight brings me nane;
The night comes to me, but my rest it is gane:
I wander my lane like a night-troubled ghaist, alone
And I sigh as my heart it wad burst in my breast. would

O had she but been of a lower degree,
I then might hae hop'd she wad smil'd upon me!
O how past descriving had then been my bliss, describing
And now my distraction nae words can express.

DUNCAN GRAY.

Duncan Gray cam here to woo,
Ha, ha, the wooing o' 't,
On blythe Yule-night when we were fou,
Ha, ha, the wooing o' 't.
Maggie coost her head fu' high, cast
Look'd asklent and unco skeigh, askance—very coy
Gart poor Duncan stand abeigh, Made—aloof
Ha, ha, the wooing o' 't.

Duncan fleech'd and Duncan pray'd, besought
Ha, ha, the wooing o' 't;
Meg was deaf as Ailsa Craig,
Ha, ha, the wooing o' 't:
Duncan sigh'd baith out and in,
Grat his e'en baith bleer't an' blin', Wept—bleared
Spak o' lowpin' o'er a linn, Spoke—jumping—waterfall
Ha, ha, the wooing o' 't.

Time and Chance are but a tide,
Ha, ha, the wooing o' 't:
Slighted love is sair to bide, hard—endure
Ha, ha, the wooing o' 't:
'Shall I, like a fool,' quoth he,
'For a haughty hizzie die? hussy
She may gae to—France for me!'
Ha, ha, the wooing o' 't.

How it comes let doctors tell,
Ha, ha, the wooing o' 't;
Meg grew sick as he grew hale, sound, healthy
Ha, ha, the wooing o' 't.
Something in her bosom wrings,
For relief a sigh she brings:
And oh! her een they spak sic things! eyes—spoke such
Ha, ha, the wooing o' 't.

Duncan was a lad o' grace,
Ha, ha, the wooing o' 't:
Maggie's was a piteous case,
Ha, ha, the wooing o' 't:
Duncan could na be her death,
Swelling pity smoor'd his wrath: smothered
Now they 're crouse and canty baith, cheerful—happy
Ha, ha, the wooing o' 't.

HERE'S TO THEM THAT'S AWA.

Here 's a health to them that 's awa,
An' here 's to them that 's awa:
And wha winna wish gude luck to our cause, will not
May never gude luck be their fa'! fall=lot
It 's gude to be merry and wise;
It 's gude to be honest and true;
It 's gude to support Caledonia's cause
And bide by the Buff and the Blue.

Here 's a health to them that 's awa,
And here 's to them that 's awa:
Here 's a health to Charlie,[1] the chief o' the clan,
Altho' that his band be but sma',
May Liberty meet wi' success!
May Prudence protect her frae evil!
May tyrants and tyranny tine i' the mist be lost
And wander the road to the devil!

Here 's a health to them that 's awa,
An' here 's to them that 's awa:
Here 's a health to Tammie,[2] the Norland laddie,
That lives at the lug o' the law!

[1] Charles James Fox. Buff and blue formed his well-known livery at the Westminster elections, and came to be an ensign of the Whig party generally.
[2] The Hon. Thomas Erskine, afterwards Lord Erskine.

Here 's freedom to him that wad read!
Here 's freedom to him that wad write!
There 's nane ever feared that the truth should be heard
But they wham the truth wad indite.[1]

Here 's a health to them that 's awa,
An' here 's to them that 's awa:
Here 's Maitland and Wycombe,[2] and [may] wha does na like 'em
Be built in a hole in the wa'!
Here 's timmer that 's red at the heart! timber
Here 's fruit that is sound at the core!
And may he that wad turn the Buff and Blue coat
Be turned to the back o' the door!

Here 's a health to them that 's awa,
An' here 's to them that 's awa:
Here 's Chieftain Macleod, a chieftain worth gowd,[3]
Tho' bred amang mountains o' snaw!
Here 's friends on baith sides o' the Firth!
And friends on baith sides o' the Tweed!
And wha wad betray Old Albion's rights,
May they never eat of her bread!

EXTEMPORE ON SOME COMMEMORATIONS OF THOMSON.

Dost thou not rise, indignant shade,
And smile wi' spurning scorn
When they wha wad hae starved thy life would
Thy senseless turf adorn?

Helpless, alane, thou clamb the brae,
Wi' mickle, mickle toil, much
And claught th' unfading garland there, caught
Thy sair-won, rightful spoil.

[1] For *indict*, a Scotch law-phrase meaning *accuse*.

[2] James Maitland, eighth Earl of Lauderdale (1759-1839), one of the sixteen peers of Scotland, and one of the founders of 'The Friends of the People.' He was at this time in France with Dr John Moore.—William Petty, Earl Wycombe, Marquis of Lansdowne, better known as Lord Shelburne (1737-1805), was also a supporter of parliamentary reform.

[3] The famous General Norman Macleod (1754-1801) of Dunvegan, Isle of Skye, M.P. for the county of Inverness (1790-96).

And wear it there! and call aloud
  This axiom undoubted—
Would thou hae nobles' patronage?
  'First learn to live without it!'

To whom hae much, shall yet be given,
  Is every great man's faith;
But he, the helpless, needful wretch,
  Shall lose the mite he hath.

O POORTITH CAULD AND RESTLESS LOVE.

TUNE—*Cauld Kail in Aberdeen.*[1]

O poortith cauld and restless love, — poverty
  Ye wrack my peace between ye;
Yet poortith a' I could forgive,
  An 'twere na for my Jeanie.

Chorus—O why should Fate sic pleasure have, — such
  Life's dearest bands untwining?
Or why sae sweet a flower as love
  Depend on Fortune's shining?

The warld's wealth, when I think on
  Its pride and a' the lave o' 't; — rest
O fie on silly coward man
  That he should be the slave o' 't!

Her e'en, sae bonie blue, betray
  How she repays my passion;
But prudence is her o'erword ay: — burden of her talk
  She talks o' rank and fashion.

O wha can prudence think upon
  And sic a lassie by him?
O wha can prudence think upon
  And sae in love as I am?

How blest the humble cotter's fate!
  He woos his artless dearie;
The silly bogles, wealth and state,
  Can never make him eerie. — frightened

[1] This song is usually sung to the tune, 'I had a horse, I had nae mair.'

W. D. M'Kay, R.S.A.

I'll meet thee on the lea-rig,
My ain kind dearie O.

PAGE 386.

GALLA WATER.

Braw, braw lads on Yarrow-braes, Handsome
  They rove amang the blooming heather;
But Yarrow-braes nor Ettrick shaws
  Can match the lads o' Galla Water.

But there is ane, a secret ane,
  Aboon them a' I loe him better; Above
And I'll be his, and he'll be mine,
  The bonie lad o' Galla Water.

Altho' his daddie was nae laird, no landholder
  And tho' I hae na meikle tocher, much dowry
Yet rich in kindest, truest love,
  We'll tent our flocks by Galla Water. watch

It ne'er was wealth, it ne'er was wealth,
  That coft contentment, peace or pleasure: bought
The bands and bliss o' mutual love,
  O that's the chiefest warld's treasure.

SONNET:

Written on the 25th January 1793, the Birth-day of the Author, on hearing a Thrush sing on a Morning Walk.

Sing on, sweet thrush, upon the leafless bough;
  Sing on, sweet bird, I'll listen to thy strain;
  See aged Winter, 'mid his surly reign,
At thy blythe carol clears his furrowed brow.

Thus in lone Poverty's dominion drear
  Sits meek Content, with light, unanxious heart;
  Welcomes the rapid moments, bids them part,
Nor asks if they bring aught to hope or fear.

I thank thee, Author of this opening day,
  Thou whose bright sun now gilds yon orient skies!
  Riches denied, thy boon was purer joys,
What Wealth could never give nor take away!

Yet come, thou child of Poverty and Care!
The mite high Heaven bestowed, that mite with thee I'll share.

LORD GREGORY.

O mirk, mirk is this midnight hour, dark
And loud the tempest's roar;
A waefu' wand'rer seeks thy tower,
Lord Gregory, ope thy door.

An exile frae her father's ha',
And a' for sake o' thee;
At least some pity on me shaw, show
If love it may na be.

Lord Gregory, mind'st thou not the grove
By bonie Irwine side,
Where first I own'd that virgin love
I lang, lang had denied.

How aften didst thou pledge and vow
Thou wad for ay be mine! would
And my fond heart, itsel sae true,
It ne'er mistrusted thine.

Hard is thy heart, Lord Gregory,
And flinty is thy breast:
Thou bolt of Heaven that flashest by,
O, wilt thou bring me rest!

Ye must'ring thunders from above
Your willing victim see;
But spare and pardon my fause Love, false
His wrangs to Heaven and me.

OPEN THE DOOR TO ME.

Oh, open the door, some pity to shew,
Oh, open the door to me, oh:
Tho' thou has been false, I'll ever prove true,
Oh, open the door to me, oh.

Cauld is the blast upon my pale cheek,
But caulder thy love for me, oh:
The frost that freezes the life at my heart
Is nought to my pains frae thee, oh.

The wan Moon is setting behind the white wave,
And Time is setting with me, oh:
False friends, false love, farewell! for mair
I 'll ne'er trouble them nor thee, oh.

She has open'd the door, she has open'd it wide,
She sees the pale corse on the plain, oh:
'My true love!' she cried, and sank down by his side,
Never to rise again, oh.

ON GENERAL DUMOURIEZ' DESERTION FROM THE FRENCH REPUBLICAN ARMY.

You 're welcome to Despots, Dumouriez;
You 're welcome to Despots, Dumouriez;
How does Dampierre do?
Aye, and Beurnonville too?[1]
Why did they not come along with you, Dumouriez?

I will fight France with you, Dumouriez;
I will fight France with you, Dumouriez;
I will fight France with you,
I will take my chance with you,
By my soul, I 'll dance a dance with you, Dumouriez.

Then let us fight about, Dumouriez;
Then let us fight about, Dumouriez;
Then let us fight about
Till freedom's spark be out,
Then we 'll be d—mned, no doubt, Dumouriez.

YOUNG JESSIE.

TUNE—*Bonie Dundee.*

True-hearted was he, the sad swain o' the Yarrow,
And fair are the maids on the banks of the Ayr;
But by the sweet side o' the Nith's winding river
Are lovers as faithful and maidens as fair:

[1] General Dumouriez (b. 1739, d. 1823 in England), after a series of victories, deserted the army of the Republic on April 5, 1793, and was only prevented by accident from betraying his troops into the hands of the enemy. Dampierre (b. 1756, d. 1793) was one of Dumouriez' generals, whom he had expected to desert along with him. Beurnonevill (b. 1752, d. 1821) was an emissary of the Convention, and Dumouriez had similar hopes of him, which, however, were disappointed. He lived to figure in the crisis of the Restoration in 1814.

To equal young Jessie seek Scotland all over;
To equal young Jessie you seek it in vain:
Grace, beauty and elegance fetter her lover,
And maidenly modesty fixes the chain.

Fresh is the rose in the gay, dewy morning,
And sweet is the lily at evening close;
But in the fair presence o' lovely young JESSIE,
Unseen is the lily, unheeded the rose:
Love sits in her smile, a wizard ensnaring;
Enthron'd in her een he delivers his law:
And still to her charms SHE alone is a stranger;
Her modest demeanor 's the jewel of a'.[1]

THE SOLDIER'S RETURN.[2]

AIR—*The Mill, Mill O.*

When wild war's deadly blast was blawn,
And gentle peace returning,
Wi' mony a sweet babe fatherless,
And mony a widow mourning;
I left the lines and tented field
Where lang I 'd been a lodger,
My humble knapsack a' my wealth,
A poor but honest sodger. soldier

A leal, light heart was in my breast, loyal
My hand unstain'd wi' plunder;
And for fair Scotia, hame again,
I cheery on did wander:

[1] In this song Burns embodied a compliment to Jessie Staig, second daughter of the Provost of Dumfries, and subsequently the wife of Major William Miller, one of the sons of the poet's former landlord. Mrs Miller must have been at this time very young, for her monument in Dumfries churchyard states that she died in March 1801, at the early age of twenty-six.

[2] 'Burns, I have been informed, was one summer evening at the inn at Brownhill with a couple of friends, when a poor wayworn soldier passed the window: of a sudden, it struck the poet to call him in and get the story of his adventures; after listening to which, he all at once fell into one of those fits of abstraction not unusual with him. He was lifted to the region where he had his "garland and singing robes about him," and the result was the admirable song which he sent you for "The Mill, Mill O!"'—*Correspondent of George Thomson.* Mill of Mannoch, beautifully situated on the Coyle, near Coylton Kirk, is supposed to have been the spot where the poet imagined the rencontre of the soldier and his sweetheart to take place.

C. Martin Hardie, R.S.A.

The Soldier's Return.

PAGE 394.

I thought upon the banks o' Coil;
  I thought upon my Nancy;
I thought upon the witching smile
  That caught my youthful fancy.

At length I reach'd the bonie glen
  Where early life I sported;
I pass'd the mill and trysting thorn meeting
  Where Nancy aft I courted:
Wha spied I but my ain dear maid,
  Down by her mother's dwelling!
And turn'd me round to hide the flood
  That in my e'en was swelling.

Wi' alter'd voice, quoth I, 'Sweet lass,
  Sweet as yon hawthorn's blossom,
O! happy, happy may he be
  That's dearest to thy bosom:
My purse is light, I've far to gang, go
  And fain wad be thy lodger:
I've serv'd my king and country lang—
  Take pity on a sodger.'

Sae wistfully she gaz'd on me,
  And lovelier was than ever;
Quo' she, 'A sodger ance I lo'ed,
  Forget him shall I never:
Our humble cot and hamely fare
  Ye freely shall partake it;
That gallant badge—the dear cockade,
  Ye're welcome for the sake o' 't.'

She gaz'd—she redden'd like a rose—
  Syne pale like ony lily Then
She sank within my arms, and cried,
  'Art thou my ain dear Willie?'
'By Him who made yon sun and sky,
  By whom true love's regarded!
I am the man; and thus may still
  True lovers be rewarded!

'The wars are o'er, and I'm come hame
  And find thee still true-hearted;
Tho' poor in gear, we're rich in love, goods
  And mair we'se ne'er be parted.' we shall

Quo' she, 'My grandsire left me gowd, gold
A mailen plenish'd fairly; farm
And come, my faithfu' sodger lad,
Thou 'rt welcome to it dearly.'

For gold the merchant ploughs the main,
The farmer ploughs the manor;
But glory is the sodger's prize,
The sodger's wealth is honor:
The brave poor sodger ne'er despise,
Nor count him as a stranger;
Remember he 's his country's stay
In day and hour of danger.

MEG O' THE MILL.

AIR—*Jackie Hume's Lament.*

O ken ye what Meg o' the Mill has gotten?
An' ken ye what Meg o' the Mill has gotten?
She 's gotten a coof wi' a claute o' siller fool—hoard
And broken the heart of the barley Miller.

The Miller was strappin, the Miller was ruddy,
A heart like a lord and a hue like a lady;
The laird was a widdifu', bleerit knurl:[1]
She 's left the gude fellow and ta'en the churl.

The Miller he hecht her a heart leal and loving, promised—loyal
The laird did address her wi' matter mair moving:
A fine pacing-horse wi' a clear chainèd bridle,
A whip by her side and a bonie side-saddle.

O wae on the siller—it is sae prevalin'!
And wae on the love that is fix'd on a mailen! farm
A tocher 's nae word in a true lover's parl, dowry—talk
But gie me my love—and a fig for the warl! world

THE LAST TIME I CAME O'ER THE MOOR.

The last time I came o'er the moor,
And left Maria's dwelling,
What throes, what tortures passing cure,
Were in my bosom swelling:

[1] Widdifu' = one who deserves to hang in a widdie or halter; bleerit knurl = blear-eyed dwarf.

Condemned to see my rival's reign,
  While I in secret languish;
To feel a fire in every vein,
  Yet dare not speak my anguish.

Love's veriest wretch, despairing, I
  Fain, fain my crime would cover:
The unweeting groan, the bursting sigh, unwitting
  Betray the guilty lover.
I know my doom must be despair:
  Thou wilt nor canst relieve me;
But, O Maria, hear my prayer,
  For pity's sake, forgive me!

The music of thy tongue I heard,
  Nor wist while it enslaved me;
I saw thine eyes, yet nothing feared,
  Till fears no more had saved me.
The unwary sailor thus, aghast,
  The wheeling torrent viewing,
Mid circling horrors yields at last
  In overwhelming ruin!

BLYTHE HAE I BEEN ON YON HILL.

TUNE—*Liggeram Cosh.*

Blythe hae I been on yon hill
  As the lambs before me;
Careless ilka thought and free, every
  As the breeze flew o'er me:
Now nae langer sport and play,
  Mirth or sang, can please me;
LESLEY is sae fair and coy,
  Care and anguish seize me.

Heavy, heavy is the task,
  Hopeless love declaring;
Trembling, I dow nocht but glow'r, do nothing—stare
  Sighing, dumb despairing!
If she winna ease the thraws will not—throes
  In my bosom swelling,
Underneath the grass-green sod
  Soon maun be my dwelling. must

LOGAN BRAES.

TUNE—*Logan Water.*[1]

O Logan, sweetly didst thou glide
That day I was my Willie's bride,
And years sin syne hae o'er us run, since then
Like Logan to the simmer sun:
But now thy flowery banks appear
Like drumlie Winter, dark and drear, clouded
While my dear lad maun face his faes must
Far, far frae me and Logan braes.

Again the merry month o' May
Has made our hills and vallies gay;
The birds rejoice in leafy bowers;
The bees hum round the breathing flowers;
Blythe, Morning lifts his rosy eye;
And Evening's tears are tears of joy:
My soul, delightless, a' surveys,
While Willie 's far frae Logan braes.

Within yon milk-white hawthorn bush,
Amang her nestlings, sits the thrush;
Her faithfu' mate will share her toil
Or wi' his song her cares beguile;
But I, wi' my sweet nurslings here,
Nae mate to help, nae mate to cheer,
Pass widow'd nights and joyless days,
While Willie 's far frae Logan braes.

O wae upon you, Men o' State,
That brethren rouse to deadly hate!
As ye make mony a fond heart mourn,
Sae may it on your heads return!
How can your flinty hearts enjoy
The widow's tear, the orphan's cry!
But soon may peace bring happy days,
And Willie hame to Logan braes!

[1] The air of 'Logan Water' is old, and there are several old songs to it. Immediately before Burns's time, John Mayne, author of 'The Siller Gun,' wrote a very pleasant song to the air, beginning:

By Logan's streams, that rin sae deep.

It was published in the *Star* newspaper, May 23, 1789. Burns having heard that song, and supposing it to be an old composition, adopted into his own song a couplet from it which he admired:

While my dear lad maun face his faes
Far, far frae me and Logan braes.

BONIE JEAN.

There was a lass, and she was fair:
  At kirk and market to be seen,
When a' our fairest maids were met,
  The fairest maid was bonie Jean.

And ay she wrought her mammie's wark,
  And ay she sang sae merrilie:
The blythest bird upon the bush
  Had ne'er a lighter heart than she.

But hawks will rob the tender joys
  That bless the little lintwhite's nest; linnet
And frost will blight the fairest flowers;
  And love will break the soundest rest:

Young Robie was the brawest lad, handsomest
  The flower and pride of a' the glen;
And he had owsen, sheep and kye oxen—cows
  And wanton naigies nine or ten. horses

He gaed wi' Jeanie to the tryste, fair
  He danc'd wi' Jeanie on the down;
And, lang ere witless Jeanie wist,
  Her heart was tint, her peace was stown. lost—stolen

As in the bosom of the stream
  The moon-beam dwells at dewy e'en,
So trembling, pure, was tender love
  Within the breast of bonie Jean.

And now she works her mammie's wark;
  And ay she sighs wi' care and pain;
Yet wist na what her ail might be
  Or what wad mak her weel again.

But did na Jeanie's heart loup light, jump
  And did na joy blink in her e'e sparkle
As Robie tauld a tale o' love,
  Ae e'enin on the lily lea!

The sun was sinking in the west,
  The birds sang sweet in ilka grove, every
His cheek to hers he fondly prest,
  And whisper'd thus his tale o' love:

'O Jeanie fair, I lo'e thee dear:
O canst thou think to fancy me?
Or wilt thou leave thy mammie's cot
And learn to tent the farms wi' me? care for

'At barn or byre thou shalt na drudge, cow-house
Or naething else to trouble thee,
But stray amang the heather-bells
And tent the waving corn wi' me.'

Now what could artless Jeanie do?
She had nae will to say him na:
At length she blush'd a sweet consent,
And love was ay between them twa.

PHILLIS THE FAIR.

TUNE—*Robin Adair.*

While larks, with little wing,
Fann'd the pure air,
Tasting the breathing Spring,
Forth I did fare:
Gay the sun's golden eye
Peep'd o'er the mountains high;
Such thy morn! did I cry,
Phillis the fair.

In each bird's careless song,
Glad, I did share;
While yon wild flowers among,
Chance led me there:
Sweet to the opening day,
Rosebuds bent the dewy spray;
Such thy bloom! did I say,
Phillis the fair.

Down in a shady walk,
Doves cooing were,
I mark'd the cruel hawk
Caught in a snare:
So kind may Fortune be,
Such make his destiny!
He who would injure thee,
Phillis the fair.

SONG.

TUNE—*Robin Adair.*

Had I a cave on some wild distant shore,
Where the winds howl to the waves' dashing roar;
There would I weep my woes,
There seek my lost repose,
Till grief my eyes should close,
Ne'er to wake more!

Falsest of womankind, canst thou declare
All thy fond-plighted vows, fleeting as air!
To thy new lover hie,
Laugh o'er thy perjury;
Then in thy bosom try
What peace is there!

BY ALLAN STREAM I CHANC'D TO ROVE.

TUNE—*Allan Water.*

By Allan stream I chanc'd to rove
While Phœbus sunk beyond Benledi;
The winds were whispering through the grove,
The yellow corn was waving ready:
I listen'd to a lover's sang,
An' thought on youthful pleasures many;
And ay the wild-wood echoes rang,
'O, dearly do I lo'e thee, Annie!

'O happy be the woodbine bower,
Nae nightly bogle make it eerie; **ghost—weird**
Nor ever sorrow stain the hour,
The place and time I met my dearie!'
Her head upon my throbbing breast,
She, sinking, said 'I 'm thine for ever!'
While mony a kiss the seal imprest—
The sacred vow we ne'er should sever.

The haunt o' spring 's the primrose-brae, **hill, bank**
The simmer joy 's the flocks to follow;
How cheery, thro' her shortening day,
Is autumn in her weeds o' yellow:

But can they melt the glowing heart,
Or chain the soul in speechless pleasure?
Or through each nerve the rapture dart,
Like meeting her, our bosom's treasure?

O WHISTLE AND I'LL COME TO YOU, MY LAD.

TUNE—*O Whistle, and I'll come to you, my Lad.*

Chorus—O whistle, and I'll come to you, my lad,
O whistle, and I'll come to you, my lad;
Tho' father and mother and a' should gae mad, go
O whistle, and I'll come to you, my lad.

But warily tent, when ye come to court me, watch
And come na unless the back-yett be a-jee; gate—ajar
Syne up the back-style, and let naebody see, Then
And come as ye were na coming to me,
And come as ye were na coming to me.

At kirk or at market, whene'er ye meet me,
Gang by me as tho' that ye car'd nae a flie; Go—fly
But steal me a blink o' your bonie black e'e, glance
Yet look as ye were na looking at me,
Yet look as ye were na looking at me.

Ay vow and protest that ye carena for me,
And *whyles* ye may lightly my beauty a wee; sometimes—undervalue—a little
But court na anither, tho' joking ye be,
For fear that she wyle your fancy frae me, lure
For fear that she wyle your fancy frae me.

ADOWN WINDING NITH I DID WANDER.

TUNE—*The Mucking o' Geordie's Byre.*

Adown winding Nith I did wander,
To mark the sweet flowers as they spring;
Adown winding Nith I did wander,
Of Phillis to muse and to sing.

Chorus—Awa' wi' your belles and your beauties,
They never wi' her can compare,
Whaever has met wi' my Phillis,
Has met wi' the queen o' the fair.

R. B. Nisbet, A R.S.A.

The Winding Nith.

PAGE 402.

The daisy amus'd my fond fancy,
  So artless, so simple, so wild;
Thou emblem, said I, of my Phillis,
  For she is simplicity's child.

The rose-bud 's the blush o' my charmer,
  Her sweet balmy lip when 'tis prest:
How fair and how pure is the lily!
  But fairer and purer her breast.

Yon knot of gay flowers in the arbour,
  They ne'er wi' my Phillis can vie:
Her breath is the breath of the woodbine,
  Its dewdrop o' diamond, her eye.

Her voice is the song of the morning,
  That wakes thro' the green-spreading grove,
When Phœbus peeps over the mountains,
  On music, and pleasure, and love.

But beauty how frail and how fleeting!
  The bloom of a fine summer's day!
While worth, in the mind o' my Phillis,
  Will flourish without a decay.

COME, LET ME TAKE THEE TO MY BREAST.

AIR—*Cauld Kail.*

Come, let me take thee to my breast,
  And pledge we ne'er shall sunder;
And I shall spurn, as vilest dust,
  The world's wealth and grandeur:
And do I hear my Jeanie own
  That equal transports move her?
I ask for dearest life alone,
  That I may live to love her.

When in my arms, wi' a' thy charms,
  I clasp my countless treasure,
I'll seek nae mair o' Heaven to share, **no more**
  Than sic a moment's pleasure: **such**
And by thy e'en sae bonie blue,
  I swear I'm thine for ever!
And on thy lips I seal my vow,
  And break it shall I never!

DAINTY DAVIE.

TUNE—*Dainty Davie.*[1]

Now rosy May comes in wi' flowers,
To deck her gay green spreading bowers;
And now comes in my happy hours,
To wander wi' my Davie.

Chorus—Meet me on the warlock knowe, fairy knoll
Dainty Davie, dainty Davie;
There I'll spend the day wi' you,
My ain dear, dainty Davie. own

The chrystal waters round us fa',
The merry birds are lovers a',
The scented breezes round us blaw,
A-wandering wi' my Davie.

When purple morning starts the hare
To steal upon her early fare,
Then thro' the dews I will repair,
To meet my faithful Davie.

When day, expiring in the west,
The curtain draws of Nature's rest,
I flee to 's arms I lo'e the best,
And that 's my ain dear Davie.

BRUCE TO HIS MEN AT BANNOCKBURN.

TUNE—*Hey, tuttie taitie.*

Scots, wha hae wi' Wallace bled, who have
Scots, wham Bruce has aften led, whom
Welcome to your gory bed,
Or to victorie!

Now 's the day, and now 's the hour;
See the front of battle lour;
See approach proud Edward's power—
Chains and slaverie!

[1] The tune is one of the oldest Scots airs; it appears in Playford's Collection, 1657. Burns first used it in 1785 for 'Rantin, rovin Robin,' Mrs Dunlop's version of which has 'Davie' for 'Robin.'

Wha will be a traitor-knave?
Wha can fill a coward's grave?
Wha sae base as be a slave?
Let him turn and flee!

Wha for Scotland's king and law
Freedom's sword will strongly draw,
Freeman stand, or freeman fa',
Let him follow me!

By oppression's woes and pains!
By your sons in servile chains!
We will drain our dearest veins,
But they shall be free!

Lay the proud usurpers low!
Tyrants fall in ev'ry foe!
Liberty 's in ev'ry blow!—
Let us do or die!

THOU HAST LEFT ME EVER.

TUNE—*Fee him, Father.*

Thou hast left me ever, Jamie! thou hast left me ever;
Thou hast left me ever, Jamie! thou hast left me ever:
Aften hast thou vowed that death only should us sever;
Now thou 'st left thy lass for aye—I maun see thee never, must
Jamie,
I 'll see thee never.

Thou hast me forsaken, Jamie! thou hast me forsaken;
Thou hast me forsaken, Jamie! thou hast me forsaken:
Thou canst love anither jo, while my heart is breaking; sweetheart
Soon my weary een I 'll close—never mair to waken, eyes—more
Jamie,
Ne'er mair to waken!

THE PRIMROSE.

TUNE—*Toddlin Hame.*

Dost ask me, why I send thee here,
This firstling of the infant year—
This lovely native of the vale,
That hangs so pensive and so pale?

Look on its bending stalk, so weak
That, each way yielding, doth not break,
And see how aptly it reveals
The doubts and fears a lover feels.

Look on its leaves of yellow hue
Bepearl'd thus with morning dew,
And these will whisper in thine ears
'The sweets of love are wash'd with tears.'

DELUDED SWAIN, THE PLEASURE.

TUNE—*The Collier's Bonny Lassie.*

Deluded swain, the pleasure
The fickle fair can give thee
Is but a fairy treasure,
Thy hopes will soon deceive thee.

The billows on the ocean,
The breezes idly roaming,
The clouds' uncertain motion,
They are but types of woman.

O! art thou not ashamed
To dote upon a feature?
If man thou wouldst be named,
Despise the silly creature.

Go find an honest fellow;
Good claret set before thee:
Hold on till thou art mellow,
And then to bed in glory.

IMPROMPTU

ON MRS RIDDEL'S BIRTHDAY, 4TH NOVEMBER 1793.

Old winter, with his frosty beard,
Thus once to Jove his prayer preferred:—
'What have I done, of all the year,
To bear this hated doom severe?
My cheerless suns no pleasure know;
Night's horrid car drags, dreary, slow;
My dismal months no joys are crowning,
But spleeny, English hanging, drowning.

'Now Jove, for once be mighty civil:
To counterbalance all this evil
Give me, and I 've no more to say,
Give me Maria's natal day!
That brilliant gift will so enrich me,
Spring, Summer, Autumn, cannot match me.'
''Tis done!' says Jove; so ends my story,
And Winter once rejoic'd in glory.

MY SPOUSE NANCY.

TUNE—*My Jo Janet.*

'Husband, husband, cease your strife,
  Nor longer idly rave, sir;
Tho' I am your wedded wife,
  Yet I am not your slave, sir.'

'One of two must still obey,
  Nancy, Nancy,
Is it man or woman, say,
  My spouse Nancy?'

'If 'tis still the lordly word,
  Service and obedience;
I 'll desert my sov'reign lord,
  And so, good-bye allegiance!'

'Sad will I be, so bereft,
  Nancy, Nancy;
Yet I 'll try to make a shift,
  My spouse Nancy.'

'My poor heart then break it must,
  My last hour I 'm near it:
When you lay me in the dust,
  Think, think how you will bear it.'

'I will hope and trust in Heaven,
  Nancy, Nancy;
Strength to bear it will be given,
  My spouse Nancy.'

'Well, sir, from the silent dead,
  Still I 'll try to daunt you;

Ever round your midnight bed
  Horrid sprites shall haunt you.'

'I'll wed another, like my dear,
  Nancy, Nancy;
Then all hell will fly for fear,
  My spouse, Nancy.'

ADDRESS

SPOKEN BY MISS FONTENELLE ON HER BENEFIT NIGHT.

Wednesday, December 4th, 1793, at the Theatre, Dumfries.

Still anxious to secure your partial favor,
And not less anxious sure this night than ever,
A Prologue, Epilogue, or some such matter,
'Twould vamp my bill, said I, if nothing better;
So, sought a Poet, roosted near the skies,
Told him, I came to feast my curious eyes;
Said, nothing like his works was ever printed;
At last, my prologue-business slily hinted.
'Ma'am, let me tell you,' quoth my man of rhymes,
'I know your bent—these are no laughing times:
Can you—but Miss, I own I have my fears,
Dissolve in pause—and sentimental tears—
With laden sighs, and solemn-rounded sentence,
Rouse from his sluggish slumbers, fell Repentance;
Paint Vengeance as he takes his horrid stand,
Waving on high the desolating brand,
Calling the storms to bear him o'er a guilty land!'

I could no more—askance the creature eyeing,
D'ye think, said I, this face was made for crying?
I'll laugh, that's poz—nay more, the world shall know it;
And so, your servant! gloomy Master Poet!
Firm as my creed, Sirs, 'tis my fix'd belief,
That Misery's another word for Grief:
I also think—so may I be a bride!
That so much laughter, so much life enjoy'd.

Thou man of crazy care and ceaseless sigh,
Still under bleak misfortune's blasting eye;
Doom'd to that sorest task of man alive—
To make three guineas do the work of five:

Laugh in Misfortune's face—the beldam witch!
Say, you 'll be merry, tho' you can't be rich.
Thou other man of care, the wretch in love,
Who long with jiltish arts and airs hast strove;
Who, as the boughs all temptingly project,
Measur'st in desperate thought—a rope—thy neck—
Or, where the beetling cliff o'erhangs the deep,
Peerest to meditate the healing leap:
Wouldst thou be cur'd, thou silly, moping elf,
Laugh at her follies—laugh e'en at thyself:
Learn to despise those frowns now so terrific,
And love a kinder—that 's your grand specific.

To sum up all, be merry, I advise;
And as we 're merry, may we still be wise.

MONODY

ON A LADY FAMED FOR HER CAPRICE.[1]

How cold is that bosom which Folly once fired!
  How pale is that cheek where the rouge lately glisten'd!
How silent that tongue which the echoes oft tired!
  How dull is that ear which to flatt'ry so listen'd!

If sorrow and anguish their exit await,
  From friendship and dearest affection remov'd;
How doubly severer, Maria, thy fate!
  Thou diedst unwept, as thou livedst unlov'd.

Loves, Graces and Virtues, I call not on you:
  So shy, grave and distant, ye shed not a tear.
But come, all ye offspring of Folly so true,
  And flowers let us cull for Maria's cold bier.

We 'll search through the garden for each silly flower,
  We 'll roam through the forest for each idle weed,
But chiefly the nettle, so typical, shower,
  For none e'er approached her but rued the rash deed.

We 'll sculpture the marble, we 'll measure the lay:
  Here Vanity strums on her idiot lyre!
There keen Indignation shall dart on his prey,
  Which spurning Contempt shall redeem from his ire!

[1] The lady referred to here and in the Epistle following was Mrs Riddel of Glenriddel.

THE EPITAPH.

Here lies now, a prey to insulting neglect,
Who once was a butterfly gay in life's beam:
Want only of Wisdom denied her respect,
Want only of Goodness denied her esteem.

EPISTLE FROM ESOPUS[1] TO MARIA.

From those drear solitudes and frowsy cells,
Where Infamy with sad Repentance dwells;[2]
Where turnkeys make the jealous portal fast,
And deal from iron hands the spare repast;
Where truant 'prentices, yet young in sin,
Blush at the curious stranger peeping in;
Where strumpets, relics of the drunken roar,
Resolve to drink, nay, half—to whore—no more;
Where tiny thieves, not destin'd yet to swing,
Beat hemp for others riper for the string:
From these dire scenes my wretched lines I date,
To tell Maria her Esopus' fate.

'Alas! I feel I am no actor here!'[3]
'Tis real hangmen real scourges bear!
Prepare, Maria, for a horrid tale
Will turn thy very rouge to deadly pale;
Will make thy hair, though erst from gipsy poll'd,
By barber woven and by barber sold,
Though twisted smooth with Harry's nicest care,
Like hoary bristles to erect and stare!
The hero of the mimic scene, no more
I start in Hamlet, in Othello roar;
Or, haughty Chieftain, 'mid the din of arms,
In Highland bonnet woo Malvina's charms:
While sans-culottes stoop up the mountain high,
And steal from me Maria's prying eye.
Blest Highland bonnet! once my proudest dress,
Now, prouder still, Maria's temples press!

[1] Æsopus was the most celebrated tragic actor in Rome in the Ciceronian period, the only peer of Roscius the comedian. He was a familiar friend of Cicero.

[2] 'In these dread solitudes and awful cells,
Where heavenly pensive contemplation dwells,' &c.
—*Epistle of Eloisa to Abelard.*

[3] Lyttelton's Prologue to Thomson's *Coriolanus*, spoken by Mr Quin.

C. Martin Hardie, R.S.A.

O my luve's like a red, red rose.

PAGE 413.

I see her wave thy towering plumes afar,
And call each coxcomb to the wordy war!
I see her face the first of Ireland's sons,[1]
And even out-Irish his Hibernian bronze!
The crafty Colonel[2] leaves the tartan'd lines
For other wars, where he a hero shines;
The hopeful youth, in Scottish senate bred,
Who owns a Bushby's heart without the head,[3]
Comes 'mid a string of coxcombs to display
That *Veni, vidi, vici*, is his way;
The shrinking Bard adown the alley skulks
And dreads a meeting worse than Woolwich hulks,
Though there his heresies in Church and State
Might well award him Muir and Palmer's fate:[4]
Still she, undaunted, reels and rattles on
And dares the public like a noontide sun.
What scandal called Maria's jaunty stagger,
The ricket reeling of a crooked swagger?
Whose spleen (e'en worse than Burns's venom, when
He dips in gall unmix'd his eager pen
And pours his vengeance in the burning line),
Who christen'd thus Maria's lyre-divine,
The idiot strum of Vanity bemus'd,
And even th' abuse of Poesy abus'd?
Who called her verse a Parish Workhouse, made
For motley foundling Fancies, stolen or strayed?

A Workhouse! Ah, that sound awakes my woes,
And pillows on the thorn my rack'd repose!
In durance vile here must I wake and weep,
And all my frowsy couch in sorrow steep:
That straw where many a rogue has lain of yore,
And vermin'd gipsies litter'd heretofore.

Why Lonsdale, thus thy wrath on vagrants pour:
Must earth no rascal save thyself endure?

[1] The poet here enumerates several of Mrs Riddel's visiting-friends. 'Gillespie' has been noted as the name of the Irish gentleman first alluded to.

[2] Colonel M'Douall of Logan, a noted Lothario. He figures also as 'Sculdudd'ry Logan's M'Douall' in the Second Heron Election Ballad.

[3] Maitland Bushby, son of John Bushby, the 'honest man.'

[4] Thomas Muir (b. Glasgow, 1765), a member of the Scottish Bar, was an active promoter of the Society of Friends of the Constitution and the People. He was tried for sedition in Edinburgh in 1793, and sentenced to fourteen years' transportation. He died abroad in 1796. Rev. Thomas Fyshe Palmer (b. in Bedfordshire, 1747) was a graduate of Cambridge and a Unitarian minister in Dundee. He was tried after Muir, convicted of sedition on equally paltry evidence, and sentenced to seven years' transportation. He survived till 1802.

Must thou alone in guilt immortal swell
And make a vast monopoly of Hell?
Thou know'st the Virtues cannot hate thee worse:
The Vices also, must they club their curse?
Or must no tiny sin to others fall,
Because thy guilt 's supreme enough for all?

Maria, send me, too, thy griefs and cares,
In all of thee sure thy Esopus shares:
As thou at all mankind the flag unfurls,
Who on my fair one Satire's vengeance hurls!
Who calls thee pert, affected, vain coquette,
A wit in folly and a fool in wit!
Who says that 'fool' alone is not thy due,
And quotes thy treacheries to prove it true!

Our force united on thy foes we 'll turn,
And dare the war with all of woman born:
For who can write and speak as thou and I?
My periods that deciphering defy,
And thy still matchless tongue that conquers all reply!

THE LOVELY LASS OF INVERNESS.[1]

TUNE—*The lovely Lass of Inverness.*

The lovely lass o' Inverness,
Nae joy nor pleasure can she see;
For e'en and morn she cries, 'Alas!'
And ay the saut tear blins her e'e; salt—blinds
'Drumossie Moor[2]—Drumossie day—
A waefu' day it was to me! woeful
For there I lost my father dear—
My father dear and brethren three.

'Their winding-sheet the bluidy clay,
Their graves are growing green to see;
And by them lies the dearest lad
That ever blest a woman's e'e!
Now wae to thee, thou cruel lord,[3]
A bluidy man I trow thou be;
For mony a heart thou has made sair sore
That ne'er did wrang to thine or thee!'

1 The first half-stanza of this song is from an old composition.
2 The battle of Culloden was fought, 16th April 1746, on Drummossie Muir.
3 The Duke of Cumberland.

A RED, RED ROSE.[1]

TUNE—*Graham's Strathspey.*

O my Luve 's like a red, red rose
  That 's newly sprung in June;
O my Luve 's like the melodie
  That 's sweetly play'd in tune.
As fair art thou, my bonie lass,
  So deep in luve am I;
And I will luve thee still, my dear,
  Till a' the seas gang dry.

Till a' the seas gang dry, my Dear,
  And the rocks melt wi' the sun;
O I will love thee still, my dear,
  While the sands o' life shall run.
And fare thee weel, my only Luve!
  And fare thee weel a while!
And I will come again, my Luve,
  Tho' it were ten thousand mile!

OUT OVER THE FORTH.

TUNE—*Charlie Gordon's welcome Home.*

Out over the Forth I look to the North:
  But what is the North and its Highlands to me?
The South nor the East gie ease to my breast,
  The far foreign land or the wild rolling sea.

But I look to the West when I gae to rest,
  That happy my dreams and my slumbers may be:
For far in the West lives he I lo'e best,
  The lad that is dear to my babie and me.

[1] This song was written by Burns as an improvement upon a street ditty, which Peter Buchan says was composed by a Lieutenant Hinches, as a farewell to his sweetheart, when on the eve of parting. Various versions of the original song are given in Hogg and Motherwell's edition of Burns, including one from a stall sheet containing 'six excellent new songs,' which Motherwell conjectures to have been printed about 1770, and of which his copy bore these words on its title, in a childish scrawl believed to be that of the Ayrshire bard, 'Robine Burns aught this buik and no other.'

LOUIS, WHAT RECK I BY THEE?[1]

TUNE—*Louis, what Reck I by Thee?*

Louis,[2] what reck I by thee?
Or Geordie[3] on his ocean?
Dyvor, beggar louns to me, — Bankrupt—worthless fellows
I reign in Jeanie's bosom!

Let her crown my love her law,
And in her breast enthrone me:
Kings and nations, swith awa! — quick—begone
Reif randies, I disown ye! — Thief-beggars

CHARLIE, HE'S MY DARLING.

'Twas on a Monday morning
Right early in the year
That Charlie came to our town,
The young Chevalier.

Chorus—An' Charlie, he 's my darling,
My darling, my darling,
Charlie, he 's my darling,
The young Chevalier.

As he was walking up the street
The city for to view,
O there he spied a bonie lass
The window looking thro'.

Sae light 's he jimped up the stair
And tirled at the pin;[4]
And wha sae ready as hersel
To let the laddie in!

He set his Jenny on his knee,
All in his Highland dress;
For brawlie well he ken'd the way — full well
To please a bonie lass.

[1] It has been conjectured, from the allusion to 'Jeanie' in this song, that it was composed by Burns on the arrival of his wife at Ellisland in 1788. This is, however, merely conjecture.

[2] The king of France. [3] The king of Great Britain.

[4] On the back of a house-door there used to be attached a risping pin—i.e. a notched rod of iron, with a loose string attached. This made a loud noise on being drawn up and down (*tirled*).

It 's up yon heathery mountain,
And down yon scroggy glen, abounding in brushwood
We daur na gang a-milking, go
For Charlie and his men.

THE COOPER O' CUDDY.

TUNE—*Bab at the Bouster.*

The Cooper o' Cuddy cam here awa,
He ca'd the girrs out o'er us a'; hoops
And our gudewife has gotten a ca'
That anger'd the silly gudeman, O.

Chorus—We 'll hide the cooper behind the door,
Behind the door, behind the door,
We 'll hide the cooper behind the door,
An' cover him under a mawn, O. basket without lid

He sought them out, he sought them in,
Wi' deil hae her! and deil hae him!
But the body he was sae doited an' blin' stupid
He wist na whare he was gaun, O. knew not—going

They cooper'd at e'en, they cooper'd at morn,
Till our gudeman has gotten the scorn;
On ilka brow she 's planted a horn,
And swears that there they shall stan', O.

SOMEBODY![1]

TUNE—*For the Sake of Somebody.*

My heart is sair, I dare na tell, sore
My heart is sair for Somebody;
I could wake a winter-night
For the sake o' Somebody.
Oh-hon! for Somebody!
Oh-hey! for Somebody!
I could range the world around
For the sake o' Somebody!

[1] 'The whole of this song was written by Burns, except the third and fourth lines of stanza first, which are taken from Ramsay's song under the same title and to the same old tune.'—STENHOUSE.

Ye Powers that smile on virtuous love,
O, sweetly smile on Somebody!
Frae ilka danger keep him free, From every
And send me safe my Somebody!
Oh-hon! for Somebody!
Oh-hey! for Somebody!
I wad do—what wad I not?— would
For the sake o' Somebody!

WILT THOU BE MY DEARIE?

AIR—*The Sutor's Dochter.*

Wilt thou be my Dearie?
When sorrow wrings thy gentle heart
O wilt thou let me chear thee?
By the treasure of my soul,
That 's the love I bear thee!
I swear and vow that only thou
Shall ever be my Dearie;
Only thou, I swear and vow,
Shall ever be my Dearie!

Lassie, say thou lo'es me! lovest
Or, if thou wilt na be my ain,
Say na thou 'lt refuse me!
If it winna, canna be
Thou for thine may chuse me,
Let me, Lassie, quickly die,
Trusting that thou lo'es me;
Lassie, let me quickly die,
Trusting that thou lo'es me!

LOVELY POLLY STEWART.[1]

TUNE—*You 're welcome, Charlie Stewart.*

O lovely Polly Stewart!
O charming Polly Stewart!
There 's ne'er a flower that blooms in May
That 's half so fair as thou art!

[1] Mary Stewart, the subject of these verses, was a girl about seventeen or eighteen years of age when they were written, having been born in 1775. She was the daughter of William Stewart, resident factor on the Rev. James Stewart Menteith's Dumfriesshire estate of Closeburn.

The flower it blaws, it fades, it fa's, blows—falls
And art can ne'er renew it;
But worth and truth eternal youth
Will gie to Polly Stewart!

May he whase arms shall fauld thy charms fold
Possess a leal and true heart! loyal
To him be given to ken the Heaven know
He grasps in Polly Stewart!
O lovely Polly Stewart!
O charming Polly Stewart!
There's ne'er a flower that blooms in May
That's half so fair as thou art!

WAE IS MY HEART.

TUNE—*Wae is my Heart.*

Wae is my heart, and the tear's in my e'e; Sorrowful
Lang, lang joy's been a stranger to me; Long
Forsaken and friendless my burden I bear,
And the sweet voice o' pity ne'er sounds in my ear.

Love, thou hast pleasures, and deep hae I loved; have
Love, thou hast sorrows, and sair hae I proved; sore
But this bruised heart that now bleeds in my breast,
I can feel by its throbbings will soon be at rest.

O if I were where happy I hae been;
Down by yon stream and yon bonie castle-green;
For there he is wand'ring, and musing on me,
Wha wad soon dry the tear frae Phillis's e'e.[1] would—from

HERE'S TO THY HEALTH, MY BONIE LASS.[2]

TUNE—*Laggan Burn.*

Here's to thy health, my bonie lass,
Gude-night and joy be wi' thee;
I'll come nae mair to thy bower-door
To tell thee that I loe thee.

[1] Mr Scott Douglas has suggested that in this song Burns may have been 'mustering all the mysteries of his art with a view to cast his glamour over and render secure the affections of Maria Riddel, whom he had recently lampooned so severely.' The last two lines, apart from the allusion to Phillis, give an air of extreme improbability to this suggestion.

[2] Mrs Begg declared this song not to be Burns's, but to be one of those familiar ditties commonly sung at rural firesides before his efforts in that way were known. But internal evidence is all in favour of Burns's authorship.

O dinna think, my pretty pink,
But I can live without thee:
I vow and swear I dinna care
How lang ye look about ye.

Thou 'rt ay sae free informing me
Thou hast nae mind to marry;
I 'll be as free informing thee
Nae time hae I to tarry.
I ken thy friends try ilka means — know—every
Frae wedlock to delay thee,
Depending on some higher chance—
But fortune may betray thee.

I ken they scorn my low estate,
But that does never grieve me;
For I 'm as free as any he,
Sma' siller will relieve me. — Little money
I count my health my greatest wealth
Sae lang as I 'll enjoy it;
I 'll fear na scant, I 'll bode nae want, — anticipate
As lang 's I get employment.

But far-off fowls hae feathers fair,
And ay until ye try them;
Tho' they seem fair, still have a care
They may prove as bad as I am.
But at twal at night, when the moon shines bright, — twelve
My dear, I 'll come and see thee;
For the man that loves his mistress weel,
Nae travel makes him weary.

ANNA, THY CHARMS MY BOSOM FIRE.[1]

TUNE—*Bonny Mary.*

Anna, thy charms my bosom fire
And waste my soul with care;
But ah! how bootless to admire
When fated to despair!
Yet in thy presence, lovely Fair,
To hope may be forgiv'n:
For sure 'twere impious to despair,
So much in sight of Heaven.

[1] Composed on a sweetheart of Alexander Cunningham—she who afterwards jilted him.

C. Martin Hardie, R.S.A.

My heart is sair, I dare na tell,
My heart is sair for somebody.

PAGE 415.

MY LADY'S GOWN THERE'S GAIRS UPON'T.[1]

My Lord a-hunting he is gane, gone
But hounds or hawks wi' him are nane;
By Colin's cottage lies his game,
If Colin's Jenny be at hame.

Chorus—My Lady's gown there 's gairs[2] upon 't,
And gowden flowers sae rare upon 't; golden
But Jenny's jimps and jirkinet stays—bodice
My Lord thinks meikle mair upon 't. much more

My Lady 's white, my Lady 's red,
And kith and kin o' Cassillis'[3] blude;
But her tenpund lands o' tocher gude dowry
Were a' the charms his Lordship lo'ed.

Out o'er yon moor, out o'er yon moss, over
Whare gor-cocks through the heather pass, moor-cocks
There wons auld Colin's bonie lass— lives
A lily in a wilderness.

Sae sweetly move her genty limbs, handsome
Like music-notes o' Lovers' hymns;
The diamond-dew is her een sae blue,
Where laughing love sae wanton swims.

My Lady 's dink, my Lady 's drest, trim
The flower and fancy o' the west;
But the Lassie that a man lo'es best,
O that 's the Lass to make him blest.

JOCKEY'S TA'EN THE PARTING KISS.

TUNE—*Jockey 's ta'en the Parting Kiss.*

Jockey 's ta'en the parting kiss,
O'er the mountains he is gane;
And with him is a' my bliss,
Nought but griefs with me remain.

[1] Stenhouse says: 'Johnson long hesitated to admit the song into his work; but, being blamed for such fastidiousness, he at length gave it a place there.'

[2] Gair, English *gore*, properly a piece inserted in a dress, evidently here meaning an ornamental part, a bright-coloured piece.

[3] The Kennedies, Earls of Cassillis, were the leading family in Carrick.

Spare my love, ye winds that blaw,
  Plashy sleets and beating rain;
Spare my love, thou feath'ry snaw
  Drifting o'er the frozen plain.

When the shades of evening creep
  O'er the day's fair, gladsome e'e,
Sound and safely may he sleep,
  Sweetly blythe his waukening be. awakening
He will think on her he loves,
  Fondly he 'll repeat her name;
For whare'er he distant roves,
  Jockey's heart is still at hame.

O LAY THY LOOF IN MINE, LASS.[1]

TUNE—*The Cordwainers' March.*

A slave to love's unbounded sway,
He aft has wrought me meikle wae; often—much woe
But now he is my deadly fae, foe
  Unless thou be my ain.

Chorus—O lay thy loof in mine, lass, hand, palm
  In mine, lass, in mine, lass,
  And swear on thy white hand, lass,
    That thou wilt be my ain. own

There 's monie a lass has broke my rest many
That for a blink I ha'e lo'ed best; instant
But thou art queen within my breast,
  For ever to remain.

CAULD IS THE E'ENIN' BLAST.

TUNE—*Peggy Ramsay.*[2]

Cauld is the e'enin' blast
  O' Boreas o'er the pool,
And dawin it is dreary dawn
  When birks are bare at Yule. birches

[1] Both this song and its predecessor have been assigned by some editors to a late period in Burns's life—when he was lying on his death-bed. For this view no valid reason is assigned.

[2] This is a version of a very old song, the title of which is quoted in *Twelfth Night*, Act II. Scene iii., by Sir Toby Belch.

Cauld blaws the e'enin' blast
When bitter bites the frost,
And, in the mirk and dreary drift, dark
The hills and glens are lost.

Ne'er sae murky blew the night
That drifted o'er the hill,
But bonie Peg-a-Ramsey
Gat grist to her mill.

THERE'S NEWS, LASSES, NEWS.

'There 's news, lasses, news,
Gude news I 've to tell!
There 's a boatfu' o' lads
Come to our town, to sell.

Chorus—The wean wants a cradle, child
And the cradle wants a cod; pillow
An' I'll no gang to my bed
Until I get a nod.'

'Father,' quo' she, 'Mither,' quo' she,
'Do what you can,
I'll no gang to my bed
Until I get a man.

'I hae as gude a craft rig croft ridge
As made o' yird and stane; earth
And waly fa' the ley-crab, ill befall—grass crop
For I maun till 't again.'

O MALLY'S MEEK, MALLY'S SWEET.

As I was walking up the street,
A barefit maid I chanc'd to meet; barefoot
But O the road was very hard
For that fair maiden's tender feet.

Chorus—O Mally 's meek, Mally 's sweet,
Mally 's modest and discreet,
Mally 's rare, Mally 's fair,
Mally 's ev'ry way compleat.

It were mair meet that those fine feet — more
Were weel lac'd up in silken shoon, — shoes
And 'twere more fit that she should sit
Within yon chariot gilt aboon. — above

Her yellow hair, beyond compare,
Comes trinkling down her swan-white neck; — trickling
And her two eyes, like stars in skies,
Would keep a sinking ship frae wreck. — from

SONG—A BOTTLE AND FRIEND.

'There's nane that's blest of human kind
But the cheerful and the gay, man,
Fal la, la,' &c.

Here's a bottle and an honest friend!
What wad ye wish for mair, man?
Wha kens, before his life may end, — knows
What his share may be of care, man?

Then catch the moments as they fly,
And use them as ye ought, man:
Believe me, happiness is shy
And comes not ay when sought, man.

THENIEL MENZIES' BONIE MARY.[1]

TUNE—*The Ruffian's Rant.*

In coming by the brig o' Dye, — bridge
At Darlet we a blink did tarry; — a brief period
As day was dawin in the sky, — dawning
We drank a health to bonie Mary.

Chorus—Theniel Menzies' bonie Mary,
Theniel Menzies' bonie Mary;
Charlie Gregor tint his plaidie, — lost
Kissin' Theniel's bonie Mary.

Her een sae bright, her brow sae white,
Her haffet locks as brown 's a berry; — side-locks
And ay they dimpl't wi' a smile,
The rosy cheeks o' bonie Mary.

[1] It has been suggested from Darlet being in Aberdeenshire that this song was inspired by Burns's northern tour.

We lap and danc'd the lee-lang day — live-long
Till Piper lads were wae and weary:
But Charlie gat the spring to pay
For kissin' Theniel's bonie Mary.

THE CAPTIVE RIBBAND.

TUNE—*Robie donna gorrach.*

Dear Myra, the captive ribband 's mine,
'Twas all my faithful love could gain;
And would you ask me to resign
The sole reward that crowns my pain?

Go bid the hero who has run
Thro' fields of death to gather fame;
Go bid him lay his laurels down
And all his well-earn'd praise disclaim.

The ribband shall its freedom lose—
Lose all the bliss it had with you,
And share the fate I would impose
On thee, wert thou my captive too.

It shall upon my bosom live
Or clasp me in a close embrace;
And at its fortune if you grieve,
Retrieve its doom and take its place.

EPPIE ADAIR.

By love and by beauty,
By law and by duty,
I swear to be true to
My Eppie Adair!

Chorus—An' O! my Eppie,
My jewel, my Eppie!
Wha wadna be happy
Wi' Eppie Adair!

A' pleasure exile me,
Dishonour defile me,
If e'er I beguile thee,
My Eppie Adair!

A FIDDLER IN THE NORTH.

TUNE—*The King of France, he rade a Race.*

Amang the trees where humming bees
  At buds and flowers were hinging, O,
Auld Caledon drew out her drone,
  And to her pipe was singing, O:
'Twas Pibroch, Sang, Strathspeys and Reels,
  She dirl'd them aff fu' clearly, O;
When there cam' a yell o' foreign squeels
  That dang her tapsalteerie, O. drove—head over heels

Their capon craws and queer 'ha, ha's,'
  They made our lugs grow eerie, O; ears
The hungry bike did scrape and fyke crew—fuss
  Till we were wae and weary, O:
But a royal ghaist,[1] wha ance was cas'd
  A prisoner aughteen year awa,
He fir'd a Fiddler in the North[2]
  That dang them tapsalteerie, O.

SONNET ON THE DEATH OF GLENRIDDEL.[3]

No more, ye warblers of the wood, no more,
Nor pour your descant grating on my soul!
Thou young-eyed Spring, gay in thy verdant stole,
More Welcome were to me grim Winter's wildest roar!
How can ye charm, ye flowers, with all your dyes?
Ye blow upon the sod that wraps my friend.
How can I to the tuneful strain attend?
That strain flows round th' untimely tomb where Riddel lies.
Yes, pour, ye warblers, pour the notes of woe,
And soothe the Virtues weeping o'er his bier!
The man of worth—and 'hath not left his peer!'—
Is in his 'narrow house' for ever darkly low.
Thee, Spring, again with joy shall others greet;
Me, memory of my loss will only meet.

[1] James I. of Scotland, detained eighteen years in the Tower by Henry IV. of England.

[2] Probably a brother of Neil Gow.

[3] Riddel was buried in Dunscore churchyard. On a plain tombstone the following inscription is cut: 'To the memory of Robert Riddell, Esq. of Glenriddell, who departed this life on the 21st day of Aprile 1794, in the 38th year of his age.' Mrs Riddel, his widow, died seven years later at Bath.

TO WILLIAM STEWART.

In honest Bacon's ingle-neuk — chimney-corner
  Here maun I sit and think, — must
Sick o' the warld and warld's folk,
  An' sick, damn'd sick, o' drink!

I see, I see there is nae help,
  But still doun I maun sink,
Till some day laigh enough, I yelp — low
  'Wae worth that cursèd drink!' — woe befall

Yestreen, alas! I was sae fu' — Yesterday—drunk
  I could but yisk and wink; — hiccup
And now, this day, sair, sair I rue — sorely
  The weary, weary drink.

Satan, I fear thy sooty claws,
  I hate thy brunstane stink, — brimstone
And ay I curse the luckless cause—
  The wicked soup o' drink. — sup

In vain I would forget my woes
  In idle rhyming clink,
For, past redemption damn'd in prose,
  I can do nought but drink.

To you, my trusty, well-tried friend,
  May heaven still on you blink!
And may your life flow to the end,
  Sweet as a dry man's drink!

YOU'RE WELCOME, WILLIE STEWART.[1]

Come, bumpers high, express your joy,
The bowl we maun renew it, — must
The tappet hen, gae bring her ben — quart measure
To welcome Willie Stewart.

Chorus—You 're welcome, Willie Stewart!
  You 're welcome, Willie Stewart!
  There 's ne'er a flower that blooms in May
  That 's half sae welcome 's thou art!

[1] This song was inscribed on a crystal tumbler, which was acquired by Sir Walter Scott and is preserved at Abbotsford.

May foes be strang and friends be slack;
  Ilk action, may he rue it; Every
May woman on him turn her back
  That wrangs thee, Willie Stewart!

THE BANKS OF CREE.

TUNE—*The Banks of Cree.*

Here is the glen and here the bower,
  All underneath the birchen shade;
The village-bell has tolled the hour,
  O what can stay my lovely maid?

'Tis not Maria's whispering call;
  'Tis but the balmy-breathing gale
Mixt with some warbler's dying fall,
  The dewy star of eve to hail.

It is Maria's voice I hear;
  So calls the woodlark in the grove
His little, faithful mate to chear:
  At once 'tis music—and 'tis love.

And art thou come? and art thou true?
  O welcome, dear, to love and me!
And let us all our vows renew,
  Along the flowery banks of Cree.

THE MINSTREL AT LINCLUDEN.

PART I.—A VISION.[1]

As I stood by yon roofless tower,
  Where the wa'-flower scents the dewy air, wall-
Where the howlet mourns in her ivy bower, owl
  And tells the midnight moon her care.

[1] 'Our poet's prudence suppressed the song of Libertie,' Dr Currie stated in a note to 'A Vision.' In the 'Self-interpreting' edition (published at Philadelphia in 1886), the editors, Messrs Hunter and Gebbie, claimed 'to be able to announce that we for the first time present to the world the perfect poem.' They conjecture that the 'Ode to Liberty' (or 'Ode for General Washington's Birthday') was the song the minstrel sang. 'A very careful study' led them to conclude 'that Burns . . . produced the two pieces as a connected whole and nearly at a sitting; but that he must have immediately afterwards seen that it would be

The winds were laid, the air was still,
  The stars they shot alang the sky;
The fox was howling on the hill,
  And the distant-echoing glens reply.

The stream adown its hazelly path
  Was rushing by the ruin'd wa's,
Hasting to join the sweeping Nith,
  Whase distant roaring swells and fa's. falls

The cauld blue north was streaming forth cold
  Her lights, wi' hissing eerie din;[1]
Athort the lift they start and shift, Athwart—firmament
  Like fortune's favors, tint as win. lost as soon as won

By heedless chance I turn'd mine eyes
  And, by the moon-beam, shook, to see
A stern and stalwart ghaist arise,
  Attir'd as minstrels wont to be.

Had I a statue been o' stane,
  His darin look had daunted me;
And on his bonnet grav'd was plain
  The sacred posy—Libertie!

And frae his harp sic strains did flow from—such
  Might rous'd the slumb'ring dead to hear;
But oh, it was a tale of woe
  As ever met a Briton's ear!

PART II.—ODE.

No Spartan tube, no Attic shell,
  No lyre Æolian I awake.
'Tis Liberty's bold note I swell:
  Thy harp, Columbia, let me take!
See gathering thousands, while I sing,
A broken chain, exulting, bring,

unsafe to publish them in that form, and therefore added a verse to the "Vision" or prelude:

He sang wi' joy his former day,
  He, weeping, wail'd his latter times;
But what he said it was nae play—
  I winna ventur't in my rhymes.

This he did to give an air of completeness to what would otherwise have appeared a fragment.' This theory is, owing to its intrinsic reasonableness, adopted here. 'The Vision' shows in itself that it was intended as prelude to another poem. Besides, the two pieces are in perfect harmony.

[1] A display of the Aurora Borealis is said to be accompanied by hissing or crackling sounds.

And dash it in a tyrant's face,
And dare him to his very beard,
And tell him he no more is fear'd—
No more the despot of Columbia's race!
A tyrant's proudest insults brav'd,
They shout a People freed! They hail an Empire sav'd!

Where is man's godlike form?
Where is that brow erect and bold,
That eye that can, unmov'd, behold
The wildest rage, the loudest storm
That e'er created Fury dared to raise?
Avaunt! thou caitiff, servile, base,
That tremblest at a despot's nod,
Yet, crouching under the iron rod,
Canst laud the hand that struck th' insulting blow!
Art thou of man's Imperial line?
Dost boast that countenance divine?
Each skulking feature answers, No!
But come, ye sons of Liberty,
Columbia's offspring, brave as free,
In danger's hour still flaming in the van,
Ye know, and dare maintain, the Royalty of Man!

Alfred! on thy starry throne
Surrounded by the tuneful choir,
The Bards that erst have struck the patriot lyre,
And rous'd the freeborn Briton's soul of fire,
No more thy England own!
Dare injured nations from the great design
To make detested tyrants bleed?
Thy England execrates the glorious deed!
Beneath her hostile banners waving,
Every pang of honour braving,
England in thunder calls 'The Tyrant's cause is mine!'
That hour accurst how did the fiends rejoice,
And Hell thro' all her confines raise th' exulting voice!
That hour which saw the generous English name
Link't with such damnèd deeds of everlasting shame!

Thee, Caledonia! thy wild heaths among,
Fam'd for the martial deed, the heaven-taught song,
To thee I turn with swimming eyes!
Where is that soul of Freedom fled?
Immingled with the mighty dead
Beneath that hallow'd turf where Wallace lies!

Hear it not, Wallace, in thy bed of death!
  Ye babbling winds, in silence sweep!
  Disturb not ye the hero's sleep
Nor give the coward secret breath!
In this the ancient Caledonian form,
Firm as her rock, resistless as her storm?
Show me that arm which, nerv'd with thundering fate,
  Crush'd Usurpation's boldest daring!
Dark-quench'd as yonder sinking star,
No more that glance lightens afar,
That palsied arm no more whirls on the waste of war.

TO MISS GRAHAM OF FINTRY.[1]

Here, where the Scottish Muse immortal lives
  In sacred strains and tuneful numbers joined,
Accept the gift; though humble he that gives,
  Rich is the tribute of the grateful mind.

So may no ruffian feeling in thy breast
  Discordant jar thy bosom-chords among!
But Peace attune thy gentle soul to rest,
  Or Love ecstatic wake his seraph song!

Or Pity's notes in luxury of tears,
  As modest Want the tale of woe reveals;
While conscious Virtue all the strain endears,
  And heaven-born Piety her sanction seals!

THE TREE OF LIBERTY.

Heard ye o' the tree o' France?
  I watna what 's the name o' 't; wot not
Around it a' the patriots dance,
  Weel Europe kens the fame o' 't. knows
It stands where ance the Bastile stood,
  A prison built by kings, man,
When Superstition's hellish brood
  Kept France in leading-strings, man.

Upo' this tree there grows sic fruit, such
  Its virtues a' can tell, man;
It raises man aboon the brute, above
  It makes him ken himsel', man.

[1] Written on the blank side of the title-page of a copy of *The Melodies of Scotland*, which the poet presented to Miss Graham of Fintry.

Gif ance the peasant taste a bit, If once
He 's greater than a lord, man,
And wi' the beggar shares a mite
O' a' he can afford, man.

This fruit is worth a' Afric's wealth, all
To comfort us 'twas sent, man:
To gie the sweetest blush o' health
And mak us a' content, man.
It clears the een, it cheers the heart, eyes
Maks high and low guid friends, man;
And he wha acts the traitor's part,
It to perdition sends, man.

My blessings aye attend the chiel fellow
Wha pitied Gallia's slaves, man,
And staw a branch, spite o' the deil, stole
Frae yont the western waves, man. From beyond
Fair Virtue watered it wi' care,
And now she sees wi' pride, man,
How weel it buds and blossoms there,
Its branches spreading wide, man.

But vicious folk aye hate to see
The works o' Virtue thrive, man;
The courtly vermin 's banned the tree
And grat to see it thrive, man; wept
King Louis thought to cut it down,
When it was unco sma', man; very small
For this the watchman cracked his crown,
Cut aff his head and a', man.

A wicked crew syne, on a time, once
Did tak a solemn aith, man, oath
It ne'er should flourish to its prime:
I wat they pledged their faith, man. warrant
Awa they gaed wi' mock parade, went
Like beagles hunting game, man,
But soon grew weary o' the trade
And wished they 'd been at hame, man.

For Freedom, standing by the tree,
Her sons did loudly ca', man;
She sang a sang o' liberty,
Which pleased them ane and a', man.

By her inspired, the new-born race
  Soon drew the avenging steel, man;
The hirelings ran—her foes gied chase
  And banged the despot weel, man.

Let Britain boast her hardy oak,
  Her poplar and her pine, man,
Auld Britain ance could crack her joke, once
  And o'er her neighbours shine, man.
But seek the forest round and round,
  And soon 'twill be agreed, man,
That sic a tree can not be found
  'Twixt London and the Tweed, man.

Without this tree, alake! this life alas!
  Is but a vale o' woe, man;
A scene o' sorrow mixed wi' strife,
  Nae real joys we know, man.
We labour soon, we labour late,
  To feed the titled knave, man;
And a' the comfort we 're to get
  Is that ayont the grave, man. beyond

Wi' plenty o' sic trees, I trow, such
  The warld would live in peace, man;
The sword would help to mak a plough,
  The din o' war wad cease, man.
Like brethren in a common cause
  We 'd on each other smile, man;
And equal rights and equal laws
  Wad gladden every isle, man.

Wae worth the loon wha wadna eat Woe be to the fellow
  Sic halesome dainty cheer, man; wholesome
I 'd gie my shoon frae aff my feet, shoes
  To taste sic fruit, I swear, man.
Syne let us pray auld England may
  Sure plant this far-famed tree, man;
And blithe we 'll sing, and hail the day
  That gave us liberty, man.[1]

[1] Originally printed in the People's Edition of Burns (1840), from a manuscript in the possession of James Duncan, Mosesfield, Glasgow. David Robertson, editor of *Whistle Binkie*, did not allow that 'The Tree of Liberty' was anything but a successful imitation of Burns's manner. He 'submitted it to a gentleman of the highest respectability, to whose opinion Burns paid great deference, and to whom he was in the habit of showing his compositions, and he had never heard the poet allude to "The Tree of Liberty."'

ON THE SEAS AND FAR AWAY.

TUNE—*O'er the Hills, &c.*

How can my poor heart be glad,
When absent from my sailor lad;
How can I the thought forego,
He 's on the seas to meet the foe?
Let me wander, let me rove,
Still my heart is with my Love:
Nightly dreams and thoughts by day
Are with him that 's far away.

Chorus—On the seas and far away,
On stormy seas and far away,
Nightly dreams and thoughts by day
Are ay with him that 's far away.

When in summer noon I faint,
As weary flocks around me pant,
Haply in this scorching sun
My sailor 's thundering at his gun:
Bullets, spare my only joy!
Bullets, spare my darling boy!
Fate do with me what you may,
Spare but him that 's far away!

At the starless, midnight hour,
When Winter rules with boundless power;
As the storms the forest tear
And thunders rend the howling air:
Listening to the doubling roar
Surging on the rocky shore,
All I can—I weep and pray
For his weal that 's far away.

Peace, thy olive wand extend!
And bid wild war his ravage end!
Man with brother Man to meet
And as a brother kindly greet:
Then may Heaven with prosp'rous gales
Fill my sailor's welcome sails,
To my arms their charge convey
My dear lad that 's far away.

CA' THE YOWES TO THE KNOWES.

Hark, the mavis' evening sang — thrush's
Sounding Clouden's woods amang;
Then a-faulding let us gang, — a (sheep) folding—go
My bonie Dearie.

Chorus—Ca' the yowes to the knowes, — Drive—ewes—knolls
Ca' them whare the heather grows,
Ca' them whare the burnie rowes, — brooklet rolls
My bonie Dearie.

We 'll gae down by Clouden side,
Through the hazels spreading wide,
O'er the waves, that sweetly glide
To the moon sae clearly.

Yonder Clouden's silent towers,
Where at moonshine midnight hours,
O'er the dewy bending flowers,
Fairies dance sae cheary.

Ghaist nor bogle shalt thou fear; — Ghost—bogy
Thou 'rt to Love and Heaven sae dear,
Nocht of Ill may come thee near, — Nothing
My bonie Dearie.

Fair and lovely as thou art,
Thou hast stown my very heart; — stolen
I can die—but canna part,
My bonie Dearie.

SHE SAYS SHE LO'ES ME BEST OF A'.

TUNE—*Oonagh's Waterfall.*

Sae flaxen were her ringlets, — So
Her eyebrows of a darker hue,
Bewitchingly o'erarching
Twa laughing e'en o' bonie blue: — Two—eyes
Her smiling, sae wyling, — enticing
Wad make a wretch forget his wo;
What pleasure, what treasure,
Unto these rosy lips to grow:

Such was my Chloris' bonie face,
  When first her bonie face I saw;
And ay my Chloris' dearest charm—
  She says she lo'es me best of a'.

Like harmony her motion,
  Her pretty ankle is a spy,
Betraying fair proportion
  Wad make a saint forget the sky:
Sae warming, sae charming,
  Her fauteless form and gracefu' air;
Ilk feature—auld Nature
  Declar'd that she could do nae mair.
Hers are the willing chains o' love,
  By conquering Beauty's sovereign law:
And still my Chloris' dearest charm—
  She says she lo'es me best of a'.

Let others love the city,
  And gaudy show at sunny noon,
Gie me the lonely valley,
  The dewy eve, and rising moon
Fair beaming, and streaming
  Her silver light the boughs amang,
While falling, recalling,
  The amorous thrush concludes his sang:
There, dearest Chloris, wilt thou rove
  By wimpling burn and leafy shaw, grove
And hear my vows o' truth and love,
  And say thou lo'es me best of a'.

SAW YE MY PHELY?[1]

TUNE—*When she cam ben she bobbit.*

Oh, saw ye my dearie, my Phely?
Oh, saw ye my dearie, my Phely?
She 's down i' the grove, she 's wi' a new Love,
  She winna come hame to her Willy.

What says she, my dearest, my Phely?
What says she, my dearest, my Phely?
She lets thee to wit that she has thee forgot, know
  And for ever disowns thee her Willy.

[1] *Quasi dicat* Phillis.—R. B.

O, had I ne'er seen thee, my Phely!
O, had I ne'er seen thee, my Phely!
As light as the air, and fause as thou 's fair,
Thou 's broken the heart o' thy Willy.

HOW LANG AND DREARY IS THE NIGHT.

TUNE—*Cauld Kail in Aberdeen.*

How lang and dreary is the night
When I am frae my Dearie;
I restless lie frae e'en to morn,
Though I were ne'er sae weary.

Chorus—For Oh, her lanely nights are lang;
And Oh, her dreams are eerie; weird, dismal
And Oh, her widow'd heart is sair,
That 's absent frae her Dearie.

When I think on the lightsome days
I spent wi' thee, my Dearie;
And now what seas between us roar,
How can I be but eerie?

How slow ye move, ye heavy hours;
The joyless day, how dreary:
It was na sae—ye glinted by— passed quickly
When I was wi' my dearie?

LET NOT WOMAN E'ER COMPLAIN.

TUNE—*Duncan Gray.*

Let not Woman e'er complain
Of inconstancy in love;
Let not Woman e'er complain,
Fickle Man is apt to rove:

Look abroad through Nature's range,
Nature's mighty law is CHANGE;
Ladies, would it not be strange,
Man should then a monster prove.

Mark the winds, and mark the skies;
Oceans ebb, and oceans flow;
Sun and moon but set to rise;
Round and round the seasons go:

Why then ask of silly Man
To oppose great Nature's plan?
We 'll be constant while we can—
You can be no more you know.

THE LOVER'S MORNING-SALUTE TO HIS MISTRESS.

TUNE—*Deil tak the Wars.*

Sleep 'st thou, or wauk 'st thou, fairest creature;
Rosy morn now lifts his eye,
Numbering ilka bud which Nature every
Waters wi' the tears o' joy:
Now through the leafy woods,
And by the reeking floods;
Wild Nature's tenants, freely, gladly stray;
The lintwhite in his bower linnet
Chants, o'er the breathing flower:
The lavrock to the sky lark
Ascends wi' sangs o' joy,
While the sun and thou arise to bless the day.

Phebus gilding the brow o' morning
Banishes ilk darksome shade,
Nature gladd'ning and adorning;
Such to me my lovely maid.
When absent frae my Fair,
The murky shades o' Care
With starless gloom o'ercast my sullen sky;
But when, in beauty's light,
She meets my ravish'd sight;
When through my very heart
Her beaming glories dart;
'Tis then I wake to life, to light and joy!

THE AULD MAN.

But lately seen in gladsome green
The woods rejoiced the day,
Thro' gentle showers the laughing flowers
In double pride were gay:

But now our joys are fled
 On winter blasts awa'. away
Yet maiden May, in rich array,
 Again shall bring them a'. all

But my white pow—nae kindly thowe head—thaw
 Shall melt the snaws of Age;
My trunk of eild, but buss or beild, senility—without bush or shelter
 Sinks in Time's wintry rage.
Oh, Age has weary days!
 And nights o' sleepless pain!
Thou golden time o' Youthfu' Prime,
 Why comest thou not again![1]

TO CHLORIS.[2]

WRITTEN ON THE BLANK LEAF OF A COPY OF THE LAST EDITION OF MY POEMS.

'Tis Friendship's pledge, my young, fair Friend,
 Nor thou the gift refuse;
Nor with unwilling ear attend
 The moralising Muse.

Since thou in all thy youth and charms
 Must bid the world adieu
(A world 'gainst peace in constant arms),
 To join the friendly few;

Since, thy gay morn of life o'ercast,
 Chill came the tempest's lour
(And ne'er Misfortune's eastern blast
 Did nip a fairer flower);

Since life's gay scenes must charm no more:
 Still much is left behind,
Still nobler wealth hast thou in store—
 The comforts of the mind!

[1] It has been assumed, quite unwarrantably, that Burns here alludes to himself. Thus we are assured: 'It seems very evident that the vigour of the poet's constitution before the close of this year, 1794, began to give way under the tear and wear of disappointed hopes and the effects of his occasional imprudent course of life.' Nothing can be clearer than that the 'Auld Man' with his 'white pow' is one of Burns's models, not Burns himself.

[2] Mrs Whelpdale (Jean Lorimer, mentioned in note to 'Craigieburn Wood,' page 368).

Thine is the self-approving glow
  Of conscious honor's part;
And (dearest gift of Heaven below)
  Thine Friendship's truest heart;

The joys refined of sense and taste,
  With every Muse to rove:
And doubly were the Poet blest,
  These joys could he improve.

COILA. *Une Bagatelle de l'Amitié.*

ESTEEM FOR CHLORIS.

Ah, Chloris, since it may not be
  That thou of love wilt hear;
If from the lover thou maun flee,
  Yet let the friend be dear.

Altho' I love my Chloris mair
  Than ever tongue could tell;
My passion I will ne'er declare—
  I'll say I wish thee well.

Tho' a' my daily care thou art
  And a' my nightly dream,
I'll hide the struggle in my heart,
  And say it is esteem.

MY CHLORIS, MARK HOW GREEN THE GROVES.

TUNE—*My Lodging is on the cold Ground.*

My Chloris, mark how green the groves,
  The primrose-banks how fair;
The balmy gales awake the flowers
  And wave thy flaxen hair.

The lavrock shuns the palace gay, **lark**
  And o'er the cottage sings:
For nature smiles as sweet, I ween,
  To Shepherds as to Kings.

Let minstrels sweep the skilfu' string,
  In lordly, lighted ha': **hall**
The Shepherd stops his simple reed,
  Blithe, in the birken shaw. **birch wood**

C. Martin Hardie, R.S.A.

Ca' the yowes to the knowes,
Ca' them whare the heather grows,
Ca' them whare the burnie rowes,
My bonnie dearie!

PAGE 433.

The princely revel may survey
  Our rustic dance wi' scorn :
But are their hearts as light as ours
  Beneath the milk-white thorn ?

The Shepherd, in the flowery glen,
  In Shepherd's phrase will woo :
The Courtier tells a finer tale,
  But is his heart as true ?

These wild-wood flowers I've pu'd, to deck pulled
  That spotless breast o' thine,
The Courtier's gems may witness love—
  But 'tis na love like mine.

SONG,

ALTERED FROM AN OLD ENGLISH ONE.

IT WAS THE CHARMING MONTH OF MAY.

TUNE—*Daintie Davie.*

It was the charming month of May,
When all the flowers were fresh and gay,
One morning by the break of day,
  The youthful, charming Chloe
From peaceful slumber she arose,
Girt on her mantle and her hose,
And o'er the flowery mead she goes,
  The youthful, charming Chloe.

Chorus—Lovely was she by the dawn,
  Youthful Chloe, charming Chloe,
 Tripping o'er the pearly lawn,
  The youthful, charming Chloe.

The feather'd people, you might see
Perch'd all around on every tree,
In notes of sweetest melody
  They hail the charming Chloe ;
Till, painting gay the eastern skies,
The glorious sun began to rise ;
Out-rivall'd by the radiant eyes
  Of youthful, charming Chloe.

LASSIE WI' THE LINT-WHITE LOCKS.[1]

TUNE—*Rothemurche's Rant.*

Now nature cleeds the flowery lea, clothes
And a' is young and sweet like thee; all
O wilt thou share its joys wi' me,
And say thou 'lt be my Dearie O?

Chorus—Lassie wi' the lint-white locks,
Bonie lassie, artless lassie,
Wilt thou wi' me tent the flocks, herd
Wilt thou be my Dearie O?

The primrose bank, the wimpling burn,
The cuckoo on the milk-white thorn,
The wanton lambs at early morn
Shall welcome thee, my Dearie O.

And when the welcome simmer-shower
Has chear'd ilk drooping little flower, every
We 'll to the breathing woodbine bower
At sultry noon, my Dearie O.

When Cynthia lights, wi' silver ray,
The weary shearer's hameward way,
Thro' yellow waving fields we 'll stray,
And talk o' love, my Dearie O.

And when the howling wintry blast
Disturbs my Lassie's midnight rest;
Enclaspèd to my faithfu' breast,
I 'll comfort thee, my Dearie O.

FAREWELL, THOU STREAM THAT WINDING FLOWS.[2]

Farewell, thou stream that winding flows
Around Eliza's dwelling;
O mem'ry, spare the cruel throes
Within my bosom swelling:

[1] Dr James Adams, who saw Chloris when she was upwards of fifty, says: 'Her countenance has been in frequent varied phraseology described as bewitchingly lovely. To me it was only very pleasing. Her hair, abundant, was of what I should at the present time indicate as a pale straw, yellowish lemon colour, of glossy sheen.'

[2] This is a new and improved version of the song beginning, 'The last time I came o'er the Moor.' The most remarkable change is the substitution of Eliza for Maria, due doubtless to the alienation of Mrs Riddel, and Burns's resentment against her.

Condemn'd to drag a hopeless chain,
  And yet in secret languish;
To feel a fire in every vein,
  Nor dare disclose my anguish.

Love's veriest wretch, unseen, unknown,
  I fain my griefs would cover;
The bursting sigh, th' unweeting groan, unwitting
  Betray the hapless lover:
I know thou doom'st me to despair,
  Nor wilt, nor canst, relieve me;
But, Oh Eliza, hear one prayer,
  For pity's sake, forgive me!

The music of thy voice I heard,
  Nor wist while it enslav'd me;
I saw thine eyes, yet nothing fear'd,
  Till fears no more had sav'd me:
Th' unwary sailor thus, aghast,
  The wheeling torrent viewing,
Mid circling horrors sinks at last
  In overwhelming ruin.

PHILLY AND WILLY.

TUNE—*The Sow's Tail.*

HE.

O Philly, happy be that day
When roving through the gather'd hay,
My youthfu' heart was stown away, stolen
  And by thy charms, my Philly.

SHE.

O Willy, ay I bless the grove
Where first I owned my maiden love,
Whilst thou did pledge the Powers above
  To be my ain dear Willy.

HE.

As songsters of the early year
Are ilka day mair sweet to hear, every—more
So ilka day to me mair dear
  And charming is my Philly.

SHE.

As on the brier the budding rose
Still richer breathes and fairer blows,
So in my tender bosom grows
 The love I bear my Willy.

HE.

The milder sun and bluer sky,
That crown my harvest cares wi' joy,
Were ne'er sae welcome to my eye
 As is a sight o' Philly.

SHE.

The little swallow's wanton wing,
Tho' wafting o'er the flowery spring,
Did ne'er to me sic tidings bring,
 As meeting o' my Willy.

HE.

The bee that thro' the sunny hour
Sips nectar in the opening flower,
Compar'd wi' my delight is poor,
 Upon the lips o' Philly.

SHE.

The woodbine in the dewy weet
When evening shades in silence meet,
Is nocht sae fragrant or sae sweet
 As is a kiss o' Willy.

HE.

Let Fortune's wheel at random run,
And Fools may tyne, and Knaves may win; lose
My thoughts are a' bound up on ane, one
 And that 's my ain dear Philly.

SHE.

What 's a' the joys that gowd can gie? gold—give
I care na wealth a single flie; fly
The lad I love 's the lad for me,
 And that 's my ain dear Willy.

CONTENTED WI' LITTLE.

TUNE—*Lumps o' Pudding.*

Contented wi' little, and cantie wi' mair, merry
Whene'er I forgather wi' Sorrow and Care, meet
I gi'e them a skelp, as they're creeping alang, slap
Wi' a cog o' gude swats, and an auld Scotish sang. cup—ale

I whyles claw the elbow o' troublesome thought; scratch
But man is a soger, and Life is a faught: struggle
My mirth and good humour are coin in my pouch, pocket
And my FREEDOM's my lairdship nae monarch dare touch.

A towmond o' trouble, should that be my fa', twelvemonth—fate
A night o' gude fellowship sowthers it a': solders
When at the blythe end of our journey at last,
Wha the de'il ever thinks o' the road he has past.

Blind chance, let her snapper and stoyte on her way; stumble—totter
Be't to me, be't frae me, e'en let the jade gae: go
Come Ease, or come Travail, come Pleasure or Pain;
My warst word is: 'Welcome and welcome again!'

CANST THOU LEAVE ME THUS, MY KATY?

TUNE—*Roy's Wife.*

Chorus—Canst thou leave me thus, my Katy?
Canst thou leave me thus, my Katy?
Well thou know'st my aching heart,
And canst thou leave me thus for pity?

Is this thy plighted, fond regard,
Thus cruelly to part, my Katy:
Is this thy faithful swain's reward—
An aching broken heart, my Katy.

Farewel! and ne'er such sorrows tear
That fickle heart of thine, my Katy!
Thou may'st find those will love thee dear—
But not a love like mine, my Katy.

A MAN'S A MAN FOR A' THAT.

Is there for honest Poverty
That hings his head, and a' that? — all that
The coward-slave, we pass him by,
We dare be poor for a' that![1]
For a' that, and a' that,
Our toils obscure, and a' that,
The rank is but the guinea's stamp,[2]
The Man 's the gowd for a' that!

What though on hamely fare we dine,
Wear hoddin grey, and a' that; — coarse home-made woollen cloth
Gie fools their silks and knaves their wine,
A Man 's a Man for a' that:
For a' that, and a' that,
Their tinsel show, and a' that;
The honest man, tho' e'er sae poor,
Is king o' men for a' that!

Ye see yon birkie ca'd a lord, — fellow
Wha struts, and stares, and a' that,
Though hundreds worship at his word,
He 's but a coof for a' that: — fool, ninny
For a' that, and a' that,
His ribband, star and a' that;
The man of independent mind
He looks and laughs at a' that.

A prince can mak a belted knight,
A marquis, duke and a' that;
But an honest man 's aboon his might— — above
Gude faith, he mauna fa' that![3] — must not
For a' that, and a' that,
Their dignities, and a' that;
The pith o' sense and pride o' worth
Are higher rank[4] than a' that!

[1] These four lines, the sense of which is often misunderstood, may be thus interpreted: 'Is there any one who hangs his head in shame at his poverty? If there is such a poor creature, we pass him by as a coward slave.'

[2] A similar thought occurs in Wycherley's *Plain-Dealer*, which Burns may have seen: 'I weigh the man, not his title; 'tis not the king's stamp can make the metal better or heavier. Your lord is a leaden shilling, which you bend every way, and which debases the stamp he bears.'

[3] 'Fa',' as a noun, means lot or share; as a verb, to get or obtain. Burns here uses the word in a violent sense—'He must not attempt or pretend to have that as a thing in his power.'

[4] So in manuscript, though usually printed 'ranks.'

Then let us pray that come it may,—
  As come it will for a' that—
That Sense and Worth, o'er a' the earth,
  May bear the gree, and a' that. supremacy
For a' that, and a' that,
  It 's comin' yet for a' that,
That Man to Man, the world o'er,
  Shall brothers be for a' that!

O LASSIE, ARE YE SLEEPING YET?

TUNE—*Let me in this ae Night.*

O lassie, are ye sleeping yet,
Or are ye waukin, I would wit? know
For Love has bound me hand and foot,
  And I would fain be in, jo. sweetheart

Chorus—O let me in this ae night, one
    This ae, ae, ae night;
  For pity's sake this ae night,
    O rise and let me in, jo.

Thou hear'st the winter wind an' weet, wet, rain
Nae star blinks thro' the driving sleet; peeps
Take pity on my weary feet,
  And shield me frae the rain, jo.

The bitter blast that round me blaws blows
Unheeded howls, unheeded fa's; falls
The cauldness o' thy heart 's the cause
  Of a' my care and pine, jo.

HER ANSWER.

O tell na me o' wind an' rain,
Upbraid na me wi' cauld disdain, cold
Gae back the gate ye cam again, way
  I winna let you in, jo.

Chorus—I tell you now this ae night,
    This ae, ae, ae night;
  And ance for a' this ae night, once for all
    I winna let ye in, jo. will not

The snellest blast, at mirkest hours, keen—dark
That round the pathless wanderer pours,
Is nocht to what poor She endures nothing
  That 's trusted faithless Man, jo.

The sweetest flower that deck'd the mead,
Now trodden like the vilest weed—
Let simple maid the lesson read,
  The weird may be her ain, jo. destiny

The bird that charm'd his summer-day,
And now the cruel Fowler's prey,
Let that to witless Woman say
  The gratefu' heart of Man, jo.

BALLADS ON MR HERON'S ELECTION, 1795.

BALLAD FIRST.

Wham will we send to London town,
  To Parliament and a' that?
Or wha in a' the country round
  The best deserves to fa' that? attain to
    For a' that, and a' that,
    Thro' Galloway and a' that,
    Where is the Laird or belted Knight
    That best deserves to fa' that?

Wha sees Kerroughtree's open yett— door
  And wha is 't never saw that?—
Wha ever wi' Kerroughtree met
  And has a doubt of a' that?
    For a' that, and a' that,
    Here 's Heron yet for a' that!
    The independent patriot,
    The honest man, and a' that.

Tho' wit and worth, in either sex,
  Saint Mary's Isle [1] can shaw that,
Wi' Lords and Dukes let Selkirk mix,
  And weel does Selkirk fa' that. become
    For a' that, and a' that,
    Here 's Heron yet for a' that!
    An independent commoner
    Shall be the man for a' that.

[1] The seat of the Earl of Selkirk.

But why should we to Nobles jeuk, bend
And is 't against the law, that?
And even a Lord may be a gowk, fool
Wi' ribban, star, and a' that.
For a' that, and a' that,
Here 's Heron yet for a' that!
A Lord may be a lousy loun, fellow
Wi' ribban, star, and a' that.

A beardless boy comes o'er the hills
Wi's uncle's purse and a' that;
But we 'll hae ane frae 'mang oursels,
A man we ken, and a' that.
For a' that, and a' that,
Here 's Heron yet for a' that!
We are na to be bought and sold
Like nowte, and naigs, and a' that. cattle—horses

Then let us drink:—'The Stewartry,
Kerroughtree's laird, and a' that,
Our representative to be':
For weel he 's worthy a' that!
For a' that, and a' that,
Here's Heron yet for a' that!
A House of Commons such as he,
They wad be blest that saw that.

BALLAD SECOND: THE ELECTION.[1]

TUNE—*Fy, let us a' to the Bridal.*

Fy, let us a' to Kirkcudbright,[2]
For there will be bickerin there: a scrimmage
For Murray's light horse are to muster,
An' O, how the heroes will swear!
An' there 'll be Murray commander,[3]
An' Gordon the battle to win:[4]
Like brothers, they 'll stan' by each other,
Sae knit in alliance and kin.

1 This ballad is composed in imitation of a rough but amusing specimen of the old ballad literature of Scotland, descriptive of the company attending a country-wedding—

Fy, let us a' to the wedding,
For there 'll be lilting there, &c.

2 Pronounced Kir-coo'-bry.

3 Mr Murray of Broughton. This gentleman had left his wife, and eloped with a lady of rank. His great wealth had permitted him to do this with comparative impunity, and even without forfeiting the alliance of his wife's relations, one of whom he was supporting in this election.

4 Mr Gordon of Balmaghie, the government candidate.

An' there 'll be black-nebbit Johnie,[1] nosed
The tongue o' the trump to them a': Jew's harp
Gin he get na Hell for his haddin, dwelling
The Deil gets nae justice ava! at all
An' there 'll be Kempleton's birkie,[2] young Kempleton
A chiel no sae black at the bane; fellow—bone
For as to his fine nabob fortune—
We 'll e'en let the subject alane.

An' there 'll be Wigton's new sheriff[3]—
Dame Justice fu' brawly has sped: bravely
She 's gotten the heart of a Bushby,
But Lord! what 's become o' the head?
An' there 'll be Cardoness, Esquire,[4]
Sae mighty in Cardoness' eyes:
A wight that will weather damnation,
For the Devil the prey would despise.

An' there 'll be Douglasses doughty,
New christening towns far and near:[5]
Abjuring their democrat doings
An' kissing the arse of a peer!
An' there 'll be Kenmure sae generous,[6]
Whase honour is proof to the storm:
To save them from stark reprobation
He lent them his name to the firm!

But we winna mention Redcastle,[7] won't
The body—e'en let him escape!
He 'd venture the gallows for siller, money
An' 'twere na the cost o' the rape! rope
An' whare is our King's Lord Lieutenant,
Sae famed for his gratefu' return?
The billie is getting his Questions[8] fellow
To say at St Stephen's the morn. to-morrow

[1] John Bushby.

[2] William Bushby of Kempleton, brother of John. He had been involved in the downfall of Douglas, Heron, & Co.'s Bank, and had subsequently gone to India, where he realised a fortune.

[3] Mr Maitland Bushby, son of John, and new appointed Sheriff of Wigtownshire. The same idea occurs in 'The Epistle of Esopus to Maria.'

[4] David Maxwell of Cardoness was created a baronet in 1804, and died in 1825.

[5] Sir William and James Douglas, brothers, of Carlinwark (which the former had changed to Castle-Douglas by royal warrant) and Orchardton.

[6] Mr Gordon of Kenmure.

[7] Walter Sloan Lawrie of Redcastle.

[8] Youth, committing his Catechism to memory.

An' there 'll be lads o' the gospel:
  Muirhead, wha 's as guid as he 's true;[1]
An' there 'll be Buittle's Apostle,
  Wha 's mair o' the black than the blue;[2] not true blue
An' there 'll be folk frae St Mary's,
  A house o' great merit and note:
The Deil ane but honors them highly, Not one
  The Deil ane will gie them his vote!

An' there 'll be wealthy young Richard,[3]
  Dame Fortune should hang by the neck:
But for prodigal thriftless bestowing,
  His merit had won him respect.
An' there 'll be rich brither nabobs;
  Tho' nabobs, yet men o' the first![4]
An' there 'll be Collieston's whiskers,[5]
  An' Quinton—o' lads no the warst![6]

An' there 'll be Stamp-office Johnie:[7]
  Tak tent how ye purchase a dram! care
An' there 'll be gay Cassencarry,[8]
  An' there 'll be Colonel Tam;[9]
An' there 'll be trusty Kerroughtree,
  Whase honour was ever his law:
If the virtues were pack't in a parcel,
  His worth might be sample for a'!

An' can we forget the auld Major,[10]
  Wha 'll ne'er be forgot in the Greys? Scots Greys
Our flatt'ry we 'll keep for some other:
  Him only it 's justice to praise!

[1] Rev. Mr Muirhead, minister of Urr (1742–1805). He was 'of Logan,' and chief of the name or Clan Muirhead.

[2] Rev. George Maxwell, minister of Buittle (1762–1807).

[3] Richard Oswald of Auchincruive, heir to the Mrs Oswald who was the subject of Burns's 'Ode.' See p. 286.

[4] Messrs Hannay.

[5] Copland of Collieston.

[6] Quintin, son of the M'Adam of Craigengillan to whom Burns in 1786 wrote a rhymed epistle. See p. 213.

[7] John Syme, distributor of stamps, Dumfries.

[8] Colonel M'Kenzie of Cassencarry.

[9] Colonel Goldie of Goldielea.

[10] Major Heron, brother of the Whig candidate.

An' there 'll be maiden Kilkerran;[1]
An' also Barskimming's guid Knight;[2]
An' there 'll be roaring Birtwhistle[3]
Yet luckily roars in the right!

An' there, frae the Niddesdale border,
Will mingle the Maxwells in droves:
Teuch Johnie,[4] Staunch Geordie,[5] and Wattie[6] Tough
That girns for the fishes an' loaves! longs
An' there 'll be Logan M'Doual[7]—
Sculdudd'ry an' he will be there! Fornication
An' also the wild Scot o' Galloway,
Sogering, gunpowther Blair![8]

Then hey the chaste interest of Broughton!
An' hey for the blessings 'twill bring!
It may send Balmaghie to the Commons—
In Sodom 'twould mak him a King!
An' hey for the sanctified Murray
Our land wha wi' chapels has stor'd;
He founder'd his horse among harlots,
But gie'd the auld naig to the Lord! nag

BALLAD THIRD: JOHN BUSHBY'S LAMENTATION.

TUNE—*The Babes in the Wood.*

'Twas in the Seventeen Hunder year
O' grace, and Ninety-Five,
That year I was the wae'est man saddest
Of onie man alive.

In March the three-an'-twentieth morn,
The sun raise clear an' bright; rose
But O, I was a waefu' man
Ere to-fa' o' the night! nightfall

[1] Sir Adam Fergusson of Kilkerran. See 'The Author's Earnest Cry and Prayer,' p. 136, where he is called 'chaste Kilkerran.'
[2] Sir William Miller of Barskimming; afterwards a judge under the designation of Lord Glenlee.
[3] Alexander Birtwhistle, Provost of Kirkcudbright.
[4] Maxwell of Terraughty, the venerable gentleman on whose birthday Burns wrote some verses. See p. 362.
[5] George Maxwell of Carruchan.
[6] Wellwood Maxwell.
[7] Captain M'Douall of Logan.
[8] Major Blair of Dunskey.

Yerl Galloway lang did rule this land — Earl
 Wi' equal right and fame,
Fast knit in chaste and holy bands
 With Broughton's noble name.

Yerl Galloway's man o' men was I
 And chief o' Broughton's host:
So twa blind beggars, on a string,
 The faithfu' tyke will trust! — dog

But now Yerl Galloway's sceptre 's broke
 And Broughton 's wi' the slain,
And I my ancient craft may try,
 Sin' honesty is gane.

'Twas by the banks o' bonie Dee,
 Beside Kirkcudbright's towers,
The Stewart and the Murray there
 Did muster a' their powers.

The Murray on the auld gray yaud — old horse
 Wi' wingèd spurs did ride:[1]
That auld gray yaud a' Nidsdale rade,
 He staw upon Nidside. — stole

An' there had na been the Yerl himsel, — An' = if
 O, there had been nae play!
But Garlies was to London gane,
 And sae the kye might stray. — cattle

And there was Balmaghie, I ween—
 In front rank he wad shine;
But Balmaghie had better been
 Drinkin' Madeira wine.

And frae Glenkens cam to our aid
 A chief o' doughty deed:
In case that worth should wanted be,
 O' Kenmure we had need.

And by our banners march'd Muirhead,
 And Buittle was na slack,
Whase haly priesthood nane could stain,
 For wha could dye the black?

[1] An obscure allusion to the lady with whom Murray had eloped—a member of the house of Johnstone, whose well-known crest is a winged spur.

And there was grave Squire Cardoness,
Look'd on till a' was done :
Sae in the tower o' Cardoness
A howlet sits at noon. **owl**

And there led I the Bushby clan :
My gamesome billie, Will, **crony**
And my son Maitland, wise as brave,
My footsteps follow'd still.

The Douglas and the Heron's name,
We set nought to their score ;
The Douglas and the Heron's name
Had felt our weight before.

But Douglasses o' weight had we :
The pair o' lusty lairds,
For building cot-houses sae fam'd,
And christenin' kail-yards. **kitchen-gardens**

And there Redcastle drew his sword
That ne'er was stain'd wi' gore
Save on a wand'rer lame and blind,
To drive him frae his door.

And last cam creepin Collieston,
Was mair in fear than wrath ;
Ae knave was constant in his mind— **One**
To keep that knave frae scaith. **harm**

THE DUMFRIES VOLUNTEERS.

TUNE—*Push about the Jorum.*

Does haughty Gaul invasion threat ?
Then let the louns beware, Sir ! **fellows**
There 's WOODEN WALLS upon our seas,
And VOLUNTEERS on shore, Sir :
The *Nith* shall run to *Corsincon*,[1]
The *Criffel*[2] sink in *Solway*
Ere we permit a foreign foe
On British ground to rally !
We 'll ne'er permit a foreign foe
On British ground to rally !

[1] A high hill at the source of the Nith.—*B.*
[2] A well-known mountain near the mouth of the Nith,

O let us not, like snarling curs,
  In wrangling be divided,
Till, slap! come in an *unco loun* — stranger fellow
  And wi' a rung decide it! — cudgel
Be Britain still to Britain true,
  Among oursels united!
For never but by *British hands*
  Maun *British wrangs* be righted! — must
    No! never but by *British hands*
    Shall *British wrangs* be righted!

The *Kettle* o' the Kirk and State
  Perhaps a *clout* may fail in 't; — patch
But deil a *foreign* tinker loun
  Shall ever ca' a nail in 't. — drive
Our FATHER'S BLUDE the *Kettle* bought! — blood
  And wha wad dare to spoil it? — who would
By Heav'ns! the sacrilegious dog
  Shall fuel be to boil it!
    By Heav'ns! the sacrilegious dog
    Shall fuel be to boil it!

The wretch that would a *Tyrant* own,
  And the wretch, his true-born brother,
Who would set the *Mob* aboon the *Throne*, — above
  May they be damn'd together!
Who will not sing 'God save the King'
  Shall hang as high 's the steeple;
But while we sing 'God save the King'
  We 'll ne'er forget THE PEOPLE!
    But while we sing 'God save the King'
    We 'll ne'er forget THE PEOPLE.

TOAST FOR THE 12TH OF APRIL.

Instead of a song, boys, I 'll give you a toast:
Here 's the Mem'ry of those on the Twelfth that we lost!—
We lost, did I say?—No, by Heav'n, that we found!
For their fame it shall live while the world goes round.
The next in succession I 'll give you: the King!
Whoe'er would betray him, on high may he swing!
And here 's the grand fabric, our Free Constitution
As built on the base of the great Revolution!

And, longer with Politics not to be cramm'd,
Be Anarchy curs'd and be Tyranny damn'd!
And who would to Liberty e'er prove disloyal,
May his son be a hangman—and he his first trial!

OH, WAT YE WHA'S IN YON TOWN?

TUNE—*We'll gang nae mair to yon Town.*

Now, haply, down yon gay green shaw — plantation
She wanders by yon spreading tree;
How blest, ye flowers that round her blaw—
Ye catch the glances o' her e'e!

Chorus—Oh, wat ye wha's in yon town
Ye see the e'enin sun upon?
The fairest dame 's in yon town
That e'enin sun is shining on.

How blest, ye birds that round her sing
And welcome in the blooming year!
And doubly welcome be the Spring,
The season to my Lucy dear!

The sun blinks blythe on yon town, — shines cheerfully
And on yon bonie braes of Ayr;
But my delight in yon town,
And dearest bliss, is Lucy fair.

Without my Love, not a' the charms
O' Paradise could yield me joy;
But gie me Lucy in my arms, — give
And welcome, Lapland's dreary sky!

My cave would be a Lover's bower
Tho' raging Winter rent the air;
And she, a lovely little flower
That I wad tent and shelter there. — would care for

Oh, sweet is she in yon town
Yon sinking sun 's gane down upon;
A fairer than 's in yon town
His setting beam ne'er shone upon.

G. O. Reid, A.R.S.A.

Last May a braw wooer cam down the lang glen,
And sair wi' his love he did deave me.

PAGE 460.

If angry Fate is sworn my foe
  And suff'ring I am doom'd to bear;
I, cureless, quit all else below,
  But spare me, spare me Lucy dear!

For while life's dearest blood is warm,
  Ae thought frae her shall ne'er depart; One
And she, as fairest is her form,
  She has the truest, kindest heart!

ADDRESS TO THE WOODLARK.

TUNE—*Where'll bonie Ann lie?* or, *Loch-Erroch Side.*

O stay, sweet warbling woodlark, stay,
Nor quit for me the trembling spray,
A hapless lover courts thy lay,
  Thy soothing fond complaining.

Again, again that tender part,
That I may catch thy melting art;
For surely that wad touch her heart
  Wha kills me wi' disdaining.

Say, was thy little mate unkind
And heard thee as the careless wind?
Oh, nocht but love and sorrow join'd
  Sic notes o' woe could wauken. waken

Thou tells of never-ending care,
Of speechless grief and dark despair:
For pity's sake, sweet bird, nae mair! no more
  Or my poor heart is broken!

ON CHLORIS BEING ILL.

TUNE—*Aye wakin' O.*

Can I cease to care,
  Can I cease to languish,
While my darling fair
  Is on the couch of anguish?

Chorus—Long, long the night,
Heavy comes the morrow,
While my soul's delight
Is on her bed of sorrow.

Every hope is fled;
Every fear is terror;
Slumber even I dread:
Every dream is horror.

Hear me, Pow'rs Divine!
Oh, in pity hear me!
Take aught else of mine,
But my Chloris spare me!

CALEDONIA.

TUNE—*Humours of Glen.*

Their groves o' sweet myrtle let Foreign Lands reckon,
Where bright-beaming summers exalt the perfume;
Far dearer to me yon lone glen o' green breckan, bracken
Wi' the burn stealing under the lang, yellow broom;
Far dearer to me are yon humble broom bowers,
Where the blue-bell and gowan lurk, lowly, unseen; daisy
For there, lightly tripping amang the wild flowers,
A-listening the linnet, oft wanders my Jean.

Tho' rich is the breeze in their gay, sunny vallies,
And cauld, Caledonia's blast on the wave;
Their sweet-scented woodlands that skirt the proud palace,
What are they?—The haunt of the Tyrant and Slave!
The Slave's spicy forests and gold-bubbling fountains,
The brave Caledonian views with disdain;
He wanders as free as the winds of his mountains,
Save Love's willing fetters, the chains o' his Jean.

'TWAS NA HER BONIE BLUE E'E WAS MY RUIN.

TUNE—*Laddie, lie near me.*

'Twas na her bonie blue e'e was my ruin;
Fair tho' she be, that was ne'er my undoing:
'Twas the dear smile when naebody did mind us,
'Twas the bewitching, sweet, stown glance o' kindness. stolen

Sair do I fear that to hope is denied me; Sore
Sair do I fear that despair maun abide me; must
But tho' fell fortune should fate us to sever, cruel
Queen shall she be in my bosom for ever!

Chloris, I'm thine wi' a passion sincerest,
And thou hast plighted me love o' the dearest!
And thou 'rt the angel that never can alter,
Sooner the sun in his motion would falter!

HOW CRUEL ARE THE PARENTS!

ALTERED FROM AN OLD ENGLISH SONG.

TUNE—*John Anderson, my Jo.*

How cruel are the parents
  Who riches only prize,
And to the wealthy booby
  Poor woman sacrifice:
Meanwhile the hapless Daughter
  Has but a choice of strife;
To shun a tyrant Father's hate—
  Become a wretched wife.

The ravening hawk pursuing,
  The trembling dove thus flies,
To shun impelling ruin
  Awhile her pinions tries;
Till of escape despairing,
  No shelter or retreat,
She trusts the ruthless falconer
  And drops beneath his feet.

MARK YONDER POMP OF COSTLY FASHION.

TUNE—*Deil tak the Wars.*

Mark yonder pomp of costly fashion
  Round the wealthy, titled bride:
But when compared with real passion
  Poor is all that princely pride.
What are their showy treasures?
What are their noisy pleasures?

The gay, gaudy glare of vanity and art:
The polish'd jewel's blaze
May draw the wond'ring gaze,
And courtly grandeur bright
The fancy may delight,
But never, never can come near the heart.

But did you see my dearest Chloris
In simplicity's array;
Lovely as yonder sweet opening flower is,
Shrinking from the gaze of day.
O then, the heart alarming,
And all resistless charming,
In Love's delightful fetters she chains the willing soul!
Ambition would disown
The world's imperial crown,
Even Av'rice would deny
His worshipp'd deity,
And feel thro' every vein Love's raptures roll.

ADDRESS TO THE TOOTHACHE.[1]

My curse upon your venom'd stang, sting
That shoots my tortur'd gooms alang gums
An' thro' my lug gies monie a twang ear
Wi' gnawing vengeance,
Tearing my nerves wi' bitter pang,
Like racking engines?

A' down my beard the slavers trickle,
I throw the wee stools o'er the mickle,
While round the fire the giglets keckle, maids—cackle
To see me loup, jump
An', raving mad, I wish a heckle heckling-comb
Were i' their doup!

When fevers burn or ague freezes,
Rheumatics gnaw or colic squeezes,
Our neebors sympathise to ease us
Wi' pitying moan;
But thee!—thou hell o' a' diseases,
They mock our groan!

[1] The only manuscript of this poem known to be in existence is in the possession of Lord Blythswood.

Of a' the num'rous human dools— griefs
Ill-hairsts, daft bargains, cutty-stools,[1] harvests—foolish
Or worthy frien's laid i' the mools,[2]—
Sad sight to see!—
The tricks o' knaves or fash o' fools— worry
Thou bear'st the gree! hast pre-eminence

Whare'er that place be priests ca' Hell,
Whare a' the tones o' misery yell,
An' rankèd plagues their numbers tell ranked
In dreadfu' raw, row
Thou, Toothache, surely bear'st the bell
Amang them a'! all

O thou grim, mischief-making chiel, fellow
That gars the notes o' discord squeel makes
Till humankind aft dance a reel
In gore a shoe-thick,
Gie a' the faes o' Scotland's weal
A towmond's toothache. twelvemonth's

FORLORN, MY LOVE, NO COMFORT NEAR.

TUNE—*Let me in this ae Night.*

Forlorn, my Love, no comfort near,
Far, far from thee I wander here;
Far, far from thee, the fate severe
At which I most repine, Love.

Chorus—Oh, wert thou, Love, but near me;
But near, near, near me;
How kindly thou wouldst chear me
And mingle sighs with mine, Love.

Around me scowls a wintry sky,
Blasting each bud of hope and joy;
And shelter, shade nor home have I,
Save in those arms of thine, Love.

Cold, alter'd friendship's cruel part,
To poison Fortune's ruthless dart—
Let me not break thy faithful heart,
And say that fate is mine, Love.

1 Stools of repentance.
2 Friends covered up beneath the churchyard mould.

But dreary though the moments fleet,
Oh, let me think we yet shall meet!
That only ray of solace sweet
Can on thy Chloris shine, Love!

LAST MAY A BRAW WOOER.

TUNE—*The Lothian Lassie.*

Last May a braw wooer cam down the lang glen, handsome—long valley
And sair wi' his love he did deave me; deafen, or bore
I said there was naething I hated like men, nothing
The deuce gae wi' him, to believe me, believe me!
The deuce gae wi' him, to believe me!

He spak o' the darts in my bonie black een, eyes
And vow'd for my love he was dying;
I said he might die when he liked—for Jean—
The Lord forgi'e me for lying, for lying!
The Lord forgi'e me for lying!

A well-stocked mailin, himsel for the laird, farm—proprietor
And marriage affhand, were his proffers:
I never loot on that I kend it, or car'd, allowed—knew
But thought I might hae waur offers, waur offers; worse
But thought I might hae waur offers.

But what wad ye think? in a fortnight or less—
The deil tak his taste to gae near her!
He up the Gateslack to my black cousin Bess,
Guess ye how, the jad! I could bear her, could bear her! jade
Guess ye how, the jad! I could bear her!

But a' the niest week as I petted wi' care, next
I gaed to the tryste o' Dalgarnock; fair
And wha but my fine, fickle lover was there,
I glowr'd as I 'd seen a warlock, a warlock, stared—wizard, bogle
I glowr'd as I 'd seen a warlock.

But owre my left shouther I ga'e him a blink, over—gave—look
Least neebours might say I was saucy:
My wooer he caper'd as he 'd been in drink,
And vow'd I was his dear lassie, dear lassie;
And vow'd I was his dear lassie.

I spiered for my cousin fu' couthy and sweet, asked—full kindly
Gin she had recover'd her hearin',
And how her new shoon fit her auld shachl't feet; shoes—misshapen
But, heavens! how he fell a-swearin', a-swearin';
But, heavens! how he fell a-swearin'.

He begged, for Gudesake! I wad be his wife,
Or else I wad kill him wi' sorrow:
So, e'en to preserve the poor body in life,
I think I maun wed him to-morrow, to-morrow; must
I think I maun wed him to-morrow.

THIS IS NO MY AIN LASSIE.

TUNE—*This is no my ain house.*

I see a form, I see a face,
Ye weel may wi' the fairest place:
It wants, to me, the witching grace,
The kind love that 's in her e'e.

Chorus—O this is no my ain lassie,
Fair tho' the lassie be:
O weel ken I my ain lassie,
Kind love is in her e'e.

She 's bonie, blooming, straight and tall,
And lang has had my heart in thrall;
And ay it charms my very saul, soul
The kind love that 's in her e'e.

A thief sae pawkie is my Jean sly
To steal a blink, by a' unseen; glance
But gleg as light are lover's e'en, quick
When kind love is in the e'e.

It may escape the courtly sparks,
It may escape the learnèd clerks;
But weel the watching lover marks
The kind love that 's in her e'e.

NOW SPRING HAS CLAD THE GROVE IN GREEN.

Now spring has clad the grove in green
And strewed the lea wi' flowers:
The furrow'd, waving corn is seen
Rejoice in fostering showers.
While ilka thing in Nature join — every
Their sorrows to forego,
O why thus all alone are mine
The weary steps o' woe.

The trout within yon wimpling burn — rippling
That glides—a silver dart,
And safe beneath the shady thorn
Defies the angler's art:
My life was ance that careless stream, — once
That wanton trout was I;
But Love, wi' unrelenting beam,
Has scorch'd my fountains dry.

The little floweret's peaceful lot
In yonder cliff that grows—
Which, save the linnet's flight, I wot,
Nae ruder visit knows—
Was mine; till Love has o'er me past
And blighted a' my bloom,
And now beneath the withering blast
My youth and joy consume.

The waken'd lav'rock warbling springs, — lark
And climbs the early sky,
Winnowing blythe her dewy wings
In morning's rosy eye;
As little reckt I sorrow's power,
Until the flowery snare
Of witching love, in luckless hour,
Made me the thrall o' care.

O had my fate been Greenland snows,
Or Afric's burning zone,
Wi' man and nature leagu'd my foes,
So Peggy ne'er I'd known!
The wretch whase doom is, 'hope nae mair,' — whose
What tongue his woes can tell;
Within whase bosom save Despair
Nae kinder spirits dwell.

O BONIE WAS YON ROSY BRIER.

TUNE—*I wish my Love were in a mire.*

O bonie was yon rosy brier
That blooms sae far frae haunt o' man;
And bonie she, and ah, how dear!
It shaded frae the e'enin sun.

Yon rosebuds in the morning dew
How pure, amang the leaves sae green;
But purer was the lover's vow
They witness'd in their shade yestreen.

All in its rude and prickly bower
That crimson rose how sweet and fair;
But love is far a sweeter flower
Amid life's thorny path o' care.

The pathless wild, and wimpling burn,
Wi' Chloris in my arms, be mine;
And I the world, nor wish, nor scorn,
Its joys and griefs alike resign.

INSCRIPTION

FOR AN ALTAR TO INDEPENDENCE AT KERROUGHTREE, THE SEAT OF MR HERON.

Thou of an independent mind,
With soul resolved, with soul resigned;
Prepar'd Power's proudest frown to brave,
Who wilt not be, nor have, a slave,
Virtue alone who dost revere,
Thy own reproach alone dost fear:
Approach this shrine and worship here.

ON THE DUKE OF QUEENSBERRY.

As I cam down the banks o' Nith
And by Glenriddel's ha', man,
There I heard a piper play
'Turn-coat Whigs, awa, man!'

Drumlanrig's towers hae tint the powers lost
That kept the lands in awe, man:
The eagle 's dead, and in his stead
We 've gotten a hoody-craw, man.

The turn-coat Duke his King forsook
When his back was at the wa', man:
The rattan ran wi' a' his clan rat
For fear the hoose should fa', man.

The lads about the banks o' Nith,
They trust his Grace for a', man:
But he 'll sair them as he sair'd the King— serve
Turn tail and rin awa, man.

VERSES ON THE DESTRUCTION OF THE WOODS NEAR DRUMLANRIG.

As on the banks o' wandering Nith
Ae smiling simmer-morn I strayed, One—summer
And traced its bonny howes and haughs, hollows—holms
Where linties sang and lambkins played, linnets
I sat me down upon a craig rocky knoll
And drank my fill o' fancy's dream,
When from the eddying deep below
Uprose the genius of the stream:

Dark, like the frowning rock, his brow,
And troubled, like his wintry wave,
And deep, as sughs the boding wind sighs, moans
Amang his caves, the sigh he gave—
'And came ye here, my son,' he cried,
'To wander in my birken shade? birchen
To muse some favourite Scottish theme
Or sing some favourite Scottish maid?

'There was a time, it 's nae lang syne, ago
Ye might hae seen me in my pride,
When a' my banks sae bravely saw
Their woody pictures in my tide;
When hanging beech and spreading elm
Shaded my stream sae clear and cool;
And stately oaks their twisted arms
Threw broad and dark across the pool;

'When, glinting through the trees, appeared
The wee white cot aboon the mill, above
And peacefu' rose its ingle reek chimney smoke
That slowly curlèd up the hill.
But now the cot is bare and cauld, cold
Its branchy shelter 's lost and gane,
And scarce a stinted birk is left birch
To shiver in the blast its lane.' alone

'Alas!' said I, 'what ruefu' chance
Has twined ye o' your stately trees? stripped
Has laid your rocky bosom bare,
Has stripped the cleeding o' your braes? clothing—banks
Was it the bitter eastern blast
That scatters blight in early spring?
Or was 't the wil'fire scorched their boughs lightning
Or canker-worm wi' secret sting?'

'Nae eastlin blast,' the sprite replied,
'It blew na here sae fierce and fell,
And on my dry and halesome banks healthful
Nae canker-worms get leave to dwell:
Man! cruel man!' the genius sighed—
As through the cliffs he sank him down—
'The worm that gnawed my bonny trees,
That reptile wears a ducal crown.'[1]

TO COLLECTOR MITCHELL.

Friend of the Poet, tried and leal, true, loyal
Wha wanting thee might beg or steal;
Alake, alake, the meikle Deil alas!—big
Wi' a' his witches
Are at it, skelpin jig an' reel rattling
In my poor pouches! pockets

[1] This piece was first printed in the *Scots Magazine* for February 1803, with a note to the effect that the verses were found, in Burns's handwriting, pasted on the back of a window-shutter in an inn or toll-house near the scene of desolation. It has been conjectured that this poem, Burns's authorship of which was doubted by Allan Cunningham in spite of internal evidence in its favour, was written in 1791, when, as the Election Ballads show, the poet was very bitter against the Duke of Queensberry. In support of this view the courteous letter Burns wrote to the Duke in 1793 has been cited. But a fresh access of detestation in 1795, caused by the cutting down of the woods at Drumlanrig and at Neidpath in Peeblesshire, is sufficient to account for a new poem embodying it.

I modestly fu' fain wad hint it, — would
That One-pound-one, I sairly want it ;
If wi' the hizzie down ye sent it, — servant-girl
　　It would be kind ;
And while my heart wi' life-blood dunted — throbbed
　　I'd bear 't in mind !

So may the Auld Year gang out moanin — go
To see the New come laden, groaning
Wi' double plenty o'er the loanin — road
　　To thee and thine :
Domestic peace and comforts crownin
　　The hale design ! — whole

POSTSCRIPT.

Ye 've heard this while how I 've been licket, — struck
And by fell Death was nearly nicket? — cut off
Grim loon! He got me by the fecket — waistcoat
　　And sair me sheuk ; — sore—shook
But by gude-luck I lap a wicket — good-luck—leaped
　　And turn'd a neuk. — corner

But by that health, I 've got a share o' 't !
And by that life, I 'm promised mair o' 't !
My hale and weel, I 'll take a care o' 't ! — health—prosperity
　　A tentier way : — more careful
Then farewell Folly, hide and hair o' 't,
　　For ance and aye !

THE DEAN OF THE FACULTY.[1]

A NEW BALLAD.

TUNE—*The Dragon of Wantley.*

Dire was the hate at Old Harlaw
　That Scot to Scot did carry ;
And dire the discord Langside saw
　For beauteous, hapless Mary.

[1] On January 12, 1796, the election of Dean of the Faculty of Advocates took place amid great excitement. Henry Erskine (1746–1817), who then held the appointment, having presided at a public meeting held to protest against the Seditious Writings Bill proposed by the government, the Tory majority of the Scottish bar resolved to oppose his reappointment, and nominated Robert Dundas of Arniston. Dundas was preferred by a majority of 123 to 38. The name of Walter Scott is found in the roll of those who opposed and voted against Erskine.

But Scot to Scot ne'er met so hot
  Or were more in fury seen, Sir,
Than 'twixt Hal and Bob for the famous job,
  Who should be the Faculty's Dean, Sir.

This Hal for genius, wit and lore
  Among the first was number'd;
But pious Bob, 'mid learning's store
  Commandment the Tenth remember'd.
Yet simple Bob the victory got
  And won his heart's desire:
Which shows that Heaven can boil the pot,
  Tho' the Deil piss in the fire.

Squire Hal, besides, had in this case
  Pretensions rather brassy;
For talents, to deserve a place,
  Are qualifications saucy.
So their worships of the Faculty,
  Quite sick of Merit's rudeness,
Chose one who should owe it all (d' ye see?)
  To their gratis grace and goodness!

As once on Pisgah purg'd was the sight
  Of a son of Circumcision,
So, may be, on this Pisgah height
  Bob's purblind mental vision.
Nay, Bobby's mouth may be open'd yet,
  Till for eloquence you hail him,
And swear that he has the Angel met
  That met the Ass of Balaam.

In your heretic sins may ye live and die,
  Ye heretic Eight-and-Thirty!
But accept, ye sublime majority,
  My congratulations hearty!
With your honors, as with a certain King,
  In your servants this is striking,
The more incapacity they bring
  The more they 're to your liking!

O THAT'S THE LASSIE O' MY HEART.

TUNE—*Morag.*

O wat ye wha that lo'es me,
And has my heart a-keeping?
O sweet is she that lo'es me,
As dews o' summer weeping,
In tears the rose-buds steeping:

Chorus—O that 's the lassie o' my heart,
My lassie, ever dearer;
O that 's the queen o' woman-kind,
And ne'er a ane to peer her. **to be her peer**

If thou shalt meet a lassie
In grace and beauty charming;
That e'en *thy* chosen lassie,
Erewhile thy breast sae warming,
Had ne'er sic powers alarming. **such**

If thou hast heard her talking,
(And thy attention 's plighted,)
That ilka body talking **every one**
But her by thee is slighted,
And thou art all-delighted.

If thou hast met this fair one,
When frae her thou hast parted,
If every other fair one
But her thou hast deserted:
And thou art broken-hearted:
O that 's the lassie o' my heart,
My lassie, ever dearer;
O that 's the queen o' woman-kind,
And ne'er a ane to peer her.

TO COLONEL DE PEYSTER.[1]

My honor'd Colonel, deep I feel
Your interest in the Poet's weal: **welfare**

[1] Colonel Arentz Schuyler de Peyster died at Dumfries in November 1822, at the age, it was believed, of ninety-six or ninety-seven. He had held the royal commission for about eighty years. In early life he commanded at Detroit, Michilimackinac, and other parts of Upper Canada, during the Seven Years' War, when he distinguished himself by detaching the Indians from the service of the French.

Ah! now sma' heart hae I to speel — climb
The steep Parnassus
Surrounded thus by bolus pill
And potion glasses.

O what a canty warld were it — happy
Would pain and care and sickness spare it,
And Fortune favor worth and merit
As they deserve,
And ay a rowth—roast beef and claret!— — plenty
Syne, wha wad starve? — Then—would

Dame Life, tho' fiction out may trick her,
And in paste gems and frippery deck her,
Oh! flickering, feeble and unsicker — uncertain
I've found her still—
Ay wavering, like the willow-wicker,
'Tween good and ill!

Then that curst carmagnole, auld Satan![1]
Watches, like baudrons by a ratton, — the cat—rat
Our sinfu' saul to get a claut on — clutch
Wi' felon ire;
Syne, whip! his tail ye'll ne'er cast saut on— — salt
He's aff like fire.

Ah Nick! ah Nick! it is na fair,
First showing us the tempting ware—
Bright wine and bonie lasses rare—
To put us daft; — wild
Syne weave, unseen, thy spider snare
O' Hell's damned waft! — woof, weaving

Poor Man, the flie, aft bizzes by, — fly—buzzes past
And aft, as chance he comes thee nigh,
Thy damn'd auld elbow yeuks wi' joy — itches
And hellish pleasure;
Already in thy fancy's eye
Thy sicker treasure! — certain

Soon, heels o'er gowdie, in he gangs, — heels-overhead—goes
And, like a sheep-head on a tangs, — tongs
Thy girnin laugh enjoys his pangs — grinning
And murdering wrestle

[1] Satan is here compared uncomplimentarily to a sansculotte of the French Revolution, with whom 'the Carmagnole' was a favourite melody.

As, dangling in the wind, he hangs
A gibbet's tassel.

But lest you think I am uncivil
To plague you with this draunting drivel, drawling
Abjuring a' intentions evil,
I quat my pen: quit
The Lord preserve us frae the Devil!
Amen! Amen!

HEY FOR A LASS WI' A TOCHER.

TUNE—*Balinamona and ora.*

Awa' wi' your witchcraft o' beauty's alarms,
The slender bit beauty you grasp in your arms;
O gie me the lass that has acres o' charms,
O gie me the lass wi' the weel-stockit farms. well-stocked

Chorus—Then hey, for a lass wi' a tocher, dowry
Then hey, for a lass wi' a tocher;
Then hey, for a lass wi' a tocher;
The nice yellow guineas for me.

Your beauty 's a flower in the morning that blows,
And withers the faster, the faster it grows;
But the rapturous charm o' the bonie green knowes, knolls
Ilk spring they 're new deckit wi' bonie white yowes. sheep

And e'en when this beauty your bosom has blest,
The brightest o' beauty may cloy when possest;
But the sweet yellow darlings wi' Geordie imprest, the king's head
The langer ye ha'e them, the mair they 're carest.

JESSY.[1]

Altho' thou maun never be mine,
Altho' even hope is denied;
'Tis sweeter for thee despairing,
Than aught in the world beside—Jessy.

[1] Jessy Lewars was the heroine of this song. It is quite characteristic of Burns, and a proof of his artistic thoroughness, to find him, even in his present melancholy circumstances, imagining himself as the lover of his wife's kind-hearted young friend, as if the position of an inamorata were the most exalted in which his fancy could place any woman he admired or towards whom he felt gratitude.

Chorus—Here 's a health to ane I loe dear,
Here 's a health to ane I loe dear;
Thou art sweet as the smile when fond lovers meet,
And soft as their parting tear—Jessy.

I mourn through the gay, gaudy day,
As, hopeless, I muse on thy charms;
But welcome the dream o' sweet slumber,
For then I am lockt in thy arms—Jessy.

I guess by the dear angel smile;
I guess by the love-rolling e'e;
But why urge the tender confession,
'Gainst fortune's fell, cruel decree—Jessy?

OH, WERT THOU IN THE CAULD BLAST.

Oh, wert thou in the cauld blast,
On yonder lea, on yonder lea,
My plaidie to the angry airt, quarter
I 'd shelter thee, I 'd shelter thee:
Or did Misfortune's bitter storms
Around thee blaw, around thee blaw,
Thy bield should be my bosom, shelter
To share it a', to share it a'.

Or were I in the wildest waste
Sae black and bare, sae black and bare,
The desert were a paradise,
If thou wert there, if thou wert there;
Or were I monarch o' the globe,
Wi' thee to reign, wi' thee to reign;
The brightest jewel in my crown
Wad be my queen, wad be my queen. Would

BUY BRAW TROGGIN:

AN EXCELLENT NEW SONG.

TUNE—*Buy Broom Besoms.*

Wha will buy my troggin,[1]
Fine election ware,

[1] Clothes and miscellaneous articles sold by vagrant traffickers called *troggers* or *trokers.*

Broken trade o' Broughton,
A' in high repair?

Chorus—Buy braw troggin fine
Frae the banks o' Dee!
Wha want troggin
Let them come to me!

Here 's a noble Earl's
Fame and high renown,[1]
For an auld sang—
It 's thought the gudes were stown. goods—stolen

Here 's the worth o' Broughton
In a needle's e'e.
Here 's a reputation
Tint by Balmaghie. Lost

Here 's an honest conscience
Might a Prince adorn,
Frae the Downs o' Tinwald—
So was never worn!

Here 's its stuff and lynin,
Cardoness's head—
Fine for a soger,
A' the wale o' lead. choice

Here 's a little wadset— mortgage
Buittle's scrap o' Truth,
Pawn'd in a gin-shop,
Quenching haly drouth.

Here 's armorial bearings
Frae the manse of Urr:
The crest, an auld crab-apple
Rotten at the core.[2]

Here is Satan's picture,
Like a bizzard-gled buzzard kite
Pouncing poor Redcastle,
Sprawlin' as a taed. toad

[1] The Earl of Galloway. Notes on the other names mentioned are appended to the 'Ballads on Mr Heron's Election.'

[2] This looks like a retort on the epigram launched by the Rev. Mr Muirhead against Burns.

Here 's the font where Douglas
Stane and mortar names,
Lately us'd at Caily
Christening Murray's crimes.

Here 's the worth and wisdom
Collieston can boast:
By a thievish midge
They had been nearly lost.

Here is Murray's fragments
O' the Ten Commands,
Gifted by Black Jock—
To get them off his hands.

Saw ye e'er sic troggin?—
If to buy ye 're slack,
Hornie 's turnin' chapman: The devil
He 'll buy a' the pack!

THE RANTIN DOG THE DADDIE O'T.[1]

O wha my babie-clouts will buy?
Wha will tent me when I cry?
Wha will kiss me whare I lie?
The rantin dog the daddie o 't.

Wha will own he did the faut?
Wha will buy my groanin-maut?
Wha will tell me how to ca 't?
The rantin dog the daddie o 't.

When I mount the creepie-chair,
Wha will sit beside me there?
Gie me Rob, I seek nae mair,
The rantin dog the daddie o 't.

Wha will crack to me my lane?
Wha will mak me fidgin fain?
Wha will kiss me o'er again?
The rantin dog the daddie o 't.

[1] 'I composed this song pretty early in life, and sent it to a young girl, a very particular friend of mine, who was at that time under a cloud.'—*R. B. in the Notes to the 'Museum.'*

TO MISS JESSY LEWARS.[1]

Thine be the volumes, Jessy fair,
And with them take the Poet's prayer:—
That Fate may in her fairest page,
With every kindliest, best presage
Of future bliss, enroll thy name:
While native worth, and spotless fame,
And wakeful caution to beware
Of ill, but chief man's felon snare;
All blameless joys on earth we find,
And all the treasures of the mind:—
These be thy Guardian and Reward!
So prays thy faithful friend, the Bard.

FAIREST MAID ON DEVON BANKS.[2]

TUNE—*Rothiemurchie.*

Full well thou knowest I love thee dear,
Couldst thou to malice lend an ear?
O did not Love exclaim 'Forbear,
Nor use a faithful lover so.'

Chorus—Fairest maid on Devon banks,
Chrystal Devon, winding Devon,
Wilt thou lay that frown aside,
And smile as thou wert wont to do?

Then come, thou fairest of the fair,
Those wonted smiles O let me share;
And by thy beauteous self I swear
No love but thine my heart shall know.

[1] Inscribed on one of three copies of the *Museum* sent by Johnson to the poet. The volumes are in the possession of Lord Rosebery.

[2] These lines were the last composed by Burns.

VERSICLES AND FRAGMENTS.

EPITAPHS.

ON THE SMALL HEADSTONE

OVER THE GRAVE OF THE POET'S FATHER IN ALLOWAY KIRKYARD.

O ye whose cheek the tear of pity stains,
Draw near with pious rev'rence, and attend!
Here lie the loving husband's dear remains,
The tender father, and the gen'rous friend;
The pitying heart that felt for human woe,
The dauntless heart that fear'd no human pride;
The friend of man—to vice alone a foe;
For 'ev'n his failings lean'd to virtue's side.'[1]

ON JAMES GRIEVE,

LAIRD OF BOGHEAD, TARBOLTON.[2]

Here lies Boghead amang the dead,
In hopes to get salvation;
But if such as he in Heav'n may be,
Then welcome—hail! damnation.

ON GAVIN HAMILTON.

The poor man weeps—here Gavin sleeps
Whom canting wretches blamed:
But with such as he, where'er he be,
May I be saved or damned!

[1] Goldsmith. [2] Boghead lies west from Lochlea.

ON ROBERT AIKEN, ESQ.

Know thou, O stranger to the fame
Of this much-loved, much-honoured name!
(For none that knew him need be told)
A warmer heart Death ne'er made cold.

ON A CELEBRATED RULING ELDER.[1]

Here souter Hood in death does sleep— cobbler
  To hell, if he 's gane thither,
Satan, gie him thy gear to keep, money
  He 'll haud it weel thegither. hold

ON WEE JOHNNY.[2]

HIC JACET WEE JOHNNY.

Whoe'er thou art, O reader, know
  That Death has murdered Johnny!
And here his body lies fu' low—
  For saul he ne'er had ony.

ON A NOISY POLEMIC.[3]

Below thir stanes lie Jamie's banes: these
  O Death, it 's my opinion
Thou ne'er took such a bleth'rin b—h garrulous
  Into thy dark dominion!

ON THOMAS KIRKPATRICK,

LATE BLACKSMITH IN STOOP.

Here lies, 'mang ither useless matters, other
Auld Thomas wi' his endless clatters. talk

[1] This epitaph is inserted in the First Common-place Book, under title, 'Epitaph on Wm. Hood, Senr., in Tarbolton.'

[2] Wee Johnny was for long supposed to be John Wilson, printer of the Kilmarnock Edition. This view is now seldom taken. In or near Mauchline there seem to have been several men of the name of John Wilson to whom these lines might have been applied with more or less appropriateness. Local tradition associates them generally with a grocer who did a little bookselling, and who was more notable for his diminutive stature than his intellectual capacity.

[3] James Humphry, a Mauchline mason.

ON JAMES SMITH.

Lament him, Mauchline husbands a',
He aften did assist ye;
For had ye staid hale weeks awa, whole
Your wives they ne'er had missed ye!

Ye Mauchline bairns, as on ye press children
To school in bands thegither,
O tread ye lightly on his grass—
Perhaps he was your father!

ON TAM THE CHAPMAN.[1]

As Tam the chapman on a day pedlar
Wi' Death forgather'd by the way, had a meeting
Weel pleas'd he greets a wight sae famous,
And Death was nae less pleas'd wi' Thomas,
Wha cheerfully lays down his pack, pedlar's bundle
And there blaws up a hearty crack: talk
His social, friendly, honest heart
Sae tickled Death, they couldna part;
Sae, after viewing knives and garters,
Death taks him hame to gie him quarters. give

ON WILLIAM MUIR, TARBOLTON MILL.[2]

An honest man here lies at rest
As e'er God with His image blest:
The friend of man, the friend of truth,
The friend of age and guide of youth;
Few hearts like his—with virtue warm'd,
Few heads with knowledge so inform'd:
If there's another world, he lives in bliss;
If there is none, he made the best of this.

1 Tam the Chapman was a Thomas Kennedy, whom Burns had known in boyhood, and whom he afterwards encountered as a pedlar, when he found him a pleasant companion and estimable man. Kennedy, in old age, was known to William Cobbett, who printed these lines, either from a manuscript or from recollection. He died in Homer, Courtland county, New York, in November 1846.

2 See note to 'Death and Dr Hornbook.'

ON A HENPECKED COUNTRY SQUIRE.[1]

As Father Adam first was fooled—
A case that 's still too common—
Here lies a man a woman ruled;
The devil ruled the woman.

ON ROBERT FERGUSSON.[2]

No sculptur'd Marble here, nor pompous lay,
No storied Urn nor animated Bust;
This simple stone directs pale Scotia's way
To pour her sorrows o'er the Poet's dust.

She mourns, sweet tuneful youth, thy hapless fate:
Tho' all the powers of song thy fancy fir'd,
Yet Luxury and Wealth lay by in State,
And, thankless, starv'd what they so much admir'd.

This humble tribute with a tear he gives,
A brother Bard—he can no more bestow;
But dear to fame thy Song immortal lives,
A nobler monument than Art can show.

ON WILLIAM CRUIKSHANK, A.M.,[3]

OF THE HIGH SCHOOL, EDINBURGH.

Honest Will to Heaven is gane,
And monie shall lament him;
His faults they a' in Latin lay,
In English nane e'er kent them. knew

ANOTHER VERSION.[4]

Now honest William 's gaen to Heaven,
I wat na gin 't can mend him: I do not know if
The fauts he had in Latin lay,
For nane in English kend them.

[1] Campbell of Netherplace, between Mossgiel and Mauchline.
[2] Only the first stanza of this is on the stone erected by Burns to Fergusson in Canongate Churchyard, Edinburgh; all three are inserted in the Second Common-place Book.
[3] Died 8th March 1795.
[4] From MS. in the Watson Collection.

ON WILLIAM NICOL.

Ye maggots, feed on Nicol's brain,
For few sic feasts ye 've gotten ; such
And fix your claws in Nicol's heart,
For deil a bit o' t 's rotten.

ON EBENEZER MICHIE,[1]

SCHOOLMASTER, CLEISH, FIFESHIRE.

Here lie Eben Michie's banes :
O Satan, an ye tak him, if
Gie him the schulin' o' your weans, children
For clever deils he 'll mak 'em !

ON GABRIEL RICHARDSON, BREWER, DUMFRIES.

Here brewer Gabriel's fire 's extinct,
And empty all his barrels :
He 's blest—if, as he brew'd, he drink—
In upright, virtuous morals.[2]

ON JOHN BUSHBY, WRITER, DUMFRIES.

Here lies John Bushby, honest man !
Cheat him, devil—if you can.[3]

ON THE AUTHOR.[4]

He who of Rankine sang lies stiff and dead,
And a green, grassy hillock hides his head :
Alas ! alas ! a devilish change indeed !

[1] Burns, walking one evening with Nicol, was introduced by him to Ebenezer Michie, schoolmaster of Cleish, who accompanied them to the poet's lodging, and a merry evening was spent. In the course of the evening Michie fell asleep, and Burns proposed to write an epitaph for him. Michie was schoolmaster first in Kettle, and afterwards in Cleish. He died in 1812, at the age of forty-six.

[2] These lines were inscribed on a crystal goblet.

[3] These lines were inscribed on a window in the Globe Tavern.

[4] Said by Stewart (1801) to have been written by Burns on his death-bed, and forwarded to Rankine immediately after the poet's death.

ON GRIM GRIZEL.

Here lies with Death auld Grizel Grim,
  Lincluden's ugly witch.
O Death, how horrid is thy taste
  To lie with such a bitch!

ANOTHER VERSION.[1]

Here lyes withe Dethe auld Grizzel Grimme,
  Lincluden's ugly witche.
O Dethe, an' what a taste hast thou
  Cann lye withe siche a bitche!

ON AN INNKEEPER, NICKNAMED 'THE MARQUIS.'

Here lies a mock Marquis, whose titles were shamm'd,
If ever he rise, it will be to be damn'd.

ON A SWEARING COXCOMB.

Here cursing, swearing Burton lies,
A buck, a beau, or 'Dem my eyes!'
Who in his life did little good,
And his last words were 'Dem my blood!'

ON A SUICIDE.

Here lies in earth a root of Hell
  Set by the Deil's ain dibble: — own—tool used for planting roots
This worthless body damn'd himsel
  To save the Lord the trouble.

ON WILLIAM GRAHAM OF MOSSKNOWE.

'Stop thief!' dame Nature call'd to Death,
As Willie drew his latest breath:
'How shall I make a fool again?—
My choicest model thou hast ta'en.'

[1] Inscribed by Burns in a MS. volume (from the Glenriddel Library) now in the possession of Lord Rosebery. It is preceded by this note: 'Passing lately through Dunblane, while I stopped to refresh my horse, the following ludicrous epitaph, which I pickt up from an old tombstone among the ruins of the ancient Abbacy, struck me particularly, being myself a native of Dumfriesshire.'

ON CAPTAIN FRANCIS LASCELLES.

When Lascelles thought fit from this world to depart,
Some friends warmly thought of embalming his heart:
A bystander whispers—'Pray don't make so much o 't—
The subject is poison, no reptile will touch it.'

EPIGRAMS.

EXTEMPORE,

PINNED TO A LADY'S COACH.

If you rattle along like your mistress's tongue,
Your speed will out-rival the dart:
But, a fly for your load, you 'll break down on the road
If your stuff be as rotten 's her heart.

NITH.

ON A NOTED COXCOMB.

[CAPTAIN WILLIAM RODDICK OF CORBISTON.]

'Light lay the earth on Billy's breast,'
His chicken heart so tender;
But build a castle on his head,
His skull will prop it under.

CLINCHER.

ON SEEING MRS KEMBLE IN YARICO.

Kemble, thou cur'st my unbelief
Of Moses and his rod:
At Yarico's sweet notes of grief
The rock with tears had flow'd.

ON W[ALTER] R[IDDEL], ESQ.

So vile was poor Wat, such a miscreant slave,
That the worms ev'n damn'd him when laid in his grave.
'In his skull there 's a famine' a starved reptile cries;
'And his heart, it is poison' another replies.

ON JEANIE SCOTT,

DAUGHTER OF THE ECCLEFECHAN POSTMASTER.

O had each Scot on English ground
Been bonnie Scott, as thou art,
The stoutest heart of English kind
Had yielded like a coward.

IMPROMPTU

ON MR BACON, OF BROWNHILL INN, DUMFRIESSHIRE.

At Brownhill we always get dainty good cheer
And plenty of bacon each day in the year;
We 've a' thing that 's nice, and mostly in season—
But why always *Bacon?*—come, tell me a reason?

ON A HENPECKED COUNTRY SQUIRE.[1]

O Death, hadst thou but spared his life
Whom we this day lament!
We freely wad exchanged the wife, — would
And a' been weel content.

E'en as he is, cauld in his graff, — grave
The swap we yet will do 't; — exchange
Tak thou the carline's carcass aff, — old woman
Thou 'se get the saul to boot. — Thou shalt

ANOTHER.

One Queen Artemisia, as old stories tell,
When deprived of her husband she lovèd so well,
In respect for the love and affection he shewed her,
She reduced him to dust, and she drank off the powder.

But Queen Netherplace, of a different complexion,
When called on to order the funeral direction,
Would have ate her dead lord, on a slender pretence,
Not to shew her respect, but—to save the expense!

[1] Campbell of Netherplace.

IN LAMINGTON KIRK.

As cauld a wind as ever blew, **cold**
A cauld kirk, and in 't but few,
As cauld a minister 's[1] ever spak—
Ye 'se a' be het or I come back! **You'll all be hot before**

ON ROUGH ROADS.

I 'm now arrived—thanks to the gods!—
Thro' pathways rough and muddy:
A certain sign that makin roads
Is no this people's study:
Altho' I 'm no wi' Scripture cramm'd,
I 'm sure the Bible says
That heedless sinners shall be damn'd
Unless they mend their *ways.*

ON THE BOOK-WORMS.[2]

Through and through th' inspirèd leaves
Ye maggots, make your windings;
But O, respect his lordship's taste,
And spare the golden bindings!

ON BEING APPOINTED TO AN EXCISE DIVISION.

Searching auld wives' barrels,
Ochon, the day
That clarty barm should stain my laurels! **muddy yeast**
But what 'll ye say?
These movin' things ca'd wives an' weans **called—children**
Wad move the very hearts o' stanes. **Would**

[1] Rev. Thomas Mitchell, described as 'an accomplished scholar.'

[2] 'Burns,' says Allan Cunningham, 'on a visit to a nobleman, was shewn into the library, where stood a Shakespeare, splendidly bound, but unread and much worm-eaten. Long after the poet's death, some one happened to open, accidentally perhaps, the same neglected book, and found the above epigram in the handwriting of Burns.'

ON A GROTTO IN FRIARS' CARSE GROUNDS.

To Riddel, much-lamented man,
This ivied cot was dear:
Wand'rer, dost value matchless worth?
This ivied cot revere.

ON MARIA RIDDEL.[1]

'Praise Woman still' his lordship roars,
'Deserv'd or not, no matter!'
But thee, whom all my soul adores,
There Flattery cannot flatter!
Maria, all my thought and dream,
Inspires my vocal shell:
The more I praise my lovely theme,
The more the truth I tell.

ON THE HENPECKED HUSBAND.

Curs'd be the man, the poorest wretch in life,
The crouching vassal to the tyrant wife!
Who has no will but by her high permission;
Who has not sixpence but in her possession;
Who must to her his dear friend's secrets tell;
Who dreads a curtain-lecture worse than hell!
Were such the wife had fallen to my part,
I'd break her spirit or I'd break her heart:
I'd charm her with the magic of a switch,
I'd kiss her maids and kick the perverse bitch.

ON A BEAUTIFUL COUNTRY-SEAT.

We grant they're thine, those beauties all,
So lovely in our eye:
Keep them, thou eunuch, Cardoness,
For others to enjoy!

[1] In a MS. in the possession of Mrs Locker-Lampson the heading is 'On my Lord Buchan's reiterating in an argument that "women must always be flattered grossly or not spoken to at all."'

ON A GALLOWAY LAIRD—NOT QUITE SO WISE AS SOLOMON.

Bless Jesus Christ, O Cardoness,[1]
With grateful lifted eyes,
Who taught that not the soul alone,
The body too shall rise:
For had He said, 'The soul alone
From death I shall deliver,'
Alas! alas! O Cardoness,
Then thou hadst lain for ever!

ON THE EARL OF GALLOWAY.[2]

I.

What dost thou in that mansion fair?
Flit, Galloway, and find
Some narrow, dirty, dungeon cave,
The picture of thy mind!

II.

No Stewart art thou, Galloway:
The Stewarts all were brave;
Besides, the Stewarts were but fools,
Not one of them a knave.

Bright ran thy line, O Galloway,
Thro' many a far-famed sire!
So ran the far-famed Roman way,
And ended in a mire.

III.

Spare me thy vengeance, Galloway![3]
In quiet let me live:
I ask no kindness at thy hand,
For thou hast none to give.

[1] David Maxwell of Cardoness. He is described in a letter to Mrs Dunlop as a 'stupid, money-loving dunderpate.' See 'Ballads on Mr Heron's Election.'

[2] Burns had an antipathy of old standing to the Earl of Galloway. It was against him that he launched invectives when Mr Syme pointed to Garlies House, across the Bay of Wigtown, in the course of their excursion in July 1793.

[3] On being informed [misinformed?] that the Earl threatened him with his resentment.

ON COMMISSARY THOMAS GOLDIE'S BRAINS.

Lord, to account who dares Thee call
  Or e'er dispute Thy pleasure?
Else, why within so thick a wall
  Enclose so poor a treasure?

TO THE HON. WM. R. MAULE OF PANMURE.[1]

Thou fool, in thy phaeton towering,
  Art proud when that phaeton is prais'd?
'Tis the pride of a Thief's exhibition
  When higher his pillory 's rais'd!

THE SOLEMN LEAGUE AND COVENANT.

The Solemn League and Covenant
  Now brings a smile, now brings a tear;
But sacred Freedom, too, was theirs:
  If thou 'rt a slave, indulge thy sneer.[2]

SECOND VERSION.

The Solemn League and Covenant
  Cost Scotland blood—cost Scotland tears;
But it sealèd Freedom's sacred cause—
  If thou 'rt a slave, indulge thy sneers.

[1] Afterwards Lord Panmure, friend of Fox, and a notorious free-liver. He settled on Mrs Burns a pension of £50. He was an officer in a regiment stationed in Dumfries when he provoked this outburst (1794) on the part of the poet.

[2] In the library of the Dumfries Mechanics' Institute is a copy of the thirteenth volume of Sir John Sinclair's *Statistical Account of Scotland* (Edinburgh, 1794). 'Under the head "Balmaghie" a notice is given of several martyred Covenanters belonging to that parish; and the rude yet expressive lines engraved on their tombstones are quoted at length. The pathos of the simple prose statement and the rugged force of the versification seem to have aroused the fervid soul of Burns, for there appears [on page 652], in his bold handwriting, the above verse pencilled on the margin by way of footnote.'—WILLIAM M'DOWALL. These seem to be the original of the inferior but much more frequently quoted lines, said by Allan Cunningham to have been 'spoken in reply to a gentleman who sneered at the sufferings of Scotland for conscience' sake, and called the Solemn League and Covenant of the Lords and People ridiculous and fanatical.'

THE KEEKIN' GLASS.[1]

How daur ye ca' me 'Howlet-face,' dare—Owl
 Ye bleár-e'ed, wither'd spectre?
Ye only spied the keekin' glass, looking-glass
 An' there ye saw your picture.

VERSES TO JOHN M'MURDO, ESQ.,

WITH A PRESENT OF BOOKS.

Oh, could I give thee India's wealth,
 As I this trifle send,
Because thy joy in both would be
 To share them with a friend!

But golden sands did never grace
 The Heliconian stream;
Then take what gold could never buy—
 An honest Bard's esteem.

ON JAMES GRACIE.[2]

Gracie, thou art a man of worth,
 O be thou Dean for ever!
May he be damn'd to Hell henceforth
 Who fauts thy weight or measure! faults

ON THE REV. DR WILLIAM BABINGTON'S LOOKS.

That there is falsehood in his looks
 I must and will deny:
They say their master is a knave,
 And sure they do not lie.

[1] 'One of the Lords of Justiciary, when holding circuit at Dumfries,' so runs a local story, 'dined one day with Mr Miller at Dalswinton. According to the custom of the times, the after-dinner libations were somewhat copious; and, on entering the drawing-room, his lordship's vision was so much affected that he asked Mr Miller, pointing to one of his daughters, who were reckoned remarkably handsome women, "Wha's yon howlet-faced thing in the corner?"' Next day, Burns, who then resided at Ellisland, happened to be a guest at Dalswinton, and, in the course of conversation, his lordship's very ungallant and unjust remark was mentioned to him. He immediately took from his pocket an old letter, on the back of which he wrote in pencil the above lines, and handed them to Miss Miller.

[2] Gracie was Dean of Guild of the burgh of Dumfries.

ANDREW TURNER.[1]

In Se'enteen Hunder 'n Forty-Nine
The Deil gat stuff to mak a swine,
An' coost it in a corner; cast
But wilily he chang'd his plan,
An' shap'd it something like a man,
An' ca'd it Andrew Turner. called

ON MARRIAGE.

That hackney'd judge of human life,
The Preacher and the King,
Observes:—'The man that gets a wife
He gets a noble thing.'
But how capricious are mankind,
Now loathing, now desirous!
We married men, how oft we find
The best of things will tire us!

TO THE BEAUTIFUL MISS ELIZA J——N,

ON HER PRINCIPLES OF LIBERTY AND EQUALITY.

How, 'Liberty!' Girl, can it be by thee nam'd?
'Equality,' too! Hussy, art not asham'd?
Free and Equal indeed, while mankind thou enchainest,
And over their hearts a proud Despot so reignest!

THANKSGIVING FOR A NATIONAL VICTORY.[2]

Ye hypocrites, are these your pranks?
To murder men and give God thanks?
Desist, for shame! Proceed no further:
God won't accept your thanks for murther.

[1] 'Being rudely called out one evening from a party of friends at the King's Arms, Dumfries, to see a vain coxcomb of an English commercial traveller, who, having a bottle of wine on his table, thought he might patronise the *Ayrshire Ploughman*, Burns entered into conversation with the man, and soon saw what sort of person he had to deal with. Before leaving, Burns was urged to give an exhibition of his powers of impromptu versifying, and, having asked the stranger's name and age, he instantly penned and handed to him the above stanza—and then abruptly quitted the room.'

[2] Adapted from lines 'on the Thanksgiving Day for Perth and Preston, 17th June 1716' (Maidment's *Scottish Pasquils*, 1868). The victory Burns celebrated was doubtless Howe's, off Ushant, 1st June 1794.

THE PHILOSOPHER'S STONE.[1]

Long have the learnèd sought, without success,
To find what you alone, O Pitt, possess!
Thou only hast the magic power to draw
A *guinea* from a *head* not worth a *straw.*

GRACES.

GRACES BEFORE MEAT.

I.

Some hae meat and canna eat,
  And some wad eat that want it: would
But we hae meat and we can eat,
  Sae let the Lord be thankit.

II.

O Thou, who kindly dost provide
  For ev'ry creature's want!
We bless Thee, God of Nature wide,
  For all Thy goodness lent.
And if it please Thee, heavenly Guide,
  May never worse be sent;
But, whether granted or denied,
  Lord, bless us with content!

III.

O Thou, in whom we live and move,
  Who mad'st the sea and shore,
Thy goodness constantly we prove
  And, grateful, would adore.
And, if it please Thee, Power above,
  Still grant us, with such store,
The friend we trust, the fair we love,
  And we desire no more.

[1] This anonymous quatrain, which appeared in the *Dumfries Weekly Journal* of 7th July 1795, was first included in the *Works* of Burns in Chambers's edition of the *Life and Works* (4 vols. 1896). Circumstantial and internal evidence is proof that it is from the pen of Burns. It refers, of course, to Pitt's tax (1795) of a guinea on each person who used hair-powder.

IV.

O Lord, when hunger pinches sore,
Do Thou stand us in stead,
And send us from Thy bounteous store,
A tup- or wether-head. Amen.

GRACES AFTER MEAT.

I.

Lord, [Thee] we thank, and Thee alone,
For temporal gifts we little merit!
At present we will ask no more—
Let William Hyslop[1] bring the spirit.

II.

O Lord, since we have feasted thus,
Which we so little merit,
Let Meg now take away the flesh,
And Jock bring in the spirit. Amen.

FRAGMENTS.

A RUMOUR.

I am a keeper of the law
In some sma' points, altho' not a';
Some people tell me gin I fa',
Ae way or ither,
The breaking of ae point, tho' sma',
Breaks a' thegether.[2]

I hae been in for 't ance or twice,
And winna say o'er far for thrice;
Yet never met wi' that surprise
That broke my rest;
But now a rumour 's like to rise—
A whaup 's i' the nest! curlew

[1] Landlord of the Globe Inn, Dumfries.

[2] 'For whosoever shall keep the whole law, and yet offend in one point, he is guilty of all.'—*James*, ii. 10.

REMORSE.

Of all the numerous ills that hurt our peace;
That press the soul, or wring the mind with anguish;
Beyond comparison the worst are those
By our own folly, or our guilt brought on.
In ev'ry other circumstance the mind
Has this to say, It was no deed of mine:
But, when to all the evil of misfortune
This sting is added, blame thy foolish self;
Or worser far, the pangs of keen remorse:
The tort'ring, gnawing consciousness of guilt—
Or guilt, perhaps, where we 've involvèd others;
The young, the innocent, who fondly lov'd us:
Nay more, that very love their cause of ruin—
O! burning Hell in all thy store of torments
There 's not a keener Lash—
Lives there a man so firm who, while his heart
Feels all the bitter horrors of his crime,
Can reason down its agonising throbs,
And, after proper purpose of amendment,
Can firmly force his jarring thoughts to peace.
O happy, happy, enviable man!
O glorious magnanimity of soul!

All villain as I am, a damnèd wretch,
A hardened, stubborn, unrepenting sinner,
Still my heart melts at human wretchedness;
And with sincere tho' unavailing sighs,
I view the helpless children of distress:
With tears indignant I behold the oppressor
Rejoicing in the honest man's destruction,
Whose unsubmitting heart was all his crime.
Ev'n you, ye hapless crew, I pity you;
Ye, whom the seeming good think sin to pity;
Ye poor, despised, abandoned vagabonds,
Whom Vice, as usual, has turn'd o'er to ruin.
Oh! but for friends and interposing Heaven,
I had been driven forth like you forlorn,
The most detested, worthless wretch among you!
O injured God! Thy goodness has endow'd me
With talents passing most of my compeers,
Which I in just proportion have abused—
As far surpassing other common villains
As Thou in natural parts has given me more.

WHEN FIRST I CAME TO STEWART KYLE.[1]

TUNE—*I had a horse & I had nae mair.*

When first I came to Stewart Kyle,
My mind it was na steady;
Where'er I gaed, where'er I rade,
A mistress still I had ay:

But when I came roun' by Mauchline toun,
Not dreadin anybody,
My heart was caught, before I thought,
And by a Mauchline lady.[2]

One night as I did wander,
When corn begins to shoot,
I sat me down to ponder,
Upon an auld tree-root:
Auld Ayr ran by before me,
And bicker'd to the seas; ran rapidly
A cushat crooded o'er me, wood-pigeon cooed
That echoed through the braes.

O raging Fortune's withering blast
Has laid my leaf full low!
O raging Fortune's withering blast
Has laid my leaf full low!

My stem was fair, my bud was green,
My blossom sweet did blow;
The dew fell fresh, the sun rose mild,
And made my branches grow;

But luckless Fortune's northern storms
Laid a' my blossoms low,—
But luckless Fortune's northern storms
Laid a' my blossoms low!

[1] Kyle is the middle of the three divisions of Ayrshire; having been at one time almost entirely covered with forest, it may have derived its name from the Celtic *coille*, a wood.

[2] If the 'Mauchline lady' was Jean Armour, this poem—a parody of the song to the music of which it was set by the author—gives support to the belief that the poet had seen and admired, if not spoken to her, in the spring or early summer of 1784.

THE NORTHERN LASS.

Tho' cruel fate should bid us part,
Far as the pole and line;
Her dear idea round my heart
Should tenderly entwine.
Tho' mountains rise, and deserts howl,
And oceans roar between;
Yet, dearer than my deathless soul,
I still would love my Jean.

Though fickle Fortune has deceived me,
She promis'd fair and perform'd but ill;
Of mistress, friends, and wealth bereav'd me,
Yet I bear a heart shall support me still.[1]

I'll act with prudence as far as I'm able,
But if success I must never find,
Then come misfortune, I bid thee welcome,
I'll meet thee with an undaunted mind.

Farewell, dear Friend! may gude luck hit you,
And 'mang her favorites admit you!
If e'er Detraction shore to smit you, threaten—attack
May nane believe him!
And ony deil that thinks to get you,
Good Lord deceive him.

Rusticity's ungainly form
May cloud the highest mind;
But when the heart is nobly warm,
The *good* excuse will find.

Propriety's cold, cautious rules
Warm fervour may o'erlook;
But spare poor sensibility
Th' ungentle, harsh rebuke.

[1] This verse is a variation of the last four lines of 'I Dream'd I Lay.'

TO DR JOHN MACKENZIE.

Friday first 's the day appointed
By the Right Worshipful anointed,
To hold our grand procession;[1]
To get a blad o' Johnie's morals,[2]
And taste a swatch o' Manson's barrels — sample
I' the way of our profession.
The Master and the Brotherhood
Would a' be glad to see you;
For me I would be mair than proud
To share the mercies[3] wi' you.
If Death, then, wi' skaith, then, — hurt
Some mortal heart is hechtin, — threatening
Inform him, and storm him, — tell him peremptorily
That Saturday you 'll fecht him. — fight

MOSSGIEL, *An. M.* 5790 [A.D. 1786]. ROBERT BURNS.

RATTLIN, ROARING WILLIE.[4]

As I cam by Crochallan,
I cannily keekit ben, — cautiously looked in
Rattlin, roarin Willie
Was sitting at yon boord-en', — end of the table
Sitting at yon boord-en',
And amang guid companie; — good
Rattlin, roarin Willie,
Ye 're welcome hame to me.

[1] St John's Day procession of the Brethren of St James's Lodge.

[2] 'Blad' means a blow or shower. Burns probably meant that Mackenzie would take advantage of the meeting of his friends to pelt them with his doctrines on morals. 'The phrase, "Johnie's morals,"' explains Mr Mackenzie in a letter to Dr Robert Chambers, in which he enclosed a copy of these verses, 'originated from some correspondence Burns and I had on the origin of morals; and "Manson's barrels" to the small beer of a very superior kind that the brethren got from him at dinner. The lines, "If death, then, wi' skaith, then," &c. were in consequence of my expressing a doubt whether I could attend the lodge on that day, from the number of patients that I had to visit at that period.'

[3] 'These Thy mercies'—*i.e.* the food and drink now before us—'which Thou in Thine Infinite Benevolence hast vouchsafed,' was an expression frequently used in a Scottish grace before meat.

[4] William Dunbar was the third son of Alexander Dunbar, of Boath, Nairnshire. He was year after year appointed the representative elder of the Nairn Town Council to the General Assembly. It is said that 'a faggot vote was created for him in Nairnshire, but being a conscientious man he "would not swear"—namely, take the trust oath that the qualification was genuine, and he renounced.'—BAIN'S *History of Nairnshire.* He died unmarried in 1807. His elder brother, James, became professor of Philosophy in King's College, Aberdeen, and an LL.D.

ON LEAVING A PLACE IN THE HIGHLANDS

WHERE HE HAD BEEN KINDLY ENTERTAINED.

When Death's dark stream I ferry o'er
(A time that surely shall come),
In Heav'n itself I 'll ask no more
Than just a Highland welcome.

The crimson blossom charms the bee,
The summer sun the swallow,
So dear this tuneful gift [1] to me
From lovely Isabella.[2]

Her portrait [*strong*] fair upon my mind,
Revolving time shall mellow;
And mem'ry's latest effort find
The lovely Isabella.

No bard nor lover's rapture this,
In fancies vain and shallow;
She is, so come my soul to bliss,
The lovely Isabella.

Sound be his sleep and blithe his morn
That never did a lassie wrang;
Who poverty ne'er held in scorn—
For misery ever tholed a pang.[3] endured

THE CREED OF POVERTY.

In Politics if thou wouldst mix,
And mean thy fortunes be;
Bear this in mind, be deaf and blind,
Let great folks hear and see.

[1] What the 'tuneful gift' was is not known.
[2] Supposed to be a Miss Isabella M'Leod.
[3] This was given on the authority of Mr G. Boyack, St Andrews, in the *Fifeshire Journal*, November 4, 1847. The last line is there printed: 'For misery *never* tholed a pang.'

WHERE ARE THE JOYS?

TUNE—*Saw ye my Father?*

Where are the joys I hae met in the morning,
That danced to the lark's early sang?
Where is the peace that awaited my wandering,
At e'enin' the wild-woods amang?

Nae mair a winding the course o' yon river,
And marking sweet flowrets sae fair;
Nae mair I trace the light footsteps o' pleasure,
But sorrow and sad-sighing care.

Is it that simmer's forsaken our vallies,
And grim surly winter is near?
No, no, the bees humming round the gay roses
Proclaim it the pride o' the year.

Fain wad I hide, what I fear to discover,
Yet lang, lang too well hae I known;
A' that has causèd the wreck in my bosom
Is, Jenny, fair Jenny, alone.

Time cannot aid me, my griefs are immortal,
Not Hope dare a comfort bestow:
Come then, enamor'd and fond of my anguish,
Enjoyment I'll seek in my woe.

In vain would Prudence with decorous sneer
Point out a censuring world, and bid me fear:
Above that world on wings of love I rise,
I know its worst and can that worst despise.

'Wronged, injured, shunned, unpitied, unredrest,
The mocked quotation of the scorner's jest,'
Let Prudence' direst bodements on me fall,
Clarinda, rich reward! o'erpays them all.

Grant me, indulgent Heaven, that I may live
To see the miscreants feel the pains they give;
Deal Freedom's sacred treasures free as air,
Till Slave and Despot be but things which were.

TO DR MAXWELL,

ON MISS JESSY STAIG'S RECOVERY.

Maxwell, if merit here you crave,
That merit I deny:
You save fair Jessy from the grave!
An ANGEL could not die!

Ah, Chloris, could I now but sit
As unconcerned as when
Your infant beauty could beget
Nor happiness nor pain.

Kist yestreen, kist yestreen,
O as I was kist yestreen,
I'll ne'er forget while the hollin grows green
The bonie sweet lassie I kist yestreen.

Ye true 'Loyal Natives,' attend to my song:
In uproar and riot rejoice the night long!
From Envy and Hatred your corps is exempt,
But where is your shield from the darts of Contempt?

WHY TELL THY LOVER?

TUNE—*The Caledonian Hunt's Delight.*

Why, why tell thy lover
Bliss he never must enjoy?
Why, why undeceive him
And give all his hopes the lie?

O why, while fancy, raptured, slumbers,
Chloris, Chloris all the theme,
Why, why wouldst thou cruel
Wake thy lover from his dream?

VERSES ON JESSY LEWARS.

I.

Talk not to me of savages
  From Afric's burning sun!
No savage e'er can rend my heart
  As, Jessy, thou hast done.

But Jessy's lovely hand in mine
  A mutual faith to plight—
Not even to view the heavenly choir
  Would be so blest a sight.

II.

Fill me with the rosy wine;
Call a toast—a toast divine;
Give the Poet's darling flame—
Lovely Jessy be her name:
Then thou mayest freely boast
Thou hast given a peerless toast.

III.

Say, sages, what 's the charm on earth
  Can turn Death's dart aside?
It is not purity and worth,
  Else Jessy had not died.

IV.

But rarely seen since Nature's birth,
  The natives of the sky!
Yet still one seraph 's left on earth,
  For Jessy did not die.

SONG.

TUNE—*Black Jock.*

My girl she 's airy, she 's buxom and gay;
Her breath is as sweet as the blossoms in May;
  A touch of her lips it ravishes quite.
She 's always good-natur'd, good-humor'd and free;
She dances, she glances, she smiles upon me:
  I never am happy when out of her sight.

* * * * * *

O WHY THE DEUCE SHOULD I REPINE?

O why the deuce should I repine,
And be an ill foreboder?
I 'm twenty-three, and five feet nine,
I 'll go and be a sodger!

I gat some gear wi' mickle care, wealth
I held it weel thegither;
But now it 's gane, and something mair—
I 'll go and be a sodger![1]

ADVICE TO THE MAUCHLINE BELLES.

O leave novels, ye Machline belles,
Ye 're safer at your spinning-wheel;
Such witching books are baited hooks
For rakish rooks like Rob Mossgiel;
Your fine *Tom Jones* and *Grandisons*,
They make your youthful fancies reel;
They heat your brains, and fire your veins,
And then you 're prey for Rob Mossgiel.

Beware a tongue that 's smoothly hung,
A heart that warmly seems to feel;
That feeling heart but acts a part—
'Tis rakish art in Rob Mossgiel.
The frank address, the soft caress,
Are worse than poisoned darts of steel;
The frank address, and politesse,
Are all finesse in Rob Mossgiel.

LEEZIE LINDSAY.

Will ye go to the Hielands, Leezie Lindsay?
Will ye go to the Hielands wi' me?
Will ye go to the Hielands, Leezie Lindsay,
My pride and my darling to be?

[1] The date April 1782 is prefixed by Currie to these extempore verses, but perhaps only under a presumption arising from the time of life indicated. Or it may be that Burns started his memorandum-book on his return to Lochlea from Irvine; 'I'm twenty-three' and the allusion to his 'gear' being 'gane and something mair' fit in with that period.

LINES TO JOHN RANKINE.

Ae day, as Death, that gruesome carl, **fellow**
Was driving to the tither warl' **other world**
A mixtie-maxtie, motley squad **miscellaneous**
And monie a guilt-bespotted lad:
Black gowns of each denomination
And thieves of every rank and station—
From him that wears the star and garter
To him that wintles in a halter: **dangles**
Ashamed himself to see the wretches,
He mutters, glow'ring at the bitches:
'By God, I 'll not be seen behint them,
Nor 'mang the sp'ritual core present them **corps**
Without, at least, ae honest man **one**
To grace this damn'd infernal clan!
By Adamhill a glance he threw:
'Lord God!' quoth he, 'I have it now:
There 's just the man I want, i' faith!'
And quickly stoppit Rankine's breath.

HER FLOWING LOCKS.

Her flowing locks—the raven's wing—
Adown her neck and bosom hing;
How sweet unto that breast to cling,
And round that neck entwine her!

Her lips are roses wet wi' dew!
O what a feast her bonie mou'!
Her cheeks a mair celestial hue,
A crimson still diviner!

HERE'S HIS HEALTH IN WATER.

Altho' my back be at the wa',
And though he be the fautor; **culprit**
Although my back be at the wa',
Yet here 's his health in water!
O wae gae by his wanton sides— **woe be to**
Sae brawly 's he could flatter; **finely**
Till for his sake I 'm slighted sair **sorely**
And dree the kintra clatter; **endure the gossip of the district**
But though my back be at the wa',
Yet here 's his health in water!

GRIM GRIZZEL.—A BALLAD.[1]

Grim Grizzel was a mighty Dame
Weel ken'd on Cluden-side; known
Grim Grizzel was a mighty Dame
O' meikle fame and pride. great

When gentles met in gentle bowers
And nobles in the ha',
Grim Grizzel was a mighty Dame,
The loudest o' them a'.

Where lawless Riot rag'd the night
And Beauty durst na gang, dared not go
Grim Grizzel was a mighty Dame
Whom nae man e'er wad wrang. would

Nor had Grim Grizzel skill alane
What Bower and Ha' require;
But she had skill, and meikle skill
In barn and eke in byre. cow-house

Ae day Grim Grizzel walkèd forth,
As she was wont to do,
Alang the banks o' Cluden fair
Her cattle for to view.

* * * * * *

THE CARES O' LOVE.

HE.

The cares o' Love are sweeter far
Than onie other pleasure; any
And if sae dear its sorrows are,
Enjoyment, what a treasure!

SHE.

I fear to try, I dare na try
A passion sae ensnaring;
For light 's her heart and blythe 's her song
That for nae man is caring.

[1] This ballad, extending to twenty verses, is from the Rosebery MS. mentioned in the note to the Epitaph on Grim Grizel. Mrs Grizzel Craik was the widow of Thomas Young of Lincluden.

PASSION'S CRY.[1]

Mild zephyrs waft thee to life's farthest shore,
Nor think of me and my distresses more.
Falsehood accurst! No! still I beg a place,
Still near thy heart some little, little trace.
For that dear trace the world I would resign:
O let me live, and die, and think it mine!

By all I loved, neglected and forgot,
No friendly face e'er lights my lonely cot:
Shunned, hated, wronged, unpitied, unredrest,
The mocked quotation of the scorner's jest;
Even the poor support of my wretched life,
Snatched by the violence of legal strife;
Oft grateful for my very daily bread
To those my Family's once large bounty fed;
A welcome inmate at their homely fare,
My griefs, my woes, my sighs, my tears they share:
(Their vulgar souls unlike the soul refined,
The fashioned marble of the polished mind!)

'I burn, I burn, as when thro' ripen'd corn
By driving winds the crackling flames are borne.'
Now, maddening wild, I curse that fatal night;
Now bless the hour that charmed my guilty sight.
In vain the Laws their feeble force oppose:
Chained at his feet they groan Love's vanquished foes;
In vain Religion meets my shrinking eye:
I dare not combat, but I turn and fly.
Conscience in vain upbraids th' unhallowed fire.
Love grasps her scorpions—stifled they expire.
Reason drops headlong from his sacred throne,
Your dear idea reigns, and reigns alone;
Each thought intoxicated homage yields,
And riots wanton in forbidden fields.

By all on high, adoring mortals know!
By all the conscious villain fears below!
By what, alas, much more my soul alarms—
My doubtful hopes once more to fill thy arms—
Even shouldst thou, false, forswear the guilty tie,
Thine and thine only I must live and die!

[1] Supposed to be spoken by Mrs Maxwell Campbell of Skerrington.

SKETCH FOR AN ELEGY.[1]

Craigdarroch,[2] fam'd for speaking art
And every virtue of the heart,
Stops short, nor can a word impart
To end his sentence,
When mem'ry strikes him like a dart
With auld acquaintance.

Black James[3]—whase wit was never laith, loath
But, like a sword had tint the sheath, lost
Ay ready for the work o' death—
He turns aside,
And strains wi' suffocating breath
His grief to hide.

Even Philosophic Smellie tries
To choke the stream that floods his eyes:
So Moses wi' a hazel-rice rod
Came o'er the stane;
But, tho' it cost him speaking twice,
It gush'd amain.

Go to your marble graffs, ye great, graves
In a' the tinkler-trash of state!
But by thy honest turf I 'll wait,
Thou man o' worth,
And weep the ae best fallow's fate one—fellow
E'er lay in earth!

A MAUCHLINE WEDDING.

When Eighty-five was seven months auld
And wearing thro' the aught, eighth
When rolling rains and Boreas bauld
Gied farmer-folks a faught; Gave—fight
Ae morning quondam Mason W[4] . . .,
Now Merchant Master Miller,
Gaed down to meet wi' Nansie B . . ., Went
And her Jamaica siller money
To wed, that day.

[1] Possibly the first sketch for the Elegy on Captain Matthew Henderson.
[2] Alexander Fergusson of Craigdarroch, hero of 'The Whistle.'
[3] Unknown. Possibly James Boswell, biographer of Johnson.
[4] William Miller, a Mauchline friend of Burns.

The rising sun o'er Blacksideen[1]
  Was just appearing fairly,
When Nell and Bess[2] got up to dress
  Seven lang half-hours o'er early!
Now presses clink and drawers jink,
  For linens and for laces:
But modest Muses only *think*
  What ladies' underdress is
      On sic a day! such

But we'll suppose the stays are lac'd
  And bonie bosoms steekit, covered
Tho' thro' the lawn—but guess the rest!
  An angel scarce durst keek it. peep
Then stockins fine o' silken twine
  Wi' cannie care are drawn up, cautious
An' garten'd tight whare mortal wight,

* * * * * *

[As I never wrote it down my recollection does not entirely serve me.]

But now the gown wi' rustling sound
  Its silken pomp displays;
Sure there's nae sin in being vain
  O' siccan bonie claes! such
Sae jimp the waist, the tail sae vast—
  Trouth, they were bonie birdies!
O Mither Eve, ye wad been grieve
  To see their ample hurdies hips
      Sae large that day!

Then Sandy,[3] wi 's red jacket braw, fine
  Comes whip-jee-woa! about,
And in he gets the bonie twa—
  Lord, send them safely out!
And auld John Trot[4] wi' sober phiz,
  As braid and braw 's a Bailie, broad
His shouthers and his Sunday's jiz wig
  Wi' powther and wi' ulzie oil
      Weel smear'd that day.

* * * * * *

[Against my Muse had come thus far Miss Bess and I were once more in unison.][5]

[1] A hill.—*R. B.*

[2] Miller's sisters, two of the 'Mauchline Belles.' Burns commenced this satirical account of the marriage because Bess Miller had huffed his 'Bardship in the pride of her new connection.'

[3] Driver of the Post-chaise.—*R. B.*

[4] Miller's father.—*R. B.*

[5] Said to have been 'enclosed in a letter [unpublished] to Mrs Dunlop, 21st August 1788.'

EXTEMPORE REPLIES TO INVITATIONS.

I.

TO CAPTAIN RIDDEL.

Dear Sir, at ony time or tide
I'd rather sit wi' you than ride,
Tho' 'twere wi' royal Geordie:
And trowth, your kindness, soon and late,
Aft gars me to mysel look blate— makes—bashful
The Lord in Heaven reward ye!

II.

The king's poor blackguard slave am I,
And scarce dow spare a minute;
But I'll be with you by and bye,
Or else the devil's in it!

III.

SIR,

Yours this moment I unseal,
And faith I'm gay and hearty!
To tell the truth and shame the deil,
I am as fou as Bartie: drunk—the Devil
But Foorsday, sir, my promise leal, Thursday—true
Expect me o' your partie,
If on a beastie I can speel climb
Or hurl in a cartie. drive

Yours, ROBERT BURNS.

MACHLIN, *Monday night*, 10 *o'clock*.

VERSICLES ON SIGN-POSTS.[1]

I.

Her face with smile eternal drest
Just like the landlord to his guest,
High as they hang with creaking din
To index out the Country Inn.

[1] 'The everlasting surliness of a lion, Saracen's head, &c., or the unchanging blandness of the Landlord welcoming a Traveller, on some Sign-posts, would be no bad similes of the constant affected fierceness of a Bully or the eternal simper of a Frenchman or a Fiddler.'—*Burns in his Second Common-place Book.*

II.

He looked
Just as your sign-post Lions do,
With aspect fierce, and quite as harmless, too.

III.

A head, pure, sinless quite of brain and soul,
The very image of a barber's poll:
Just shows a human face and wears a wig
And looks, when well-friseur'd, amazing big.

VERSES

WRITTEN ON THE REVERSE SIDE OF A WOODEN PLATTER IN MRS DAVID WILSON'S LITTLE INN AT ROSLIN.

My blessings on you, sonsy wife; buxom
I ne'er was here before;
You 've gi'en us walth for horn and knife, wealth—spoon
Nae heart could wish for more.

Heaven keep you free frae care and strife, from
Till far ayont fourscore; beyond
And while I toddle on thro' life, walk
I 'll ne'er gang by your door. go

LINES

WRITTEN ON A BANK-NOTE.[1]

Wae worth thy power, thou cursèd leaf, woe worth
Fell source o' a' my woe and grief;
For lack o' thee I 've lost my lass,
For lack o' thee I scrimp my glass: stint
I see the children of affliction
Unaided, through thy cursed restriction:
I 've seen the oppressor's cruel smile
Amid his hapless victim's spoil;
And for thy potence vainly wished,
To crush the villain in the dust:
For lack o' thee, I leave this much-lov'd shore,
Never, perhaps, to greet old Scotland more. R. B.

KYLE.

[1] 'The above verses, in the handwriting of Burns, are copied from a bank-note in the possession of Mr James F. Gracie of Dumfries. The note is of the Bank of Scotland, and is dated so far back as 1st March 1780.'—MOTHERWELL. The verses appear to have been first published in *The Morning Chronicle* of 27th May 1814; they appeared in the *Scots Magazine* for September of the same year.

WRITTEN

ON A BLANK LEAF OF A COPY OF THE 'POEMS.'[1]

Once fondly lov'd, and still remember'd dear,
Sweet early object of my youthful vows,
Accept this mark of friendship, warm, sincere,
Friendship! 'tis all cold duty now allows.

And when you read the simple artless rhymes,
One friendly sigh for him, he asks no more,
Who, distant, burns in flaming torrid climes,
Or haply lies beneath th' Atlantic roar.

LINES

WRITTEN ON THE WINDOW OF A ROOM IN STIRLING.

Here Stewarts once in glory reigned,
And laws for Scotland's weal ordained;
But now unroofed their palace stands,
Their sceptre 's swayed by other hands;
Fallen, indeed, and to the earth
Whence grovelling reptiles take their birth,
The injured Stewart line is gone,
A race outlandish fills their throne;
An idiot race, to honour lost;
Who know them best despise them most.

Rash mortal, and slanderous Poet, thy name
Shall no longer appear in the records of fame;
Dost not know that old Mansfield, who writes like the Bible,
Says the more 'tis a truth, Sir, the more 'tis a libel?[2]

[1] Burns included these verses in the collection he made for Captain Riddel, with the note—'Written on the blank leaf of a copy of the first edition of my Poems, which I presented to an old sweetheart then married. 'Twas the girl I mentioned in my letter to Dr Moore, where I speak of taking the sun's altitude. Poor Peggy! Her husband is an old acquaintance and a most worthy fellow. When I was taking leave of my Carrick relations, intending to go to the West Indies, when I took farewell of her, neither she nor I could speak a syllable. Her husband escorted me three miles on my road, and we both parted with tears.' 'Kirkoswald Peggy' had married John Neilson, farmer of Monnyfee, in the same parish, towards the end of 1784.

[2] Allan Cunningham stated that some one cautioned Burns that the inscription would do him no good. 'I shall reprove myself,' he replied, and proceeded to aggravate his offence by adding these four lines.

LINES

WRITTEN UNDER THE PORTRAIT OF MISS REBEKAH CARMICHAEL WHICH SERVED AS A FRONTISPIECE TO HER 'POEMS.'

Curse on ungrateful man, that can be pleas'd
And yet can starve the author of the pleasure.
O thou, my elder brother in misfortune,
By far my elder brother in the muse,
With tears I pity thy unhappy fate!
Why is the bard unfitted for the world,
Yet has so keen a relish of its pleasures?

LINES

WRITTEN ON THE BACK OF A SKETCH.

Dear ——, I 'll gie ye some advice,
You 'll tak it no uncivil:
You shouldna paint at angels, man,
But try and paint the Devil.
To paint an angel 's kittle wark, difficult
Wi' Nick there 's little danger;
You 'll easy draw a lang-kent face, long-known
But no sae weel a stranger.[1]

VERSES

WRITTEN ON A WINDOW OF THE GLOBE TAVERN, DUMFRIES.[2]

I.

The greybeard, old Wisdom, may boast of his treasures;
Give me with gay Folly to live!
I grant him his calm-blooded, time-settled pleasures,
But Folly has raptures to give.

II.

My bottle is a holy pool
That heals the wounds o' care an' dool, sorrow
And pleasure is a wanton trout,
An ye drink it, ye 'll find him out. If

[1] When Burns was in Edinburgh he was introduced by a friend to a well-known painter, whom he found in his studio engaged on a picture of Jacob's dream; after minutely examining the work, he wrote the above verse.

[2] The panes are in the possession of Mr J. P. Brunton, Galashiels.

VERSES

WRITTEN ON A WINDOW OF THE INN AT CARRON.

We cam na here to view your warks, came not—works
In hopes to be mair wise, more
But only, lest we gang to hell, go
It may be nae surprise :

But when we tirl'd at your door, knocked
Your porter dought na hear us ; could not
Sae may, shou'd we to hell's yetts come, gates
Your billy Satan sair us ! crony—serve

LINES

WRITTEN ON A WINDOW-PANE AT WHIGHAM'S INN, SANQUHAR.

Envy, if thy jaundiced eye
Through this window chance to spy,
To thy sorrow thou shalt find
All that 's generous, all that 's kind :
Friendship, virtue, every grace,
Dwelling in this happy place.

ON MR M'MURDO.

INSCRIBED ON A PANE OF GLASS IN HIS HOUSE.

Blest be M'Murdo to his latest day !
No envious cloud o'ercast his evening ray ;
No wrinkle furrowed by the hand of care,
Nor ever sorrow add one silver hair !
Oh, may no son the father's honour stain,
Nor ever daughter give the mother pain !

EXCISEMEN UNIVERSAL.

WRITTEN ON A WINDOW.[1]

Ye men of wit and wealth, why all this sneering
'Gainst poor Excisemen ? Give the cause a hearing :
What are your Landlords' rent-rolls ? Taxing ledgers :
What Premiers ? What even Monarchs ? Mighty Gaugers !
Nay, what are Priests (those seeming godly wise-men) ?
What are they, pray, but Spiritual Excisemen !

[1] In the King's Arms Inn, Dumfries, in consequence of overhearing a gentleman speak despitefully of the officers of Excise.

OLD SONGS IMPROVED BY BURNS.

O WHARE DID YOU GET THAT HAUVER MEAL BANNOCK?

TUNE—*Bonie Dundee.*

[The first of the following verses is from an old homely ditty, the second only being the composition of Burns.]

O whare did you get that hauver meal bannock? — oatmeal
O silly blind body, O dinna ye see?
I gat it frae a brisk young sodger laddie,
Between St Johnston and bonie Dundee. — Perth
O gin I saw the laddie that gae me 't! — if—gave
Aft has he doudl'd me upon his knee; — dandled
May Heaven protect my bonie Scots laddie
And send him safe hame to his babie and me!

My blessin's upon thy sweet wee lippie,
My blessin's upon thy bonny e'e-bree! — eyebrow
Thy smiles are sae like my blythe sodger laddie, — gay
Thou 's aye the dearer and dearer to me!
But I'll big a bower on yon bonie banks, — build
Where Tay rins wimplin' by sae clear; — meandering
And I'll cleed thee in the tartan sae fine — clothe
And mak thee a man like thy daddie dear.

TO THE WEAVER'S GIN YE GO.

[All of this song but the chorus is by Burns. He may have written the first rough draft of it when he heard the report in 1786, that Jean Armour was about to desert him for Robert Wilson, the Paisley weaver.]

My heart was ance as blythe and free
As simmer days were lang;
But a bonie, westlin weaver lad — west-country
Has gart me change my sang. — made

Chorus—To the weaver's gin ye go, fair maids, if
To the weaver's gin ye go;
I rede you right, gang ne'er at night advise—go
To the weaver's gin ye go.

My mither sent me to the town,
To warp a plaiden wab;
But the weary, weary warpin o 't
Has gart me sigh and sab.

A bonie, westlin weaver lad
Sat working at his loom;
He took my heart as wi' a net,
In every knot and thrum.

I sat beside my warpin-wheel,
And ay I ca'd it roun';
But every shot and every knock,
My heart it gae a stoun.

The moon was sinking in the west,
Wi' visage pale and wan,
As my bonie, westlin weaver lad
Convoy'd me thro' the glen.

But what was said, or what was done,
Shame fa' me gin I tell; fall on
But Oh! I fear the kintra soon country
Will ken as weel 's mysel!

I AM MY MAMMY'S AE BAIRN.

TUNE—*I 'm owre young to Marry yet.*

I am my mammy's ae bairn, one child
Wi' unco folk I weary, sir; strange
And if I gang to your house,
I 'm fleyed 'twill make me eerie, sir. afraid

Chorus—I 'm owre young to marry yet; too
I'm owre young to marry yet;
I'm owre young—'twad be a sin
To tak me frae my mammy yet.

Hallowmass is come and gane, All Saints' Day
The nights are lang in winter, sir;
And you and I in ae bed,
In troth, I dare na venture, sir.

Fu' loud and shrill the frosty wind
Blaws through the leafless timmer, sir; wood
But if ye come this gate again, way
I 'll aulder be gin summer, sir. before

THE LAD THEY CA' JUMPIN JOHN.

Her daddie forbad, her minnie forbad,
Forbidden she wadna be:
She wadna trow 't, the browst she brew'd,
Wad taste sae bitterlie.

Chorus—The lang lad they ca' Jumpin John
Beguil'd the bonie lassie,
The lang lad they ca' Jumpin John
Beguil'd the bonie lassie.

A cow and a cauf, a yowe and a hauf, sheep
And thretty gude shillins and three;
A vera gude tocher, a cotter-man's dochter, dowry
The lass wi' the bonie black e'e.

UP IN THE MORNING EARLY.

TUNE—*Cold blows the Wind.*

[Written on the basis of an old song, the chorus of which is here preserved.]

Cauld blaws the wind frae east to west,
The drift is driving sairly;
Sae loud and shill 's I hear the blast—
I 'm sure it 's winter fairly.

Chorus—Up in the morning 's no for me,
Up in the morning early;
When a' the hills are covered wi' snaw,
I 'm sure it 's winter fairly.

The birds sit chittering in the thorn, — shivering
A' day they fare but sparely ;
And lang 's the night frae e'en to morn—
I 'm sure it 's winter fairly.

DUSTY MILLER.

Hey the dusty Miller,
And his dusty coat,
He will win a shilling,
Or he spend a groat. — Ere

Dusty was the coat,
Dusty was the colour,
Dusty was the kiss
That I gat frae the Miller.

Hey, the dusty Miller,
And his dusty sack ;
Leeze me on the calling — Commend me to
Fills the dusty peck :

Fills the dusty peck,
Brings the dusty siller ; — money
I wad gie my coatie
For the dusty Miller.

THERE WAS A LASS.

TUNE—*Duncan Davison.*

[Burns wrote 'Mary Morison' to the same tune. It is probable that this song is almost entirely his.]

There was a lass, they ca'd her Meg,
And she held o'er the moors to spin ;
There was a lad that followed her,
They ca'd him Duncan Davison.
The moor was driegh, and Meg was skeigh, — tedious—timorous
Her favour Duncan could na win ;
For wi' the rock she wad him knock, — distaff
And ay she shook the temper-pin. — pin of spinning-wheel

As o'er the moor they lightly foor, went
A burn was clear, a glen was green,
Upon the banks they eased their shanks, rested their limbs
And ay she set the wheel between:
But Duncan swore a haly aith, oath
That Meg should be a bride the morn; next day
Then Meg took up her spinnin-graith, implements
And flang them a' out o'er the burn. across

We will big a wee, wee house, build
And we will live like king and queen;
Sae blithe and merry 's we will be
When ye set by the wheel at e'en. put away
A man may drink, and no be drunk;
A man may fight, and no be slain;
A man may kiss a bonie lass,
And ay be welcome back again.

THE PLOUGHMAN.

[Of this piece, the last two verses only are by Burns. For the longer song, including them, reference may be made to the *Museum*.]

The ploughman he 's a bonie lad,
His mind is ever true, jo,
His garters knit below his knee,
His bonnet it is blue, jo.

Chorus—Then up wi 't a', my ploughman lad,
And hey my merry ploughman;
Of a' the trades that I do ken,
Commend me to the ploughman.

I hae been east, I hae been west,
I hae been at St Johnston; Perth
The boniest sight that e'er I saw
Was the ploughman laddie dancin'.

Snaw-white stockins on his legs,
And siller buckles glancin';
A gude blue bonnet on his head,
And oh, but he was handsome.

LADY ONLIE.

Tune—*The Ruffian's Rant.*

[It has been assumed from the allusion to 'Bucky' that Burns was inspired by his northern tour to put some of his genius into a local song.]

A' the lads o' Thornie-bank,
When they gae to the shore o' Bucky,
They 'll step in an' tak a pint
Wi' Lady Onlie, honest Lucky! — an elderly woman, landlady

Chorus—Lady Onlie, honest Lucky,
Brews gude ale at shore o' Bucky;
I wish her sale for her gude ale,
The best on a' the shore o' Bucky.

Her house sae bien, her curch sae clean, — comfortable—head-kerchief
I wat she is a dainty chuckie; — trow—darling
And cheerlie blinks the ingle-gleed — chimney-flame
O' Lady Onlie, honest Lucky!

TO DAUNTON ME.

The blude-red rose at Yule may blaw,
The simmer lilies bloom in snaw,
The frost may freeze the deepest sea;
But an auld man shall never daunton me. — tame

Refrain—To daunton me, to daunton me,
An auld man shall never daunton me.

To daunton me, and me sae young,
Wi' his fause heart and flatt'ring tongue,
That is the thing you shall never see,
For an auld man shall never daunton me.

For a' his meal and a' his maut,
For a' his fresh beef and his saut,
For a' his gold and white monie,
An auld man shall never daunton me.

His gear may buy him kye and yowes, wealth—cows—sheep
His gear may buy him glens and knowes; knolls
But me he shall not buy nor fee,
For an auld man shall never daunton me.

He hirples twa-fauld as he dow, limps double—can
Wi' his teethless gab and his auld beld pow, mouth—bald
And the rain rains down frae his red blear'd e'e;
That auld man shall never daunton me.

TO A BLACKBIRD.

[Written in the beginning of 1788 to supplement a song by Clarinda, which he sent to Johnson to fit an old melody called 'The Banks of Spey.']

For thee is laughing nature gay;
For thee she pours the vernal day:
For me in vain is nature drest,
While joy's a stranger to my breast!

THE WINTER IT IS PAST.

[The second of these verses is from the hand of Burns.]

The winter it is past, and the summer comes at last,
And the small birds, they sing on ev'ry tree;
Now ev'ry thing is glad, while I am very sad,
Since my true love is parted from me.

The rose upon the brier, by the waters running clear,
May have charms for the linnet or the bee;
Their little loves are blest, and their little hearts at rest,
But my true love is parted from me.

MY HOGGIE.

What will I do gin my Hoggie[1] die, if
My joy, my pride, my Hoggie?
My only beast, I had nae mae, no more
And vow but I was vogie. vain

[1] '*Hoggie,* a young sheep after it is smeared and before it is first shorn.'—STENHOUSE.

The lee-lang night we watch'd the fauld, live-long—fold
  Me and my faithfu' doggie;
We heard nocht but the roaring linn, waterfall
  Among the braes sae scroggie.[1] slopes

But the houlet cry'd frae the castle wa', owl
  The blitter frae the boggie; mire-snipe
The tod reply'd upon the hill— fox
  I trembled for my Hoggie.

When day did daw, and cocks did craw, dawn
  The morning it was foggie;
An unco tyke lap o'er the dyke, strange dog
  And maist has killed my Hoggie. almost

THE BONIE MOOR HEN.

[This song was based on an old 'Crochallan' ditty.]

The heather was blooming, the meadows were mawn,
Our lads gaed a-hunting, ae day at the dawn,
O'er moors and o'er mosses and mony a glen.
At length they discover'd a bonie moor-hen.

Chorus—I rede you, beware at the hunting, young men;
  I rede you, beware at the hunting, young men;
  Take some on the wing, and some as they spring,
  But cannily steal on a bonie moor-hen. cautiously

Sweet brushing the dew from the brown heather bells,
Her colours betray'd her on yon mossy fells;
Her plumage outlustr'd the pride o' the spring,
And O! as she wanton'd sae gay on the wing.

Auld Phœbus himsel, as he peep'd o'er the hill,
In spite at her plumage he tryèd his skill;
He levell'd his rays where she bask'd on the brae— slope
His rays were outshone, and but mark'd where she lay.

They hunted the valley, they hunted the hill,
The best of our lads wi' the best o' their skill;
But still as the fairest she sat in their sight,
Then, whirr! she was over—a mile at a flight.

[1] Covered with stunted bushes.

I LOVE MY LOVE IN SECRET.

[Based on an old rude song.]

My Sandy gied to me a ring,
Was a' beset wi' diamonds fine;
But I gied him a far better thing,
I gied my heart in pledge o' his ring.

Chorus—My Sandy O, my Sandy O,
My bonie, bonie Sandy O:
Tho' the love that I owe, to thee I dare na show,
Yet I love my love in secret, my Sandy O.

My Sandy brak a piece o' gowd,
While down his cheeks the saut tears row'd;
He took a hauf an' gied it to me,
And I'll keep it till the hour I die.

MY LOVE SHE'S BUT A LASSIE YET.

[Stenhouse says the title and the last four lines of this song are old, and that the remainder is by Burns.]

I rue the day I sought her, O,
I rue the day I sought her, O;
Wha gets her needs na say he 's woo'd,
But he may say he has bought her, O.

Chorus—My love, she 's but a lassie yet,
My love, she 's but a lassie yet;
We 'll let her stand a year or twa,—
She 'll no' be hauf sae saucy yet.

Come draw a drap o' the best o 't yet,
Come draw a drap o' the best o 't yet;
Gae seek for pleasure whare ye will,
But here I never miss'd it yet.

We 're a' dry wi' drinkin o 't,
We 're a' dry wi' drinkin o 't:
The minister kiss't the fiddler's wife.
He could na preach for thinkin o 't.

THE CAPTAIN'S LADY.

[Based on an old song popular in the time of the Duke of Marlborough. Stenhouse says these words are by Burns.]

When the drums do beat,
And the cannons rattle;
Thou shalt sit in state,
And see thy love in battle.

Chorus—O mount and go,
Mount and make you ready;
O mount and go,
And be the Captain's Lady.

When the vanquish'd foe
Sues for peace and quiet;
To the shades we 'll go,
And in love enjoy it.

CARLE, AN THE KING COME.

[Based on old song of the Cromwellian period.]

An somebody were come again,
Then somebody maun cross the main; must
And every man shall hae his ain,
Carle, an the King come. Old fellow

Chorus—Carle, an the King come,
Carle, an the King come;
Thou shalt dance and I will sing,
Carle, an the King come.

I trow we swappet for the warse, exchanged
We gae the boot and better horse; something to boot
And that we 'll tell them at the cross,[1]
Carle, an the King come.

Coggie, an the King come, Cup
Coggie, an the King come,
I 'se be fou and thou 'se be toom, I'll—drunk—empty
Coggie, an the King come.

[1] Probably the market-cross, where proclamations are made, and natural locale of a defiance.

FIRST WHEN MAGGY WAS MY CARE.

TUNE—*Whistle o'er the Lave o't.*

[In this song Burns improved upon some wittily indelicate verses preserved in Herd's collection.]

First when Maggie was my care,
Heaven I thought was in her air;
Now we 're married—speir nae mair— inquire
Whistle o'er the lave o 't. rest

Meg was meek, and Meg was mild,
Bonie Meg was Nature's child;
Wiser men than me 's beguiled—
Whistle o'er the lave o 't.

How we live, my Meg and me,
How we love, and how we gree, agree
I care na by how few may see— do not care
Whistle o'er the lave o 't.

Wha I wish were maggot's meat,
Dish'd up in her winding-sheet,
I could write—but Meg may see 't—
Whistle o'er the lave o 't.

JAMIE, COME TRY ME.

If thou should ask my love,
Could I deny thee?
If thou would win my love,
Jamie, come try me.

Chorus—Jamie, come try me;
Jamie, come try me;
If thou would win my love,
Jamie, come try me.

If thou should kiss me, love,
Wha could espy thee?
If thou wad be my love,
Jamie, come try me.

AWA, WHIGS, AWA!

TUNE—*Awa, Whigs, awa.*

[The second and last stanzas are certainly by Burns; the rest is said to be an improvement on an old Jacobite song, which has not, however, been recovered.]

Our thrissles flourish'd fresh and fair, thistles
And bonie bloom'd our roses;
But Whigs cam' like a frost in June,
An' wither'd a' our posies.

Chorus—Awa, Whigs, awa!
Awa, Whigs, awa!
Ye 're but a pack o' traitor louns, fellows
Ye 'll do nae good at a'.

Our ancient crown 's fa'en in the dust—
Deil blin' them wi' the stoure o 't; dust
And write their names in his black beuk,
Wha gae the Whigs the power o 't.

Our sad decay in church and state
Surpasses my descriving;
The Whigs cam' o'er us for a curse,
And we hae done wi' thriving.

Grim vengeance lang has ta'en a nap,
But we may see him waukin;
Gude help the day when Royal heads
Are hunted like a maukin! hare

WHARE HAE YE BEEN?

TUNE—*Killiecrankie.*

['The chorus of this song is old; the rest of it was written by Burns.'—STENHOUSE.]

Whare hae ye been sae braw, lad? fine
Whare hae ye been sae brankie, O? gay
Oh, whare hae ye been sae braw, lad?
Cam ye by Killiecrankie, O?

Chorus—An ye had been whare I hae been,
Ye wad na been sae cantie, O; merry
An ye had seen what I hae seen,
On the Braes o' Killiecrankie, O.

I faught at land, I faught at sea;
At hame I faught my Auntie, O;
But I met the devil an' Dundee,
On the Braes o' Killiecrankie, O.

The bauld Pitcur[1] fell in a furr, furrow
An' Clavers got a clankie, O; sharp blow
Or I had fed an Athole gled, kite
On the Braes o' Killiecrankie, O.

CA' THE YOWES TO THE KNOWES.

[The verses within brackets are old, with only a few touches of improvement by Burns. See original version, p. 433.]

As I gaed down the water-side,
There I met my shepherd lad,
He rowed me sweetly in his plaid, rolled
And he ca'd me his dearie.

Chorus—Ca' the yowes to the knowes, Drive—ewes—knolls
Ca' them where the heather grows,
Ca' them where the burnie rows, rolls
My bonie dearie.

Will ye gang down the water-side, go
And see the waves sae sweetly glide?
Beneath the hazel spreading wide,
The moon it shines fu' clearly.

[Ye sall get gowns and ribbons meet,
Cauf-leather shoon upon your feet,
And in my arms thou 'lt lie and sleep,
And ay sall be my dearie.

If ye 'll but stand to what ye 've said,
I 'se gang wi' thee, my shepherd lad,
And ye may row me in your plaid,
And I sall be your dearie.]

[1] The battle of Killiecrankie was fought July 17, 1689. David Hallyburton of Pitruc (an estate in Forfarshire) was with Claverhouse throughout the campaign, and fell with him in the battle.

While waters wimple to the sea, wander
While day blinks in the lift sae hie, shines—sky—high
Till clay-cauld death shall blin' my e'e,
Ye sall be my dearie.

YOUNG JOCKIE.

TUNE—*Young Jockey.*

[Stenhouse says that, excepting three or four lines, the whole of this song is the production of Burns.]

Young Jockie was the blythest lad
In a' our town or here awa': in this neighbourhood
Fu' blythe he whistled at the gaud,[1]
Fu' lightly danc'd he in the ha'.
He roos'd my een, sae bonie blue, praised
He roos'd my waist, sae genty sma'; elegantly
An' ay my heart cam to my mou',
When ne'er a body heard or saw.

My Jockie toils upon the plain,
Thro' wind and weet, thro' frost and snaw:
And o'er the lea I leuk fu' fain, look—fondly
When Jockie's owsen hameward ca'. oxen—drive
An' ay the night comes round again,
When in his arms he takes me a';
An' ay he vows he 'll be my ain,
As lang 's he has breath to draw.

COCK UP YOUR BEAVER.

[Based on an English song ridiculing Scotsmen who settled in London after the accession of James VI. to the throne of England.]

When first my brave Johnie lad came to this town
He had a blue bonnet that wanted the crown;
But now he has gotten a hat and a feather,—
Hey, brave Johnie lad, cock up your beaver!
Cock up your beaver, and cock it fu' sprush; spruce
We 'll over the border and gie them a brush;
There 's somebody there we 'll teach better behaviour,
Hey, brave Johnie lad, cock up your beaver!

[1] The driver of the plough-horses carried a rod or gaud.

BONIE LADDIE, HIGHLAND LADDIE.

I hae been at Crookieden,[1]
  My bonie laddie, Highland laddie,
Viewing Willie and his men,
  My bonie laddie, Highland laddie.
There our foes that burnt or slew
  My bonie laddie, Highland laddie,
There, at last, they gat their due,
  My bonie laddie, Highland laddie.

Satan sits in his black neuk, corner
  My bonie laddie, Highland laddie,
Breaking sticks to roast the Duke,[2]
  My bonie laddie, Highland laddie.
The bloody monster gae a yell,
  My bonie laddie, Highland laddie,
And loud a laugh gaed round a' hell,
  My bonie laddie, Highland laddie.

EPPIE M'NAB.

O saw ye my dearie, my Eppie Macnab?
O saw ye my dearie, my Eppie Macnab?
She 's down in the yard, she 's kissin' the laird,
She winna come hame to her ain Jock Rab.
O come thy ways to me, my Eppie Macnab;
O come thy ways to me, my Eppie Macnab;
Whate'er thou has dune, be it late, be it sune,
Thou 's welcome again to thy ain Jock Rab.

What says she, my dearie, my Eppie Macnab?
What says she, my dearie, my Eppie Macnab?
She lets thee to wit, that she has thee forgot,
And for ever disowns thee, her ain Jock Rab.
O had I ne'er seen thee, my Eppie Macnab!
O had I ne'er seen thee, my Eppie Macnab!
As light as the air, and fause as thou 's fair,
Thou 's broken the heart o' thy ain Jock Rab.

[1] A cant name for hell. [2] Cumberland.

WHA IS THAT AT MY BOWER DOOR?

TUNE—*Lass, an I come near thee.*

[It has been suggested that either James Findlay, the Excise officer at Tarbolton, who, in 1788, trained Burns for his official duties, or a relative, may have been the hero of this amended song.]

Wha is that at my bower-door?
  O wha is it but Findlay:
Then gae your gate, ye 'se nae be here; go your way—you shan't
  Indeed maun I, quo' Findlay. must
What maks ye, sae like a thief?
  O come and see, quo' Findlay.
Before the morn ye 'll work mischief;
  Indeed will I, quo' Findlay.

Gif I rise and let you in; If
  Let me in, quo' Findlay:
Ye 'll keep me waukin wi' your din;
  Indeed will I, quo' Findlay.
In my bower if ye should stay;
  Let me stay, quo' Findlay:
I fear ye 'll bide till break o' day;
  Indeed will I, quo' Findlay.

Here this night if ye remain;
  I 'll remain, quo' Findlay:
I dread ye 'll learn the gate again; way
  Indeed will I, quo' Findlay.
What may pass within this bower;
  Let it pass, quo' Findlay:
Ye maun conceal till your last hour;
  Indeed will I, quo' Findlay.

THE TITHER MORN.

To a Highland air.

The tither morn, when I forlorn other
  Aneath an aik sat moaning, oak
I did na trow, I 'd see my jo, sweetheart
  Beside me, 'gain the gloaming. before
But he sae trig, lap o'er the rig, neat—ridge
  And dawtingly did cheer me, caressingly
When I, what reck, did least expec'
  To see my lad so near me.

His bonnet he a thought ajee — awry
  Cocked sprush when first he clasped me; — spruce
And I, I wat, wi' fainness grat, — fondness
  While in his grips he pressed me.
Deil tak the war! I late and air — early
  Hae wished, since Jock departed;
But now as glad I'm wi' my lad,
  As short syne broken-hearted. — not long since

Fu' aft at e'en wi' dancing keen,
  When a' were blithe and merry,
I cared na by, sae sad was I,
  In absence o' my dearie.
But, praise be blest, my mind 's at rest,
  I'm happy wi' my Johnny:
At kirk and fair, I 'se aye be there, — I'll
  And be as canty 's ony. — cheerful

AS I WAS A-WANDERING.

TUNE—*Rinn Meudial mo Mhealladh.*

[Burns has here merely made some changes upon an old song.]

As I was a-wandering ae midsummer e'enin',
  The pipers and youngsters were making their game;
Amang them I spied my faithless fause lover, — false
  Which bled a' the wounds o' my dolour again.

Chorus—Weel, since he has left me, may pleasure gae wi' him;
  I may be distressed, but I winna complain; — won't
I flatter my fancy I may get anither,
  My heart it shall never be broken for ane.

I couldna get sleeping till dawin for greetin', — dawn—weeping
  The tears trickled down like the hail and the rain:
Had I na got greetin', my heart wad ha' broken,
  For oh! love forsaken 's a tormenting pain.

Although he has left me for greed o' the siller, — money
  I dinna envy him the gains he can win;
I rather wad bear a' the lade o' my sorrow — load
  Than ever hae acted sae faithless to him.

THE WEARY PUND O' TOW.

TUNE—*The Weary Pund o' Tow.*

[Here Burns very greatly improved a very old song.]

I bought my wife a stane o' lint — flax
As gude as e'er did grow;
And a' that she has made o' that,
Is ae puir pund o' tow.

Chorus—The weary pund, the weary pund,
The weary pund o' tow; — yarn
I think my wife will end her life
Before she spin her tow.

There sat a bottle in a bole, — recess in wall
Ayont the ingle lowe, — fireplace—flame
And ay she took the tither souk, — another mouthful
To drouk the stourie tow.[1]

Quoth I, For shame, ye dirty dame,
Gae spin your tap o' tow!
She took the rock, and wi' a knock — distaff
She brake it o'er my pow. — head

At last her feet—I sang to see 't—
Gaed foremost o'er the knowe; — knoll
And or I wad anither jad — wed
I 'll wallop in a tow. — hang in a halter

WHEN SHE CAM BEN SHE BOBBET.

O when she cam' ben she bobbet fu' low,
O when she cam' ben she bobbet fu' low;
And when she cam' ben she kiss'd Cockpen,[2]
And syne she deny'd she did it at a.' — then

And was na Cockpen right saucy witha',
And was na Cockpen right saucy witha',
In leaving the daughter o' a lord,
And kissin' a collier lassie, an' a'.

[1] To quench the thirst caused by the dust given off by the flax.

[2] The allusion in this song to Cockpen, a village a few miles to the south of Edinburgh, may have inspired Lady Nairne's ballad 'The Laird o' Cockpen.'

O never look down, my lassie, at a',
O never look down, my lassie, at a';
Thy lips are as sweet, and thy figure complete,
As the finest dame in castle or ha'.

Tho' thou hast nae silk and holland sae sma',
Tho' thou hast nae silk and holland sae sma';
Thy coat and thy sark are thy ain handywark— shirt
And Lady Jean was never sae braw. fine

MY COLLIER LADDIE.

TUNE—*The Collier Laddie.*

[Burns, in his Notes, speaks of this song as an old one with which he had had nothing to do. As it appears, however, in no other collection, and is found in his handwriting among Johnson's manuscripts, Mr Stenhouse infers that the greater part of it is his own composition.]

Whare live ye, my bonie lass?
And tell me what they ca' ye; call
My name, she says, is mistress Jean,
And I follow the Collier laddie.

See you not yon hills and dales
The sun shines on sae brawlie! brightly
They a' are mine, and they shall be thine
Gin ye'll leave your Collier laddie. If

Ye shall gang in gay attire,
Weel buskit up sae gaudy; dressed
And ane to wait on every hand
Gin ye'll leave your Collier laddie.

Though ye had a' the sun shines on
And the earth conceals sae lowly,
I wad turn my back on you and it a'
And embrace my Collier laddie.

I can win my five pennies in a day,
And spend at night fu' brawlie, finely
And make my bed in the collier's neuk corner
And lie down wi' my Collier laddie.

Loove for loove is the bargain for me,
Though the wee cot-house should haud me; hold
And the world before me to win my bread,
And fair fa' my Collier laddie. blessings on

GANE IS THE DAY.

TUNE—*Guidwife, count the Lawin.*

Gane is the day, and mirk 's the night, dark
But we 'll ne'er stray for faute o' light,
Gude ale and brandy 's stars and moon,
And blude-red wine 's the rysing sun.

Chorus—Then gudewife, count the lawin, reckoning
The lawin, the lawin;
Then gudewife, count the lawin,
And bring a coggie mair. cup

There 's wealth and ease for gentlemen,
And simple folk maun fecht and fen; must make a shift
But here we 're a' in ae accord,
For ilka man that 's drunk 's a lord. every

My coggie is a haly pool holy
That heals the wounds o' care and dool; sorrow
And Pleasure is a wanton trout,
An ye drink it a', ye 'll find him out.[1]

IT IS NA, JEAN, THY BONIE FACE.

TUNE—*The Maid's Complaint.*

It is na, Jean, thy bonie face
Nor shape that I admire,
Although thy beauty and thy grace
Might weel awauk desire.
Something, in ilka part o' thee,
To praise, to love, I find;
But dear as is thy form to me,
Still dearer is thy mind.

Nae mair ungenerous wish I hae,
Nor stronger in my breast,
Than, if I canna mak thee sae,
At least to see thee blest.
Content am I, if Heaven shall give
But happiness to thee:
And as wi' thee I 'd wish to live,
For thee I 'd bear to die.

[1] Burns wrote this last stanza on one of the windows of the Globe Inn.

YE JACOBITES BY NAME.

TUNE—*Ye Jacobites by Name.*

Ye Jacobites by name, give an ear, give an ear;
Ye Jacobites by name, give an ear;
Ye Jacobites by name,
Your fautes I will proclaim, faults
Your doctrines I maun blame— must
You shall hear.

What is Right and what is Wrang, by the law, by the law?
What is Right and what is Wrang by the law?
What is Right and what is Wrang?
A short sword, and a lang,
A weak arm, and a strang,
For to draw.

What makes heroic strife, famed afar, famed afar?
What makes heroic strife famed afar?
What makes heroic strife?
To whet th' assassin's knife,
Or hunt a Parent's life
Wi' bluidy war.

Then let your schemes alone, in the state, in the state;
Then let your schemes alone in the state;
Then let your schemes alone,
Adore the rising sun,
And leave a man undone[1]
To his fate.

THE CARLS O' DYSART.

TUNE—*Hey, ca' through.*

[Written upon the basis of an old Fifeshire boat-song.]

Up wi' the carls o' Dysart, old men
And the lads o' Buckhaven,
And the kimmers o' Largo, gossips
And the lasses o' Leven.

[1] Mr Andrew Lang has pointed out that the 'man undone,' if Henry, Cardinal Duke of York, is intended, had, of course, no party, except the Laird of Gask, in 1792, when the song was published.

Chorus—Hey, ca' thro', ca' thro', press on
For we hae mickle ado; much
Hey, ca' thro', ca' thro',
For we hae mickle ado.[1]

We hae tales to tell,
An' we hae sangs to sing;
We hae pennies to spend,
And we hae pints to bring.

We 'll live a' our days,
And them that comes behin',
Let them do the like,
And spend the gear they win. wealth

LADY MARY ANN.

TUNE—*Craigton's Growing.*

['Modelled by Burns from an ancient ballad entitled *Craigstone's Growing.*'—STENHOUSE. The ballad, the original of which, with the music, Burns is said to have taken down from a lady's recitation in the course of his Highland tour, is said to have been founded on an incident in real life. The young Urquhart of Craigstone was married, while yet a lad, to Elizabeth, the daughter of his guardian, the laird of Innes, who wished to secure his estates.]

Oh, Lady Mary Ann looks o'er the Castle wa';
She saw three bonie boys playing at the ba';
The youngest he was the flower amang them a'—
My bonie laddie 's young, but he 's growin' yet.

O father! O father! an' ye think it fit,
We 'll send him a year to the college yet:
We 'll sew a green ribbon round about his hat,
And that will let them ken he 's to marry yet.

Lady Mary Ann was a flower in the dew,
Sweet was its smell, and bonie was its hue;
And the langer it blossom'd the sweeter it grew:
For the lily in the bud will be bonier yet.

Young Charlie Cochrane was the sprout of an aik; oak
Bonie and bloomin', and straught was its make:
The sun took delight to shine for its sake,
And it will be the brag o' the forest yet.

[1] 'These lines are the refrain of the singers as they kept time to the tune with their oars.'—*A History of Fife and Kinross*, by Æ. J. G. Mackay.

The simmer is gane when the leaves they were green,
And the days are awa' that we hae seen;
But far better days I trust will come again,
For my bonie laddie 's young, but he 's growin' yet.

KENMURE'S ON AND AWA.

TUNE—*O Kenmure 's on and awa', Willie.*

[This song is supposed to be one of those which Burns only improved from old versions. William Gordon, sixth Viscount of Kenmure, raised a body of troops for the Pretender in 1715, and had the chief command of the insurgent forces in the south of Scotland. Taken at Preston, he was tried and condemned to be beheaded, which sentence was executed on the 24th of February 1716. His forfeited estate was bought back by his widow, and transmitted to their son. By the son of that son—afterwards Viscount of Kenmure in consequence of the restoration of the title—Burns was on one occasion entertained at his romantic seat, Kenmure Castle, near New Galloway.

O Kenmure 's on and awa, Willie!
O Kenmure 's on and awa!
And Kenmure's lord 's the bravest lord
That ever Galloway saw.

Success to Kenmure's band, Willie!
Success to Kenmure's band;
There 's no a heart that fears a Whig
That rides by Kenmure's hand.

Here 's Kenmure's health in wine, Willie!
Here 's Kenmure's health in wine;
There ne'er was a coward o' Kenmure's blude,
Nor yet o' Gordon's line.

O Kenmure's lads are men, Willie!
O Kenmure's lads are men;
Their hearts and swords are metal true—
And that their foes shall ken.

They 'll live or die wi' fame, Willie!
They 'll live or die wi' fame;
But sune, wi' sounding victorie,
May Kenmure's lord come hame!

Here 's him that 's far awa, Willie!
Here 's him that 's far awa!
And here 's the flower that I loe best—
The rose that 's like the snaw!

SUCH A PARCEL OF ROGUES IN A NATION.

TUNE—*A Parcel of Rogues in a Nation.*

[Burns here greatly improved a song directed against the Union between Scotland and England and the Scottish politicians who favoured it.]

Fareweel to a' our Scotish fame,
Fareweel our ancient glory,
Fareweel even to the Scotish name
Sae famed in martial story.
Now Sark rins o'er the Solway sands
And Tweed rins to the ocean,
To mark where England's province stands—
Such a parcel of rogues in a nation!

What force or guile could not subdue
Through many warlike ages
Is wrought now by a coward few
For hireling traitors' wages.
The English steel we could disdain,
Secure in valour's station;
But English gold has been our bane—
Such a parcel of rogues in a nation!

O would, ere I had seen the day
That treason thus could fell us,
My auld gray head had lien in clay lain
Wi' Bruce and loyal Wallace!
But pith and power, till my last hour,
I 'll mak this declaration:
We 're bought and sold for English gold—
Such a parcel of rogues in a nation!

THE CARL OF KELLY BURN BRAES.

TUNE—*Kellyburn Braes.*

[An old set of traditionary verses entitled 'The Farmer's Old Wife,' which is given at p. 204 of Robert Bell's *Ancient Poems, Ballads, and Songs of the Peasantry of England*, modified by Burns.]

There leevit a carl on Kelly Burn Braes,[1] old man
(Hey, and the rue grows bonie wi' thyme,)
And he had a wife was the plague o' his days;
And the thyme it is wither'd, and rue is in prime.

[1] The Kelly Burn is the northern boundary of Ayrshire, dividing the parish of Largs from Renfrewshire, and falls into the Firth of Clyde at Kelly Bridge.

Ae day as the carl gaed up the lang glen,
(Hey, and the rue grows bonie wi' thyme,)
He met wi' the Deil; wha said, 'How do you fen?' contrive to live
And the thyme it is wither'd, and rue is in prime.

'I've got a bad wife, sir; that's a' my complaint;
(Hey, and the rue grows bonie wi' thyme,)
For, saving your presence, to her ye're a saint:
And the thyme it is wither'd, and rue is in prime.'

'It's neither your stot nor your staig I shall crave, bullock—stallion
(Hey, and the rue grows bonie wi' thyme,)
But gie me your wife, man, for her I must have,
And the thyme it is wither'd, and rue is in prime.'

'O welcome, most kindly,' the blythe carl said,
(Hey, and the rue grows bonie wi' thyme,)
'But if ye can match her, ye're waur than ye're ca'd, worse
And the thyme it is wither'd, and rue is in prime.'

The devil has got the auld wife on his back;
(Hey, and the rue grows bonie wi' thyme,)
And, like a poor pedlar, he's carried his pack;
And the thyme it is wither'd, and rue is in prime.

He's carried her hame to his ain hallan-door; porch
(Hey, and the rue grows bonie wi' thyme,)
Syne bade her gae in, for a b—— and a ——,
And the thyme it is wither'd, and rue is in prime.

Then straight he makes fifty, the pick o' his band,
(Hey, and the rue grows bonie wi' thyme,)
Turn out on her guard in the clap o' a hand;
And the thyme it is wither'd, and rue is in prime.

The carlin gaed thro' them like ony wud bear, old woman—mad
(Hey, and the rue grows bonie wi' thyme,)
Whae'er she gat hands on cam' near her nae mair;
And the thyme it is wither'd, and rue is in prime.

A reekit wee devil looks over the wa'; smoked
(Hey, and the rue grows bonie wi' thyme,)
'Oh, help, maister, help, or she'll ruin us a',
And the thyme it is wither'd, and rue is in prime.'

The Devil he swore by the edge o' his knife,
(Hey, and the rue grows bonie wi' thyme,)
He pitied the man that was tied to a wife;
And the thyme it is wither'd, and rue is in prime.

The Devil he swore by the kirk and the bell,
(Hey, and the rue grows bonie wi' thyme,)
He was not in wedlock, thank Heav'n, but in hell;
And the thyme it is wither'd, and rue is in prime.

Then Satan has travell'd again wi' his pack;
(Hey, and the rue grows bonie wi' thyme,)
And to her auld husband he 's carried her back;
And the thyme it is wither'd, and rue is in prime.

'I hae been a Deevil the feck o' my life, greater part
(Hey, and the rue grows bonie wi' thyme,)
But ne'er was in hell till I met wi' a wife;
And the thyme it is wither'd, and rue is in prime.'

THE SLAVE'S LAMENT.

['The words and the music of this song were communicated by Burns for the *Museum*.'—STENHOUSE. 'I believe that Burns took the idea of his verses from the "Betrayed Maid," a ballad formerly much hawked about in Scotland.'—C. K. SHARPE. One might have hesitated to assign this song to Burns; but certainly his authorship of it is much fortified by its resemblance to another song of his, entitled 'The Ruined Farmer—"It's O, Fickle Fortune, O!"' which seems to have been formed on the same model.]

It was in sweet Senegal that my foes did me enthral,
For the lands of Virginia, ginia O;
Torn from that lovely shore, and must never see it more,
And alas! I am weary, weary, O!

All on that charming coast is no bitter snow or frost,
Like the lands of Virginia, ginia O;
There streams for ever flow, and there flowers for ever blow,
And alas! I am weary, weary, O!

The burden I must bear, while the cruel scourge I fear,
In the lands of Virginia, ginia O;
And I think on friends most dear, with the bitter, bitter tear,
And alas! I am weary, weary, O!

JOCKY FOU AND JENNY FAIN.

[Burns made these lines of his own the middle portion of a song in the *Tea-table Miscellany*, called 'Jocky Fou and Jenny Fain,' which Johnson included in his *Museum.*]

Ithers seek they ken na what,
Features, carriage and a' that;
Gie me loove in her I court,
Loove to loove maks a' the sport.

Let loove sparkle in her e'e;
Let her lo'e nae man but me;
That 's the tocher gude I prize, dowry
There the luver's treasure lies.

HAD I THE WYTE? SHE BADE ME!

Had I the wyte? had I the wyte? Was I to blame?
Had I the wyte? she bade me!
Had I the wyte? had I the wyte?
Had I the wyte? she bade me!
Had I the wyte? had I the wyte?
Had I the wyte? she bade me;
She watch'd me by the hie-gate-side,
And up the loan she shaw'd me. milking-place

And when I wad na venture in,
A coward loon she ca'd me;
And when I wad na venture in,
A coward loon she ca'd me;
And when I wad na venture in,
A coward loon she ca'd me;
Had Kirk and State been in the gate,
I 'd lighted when she bade me!

Sae craftilie she took me ben, in
And bade me mak nae clatter;
'For our ramgunshoch, glum goodman surly
Is o'er ayont the water:'
Whae'er shall say I wanted grace,
When I did kiss and dawte her, caress
Let him be planted in my place,
Syne say I was a fautor. Then—culprit

Could I for shame, could I for shame,
Could I for shame refus'd her?
And wad na Manhood been to blame,
Had I unkindly us'd her?
He claw'd her wi' the ripplin-kame, flax-dressing comb
And blae and bluidy bruis'd her: blue
When sic a husband was frae hame,
What wife but wad excus'd her?

I dighted aye her een sae blue, wiped—eyes
And bann'd the cruel randy:
And weel I wat her willin' mou' wot
Was e'en like succar-candie.
At gloamin-shote it was, I wat, twilight
I lighted on the Monday;
But I cam' through the Tiseday's dew,
To wanton Willie's brandy.

YOUNG JAMIE, PRIDE OF A' THE PLAIN.

TUNE—*The Carlin o' the Glen.*

[Stenhouse regards this song, the original of which is in the British Museum, as an unclaimed production of Burns. The rather fanciful suggestion has been thrown out that 'it may have been one of those pastorals which the poet composed with a view to conciliate the temper and melt the coldness of Maria Riddel, whose lyrical tastes were very Arcadian.']

Young Jamie, pride of a' the plain,
Sae gallant and sae gay a swain;
Thro' a' our lasses he did rove,
And reigned resistless King of Love:
But now wi' sighs and starting tears,
He strays amang the woods and breers;
Or in the glens and rocky caves
His sad complaining dowie raves: doleful

I wha sae late did range and rove,
And chang'd with every moon my love,
I little thought the time was near,
Repentance I should buy sae dear.
The slighted maids my torments see,
And laugh at a' the pangs I dree; suffer
While she, my cruel, scornful Fair,
Forbids me e'er to see her mair!

O CAN YE LABOR LEA, YOUNG MAN.

I fee'd a man at Martinmas, hired
Wi' airle pennies three; earnest
But a' the faut I had to him,
He could na labor lea.

Chorus—O can ye labor lea, young man? till grass-land
O can ye labor lea?
Gae back the gate ye cam again, way
Ye 'se never scorn me.

O clappin 's gude in Febarwar,
An' kissin 's sweet in May;
But what signifies a young man's love,
An it does na last for ay?

O kissin' is the key o' luve,
An' clappin is the lock;
An' makin o 's the best thing yet,
That e'er a young thing gat.

COMING THROUGH THE RYE.

TUNE—*Coming through the Rye.*

Coming through the rye, poor body,
Coming through the rye,
She draiglet a' her petticoatie, wet
Coming through the rye.

Chorus—Jenny 's a' wat, poor body,
Jenny 's seldom dry;
She draiglet a' her petticoatie,
Coming through the rye.

Gin a body meet a body If
Coming through the rye,
Gin a body kiss a body,
Need a body cry?

Gin a body meet a body
Coming through the glen,
Gin a body kiss a body,
Need the world ken?

THE LASS O' ECCLEFECHAN.

TUNE—*Jacky Latin.*

Gat ye me, O gat ye me,
  O gat ye me wi' naething;
Rock an' reel, and spinning-wheel, distaff
  A mickle quarter bason.
Bye attour, my Gutcher has Over and above—grandsire
  A heich house and a laich ane,
A' forbye my bonny sel', besides
  The toss o' Ecclefechan. toast

O haud your tongue now, Lucky Laing;
  O haud your tongue and jauner; prattle
I held the gate till you I met, went (the right) way
  Syne I began to wander: Then
I tint my whistle and my sang, lost
  I tint my peace and pleasure;
But your green graff, now, Lucky Laing, grave
  Wad airt me to my treasure. direct

THE LASS THAT MADE THE BED TO ME.

[Burns contributed this song to Johnson's fifth volume. It was founded on an old ballad, 'The Cumberland Lass,' preserved by Tom D'Urfey, and composed, as Burns himself says, on 'an amour of Charles II. when skulking in the north about Aberdeen in the time of usurpation.']

When Januar' wind was blawin cauld,
  As to the North I took my way,
The mirksome night did me enfauld,
  I knew na whare to lodge till day:
By my gude luck a maid I met,
  Just in the middle o' my care,
And kindly she did me invite
  To walk into a chamber fair.

I bow'd fu' low unto this maid,
  And thank'd her for her courtesie;
I bow'd fu' low unto this maid,
  An' bade her make a bed to me;
She made the bed baith large and wide,
  Wi' twa white hands she spread it doun;
She put the cup to her rosy lips,
  And drank—'Young man, now sleep ye soun'.'

Chorus—The bonie lass made the bed to me,
The braw lass made the bed to me, fine
I'll ne'er forget till the day I die,
The lass that made the bed to me.

She snatch'd the candle in her hand,
And frae my chamber went wi' speed;
But I call'd her quickly back again,
To lay some mair below my head:
A cod she laid below my head, pillow
And servèd me with due respect,
And, to salute her wi' a kiss,
I put my arms about her neck.

'Haud aff your hands, young man!' she said,
'And dinna sae uncivil be;
Gif ye hae ony luve for me, If
O wrang na my virginitie.'
Her hair was like the links o' gowd,
Her teeth were like the ivorie,
Her cheeks like lilies dipt in wine,
The lass that made the bed to me:

Her bosom was the driven snaw,
Twa drifted heaps sae fair to see;
Her limbs the polish'd marble stane,
The lass that made the bed to me.
I kiss'd her o'er and o'er again,
And aye she wist na what to say:
I laid her 'tween me and the wa';
The lassie thocht na lang till day.

Upon the morrow when we raise,
I thank'd her for her courtesie;
But ay she blush'd and ay she sigh'd,
And said, 'Alas, ye've ruin'd me.'
I clasp'd her waist, and kiss'd her syne, then
While the tear stood twinkling in her e'e;
I said, 'My lassie, dinna cry,
For ye ay shall make the bed to me.'

She took her mither's holland sheets,
An' made them a' in sarks to me;
Blythe and merry may she be,
The lass that made the bed to me.

The bonie lass made the bed to me,
The braw lass made the bed to me;
I'll ne'er forget till the day I die
The lass that made the bed to me.

THE CARDIN' O'T.

TUNE—*Salt-fish and Dumplings.*

I coft a stane o' haslock woo', — bought—soft wool from neck of sheep
To make a wab to Johnie o't; — web
For Johnie is my only jo; — sweetheart
I lo'e him best of onie yet.

Chorus—The cardin' o't, the spinnin' o't,
The warpin' o't, the winnin' o't; — winding
When ilka ell cost me a groat, — every
The tailor staw the lynin' o't. — stole—lining

For though his locks be lyart grey, — mixed black and gray
And though his brow be beld aboon; — bald above
Yet I hae seen him on a day,
The pride of a' the parishen.

THE HIGHLAND LADDIE.

TUNE—*If thou'lt play me fair play.*

['Compiled by Burns from some Jacobite verses, entitled "The Highland Lad and the Lowland Lassie."'—STENHOUSE.]

The boniest lad that e'er I saw,
Bonie laddie, Highland laddie,
Wore a plaid, and was fu' braw, — gay
Bonie Highland laddie.
On his head a bonnet blue,
Bonie laddie, Highland laddie;
His royal heart was firm and true,
Bonie Highland laddie.

Trumpets sound, and cannons roar,
Bonie lassie, Lowland lassie;
And a' the hills wi' echoes roar,
Bonie Lowland lassie.

Glory, honour, now invite,
  Bonie lassie, Lowland lassie,
For freedom and my king to fight,
  Bonie Lowland lassie.

The sun a backward course shall take,
  Bonie laddie, Highland laddie,
Ere aught thy manly courage shake,
  Bonie Highland laddie.
Go! for yourself procure renown,
  Bonie laddie, Highland laddie;
And for your lawful king his crown,
  Bonie Highland laddie.

SAE FAR AWA.

TUNE—*Dalkeith Maiden Bridge.*

O sad and heavy should I part,
  But for her sake sae far awa';
Unknowing what my way may thwart,
  My native land sae far awa'.
Thou that of a' things Maker art,
  That formed this Fair sae far awa',
Gie body strength, and I 'll ne'er start
  At this my way sae far awa'.

How true is love to pure desert,
  So love to her sae far awa';
And nought can heal my bosom's smart,
  While, oh, she is sae far awa'.
Nane other love, nae other dart,
  I feel, but hers sae far awa';
But fairer never touch'd a heart,
  Than hers, the Fair sae far awa'.

I'LL AY CA' IN BY YON TOWN.

There 's nane sall ken, there 's nane sall guess,
  What brings me back the gate again, — way
But she my fairest faithfu' lass,
  And stowlins we sall meet again. — by stealth

Chorus—I 'll ay ca' in by yon town,[1] call at
And by yon garden green again;
I 'll ay ca' in by yon town,
And see my bonie Jean again.

She 'll wander by the aiken tree, oak
When trystin' time draws near again; meeting
And when her lovely form I see,
O haith, she 's doubly dear again. In truth

THE HIGHLAND BALOU.

[Stenhouse says Burns obtained the words as well as the music of this song in the course of his Highland tour, and translated the former into Lowland Scotch.]

Hee balou, my sweet wee Donald,
Picture o' the great Clanronald;
Brawlie kens our wanton Chief Well
Wha gat my young Highland thief.

Leeze me on thy bonie craigie, I dote on—neck
An thou live, thou 'll steal a naigie, horse
Travel the country thro' and thro',
And bring hame a Carlisle cow.

Thro' the Lawlands, o'er the Border,
Weel, my babie, may thou furder! further
Harry the louns o' the laigh Countrie, low
Syne to the Highlands hame to me. Then

BANNOCKS O' BARLEY.

TUNE—*The Killogie.*

[Based by Burns on a Jacobite song, and almost, if not altogether, rewritten.]

Wha in a brulyie broil
Will first cry a parley?
Never the lads wi'
The bannocks o' barley!

[1] 'Town' is probably used here in the Scotch sense, and may mean a farm-steading or a clump of cottages round or near a country house.

Chorus—Bannocks o' bear-meal,
Bannocks o' barley;
Here 's to the Highlandman's
Bannocks o' barley!

Wha in his wae-days — adversity
Were loyal to Charlie?—
Wha but the lads wi'
The bannocks o' barley?

IT WAS A' FOR OUR RIGHTFU' KING.

TUNE—*It was a' for our rightfu' King.*

[There is some doubt as to the authorship of this singularly beautiful song, which Burns sent to Johnson in his own handwriting. Allan Cunningham was of opinion that Burns 'rather beautified and amended some ancient strain which he had discovered than wrote it wholly from his own heart and fancy.' In this view he was supported by David Laing. The third verse is to be found in an old stall-ballad called 'Molly Stuart,' which is, however, of uncertain date. Sir Walter Scott, under the belief that the stanza was old, reproduced it in 'Elspeth's Daughter' in the *Antiquary*. Into his song 'A weary lot is thine, fair maid,' in *Rokeby*, he introduces this verse:

He turned his charger as he spake,
Upon the river shore;
He gave his bridle reins a shake,
Said 'Adieu for ever more, my love,
And adieu for ever more.'

It is tolerably safe to say that whatever virtue the song has has been given to it by Burns.]

It was a' for our rightfu' King
We left fair Scotland's strand;
It was a' for our rightfu' King
We e'er saw Irish land,
My dear;
We e'er saw Irish land.

Now a' is done that men can do,
And a' is done in vain;
My Love and Native Land farewell,
For I maun cross the main, — must
My dear;
For I maun cross the main.

He turn'd him right, and round about
Upon the Irish shore;
And gae his bridle reins a shake,
With adieu for evermore,
My dear;
With adieu for evermore.

The soger frae the wars returns,
  The sailor frae the main;
But I hae parted frae my love,
  Never to meet again,
    My dear;
  Never to meet again.

When day is gane, and night is come,
  And a' folk bound to sleep,
I think on him that 's far awa',
  The lee-lang night, and weep, live-long
    My dear;
  The lee-lang night, and weep.

THE HIGHLAND WIDOW'S LAMENT.

['This pathetic ballad was wholly composed by Burns for the *Museum*, unless we except the exclamation, "Och-on, och-on, och-rie!" which appears in the old song composed on the massacre of Glencoe, inserted in the first volume of the *Museum*.'—STENHOUSE.]

O, I am come to the low Countrie,
  Och-on, och-on, och-rie!
Without a penny in my purse,
  To buy a meal to me.

It was na sae in the Highland hills,
  Och-on, och-on, och-rie!
Nae woman in the Country wide
  Sae happy was as me.

For then I had a score o' kye, cattle
  Och-on, och-on, och-rie!
Feeding on yon hill sae high,
  And giving milk to me.

And there I had threescore o' yowes, sheep
  Och-on, och-on, och-rie:
Skipping on yon bonny knowes, knolls
  And casting woo' to me.

I was the happiest of the Clan,
  Sair, sair may I repine;
For Donald was the brawest lad, finest
  And Donald he was mine.

Till Charlie Stewart cam at last,
  Sae far to set us free;
My Donald's arm was wanted then,
  For Scotland and for me.

Their waefu' fate what need I tell?
  Right to the wrang did yield:
My Donald and his Country fell
  Upon Culloden's field.

Och-on, O Donald, oh!
  Och-on, och-on, och-rie!
Nae woman in the warld wide
  Sae wretched now as me.

WEE WILLIE GRAY.

[Written by Burns in imitation, and to the tune, of an old nursery song called 'Wee Totum Fogg.']

Wee Willie Gray, and his leather wallet,
Peel a willow-wand, to be him boots and jacket;
The rose upon the breer will be him trews and doublet,
The rose upon the breer will be him trews and doublet.

Wee Willie Gray, and his leather wallet,
Twice a lily-flower will be him sark and cravat; shirt
Feathers of a flee wad feather up his bonnet,
Feathers of a flee wad feather up his bonnet.

O GUDE ALE COMES.

[Based on old song.]

O gude ale comes, and gude ale goes,
Gude ale gars me sell my hose, makes
Sell my hose and pawn my shoon;
Gude ale keeps my heart aboon. above

I had sax owsen in a pleugh,
And they drew a' weel eneugh,
I sell'd them a' just ane by ane;
Gude ale keeps the heart aboon.

O AY MY WIFE SHE DANG ME.

TUNE—*My Wife she dang me.*

On peace an' rest my mind was bent,
And fool I was, I married;
But never honest man's intent
Sae cursedly miscarried.

Chorus—O ay my wife she dang me, discomfited
And aft my wife she bang'd me; beat
If ye gie a woman a' her will,
Gude faith, she 'll soon o'ergang ye. master

Some sairie comfort at the last, sorry bit
When thir days are done, man;
My pains o' hell on earth are past,
I 'm sure o' bliss aboon, man. above

O STEER HER UP.

TUNE—*O steer her up, and haud her gaun.*

[The first four lines of this song are part of an old song which appears in D'Urfey's Collection.]

O steer her up, and haud her gaun— stir—keep her going
Her mother 's at the mill, jo,
And gin she winna take a man, if
E'en let her tak her will, jo:
First shore her wi' a gentle kiss, threaten
And ca' anither gill, jo; call
And gin she take the thing amiss,
E'en let her flyte her fill, jo. scold

O steer her up, and be na blate, bashful
And gin she tak it ill, jo,
Then leave the lassie till her fate,
And time nae langer spill, jo:
Ne'er break your heart for ae rebute, one rebuff
But think upon it still, jo;
Then gin the lassie winna do 't,
Ye 'll find another will, jo.

SWEETEST MAY.

Sweetest May, let love inspire thee;
Take a heart which he designs thee;
As thy constant slave regard it;
For its faith and truth reward it.

Proof o' shot to birth or money, Proof against the attractions of
Not the wealthy but the bonny;
Not high-born, but noble-minded,
In love's silken band can bind it.

THERE WAS A BONIE LASS.

There was a bonie lass, and a bonie, bonie lass,
And she lo'ed her bonie laddie dear,
Till war's loud alarms tore her laddie frae her arms,
Wi' monie a sigh and a tear.

Over sea, over shore, where the cannons loudly roar,
He still was a stranger to fear;
And nought could him quail, or his bosom assail,
But the bonie lass he lo'ed sae dear.

CROWDIE.

['The first verse of this song is old; the second was written by Burns'—STENHOUSE.]

O that I had ne'er been married,
I wad never had nae care;
Now I've gotten wife an' weans, children
And they cry crowdie evermair. oatmeal pudding

Chorus—Ance crowdie, twice crowdie,
Three times crowdie in a day;
Gin ye crowdie ony mair, If
Ye'll crowdie a' my meal away.

Waefu' Want and Hunger fley me, terrify
Glowrin' by the hallan en'; staring—cottage door
Sair I fecht them at the door,
But aye I'm eerie they come ben. fear lest—come in

INDEX OF FIRST LINES.

Edinburgh:
Printed by W. & R. Chambers, Limited.